Brief Table of Contents

W9-ANH-177

Intersections

A Thematic Reader for Writers

Intersections
A Thematic Reader for Writers

Emily Isaacs
Montclair State University

Catherine Keohane
Montclair State University

bedford/st.martin's
Macmillan Learning
Boston | New York

For Bedford/St. Martin's

VICE PRESIDENT, EDITORIAL, MACMILLAN LEARNING HUMANITIES: Edwin Hill

EDITORIAL DIRECTOR, ENGLISH: Karen S. Henry

SENIOR PUBLISHER FOR COMPOSITION, BUSINESS AND TECHNICAL WRITING,
    DEVELOPMENTAL WRITING: Leasa Burton

EXECUTIVE EDITOR: Karita dos Santos

SENIOR DEVELOPMENTAL EDITOR: Jill Gallagher

EDITORIAL ASSISTANT: Julia Domenicucci

SENIOR PRODUCTION EDITOR: Ryan Sullivan

MEDIA PRODUCER: Sarah O'Connor

PRODUCTION SUPERVISOR: Robert Cherry

EXECUTIVE MARKETING MANAGER: Joy Fisher Williams

COPY EDITOR: Jamie Nan Thaman

INDEXER: Schroeder Indexing Services

SENIOR PHOTO EDITOR: Martha Friedman

PERMISSIONS MANAGER: Kalina K. Ingham

SENIOR ART DIRECTOR: Anna Palchik

TEXT DESIGN: Parallelogram Graphics

COVER DESIGN: William Boardman

COVER ART: *Cove,* painting by Julia Ricketts

COMPOSITION: Jouve

PRINTING AND BINDING: BR Printers

Copyright © 2017 by Bedford/St. Martin's.

All rights reserved. No part of this book may be reproduced, stored in a retrieval system,
or transmitted in any form or by any means, electronic, mechanical, photocopying, recording,
or otherwise, except as may be expressly permitted by the applicable copyright statutes or
in writing by the Publisher.

Manufactured in the United States of America.

1 0 9
f e d c b

For information, write: Bedford/St. Martin's, 75 Arlington Street, Boston, MA 02116
(617-399-4000)

ISBN 978-1-319-00496-5 (Student Edition)
ISBN 978-1-319-04741-2 (Instructor's Edition)

Acknowledgments

*Text acknowledgments and copyrights appear at the back of the book on pages 465–68, which
constitute an extension of the copyright page. Art acknowledgments and copyrights appear on
the same page as the art selections they cover.*

About the Authors

Emily Isaacs (BA, Colby College; PhD, University of Massachusetts Amherst) has taught composition for thirty years, first in Massachusetts, very briefly at a state penitentiary, and, for the last twenty years, at Montclair State University in New Jersey. She has taught a wide variety of students at various levels, with a focus on less prepared students who are anxious to catch up to their peers. Emily developed the award-winning Writing Program at Montclair State, and served as a campus leader in pedagogical innovations, writing assessment, and individualized learning pedagogies. Emily's scholarship is in the area of writing studies, with  publications in *College English*, *Pedagogy*, *Writing Center Journal*, *Writing Program Administration*, and several edited books. She is the coauthor of *Public Writing: Student Writing as Public Text*, and the author of the forthcoming book *Writing at the State U* (Utah State University Press). Emily is a steadfast believer in teaching all students the creative, intellectual processes that writers follow to succeed, but also sees the importance of providing explicit instruction in the conventions of academic and disciplinary writing.

Catherine Keohane (BA, Columbia University; PhD, Rutgers University) has taught composition for more than twenty years, both at four-year and two-year institutions, working with students at every level. She earned her PhD in English literature from Rutgers University and now teaches at Montclair State University, having also taught at Bergen Community College. With a background in eighteenth-century literature, Catherine now splits her teaching between composition and literature. At Montclair State, she served as Director for Writing Placement and also participated in a review of the basic writing curriculum, helping to restructure  the course and coauthoring a custom textbook. She has published articles in *ELH*, *Writing Program Administration*, *Studies in the Novel*, and *Studies in Eighteenth-Century Culture*, and has presented papers at conferences including MLA, CCCC, and ASECS. Her scholarship includes literary studies, writing assessment, outcomes assessment, and teaching difficult texts. Catherine sees the goal of college composition classes at all levels as engaging in the crucial work of developing not only students' critical reading and writing skills but also their confidence in their ability and right to join in conversation with other writers.

Preface for Instructors

Intersections—it's an evocative term, one that brings to mind meeting points, crossroads, and overlaps. As its title indicates, *Intersections: A Thematic Reader for Writers* brings together fresh, engrossing, and relatable readings with a broad range of flexible reading and writing instruction. Modular toolkits on key reading and writing topics—such as note taking, summarizing, outlining, peer review, MLA documentation, and grammar—allow for the intersection of reading with writing, classroom discussion with independent study, and critical thinking with creative expression.

In writing classrooms where students' needs are increasingly diverse and evershifting, it can be difficult to address all of the skills necessary to help your students excel, both in this course and beyond. That's where *Intersections* comes in. Developed out of our combined experience as writing teachers, *Intersections* offers timely readings on themes students care about, keeping them interested and helping them think deeply about their world. The readings are combined with toolkit activities and tutorials, which offer the right amount of instruction for students with the flexibility instructors need.

We wrote *Intersections* with two audiences in mind—students who are becoming college writers and the teachers who are supporting them. One of the primary struggles for instructors of college writing, both in developmental and composition classrooms, is the wide range of background knowledge and skills their students bring. You may very well have a future English major sitting beside a part-time student and full-time parent for whom English is a second language. The toolkits in *Intersections* are designed to help bridge those gaps, giving instructors strategies for addressing the needs of individual students without overwhelming them. Toolkits may be assigned to an entire class as they work through an assignment. Or if an ELL student is grappling with subject-verb agreement, for example, an instructor can direct that student to Toolkit 6.5, "Subject-Verb Agreement," for additional guidance. The toolkits are designed for use with any of the readings and assignments in the book, allowing for complete and easy customization of the course. In addition, students can easily find the help they need as they work on assignments independently outside of the classroom.

The readings in *Intersections* represent a range of lengths, difficulty, and topics so that students are both challenged and engaged. The reading selections also testify to our belief that emerging writers can—and should—write thoughtfully not just about themselves but also about the world around them. Themes such as immigration, American sports culture, gender identity, and disabilities offer a wealth of opportunity for stimulating classroom discussions and written expression. All along the way, students are supported through reading glosses, as well as pre- and post-reading assignments that help them home in on key elements such as main ideas, author bias, and essay structure. Students can further sharpen their reading skills with the reading toolkits in Chapter 3, which cover note taking, reverse outlining, reading visuals, and strategies for overcoming "reader's block."

Core Features

The Basics: Reading and Writing Instruction

The first two chapters provide the building blocks of reading and writing instruction, offering key terms and definitions, essential reading and writing strategies, and a walk-through of a student's writing process, including brainstorming, drafting, and revision.

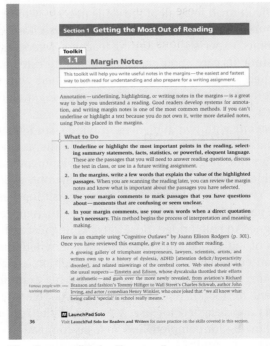

The first toolkit in Chapter 3

Modular, Customizable Toolkits

The toolkits chapter forms the central component of direct instruction in *Intersections*: a collection of pedagogical materials and activities designed to assist emerging writers with critical reading and American academic writing. The toolkits for reading and writing assist students by directly addressing many of the *specific* areas that pose challenges to many college writers. These toolkits, organized in six sections—"Getting the Most Out of Reading," "Generating Writing," "Organizing Writing," "Revising Writing," "Following Writing Rules and Conventions," and "Polishing Sentences"—are designed to be used with the reading and writing assignments found in the text, but can also function as stand-alone assignments or in conjunction with material that an instructor has selected independently. Numbering more than eighty, the toolkit exercises provide students with hands-on practice in such competencies as active reading, outlining, summarizing, evaluating arguments, planning, drafting theses, tackling revision, and addressing editing challenges such as run-ons and vague pronouns.

Fresh, Provocative, and Relevant Readings

Experience tells us that students read more carefully and write better when they are interested in the topic. Our thematic chapters, featuring forty-eight readings in all, aim to engage students while also allowing them to develop core skills that they can take to their other courses; these themes mix classic topics (for example, issues of language and immigration) with less commonly taught topics that speak to the interests of diverse student populations (for example, issues of disabilities and of sports in American culture).

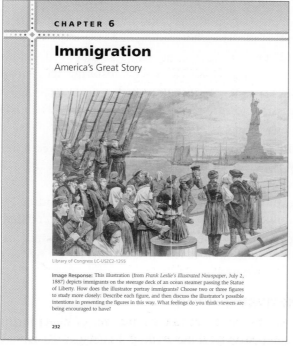

CHAPTER 6

Immigration
America's Great Story

Library of Congress LC-US2C2-1255

Image Response: This illustration (from *Frank Leslie's Illustrated Newspaper*, July 2, 1887) depicts immigrants on the steerage deck of an ocean steamer passing the Statue of Liberty. How does the illustrator portray immigrants? Choose two or three figures to study more closely: Describe each figure, and then discuss the illustrator's possible intentions in presenting the figures in this way. What feelings do you think viewers are being encouraged to have?

232

The image and image response for Chapter 6

Each thematic chapter opens with an **image** and an **image response** assignment to pique interest and get students thinking about the chapter's theme, followed by an **introduction** that provides historical and cultural context. Chapters include readings of varied styles and length. Their authors—including blogger Lauren Shields (recounting her modest-dress experiment), writer Jose Antonio Vargas (writing about being an undocumented immigrant), academics Russell John Rickford and John Russell Rickford (writing about black English), journalist Cyd Zeigler (profiling college basketball player Derrick Gordon), professional athlete Mike Matheny (offering his vision for youth sports), and novelist Alice Randall (sharing her struggles with weight)—model a range of approaches and genres, including journalistic reports, narratives, analyses, and arguments.

Readings within chapters are divided into two clusters, providing teachers with options in designing their courses. Every reading offers pre- and post-reading activities and questions designed to engage students and to assess their comprehension, while also moving them to critical inquiry and writing.

Guided Reading Support

Students become successful writers when they understand what they have read. Each selection in *Intersections* includes the following support:

- **"Before You Read"** activities prompt students to start thinking about the topic early, giving them an entry point into the reading.
- **Headnotes** about the author provide important biographical context for the reading so that students aren't reading in a vacuum.
- **"As You Read"** tasks help students focus as they read, asking them to underline, highlight, and make lists as they go, fostering active reading skills.
- **Marginal glosses** explain vocabulary and cultural references that may be otherwise inaccessible to students of various backgrounds and ages.
- **Pull quotes** help students identify key points.
- **"Mapping the Reading"** questions focus on reading comprehension and rhetorical analysis, ensuring that students have grasped the main ideas of what they've just read.
- **"Discussing and Thinking Critically about the Reading"** questions prompt students to think more deeply about the selection and related issues.
- **"Navigating the Intersections"** assignments engage students in critical thinking by making connections between selections or asking for further investigation into questions raised.

Model Student Writing

The **Appendix** provides five sample student essays, each illustrating a different genre and fully annotated to show writing strategies and conventions, including updated MLA citation style.

440 ◆ **Appendix** Annotated Student Essays

For this **analytical essay**, Selena Alvarez responds to an assignment asking her to describe and analyze the standard of beauty in her society, drawing on personal observations and sources. She brainstormed ideas and decided to focus on the role of the media in creating restrictive models of beauty. She wrote three drafts, the final of which we present here. In this final draft, Alvarez analyzes, or breaks down, how standards of beauty are established within a society, focusing especially on the media's part in shaping people's ideas.

Heading includes writer's name, instructor's name, course title, and date of assignment, all double-spaced. (For more on document formatting, see Toolkit 5.1.)

Centered title, indicating Alvarez's focus. (For more on titles, see Toolkits 5.2 and 5.3.)

Introductory paragraph begins with the broad topic of beauty standards and then narrows to the connection between beauty and weight. (For more on introductions, see Toolkit 2.7.)

Here, Alvarez first questions why thinness is valued and then proposes an answer.

Thesis statement, which Alvarez will support with examples. (For more on thesis statements, see Toolkit 2.4.)

First body paragraph, focusing on the Internet.

Alvarez 1

Selena Alvarez
Professor Keohane
Introduction to College Writing
March 6, 2017

Beauty according to Society

For many generations, there has been a specific description of what beauty really is. This description defines the way beauty should look and be expressed. The mainstream representation of beauty in the media has to do with thinness. People others usually confirm as beautiful are those who appear thin. Little girls have grown up to believe that a Barbie doll is perfect. There was never a doll made to look a little overweight. As females grew older, they wanted to be like that Barbie doll they once had. In my household, everyone I live with is always telling me that they envy my flat stomach. They constantly tell me how lucky I am or how they envy my petite body shape. Why is it that they believe that being thin is something to envy or cherish? The fear of judgment may be the answer to this question. Society seems to constantly make fun of obesity as if it were horrible for a person to be overweight. The media creates and promotes the standards of beauty that lead to negative judgments that make it hard for those who look different.

Today we observe teenagers all over the world using the Internet on a daily basis. Not only do they use the Internet for communication and

Sample student essay from the Appendix

Support for Students and Instructors

Student Resources

Pairing *Intersections* with *LaunchPad Solo for Readers and Writers* helps students succeed at their own pace. Available free when packaged with *Intersections*, *LaunchPad Solo for Readers and Writers* provides you with a quick and flexible solution for targeting instruction on critical reading, the writing process, grammar, mechanics, style, and punctuation. By combining formative and summative assessments with opportunities to study, practice, and review specific skills, *LaunchPad Solo for Readers and Writers* helps students gain confidence as they work through sequenced units that guide them from concept to mastery.

To order *Intersections* packaged with *LaunchPad Solo for Readers and Writers*, please use ISBN **978-1-319-08266-6**.

LearningCurve for Readers and Writers. LearningCurve, Bedford/St. Martin's adaptive quizzing program, quickly learns what students know and helps them practice what they don't yet understand. Game-like quizzing motivates students to engage with their course, and reporting tools help teachers discern their students' needs.

Please note: *LearningCurve for Readers and Writers* is included with *Launch-Pad Solo for Readers and Writers*.

Free Instructor Resources

The **Instructor's Edition** of *Intersections* includes the Instructor's Manual for *Intersections*, bound right in with the book. The Instructor's Manual provides helpful information and advice on teaching with *Intersections*, including sample syllabi, Lexile measures for the readings in the book, additional essay and discussion prompts, suggested responses for the questions in the book, and ideas for how to integrate this book in your classroom. Please use ISBN **978-1-319-04741-2**.

Join Our Community! At Bedford, providing support to teachers and their students who choose our books and digital tools is our first priority. The Bedford/St. Martin's English Community is now our home for professional resources, featuring Bedford *Bits*, our popular blog site offering new ideas for the composition classroom and composition teachers. Connect and converse with a growing team of Bedford authors and top scholars who blog on *Bits*: Barclay Barrios, Steve Bernhardt, Susan Bernstein, Traci Gardner, Elizabeth Losh, Andrea Lunsford, Miriam Moore, Jack Solomon, Elizabeth Wardle, and Donna Winchell, among others. In addition, you'll find an expanding collection of resources that support your teaching. Download titles from our professional resource series to support your teaching, review projects in the pipeline, sign up for professional development webinars, start a discussion, ask a question, and follow your favorite members. Visit **community .macmillan.com** to join the conversation with your fellow teachers.

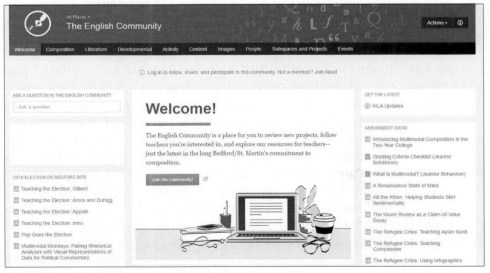

The Bedford/St. Martin's English Community

Acknowledgments

We thank the wonderful, smart people at Macmillan who have helped guide our book through its development to completion, including Alexis Walker, Edwin Hill, Vivian Garcia, Karita dos Santos, Leasa Burton, Joy Fisher Williams, Christina Shea, Julia Domenicucci, Kalina Ingham, Martha Friedman, Pablo D'Stair, and Ryan Sullivan. We especially thank our editor, Jill Gallagher, for her cheerful guidance and engagement in our project.

We thank our colleagues at Montclair State University who provided feedback on the book, including Kristen Anderson, Nikki Bosca, Claudia Cortese, Leslie Doyle, Tavya Jackson, Franc Lacinski, Peggy McGlone, Carrie O'Dell, Tatum Petrich, Jessica Restaino, Jill Rosenberg, and Fran Shultz. We thank all those at Montclair State University who help provide students and instructors with a supportive environment for the teaching and learning of writing. We thank students Joseph De-Guzman, Vera Lentini, Maria Luque, and Zachary Rosenblum. We thank our many composition students who inspired us to develop and refine the activities we share in this book.

We would also like to thank the following instructors, who provided valuable feedback and suggestions throughout the development process of this book: Brenda Ashcroft, Virginia Western Community College; Beau Boudreaux, Tulane University; Osen Bowser, Community College of Baltimore County; Carolyn Calhoon-Dillahunt, Yakima Valley Community College; Cheryl Cardoza, Truckee Meadows Community College; Bethany Davila, University of New Mexico; Marie Eckstrom, Rio Hondo College; James Fairchild, Maharishi University of Management; Kate Falvey, City University of New York and New York City College of Technology; Carrie Finestone, Middlesex Community College; Edward Glenn, Miami Dade College; Kyle Goehner, Community College of Baltimore County; Regina Golar, Judson College; Sharon Hayes, Community College of Baltimore County; Robert Huxell, Cincinnati State University; Brent Kendrick, Lord Fairfax Community College; Janet Kirchner, Southeast Community College; Loren Kleinman, Passaic County Community College; Julie Kratt, Cowley Community College; Kathryn Lane, Northwestern State University; Mary Leonard, Wytheville Community College; Dennis Lynch, Elgin Community College; Carol Martinson, Polk State College; Gail Marxhausen, Lone Star College; Gwen McIntyre, Atlantic Cape Community College; Josie Mills, Arapahoe Community College; Linda Mininger, Harrisburg Area Community College; Lisa Mott, Santa Rosa Junior College; Caryn Newberger, Austin Community College; Chris Nordquist, Arapahoe Community College; Carla Nyssen, California State University, Long Beach; Brit Osgood-Treston, Riverside Community College; Jennifer Pacheco, Olympic College; Taunya Paul, York Technical College; Robert Pontious, Brunswick Community College; Lynn Reid, Fairleigh Dickinson University; Carolee Ritter, Southeast Community College; Claire Roof, Ivy Tech Community College; Phip Ross, Southeast Community College; Rebecca Samberg, Housatonic Community College; Danielle

Santos, North Shore Community College; Stacey Stover, Austin Community College; Jennifer Taylor, Northern Virginia Community College; Kerry Taylor, Anne Arundel Community College; Jacqueline Tiermini, Finger Lakes Community College; Jeremy Trabue, Chemeketa Community College; Karen Uehling, Boise State University; Greg Underwood, Pearl River Community College; Michelle Van de Sande, Arapahoe Community College; and Carol Zitzer-Comfort, California State University, Long Beach.

Lastly, we thank our families for their support, encouragement, and understanding as we wrote this book.

Emily Isaacs
Catherine Keohane

Teaching with *LaunchPad Solo for Readers and Writers*

Pairing *Intersections* with *LaunchPad Solo for Readers and Writers* helps students succeed at their own pace.

Available free when packaged with *Intersections*, *LaunchPad Solo for Readers and Writers* can help you integrate skills-based practice into your teaching with *Intersections*, allowing you to more efficiently track students' progress with reading, writing, and grammar skills in an active learning arc that complements the book.

To package *LaunchPad Solo for Readers and Writers* with *Intersections*, use ISBN **978-1-319-08266-6**.

Assigning a project for which students will need to develop a strong thesis?

Start with the thesis statements unit in *LaunchPad Solo for Readers and Writers* to assess what students know.

Before turning to Chapter 2, "Breaking It Down: An Approach to Successful College Writing," in *Intersections*, have students complete the **pre-test** to get a sense of students' background knowledge of the topic. With this insight, you can meet them where they are.

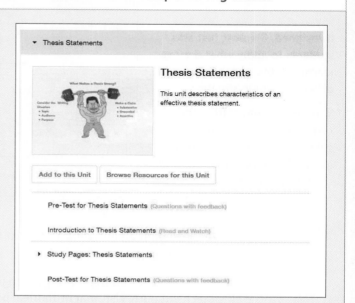

Then, from *Intersections*, assign appropriate toolkits based on the results of the pre-test.

For example, if the pre-test shows many students cannot identify thesis statements, you might spend class time on Toolkit 2.4, "Drafting a Thesis," as they work on drafts.

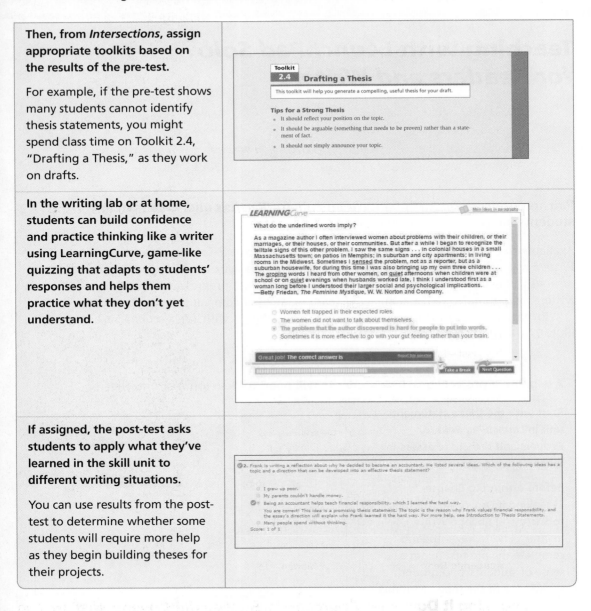

Toolkit 2.4 Drafting a Thesis

This toolkit will help you generate a compelling, useful thesis for your draft.

Tips for a Strong Thesis
- It should reflect your position on the topic.
- It should be arguable (something that needs to be proven) rather than a statement of fact.
- It should not simply announce your topic.

In the writing lab or at home, students can build confidence and practice thinking like a writer using LearningCurve, game-like quizzing that adapts to students' responses and helps them practice what they don't yet understand.

LEARNING Curve — Main Ideas in paragraphs

What do the underlined words imply?

As a magazine author I often interviewed women about problems with their children, or their marriages, or their houses, or their communities. But after a while I began to recognize the telltale signs of this other problem. I saw the same signs . . . in colonial houses in a small Massachusetts town; on patios in Memphis; in suburban and city apartments; in living rooms in the Midwest. Sometimes I sensed the problem, not as a reporter, but as a suburban housewife, for during this time I was also bringing up my own three children . . . The groping words I heard from other women, on quiet afternoons when children were at school or on quiet evenings when husbands worked late, I think I understood first as a woman long before I understood their larger social and psychological implications.
—Betty Friedan, *The Feminine Mystique*, W. W. Norton and Company.

○ Women felt trapped in their expected roles.
○ The women did not want to talk about themselves.
⊙ The problem that the author discovered is hard for people to put into words.
○ Sometimes it is more effective to go with your gut feeling rather than your brain.

Great job! The correct answer is   Report this question

Take a Break   Next Question

If assigned, the post-test asks students to apply what they've learned in the skill unit to different writing situations.

You can use results from the post-test to determine whether some students will require more help as they begin building theses for their projects.

2. Frank is writing a reflection about why he decided to become an accountant. He listed several ideas. Which of the following ideas has a topic and a direction that can be developed into an effective thesis statement?

○ I grew up poor.
○ My parents couldn't handle money.
⊙ Being an accountant helps teach financial responsibility, which I learned the hard way.
   You are correct! This idea is a promising thesis statement. The topic is the reason why Frank values financial responsibility, and the essay's direction will explain why Frank learned it the hard way. For more help, see Introduction to Thesis Statements.
○ Many people spend without thinking.
Score: 1 of 1

For more information about *LaunchPad Solo for Readers and Writers*, visit **macmillanlearning.com/readwrite**.

To sign up for WebEx trainings with pedagogical specialists and to access round-the-clock tech support, visit **macmillanlearning.com/catalog/training.aspx**.

Table of Contents

3 Toolkits for Reading and Writing / 35

What Are Toolkits?   35

4 Language and Identity: Are We Made with Words? / 168

Language and Identity

Rafael Campo, "The Way of the Dinosaurs" 172

"By learning English, I hoped I would someday forget Spanish completely. In fact, I believed that only by *unlearning* Spanish could I finally leave Cuba behind and become truly American."

Arthur Chu, "Breaking Out the Broken English" 178

"The accent of our parents is the accent of the grimy streets of Chinatown with its mahjong parlors and fried food stalls and counterfeit jewelry, so we work to wipe away all traces of that world from our speech so we can settle comfortably into our roles as respectable middle-class doctors, lawyers, engineers, hundreds of miles from Chinatown."

Tracy López, "Non-Spanish-Fluent Latinas: 'Don't Judge Us'" 182

"For U.S. Latinos, not speaking Spanish is often a source of insecurity or even shame. Lacking Spanish fluency brings with it judgment from other Latinos in the community as well as a loss of opportunity."

Linguistic Profiling

Patricia Rice, "Linguistic Profiling: The Sound of Your Voice May Determine If You Get That Apartment or Not" 186

"Many Americans can guess a caller's ethnic background from their first hello on the telephone. However, the inventor of the term 'linguistic profiling' has found . . . that when a voice sounds African-American or Mexican-American, racial discrimination may follow."

failure from an early age. They embraced the 'cognitive quirks' that made school and sometimes relationships tough, but also made them charming."

"I was finding it harder and harder to cope with everything, and my resolve was wearing very thin. The school was keeping a close, watchful eye on me, and to everyone, I became a spectacle. I was reduced to this 'thing' that could explode at any moment."

"I'm right here fathering my son. I want to love him, not change him. My son skipping and twirling in a dress isn't a sign that a strong male figure is missing from his life; to me it's a sign that a strong male figure is fully vested in his life and committed to protecting him and allowing him to grow into the person who he was created to be."

"In a society that still often expects men to be tough and rugged and women to be gentle and pretty, embracing their inner tomboy allows females to stand out and be rewarded for activities, rather than appearance or demeanor."

"Since then, the awareness that I was in the wrong body, living the wrong life, was never out of my conscious mind—never, although my understanding of what it meant to be a boy, or a girl, was something that changed over time."

"What's more masculine: being a strong, silent, unemployed absentee father, or actually fulfilling your half of the bargain as a breadwinner and a dad?"

"[M]en are simultaneously accused of being lacking in chivalry, while also insulting women with chivalry. Some women also feel pulled between rejecting chivalry out of allegiance with feminism, and embracing it because it makes some men feel more comfortable."

"So here's the simple question with no simple answer: Is chivalry sexist?"

"At a time when black girls' lives and looks are under assault, our daughters deserve no less than to grow up with the same life-affirming benefits that sports have provided our sons and that have propelled Mo'ne into the stratosphere. If her example encourages other black girls and women to get in the game, that could be her greatest accomplishment of all."

Rhetorical Table of Contents

Narration

Description/Informative

Cause and Effect

Classification

Definition

Argument

Intersections

A Thematic Reader for Writers

Getting Active

An Approach to Successful College Reading

In This Chapter

Introduction: Getting Active

Have you ever read carefully for thirty minutes and then realized you didn't remember anything you just read? What about when you've read hundreds of words but can't come up with a sentence of your own to explain what those words communicated?

If you've ever found yourself in either of these situations, you are like millions of students who discover that reading for college is hard and requires new habits and strategies.

At the core, successful college readers are active, not passive.

Let's explain by way of a comparison: Think for a moment of academic reading as an active experience, like playing soccer, instead of a viewing experience, like watching soccer on television. What is the difference? *Watching* a player on the U.S. men's national soccer team position his body, pull back his leg, and strike the ball with the right force and direction to drive it over the goalie's head and into a top corner is amazing, but it doesn't much help you repeat this performance with your own team. *Playing* or *practicing* soccer every day, however, allows you to learn how to get in the right position to strike the ball with appropriate force and accuracy. Much (though not all) of what the successful athlete does well is learned by practice, and practice over time makes difficult, highly skillful movements look natural and easy.

Reading well is a lot like playing sports well: It requires frequent practice — not only playing in the big game but also doing practice drills. To improve your overall reading skills, you can simply read frequently and for many hours at a time. But to practice and improve your reading skills *for college*, you need to become an *active, critical reader*; this chapter offers strategies for doing so.

Reading Terms

To get started, it's useful to become familiar with terms that college professors use when they talk about reading. These terms are also used throughout *Intersections*.

Text: High school teachers often talk about stories, essays, or books, and although these terms are also used by college professors, frequently a professor will refer to a "text" instead. *Text* is an umbrella term that is used to label any kind of item that is read, viewed, listened to, or otherwise "studied." A text can be an essay, a story, an article, a poem, a video, a blog post, an audio file, and so on. Instructors may refer to a "reading" to mean a text, as we often do in *Intersections*.

Note on terminology: It is best to use the term *story* only when referring to fiction or a narrative. Although we often hear references to "news stories" when discussing the media, a nonfiction *essay* is not a story. In addition, a *passage* refers to a part of a whole; thus, it is inappropriate to refer to a whole essay as a passage.

Genre: A category or type of text, sometimes referred to as a *mode*. There are *musical genres* (jazz and classical, for example), *film genres* (horror and comedy, for example), *literary genres* (confessional poetry and science fiction, for example), and *essay genres*. Following are the essay genres, broadly defined, that you will be asked to read in *Intersections*:

> **Narrative:** An essay that presents a nonfiction personal story about the author or someone else, and that typically makes its points indirectly, through the story itself.

> **Report:** An essay that provides a summary of information and findings, and often presents recommendations about a particular subject or problem.

> **Analysis:** An essay that provides an examination of information or an issue. This examination may take the form of comparison, of explaining cause and effect, of process analysis, or of another method that breaks down the issue.

> **Argument:** An essay that takes a position on a subject of debate or disagreement, and supports that position by presenting evidence and discussion. It may also attempt to persuade or convince readers to accept that position.

Thesis: An overarching, all-encompassing point, claim, or argument that a writer makes. The thesis explains the position that a writer has taken and will attempt to prove. A thesis is always present in argumentative essays and sometimes present in narrative or descriptive essays. A thesis is seldom found in reports.

Main idea: The concept, idea, point, or unifying topic that organizes an essay or a report. It is similar to a thesis in that it unifies a text, but it is different in that it does not state a position. Although less common, some narratives may include a main idea.

Supporting claim: One of several smaller claims made in an essay that support a thesis or that relate to a main idea. A claim is a statement that is accompanied by evidence or support.

Supporting point: The information, example, quotation, or data point that is presented to support a thesis or a supporting claim.

Topic sentence: A sentence provided early in a paragraph that indicates the point or focus of the paragraph, providing readers with a good idea of the areas covered within the paragraph. Not all well-written paragraphs have a topic sentence, but many do.

Inference or prediction: An educated guess. Successful readers make informed, reasonable guesses before beginning to read — and even while reading, in anticipation of an upcoming section.

Point of view—first person, second person, and third person: The perspective from which authors choose to present their subject. The two most common points of view are **first person** (*I* or *we*) and **third person** (*he, she, they, one,* and *it*); the least common is **second person** (*you*). Often, genre will influence a writer's choice of point of view. For example, personal narratives are often written in first person because the writer is recounting his or her own experiences, and first person puts the emphasis on the writer. (When used in other genres, first person is often considered too informal.) As with other, more formal pieces of writing, reports and arguments are often written in third person, allowing the focus to be on the information being presented instead of on the writer. Second person is the least frequently used point of view, and it is sometimes considered too informal for academic writing. Because it places emphasis on the reader, it is often used in pieces that offer advice or directions (note that we use second person in this textbook as part of our effort to directly address students).

The Case for Reading outside of School

If there is anything that educators agree on, it's that students need to read more. The more you read, the better you read; the better you read, the better you write. Reading regularly makes learning easier and faster, and it makes the energy spent on learning more effective. Reading more improves your spelling, grammar, and vocabulary. If you don't enjoy reading, these are hard truths to swallow, but it doesn't change the fact that reading is the most important skill that you can develop, and even master, to improve your performance in school. Successful college students not only read frequently but also practice daily, in the same way that an athlete practices daily.

There are two pieces of good news.

First, if you've never been a reader, it is not too late. There are countless examples of successful people who became readers as adults: Malcolm X, a minister and leader of the civil rights movement of the 1950s and 1960s; Jim Adkins, front man for the rock band Jimmy Eat World; and Chris Stewart, Major League Baseball catcher, to name a few. Another, the director, actor, and writer Woody Allen, has said, "I didn't start reading until I was in my late teens, because I never liked to read. . . . I read because it's important to read. Every now and then something gives me pleasure, but mostly it's a chore for me to read" (9). Allen points to the value of reading even in cases where it is not pleasurable.

Second, for the purposes of becoming a better writer and a more capable student, it does not matter what you read—although to build your English reading skills, it is important to read texts written in English. You do not have to be a regular or avid reader of the *New York Times* or Shakespeare, or the latest winner of the Nobel Prize in Literature. You can read James Patterson, Nora Roberts, *Sports Illustrated*, the local newspaper, or your favorite entertainment blog. If you like fiction but find long novels hard to get through, try short stories or even flash or hint fiction (very short fiction, catered to a generation of people whose available time comes in small bursts). If you don't like fiction, nonfiction may be more appealing: Try biography, self-help, or memoir. If you have an interest in current events, sign up for a "news alert" on your phone so that you can read articles selected just for you. The number one priority is to get yourself to read more (of just about anything) and to read regularly.

Regardless of what you decide to read, make a plan to read regularly, even daily. If you ride public transportation, commit to reading for at least one leg of your commute. If you watch television to fall asleep, read every other night instead. Regular fifteen-minute bouts of reading will do more to improve your learning abilities, your reading comprehension, and your writing skills than just about anything else you could do. Once you get started, it will become easier. Reading can become a habit of which you can be proud.

Reading for College

What we advise for general reading development—reading regularly to improve your writing, fluency, vocabulary, grammatical strength, and overall abilities as a learner—is different from reading for college courses. Whereas you can read whatever you find most interesting or entertaining to build your general reading ability, you often have no choice in what you read for school. Professors assign readings, and you have to read and understand them.

Moving beyond Passive Reading

Many students complete the assigned reading but seem to get little or nothing out of the process. In such situations, they may have been reading passively: looking at the words but not processing them or taking steps to make sense of them. Passive readers have trouble recalling the main point, supporting points, or interesting details. When asked, "What's your view of the author's point?," the passive reader has trouble responding and typically says "I don't know" or "I agree, I guess." Of course, there are situations in which passive reading is appropriate—for example, when reading a blog post or a short story for pleasure, or other times when you won't need to use the information further. All too often, however, passive reading habits carry over into school situations, where they are extremely unhelpful. You cannot succeed in college simply by participating in class, completing assignments, and passing exams. Success in college is dependent on your ability not just to read what you're assigned but also to retain and draw on what you've learned from that reading.

Intersections is designed to help you become an active reader who retains information for use in class discussions, homework, and future writing assignments. We have provided questions, activities, and informational glosses designed to engage you in the readings and to help you practice active and critical reading so that you will start to feel more like the seemingly natural soccer player described at the beginning of this chapter.

For college reading assignments, you have to be an active and critical reader. In addition to the questions that accompany each reading in this book, activities to help focus and develop your academic reading skills are available in Toolkit section 1, "Getting the Most Out of Reading." Moreover, later in this chapter we present strategies to help make reading more productive. Successful readers will use some of these strategies as they read, selecting those they find most useful personally as well as those they feel are most helpful for a specific reading assignment. Try them out to see which ones work best for you.

Strategies for Academic Reading: Be Active, Be Critical

Good readers not only have to read a great deal but also, and more importantly, have to learn how to read actively rather than passively. Whereas passive readers have trouble recalling what they have read, active readers are able to summarize the reading (recall the main and supporting points) and describe a few striking key details. Just as importantly, active readers form an initial response to a reading, including points of agreement and disagreement, simply because they have been more active while reading. If we were to look at both an active and a passive reader, we'd see that the active reader is moving: taking notes; underlining key words, phrases, and sentences; and writing down questions. In contrast, the passive reader is sitting there, doing no more than turning the page.

We are especially likely to fall into passive reading when we're distracted or when we're faced with difficult texts — those filled with vocabulary or ideas that are new or unfamiliar. As writing teachers, we can admit to coming across certain articles — those on accounting, for example — full of words and concepts that are difficult for us to understand if we read passively. To understand an accounting article, we have to use deliberate strategies to break down the reading, making it memorable and understandable. When we — or you — encounter a difficult or unfamiliar text, it is time to pull out some serious academic reading strategies.

Along with reading actively (paying careful attention and working hard to understand and remember what you have read), you also need to read critically. That is, you need to push a little further, ask questions, and not accept an author's assertions or points without giving them some thought. Think of critical readers as doubters, skeptics, or people who simply want to know more. To be a good student, you need to adopt both an active and a critical approach to reading; in other words, you need to engage in academic reading.

Academic Reading Strategy 1: Read Aloud

If you realize you are not retaining or remembering what you are reading, try reading aloud for a while. Reading aloud helps you approach the ideas more closely. Reading aloud makes you slow down and focus, and this makes the words clearer, as they literally enter your brain through a different channel. When you read aloud, you essentially digest each word twice — when you speak it and when you hear it — increasing your comprehension.

Another way to take advantage of the benefits of reading aloud is to use a device that will do this for you. Many electronic readers have a feature that allows the machine to "read aloud" to you. This is most effective if you are closely following along with the text as well.

Academic Reading Strategy 2: Forecast — Predict, Guess

A good reader makes an informed guess about a text before reading it. As you prepare to read, ask yourself, "What do I think this reading will be about? What do I expect?" The following sources often provide clues to the answers; be sure to review them before beginning to read.

    Title: What does it suggest? What does it make you expect from the reading?

    Table of contents or chapter introduction: In most textbooks that contain readings, the authors of the book summarize each reading in the chapter introduction or in the table of contents. In *Intersections*, we offer a short quotation from each reading in the table of contents to provide an overview. These quotations provide a forecast of what the readings will be about.

For example, consider Chapter 4's "Non-Spanish-Fluent Latinas: 'Don't Judge Us,'" by Tracy López. Here is a guess based on the title of this essay: "I think the author will talk about how she and other people like herself — people who aren't fluent in Spanish, I am guessing — shouldn't be judged negatively by Latinas who are fluent."

You might find yourself with a question about the reading already. For example, in this case, you might wonder why the author is talking only about Latinas (women) and not also Latinos (men). It is useful to have questions about a reading right from the beginning.

As you read, you may find that sometimes your guesses are wrong. For example, while reading "Non-Spanish-Fluent Latinas: 'Don't Judge Us,'" you will discover that López does not offer personal experience as evidence, but that she does talk about how some Spanish-speaking Latinas criticize Latinas who do not speak Spanish. Even if pre-reading guesses are wrong, they are still valuable in that they help you get more involved as you read.

Academic Reading Strategy 3:
Profile the Author

Inexperienced students often do not pay attention to who has written what they're reading, whereas experienced students know that having some knowledge of the author may help with comprehension. Therefore, always make sure you notice who has written what you are reading. (If there is more than one author, notice that as well.) Doing so will also help you during class discussion or when writing about the reading because it is much clearer and more effective to refer to authors by name rather than as "he," "she," or "they."

After noting who the author is, you should figure out the author's credibility or authority. Why should you pay attention to this author's words? What expertise does the author bring to the topic? Does the expertise come from personal experience, research, or professional position? Is the author the source of the information? Or is the author a reporter — a professional writer — whose job is to report on other people's experiences or research?

To profile an author in this book, look at the headnote paragraph that comes before the reading. What are the author's personal facts? What does the author do for a living? What other information is provided? What clues might all this information provide about the reading? For example, look at the headnote about Tracy López on page 182. The first sentence begins: "A self-described 'gringa' (white girl), Tracy López is a bilingual freelance writer and novelist . . ." "Gringa" means a woman of non-Hispanic origin, so this information indicates that López is not writing about herself. Reading further, you might notice that López is interested in Latin American culture, is married, and has children. Based on this information, you can guess that even though she is not writing from personal experience (because she isn't a Latina), she might be writing about her family's experience, or perhaps the reading has something to do with Latin American life more generally, since she is very interested in that topic. Knowing something about the author helps you predict his or her perspective or focus and improves your ability to understand what you read.

Academic Reading Strategy 4:
Pre-read—Skim in Advance

Spend a few minutes skimming through a reading before beginning to read closely. Read any section headers and look at any images, charts, or other visuals. After you've reviewed these, quickly summarize them for yourself, putting the author's basic points in your own words. These are like headlines, telling you the basic point of the reading. Pre-reading these "headlines" makes reading and remembering easier.

Academic Reading Strategy 5:
Ask Yourself, "What Do I Already Know?"

Looking at the title and pre-reading the text may give you a sense of the topic. Before reading closely, think about what you might already know about the topic. You can use this prior knowledge to ask questions of the reading. For example, Chapter 7 includes a narrative essay by Temple Grandin titled "Autism and Visual Thought." You likely know a little something about autism. Consider what you already know—in this case, that autistic people have difficulty with social behaviors but often have great memories. As you read, consider whether the reading addresses this issue or any others that you have prior knowledge about.

Academic Reading Strategy 6:
Look for Key Signaling Words

Writers often try to flag important points with words that tell readers to pay special attention; therefore, finding these words can help you identify an essay's main points. Writers use a variety of signaling language to guide readers to their most important ideas; these words and phrases include the following:

Therefore	*In conclusion*
Thus	*Consequently*
Accordingly	*The point being that*
In closing	

Writers don't always use these exact words, but they choose language that similarly conveys urgency or summary. For example, in Chapter 8's "Why We Need to

Reimagine Masculinity," Andrew Romano begins his third-to-last paragraph with "It's clear that we've arrived at another crossroads—only today the prevailing codes of manhood have yet to adjust to the changing demands on men" (p. 333). This is an important sentence because Romano is summarizing a point he has been trying to make over the previous few paragraphs. The words that indicate that Romano is summarizing a central idea here are "It's clear that we've arrived at another crossroads." Although these words do not appear on the preceding list, they still announce that Romano is making a major statement to which he wants you to pay close attention. In this case, his point is that "today the prevailing codes of manhood have yet to adjust to the changing demands on men."

Academic Reading Strategy 7:
Annotate (Take Notes) and Write Questions

Writing forces you to wake up and make meaning of what you are reading. The easiest way to use writing to read better is to take notes and write down questions as you read. You can jot down these notes and questions on a separate piece of paper or even in the margins of the book (if you own it). What you're doing is being a skeptic, someone who does not blindly accept what they have read without first evaluating it. For example, in the margins of Grandin's article, we wrote these annotations:

> *How different are verbal and "visual spatial skills"?*
> *What problems might there be with visual thinking?*
> *What are abstract concepts? How do these relate to doors and gates?*

For a fuller discussion of annotation, see Toolkit 1.1 (p. 36).

Academic Reading Strategy 8:
Identify the Genre of the Reading to Evaluate It

As discussed in the "Reading Terms" section of this chapter (p. 2), a genre is a type of text: narrative, opinion, government report, historical analysis research report, news report, news analysis, poem, and so on. Because genre shapes what a writer does, identifying the genre of a text will provide you with useful clues about what to expect and about how you should respond to the reading. For example, reading the first sentence of "Autism and Visual Thought" (p. 280), you will discover that Grandin writes in the first person ("I" form): "I think in pictures." Reading further confirms that the text is written from the perspective of someone who is autistic, as the author offers her experiences and story to explain how she thinks through visualization, allowing you to recognize that her text is a narrative.

Genres are often very different from one another, and there are different criteria for judging their effectiveness or persuasiveness (or ineffectiveness or lack of persuasiveness). Let's consider four genres that you will find frequently in *Intersections*.

Narratives. In a narrative, the writer tells some part of his or her own story (or that of someone else), typically for the purpose of making a point about him- or herself or about a social or political issue. Narratives are subjective — or personal. Narratives are usually entertaining, full of details and drama, and intended to inspire readers' emotions. Thus, the writer's authority is personal, and the text's persuasiveness is tied to the facts of the story, the strength of the writing, and the writer's capacity to generate readers' sympathy. Examples of narratives in *Intersections* include Rafael Campo's "The Way of the Dinosaurs" (p. 172) and Alice Randall's "My Soul to Keep, My Weight to Lose" (p. 206).

Reports. In a report, the writer's primary responsibility is to convey information, and the author may or may not intend to be persuasive or even to try to make a point. A report is typically full of facts, description, data, and statistics, and the writing may be neutral or even dry. Report writers typically work to be objective. The writer's authority is not personal but is based on the quality and relevance of the information or data offered as well as its presentation. Examples of reports in *Intersections* include news articles such as Patricia Rice's "Linguistic Profiling: The Sound of Your Voice May Determine If You Get That Apartment or Not" (p. 186) and research articles such as Joe DeGuzman's "Targets of Caricature: Irish Immigrants in Nineteenth-Century America" (p. 241).

Analyses. In an analysis, the writer's task is to analyze — dissect, break down, examine — an issue by looking at its parts. An analysis contains information or evidence that is discussed in order to understand an issue. The writer's authority is based on the quality of the discussion and the persuasiveness of the analysis. Examples of analyses in *Intersections* include Rosemary Mahoney's "Why Do We Fear the Blind?" (p. 297) and Theodore R. Johnson III's "Chivalry, Feminism, and the Black Community" (p. 335).

Arguments. In an argumentative essay, the writer attempts to convince readers to consider or adopt a perspective on an issue. The writer's persuasiveness is best judged by the quality and relevance of the evidence and discussion offered to support that point, though writing style is hard to ignore. Examples of arguments in *Intersections* include Andrew Romano's "Why We Need to Reimagine Masculinity" (p. 329) and Mary Jo Kane's "Sex Sells Sex, Not Women's Sports" (p. 362).

Paying attention to genre as you read will help you know how, and on what criteria, you should evaluate the text. For example, it would be unfair to criticize a report for failing to present an argument, but it would be very reasonable to criticize an argument for not having a clear thesis.

Academic Reading Strategy 9:
Outline

Track what you are reading by creating a reading outline on a separate sheet of paper. This is especially helpful with difficult readings that you get distracted from or can't read all at once. As you read, be attentive to when the writer is making a point or claim that you understand, and write down a few words that summarize the point. You can review your outline when you get lost, as well as when you're trying to remember what you've read. For example, while reading "Autism and Visual Thought" (p. 280), you might start with the following:

- *Author Grandin is autistic and thinks in pictures to do her job with livestock*
- *Built cattle equipment because of autism-related abilities*
- *Autistics think in pictures*
- *Thinking this way helps her understand animals*

An outline that includes a short phrase or sentence for each paragraph essentially captures the text, showing how points develop and connect to one another.

Academic Reading Strategy 10:
Underline or Highlight

Underlining or highlighting can be especially useful when you want to identify and keep track of key points, terms, or examples in the text. Underlining and highlighting are often combined with other forms of annotation (marking the text); see Toolkit 1.1 for an annotation activity (p. 36). Any highlighting or underlining should be done carefully so that it makes important things stand out; this does not work if whole paragraphs are underlined or highlighted. Following are two methods of strategic underlining or highlighting:

Underline or highlight for summary: Many writers summarize what they are stating once or twice in each paragraph — at the beginning, at the end, or both. When you read a paragraph and find yourself confused, go back and look for a summary sentence, underlining or highlighting it.

Underline or highlight for key points: As you read, underline or highlight points, examples, and key words that stand out to you as being important or that you want to be able to return to easily later.

To demonstrate these methods, we present the first four sentences that we underlined when we read Temple Grandin's essay. These sentences were selected because they presented a key point or a summary:

Key Point: Words are like a second language to me.

Summary: Visual thinking has enabled me to build entire systems in my imagination.

Key Point: I value my ability to think visually, and I would never want to lose it.

Summary: One of the most profound mysteries of autism has been the remarkable ability of most autistic people to excel at visual spatial skills while performing so poorly at verbal skills.

Academic Reading Strategy 11:
Take Two-Column Quick Notes

While reading, make notes to keep track of what the author is saying and also what you are thinking. Divide a sheet of paper or computer document into two columns. In one column, make note of the author's points; in the second column, make note of your responses to those points.

NOTES ON RODGERS'S "COGNITIVE OUTLAWS" (P. 301)	
Author's Points	*My Response*
Lots of famous, talented people with dyslexia	*What about all the dyslexics who DON'T succeed at all?*
Do they succeed "in spite of the disability or because of it"?	*LOVE THIS: Great strength comes from great weakness.*
Her source Shaywitz argues: "They learn to think outside the box."	*Is there real evidence?*

Here's a tip: After you read each paragraph of a text, pause to ask yourself, "Is there a point here I need to remember?" If so, write it down in the "Author's Points" column along with a note about your response in the other column. If you think the paragraph is an elaboration or illustration of an earlier point, no notes are needed, so read on.

Academic Reading Strategy 12:
Identify an Author's Bias, Blind Spot, or Prejudice

As you read, pay attention to the types of information the writer presents, how the writer discusses the information, and whether the author displays some bias, blind spot, or prejudice that might call into question the persuasiveness of the essay or the credibility of the author. For example, in a report, does the writer present just one side of an issue? In an argument, does the writer fail to acknowledge other points of view? In a narrative, does the writer seem to leave out important details, making you feel as though you are not getting the true story? Cases like these all suggest a writer who has a bias, blind spot, or prejudice. Typically, report writers who present more than one side of an issue and argument writers who acknowledge other points of view are trying not to be biased.

After Reading: Preparing to Discuss the Reading in Class

Whenever you are assigned a reading, you should know there is a good chance that your professor will want to discuss that text in class. Quite often, a reading is assigned for the purpose of provoking class discussion. Your instructor is hoping that you will come to class ready to speak, and expecting you to express interest and excitement about the reading. If your teacher has not assigned you any questions, and if this state of readiness does not come naturally to you, you will need to prepare a little more for class. Consider the following generic questions as a practice tool before class:

- What did you like most about the reading?
- What is the author's main idea or point of view?
- What problem / frustration / irritation / disagreement do you have with the author?
- What point or idea was confusing or unclear?
- What did you learn from this reading that you didn't know before?

By asking yourself several of these questions in advance of class, you will be ready when your instructor turns to you and asks, "What did you think of the reading?" As a prepared student, you will know that the answer is not "I liked it" (or worse, "It was boring"), and will instead be able to offer an informed comment based on one of your practice questions.

Good Reading Habits

While these reading strategies will help you develop your academic reading skills, adopting good reading habits will enable you to read more efficiently and effectively.

First, make the environment work for you rather than against you. Reading speed and comprehension decrease in the presence of noise and visual distractions, and also when the reader is tired, preoccupied, hungry, or under the influence of drugs or alcohol. No one can read well with a video "in the background," while friends are talking nearby, or when checking his or her phone every two minutes. People can't comprehend what they are reading if they have to keep waking themselves up. Therefore, to be a better, more productive reader, you need to put yourself in the right environment — one that is quiet and visually calm — and be awake and alert. If you are too tired, it's better to go to sleep and wake up in a few hours or early the next morning. You read much better when you are fresh.

Second, manage your temptations. Many temptations can distract you from reading or other tasks: checking social media, socializing, eating, shopping online, watching videos, and so on. You cannot read well when participating in any of these activities at the same time. Our advice is not to try to give up all temptations completely but rather to manage temptation by scheduling regular breaks from reading (or writing) so that the temptations work as a reward. How long someone can productively read varies from person to person, but the guide shown in the figure at right has worked well for many of our students.

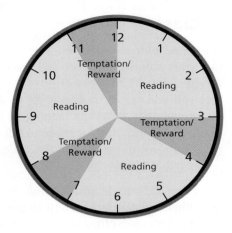

The point here is to break up difficult tasks into manageable chunks, and to reward yourself for what is truly hard work. You may have experienced some version of this reward system being used by teachers or supervisors; the only difference here is that you need to be in charge of yourself. Using a timer on your phone works well, making it easier for you to stay on task for the full amount of time you have allotted yourself.

Finally, plan your time wisely, making sure to leave enough time for your work. Unsuccessful students greatly underestimate how long it takes to complete a reading task. In fact, we all read at different rates. Narrative and descriptive texts typically allow for the quickest reading, while reports and analytic articles — that is, most of what you need to read for college classes — take much longer. In general, the average adult reads 250 words per minute (WPM), the average college student reads 300 WPM, and speed readers can read 675 WPM.

What is your reading rate?

Knowing your rate will allow you to plan how much time you need to complete your assigned reading. If you go to an online search engine and type in "find out your reading rate," you will find many programs that will allow you to figure out your rate. Or you can take this short test to figure out your reading rate for non-narrative reading: Turn to the beginning of Chapter 2 (p. 16), set a stopwatch timer for two minutes, and start reading. When the timer goes off, stop reading and mark where you stopped. Then go back and count the number of lines of text you read. On average, this book has sixteen words per line, so multiply sixteen by the number of lines you've read. Then divide that number by two, and you have your WPM.

> Number of lines you read _____ × 16 ÷ 2 = your reading rate.

On average, each page of this textbook contains 440 words. Multiply the number of pages you need to read by the number of words per page, and then divide the total number of words by your WPM to estimate how long you should plan to read. You should plan an extra minute for every page so that you can think, underline, or make a note.

Number of pages to read _____ × 440 ÷ your WPM = _____
(amount of minutes you will need to read, not including extra annotation
minute).

Amount of minutes _____ + number of pages to read _____ =
ideal number of minutes you should set aside to complete the reading.

These calculations will give you a rough estimate of how long you should
expect to read. Of course, some texts will take less time to read, while others might
take more. An argument that presents a lot of evidence, for example, might take you
longer to read than a narrative.

Remember: Reading actively and critically takes practice, but like the soccer player's impressive ball-management skills, reading becomes easier with practice. What's
more, you will find that writing becomes easier, too, as we discuss in Chapter 2.

Academic Reading Strategies at a Glance

1. Read aloud
2. Forecast—predict, guess
3. Profile the author
4. Pre-read—skim in advance
5. Ask yourself, "What do I already know?"
6. Look for key signaling words
7. Annotate (take notes) and write questions
8. Identify the genre of the reading to evaluate it
9. Outline
10. Underline or highlight
11. Take two-column quick notes
12. Identify an author's bias, blind spot, or prejudice

Work Cited

Allen, Woody, and Stig Bjorkman. *Woody Allen on Woody Allen: In Conversation
with Stig Bjorkman.* Grove, 2005.

CHAPTER 2

Breaking It Down

An Approach to Successful College Writing

In This Chapter

Introduction: Breaking It Down

At first glance, an academic writing assignment appears straightforward. For example, consider this assignment: "Write a 3- to 4-page paper in which you take a position on the issues discussed by the authors we have read." This type of assignment, typically known as a position paper, issue paper, or response paper, is common in college classes. While this task sounds manageable enough, many writers struggle to complete it.

This writing assignment is difficult because behind the one-sentence instructions are dozens of unspecified tasks, starting with the first task, which is to overcome the instinct for procrastination. Most writers—students but also professors and professionals—procrastinate, coming up with a million things to do before finally placing fingers on a keyboard or putting pen to paper. It is the most common and perhaps most difficult problem that people have with writing: sitting down to do it.

Writers procrastinate because most assignments do not come with a set of directions that they can follow one by one in the same way they might complete a homework assignment that asks them to answer questions 1 through 20. Writing a paper is too complicated to tackle in the same mechanical way someone might sort and fold the laundry or answer a series of questions about a reading assignment. With a writing assignment, it is not at all obvious how to complete the job, and it takes energy, experience, and knowledge to break the assignment down well enough to complete the job. Yet that is exactly what needs to be done.

"Break it down" is the advice and direction that we offer again and again as writing teachers, and you will see this direction throughout *Intersections*. In this book, we are *breaking it down* for you, helping you figure out how to develop the skills to perform the many tasks that are required but not specified in the seemingly straightforward assignments that college students face every semester.

Successful students and professional writers have figured out how to break down their writing tasks so that they can do their best work. In breaking down the process, writers become less anxious, less likely to procrastinate, and more able not only to get started but also to finish. The strategies and assignments offered in *Intersections* are designed to provide specific direction, instruction, and support for writing academic papers that are original and compelling in their ideas, but that also follow academic rules and conventions for writing. The toolkits, activities, and questions in *Intersections* provide guidance to help writers take action when they feel like giving up.

In this chapter we offer an overview of strategies that allow students to become successful academic writers, ending with our list of the essential elements of academic essays. Based on the five elements required in most academic writing, this list will help you review and check your work. It's a list we have in our heads as writers, readers, and teachers, and one we hope you will adopt to guide and support your writing as well.

Writing Terms

It's useful to review or become familiar with some of the terms that writing instructors use when talking about writing and the writing process. These terms are also used throughout *Intersections*.

The writing process: The many activities or steps that a writer can use to go from an assignment or idea to a final, finished text: prewriting, drafting, revising, and editing, for example. The phrase *writing process* emphasizes that there are many steps, and that good writers do not simply sit down and write a "final" essay all at once. Rather, they break down the larger task and take it step by step. The writing process is recursive, which is to say that writers often find they have to repeat earlier activities; for example, you may return to brainstorming after you have drafted your entire essay. It is also nonlinear, which means that writers do not typically write an essay in order, introduction straight through to conclusion.

Prewriting: A term used to describe the activities that writers engage in before they actually draft their essay. Writers can brainstorm ideas through freewriting, answering questions about a reading, making lists, creating graphic organizers (such as bubble maps), or writing an outline, to name just a few methods. It is valuable to try out lots of different ways for generating ideas through prewriting, as most writers find they need different methods at different times. Prewriting activities that successful writers often use include:

Freewriting: An activity that pushes writers to start writing, even when they feel they have nothing to say or don't know what to say. Freewriting is almost magical, drawing out ideas and thoughts from the unconscious by allowing total freedom in terms of topic, structure, punctuation, and even the expectation to finish a thought. What makes freewriting work is mechanical. When freewriting, you commit to writing—moving your pencil and forming words even when you don't know what to write.

Writing briefly: A signature method of *Intersections*, an activity that is designed to uncover ideas that the writer didn't know he or she had. Although related to freewriting, the writing briefly method has you write in response to a prompt and stay focused on that prompt (e.g., What is good writing?). As with freewriting, you simply write down everything that comes into your head, not worrying about whether what you write is elegant, clear, or "good enough." Turn off the doubting, judgmental voice in your head and just write to the prompt—that's the only requirement. The point is to generate lots of material and to use the act of writing to discover what you know and think.

Brainstorming: An activity that takes many forms but is essentially any kind of writing you do to generate more ideas. Some people like to use graphic organizers (charts or graphs that use visuals to represent ideas), while others like making lists of words and phrases, or of key ideas, points, and examples.

Outlining: Involves planning for a writing task by writing down or listing each topic and subtopic (or point and subpoint) in a linear form that directs writing from the introduction to the conclusion.

Drafting or generating writing: A process that involves writing sentences, paragraphs, and the entire essay without worrying about getting it all right, as there will be time to rewrite later. Drafting is about pushing ahead, getting ideas out, and not giving up. It's about trying out ideas and seeing which ones are worth keeping. When you draft, you get from the beginning all the way to the end; however, the draft you have written is *not* the final draft.

Revising: The process of rewriting your essay significantly to change or improve its focus, development, organization, and clarity. Good revision work requires cutting out phrases, sentences, and even paragraphs, and also adding new ones. It often involves moving essay parts around. For most student writers, *a successfully revised essay is at least 50 percent different* from how it appeared at the first draft stage.

Editing: In the editing phase, writers focus on clarity, correctness, and even elegance, looking closely at sentences and words. During editing, writers attend to grammar, mechanics, and the rules of writing.

Peer review: The process of having an essay reviewed by a classmate or another reader who is willing to give feedback. Peer reviews can be written or oral, formal or informal, focused on a specific concern or open to whatever a writer would like feedback on. Peer review feedback helps a writer revise his or her draft.

Thesis: The point a writer makes, also called an argument or a claim. The thesis must be a point that is arguable and about which there can be some disagreement or debate. In other words, it needs to be proven. For example: *Cats meow* is not a thesis (there is no debate), but *Cats meow because they are neurotic animals* is a thesis (a position that is definitely up for debate). A writer's thesis is typically focused enough to be stated in one sentence, often called the *thesis statement*. In academic writing, writers often find it useful to place the thesis at the end of the introductory paragraph. A thesis is required in argument essays.

Focus: The guiding purpose, question, topic, or argument of a piece of writing that runs through the paragraphs, tying them together. If an essay has a consistent focus, it has **unity**. In an argument essay, the focus is related to the thesis.

Development: Involves the expanding of ideas, paragraphs, and whole essays through description, details, examples, evidence, or discussion. To write a developed paragraph or essay is to go beyond first thoughts, memorized facts, or prior beliefs.

Discussion: Explaining, reflecting, and reasoning to go beyond the superficial or obvious. This is the thinking part—where you *make meaning* rather than just describe or summarize what someone else means. Discussion involves explaining how you are viewing or interpreting your examples, and how you see your evidence working to support your thesis or guiding purpose.

Organization: The arrangement of an essay's sentences, paragraphs, and ideas in a logical, clear, and pleasing order that makes sense to readers.

Clarity: The clear expression of ideas with respect to vocabulary and grammar, and to following the rules and conventions expected by an academic community. It involves editing for **coherence**—that is, making sure that sentences are clear and correct, and can be understood by readers.

Writing conventions: The rules that writers within a specific community follow. For example, it's a rule that we capitalize the first letter of the first word in a sentence, and end the sentence with a period. You have likely memorized and internalized these and many other rules. However, not all communities of writers follow the same writing rules. For example, the rules for writing song lyrics are

different from the rules for writing an academic essay. And scientists write differently than do literary scholars. Within academic writing, however, there are some
widely agreed upon conventions and rules that your teachers and *Intersections* will
help you master.

The Shape of an Academic Essay

Unless given other directions, students can assume that they should follow the
conventions for academic writing when structuring essay and paper assignments.
Academic writing is a genre — or style — that has its own set of conventions or
expectations. That is, readers of academic writing expect to find a certain shape,
style, and level of formality. In terms of shape or structure, readers expect to find
the following:

- An introduction, which presents the topic and provides the primary focus or
thesis (the point the writer will prove in the essay)
- Body paragraphs, which provide supporting evidence and discussion
- A conclusion, which wraps up the essay
- Appropriate citation of sources

Editing your writing for appropriate style and level of formality is usually easier
to do after the essay shape is established (we discuss editing later in this chapter).
We suggest that during the drafting and revision stage, you reread and rewrite your
essay to make sure it has the shape and content it needs.

Drawing on the sample essay "Reforming Social Media," by student Miryam
Abraham (p. 445), we see an example of the basic *shape* of an academic essay.

The **introduction**, usually a paragraph long, introduces the topic, the main
examples, and the focus or thesis. In the introduction, you provide the framework
that guides your readers through the essay. The introduction creates expectations
regarding the essay, including what it will be about and what it will do.

Here is Miryam's introduction:

> "Don't judge a book by its cover" is a saying we have all heard at least once in
> our lives. With the current technological advancements of the Internet world, we
> have more than just a cover to judge each person by, because social media has led
> to oversharing. The use of social media, and the exposure of people's lives online,
> leaves plenty of open-ended opinions and ideas that can be summed up about each
> person. Also, it can lead to judgments of what's portrayed as one's online life. In
> articles by Andrea Shea and Julian B. Gewirtz and Adam B. Kern, the authors have
> voiced their opinions about the somber effects of social media today. Oversharing
> on social media can lower one's self-esteem and lessen one's privacy. However,
> regulations can help prevent further damages caused by the social networking and
> online hysteria that have taken over so many lives.

In this introduction, Miryam makes the following clear:

- **Topic:** oversharing on social media

- **Examples that will be used:** articles by Shea and by Gewirtz and Kern, negative judgments by others, lowered self-esteem, and privacy concerns

- **Thesis:** "Oversharing on social media can lower one's self-esteem and lessen one's privacy. However, regulations can help prevent further damages caused by the social networking and online hysteria that has taken over so many lives."

The **body paragraphs** offer evidence that supports the focus or thesis and include discussion of that evidence. In the body paragraphs, you provide examples and explain how they support your thesis or guiding purpose.

In this body paragraph, Miryam provides support for her assertion that online sharing can be harmful through **expansion** of — writing more about — this point.

> In this age of modern technology, connections can be a fingertip away. With social media being so available to almost anyone, anywhere, it's almost impossible to be unidentified. With the ease of locating anyone, there is a lack of privacy, and social media can be a disadvantage to those who may have outdated information online. In the article written by Julian B. Gewirtz and Adam B. Kern titled "Escaping Digital Histories," the authors bring up a point about the younger generations and the problems they will face with the social media epidemic. They argue that people may change their views, their beliefs, or their appearance as they age or mature and then forget to update these changes online. Therefore, the writers pinpoint that "these misrepresentations matter because they can shape unfair opinions or even cause unnecessary harm" (Gewirtz and Kern 400). This dilemma creates a need for encouraging new laws to help manage these websites and to help protect one's past from seeping into one's future. Preventive measures such as limiting how many posts each person can add each day would help resolve the issue of oversharing. They would help social media sites contain less information for viewers and protect people from losing out on employment opportunities. These new laws could also better shape the children of the future.

In this body paragraph, Miryam does the following:

- Expands on the problem of oversharing by raising the issue of misjudgment based on outdated posts
- Refers to and quotes points made by Gewirtz and Kern
- Finishes the paragraph by tying this example to her argument that the problems linked to oversharing can be solved by limiting posts

The **conclusion**, often presented as a separate paragraph in an academic essay, is your last chance to make your point. Together with the introduction, the conclusion frames your argument, helping your readers process the information you've presented in your essay. A successful, strong conclusion does more than summarize your essay. Your readers should feel as if they have gotten somewhere after reading your essay, and they should have a deeper understanding of the topic as well. Conclusions should feel *conclusive*; thus, they are not the place to raise new ideas.

Miryam takes a reflective strategy in her conclusion, choosing language that is definitive and forceful to help drive home her argument.

> Finally, social media websites are windows that have been opened wide for anyone to peer into, enabling viewers to pry into others' personal affairs. When the world of technology came about, no one knew that social media was going to take over with the popularity and the push it did. However, while social media can be useful for connecting people, those connections can have horrible effects, especially in terms of lack of privacy and lowering self-esteem. Like with everything else in this world, too much of a good thing can easily turn bad. New regulation to lessen the vast and widening oversharing of information would be a benefit for all those who feel negative about their lives online. Privacy is a major concern, and the reduction of social media in each home that would result from regulation would benefit the entire family by exposing them to less negative attention. Because oversharing is a threat to privacy and self-esteem, preventive measures should be enforced.

Miryam concludes her essay by doing the following:

- Pulling together the main supporting examples (the problems associated with oversharing)
- Reminding readers of her proposed solution (limiting posts)

Citation involves giving credit to sources for direct quotations and for ideas. There are several common academic citation styles (MLA, APA, and *Chicago*, for example), and different fields or disciplines use different citation styles. Miryam is using MLA style, and you will notice she gives a parenthetical page reference after the quotation in her body paragraph. Her essay also includes a Works Cited list (see p. 449 in the Appendix as well as Toolkit 5.13 on p. 134 for more on this citation style).

Clarity and Style

After attending to the shape of your writing, you need to attend to writing conventions: the grammatical, mechanical, and punctuation rules and guidelines that provide for clear communication between writers and readers. Examples of writing conventions that help with clarity include complete sentences, correct punctuation, consistent verb tense, and correctly italicized titles.

Often, there isn't enough time in class to go over many of these writing conventions in detail, in part because what each student needs to be taught varies. We try to do much of this teaching in Toolkit sections 5 and 6 of Chapter 3 by targeting specific conventions that we have found to be most difficult for students to master. Beyond the toolkits, a good handbook (for example, *A Writer's Reference*, by Diana Hacker and Nancy Sommers) will provide even more instruction about these surface-level conventions that enable you to write with clarity and style.

Consistently writing with clarity and style is a challenge; consequently, many writers give up on trying to be clear, declaring themselves "no good," as though there's nothing that can be done. That's wrong. All writers can become clearer and more expressive, and better able to follow the conventions of academic writing. You are likely to become able to express your ideas more clearly simply by writing and reading more, but you can significantly speed up improvement by being willing to reread and edit your own writing, and to take on one clarity problem at a time. In this course, you will likely be asked to work on your most glaring and frequent clarity problem first. Then, one problem solved, you'll be ready for the next one, and your writing will soon be noticeably clearer and better.

What Is Academic Writing?

Students often struggle with academic writing because it requires two qualities that appear to be contradictory, or opposites of each other:

Successful writing follows conventions and rules.

Successful writing requires original, deep thinking.

Some teachers may appear to value one quality more highly than the other, but it's important to be able to both follow the rules and use your own critical thinking. Students can be confused by writing assignments that emphasize either conventions and rules *or* original, deep thinking. We'll take a little time to compare these two types of assignments:

Formula Assignment: Convention and Rule Focused	Formless Assignment: Original, Deep-Thinking Focused
Write a five-paragraph essay that introduces and supports a thesis. In the first paragraph, write five sentences that generally address the topic, state your position, and provide three reasons for your point of view, ending with a thesis statement. Write three body paragraphs that each take up one of these reasons. Begin each body paragraph with a topic sentence that outlines its purpose, and use the four remaining sentences to explain why the reason covered in that paragraph supports your position. In the conclusion, wrap up the essay by restating the three reasons from the thesis statement.	Think long and deeply about the topic and the discussions we have had about it. Freewrite, brainstorm, and consider how your own perspective on the topic might be best expressed. There is no right answer here, but the best essays demonstrate deep engagement and thoughtfulness.

Focused only on conventions and rules, **formula assignments** are deceptively simple because they provide a rigid pattern—or formula—to follow. Imagine the essay in which you had the thesis statement "Dogs are man's best friend." You could likely write that essay without doing much real thinking at all—reason one: dogs are friendly; reason two: dogs are forgiving; reason three: dogs are loyal. Plug that into the assignment's directions, and you've got an essay written in very little time. The only problem is that the result is an overly simplistic essay that is probably very boring for both writer and reader. The formula approach flattens writing to a point where it's really just filling in the blanks, leaving no room for genuine thought.

On the other hand, **formless assignments** focus only on deep, original thinking, with no instruction on form. Experienced writers are able to handle such an assignment. Essentially, to address the sample assignment, you need to fill in the missing and unstated steps that are necessary to get to the point where you can write an essay that "demonstrate[s] deep engagement and thoughtfulness." Most writers, however, will struggle with this assignment, writing an essay that is missing some basic elements: The essay may lack focus or organization, be unevenly developed, or be essentially unclear. The formless assignment approach provides no structure to follow.

We are probably guilty of poking a little fun at these assignments, but we do so to make a point: Pretending that teachers have no expectations for how students should approach an assignment and pretending that good writing can be created by formula are equally limiting. Good writing is neither that free of form nor that formulaic. In fact, good writing lies between: It follows conventions and rules that a community of readers recognizes and values while allowing the writer enough freedom to say something interesting and worthwhile.

Despite appearances, formless assignments that emphasize original, deep thinking assume that you know to follow conventions and rules, too, whereas assignments that emphasize conventions and rules assume that you know that original, deep thinking is also required. You need to know how to fill in the gaps of these assignments, either providing the deep, original thinking that isn't specifically called for or following the conventions and rules that are not specified.

As students, you benefit from direct, explicit instruction both in original thinking and in the conventions that readers expect writers to follow; you benefit, in other words, from being asked thought-provoking questions *and* from being given information about the conventions of academic writing. *Intersections* is designed to help you by offering both.

Process Writing 101: Writing in College

Although it may appear as though accomplished writers produce good writing naturally, in fact, they do so because of practice, revision, and good habits. Writing teachers and researchers have developed a way to teach writing called the process writing approach. Advocates of process writing believe that complicated and difficult tasks (like writing essays) require that we break down the larger task into lots of little tasks, many of which are discussed under "Writing Terms" at the beginning of the chapter (p. 17). Beyond this basic principle, advocates of process writing have identified several attributes or qualities of successful writers: Successful writers read; they accept the nonlinear, recursive nature of writing (i.e., that final essays are *not* written straight from the first to the last word); they rewrite; they share their work and receive feedback on it; and they edit for clarity.

Successful Writers Read

To be a good writer, you have to spend time reading other people's writing, as well as rereading and revising what you have already written. As we discussed more fully in Chapter 1, good writers are not passive readers who have trouble remembering what they have read. Rather, they are *active, thinking, critical* readers.

Original ideas do not usually come entirely from a person's imagination but are inspired by or developed in response to the ideas of others. College courses—and *Intersections*, as well—heavily use reading to support learning. Writing instructors have found that students are inspired and provoked into thinking new ideas by reading, viewing, listening to, and thinking deeply about others' ideas.

Successful Writers Accept the Nonlinear, Recursive Nature of Writing

The nonlinear nature of successful writing: Even though it is hard, successful writers understand and accept that a page of good writing isn't generated in the order that it's read—that is, first word to final word, one right after the other. Effective writers realize they can and usually must work out of order, often doubling back to rewrite a section, paragraph, or sentence. Successful writers might start with the introduction but, just as likely, might start by writing an analysis of a point raised in one of the readings, something that will wind up as a body paragraph. Writing in a nonlinear way also means that writers who embrace this approach can skip ahead to a new section when they get stuck, thus keeping up the flow, confident in the knowledge that they can return later to the part that is frustrating them.

The recursive nature of successful writing: Successful writers also understand and accept that final drafts are very different from early drafts—that is, that much, if not most, of the writing and actual ideas that a writer begins with are ultimately replaced with better writing and ideas. Effective writers often start with activities designed to get ideas on paper so that they can be evaluated, developed, and—in some cases—discarded. These activities, presented in Chapter 3, help with generating, drafting, organizing, and revising writing. Because high-quality final products are the result of a recursive writing process, writers don't always approach the steps of writing in a seemingly logical order: generating writing, then outlining, then drafting. Sometimes they mix it up, and often they revisit activities in the course of writing—for example, brainstorming again after writing the first draft.

The Writing Process in Action: An Example

The following is an example of how a student might successfully use process writing to approach an essay question inspired by the readings in Chapter 5: "Why are Americans today struggling more than ever with obesity?"

The student writer, Janelle, has read a few articles on this topic and is now faced with the task of writing a first draft. Observe how Janelle goes about writing this first draft, which she spends about an hour on: She's very casual, she makes lots of mistakes, and she leaves big holes that she'll fill in later; however, she still manages to begin to answer the question by regularly reminding herself of it and by pushing through to a possible conclusion. Here's a look inside Janelle's thought process as she drafts her essay:

I'll start with generating writing about the question—why are we obese?—just quick and fast to see if I have any ideas.

I'll try generating writing by brainstorming a list:

"*Why are we obese?*"

- because we don't walk to school, or walk as much anyway
- because we don't have to work physically at home—have washing machines, don't have farms or vegetable gardens, have machines that do it
- because we have more junk food [is that true? Can I find a stat? Could quote that article in the book] and junk food is cheaper than healthy food
- because of bigger portion sizes and juice—one of the readings said that juice was terrible; that people think it's good for them, but it's not
- because it's not embarrassing to be a little fat—everyone else is, too
- because we live in a very stressed world, and food makes us feel better!

Okay, now I'll go ahead and write. Ran out of brainstorming ideas, got an idea for a beginning.

Draft Beginning

I saw a documentary on television [*title? Don't remember*] about school integration in the South [*?*] and even though the main story was about racial discrimination, the big thing I kept noticing was how skinny all the people were. This documentary was shot in the 1940s [*check date*]. The kids and teenagers were all skinny. Not unhealthy, but they didn't have any extra weight on them. In comparison, today when you walk through a school, you see some skinny kids but lots of chubby ones, and even some very heavy ones.

[*What's the question again? What am I supposed to say? Oh yes, why are Americans struggling with obesity; oh no, am I off topic?*]

I myself am somewhere in the middle, and I don't think anyone would think I was really fat. But maybe if I lived back in the days of the documentary, I'd be the fattest one in the room! So yes, definitely, Americans are fatter than they used to be. Statistics [*find one!*] show that, but so does just looking at pictures or film from the past.

Why are we fatter? Why are we obese? [*take out these questions later*]

Although I have recently learned that there's an "obesity epidemic," and I have always noticed that a lot of people are getting really big, honestly, I have never really thought about why this happened. Here's what I think now. [*I know I need more here, but can't think of what . . .*]

[*list of reasons—doesn't have to be three!, and not sure what order, but I'll use my ideas from brainstorming here*]

What I really think is that the biggest reason why we are overweight now more than in earlier times is because of how little most of us move. I know that I lived a life of little moving, that is until I got to college, where we have to walk all the time. At home I would go everywhere by car, and almost always I was able to park close to where I wanted to go. Gym was once a week, and we often had a health lecture or saw a movie. And once a week is not enough anyway. The only people who move a lot are student-athletes, and really, most of us aren't that. What I notice now that I am in college is that I walk a lot more. I don't have a car. My dorm is at least ten minutes from my classes, and sometimes even more. Waiting for the shuttle bus takes more time than walking, so I just walk. I probably walk for 30 or 40 minutes a day. While I haven't lost weight yet, I notice I can walk better, and I think that if I were to change my eating just a little I could actually lose weight, and certainly be in better health.

[*something needed here to connect*]

What I really think is that we as a society should redesign the way children and adolescents, and even adults, travel. There should be much more walking built into our daily lives, much less driving in cars. [*say more here, give examples?*] For every hour a person walks, xx calories are burned [*check the article we read in class*], and so that would mean xx calories a week if you walked every day, and xx calories a year. There are 2,000 calories in a pound [*I think, check*], so that would mean a person would either lose xx pounds every year, or be able to eat an extra xx calories every day without gaining weight! Walking is definitely the best way to solve the obesity epidemic because it's something just about everyone can do, it doesn't cost any money, and it really works.

The only problem is with time: Who has time to walk? Between work and school and family, it's hard to find time to walk.

Janelle isn't finished with her essay, but she has accomplished a great deal in this first draft. What's important to notice is that she has successfully generated writing to get the ideas going, drafted through to the end, and come up with a tentative conclusion. She has worked on the question, and some of what she has written is likely to show up in the final draft. Other parts won't, and certainly she needs to fill in and develop her essay with more information.

Notice that one of her strategies is to put in "xx," blanks, and little notes to herself as placeholders for the information she needs to get or think about further. If Janelle were to stop writing her draft in order to go look up, for example, how many calories are burned from an hour of walking, she would probably completely forget her point. There's also the potential for distraction; while she is searching for the calorie information, she may end up checking her e-mail or looking at Instagram, losing the flow of writing. This means she wouldn't get her idea out before her energy for writing was used up. A lot can be written if you push through the "stuck" spots by skipping them and returning to them later. Writers who do this are showing their awareness of the recursiveness of the writing process. They know that successful writers don't write the first word first and the last word last but rather go through the draft many times, developing it more each time they work on it.

Successful Writers Rewrite

We all wish that we could get away without having to rewrite, and that our first draft would come out good enough to stand as the final draft. However, those moments when our brain just pours out the ideas right onto the page — reasonably, logically, and clearly — are very rare; thus, effective writers should plan on revising, often more than once. College writing tasks are typically not suited to a one-draft approach, instead requiring drafting, rethinking, and rewriting.

Albert Einstein once responded to a question about where his laboratory was by pointing to his pen: "Here," he said. Einstein was telling the reporter that his genius didn't just come from his head or from a well-equipped laboratory; it also came from writing. Through the process of trying to express his thoughts in writing, Einstein was able to make sense of what he thought. That's why successful writers have to learn how to rewrite. Rather than giving up, writers who persevere realize that more often than not, good writing is not produced in a single session but is drafted and rewritten many times. Things are added, cut, moved, reworded, and explained. The first sentence in the final version may be the sentence that was actually written last. A general rule of thumb is that you have to write 500 or more words (about two pages) to end up with 250 words that are worth keeping in the final draft. Rewriting allows you to go back and fill in the "stuck" spots and to replace weak ideas with better ones.

Let's return to Janelle. When Janelle begins writing her essay, she doesn't have a set point to prove, but through the process of brainstorming and drafting, she figures out that she can argue that actions need to be taken to encourage people to engage in more physical activity, like walking. This idea can be developed into her thesis.

Let's focus on how Janelle rewrites the first paragraph of her draft. In the draft that follows, the underlined sections represent new writing, and the crossed-out section represents writing that Janelle has cut. We can see that Janelle adds and deletes parts as she realizes that she has to focus on obesity (and not get distracted by the documentary) and actually address the essay question in her introduction.

> <u>As a twenty-one-year-old woman, I have spent lots of time thinking about my weight and wishing I could lose some of it, but I haven't really thought much about obesity as a national health problem. I saw it as a personal problem. But recently, I had the opportunity to see film footage of Americans from 1960, and I was shocked by how different the people were.</u> ~~I saw a documentary on television~~ [*title? **Don't remember***] ~~about school integration in the South~~ [*?*] ~~and even though the main story was about racial discrimination, the big thing I kept noticing was how skinny all the people were. This documentary was shot in the 1940s~~ [***check date***]. The kids and teenagers were all skinny. Not unhealthy, but they didn't have any extra weight on them. In comparison, today when you walk through a school, you see some skinny kids but lots of chubby ones, and even some very heavy ones. <u>How did we get so much bigger, and how can we as Americans change for the better? We're big because we don't have to move much anymore, and that sedentary lifestyle is a major part of the reason Americans are suffering from an obesity case. The answer is for us to "get moving," as Michelle Obama said.</u>

As you can see, Janelle's draft has changed greatly.

First, Janelle realizes that she has to lead her readers into her topic with what is often called a **hook**. A hook is exactly what it sounds like: a bit of writing that engages readers, bringing them into the topic. There are many kinds of hooks. For this essay, Janelle works to establish her personal relationship to the topic of obesity, which draws readers in and encourages them to think about their own personal relationship to the topic. This works!

Second, Janelle realizes that writing too much about a documentary on school integration and racial discrimination is a distraction from her main topic. Racial discrimination and school integration are huge and important topics that Janelle can't just refer to briefly and then drop; moreover, they are off topic for her essay on obesity. What is important for Janelle's essay is that the documentary helped her realize that Americans used to be much thinner; therefore, she revises those sentences to keep readers focused on her main point: recognizing that obesity has become a real problem.

Third, Janelle realizes that she needs to establish the focus and plan for her essay by introducing the question that drives the essay (in this case, the one provided by the instructor) and its answer. Notably, she doesn't use the exact language of the essay question, and in her answer, she is clear about her point. From this paragraph, Janelle — and her readers — know what will come next.

Committing to rewriting is the best thing you can do for yourself as a writer. Once you are a committed rewriter, you can write a first draft without the pressure of having to be perfect, and the great advantage of a quickly written first draft is that it helps you figure out what you want to say, which then allows you to rewrite productively. A roughed-out first draft — like the one Janelle wrote — is useful, but it is not something you can submit to your teacher as a final draft. Instead, it's a tool that enables you to learn and discover what you need to do when you rewrite, thereby allowing that second draft to take shape. Typically in the second draft, a writer establishes the essay's *focus* and *develops* the major parts of the essay.

Successful Writers Share Their Work and Receive Feedback on It

Figuring out how to rewrite a draft to the point where it has the right shape and content can be challenging. Most writers can reread their draft and come up with some solutions by reviewing the assignment and our list of the essential elements of academic essays (p. 34), but they often get stuck because they can't see their own writing clearly. Either they are simply too invested in what they've written and don't want to make changes, or they've run out of ideas.

The solution to this problem is to get feedback. Successful writers are able to write more and to write better after receiving feedback from others — including teachers, classmates, and writing center tutors. As a writer, you need to make sure that your ideas are coming across clearly and that your readers understand the point you are trying to make. This is where sharing work and receiving feedback is crucial. Feedback allows you to understand how others read your work and what you need to do to improve it. For example, you might have a terrific point, but if you present it in a way that is underdeveloped, no one else will grasp how great the point is. Feedback gives you a new perspective on your ideas: Readers may recognize that a great idea in paragraph 3 could be used as the thesis, notice that an example doesn't work to support the point without more explanation, or alert you to places where sentence structure is confusing.

The most common form of feedback is **peer review**. As a college writer, you will likely be asked to share your work with your peers as well as to offer feedback on others' work. While getting feedback on your work is very helpful, giving feedback also trains you as a writer. Being able to raise questions and identify places for revision in the work of others develops your ability to thoughtfully revise your own work. Thus, by reading and commenting on a peer's essay, you learn how to better write your own — and that's true whether the essay is very good (and therefore a model) or weak (and therefore one that illustrates traps to avoid).

The peer review process works best — and is most useful to parties on both sides — when writers are open to giving and receiving constructive criticism. Although it is nice to have someone say "Your essay is great!," such a comment doesn't offer much specific help: What's great? everything? the example given in paragraph 3? the conclusion? Constructive criticism involves being honest and specific: providing praise for specific strengths, directing attention to weak spots, and offering suggestions for what needs revision. In Toolkit section 4, "Revising Writing," you will find several peer review activities that you can use to give and receive feedback on writing (pp. 94–102).

Successful Writers Edit for Clarity

Once a draft is revised for shape and content — meaning it is focused, developed, and organized — it is time to edit for clarity. Editing is the process of making small but important changes at the phrase, word, punctuation, and even formatting level. In the editing stage, you deal with surface-level problems, such as punctuation, sentence structure, and word choice. Spelling, of course, is important, but true editing for clarity involves more than spell-checking. Simply put, it's about ensuring that the writing makes sense by taking on the perspective of a reader.

Student writers too often avoid or rush through this step of the writing process, which is a mistake. The essay may not be perfect, but reading and editing it for surface-level problems will lead you to make many small but important improvements and produce a better draft.

Editing requires three things — willingness, knowledge, and the ability to reread your own writing slowly and attentively, often looking for specific issues like comma usage or fragments. You have to be willing to take on the task of editing. *Intersections* and your teacher can help with the second part, which is knowledge of what is expected of academic writing. And Toolkit sections 5 and 6 in Chapter 3 provide tips for performing focused rereading of your own writing that allows you to edit to follow specific rules and conventions.

As a college student, you will need to learn the surface-level rules of academic writing, many of which may not be explicitly taught. We try to do much of this teaching in the toolkits chapter by helping you learn what the rules are. Similarly, a good writing handbook will provide even more instruction about these surface-level rules. Most rules of academic writing are about being clear or formal. For example, did you know that in academic writing you should never refer to a published writer by just his or her first name, and that if you are writing about a book or an article, you need to include its title the first time you mention it?

So, avoid writing:

> **Toni is a Pulitzer Prize–winning author whose book about a girl who hated her brown-colored eyes teaches readers about internalized racism.**

Instead, write:

> **Toni Morrison is a Pulitzer Prize–winning author whose book about a girl who hated her brown-colored eyes, *The Bluest Eye*, teaches readers about internalized racism.**

After the first reference, you refer to the author by last name only. (Here's a trick to help you remember: You are not on a first-name basis with the author.)

This is just an example of two of the conventions that writers are expected to know and follow. Your job as a college student is to learn and apply all the rules and conventions of academic writing.

For whatever writing task you are working on, from an essay to a text message, the level of formality is situational — that is, you adjust it to fit the situation at hand. So, just as you likely wouldn't talk to your grandmother the same way you talk to your friends, you need to be more formal in your academic writing — it's not a block party but a party at the White House. You change the level of formality of your speech to meet the situation, and you need to make similar adjustments for different writing situations.

Many students learn to really like editing. In a way, it's easier work than drafting and revising because surface work doesn't require total rethinking. You are looking at words and phrases rather than paragraphs or the whole essay. Here are some tricks for editing more successfully:

1. Read your essay aloud to force yourself to go more slowly and catch errors.

2. Read one sentence at a time, *from the end of the essay to the beginning*, to force yourself to pay attention to each sentence individually.

3. Print your essay and edit it on paper to *see* the words differently.

Using these methods will encourage you to pay attention, allowing you to see more errors, which you can then correct.

Genres: Types of Assignments

College writing assignments can take many forms, from a basic summary of an article to an argumentative essay that offers and supports the writer's point. In *Intersections*, we focus on some of the most common types of essays:

- Reflective
- Informative
- Analytical
- Argumentative

Reflective writing assignments can take a few forms. Some reflective writing assignments ask you to offer your own **narrative** — that is, to share a personal experience that is somehow connected to or inspired by the reading. Other reflective writing assignments, sometimes called **response papers**, may ask you to share your reaction to a reading, whether that reaction is agreement, disagreement, pleasure, concern, surprise, or something else. The goal of reflective writing assignments is to offer some reflection — or thought — about a topic.

Informative writing assignments provide just that — information. They can take the form of **reports**, **summaries**, and **descriptions**. Some informative writing assignments might ask you to summarize a reading or a set of readings. Others might ask you to do research and present information about a topic or an issue. Some assignments might ask you to provide a detailed description. The common goal of informative writing assignments is to offer readers a clear, rich understanding of the topic at hand. In short, the goal is to help readers learn something by informing them.

Analytical writing assignments involve looking closely at an issue, perhaps by dividing it into subtopics and figuring out how they all connect to one another. In short, analysis involves figuring out relationships between ideas and examples. Some analytical strategies are **comparing and contrasting**, and **causal analysis** (explaining cause-and-effect relationships). The shared goal of analytical writing assignments is to break down and explain something in order to help readers understand it more deeply.

Argumentative writing assignments ask writers to offer and support a main point using evidence and explanation. More than just explaining or informing readers about an issue, these assignments set out to prove a point and to convince or persuade readers to adopt or at least consider a particular perspective or idea.

You will find samples of these four common types of assignments in the Appendix (p. 439). A note on terms: Instructors across the country and likely even at your institution do not define types of writing assignments in exactly the same way, so it is important that you read the assignment carefully and ask questions about the type of essay that is expected.

Essential Elements of Academic Essays: Focus, Development, Discussion, Organization, and Clarity

In our teaching of college writing, we have identified five elements that are important in most academic writing assignments — focus, development, discussion, organization, and clarity — defined in the earlier "Writing Terms" section. You can use these elements to help shape your work and as a supplement to specific assignments given by instructors. Although some assignments may require modification of the list, our students have found this list of essential elements to be very helpful as they plan, draft, revise, and edit their work.

The toolkits in Chapter 3 offer support for these elements by breaking them down into smaller steps.

Essential Elements of Academic Essays

Focus: The essay has and keeps a focus—thesis, question, or purpose—through every paragraph of the essay. The focus is briefly stated in the introduction; in argument essays, the focus is tied to the thesis statement.

Development: The essay provides description, details, examples, evidence, or reflection to support the focus (thesis, question, or purpose) of the essay. The essay uses this information to go beyond first thoughts, memorized facts, or statements of beliefs.

Discussion: The essay *makes meaning* (through explaining, reasoning, or analyzing), going beyond the superficial or obvious.

Organization: The essay's ideas and paragraphs flow in a logical, clear, and pleasing order that makes sense to readers.

Clarity: The essay follows the rules and conventions expected by an academic community, making the essay readable and clear.

CHAPTER 3

Toolkits for Reading and Writing

In This Chapter

What Are Toolkits?

Toolkits are a collection of resources and activities designed to assist college writers with the practices of American academic reading and writing. The chapter is broken up into separate sections on active and critical reading, brainstorming and generating drafts, organization, revision, and editing for correctness and for polish. Toolkits take the form of activities and tutorials that guide you through a series of informative questions and resources.

The toolkits are designed to be used with any of the reading and writing assignments in *Intersections*, and they do not need to be completed in order. Your instructor may assign a toolkit to the whole class for homework or in-class work, or you might be assigned a specific toolkit based on your writing and development needs.

Writing is challenging and multifaceted, and these toolkits, which many students have found helpful, are designed to break down challenges and focus attention on specific areas for improvement.

Toolkit
1.1 **Margin Notes**

This toolkit will help you write useful notes in the margins—the easiest and fastest way to both read for understanding and also prepare for a writing assignment.

Annotation—underlining, highlighting, or writing notes in the margins—is a great way to help you understand a reading. Good readers develop systems for annotation, and writing margin notes is one of the most common methods. If you can't underline or highlight a text because you do not own it, write more detailed notes, using Post-its placed in the margins.

What to Do

1. **Underline or highlight the most important points in the reading, selecting summary statements, facts, statistics, or powerful, eloquent language.** These are the passages that you will need to answer reading questions, discuss the text in class, or use in a future writing assignment.

2. **In the margins, write a few words that explain the value of the highlighted passages.** When you are scanning the reading later, you can review the margin notes and know what is important about the passages you have selected.

3. **Use your margin comments to mark passages that you have questions about—moments that are confusing or seem unclear.**

4. **In your margin comments, use your own words when a direct quotation isn't necessary.** This method begins the process of interpretation and meaning making.

Here is an example using "Cognitive Outlaws" by Joann Ellison Rodgers (p. 301). Once you have reviewed this example, give it a try on another reading.

> A growing gallery of triumphant entrepreneurs, lawyers, scientists, artists, and writers own up to a history of dyslexia, ADHD [attention deficit / hyperactivity disorder], and related miswirings of the cerebral cortex. Web sites abound with the usual suspects—Einstein and Edison, whose dyscalculia throttled their efforts at arithmetic—and gush over the more newly revealed, from aviation's Richard Branson and fashion's Tommy Hilfiger to Wall Street's Charles Schwab, author John Irving, and actor / comedian Henry Winkler, who once joked that "we all know what being called 'special' in school really means."

Famous people with learning disabilities

LaunchPad Solo

Visit **LaunchPad Solo for Readers and Writers** for more practice on the skills covered in this section.

What drives a man who couldn't pass algebra to master physics and change our view of the universe? What compels a novelist who failed to decipher *Moby-Dick* to put words on a page for a living? Do they achieve in spite of the disability or because of it? Do dyslexia and similar afflictions rob the left brain, dominated by "logical" cognition processes that manage reading and other learning skills favored in school, but pay the right hemisphere, in which neurons instantiate more inventive, ambitious, and creative processes?

It's not yet clear whether dyslexics make lemonade by figuring out ways around their reading problems or actually come pre-equipped with compensatory strengths. But the issue matters to many. An estimated one in ten children in the United States is dyslexic, and for most, their stories bog down in stigma.

"The pain begins the first day in school when kids realize they can't do what others do so easily," says Sally Shaywitz, a pediatric neurologist at Yale, cofounder of its Center for Dyslexia and Creativity, and researcher of the reading disability that accounts for 80 to 90 percent of all learning problems. She believes the learning disabled are an unmined treasure with great potential value to society.

Shaywitz has evidence that their inability to decode letters on a page is often accompanied by "a sea of strength" in analytic thinking, reasoning, and creativity. Perhaps because they are forced to concentrate harder on particular problems, find work-arounds, and seek alternate ways to sort through chaff, they solve problems more easily, less distracted by irrelevant details. "They learn to think outside the box," she insists, "because they never fit inside."

Are those with learning disabilities more capable because of their disabilities? Or is it unrelated?

Repeats the key issue of possible connection

1 in 10 children has dyslexia

Biggest problem for dyslexics is STIGMA

80%–90% of all learning problems come from dyslexia

Researcher finds that dyslexics have "a sea of strength"— thinking, reasoning, and creativity

Good quote to explain why people with dyslexia are so talented

Toolkit 1.2 Outlining

> This toolkit will help you understand and evaluate what you are reading as well as prepare to write about the text.

Outlining a reading can help you better understand it. Outlining encourages critical reading, allowing you to see how the author structured the text, and in doing so potentially revealing places that are well supported, off topic, or poorly supported.

What to Do

1. **Read the text more than once, looking for the author's key points and examples.**

2. **Informally outline the movement of the reading by listing the main points, sections, examples, and occasionally a key quotation.** One way to do this is by writing a short summary (a sentence or a phrase) of each paragraph or

section. (If the reading does not already have labeled sections, you can create your own, as in the example that follows.)

3. **When you are done, evaluate your outline to see what points the author has made, whether the author has offered supporting evidence, and whether the author has stayed on topic.**

Here is an example of step 2 using "My Soul to Keep, My Weight to Lose" by Alice Randall (p. 206). Once you have reviewed this example, write your own outline for another reading.

Outline of "My Soul to Keep, My Weight to Lose" by Alice Randall

1. Introduction
   a. Tells the story of realizing that she didn't know how much she weighed
   b. Connects with Booker T. Washington's *Up from Slavery* narrative
   c. Asks, "How far up was I from my own slavery if I didn't get down from my obesity?" (206)

2. Race-specific: mind matters most (not body)
   a. Grandfather tells her what's in her head is most important because it is the one thing that racists in America can't take away from you
      i. Mentions obesity among many black women

3. Reflects on reasons why she is overweight
   a. Most out of her control (oversized portions, advertising, and low wages)
   b. In her control:
      i. Idolizing grandmother, Dear, who was also obese
      ii. Defiance against dominant aesthetics: large, loud, and proud
      iii. Caring for other people instead of herself

4. Work schedule example
   a. 360 days a year
   b. 7:00 a.m. to 2:00 a.m.
   c. Raised a daughter, sent her to Harvard, wrote 4 books, got obese
   d. "I thought self-sacrifice was the central part of being grown" (208)

5. Black women and obesity
   a. 25% of black women over 55 have diabetes
   b. 80% of black women are overweight

6. Learned that to be healthy can be a priority
   a. Staying fit by walking and sleeping is sacred
   b. Being healthy can be part of the civil rights movement—it's the next step in freeing the black race from the damage of slavery

Toolkit
1.3 Summarizing

This toolkit will help you summarize an article that you have read.

A summary is a restatement in your own words of another writer's material. Summaries can serve a variety of purposes in college writing. One purpose is to demonstrate how well you have understood the material, which is the goal of writing a reading summary. Essentially, a summary serves as a condensed version of the reading. For other uses of summary, see Toolkits 2.5 and 2.11.

What to Do

1. **In the first sentence of your summary, clearly identify the article's title, its author, and its thesis or main focus.**

2. **Present the article's ideas fairly and accurately.**

3. **Follow the order of the article, focusing on the author's main ideas.** Don't overemphasize a minor section or otherwise misrepresent the author's ideas.

4. **Present the author's ideas primarily using your own words.** You may choose to use a few quotations as well (be sure to use quotation marks appropriately; see Toolkit 5.10 for more on formatting quotations).

5. **Use signal phrases (e.g., "Chu observes"; "Vargas asserts") to make it clear that these are not your own ideas.** (See Toolkit 5.9 for more about signal phrases.) Use the present tense when referring to what the author writes.

6. **Do not include your own ideas or opinions about the article or its topic when writing a reading summary.**

Here is an example using "Escaping Digital Histories" by Julian B. Gewirtz and Adam B. Kern (p. 399). Once you have read this example, read a different piece from Chapters 4–11 of this book; then, following the guidelines presented here, write a summary of your own.

Summary of "Escaping Digital Histories" by Julian B. Gewirtz and Adam B. Kern

In "Escaping Digital Histories," recent college graduates Julian B. Gewirtz and Adam B. Kern write from the perspective of young people who have grown up with the Internet and have never lived without social media and the presence of selfies, embarrassing videos, and thoughtless online comments. They discuss how their generation will have to deal with having their lives recorded, viewed, and even misinterpreted by both friends and potential employers for the rest of their lives. They state, "A fact of being a young person today is that our data are out there forever, and we must find ways to deal with that" (400). Gewirtz and Kern propose that the solution to this problem is for society to pass a "cultural treaty" and to stop judging and caring about the often stupid things people said and did when they were young (400).

Toolkit

1.4 **Decoding Vocabulary**

This toolkit offers fast solutions for figuring out unfamiliar words.

You do not always need to know the exact dictionary definition of a word to understand its meaning; good readers often decode — figure out — a "good enough" meaning of the unfamiliar words they encounter as they read. You will still need to look up some definitions, but most of the time you can figure out enough of a word's meaning by looking at the context, which simply means rereading the words that surround the unknown word.

What to Do

1. **Look for a definition.** Authors may give the meaning of an unfamiliar word right in the sentence itself. For example, *pedagogy* is defined in this sentence: "My pedagogy, or theory of teaching, has been informed by years of teaching in China."

2. **Look for a synonym.** Authors may include synonyms, or similar words, next to challenging vocabulary. Authors often announce difficult synonyms with phrases such as *in other words* or *that is*, or by the use of the word *or*. For example, *ferocious* is defined by synonyms in this sentence: "The child was cruel and extremely aggressive — in other words, ferocious."

3. **Look for antonyms or contrasting words.** Writers frequently set up contrasts, and finding these contrasts will make it easier to understand challenging vocabulary. For example, see how *inarticulate* is set up as a contrast to *crystal clear* in the following sentence: "While the first speaker in the debate was essentially inarticulate, the second speaker was crystal clear, explaining complex political realities in plain English."

4. **Look for examples or illustrations of unknown words for clues as to the meaning of these words.** For example, *polysyllabic* isn't defined in this sentence, but the list of examples provides a pretty good clue: "Polysyllabic words such as *attention*, *hyperbolic*, and *possibility* are difficult for people who have speech impediments."

5. **Still stuck? Evaluate the importance of knowing the meaning of the unfamiliar word.** If it is used frequently in the reading or is obviously important to the writer's main idea, take the time to look it up in the dictionary.

For example, in Chapter 8's "Chivalry Isn't Dead, but It Should Be," Hailey Yook uses the word *subtle* three times. She first uses it at the beginning of the third paragraph: "Besides the obvious stuff, we're beginning to notice the subtle, underlying gender stereotypes in previously disregarded aspects of everyday life, such as the media" (p. 339). From this sentence, we can decode the meaning of *subtle* by noticing the contrast Yook sets up (*subtle* vs. *obvious stuff*) and the synonyms she uses (*underlying*). Double-checking our decoding, we find that according to *Merriam-Webster.com*, *subtle* means "hard to notice or see: not obvious." This connects to Yook's main idea that we need to pay attention to the types of sexism that may not be obvious.

Toolkit 1.5 Finding the Main Idea

> This toolkit will help make sure you can identify, remember, and articulate the main idea of a reading, something that many busy college students forget to do.

Sometimes college students are too focused on simply finishing their homework to stop to make sure they are getting enough out of their reading assignment. That is, they do not spend time digesting and understanding the reading, and instead just plow through it, word after word. Unfortunately, all that work and time spent isn't profitable. For every essay or book you read, you should be able to answer the question, What was the main idea?

The main idea is simply the author's position or point of view about a topic. In short, TOPIC + POINT OF VIEW = MAIN IDEA.

Ask yourself:

What is the topic?

What is the author's point of view on the topic? (Sometimes asking, "What is the author's position?" is more appropriate or helpful.)

Here's some help. After finishing a reading assignment, work through the following suggestions until you are satisfied that you have the main idea.

What to Do

1. **See if you already know the main idea.** Immediately after you finish reading the article, attempt to write one sentence in which you state the topic and the position or point of view of the author(s). For example, here is one sentence that explains the topic and point of view held by Gewirtz and Kern

in "Escaping Digital Histories": The authors believe that young people need to teach the world how to be forgiving and relaxed about other people's digital histories, recognizing that we are in a new age and that everyone makes mistakes.

2. **If you are not able to come up with one sentence, go through the article again, rereading only your highlighting or underlining to refresh your memory.** Attempt the one-sentence statement of the topic and author's point of view again.

3. **Still stuck? Reread the title and the first and last paragraphs of the assigned reading.** In at least one of these two paragraphs, authors are likely to state their main ideas clearly. Try again.

4. **If you are still stuck, read the article again, marking those places where the author presents a claim or expresses an opinion about the topic.** Review the places you have marked to see if one of them might contain the main idea.

Toolkit
1.6 Decoding Genres

> This toolkit will help you understand what to expect from a text and how to evaluate it.

A genre is a type or category of writing. Some common examples are **narrative**, **description**, **opinion**, **government report**, **historical analysis**, **research report**, **news report**, **news analysis**, **and poem**. Recognizing the genre of a text allows you to ask the right questions to decode it; for example, you should not expect a report to have an argument, but you should expect an argument to try to persuade you of something.

Labeling writing by genre is useful for understanding what you're reading, though it must be noted that many texts will not fit entirely into one genre definition or another.

Following are some questions to ask yourself as you attempt to label a text you are reading.

Type of Information

1. Does the author **tell a story** about him- or herself or someone else? Does this story take up most of the essay? If so, you are most likely reading **a narrative**.

2. Does the author **provide information** from interviews, reports, surveys, or other outside sources? If so, you are likely reading **a report or an informative piece**, **an analysis**, or **an argument or a persuasive piece**.

Presence or Absence of Discussion

1. Does the author **provide information** from interviews, reports, surveys, or other outside sources **in a neutral approach**, without offering her or his own commentary? Does it seem similar to a newspaper article? If so, you are most likely reading **a report or an informative piece**.

2. Does the author **provide information** from interviews, reports, surveys, or other outside sources and **also explain the information** or topic? Does the explanation take the form of comparison, cause and effect, or another method that attempts to break down and explain the issue? If so, you are most likely reading **an analysis**.

3. Does the author **take sides or try to prove a claim**? Does the author offer evidence and discussion in an attempt to back up his or her main point? Is the author trying to persuade you of something? If so, you are most likely reading **an argument or a persuasive piece**.

What to Do

1. **Select a chapter you have read, and label each of the readings in that chapter by answering the preceding questions.**

2. **Explain your reasoning.**

3. **Which readings were difficult to classify, and why?**

4. **Share your labels with a peer to confirm that you have a good understanding of genre.**

Toolkit
1.7   # Decoding Narratives

This toolkit will help you understand what a narrative is and how to read one.

Narratives tell a story, usually to make a point or to help readers understand something. To critically read a narrative, you must move beyond basic enjoyment of the story to consider what purpose the author might have in sharing the story with readers.

What to Do

After reading a narrative from *Intersections* — such as Lauren Shields's "My Year of Modesty" (p. 226), Firoozeh Dumas's "The 'F Word'" (p. 257), or Udoka Okafor's "On Living with Depression, and the Dangers of Our Culture of Silence" (p. 308) — answer the following questions:

1. What is the topic of the narrative? That is, what is it about?

2. What incident(s) or experience(s) does the author focus on in this narrative? What makes them important to the author?

3. Mark some of the most vivid details in the narrative. What makes them stand out?

4. How does the author present him- or herself and other people in the narrative? That is, what insights do we get into the personalities, beliefs, and concerns of the people described in the narrative?

5. What is the tone of the narrative (e.g., neutral, sad, distant, nostalgic, happy, funny)? How does the tone help us figure out the author's view of the events?

6. Who is the author's target audience? How can you tell? How might this influence the author's choices in writing the narrative?

7. What reflections or commentary does the author offer? What does the author want us to learn from these personal experiences? What broader relevance do these experiences have (i.e., relevance not just to the author but to other people, including readers)?

Toolkit
1.8 **Decoding Reports**

This toolkit will help you critically read an informative text.

Reports and informative texts are meant to inform. Critical readers will evaluate them on the quality of the information provided. Although informative texts may seem straightforward, as a critical reader you need to figure out what information to hold on to and remember.

What to Do

After reading an informative text from *Intersections* — such as Patricia Rice's "Linguistic Profiling" (p. 186) or Andrea Shea's "Facebook Envy" (p. 381) — answer the following questions:

1. What is the topic of the report? That is, what is it about?

2. What is the problem, issue, or situation that has prompted the writing of this text?

3. Who is the author's target audience? How can you tell? How might this influence the author's choices in writing the report?

4. What kind of information does the author provide (e.g., information from people the author has interviewed? surveys or other studies? research? books or articles?)?

5. How credible are these sources?

   a. Are the sources relevant (on topic)?

   b. Are they reliable? (If the source is a study, for example, are the people who conducted the study experts in their fields?)

   c. Are they recent? (If the report is about contemporary attitudes toward texting in class, for example, is the information recent rather than from five years ago?)

6. Although reports are typically neutral in tone, is there any open or hidden bias? For example, does the writer offer information about both sides of an issue? If the writer interviews people, does he or she interview people with differing opinions? If you answered "no" to either of the last two questions, you may have detected bias. Ask yourself: Does this bias affect the writer's credibility? Or is this bias appropriate given the author's audience?

Toolkit
1.9 **Decoding Analyses**

This toolkit will help you critically read analytical texts by identifying the main point and evaluating whether it is effective.

Analytical texts dissect and explain. Like reports, they offer information; unlike reports, they discuss that information, helping readers understand a topic more deeply, often through strategies such as comparison or cause-and-effect analysis.

What to Do

After reading an analytical text from *Intersections*—such as Sharon Haywood's "How Body Modification Ended the War against My Body" (p. 221) or Rosemary Mahoney's "Why Do We Fear the Blind?" (p. 297)—answer the following questions:

1. What is the topic of the analysis? What issue or problem is the author exploring?

2. What is the author's purpose or point in writing this analysis?

3. Who is the author's target audience? How can you tell? How might this influence the author's choices in writing the analysis?

4. What kind of information does the author provide (e.g., information from people the author has interviewed? surveys or other studies? research? books or articles? personal experiences)?

5. How credible are these sources?

   a. Are the sources relevant (on topic)?

   b. Are they reliable? (If the source is a study, for example, are the people who conducted the study experts in their fields?)

    c. Are they recent? (If the analysis is about contemporary attitudes toward texting in class, for example, is the information recent rather than from five years ago?)

6. Locate those moments where the author explains or discusses the information.

    a. How does the author interpret the information?

    b. Does the explanation make sense? Are you convinced? Why or why not?

    c. In what other ways could the information be viewed?

Toolkit

1.10 **Decoding Arguments**

> This toolkit will help you critically read argumentative or persuasive texts by identifying the main point and evaluating whether the author supports it effectively.

An argumentative or persuasive text attempts to prove a claim or point, offering evidence and discussion in support. Critical readers do not accept a writer's argument without first evaluating its merits.

What to Do

After reading a persuasive text that makes an argument from *Intersections* — such as Casey Gane-McCalla's "Athletic Blacks vs. Smart Whites" (p. 359), Andrew Romano's "Why We Need to Reimagine Masculinity" (p. 329), or Abigail Saguy's "Why We Diet" (p. 210) — answer the following questions:

1. What is the topic of the argument?

2. What is the writer's thesis, argument, or position? In other words, what is the writer trying to prove or convince you of? Find the sentences in the text that make the writer's project most clear.

3. Who is the author's target audience? How can you tell? How might this influence the author's choices in writing the argument?

4. What evidence or examples does the author offer in support of the thesis? List or summarize them briefly.

5. How effective are the explanation and examples in supporting the thesis?

6. What other positions might be taken on this issue? Has the writer mentioned or disproved them?

7. Overall, based on your analysis, how convincing is the writer's argument? What is the strongest part, and why? What is the weakest part, and why?

Toolkit
1.11 Decoding Voices

> This toolkit will help you read more closely and better understand a writer's main point and use of sources.

Authors often summarize and quote other sources to provide support and illustrations for their own points. What may seem surprising, however, is that authors also summarize and quote sources that offer different, even contradictory, ideas.

Because authors can summarize or quote writers they agree and disagree with, readers need to recognize the difference between authors' original ideas and the ideas of their sources. Readers need to pay attention to the clues that writers provide: signal phrases ("as Rodriguez correctly notes" and "as Tan mistakenly argues," for example) or other words (e.g., "however") often provide these clues. Sometimes these clues are missing, and readers need to pay careful attention as they read.

What to Do

1. **Select a text from *Intersections* that includes several quotations or discussions of other writers' ideas, and read it closely and carefully.** You might try Tracy López's "Non-Spanish-Fluent Latinas: 'Don't Judge Us'" (p. 182), Sharon Haywood's "How Body Modification Ended the War against My Body" (p. 221), or Sarah Showfety's "Field Guide to the Tomboy" (p. 320), all of which draw on a variety of sources. As you do so, use different-colored highlighters or pens to identify (1) **where the writer, whom we will call the primary author, expresses his or her own views**; and (2) **where the primary author is presenting (through summary or quotation) the ideas of others**. For example, use yellow to highlight the primary author's ideas and green to highlight sources' ideas.

2. **Looking back at those passages where the primary author presents his or her own views, make a list of those ideas, beliefs, or positions, using as many lines as needed.**

   a. The primary author thinks / believes / states _____.

   b. The primary author thinks / believes / states _____.

   c. The primary author thinks / believes / states _____.

   Based on your list, what is the primary author's main idea?

3. **Next, look back at those places where the primary author presents the ideas of others — his or her secondary sources — and make a list of those, using as many lines as needed.**

   a. The secondary source (named ____ ____) thinks / believes / states _____.

   b. The secondary source (named ____ ____) thinks / believes / states _____.

   c. The secondary source (named ____ ____) thinks / believes / states _____.

4. **Decide whether the primary author agrees or disagrees with each of the secondary source ideas listed in step 3.**

   a. The primary author agrees with the secondary source (named ____ ____).

   b. The primary author agrees with the secondary source (named ____ ____).

   c. The primary author disagrees with the secondary source (named ____ ____).

5. **Reflect:** How did the primary author use other sources to support her or his point? What was most effective or ineffective?

Toolkit
1.12 **Decoding Visual Texts**

> This toolkit will guide you in analyzing a visual text, going beyond reaction and first impressions.

Visual texts, like written texts, may not have been designed to be studied and "read" closely, but college professors across disciplines have come to expect these skills of students. Thus, when critically reading a visual text, you need to study it closely and comprehensively, rather than passively. You need to actively read and study the visual text. The goal is to look beyond the obvious to observe repetition, themes, and messaging.

What to Do

1. **Annotate — make margin notes about — the visual text.** (See Toolkit 1.1 for tips on annotation.)

2. **Write a one- to two-sentence description of the visual text.** Use enough detail that someone who has not seen the text can visualize it.

3. **Ask yourself the following questions:**

   a. What is the announced or apparent purpose of the visual text?

   b. Who is the target audience? How can you tell? How might this influence the visual text's design?

   c. What is the mood or tone of the visual text? What specific clues from the visual text help you figure out this mood?

4. **Look at the design of the visual text and consider:**

   a. What is given prominent position? What is in the background?

   b. What does the positioning, angling, and placement of the elements suggest in terms of importance?

5. **Pay attention to any words that appear.** How do the words work in relation to the images?

6. **Study the text for signs and symbols.** What role do these signs and symbols play in conveying meaning?

7. **Look specifically at the background.** What does the background of the visual text tell you?

8. **Having studied the visual text through these questions, consider the following:** What theme or themes are present in the visual text? What issue, idea, or concept is the visual text actually about?

Once you have reviewed the following example, decode another visual text, such as one of the images in the introductions to Chapters 4–11.

Example

One woman looks happy and maybe admiring; the other, serious. They are pretty and wear makeup as they gaze upward toward the artist.

Use of word "girl" seems dated. When was this poster created? Uniforms and hairstyles seem to be from 1940s, WWII?

"Free" is emphasized.

High school graduates = target audience.

John Parrot/Stocktrek Images/Getty Images

1. See annotations on page 49. (See Toolkit 1.1.)

2. The image promotes the U.S. Cadet Nurse Corps by presenting sketches of two young women dressed in cadet nurse uniforms and indicating the benefits of lifetime education.

3. In general:

   a. The visual text is trying to recruit cadet nurse candidates.

   b. The target audience is young women who are high school graduates and are interested in nursing and free education. This is obvious from the picture and the information provided, as well as from the line "Be a Cadet Nurse: The Girl with a Future." The creators used these words and the image to capture young women's attention.

   c. The tone is positive and serious. The words are positive: "The Girl with a Future." The woman in the back has a serious look on her face, while the other one looks a little scared, but happy.

4. The design of the visual text:

   a. The sketches of the young women take up half the text. "Cadet Nurse" is in much larger type and also attracts attention.

   b. The angling of the information box in the bottom left corner suggests that the information is secondary. The word "free" is in capital letters and italics, drawing more attention to it.

5. The words provide more information and also indicate the purpose of the ad (recruitment).

6. There are no signs or symbols.

7. The background is all white, blank, focusing viewers' attention on the foreground.

8. The image is trying to convince young women to join the cadet nurses. It tries to persuade them by showing pretty women in nice uniforms and by explaining the benefits (future career, free education).

Toolkit 1.13 Evaluating Arguments

> With this toolkit, you can evaluate whether a writer's argument is reasonable, valid, and well supported.

A reasonable argument makes a claim about a debatable issue, one that requires discussion and proof. The argument presents reasons (supporting claims), supporting evidence, and responses to counterarguments (arguments that counter, or go against, other arguments).

What to Do

1. After reading an argument, sum up the writer's thesis or main argument about the topic in one or two sentences.

2. In a numbered list, identify the supporting claims, or reasons, that the writer gives for making this argument (Reason 1, Reason 2, and so on).

3. **Evaluate these reasons or supporting arguments.** How well do they support the main argument or thesis — that is, are they relevant? on topic? valid? Briefly explain why or why not.

4. **In a numbered list, briefly summarize the evidence that the writer uses.** (This will be easiest if you read through the article and list each piece of evidence in the order it appears.) For each, write down a phrase or sentence that summarizes the evidence (Evidence 1, Evidence 2, and so on).

5. **Evaluate this evidence in terms of whether it truly supports the argument.** Using a chart like the one that follows, decide if the evidence supports the reasons (or supporting claims) you listed in step 2, checking the appropriate box.

	Supports Reason 1	Supports Reason 2	Supports Reason 3	Supports Reason 4	Off Topic (doesn't support any reason)
Evidence 1					
Evidence 2					
Evidence 3					
Evidence 4					
Evidence 5					
Evidence 6					

6. **Reviewing your chart, consider how well the evidence supports the argument and its reasons.**

7. **Consider the effect of any off-topic evidence.** Does it weaken the overall argument? Why or why not? Does it outweigh the relevant evidence? How or how not?

8. **Overall, based on your analysis, consider:**
   a. How convincing is the writer's argument?
   b. What is the strongest part, and why? What is the weakest part, and why?

Toolkit
1.14

Overcoming Reader's Block

This toolkit provides strategies to help you get through reading assignments.

Reader's block is almost as common as writer's block. You set aside time to read, open your textbook, and then, fifteen to thirty minutes later, you find you really haven't read more than a few sentences. You know you need to, but you just can't — or won't or don't. And there you are, thirty minutes gone, no closer to done.

To get through a tough reading, you need to rid yourself of distractions, break the task down into smaller ones, write summarizing notes, and offer yourself rewards for completing small tasks.

What to Do

1. **Rid yourself of distractions.** Turn your phone off or hide it. Turn off distracting media. Remove yourself from a group situation, and sit in a quiet place.

2. **Break up the task.** Measure out what you need to do, and break it into five-minute chunks. If you are an average reader, a page in this textbook should take you between two and three minutes to read. Mark up your text with lines that indicate beginnings and endings. You might try giving yourself a break every time there is a new header.

3. **Go ahead and read, making sure to underline.**

4. **When you get to a break spot, write a one-sentence summary.**

5. **After you've written your summary, give yourself a two- to three-minute reward:** Check your phone, view a short YouTube video, or stare into space — but only for two to three minutes! Seriously consider using a timer; it will help you stay disciplined.

Still Stuck? Try These Ideas

1. **Find a reading partner.** Read two- to three-minute chunks aloud or silently, and then share your summaries.

2. **Read aloud to yourself.** By reading aloud you become more alert, and you can process the information through both reading and hearing.

3. **Change your location.** If you are used to reading in bed, move to a desk. Try the library — seeing other people reading diligently should inspire you. If quiet makes you sleepy, find yourself a place with light noise, like a café or the student center.

4. **Change the time.** If you are always doing your homework in the afternoon and are struggling to stay awake, do it in the morning or after dinner.

Toolkit 2.1 Basic Brainstorming

This toolkit will help you get started on an essay assignment by unearthing ideas that you didn't even know you had.

What to Do

To benefit from this activity, follow the directions without skipping steps.

1. **Rewrite the assignment or question.** Read the essay question or prompt, and then remove the question or prompt from sight while you rewrite it in your own words. If you get stuck, go back and reread the assignment, but *do not* read it while you are writing it in your own words.

2. **Directed freewrite.** Reread what you wrote in step 1. Then write a response for five minutes straight. If you are using a pen, do not lift the tip from the page for the full five minutes, no matter how empty of words you may feel. Force yourself to write. If you feel as though you are running out of words, write down a few easy ones repeatedly, such as, "I don't know what to write, I don't know what to write, I don't know what to write." You will find that your brain tires of the repetition and other, better words will start to flow.

3. **Reread what you wrote in step 2, and highlight or underline the words or phrases that have potential.** Those are the words that begin to significantly address the essay assignment. Use some of these words and phrases to begin drafting your essay. You may find that these have potential as part of the introduction or as body paragraphs.

Once you have reviewed the following example, drawn from a writing assignment developed for Chapter 7, begin to brainstorm for your own assignment.

THE ASSIGNMENT: WRITE A PROFILE. This assignment invites you to write an essay that profiles a person with a disability, using the profile to examine the issue of disability and, in particular, to consider whether human *disabilities* can be linked to valuable special human *abilities*.

1.   I have to write a description of a person with a disability. I have to use this profile to think about whether abilities and disabilities are connected.

LaunchPad Solo

2. Is there a link between disabilities and abilities? I have no idea. . . . Hmm. I don't know what to write. . . . Who can I write about? Someone with a disability who might also have some special talent. Can't think of anyone. No wait! What about Tom Lewis? He is a golfer and he is dyslexic. He was terrible in school, and it was embarrassing to him, I think. I read it in the article I found. I don't know if it was connected, but he definitely has both a big ability and a real disability. I wonder if this one works. In the article it said a lot about his embarrassment over his disability. Is he an overachiever in golf to make up for not being good in school? Maybe. His parents supported him in golf, and maybe they saw it as making up for bad grades. Should connect it to a reading. . . . One of the assigned articles quotes an expert who asks this question about the connection. Check to see if I can link it to Tom Lewis. Could try to go for something like . . . no one is good at everything, so why can't people who have a weakness in one thing be strong in another?

3. Is there a link between disabilities and abilities? I have no idea. . . . Hmm. I don't know what to write. . . . Who can I write about? Someone with a disability who might also have some special talent. Can't think of anyone. No wait! What about Tom Lewis? He is a golfer and he is dyslexic. He was terrible in school, and it was embarrassing to him, I think. I read it in the article I found. I don't know if it was connected, but he definitely has both a big ability and a real disability. I wonder if this one works. In the article it said a lot about his embarrassment over his disability. Is he an overachiever in golf to make up for not being good in school? Maybe. His parents supported him in golf, and maybe they saw it as making up for bad grades. Should connect it to a reading. . . . One of the assigned articles quotes an expert who asks this question about the connection. Check to see if I can link it to Tom Lewis. Could try to go for something like . . . no one is good at everything, so why can't people who have a weakness in one thing be strong in another?

Toolkit
2.2 **Directed Brainstorming**

> This toolkit will help you uncover and express your point of view and its relation to other writers' ideas.

Frequently, writing assignments ask you to express your point of view. This toolkit will get you started on this task by helping you uncover and articulate your own beliefs, and then contextualize your point of view among those of other writers you have been reading.

What to Do

1. **Create a belief list.**

   a. Looking at the essay assignment, write down six direct sentences that express beliefs that you hold that relate to the essay topic. For example, if the essay topic is animal rights, a writer might start like this:

      1. I love animals!
      2. I believe animals need to be protected.
      3. I believe humans are more important than animals.
      4. I believe it is sad but worth it to kill an animal to save a human.
      5. I believe animals should not be given hormones.
      6. I believe people should only buy organic meat.

   b. Reread your list, and then underline the sentences that best express your beliefs.

2. **Consider other positions.**

   a. Identify two authors you have read for this assignment who you think might be good to use in your essay.

   b. Write a belief list of at least five sentences per author. For example:

      1. Author 1 [use name — e.g., Jane Smith] believes the American food industry is cruel to animals.
      2. Author 1 believes the food industry also produces unhealthy food. . . .

      1. Author 2 [use name — e.g., John Jones] believes that everyone needs to eat less meat for the planet to survive.
      2. Author 2 believes that humans would be healthier if we treated livestock better. . . .

3. **Begin writing.**

   a. Begin writing your essay by expressing your beliefs (using some of what you wrote for step 1).

   b. Then, for each of your authors, first explain what they believe (from step 2), and then respond to their beliefs with your own ideas.

For example:

Animals should be protected from cruelty in the food industry. Jane Smith explains the various ways in which the food industry is cruel to animals. She especially focuses on the use of hormones. These can be cruel to animals because _____. Smith is right to point out the negative effects of these hormones on animals. We can help prevent animal cruelty by buying organic meat and not buying meat from animals that were given hormones.

Toolkit
2.3 Outlining and Planning

This toolkit will show you how to create an outline, which can help you both expand your idea of what you want to write and also develop a plan to use during the drafting process.

What to Do

1. **Read the assignment several times, and complete some prewriting activities** (such as those offered in Toolkits 2.1 and 2.2). You can also simply generate ideas on your own by freewriting, brainstorming, or discussing your ideas with a peer.

2. **Think about what you'd like your thesis or main point to be.** If you don't know what you want to say yet, go back to prewriting activities. When you have a basic point or thesis in your head, you are ready to outline.

3. **Begin your outline.** When you outline, the heading defines the topic of each section, and the subheadings provide direction; additional subheadings may be used to break down a subheading even more.

4. **Select an outline format.** It's traditional to use a mix of letters and numbers to indicate level of generalization, and it's likely that your word processor will automatically put them in the order shown in the example that follows. If you are comfortable using another method of outlining, that's fine, too.

5. **Complete your outline, using the following one as an example.** Remember that the outline is a guide, not a rulebook. As you draft and revise, you will likely discover that some parts are unnecessary and that other points will need to be added.

Here is an example of an outline that was written after some prewriting and initial research in response to a writing assignment developed for Chapter 7.

THE ASSIGNMENT: WRITE A PROFILE. This assignment invites you to write an essay that profiles a person with a disability, using the profile to examine the issue of disability and, in particular, to consider whether human *disabilities* can be linked to valuable special human *abilities*.

1. LINK BETWEEN ABILITY AND DISABILITY
   a. Introduce the question of whether or not there's a link
      i. Find a quote from a reading where the writer asks the question cleverly—from "Cognitive Outlaws"
   b. Sketch out my plan—discussing Tom Lewis, connection to "Cognitive Outlaws"

    c.   Identify and briefly describe Tom Lewis, dyslexic golfer

    d.   Present my position: how Tom Lewis persuades me that his dyslexia helped him become an overachiever in what he was good at—he had to prove himself in golf because he was so unsuccessful in school

2.   TOM LEWIS IN SCHOOL

    a.   His story in school—humiliation; use quote from article I found

    b.   Importance of support from his parents

    c.   Relate to other dyslexics who struggle in school—how common it is (Rodgers article)

3.   TOM LEWIS AND GOLF CAREER

    a.   How he discovered golf and how good he was at it

    b.   Amateur career—big wins (Rookie of the Year)

    c.   Professional career—big wins

4.   ANALYZING TOM LEWIS

    a.   Discuss what Lewis says about link between his dyslexia and golf achievements—use quote

    b.   Discuss what the psychiatrist in the Rodgers article says

    c.   Explain how it makes sense to me that Lewis would want to prove himself—prove that he could succeed at something after being so terrible at school

5.   MY REFLECTION

    a.   No one is awesome at everything, so it makes sense that a weakness would come with a strength

    b.   Use myself as an example

    c.   What made Tom Lewis and me able to succeed was that our parents believed in us and told us we could be great even though we were getting bad grades in school

---

Toolkit
2.4 **Drafting a Thesis**

This toolkit will help you generate a compelling, useful thesis for your draft.

Tips for a Strong Thesis

- It should reflect your position on the topic.

- It should be arguable (something that needs to be proven) rather than a statement of fact.

- It should not simply announce your topic.

- It should not be an opinion—that is, a mere statement of personal preference.

- It should not be too broad or too narrow for the assignment.

- It should include some specifics.

- It should not be a question but rather the answer to a question.

- It should be one or, occasionally, two sentences in length.

What to Do

1. **Write briefly on your topic.** What are your views and ideas about the topic? What do you want to prove about your topic?

2. **Choose some of the most promising ideas from your freewrite, and then use them to write one or two sentences that indicate your topic and your argument—your position—about it.**

3. **List all your reasons—your support—for making this argument.** Review your list, and identify your most important and persuasive reasons.

4. **Combining information from steps 2 and 3, draft a thesis that indicates your topic, your argument, and your major reasons for making it.**

5. **Review the following lists of examples and ask yourself:** Is your draft thesis a weak thesis? What can you do to make it stronger?

6. **Use your ideas from step 5 to write a second draft of your thesis.**

Weak Examples

- *If someone posts a photo online, it stays there forever, making a digital history.* [Too factual]

- *I don't think people should be judged by what they post online.* [An opinion, not an argument]

- *In this essay, I will write about why people should not be judged on their digital histories.* [An announcement of the topic rather than a statement of the point to be argued]

- *Digital histories create problems.* [Too broad]

- *Are digital histories dangerous?* [A question]

Better Examples

- *Since someone's digital history can contain information that is outdated or that was posted solely for entertainment reasons, employers should not use digital searches to make final decisions about job applicants.* [Good. Thesis presents the writer's claim—that employers should not judge applicants on their digital histories—and offers some reasons: that these histories are outdated or meant for entertainment. It projects a clear sense of the paper's topic and argument.]

● *Until society becomes more forgiving of youthful mistakes, teens and young adults should be careful about what they post online to protect themselves from negative judgments from potential employers and possible dates.* [Good. Thesis presents the writer's claim (certain groups of people need to be careful) and a reason (avoiding judgment), as well as the context that creates this problem (society is unforgiving).]

● *Oversharing on social media can lower one's self-esteem and lessen one's privacy. However, regulations can help prevent further negative damages caused by the social networking and online hysteria that has taken over so many lives.* [Good. Thesis presents the writer's claim—that oversharing on social media causes problems that can be solved by regulation.]

Although you should now have a working thesis, your ideas will likely grow and change as you work on your essay, so make sure to revise your thesis to reflect your final, more developed thoughts.

Toolkit 2.5 Directed Summaries

> This toolkit will help you write a directed summary of another writer's article that will provide readers with valuable context for your own ideas.

A summary is a restatement in your own words of another writer's material. Although a summary can help you understand something you have read (see Toolkit 1.3), it can also provide you with useful material for your essay, particularly when it is combined with discussion or analysis. You can include a summary to support your own point or to provide you with specific material to argue against. A *directed summary* builds on a basic summary by combining it with discussion or analysis. It can be a part of an effective body paragraph.

Directed Summary Basics

● Write one or two sentences that introduce how the example or information you will summarize connects to your argument or guiding question (it may become the topic sentence in your paragraph).

● In the first sentence of your summary, clearly identify the reading, its author, and its thesis or main focus.

● Present the reading's ideas fairly and accurately.

- Follow the order of the reading, focusing on the author's main ideas. Don't overemphasize a minor section or otherwise misrepresent the author's ideas.

- Present the author's ideas primarily using your own words; you may choose to use a few quotations as well, indicating the quoted language appropriately. (See Toolkits 2.6 and 5.10 for more about quoting.)

- Use signal phrases (e.g., "Chu observes"; "Vargas asserts") to make clear that these are not your own ideas. (See Toolkit 5.9 for more about signal phrases.) Use the present tense when referring to what the author writes.

- Write three to four sentences of discussion or analysis *after* the summary to explain its connection to your argument or guiding question.

What to Do

1. **Choose a reading from *Intersections* that will support your thesis or guiding question.** Make some quick notes about how the reading relates to your thesis or question.

2. **Write a summary of the essay, following the basics of directed summaries.**

3. **Include this summary as part of a body paragraph in your essay.** In this paragraph, use the summary to support the main point or thesis of your essay by directing it toward that point.

Here's an example of a directed summary.

First sentence introduces topic of digital histories and forgiveness

Second sentence begins summary

Discussion relating summary to topic of digital histories and forgiveness

Many people face difficulties because of things they posted online in the past, but society needs to become more forgiving of poor decisions that do not harm anyone. In "Escaping Digital Histories," recent college graduates Julian B. Gewirtz and Adam B. Kern write from the perspective of young people who have grown up with the Internet and have never lived without social media and the presence of selfies, embarrassing videos, and thoughtless online comments. They discuss how their generation will have to deal with having their lives recorded, viewed, and even misinterpreted by both friends and potential employers for the rest of their lives. Gewirtz and Kern propose that the solution to this problem is for society to pass a "cultural treaty" and to stop judging and caring about the often stupid things people said and did when they were young. Gewirtz and Kern make a good point about how we as a society should rethink how we judge the information we find online. We need to recognize that sometimes young people will post comments or silly pictures without thinking about the negative impression they create. We need to accept that people will make silly mistakes and not hold it against them.

Toolkit
2.6 **Quote Sandwiches**

This toolkit will help you connect quotations to the point you are making by building a quote sandwich, rather than just dropping quotations into your essay.

For some assignments, you may be asked to use quotations from sources you have read. Quotations can serve several purposes in academic writing:

- Provide support for your thesis
- Offer an example or evidence
- Provide ideas for you to argue against
- Provide ideas that you can apply to other examples
- Show your awareness of other arguments (opposing arguments)

Effective quotations are integrated clearly into essays. They are not simply dropped in carelessly, with readers left to make the connection. Without the writer's help, readers can make the wrong connection or fail to recognize a connection at all.

Successful writers guide their readers to understand the relevance and value of a quotation. One way to do this is to use a quote sandwich with the quotation as the filling—the peanut butter or bologna—and your introduction to the quotation and your discussion of the quotation as the two pieces of bread.

Quote Sandwich Recipe

1. **The top piece of bread prepares readers for the quotation by:**

   - giving an introduction to the topic or argument of the writer you are quoting and its connection to your claim or topic;

   - introducing the writer and article using a signal phrase. (For more on signal phrases, see Toolkit 5.9.)

2. **The filling is the quotation itself.**

3. **The bottom piece of bread is made of restatement and discussion (or analysis).** The restatement makes clear how you have interpreted the material; this might take the form of an "in other words" or "that is" statement. The discussion (sometimes called analysis) is where you make clear how you are *using* the material to support your point and how it relates to your overall argument, guiding question, or thesis and, where relevant, to other points in your essay.

Here's a sample quote sandwich:

Summary and introduction of source by title and author's name

Relevance of quotation to writer's point

Signal phrase ("As she explains"), followed by quote

Writer's restatement and explanation

In "Autism and Visual Thought," Temple Grandin describes the process of thinking in pictures as involving a library of video images in her mind. While this thought process has been beneficial in her work designing equipment for handling cattle, thinking in pictures also has its drawbacks. As she explains, "If I let my mind wander, the video jumps in a kind of free association from fence construction to a particular welding shop where I've seen posts being cut and Old John, the welder, making gates. If I continue thinking about Old John welding a gate, the video image changes to a series of short scenes of building gates on several projects I've worked on" (281). In other words, Grandin's associational thought process has the potential to distract her from what she should be focusing on. This is one way that thinking in pictures can be a disadvantage.

What to Do

In your essay draft, find one body paragraph where you use a quotation. If you haven't used any quotations yet, add one to a body paragraph now. Then, evaluate how well you have built a frame, or sandwich, around the quotation.

1. **Look at your top piece of bread:** Do you provide an introduction that indicates the quotation's relevance to your point? Do you use a signal phrase?

2. **Evaluate the quotation itself:** Have you quoted enough? too much? Does the quotation truly help you illustrate your point? Or should you find another?

3. **Look at your bottom piece of bread:** Do you explain what the quotation means? Do you explain how it is connected to your point?

4. **Revise the paragraph, incorporating any missing elements, strengthening weaker points, and expanding your paragraph as necessary.**

5. **Following the same steps, evaluate your use of another quotation (likely in a different paragraph).**

Toolkit 2.7

Drafting the Introduction

This toolkit will help you write a first draft of your introductory paragraph.

An essay's introduction prepares readers for the rest of the paper. An introduction engages readers and introduces the topic, thesis (in thesis-driven papers), or guiding question (in exploratory papers), and finally, the introduction suggests the path that the writer will take throughout the paper.

Components of a Traditional Introduction

A traditional introduction for an argument or a persuasive essay has three principal components:

1. **An introduction of the topic,** which includes the case for why the topic is important, interesting, or otherwise worth paying attention to

2. **An overview of the main issues and examples** that will be explored in the paper; that is, a view of how the topic of the essay is going to be explored, addressed, supported, or argued

3. **The thesis statement** — a claim that the writer makes about the topic under discussion

See Selena Alvarez's essay in the Appendix (p. 440) for an example of a traditional introduction.

Alternatives to the Traditional Introduction

When you are writing an essay that is exploratory, descriptive, narrative, analytic, or following any other non-argument genre, you may find that a traditional introduction is not ideal. Furthermore, for some writers and readers of argument or persuasive essays, veering from the traditional path has advantages in terms of engaging readers, or what journalists refer to as "hooking" the reader. Here are some variations you might consider:

1. Think of the introduction as a movie preview rather than a summary: It might be advantageous to keep some of your breakthrough insights as a surprise, to keep readers engaged and excited by your ideas. In *Intersections*, we see this approach taken by Theodore R. Johnson III in the first paragraph of "Chivalry, Feminism, and the Black Community" (p. 335).

2. Focus on the reader: A good introduction can serve to transport your reader from where he or she is literally and psychologically to the "place" of your topic and the focus of your inquiry. For a good example of this approach, see Ellen Welty's "Are Your Words Holding You Back?" (p. 196).

3. Begin with a vivid anecdote or an intriguing example that gets right to the heart of the issue you are addressing in your essay. For an example of this approach, look at the introduction to Chapter 11 (p. 409) or Firoozeh Dumas's "The 'F Word'" (p. 257). When writers start with a story or an example, they follow it up by connecting the story to the main point of the essay.

4. Begin with a surprising statement, a thought-provoking question, or a contradiction or paradox. For a good example, look at Bob Ryan's "I Can Hardly Believe It's Legal" (p. 355) or Josh Rose's "How Social Media Is Having a Positive Impact on Our Culture" (p. 377).

5. Provide a brief historical review of the topic. This is a tactic that often works, though it has its pitfalls, as the writer needs to provide historical notes that aren't too obvious while also being brief. For an example, look at Andrew Romano's "Why We Need to Reimagine Masculinity" (p. 329).

What to Do

1. **Focus on the specifics of your current assignment to select an approach.** Reread the assignment and any directions your teacher gave you about writing introductions. For example, are you expected to write a traditional introduction, or is an alternative approach appropriate in this instance?

2. **Draft an introduction.** If you decide a traditional approach is called for, draft a paragraph that contains the three principal components: introduction of the topic, an overview of what the essay will cover, and your thesis. If you decide that a traditional approach is not called for, review the alternatives and choose one.

3. **Try again.** Put aside what you have written and do it again, starting from scratch. The purpose here is to force yourself to go through the process twice. Inexperienced writers too often commit themselves to their initial draft introduction, locking themselves into a path that isn't promising. Writing two introductions gives you another option, and one will certainly emerge as the better choice.

Toolkit
2.8 Drafting the Conclusion

> This toolkit will help you draft a conclusion that is more than a rehash of the introduction or body of the essay.

Essays that end with a flat, brief rehash of the main points are often disappointing. The only thing worse is when essays do not have conclusions at all, making readers wonder if a page was lost. These two problems are more common than you would think. Writing good conclusions is hard because by the time we get to them, we are tired of writing. Therefore, it is helpful to draft the conclusion at the beginning of a writing session, rather than at the end.

Components of a Conclusion

Conclusions are hard to write because it's much clearer what conclusions shouldn't contain than what they should. Nonetheless, good conclusions do have the following characteristics:

1. **They provide a sense of closure to the reader,** though they vary in how they achieve that goal.

2. **They leave readers with a final message,** typically by reiterating the thesis in different words or addressing the focusing question or primary purpose.

3. **They usually emphasize their final message by briefly summarizing highlights from the body of the paper** that best speak to this final message.

4. **They reach beyond the summary,** typically using one or more of the following tactics.

Conclusion Tactics

1. **Use the conclusion to form a bridge from your topic to the imagined life of your readers.** For example:

> As I sit in the living room typing this essay on the laptop on my knees, with my tablet on one side of me, open to the blog I have referenced, and my phone on the other, waiting for texts or other social news, I have to admit that the role of social media in adolescent lives is not just an academic issue but a personal one for me, and likely for college students all over the country.

2. **Return to the introduction.** In your introduction, you may have included an anecdote or a specific example that you can return to now that readers have benefited from your discussion of the issue related to the anecdote or example. See Alice Randall's "My Soul to Keep, My Weight to Lose" (p. 206) for a good example.

3. **Indicate the broad implications or significance of your conclusion.** That is, address the "So what?" question. What is the implication of the ideas you have been discussing? What is the larger significance? For example:

> Seeing disability without the "dis" allows us to recognize humans as simply highly diverse in their abilities, and in this diversity, we are collectively able to imagine many more solutions to our problems than if we rely only on those of us that are traditionally abled.

4. **Offer a recommendation or make a call to action** by doing one of the following:

   a. Proposing a course of action that readers might take

   b. Proposing a solution for the issue you have been discussing

   c. Suggesting a question for further investigation

   For example:

> The research data that has been amassed detailing the many ways that dieting simply does not work is hard to argue against. I've tried dieting, you've tried it, we've all tried it, but dieting doesn't work. Does this mean we should just give up and accept obesity and its consequences? Absolutely not. Instead, what we can do is follow Michelle Obama and think not about dieting and becoming smaller

but about becoming healthier by eating more (not less) of what is good for us, and by moving more. By creating a culture where healthy eating and living, through walking and physical activity, is normal, we won't become skinny, but we can become healthy.

5. **Emphasize your main message with a short quotation, anecdote, or example.** Your selection must fit in well with the text; otherwise, it will appear thrown in. Be sure that you have the last word: Don't use a quotation to end the conclusion. For example:

> Daniel Kish has been blind since he was a baby, yet he climbs dangerous peaks and rides bicycles in the streets of a big city, bringing home the truth of T. S. Eliot's words, "Only those who risk going too far can possibly find out how far one can go." It is Kish's willingness to push boundaries that has allowed him to excel.

What to Do

1. **Focus on the specifics of your current assignment.** Reread the assignment and any directions your teacher has given about writing conclusions. Doing so will help you know what is expected of your conclusion.

2. **Ask yourself what you want readers to know or understand from your essay.** Write a few sentences capturing this intention.

3. **Selecting two or even three of the suggested conclusion tactics, push yourself to draft several full conclusions so that you can compare different approaches.** Make sure your conclusions express what you have written in step 2.

4. **After you draft, review the list of components of a conclusion to make sure you have these components covered.**

Toolkit
2.9 **Comparing and Contrasting Ideas**

This toolkit will help you compare and contrast the ideas of two authors.

An important skill that good writers have is the ability to read two or more texts and recognize points of similarity *and* difference, and to write clearly about them. They also recognize that writers may agree on some points even though they disagree on others.

Note: Although many people refer to the process of "comparing and contrasting," the definition of *comparison* is looking for similarities *and* differences. If you are asked to "compare" two articles, look for both similarities and differences.

What to Do

1. **Read two articles on related topics** (e.g., two articles from one chapter of *Intersections*).

2. **List three similarities and three differences that you observe in the authors' positions or focuses.**

3. **For each similarity and difference you listed in step 2, write one or two sentences that indicate the topics and the two writers' positions.** For example:

   Difference #1: Whereas Alice Randall believes that losing weight can be an act of self-love and self-caring, Abigail Saguy views dieting as destructive, the result of social pressure and a culture that stigmatizes people who aren't thin.

4. **Write a few sentences to explain the most interesting difference that you see in the two writers' positions.**

5. **Write a few sentences to explain the most interesting similarity that you see in the two writers' positions.**

6. **Write one sentence in which you indicate how the writers agree yet also disagree.**

7. **Decide if the writers' disagreements outweigh their points of agreement, or vice versa. Then, use sentence structure to emphasize whether their agreement or their disagreement is more important.** That is, put the more important element in the main clause and the less important element in a subordinate clause. For example, if you believe the similarities outweigh the differences, use a structure like this:

   While the authors disagree about _____, more importantly they agree that
   _____.

   Do the reverse if you believe the differences are more important:

   Although the writers agree that _____, this agreement is outweighed by their disagreement over _____.

8. **Finally, write a comparison and contrast of the two writers' ideas (two to three paragraphs in length).** For an extended example, see Mariia Cosmi's essay in the Appendix (p. 450).

Toolkit
2.10 Making Connections between Texts

This toolkit will help you discuss and analyze the ideas of two writers by using a concept or an idea from one reading to understand another reading.

Making connections by using one author's concept or idea to discuss and analyze an example presented by another author can be a powerful writing strategy. That is, rather than just writing about two authors separately in different paragraphs, you make connections between their ideas in one or more paragraphs.

Making connections begins with comparison and contrast, or recognition of a relationship between the texts; however, rather than stopping after you have discovered similarities or differences between two writers, you use your discovery of a difference or similarity to understand something new or deeper about the texts. In other words, you use the concept or idea of the one author to understand the example of the second author. Making connections can also help you develop a stronger, sharper thesis.

What to Do

1. **Find a concept or an idea that interests you in one of the assigned course readings.** Choose a direct quotation that explains the concept or idea, and then explain in your own words what the author means.

   Quote: _____

   Explanation: _____

2. **Choose an example from another assigned course reading that you believe is somehow related to the concept or idea.** Quote and then explain this second author's example.

   Quote: _____

   Explanation: _____

3. **List similarities and differences between the two quotations.**

Similarities	Differences

4. **Drawing on some of what you discovered in step 3, write a "connection"— three or four sentences that use the first author's concept to understand and discuss the second author's example.** Your goal here is deeper understanding of the second author's example. (If you can't come up with three or four sentences, try a different connection.)

5. **Write a sentence that asserts the point the first author's concept or idea helped you make about the second author's example.** This should be a point that you can turn into the topic sentence or claim of a paragraph.

6. **Finally, write a paragraph or two that puts all the information from steps 1–5 together.** You will probably need to reorder the sentences you wrote in steps 1–5 as well as add more detail. Make sure to write a clear topic sentence and include a quotation from both texts.

Here is an example that works with John F. Kennedy's "Why They Came" (p. 236) and Isabel Wilkerson's "The Epic Story of America's Great Migration" (p. 250).

> The experiences and motives of immigrants to the United States and African Americans moving within the country share unexpected similarities. In the essay "Why They Came," John F. Kennedy writes of the Irish and other nineteenth-century European immigrants who endured hardship and challenge to make new lives for themselves in a new land. He argues that these Europeans immigrated for three primary reasons: "religious persecution, political oppression, and economic hardship" (238). He also reminds readers of the truly desperate situations that people who ultimately choose immigration are typically in. Today, in comparison to European Americans who often talk about their immigrant ancestors, African Americans seem to have a very different story that is bound up in the involuntary experience of slavery. However, Isabel Wilkerson describes a part of African American history that is surprisingly similar to the European American immigration history. Between 1915 and 1970, "some six million black southerners left the land of their forefathers and fanned out across the country for an uncertain existence in nearly every other corner of America" (251). Similar to their European immigrant counterparts, African Americans from the U.S. South fled their homeland because of political oppression, economic hardship, and racial (as opposed to religious) persecution. Further, similar to the European immigrants, these African Americans experienced economic success, but also more hardship, discrimination, and the need for much hard work. Kennedy's words of admiration for European immigrants clearly apply just as well to these American migrants: "Little is more extraordinary than the decision to migrate, little more extraordinary than the accumulation of emotions and thoughts which finally leads a family to say farewell to a community where it has lived for centuries, to abandon old ties and familiar landmarks" (236).

Toolkit
2.11 Thinking with and against Other Writers

This toolkit will help you better integrate other writers' ideas into your essay by creating a bridge sentence between another writer's ideas and your own ideas.

In your college writing assignments, you may be asked to work with the ideas of other writers. Sometimes you will accept these ideas, sometimes you will reject them, and other times you will accept certain parts and reject others. This exercise asks you to think with, against, or both with and against another writer by choosing from among the bridge sentences presented in the following list.

What to Do

1. **After reading an article, summarize the writer's ideas about the issue(s).** (See Toolkits 1.3 and 2.5 for more on writing summaries.)

2. **Write briefly about your position or reaction to the issue(s) the article raises.**

3. **Compare your responses to steps 1 and 2, and decide if you accept, reject, or partly accept and partly reject the views of the writer.** Make some notes about your position.

4. **Choose the bridge sentence from the following list that most closely reflects your point of view, and fill in the blanks.** Insert the writer's name where "the writer" appears, and use the appropriate pronoun instead of "he or she" or "his or her." Add this bridge sentence after the summary you wrote for step 1.

   Thinking with Other Writers (Acceptance):

   a. _____ [The writer] makes a good point about _____. This point is important because _____.

   b. _____ [The writer] correctly argues _____ because _____.

   Thinking against Other Writers (Rejection):

   c. _____ [The writer] incorrectly argues _____ because _____.

   d. _____ [The writer] unconvincingly argues _____ because her or his evidence is weak. Specifically, the evidence about _____ is weak because _____.

   Thinking with *and* against Other Writers (Partial Acceptance and Rejection):

   e. Although _____ [the writer] is right to argue _____, he or she does not take into account another important issue: _____ _____.

   f. Although_____ [the writer's] point about_____ is not convincing, she or he makes an effective argument concerning _____.

5. **Following the bridge sentence, write three or four additional sentences to explain your position.**

Here is an example using "Escaping Digital Histories" by Julian B. Gewirtz and Adam B. Kern (p. 399).

In "Escaping Digital Histories," Julian B. Gewirtz and Adam B. Kern point out the dangers of a permanent digital record of someone's ideas, suggesting that ——— the information available may not provide an accurate idea of the person. They offer a hypothetical example: "Say that as an opinionated sixteen-year-old, someone wrote polemical public posts about her opposition to abortion. Her views shifted during college, but she never posted an announcement of that. Then, ten years later, she applies to teach under a pro-choice principal. The principal checks Facebook, sees her history—and then glances to his five other equally qualified applicants" (400). In this case, the principal was judging this job applicant based on outdated information. Gewirtz and Kern make a good point ——— that society needs to rethink how we use the information that is found in digital histories. This point is important because it makes us think about other ways that this situation could have played out. Because the post was so old, the principal could have asked her if her views had changed. The applicant also could have done a search of her name to see if she needed to correct any old information that might be giving people the wrong impression of her.

— Summary of article

— Bridge between summary of article and paragraph writer's thoughts

Further explanation of writer's view

Toolkit 2.12

Discussion and Analysis

This toolkit will help you improve your essay by expanding the areas of discussion and analysis, producing a richer, longer, and more thoughtful essay.

When writers include substantial discussion or analysis in their essays, they develop their ideas more fully and richly. Developing discussion in your essays allows you to write more about the evidence you have, rather than feeling as though you need to add new examples to meet the length requirement. (Evidence usually consists of summaries, quotations, or examples.) Discussion, sometimes called analysis or explanation, explains how you view or interpret your examples, and how you see your evidence working to support your thesis or guiding question.

What to Do

1. **Use two different-colored highlighters or fonts to identify the following places in your essay draft:** Use one color to mark those places where you provide evidence through summary, quotation, or example, and another to mark those places where you discuss or explain that evidence.

2. **Look at the draft to evaluate the proportion or balance between evidence and discussion.** Things to consider:

   • Are the two colors used in a balanced way (is there roughly an equal amount of each color), or is there a lot more of one color than the other?

If you notice that your essay is primarily the color of evidence, revise your draft by adding discussion after each example.

- Do you notice yourself combining evidence and discussion in the same paragraph, or are the two colors kept in separate paragraphs? It is usually most effective to combine evidence and discussion of it in the same paragraph. Revise to combine evidence and discussion, where necessary.

Here are some phrases that can help you create new sentences that will add to your discussion of your evidence:

- _____ happens because
- _____ is important because
- _____ shows
- _____ proves
- _____ suggests
- _____ could mean that
- _____ disproves
- _____ challenges

Here's an example of step 1 from the "What to Do" list above:

Many people face difficulties because of things they posted online in the past, but society needs to become more forgiving of poor decisions that do not harm anyone. In "Escaping Digital Histories," recent college graduates Julian B. Gewirtz and Adam B. Kern write from the perspective of young people who have grown up with the Internet and have never lived without social media and the presence of selfies, embarrassing videos, and thoughtless online comments.

Evidence: summary

They discuss how their generation will have to deal with having their lives recorded, viewed, and even misinterpreted by both friends and potential employers for the rest of their lives. Gewirtz and Kern propose that the solution to this problem is for society to pass a "cultural treaty" and to stop judging and caring about the often stupid things people said and did when they were young. This suggestion is important because as a society we should rethink how we judge the information we find online. We need to recognize that

Discussion

sometimes young people will post comments or silly pictures without thinking about the wrong impression they create. We need to accept that people will make silly mistakes and not hold it against them.

Toolkit
2.13 # Overcoming Writer's Block

> This toolkit provides strategies for when you have a draft due and you have nothing written.

That feeling of panic and despair that comes when a deadline looms and you are faced with a blank screen is one all writers have felt, some more frequently than others. Do not give up and abandon the project as hopeless: Something written is always better than nothing written.

Your writer's block is likely a problem of seeing the assignment as one big task, instead of seeing the individual steps needed to get the job done. But there are steps you can take, one by one, that will help you move past writer's block. Sometimes these steps are more obvious than others, and sometimes an assignment requires that you develop the steps on your own.

What to Do

1. **Reread the writing assignment.** You may have to do this five or six times. Often an assignment has directions that actually imply a set of steps. As an example, consider the following writing assignment, which is based on the readings in Chapter 5.

    > A fundamental human value is that a person should not be judged by his or her appearance. This is a value that is reflected in cliché ("Don't judge a book by its cover"), popular culture (*Shrek*), and classic literature (Victor Hugo's *The Hunchback of Notre Dame*). But while this value is widely upheld *in theory*, we seem to have trouble following the value in practice. For this writing assignment, your job is to analyze why people *do* judge by appearance in particular situations (e.g., in the case of the obese, the tattooed, the pierced, the ultrathin, or those who dress revealingly). You should choose your own case (or cases) to help you explain — not justify, just simply explain — why people violate this fundamental human value.

    The assignment follows this basic pattern:

    - First, a statement about the topic: *A fundamental human value is that a person should not be judged by his or her appearance.*

    - Second, a statement that reveals a problem with that statement: *But . . . we seem to have trouble following the value in practice.*

    - Third, the question: *Why do people judge some people by appearance?*

    - Fourth, the directions: *Choose your own case (or cases) to help you explain . . . why people violate this fundamental human value.*

As a to-do list, this is not perfect, but it can get you a draft. Follow the assignment pattern to start your draft. Looking at the pattern reveals that the writer's job is to discuss the topic, articulate a response to the question, analyze an example of people who are judged by appearance, describe their situation, and then explain what this example reveals about why people violate the shared value.

2. **Do the easiest part first.** Most writers find narrating (telling a story), describing, and summarizing easiest, and fortunately, most assignments require writers to do some narrating, describing, or summarizing. Reviewing the assignment, find this part of the essay and just work on that, not worrying about the rest of the assignment. For example, in the preceding sample assignment, students are asked to describe a case of a group of people who are judged on their appearance; therefore, a writer could start writing that part first (in short, starting with a body paragraph rather than the introduction).

3. **Write a quotation response.** Many assignments will require that you work with a particular reading. If this is the case, then you can go back to the reading and find important or memorable lines and use those to begin your writing process. First, select three notable passages from the reading that you could quote. If you have already highlighted or annotated the reading, read through the marked passages to select three that seem to be the most interesting or important. If you haven't marked the reading, reread and annotate it now. Along with highlighting summaries and facts, identify profound, powerful, or provocative statements. Open a page in your word processor and type up the statements you have selected. Then, respond to each quotation, following these guidelines:

   a. Rephrase and summarize the quotation in your own words: "The author claims/describes/notes _____."

   b. Express your reaction: agreement, disagreement, or another response.

   c. Support your agreement, disagreement, or other response with further discussion and reasons: What makes you react as you do?

4. **Write a five- to seven-sentence draft.** The length of essays—the required word or page count—paralyzes some writers. Ignore length for a bit, and take on the quickie, five- to seven-sentence draft. The idea is to have sentences stand in for paragraphs so that you can quickly sketch out the whole draft, providing a skeletal shape for your essay that will give you confidence to write out the details. Thus, for each paragraph that you will eventually have to write, compose just one sentence. The sentences can be unoriginal, clumsy, or even a rehash of the assignment—they are just a tool for getting you started. Taking this approach will allow you to sketch out your full essay in the time it would take to write one paragraph. For example, when faced with

the sample essay assignment of this toolkit, you might compose the following sentences:

1. *Right from when we are little kids, adults always tell us that we shouldn't judge other people by what they look like.*

2. *Every day I hear people making judgmental comments.*

3. *Why do people judge others by their appearances when we are all taught that it is morally wrong to do that?*

4. *A group of people I see being judged harshly is made up of people with face piercings.*

5. *I think people think judging piercers is OK because piercers are not born with piercings but choose to get them.*

6. *I think it's human instinct to be judgmental of people who look different from us.*

7. *But humans can improve on these issues. Once people see the pain that judgment causes — like racist judgment — they learn how not to be so judgmental.*

Once you have written the five- to seven-sentence draft, develop each sentence into a paragraph to form a draft of the full essay.

5. **What not to do:** Desperate writers can fall into academic dishonesty or plagiarism easily and quickly, sometimes before they have time to regret it. Be wary of this danger, particularly when using search engines. If you enter your topic into a search engine, you will find essays that others have written, which you can copy or purchase. Don't do it. This is dangerous because it's so tempting, but it's easy to get caught. Teachers know how to use search engines, too. What is more, these essays are often terrible: simpleminded, predictable, and without any personality. Besides being easy to spot, they are simply a bad option. Academic dishonesty is punishable by failing grades and, worse, expulsion.

Toolkit

3.1 **Keys to Organization**

This toolkit will help you figure out the best way to structure a fully drafted essay by introducing the keys to organization, which are expanded on throughout the rest of this section.

What to Do

1. **Clarify what you are attempting to argue or prove.** Put aside your draft and write yourself a note explaining what your essay is about—that is, what you want readers to understand.

2. **Break it down.** Looking at what you wrote for step 1, make a list of what you need to do to accomplish your goals. For example, how might your thesis be broken down into separate parts? What do you need to do for each part?

3. **Plan.** Looking at what you have listed for step 2, what might be a logical way to order this work? Some basic organizational patterns include **chronological order**, **comparison and contrast**, **cause and effect**, and **order of increasing importance**. Would any of these organizational patterns work for your essay?

4. **Convey the pattern you choose to your readers** (through **paragraph order**, **topic sentences**, and **transitional expressions**).

   - **Paragraph order.** Look at how you have ordered your body paragraphs. Are you building from the smallest, least important point to the largest, most important one? Are you deliberately saving surprising new information for the end? If so, is that effective?

   - **Topic sentences.** Make sure each of your body paragraphs includes a topic sentence (typically the first sentence of a paragraph) that indicates what the paragraph is setting out to do. The topic sentence functions like the thesis of the paragraph, and it is sometimes called a supporting claim. Make sure that all the topic sentences relate back to the thesis or main point. (See Toolkit 3.7 for more about topic sentences.)

   - **Transitional expressions.** These words and phrases help convey to readers how the parts of your essay are related. In a cause-and-effect essay, you could use phrases like *as a result*, *because*, or *consequently* to indicate that you have moved from talking about a cause to considering its effect. (See Toolkits 3.8 and 3.9 for more information about transitions.)

LaunchPad Solo

76   Visit **LaunchPad Solo for Readers and Writers** for more practice on the skills covered in this section.

Toolkit
3.2 **Clustering**

This toolkit will enable you to see and make connections between ideas early in your writing process through clustering.

Clustering refers to a free-style, nonlinear form of brainstorming that is helpful to many writers who find outlining too restrictive and freewriting too open. It is also useful for people who think visually or who are working on a group project. Like freewriting, clustering is about generating lots of ideas — more than you will actually use — and turning off the critic in your head.

What to Do

1. **Write down your main idea or topic in the center of a sheet of paper, and draw a circle around it.**

2. **Arrange your current ideas and examples in branches leading out from the center.**

3. **Use lines and other visual cues to demonstrate connections between all the subtopics.**

Here is an example of clustering for an essay on beauty and body image:

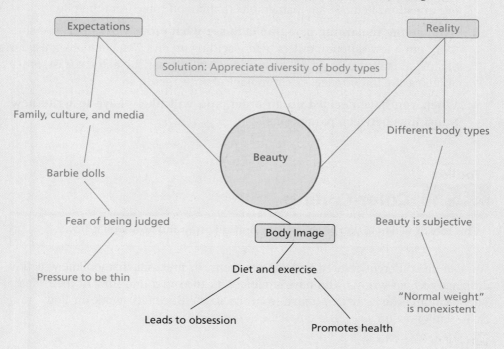

3.3   Scissors and Tape

> In this toolkit, writers who are struggling to figure out how to structure their essays will learn how to cut up their writing into chunks and then rearrange them to try out new ways to organize their essay.

Scissors-and-tape revision is a technique that was developed long before computers were invented, when people wrote out drafts of essays in longhand. They would then use scissors to cut the essay up before reorganizing it and taping it back together. Today, even though writers can easily reorganize paragraphs and other chunks of writing on the computer, often the computer limits our view. The screen is only so big, making it difficult to see the whole essay at once.

The object of this exercise is to radically reimagine the possible order of your ideas.

What to Do

1. **Print out your draft, single-sided, and then cut it apart with scissors so that each paragraph is separate.** Shuffle these smaller pieces of paper so that they are out of their original order. This seems odd, but it's crucial to the goal of truly rethinking organization.

2. **Read each paragraph separately, testing its relevance to the thesis or guiding question.** Remove any paragraphs that are off topic from the pile.

3. **Arrange the remaining paragraphs to see what order works best.** Be sure to try out a few different orders before settling on one. You could even use an organizational strategy (e.g., cause and effect, comparison and contrast, order of increasing importance, or chronological order) to do so.

4. **When you have decided on an order, you will likely have to write new transitions between paragraphs.**

Toolkit
3.4   Color-Coding

> This toolkit will help you visualize your drafted essay and how well it flows.

You can use different-colored highlighters, pens, or fonts for this toolkit, which is designed to help writers who have trouble with the order and flow of their ideas. This technique helps writers move from the vague directive "work on flow" to a clear plan of action.

What to Do

1. **Make a list of the ideas in your essay, and assign each one a color.**

2. **Using different-colored highlighters, pens, or fonts, work through your draft, marking each idea in its assigned color.**

3. **When you are done, evaluate what you have:**

   - Do you see a mix of colors within the body paragraphs? If so, consider whether you should reorganize so that each color / idea has its own paragraph or series of paragraphs.

   - Do you see that the colors of paragraphs alternate (e.g., paragraph 2 is yellow, paragraph 3 is green, paragraph 4 is yellow)? If so, consider whether it would make sense to put the same-colored paragraphs in sequence (e.g., put the two yellow paragraphs in sequence).

   - What else does the color-coding help you see about your essay in terms of the amount of attention you give to each idea? For example, if you notice that one color is used much less than the others, decide if you should cut or develop that idea.

4. **Make notes about how to reorder your paragraphs to create a clearer, more logical order.**

5. **When you have figured out a good sequence, you will likely have to write new transitions between paragraphs.**

Toolkit 3.5 Reverse Outline

> This toolkit will help you see and evaluate what you have done in a draft and make a plan for revision.

Organizing writing so that it is clear for readers can be difficult. The problem is that we can't always see what we've written accurately, and therefore we can't see what may be confusing or ineffective for our readers.

The reverse outline records what you have written so that you can really *see* it. What makes this a reverse outline is that you are not outlining what you *intend* to write but rather recording in detail what you *actually wrote*. There's usually a difference!

What to Do

1. **Number the paragraphs in your draft.**

2. **On a separate piece of paper (or in a new document window), begin your reverse outline, making sure you can see your draft while you write the outline.** Set up your reverse outline in the following format, using as many rows as needed for your draft:

Reverse Outline

Essay Title: _____

Paragraph #	What Was Said	Notes to Self
1		
2		
3		
4		
5		
6		

3. **Read your draft, pausing after each paragraph to ask yourself two simple questions: What was said here? What was this paragraph about?** Write those notes in the blanks under "What Was Said" in the reverse outline.

4. **In the third column, "Notes to Self," write a note to yourself about any problems or strengths in the paragraph, and what—if anything—needs to be done.**

   Here is an example for an essay related to readings in Chapter 6. The writer is making the case that full fluency in English should not be a requirement for citizenship.

Reverse Outline

Essay Title: Just Enough English

Paragraph #	What Was Said	Notes to Self
1	Makes claim that immigrants are able to survive without learning very much English. Gives example of grandmother who lives in her own apartment and is fine.	Strong statements, some off-topic sentences; example of grandmother may not fit in the intro.
2	Says that grandmother wouldn't survive without children and grandchildren who translate for her a lot.	Not sure this example proves my point.

Paragraph #	What Was Said	Notes to Self
3	Describes Wong's essay and says that her parents are succeeding without great English skills.	Example and paragraph are good.
4	Uses Department of Homeland Security English test for citizenship to show that citizens don't need to know English very well. Also tells a story of someone who passed the immigration test even though he doesn't speak English well.	Need to fix the citation. Paragraph just stops. Does it fit with the thesis enough?
5	Human Rights Case article discussion. Talks about how completely sad and horrible these stories of illegal immigrants are—that these people need "a break."	Is this example off topic? Think so. ☹
6	Points out that it is still important for immigrants to learn English— that it helps in getting ahead for most people.	Good point, but bad ending for essay. Goes off topic a bit.

5. **Write up a plan for revision.** Study your reverse outline, or review it with someone else. Answer the following questions carefully.

   a. What is missing? What needs to be added?

   b. Where do you go off topic?

   c. What parts need to be cut out entirely?

   d. What more needs to be said to make your thesis persuasive or to support your main point?

   e. What needs to be done to make the order of ideas and paragraphs more logical? Which paragraphs need to be reordered, and how?

   f. What else needs to be done to improve the essay?

   Here's an example of a plan for revision, drawing from the reverse outline of the essay draft "Just Enough English":

   - I will cut out *paragraphs 2 and 5.*

   - I will *move paragraph 4* so that it becomes the 2nd paragraph. Writing about the official test for English citizenship is very persuasive, and so it would be better to use it sooner.

   - Then I will talk about Wong (which will stay as paragraph 3), but add in more quotes that show that her parents are OK without knowing English well.

   - Next, need to add some more examples for my thesis.

- After discussing the importance of English (now paragraph 6), need a new paragraph that makes a point about how many native speakers are unsympathetic to people who don't speak English, and how it is not justified or fair.

6. **Go back to the draft and rewrite, using the plan you have just prepared.** This is the time to add, cut, and revise, not just edit.

Toolkit
3.6 **Purpose Outline**

This toolkit will help you evaluate how well your essay stays focused on your point.

The purpose outline is typically used during the revision process; it helps writers examine their own writing for content, organization, and effectiveness. This outline can be used to evaluate the relevance of your ideas to the thesis, as well as to ensure that you have conveyed that relevance to readers. While other outlines are focused on topics and ideas, the purpose outline is interested in *what you say* in the essay and *why*. That is, this outline asks you to list your ideas and examples, and also to evaluate the *purpose* they serve in your essay.

The purpose outline will help with discussion, development, and organization. If you have trouble determining an example's purpose, for instance, this is a sign that the example may not be relevant to your argument or that its relevance needs to be developed. You can also see whether the movement between paragraphs needs to be smoothed out or if there are gaps in your argument that need to be filled in.

What to Do

1. **Write your thesis statement or guiding question at the top of a sheet of paper or a new document, and then create three columns.** Label them "Summary of Paragraph," "Purpose of Paragraph and Connection to Thesis / Question," and "Plan for Revision."

2. **In the first column, make a reverse outline by briefly summarizing each paragraph.**

3. **In the second column, answer the following questions for each paragraph:**
   a. What purpose does this paragraph serve in my essay?
   b. How does it relate to the thesis or guiding question?
   c. Is the purpose clearly expressed in a topic sentence?

4. **In the third column, evaluate your outline, making notes based on your review of the following:**

   a. Are there any paragraphs whose purpose you could not explain? Determine whether you need to revise them so that they serve a purpose or simply cut them.

   b. Evaluate your outline more generally. Have you said everything you need to say to support your thesis or guiding question? Have you said everything you wanted to say?

   c. Do you need to take out any information?

   d. Look at the order of your points: Would your essay be more clear or logical if you moved any of the paragraphs?

   e. Is the purpose of each body paragraph clearly expressed? Where do you need to add or revise a topic sentence or explanation to make the connection and relevance clear?

5. **Review the to-do list you've created in column 3 and get to work: Revise that essay.**

This sample purpose outline was drawn from a draft based on Chapter 8 and written in response to the following question:

The Advantage of Gender Roles: While many of the authors collected here appear to argue that traditional gender roles are limiting and should be abandoned, many other people celebrate gender roles. What's so great about gender roles? Make an argument for or against the value of gender roles: How does having specific gender roles support or work against individuals, families, or social groups? To make this argument, you will need to consider those who disagree with you, and use a counterargument to refute their claims.

Thesis: *Traditional gender roles are only good if they suit us as individuals*

Summary of Paragraph	Purpose of Paragraph and Connection to Thesis/Question	Plan for Revision
How lots of people are flexible about gender, but still most people are very gendered—that is, very feminine or very masculine, as traditionally defined.	This paragraphs sets up essay. Connected to thesis, though the thesis isn't stated.	Add in thesis, and plan for how I will support the thesis.
About Matt Duron's son's interest in the female gender; ironically, the son is very traditional in his view of gender, even if it is not the gender he was "assigned"!	Connected—though it isn't said exactly how.	Tie this paragraph more directly to the thesis. Add a topic sentence.

(Continued)

(Continued)

Summary of Paragraph	Purpose of Paragraph and Connection to Thesis / Question	Plan for Revision
About me: As a girl, I've always enjoyed being a girlie girl, even while being a good student and serious person. For me, the traditional gender role — with some exceptions — is very appealing.	Makes the point about how the traditional gender role is appealing.	Is this in the right place? Right in the middle? Should be first or last body paragraph. Last!
About Jennifer Finney Boylan: She was very uncomfortable as a boy her whole life, but she found a lot of happiness once she became a traditional girl.	This paragraph shows that gender roles do matter. Boylan doesn't reject gender; she just says that she was assigned the wrong one.	Move this up and compare with C. J. Duron.
		No conclusion! Need to figure out how to weave in main thesis throughout.

Toolkit
3.7 Topic Sentences

> This toolkit will help you evaluate paragraphs and improve your use of topic sentences as a way to sharpen your essay's focus.

The topic sentence does a job similar to that of the thesis: If the thesis expresses the main point or argument of a whole essay, the topic sentence indicates the main point or argument of a single paragraph. The topic sentence supports — helps prove — the thesis, so all the topic sentences should be related to the thesis. If you are writing in a non-argument genre, the topic sentence will still serve to introduce the main point of the paragraph.

We can ask similar questions when evaluating a topic sentence as when evaluating a thesis: Is it arguable? Is it too narrow? Is it too broad? The topic sentence should introduce the point you are trying to prove in the body paragraph, not only introduce your example.

Weak topic sentence (introduces only the example)

In "Escaping Digital Histories," Julian B. Gewirtz and Adam B. Kern discuss how today's young people face potential future problems because of what they have posted online.

While this would be a good way to introduce an example within a body paragraph, it's not a great way to introduce your paragraph's point.

Stronger topic sentence (introduces arguable claim)

Because they offer information that may be out of date, digital histories may be used to form incorrect ideas about people.

Topic sentences are usually placed as the first sentence in a paragraph.

What to Do

Evaluate your use of topic sentences.

1. **For each body paragraph, underline the sentence that expresses the claim or point the paragraph is going to prove.** If there is no sentence that does this, add one.

2. **Evaluate each topic sentence:**

    a. Does it indicate the main point of the paragraph? (Make sure it doesn't just introduce your example but rather introduces your *claim or point* about your example.)

    b. Is the topic sentence arguable? Does it require support and explanation? If so, good. If not, revise so that it is arguable.

    c. Is the topic sentence related to the thesis? If not, consider whether the paragraph is on topic. If the paragraph isn't proving something related to the thesis, it likely needs to be cut or revised.

    d. Does the topic sentence indicate the organizational strategy you are using? (Not all topic sentences will do this, but many will.) If you are organizing a cause-and-effect essay, for example, the topic sentence could convey the strategy by using such phrases as *because* and *as a result of*.

    e. Can you make the topic sentence the first sentence in the paragraph?

Bonus: You can also use this exercise to check your essay's organization. Read your thesis and then read your topic sentences to see if they flow logically.

Toolkit 3.8 A Checklist for Transitional Expressions

This toolkit will help you review a draft for transitional words and phrases, which make clear connections between sentences and greatly improve the readability and organization of an essay.

Most writers have heard of transitional words and phrases, yet many student writers are either not using them frequently enough or not using a great enough variety of them. When a writer wants to make clear to readers what the relationship between one idea and the next is, transitional words and phrases are very useful. As shown in the following lists, there are three common types of transitional words or phrases. While you can find even more if you search "transitional words and phrases" in a search engine, these lists can get you started.

To demonstrate cause and effect	To link ideas that are similar	To link ideas that are in conflict or opposition
Therefore	*Again*	*However*
Thus	*In addition*	*In contrast*
So	*At the same time*	*On the contrary*
It follows	*Similarly*	*On the other hand*
Then	*Likewise*	*Nonetheless*
As a result	*Furthermore*	*In reality*
Consequently	*First*	*In fact*
	Second	

What to Do

1. **Choose two different-colored highlighters** (we refer to yellow and orange in the directions, but any other colors would be fine).

2. **Analyze your use of transitional words and phrases.** Review your draft, and yellow-highlight all the times you use a transitional word or phrase to mark a transition from one idea to another.

3. **List the specific words and phrases you used, noting how many times you used each.**

4. **With the orange highlighter in hand, read your draft and make a mark between the sentences that do not use transitional words or phrases to connect them.**

5. **Now you are ready to revise your draft, with the following goals:**

   a. Inserting transitional words or phrases where they are absent and needed (by reviewing the orange highlighted spots and then adding transitions where your ideas shift or where you need to establish a connection between ideas).

   b. Diversifying your transitional words and phrases by replacing overly used words with new ones (by reviewing those highlighted in yellow).

Coherence between Paragraphs

> If your essay lacks "flow," is "choppy," or "jumps around," this toolkit will help you revise for coherence between paragraphs.

Writers must lead readers from one paragraph to the next. Readers cannot see inside writers' heads, so when writers do not make it obvious how one idea leads to the next, readers get lost.

To provide readers enough support, writers need to be more explicit in providing transitions between paragraphs by crafting transitional sentences and using transitional words. Toolkit 3.8 provides some help with transitional expressions, whereas this toolkit focuses on writing whole sentences to provide transitions from one paragraph to the next.

First, a demonstration: In the following excerpt from Chapter 2, the underlined sentences and phrases at the beginnings and ends of each paragraph work together. As writers, we always check these two sentences to make sure the connection between ideas is very close. Sometimes the ideas are so close that no extra words need to be added, but more often we need to repeat key words or phrases.

At first glance, an academic writing assignment appears straightforward. For example, consider this assignment: "Write a 3- to 4-page paper in which you take a position on the issues discussed by the authors we have read." This type of assignment, typically known as a position paper, issue paper, or response paper, is common in college classes. While this task sounds manageable enough, many writers struggle to complete it.

This writing assignment is difficult because behind the one-sentence instructions are dozens of unspecified tasks, starting with the first task, which is to overcome the instinct for procrastination. Most writers — students but also professors and professionals — procrastinate, coming up with a million things to do before placing fingers on a keyboard or putting pen to paper. It is the most common, and perhaps most difficult, problem that people have with writing: sitting down to do it.

Writers procrastinate because most assignments do not come with a set of directions that they can follow one by one, in the same way they might complete a homework assignment that asks them to answer questions 1 through 20. Writing a paper is too complicated to tackle in the same mechanical way someone might sort and fold the laundry or answer a series of questions about a reading assignment. With a writing assignment, it is not at all obvious how to complete the job, and it takes energy, experience, and knowledge to break the assignment down well enough to get the job done. Yet that is exactly what needs to be done.

The connecting idea here is the difficulty of writing assignments. In the first paragraph, the topic is introduced, ending with a statement of a problem, allowing the second paragraph to begin by addressing the problem and repeating the subject and the new idea.

The connecting idea here is procrastination. The second paragraph establishes that writers procrastinate, and the third paragraph establishes why. The transition repeats the problem and addresses an implied question, Why do writers procrastinate?

The connecting idea here is the notion of "breaking it down." The third paragraph establishes that breaking an assignment down is key to success, and the fourth paragraph explains this advice.

"Break it down" is the advice and direction that we offer again and again as writing teachers, and you will see this direction throughout *Intersections*. In this book, we are *breaking it down* for you, helping you figure out how to develop the skills to perform the many tasks that are required but not specified in the seemingly straightforward assignments that college students face every semester.

Before moving to your own draft, take a look at the following two paragraphs, which fail to connect. Revise this writing sample so that it transitions better: You can cut words, move them around, and add additional text.

There are countless famous achievements that came from an idea that was developed from intellectual inspiration—Charles Darwin's theory of evolution, J. K. Rowling's creation of Harry Potter, or Gandhi's development of a mass movement of nonviolent protest. Crucial to the development of their ideas was that rapid synapse firing that we all experience when we're truly inspired. This should be a goal of yours when you are writing: to think so deeply that you surprise yourself with the inspired ideas that your intellect generates.

We get provoked into thinking new ideas by reading, viewing, listening, and experiencing others' ideas. That's the start, anyway. Then, crucially, at some point we have to bring our ideas out and develop them. Albert Einstein once responded to a question about where his laboratory was by pointing to his pen—"Here," he said. Einstein was telling the reporter his genius didn't all come from his head or from a well-equipped laboratory: What he had to do was engage in writing, in trying to express his thoughts in writing in order to figure out what it was that he thought.

What to Do

Here we have detailed several methods for establishing paragraph-to-paragraph transitions. Review these closely before returning to your own draft to revise for paragraph transitioning.

1. **Topic introduction / topic expansion method**—for when you are funneling down into a topic, from broad to narrow, or when you want to elaborate on an idea.

   - End one paragraph with a summary of the point of the paragraph and an introduction of the upcoming topic. For example: *The Irish immigrants were made fun of not only for their religion but also for their reputation for being big drinkers.*

   - Begin the next paragraph by discussing this topic: *DeGuzman provides many images from popular magazines and newspapers that depict the Irish as drunk and incompetent as a result, a depiction that must have made Irish immigrants furious.*

Most of the time, writers organize paragraphs by topics or subtopics, and transitions between paragraphs are provided by a brief introduction of the new topic or subtopic at the close of one paragraph. Repeating key words or concepts is one useful strategy.

2. **Continue a narrative thread**—for when you are simply continuing a story, but you want to break it up so that it's not too long and you can provide some reflection.

   - End a paragraph with a reflective statement, even a mild one. For example: *I was getting myself in a lot of trouble in school, but I don't think I even knew it.*

   - Begin the next paragraph by connecting to the reflective theme—in this case, the theme of trouble: *Fourth grade should have been a turning point, but instead I continued my downward spiral, helped in no part by my assignment for Mr. Brooks's class.*

3. **Topic sentence method**—when your essay is organized by category, use your topic sentences to indicate the relationship between paragraphs.

   - Write topic sentences that show paragraphs' relationships to each other. For example, begin one body paragraph, *One source of body-image pressure on boys is the media.*

   - Begin the next paragraph, *Another source of pressure on boys' body image is athletes' endorsements of protein supplements.*

4. **Question/answer: explicit**

   - End one paragraph with a question.
   - Begin the next paragraph with an answer.

5. **Question/answer: implicit or indirect**

   - End one paragraph with a strong, assertive, or provocative statement that makes readers ask a question in their heads.
   - Begin the next paragraph with an answer.
   - See the second and third excerpted paragraphs from Chapter 2 for an example of this method (p. 87). (Implicit question: Why do writers procrastinate?)

Toolkit 3.10	Organizing Your Comparison-and-Contrast Essay

This toolkit will help you organize your comparison-and-contrast essay.

There are two common methods for structuring a comparison-and-contrast essay: a basic approach, which is a good starting point, and a more advanced approach, which you should aim for as you become a more accomplished writer.

Basic Approach: Writer-by-Writer Method

In the first method, you look at your writers' examples writer by writer (one writer at a time). You present the ideas of your first writer, and then the ideas of your second writer. See this example on the topic of immigration:

Section about Writer A

Writer A's views on immigration policy

Writer A's views about immigration's impact on the economy

Section about Writer B

Writer B's views on immigration policy

Writer B's views about immigration's impact on the economy

More Advanced Approach: Point-by-Point Method

In the second method, you look at your examples point by point (one point or issue at a time). See this example on the same topic:

Section about immigration policy

Writer A's views on immigration policy

Writer B's views on immigration policy

Section about immigration's impact on the economy

Writer A's views about immigration's impact on the economy

Writer B's views about immigration's impact on the economy

What to Do

1. **Review a comparison-and-contrast essay you have drafted** (perhaps the two- to three-paragraph draft you wrote for Toolkit 2.9). Identify which method you are currently using: writer by writer or point by point.

2. **Write a new version of your essay, this time using the other method.** (So, if you wrote a writer-by-writer comparison, now write a point-by-point version, and vice versa.) Make sure to use some transitional expressions

(see Toolkits 3.8 and 3.9) to help indicate the relationship between ideas and examples.

3. **Now, evaluate the two versions.** Which seems more effective for this particular comparison? Explain why.

Toolkit 3.11 Paragraph Makeover

This toolkit will help you identify and sort out jumbled ideas within an individual paragraph.

Rather than focusing on the overall organization of your essay, this toolkit directs your attention to individual paragraphs. It asks you to think about similar issues of order, focus, and transition but this time at the paragraph level.

What to Do

1. **Look at one paragraph from your essay.**

2. **Write down or highlight the paragraph's main idea so that you can keep it in mind as you work.**

3. **Read each sentence of the paragraph by itself, asking whether it is relevant to the main idea of the paragraph.** If it is not relevant, cut the sentence now.

4. **After cutting irrelevant sentences, go through the paragraph again, sentence by sentence, this time looking for logic and flow:** Does each sentence move logically one after the other? Do the ideas alternate? Would it make sense to put them in a different order? If so, reorder the sentences now.

5. **Locate any transitional expressions in the paragraph.** If there aren't any, where might you add a few so that readers can better see the relationship and movement between your ideas? Add some now.

6. **Identify places where you need to add more information or explanation to fill in any gaps in logic or flow.** Add that information or explanation now.

7. **Reread your new version, repeating steps 3–6 as needed.**

Toolkit
4.1 Tackling Revision

This toolkit will help you evaluate your draft for revision by reviewing the major components of thesis-driven essays. You can work on the whole toolkit for a thorough review, or you can choose one or more parts to focus on particular aspects of your essay.

What to Do

After you have written a draft of an essay, use the following questions and strategies to revise it, remembering that good writers typically revise — make cuts and additions to — at least 25 percent of their drafts each time they undertake a major revision.

For additional help on any of these areas, refer to the suggested toolkits (in parentheses).

Introduction (Establishing Focus)

1. Without copying from your draft, write down your thesis in one or two clear sentences. Remember: Your thesis is your statement of the topic and your position on that topic.

2. Go to your draft and read your first paragraph closely. What does it *suggest* you will argue in your essay?

3. Compare what you wrote for steps 1 and 2:

   - Do they match? That is, do the thesis and the draft introduction have the same focus? (Toolkit 4.11 or 4.14)

   - Which point is stronger and worth arguing? Make sure your thesis is not a statement of fact or something too broad, general, or vague that will leave you with nothing to prove in the essay. Keep the stronger version of your thesis, revising it as is helpful. This will be your new thesis. (Toolkit 2.4)

Development

1. Quickly outline or list the major examples in the body paragraphs.

   - Test the examples against the new thesis: Is each relevant and on topic? Cut or revise any that aren't.

LaunchPad Solo

92 Visit **LaunchPad Solo for Readers and Writers** for more practice on the skills covered in this section.

- For the supporting examples, check to make sure that you have explained their relevance in the essay. (Toolkit 2.5 or 2.12)

2. Look at how you use quotations.

- Are they just "stuck in," without contributing much to the essay, or do you discuss their relevance and actively use them to make the case for your main idea?

- If quotations are just stuck in, add some explanation of how they support your point. (Toolkit 2.6)

Discussion (More Than Summary)

1. Go through your essay, paragraph by paragraph, noting (highlighting works well) where you summarize an example.

2. Next, go back through your essay and look at what follows these moments of summary. Do you discuss the example?

3. If you don't discuss the example, either add the necessary explanation that links it to your point, or cut the summary if the details are not relevant to your argument. (Toolkit 2.12)

Organization

1. Check that each body paragraph has a single idea that relates to the thesis. (Toolkit 3.5 or 3.6)

2. Split up paragraphs that contain too many ideas.

3. Revise or cut any paragraphs that do not relate to your thesis. (Toolkit 3.5 or 3.6)

4. Make sure each body paragraph includes a topic sentence that introduces the paragraph's idea. (Toolkit 3.7)

5. Check if each paragraph flows from the previous paragraph, adding transitions where necessary. (Toolkits 3.8 and 3.9)

6. Consider whether the paragraphs are clearly organized, reordering if needed. (Toolkit 3.3, 3.4, 3.5, or 3.6)

Conclusion (Reestablishing Focus)

1. Is there a conclusion? If not, add one. (Toolkit 2.8)

2. Does the conclusion relate to the thesis and overall body of the essay? Revise it to make it relevant to the rest of the essay. (Toolkit 4.15)

3. What do you want readers to learn from your essay? Make sure this is expressed in the conclusion.

Clarity

1. Read each sentence separately, asking yourself the following questions and revising as necessary:

   ● Does the sentence say what you intended? (Toolkit 6.14)
   ● Does it make sense?
   ● Is it truly relevant to the topic?
   ● Is it grammatically correct?

2. Proofread for your personal pattern of sentence-level errors (e.g., fragments, run-ons, comma splices, *they're/their/there* usage, or *to/two/too* issues). (Toolkits 5.14, 5.15, and 6.15)

Toolkit
4.2 **Peer Review Guidelines**

This toolkit provides an introduction to the peer review process and is a good place to start if you are new to peer review.

During peer review, a writer has his or her draft reviewed by a classmate or another reader who is willing to give feedback to help the writer revise the draft.

Peer review serves two main purposes. First, it provides the writer with a different perspective on the draft—fresh eyes that can more easily and objectively identify passages that do not make sense, that seem out of place, or that are especially effective. Second, it improves reviewers' ability to thoughtfully revise their own work through the practice of raising questions and identifying places for revision in the work of others.

Peer review can take many forms, and we offer several options in the following toolkits; your instructor may provide additional directions.

What to Do

1. **Address the writer directly in your comments.** For example, a comment would read something like, "I had trouble following *your* second paragraph because . . . ," not "The writer's second paragraph was hard to follow because . . ." You can think of yourself as writing a letter directly to the writer.

2. **Be honest as a responder (and expect and accept honesty from your responders).** Point out passages that are good as well as passages that need revision.

3. **Offer specific, constructive criticism and suggestions.** "I liked it" and "I didn't like it" are not helpful comments because they don't let the writer know the specific strong and weak points of the essay or provide suggestions for what needs to be revised.

4. **Consider the following issues:**

   - How well the writer seems to have understood both the assignment and the readings

   - The strengths of the draft

   - Where the draft needs most improvement

   - What the apparent focus is

   - Where the argument seems to trail off or go nowhere

   - Where the argument can be expanded

   - Which word choices and phrasing are particularly fitting, and which are vague or confusing

5. **Ask questions.** If possible, leave some time at the end of the peer review session so that you and your classmates can read each other's comments and ask for clarification.

6. **Use feedback productively.** See Toolkit 4.9 for strategies on revising with feedback.

Toolkit 4.3 "Basic Checklist" Peer Review

> This toolkit will help you provide feedback for others using the Essential Elements of Academic Essays as a guide.

In this peer review, the elements highlighted in the Essential Elements of Academic Essays will help direct the reader's response to the writer's essay. Before responding to the following lists of questions, both writer and reader should review the Essential Elements of Academic Essays, found on page 33.

What to Do

Use a separate document or sheet of paper for those comments that can't be written on the essay itself.

Focus

- What is the writer's thesis, guiding question, or purpose? Copy it down so that the writer knows what you have identified.
- Does each paragraph focus on this thesis, guiding question, or purpose? Identify those passages where you see the writer drifting off topic.

Development

- How effectively does the writer support the points being made?
- What examples does the writer offer to support the thesis, main point, or guiding question?
- Which examples do you like best, and why?
- Which examples need to be revised or cut? Why?
- Which examples are unclear in terms of how they relate to the main point?
- Where is more evidence needed for you to understand or accept the writer's point?

Discussion

- How effectively does the writer explain, reflect on, and analyze the examples, evidence, or description presented?
- Identify where you see the writer going beyond the obvious or superficial reaction or observation in productive ways.
- Identify where the writer needs to add more discussion in order to go beyond the superficial or obvious.
- Where could you use more explanation to understand or accept the writer's points?

Organization

- How clear is the logic or flow of the essay? Note those areas where the order of ideas is unclear.
- How well does each paragraph flow into the next? Note any passages where the flow feels abrupt or confusing.

Clarity

- Highlight or mark a few sentences that are particularly powerful to give the writer a sense of what is working well.
- Highlight or mark those sentences that are unclear or that have grammar or word choice problems.

Peer Review for Essay Development

This peer review toolkit will help you provide other writers with feedback for developing or expanding their essays.

You will need a partner for this toolkit.

What to Do

1. **After reading your partner's draft once, reread it and underline the most interesting phrases, sentences, or ideas.** You should be able to find at least three things to underline.

2. **Try to identify the thesis or main point.** What is the writer trying to say or prove? Quote or summarize it. If you cannot find a specific sentence, write what you feel is the *unstated* or *implicit* thesis.

3. **Use brackets to mark off any parts of the draft that you find confusing or unclear.**

4. **List the specific points that the writer makes to support his or her thesis.** Then, after each specific point, write a question or two that will help the writer say more. You might ask a question that challenges the writer to expand or clarify, or one that encourages the writer to give more examples or explanation.

   First Supporting Point: _____

   Question(s) about First Supporting Point: _____

   Second Supporting Point: _____

   Question(s) about Second Supporting Point: _____

   Continue the list to cover all the points the writer uses.

5. **Give the writer another idea for how to prove the main point.** That is, suggest another example or something from the readings that the writer might use to support the main point.

6. **Offer one final suggestion, or ask one final question.** Address another aspect of the essay that you feel needs some attention.

Summary Peer Review

This peer review toolkit will enable you to get feedback that will help you under-stand how your essay is coming across.

You will need a partner for this toolkit.

What to Do

1. **Read your partner's essay carefully.**

2. **Write a one-paragraph summary of your partner's essay.** Point out the the-sis, note the examples and supporting points, and indicate the organization. (In other words, provide a condensed version of the essay so that the writer can see if his or her ideas came across accurately and clearly.)

3. **Exchange summaries, and read your partner's summary of your essay.** The summary will let you see whether or not the point(s) you wished to make was recognized and understood in the way you intended.

4. **Respond in writing to your partner's summary of your essay.** How accu-rately does the summary reflect your intentions and ideas? What has your partner understood clearly? What has your partner misread or not understood in the way you intended? What does the summary help you realize about your essay?

5. **Plan your revision.** What will you do to improve your essay?

Conversational Peer Review

This toolkit provides a method for receiving feedback that is relaxed, open, and natural.

The most natural and free-form method for getting helpful feedback on a draft is through conversational peer review groups. This method has the advantage of being fun, though for it to work well, writers need to take clear written notes to work from later.

Conversational peer review works best in groups of three, though groups of two or four can work as well.

What to Do

Each writer should come to a session with drafts to share with each member of the group. Members of the group will take turns playing the writer role. Instructions for both the writer and listeners follow; everyone in the group should read these directions before getting started.

Writer	Listener(s)
1. State what you are most happy about with the draft and what you are most worried about. Be brief—just a minute or two.	**1.** After the writer tells you about the draft, make a note about what he or she is most pleased and most concerned about, so that you can offer help where it is needed.
2. Read the draft aloud without pausing.	**2.** As the writer reads aloud, make quick margin comments on your copy of the draft, noting where the draft strikes you as being strong, needing more, raising a question, or having a problem in one way or another.
3. When you have finished reading, give your listeners five minutes to finish their notes.	**3.** Once the writer has finished reading the essay, look at your notes to identify the following: • The most significant ways in which the draft is strong • The places where it needs more • The moments that raised questions • The most significant writing problem
4. Work through the following questions, asking listeners each question and taking notes while they speak. Do not forget to take notes! • Where is my draft strongest? • Where do I need more? • Where do you have questions about what I have written? • What is the biggest problem with my draft?	**4.** Once you have finished these notes, tell the writer what you have identified, allowing the writer time to ask you follow-up questions and to write down what you have said.

<table>
<tr><td>

Toolkit
4.7
</td><td>

Peer Review for Narratives
</td></tr>
</table>

This toolkit is for use with narrative assignments.

Peer review is very helpful with narrative writing, as writers frequently have difficulty objectively viewing the strengths and weaknesses of essays that reflect their own lives and experiences. This peer review is designed for use with a narrative assignment that requires the narrative to have an explicit point and not simply tell a story.

You will need a partner for this toolkit.

What to Do

1. **Read your partner's essay and ask yourself the following questions:**
   a. What is the greatest strength of this narrative?
   b. What main idea does the narrative focus on? What is the writer's goal in sharing the narrative with readers?

2. **Identify the passage where the writer expresses the narrative's main idea directly.** If you can't find one, suggest a passage where you think an explicit expression of the main idea could be usefully added.

3. **Consider how the writer uses examples.** Is the narrative focused on one example or many examples? Would the narrative benefit from either cutting or adding examples? Which, if any, of the current examples need more development?

4. **Evaluate how details are used.** Where would more details be useful so that readers can better understand the situation being described?

5. **List or otherwise mark on the draft those passages in which the writer reflects on the meaning of the example(s) being shared.** Where do you need more explanation to follow the writer's point clearly?

6. **Share any other suggestions you have.**

<table>
<tr><td>

Toolkit
4.8
</td><td>

Peer Review for Clarity
</td></tr>
</table>

This toolkit uses peer review to identify and correct problems with clarity and proofreading.

We are all less capable of proofreading and finding mistakes and weak areas in our own prose than we are at proofreading and finding weaknesses in others' prose. Although sharing drafts for proofreading is unlikely to ensure that writers' prose will become error-free and fully polished, it is sure to lead to improvements.

You will need a partner for this toolkit.

What to Do

For this toolkit, it is best to use a highlighter and a pencil — a highlighter for identifying unclear prose, and a pencil for making notes about potential problems.

1. **Read your partner's whole essay all the way through** *twice.* The first time, read from beginning to end; the second time, read from the last sentence to the first sentence. Although this second method may seem odd, reading the essay backward one sentence at a time helps readers to notice sentence-level mistakes.

2. **As you read, pay attention to the flow of each sentence, looking for any places where the sentence structure, grammar, punctuation, or words themselves seem wrong or awkward.** Resist the urge to make corrections; rather, highlight and make a pencil note on the side indicating the nature of the problem. See the following examples:

   > The young boy had many problems so many that it was hard to believe he — Punctuation
   > would become so successful.

   > Following the Takeover of the High School, sixty children were suspended. — Capitalization

   > Since words are used without any restrictions or rules.
   >   — Sentence problem

   > Some people think there is nothing wrong with using a "cursing word" it just — Sentence problem
   > becomes a habit.

   Here are some words and short phrases to use in the margins to describe common problems in general terms:

   - *Capitalization* or *cap*
   - *Spelling*
   - *Quote problem* — for any problem with a quotation: missing punctuation, inaccurate quoting, mistake in spacing, or missing citation
   - *Word choice* or *WC* — when the word appears incorrect or poorly chosen
   - *Sentence problem* — for fragments, run-ons, and comma splices
   - *Punctuation* — when punctuation marks are missing or misused
   - *Confusing* — when you aren't sure of the problem or find it difficult to explain

3. **When you are done, exchange papers so that each writer has his or her own paper back.**

4. **Review your partner's notes on your draft, and fix each of the highlighted areas.** If you disagree with or don't understand any of the notes, ask the reader to explain further, or double-check your grammar handbook before correcting.

5. **Look at your partner's notes in the margin of your draft, and determine if any markings are repeated.** If so, the reader may have noted a pattern error. Write down any problems that were noted a few times, and consult another toolkit (sections 5 and 6 would be helpful) or your grammar handbook to find out more about these issues.

Toolkit
4.9 **Using Feedback to Revise**

This toolkit will help you evaluate and use the peer review feedback you received to support revision of your essay.

What to Do

1. **Review the feedback you received, and summarize it in your own words.** Then write briefly about your initial reaction to the feedback. What surprised you about it? What most pleased you? What concerned you about the feedback?

2. **Review what your reader(s) identified as your thesis.** Is this what you intended? If your answer is no, you have two options:

   • Change the thesis. Did your reader(s) see a potential thesis that you didn't realize? If so, consider whether this should become your new thesis.

   • Strengthen the thesis. If reader(s) did not understand your thesis but you want to keep the general idea, consider how you can revise both your thesis and the essay itself to make your intended thesis clearer:

      • How might you revise the content of the thesis?

      • How might you reword the thesis?

      • Does the thesis need to be moved? If so, where?

      • How might you revise body (supporting) paragraphs? Where do you need to add or remove examples to make the thesis clearer? What about adding more explanation and discussion of how the examples connect to the thesis?

3. **Look at any passages that were marked.** These may be places for you to expand and develop, or to add more explanation.

4. **Look at any questions your reader(s) raised.** How would you answer them? How can you work those answers into your draft?

5. **Look at any sentence-level issues that your reader(s) noted.** These are places where wording, sentence structure, or grammar may be creating a lack of clarity.

6. **Consider the other suggestions offered by your reader(s).** How might you address them to help improve your essay?

7. **Based on all the comments and your notes, write a plan to incorporate the suggestions as you revise.**

Toolkit
4.10 **Deep Revision Strategies**

Use this toolkit when you have a draft and are struggling to revise it.

What to Do

1. **Silently read your draft.** Pretend you are someone else and read to yourself, paying attention to what is being communicated. Read like a reader, not like a writer.

2. **Put your draft aside, and then choose one or more of the following options, which work to loosen you up, shifting your approach and perspective on your topic to generate new ideas and prose:**

   - *Option 1.* Write a one- or two-paragraph letter to a respected elder — or a young child — in your life. In this letter, explain to your chosen audience what you have written about in your draft. Explain what your point is and how you made it.

      - Reread what you have just written. Think for a moment, and then revise the thesis or guiding question from your draft — that is, the idea or point that you are trying to get across — based on your new discoveries.

      - Rewrite your new thesis or guiding question at the top of a fresh page. Then, write a paragraph in which you discuss the topic and explain why it would be useful for someone — even yourself — or perhaps a population of people (e.g., students, teenage girls, teachers, native speakers, or legislators) to think about or act on your topic.

   - *Option 2.* Write about a surprising idea, fact, or point of view that is raised by your topic. What's very funny, intriguing, odd, or shocking about your topic or point of view? You might start with this structure: *Although many may have thought _____, in fact, the truth is _____.*

- *Option 3*. Write some dialogue between key characters in your essay. Imagine what they would say to each other if they were in a room together.

- *Option 4*. Go back to your inspiration for this essay — the central event, issue, experience, or fact that you are writing about.

  - Jot down details and features that you did not include in your draft.

  - Review what you wrote, and underline those details and features that will work well in your draft.

  - Write a paragraph about one or two of the underlined details and features.

- *Option 5*. Write a new conclusion. A conclusion often asks readers to do something, to understand something, or to act or think differently. What are you asking of your readers? Offer a clear explanation to them.

3. **When you are done working through the option(s), look at your draft again and make a plan for revision.** What can you cut from your original draft? What can you add from the new writing and thinking you've done about your topic?

Toolkit
4.11 **Revising Your Thesis**

> This toolkit will help you revise your thesis so that it is stronger and more relevant to your draft.

During the drafting process, your ideas will likely change and grow. Therefore, good writers almost always revise their thesis to reflect this change in thinking. Following are some strategies to help you assess and revise your thesis.

What to Do

Take Inventory of Your Ideas

1. **For reference, write down your working thesis.** If your draft does not yet have a thesis, work on adding one first. If you are stuck, try to describe your project: *In this essay, I am arguing/explaining/expressing/showing* _____. Your draft thesis will likely come from the fill-in-the-blank section of that sentence.

2. **Read the body of your essay, making a list of the major ideas and examples.**

3. **Look at what you wrote for steps 1 and 2.** Do they match? That is, are the major ideas and examples in your essay relevant to the thesis? Does the essay prove what the thesis says it will prove, or does it prove something else?

If what you wrote for steps 1 and 2 do *not* match, decide whether you need to revise the essay to match the thesis or whether you should revise the thesis to match the body. Jot down some notes about what you need to do, and if necessary, sketch out a revised version of your thesis.

4. **If you have a draft conclusion, write down the version of your main idea presented there.**

5. **Compare the conclusion's version of your main idea to your working thesis.** Which one is better? Revise the weaker version to match the stronger one, without repeating the same sentence in both places.

Sharpen Your Expression

1. **If necessary, revise your thesis to take a stand and make a claim.** In a persuasive (argument) essay, a thesis should take a clearly defined stand or position, making a claim that needs to be proven. This means that the thesis should not be an obvious point or fact; rather, it should be a point that requires discussion, proof, and support.

   Example of an obvious thesis that needs revision: If someone posts a photo online, it stays on the web forever, making a digital history.

2. **Make sure that your thesis is *not* actually an announcement of your topic.**

   Example of an announcement thesis that needs to be revised: In this essay, I will write about why people should not be judged on their digital histories.

3. **Check that the thesis is not too narrow, too limited, or too broad.** If it is too narrow or too broad, try to reword it.

   Example of a thesis that is too broad and needs to be revised: Digital histories cause many problems for people.

4. **Check the wording of your thesis to make sure it is not too vague or generic.** If it is, rephrase it for greater clarity and accuracy. Vague words include *similar*, *different*, and *people*.

   Example of a thesis that has generic words (underlined) and needs to be revised: Because digital histories can contain useless information, people should not use them to make final decisions about others.

5. **Check the placement of your thesis.** In college writing, the thesis is often the last sentence of the introduction. If you can place it there, you will make it easier for readers to identify it. (Sometimes for rhetorical effect, writers choose to place the thesis in another location.)

At this point, you should have a sharpened and refined thesis. Keep in mind that you may need to revise the thesis even further before the final draft. You can run your thesis through some or all of these steps again at any point in the drafting and revision process.

Toolkit

4.12 **Strengthening Evidence and Examples**

> This toolkit will help you evaluate the way you use evidence and examples in your draft with the goal of doing so more effectively.

There is a difference between *including* examples or evidence in your essay and *using* that evidence effectively. Effective use involves discussing and connecting the evidence to your main point, not just providing the information.

What to Do

1. **First, write briefly:** What do you want your readers to understand when they are finished reading your essay? Why?

2. **Make sure that what you want your readers to understand is expressed in your thesis, rewriting it if necessary.**

3. **Consider how your essay uses examples or evidence to help readers understand your main point.**

   a. Read through your draft, marking those places where you incorporate examples or evidence from other sources (use a highlighter or colored font).

   b. Make a quick list of these highlighted places.

   c. For each example on your list, write two or three sentences explaining how the example supports the thesis. (If you can't write anything that explains the connection, consider replacing or cutting the example.)

4. **Now consider how your essay uses discussion to help readers understand your point.**

   a. Read through your draft again, marking those places where you have discussion or explanation (use a different highlighter or colored font than you used for step 3).

   b. Evaluate the balance (or imbalance) between evidence and discussion by looking at the two colored sections.

      ● Do you have a lot of one color but not the other? If so, can you add more to balance out the discussion, for instance?

      ● Does discussion come in the same paragraph as the evidence, or are they presented separately?

      ● If they are separate, consider combining the sections.

   c. Does the discussion reflect what you wrote for step 3c? If not, include that information in your essay after each example.

5. **Next, look at your draft to see if you have explained the connections between the examples or evidence and your main focus.** Make a note to yourself about the examples that need more work, or add the discussion or other clarification right now.

6. **Make a plan for revision:**
   - Where do you need to add relevant evidence?
   - Where do you need to add more or better discussion?
   - Where do you need to cut evidence or discussion that is off topic?

Toolkit

4.13 **Connecting Reasons and Evidence**

> This toolkit will help you evaluate and improve your use of evidence by ensuring that its relation to your argument is clear.

A successful argument takes a stance on a debatable issue, presenting reasons and supporting evidence.

What to Do

1. **Summarize your argument in one or two sentences.**

2. **In a numbered list, indicate your reasons for making this argument** (Reason 1, Reason 2, and so on).

3. **Test whether your reasons truly support the thesis — are they relevant? on topic? valid?** Make a simple chart to help you keep track:

	Relevant	Needs Tweaking to Be Relevant	Off Topic	Notes
Reason 1				
Reason 2				
Reason 3				
Reason 4				

Make some notes as to which reasons are relevant, which need some revision to be relevant, and which are off topic and need to be cut.

4. **Check your evidence for relevance to your reasons, body paragraph by body paragraph.** Number the body paragraphs in your draft. Then, in the "Evidence

presented" column, write down a phrase or sentence that indicates the evidence presented in each paragraph.

	Evidence Presented	Relevant to Reason 1	Relevant to Reason 2	Relevant to Reason 3	Notes
Body paragraph 1					
Body paragraph 2					
Body paragraph 3					
Body paragraph 4					

5. **Next, test your evidence, piece by piece, to see whether it supports the thesis or main point and fits the reasons you offered.** Make some notes on your chart as to how you need to revise the evidence to better fit the reasons, or vice versa, or where you need to make cuts.

6. **Sum up your findings.** In which paragraphs do your evidence and reasons connect well? In which paragraphs do you need to make the connection clearer? What evidence or reasons should you cut because they are off topic?

Toolkit 4.14 Fixing Common Mistakes in Introductions

This toolkit will help you rewrite introductions by identifying and removing frequently made mistakes.

What to Do

As you complete your revision process, you will very likely need to revise your introduction for greater effectiveness. Go through the following checklist to identify weaknesses in your introduction that you need to address (by adding, changing, and cutting).

Introductions: Frequently Made Mistakes to Avoid

1. **Writing too many or too few sentences.** Two or three sentences is likely too short, whereas more than eight sentences is likely too long.

2. **Including a dictionary definition.** Although this is a popular move, it uses a shortcut rather than doing the real work of introducing your topic.

3. **Making sweeping generalizations.** While in early drafts many writers use sweeping generalizations as a way to get started; these should be replaced later. These tempting phrases tend to result in statements that are certainly true but are so broad that they are virtually meaningless. For example:

    Since the beginning of time

    Throughout history

    In society today

4. **Making vague and general statements that no one would disagree with.** These placeholder sentences help writers get started, but they need to be cut or significantly revised in later drafts. For example:

    Immigrants have always had a hard time when first arriving in a new country.

    Sports have always played an important role in American society.

5. **Quoting too much.** If you have a quotation in your introduction, keep it short—not more than one sentence in length.

6. **Restating the question or assignment.** Although your introduction may share some similarities with the question, if it seems as though you are parroting the textbook or your instructor, rewrite.

7. **Referring to a reading without proper identification of the author's name or text title.** For example, not *The article presents* . . . but *Amy Tan's "Personal Errata" presents* . . .

8. **Downgrading your authority or using an overly conversational tone.** Student writers sometimes put themselves down in their introductions, and these put-downs should be removed. For example:

    Despite my young age and unfamiliarity with this topic

    I'm not really sure, but I believe

    In my humble opinion

    You may be thinking that I'm not the kind of person who would know anything about discriminatory language, but actually

9. **Hiding or burying your thesis.** If you are writing a persuasive essay (an argument), readers will expect that the last sentence of the introduction is your thesis. Unless there is good reason not to do so, you should place it there to prevent any reader confusion.

10. **Losing link to the body of your essay.** Sometimes during revision, an essay goes in a different direction than was initially planned. Make sure to revise the introduction so that it is relevant to the overall essay and not just to an earlier version of it.

Fixing Common Mistakes in Conclusions

This toolkit will help you rewrite conclusions by identifying and removing frequently made mistakes.

What to Do

As you complete your revision process, you will very likely need to revise your conclusion for greater effectiveness. Go through the following checklist to identify weaknesses in your conclusion that you need to address (by adding, changing, and cutting).

Conclusions: Frequently Made Mistakes to Avoid

1. **Not writing a conclusion.** Make sure that your final paragraph truly is a conclusion. A conclusion typically helps readers understand something about the issue that has been discussed in the essay.

2. **Giving your main point or thesis only in your conclusion (when it should also be included in your introduction).** Sometimes writers don't figure out what their thesis or main point is until the end of drafting; as a result, the draft conclusion could be moved and turned into a great introduction.

3. **Restating the introduction.** In college writing, it isn't enough for your conclusion to rehash your introduction. Although you should address the main topic and refer to the major issues or themes you have mentioned in your introduction, the wording needs to be different, and the conclusion needs to go far beyond restatement. (For strategies, see Toolkit 2.8.)

4. **Adding a quotation or proverb** (a short saying of general truth or piece of advice) that does not apply specifically to your essay or is too obvious. For example:

   Shoot for the moon, and even if you miss, you'll land among the stars.

   Don't judge a book by its cover.

   People in glass houses shouldn't throw stones.

   Laughter is the best medicine.

   Beauty is in the eye of the beholder.

5. **Using obvious "conclusion language."** This rule varies by field or discipline, but in the humanities (such as English or writing classes), phrases like *In conclusion*, *In summary*, and *In closing* are typically frowned on.

6. **Introducing a new topic, idea, or evidence.** If these are important, move them to the body of the essay. If not, cut them. The conclusion should finish, not start, something.

7. **Undercutting your authority.** Resist the urge to express concerns about not knowing enough. For example, *Given what I have been able to learn about this topic*, or *Although I have never played competitive sports . . .*

8. **Using the conclusion to communicate personally to your instructor.** Do not use the conclusion to write a personal note to your professor about how you're feeling about the essay. For example, *Although I was rushed for time due to family complications and other issues, I have learned much about . . .*

9. **Ending with a quotation.** Do not let someone else have the last word in your essay.

Toolkit
4.16 # Should You Abandon a Draft?

This toolkit will help you decide if you should abandon a draft and start another one, or keep on revising.

Every once in a while, revising a draft is just unproductive. You've been working on it so long — moving parts around, trying to improve it without success, staring at the screen but not writing — that you have become tired of it. Or maybe your ideas have changed since you started writing, and you want to try a different direction or angle.

How can you tell if a draft is messy and incomplete but ready to be repaired, or if it is beyond help and destined for the recycle bin? It's a hard decision to make.

What to Do

1. **Putting your draft aside and out of your mind, reread the essay question or assignment.**

2. **Set a timer for twenty minutes, and then begin to sketch out a totally new approach:** a new topical focus, a new example to develop, a new argument, and so on. Use your favorite method for generating writing (from Toolkit section 2), and make sure you work for the full twenty minutes, simply generating writing for a new essay.

3. **Step back and compare the two drafts.** Which one holds more hope? Which one has signs of life? Select the one that inspires you and makes you feel hopeful.

4. **If you are still struggling, ask a peer or an instructor to review both drafts and offer an opinion on which one has more potential.** Then decide which one to work on.

This toolkit will help you correctly format documents in MLA style.

Although individual instructors will often have specific requests about formatting or headings, the following list should start you on your way toward a well-designed document based on MLA format. In composition courses, MLA (Modern Language Association) documentation style is the most commonly used set of rules for citing sources and formatting papers, though across the disciplines several other styles are used, with APA (American Psychological Association) and *Chicago* (*Chicago Manual of Style*/CMS) being especially common. A well-formatted paper matters because it shows respect for readers and other writers.

Breaking the rules of basic document design isn't worth the small pleasure it may give you to use a wild, cursive-style font or otherwise make your document look unique and special. It is better to personalize through your words, not your formatting.

For examples of documents using MLA format, see the Appendix.

Tip: You may find it helpful to create a template for your essays that defaults to the correct font, spacing, and so on.

What to Do

1. **Choose the right font and font size.** Best bet: Times New Roman, 12 point.

2. **Choose the right margins.** Only one is acceptable here: one-inch margins all around. (This is the default setting on most word processing programs, but you should double-check yours just in case.)

3. **Choose the right line spacing.** In MLA format, the whole paper, including the heading and Works Cited list, is double-spaced (2.0). Do not include additional space between paragraphs (check your word processing program's default setting on this). Don't be tempted to "lengthen" your paper by adjusting the spacing to 2.5, by increasing the margins, or by adding extra space before or after paragraphs. These are strategies that instructors dislike.

4. **Include a header.** In the top right corner of every page, use a header with your last name and the page number—for example, *Rivas 1*. The header should have a half-inch margin from the top. (Rather than typing a header in on every page, use the Header function of your word processing program, which will allow you to insert a code for the page number so that it automatically updates.)

LaunchPad Solo

112   Visit **LaunchPad Solo for Readers and Writers** for more practice on the skills covered in this section.

5. **Use a heading.** Starting at the left margin of the first page, place your name, your instructor's name, the course title, and the date that the assignment is submitted on separate lines. Make sure you spell your professor's name correctly (double-check this!). Like the rest of your paper, this information should be double-spaced.

6. **Include a title below the heading, centering it on its line.** Do not add extra space before or after your title; simply double-space.

7. **Format your title without dressing it up.** This means that you should <u>not</u> use *italics*, **bold** font, or "quotation marks." You should <u>not</u> enlarge the font or use special highlighting of any sort. Capitalize correctly—typically, by capitalizing all words except articles and prepositions in any position other than the first or last. (For more information on capitalization, see Toolkit 5.4.)

8. **Begin each paragraph by indenting a half inch.**

9. **Space words correctly.** Make sure to use the correct amount of space between words. When there is too much white space at the end of a line, it's usually because there is an extra hard return (¶) in the page. To check your spacing, you need to choose the option on your word processing program to show all nonprint characters so you can spot any inappropriate hard returns or other spacing issues. This is what you'll see (note that we have highlighted the errors):

→ Not···everyone·cares··how·they·space·their·papers··, → but my¶ teacher really does!

Simply go through the paper and remove extra spaces, tabs, and returns, and add necessary ones.

10. **Use proper capitalization.** Begin each sentence with a capitalized word. Make sure to capitalize the names of any people you mention. Be careful not to capitalize any words that should be lowercase. (For more information on capitalization, see Toolkit 5.4.)

Toolkit 5.2

The Good-Enough Title

> This toolkit will help you generate a good essay title, something that is more important than many writers imagine.

Why Titles Matter

Any good realtor knows that making the front of a home look beautiful creates curb appeal; in the same way, a good title creates appeal for an essay. Readers look at titles not only out of interest but also to quickly find out what is to come.

What Titles Need

At a minimum, titles need to (1) indicate a topic or subject, and (2) indicate the author's point of view or angle on this topic or subject.

With these two requirements met, you should have a perfectly good title that will serve your academic writing needs.

How Titles Should Look

Here are the MLA guidelines for titles:

1. Always capitalize the first and last words of your title and subtitle, if there is one.

2. Capitalize all other words in the title except:

   a. articles (*a*, *an*, and *the*)

   b. prepositions (e.g., *of*, *on*, *in*, *for*)

   c. coordinating conjunctions (*and*, *but*, *for*, *nor*, *or*, *so*, and *yet*)

3. Do not use quotation marks around your title. Do not use bold or italic font for your title.

4. Use a colon (:) between your title and subtitle (if you have one).

Here are a few examples of successfully formatted titles:

Toolkits for Reading and Writing

Breaking It Down: An Approach to Successful College Writing

Where Are Digital Histories Taking Us To?

What to Do

1. **Rate the titles below:** 3 stars for good, 2 stars for OK, and 1 star for bad.

Paper Title	Star Rating
Advertising	
_____ [no title]	
The Best of the Worst: Reading Women's Magazines	
Calvin Klein's Obsession	
The World of Sports	
Unit 2 Essay	
Sports and Society	
Managing Digital Histories	
Digital Histories and the Job Hunt	

Paper Title	Star Rating
A Korean-American Perspective	
Challenges for Koreans Coming to America in the Twenty-First Century	
Facebook This: Communication Isn't Shouting	
My View on Facebook	
Social Media and Today's Generation	

Briefly explain your ratings. What was especially good about those titles you awarded three stars? What was the problem with your one-star titles? What were the strengths and weaknesses of your two-star titles?

2. **Take the best titles from the preceding list and try imitating them for your own topic.** Change the nouns and verbs, but keep the general formula. For example:

    The Best of the Worst: _____ing (*verb*) _____ (*noun: your topic*)

3. **Brainstorm five possible titles.** Be sure to follow the two basic rules: Identify your topic and indicate your point of view on that topic.

    a. _____

    b. _____

    c. _____

    d. _____

    e. _____

4. **Choose the best title for your essay.**

Toolkit 5.3 **A Better Title**

This toolkit will help you generate a powerful title for your essay.

As discussed in Toolkit 5.2, at a minimum, titles need to (1) indicate a topic or subject, and (2) indicate the author's point of view or angle on this topic or subject.

Meeting the minimum requirements should produce an acceptable title but not a great one. Once you have an acceptable title, however, it's not that hard to spend a little more time trying to improve it. Sometimes writing a great title comes from a process of starting with a dull one and brainstorming up to a great one.

Great titles typically do one of the following:

1. Amuse readers with a clever turn of phrase or play on words

2. Engage readers emotionally: For example, make readers feel angry (though not at the writer!) or compassionate

3. Provide a compressed or condensed version of the thesis or claim

What to Do

1. **Collect some data about your essay:**
   a. What is your topic, most broadly?
   b. More narrowly, what is your focused topic?
   c. What is your most vivid example?
   d. What is your basic point?
   e. What is your point of view on your topic?

2. **Reread your answers, highlighting or underlining words and phrases that jump out at you.**

3. **Use those words and phrases to compose a title that combines your topic (information from your responses to a, b, or c in step 1) with your point or perspective (information from d or e in step 1).**

Here's an example of the process of generating a great title:

a. What is your topic, most broadly?

   Language and identity

b. More narrowly, what is your focused topic?

   Language can be part of someone's identity, but it's not the main part.

c. What is your most vivid example?

   Latinas who don't speak Spanish but still follow other aspects of their culture (like food).

d. What is your basic point?

   Speaking a language does not make someone have an identity. It is not a requirement. Speaking Spanish doesn't make someone Latina.

e. What is your point of view on your topic?

   I think people need to be more aware that language doesn't define people.

Here's an example showing the evolution of the title-generating process:

   How Language Connects to Identity (dull)

   Language Is Not Identity (somewhat better)

   Don't Judge People on Their Language (better)

   You Don't Have to Speak Spanish to Be Latina (better)

   Identity Has No Language Requirement (best)

Toolkit
5.4 Capitalization

This toolkit will help you identify and correct capitalization problems.

In contrast to informal writing situations like texting, the rules for capitalization in formal writing are more fixed.

- Capitalize the first word in every sentence.

- Capitalize the pronoun *I*.

- Capitalize proper names (names of people, places, and specific things — e.g., languages, religions, companies, trade names, particular courses, months, and days of the week); don't capitalize common nouns. Here are some examples:

Proper nouns (capitalize)	Common nouns (don't capitalize)
Spanish	a language
Florida State University	a university
Hudson River	a river
Bolivia	a country
Writing I	a writing course
February	last month
Twitter	a social media site

- Capitalize the first and last words in titles and subtitles of books, articles, and other works, and all other words except articles, prepositions, and coordinating conjunctions. Here are examples of properly capitalized titles:

  The Grapes of Wrath

  Romeo and Juliet

  "Linguistic Profiling: The Sound of Your Voice May Determine If You Get That Apartment or Not"

  "One Man Explains Why He Swears by Wearing Spanx"

Note: Italicize the titles of books and long works, and use quotation marks around the titles of articles, songs, and other shorter works.

- Capitalize titles when used as parts of names: *Dr. Garcia*, but not *I went to see the Dr.*

- Capitalize some abbreviations (typically those used as names of government agencies, stations, states, or companies).

  CIA, DEP, CNN, CA, GE

- Capitalize the first word of an independent clause (a clause that could stand as a separate sentence) that follows a colon (:).

  The advertising campaign sent a clear message: Women are sexual objects.

What to Do

Review your draft, looking for examples of the categories just described to check and correct your use of capitalization.

Toolkit

5.5 **Punctuation Basics**

This toolkit will help you review rules for using periods, question marks, exclamation points, semicolons, colons, and quotation marks.

See Toolkit 5.6 for commas and Toolkit 5.7 for apostrophes.

The Period [.]

● Use a period at the end of every sentence.

● Use a period after certain abbreviations:

Mon., etc., Prof. Green

Note: If your sentence ends with an abbreviation, do not add a second period.

Successful writers always leave time to proofread for punctuation, fragments, word choice, etc.

The Question Mark [?]

● Use a question mark at the end of sentences that are asking questions:

Did you understand the assignment the teacher gave out today?

● Do not use a question mark at the end of sentences that report on questions (indirect questions):

The teacher asked whether students understood the assignment she gave out earlier in the class.

The writers question if gender stereotypes should be revised.

The Exclamation Point [!]

● Use an exclamation point to indicate special emphasis and excitement; note that it is rarely used in formal writing, however:

All his students grasped punctuation basics!

The Semicolon [;]

- Use a semicolon to divide independent clauses (clauses that could stand as separate sentences):

    Properly punctuating sentences helps readers process your ideas more clearly; faulty punctuation can lead to confusion.

- Use a semicolon to separate independent clauses that are connected by a transitional expression, such as *for example*, *however*, *therefore*, *similarly*, and *in contrast*:

    Properly punctuating sentences helps readers process your ideas more clearly; in contrast, faulty punctuation can lead to confusion.

- Do not use a semicolon to introduce a list:

    Incorrect: Jerome decided to ask guests to bring appetizers to his party, such as; chips, cheese, dip, and little pizzas.

- Do not use a semicolon between an independent and a dependent clause (in some cases, as in the following example, you should use a comma instead):

    Incorrect: Because many immigrants come to the United States in search of job opportunities; Americans fear immigrants will take all the jobs and leave them with none.

The Colon [:]

- Use a colon to introduce a statement, summary, phrase, or word that you want to draw attention to. Note that the colon must come after an independent clause (but unlike the semicolon, there does not have to be an independent clause on both sides of the colon):

    Jeff has two main goals for today: understanding punctuation and finishing his essay.

    Reading well is a lot like playing sports well: It requires frequent practice.

- Use a colon to introduce a list (unless it begins with *including*, *such as*, and in some cases *for example*):

    Correct: Playing sports allows athletes to develop many skills: focus, discipline, and leadership.

    Incorrect: Playing sports allows athletes to develop many skills, such as: focus, discipline, and leadership.

- Use a colon to introduce some quotations. When *both* the quotation and what comes before it are independent clauses, use a colon to separate them.

    Correct: In "Why They Came," John F. Kennedy imagines the difficult journey many immigrants to the United States faced: "They huddled in their hard, cramped bunks, freezing when the hatches were open, stifling when they were closed. The only light came from a dim, swaying lantern. Night and day were indistinguishable.

But they were ever aware of the treacherous winds and waves, the scampering of rats and the splash of burials" (237).

Incorrect: In "Why They Came," John F. Kennedy imagines that many immigrants journeying to the United States: "huddled in their hard, cramped bunks, freezing when the hatches were open, stifling when they were closed" (237).

- Use a colon between a title and a subtitle:

  Intersections: A Thematic Reader for Writers

- Use a colon when using figures for times:

  Class starts promptly at 10:00.

- Do not use a colon between a preposition and its object or between a verb and its object:

  Incorrect: The apartment came with: furniture and heat.

  Incorrect: For his party, Jerome asked his friends to bring: chips, dip, cheese, and little pizzas.

Quotation Marks [" "]

- Use quotation marks around short, direct quotations (places where you copy the exact words of another). Make sure to use quotation marks at both the beginning and the end of the quoted material. (For more information about formatting quotes, see Toolkit 5.10.)

  In her essay exploring the reasons people diet, Abigail Saguy notes that "studies have documented weight bias in employment, healthcare, education and public spaces — unequal treatment based on stereotyping fat people as lazy, unmotivated, sloppy and lacking in self-discipline and competence" (211).

- *Special case:* If the quotation you are using includes internal quotation marks, change them to single quotes and put double quotation marks at the beginning and end of the quotation.

  Source: Black athletes are usually given credit for their "natural athleticism," while whites are credited for their "hard work," "discipline," and "knowledge of the game."

  Quoted version: Reflecting on sports stereotypes, Gane-McCalla writes, "Black athletes are usually given credit for their 'natural athleticism,' while whites are credited for their 'hard work,' 'discipline,' and 'knowledge of the game'" (360).

- Use quotation marks around the titles of short works, such as articles, short stories, poems, songs, and blog posts.

  "Why We Diet"

- Use quotation marks around (or italics for) words discussed as words.

  In "The B Word," Shanelle Matthews explains her concerns about the increased use of "bitch."

- Quotation marks and other punctuation: Commas go inside closing quotation marks; semicolons and colons go outside. Periods go inside closing quotation marks, except in cases where the quotation is followed by an MLA-style parenthetical reference. (See Toolkit 5.13 for more on MLA documentation style.)

  > Sports lingo has slipped into everyday language as we talk of "a whole new ballgame," "striking out," "Monday morning quarterbacks," "slam dunks," and "sucker punches."

Toolkit 5.6

Comma Tips and Tricks

> This toolkit explains some of the most important ways to use commas.

Commas separate components (words, phrases, and clauses) within sentences. In this way, they help pace how readers move through your sentence, assisting with comprehension.

What follows is an explanation of the key places where commas should and should not be used. You can learn more about other uses of the comma in a grammar handbook or online grammar resource.

Key Places to Use Commas

- After an introductory word, phrase, or clause:

  Introductory word: However, all students must pay their tuition bills before they will be allowed to play sports.

  Introductory phrase: Before reaching the summit, the climbers were forced by a storm to turn back.

  Introductory dependent clause: Because many immigrants come to the United States in search of job opportunities, nativists fear immigrants will take all the jobs and leave them with none.

- In a series or list containing three or more items:

  Mary Beth, Ann Marie, Sue, and Amy are roommates this semester.

- Before a coordinating conjunction (*and, but, for, nor, or, so,* or *yet*) that links two independent clauses:

  Putting commas into sentences can be tricky and challenging, but it can also be fun.

- To set off extra information or material that interrupts the main part of your sentence:

  Cape May, located at the tip of New Jersey, is a favorite spot for birding.

  Tomorrow, I believe, is the last day to register for spring semester classes.

Tip: Read the sentence without the material between the commas; if the sense is not changed significantly, keep the pair of commas to set off the material. If the sense is changed, take out both commas.

Key Places *Not* to Use Commas

- Before a concluding dependent clause or phrase that is essential to the meaning of the sentence:

  ESSENTIAL DEPENDENT CLAUSE
  A storm forced the climbers to turn back/before reaching the summit.

- In a series or list containing two items:

  Mary Beth/and Ann Marie are roommates this semester.

- To set off material that provides information needed to understand the main part of the sentence:

  Students/who are athletes/must maintain a 2.5 GPA.

  Tip: Read the sentence without the material in question; if the sense is not changed significantly, keep the pair of commas to set off the material. If the sense is changed, take out both commas.

  In this example, it is not all students who must maintain a 2.5 GPA but students who are athletes. This means that "who are athletes" is essential to the meaning and should not be set off with commas.

The possessive: the noun that "possesses" or "owns" the object

- After *such as*:

  Jerome decided to ask guests to bring appetizers to his party, such as/chips, cheese, dip, and little pizzas.

- Between a possessive and its object:

The object: the noun that is "possessed" or "owned" by the possessive

  In Shakespeare's/*Romeo and Juliet*, we meet a pair of star-crossed lovers.

- To separate a subject and verb, or a verb and its object:

  SUBJECT   VERB
  Putting <u>commas</u> in sentences/can <u>be</u> tricky but rewarding.

  VERB   OBJECT
  After reading the draft, we <u>realized</u>/that the writer needs to review how to use commas properly.

- After *although*:

  Although/many people believe that *however* and *although* can always be used interchangeably, this is not the case.

- Before *every* quotation—use a comma before a quotation only in those cases where it makes grammatical sense in your sentence.

  After hearing two fifth-grade classmates saying that he was fat, Kevin Fanning/ "was immediately overcome with self-consciousness about [his] appearance" (217).

What to Do

1. **Read your draft aloud, making an exaggerated pause at those places where you currently have commas.** Ask yourself, "Does the pause feel natural there?" "Do I really want to separate the ideas there?" Check these instances against the "Key Places to Use Commas" and the "Key Places *Not* to Use Commas" lists, deleting any misplaced commas.

2. **Read your draft aloud again, this time listening for places where you naturally pause but do not have commas.** Check to see if any of those places fall under the "Key Places to Use Commas" list, adding commas where necessary.

3. **Next, reread your draft silently and look at each sentence closely.**

   a. Check to see that you have a comma after introductory material.

   b. Check those places where you have coordinating conjunctions (*and*, *but*, *for*, *nor*, *or*, *so*, or *yet*). If you have an independent clause (a clause that could stand alone as a complete sentence) on each side of the coordinating conjunction, make sure you have a comma before the conjunction; if you don't have an independent clause on each side of the coordinating conjunction, you probably don't need the comma.

   c. Find your subject-and-verb pairs. Make sure you don't have single commas between them. It is likely that you should have either two commas (a pair) or none.

Toolkit
5.7

The Apostrophe Explained

This toolkit will help you learn to edit for apostrophe use.

Key point to remember: Apostrophes are used to form possessives and contractions, but they are not used to make single nouns (e.g., *car*) into plural nouns (e.g., *cars*, not *car's*).

Possessives

Possessives are nouns or pronouns that show ownership (e.g., in the phrase *John's car*, "John's" is the possessive). To form a possessive of a noun, we typically use an apostrophe or an *'s*, depending on the form of the word:

● For singular nouns, add an *'s* to form the possessive:

  Giancarlo's book, Thomas's pen.

- For plural nouns that end in *s*, add an apostrophe to form the possessive:

  the students' essays, the sisters' dog

- For plural or collective nouns that don't end in *s*, add an *'s*:

  the women's coats, the people's choice

- *Exception:* Possessive pronouns do not have apostrophes:

  my, yours, his, hers, its, ours, theirs, whose

Tip: Watch for the mistake of writing a word as a plural when you intend to indicate possession. For example:

  This societies culture is heavily invested in the arts.

"Societies" here should be "society's." As indicated in this example, the word *this* followed by a plural noun suggests that checking is needed.

Tip: Watch for two nouns side by side, and check to see if the first should be a possessive.

  Wrong: The writer name

  Wrong: The writers name

  Correct: The writer's name

Contractions

Apostrophes stand in for missing letter(s) in contractions. For example:

  it's: it is

  don't: do not

  you're: you are

  should've: should have

  who's: who is

Tip: When proofreading, test for correctness by substituting the full version of the contraction to check for sense. This is especially helpful with the forms that are easily confused: *you're / your, it's / its, their / there / they're, who's / whose.*

OK ———

Not OK ———

  Example: Because it's a sunny day, they put the dog on it's leash and took a walk.

  Tested: Because it is a sunny day, they put the dog on it is leash and took a walk.

  Corrected: Because it's a sunny day, they put the dog on its leash and took a walk.

  Example: Whose coming to hear the guest speaker tomorrow?

So "whose" is
not OK

  Tested: Who is coming to hear the guest speaker tomorrow?

  Corrected: Who's coming to hear the guest speaker tomorrow?

Not for Plurals or Verbs

Do not use apostrophes to form plurals or to form verbs that are not contractions.

> The ~~girl's~~ girls were running down the street to catch the ice cream truck.

> He ~~see's~~ sees the ice cream truck coming down the street.

What to Do

1. **Review all the apostrophes you've used in your writing to make sure each one is forming either a possessive or a contraction.** If an apostrophe is forming a plural or is in a verb that is not a contraction, delete the apostrophe.

2. **Look for any places where you might need to add an apostrophe.**

   a. For possible possessives, look for two nouns that sit side by side, checking to see if the first needs to be a possessive.

   b. For possible contractions, look for places where you may have mistyped or miswritten a contraction without the apostrophe.
   Hint: Search for things like *cant* or *dont*.

   c. Check your use of any frequently confused words, such as *its/it's* and *they're/their/there*, to make sure that you have chosen the proper one.

Toolkit
5.8   # How to Refer to Authors and Texts

> This toolkit will help you correctly refer to authors and texts in your writing.

Here are the conventions for referring to authors and texts in academic writing:

1. **The first time you refer to an author in your text, use the author's full name.** If the author uses a middle initial or name, include it the first time as well:

   > Jose Antonio Vargas, Patricia Rice, Lindy West, Casey Gane-McCalla

2. **After that, simply use the author's last name:**

   > Vargas, Rice, West, Gane-McCalla

If there are two authors, include both authors' names:

> **First reference:** Julian B. Gewirtz and Adam B. Kern

> **Subsequent references:** Gewirtz and Kern

If there are three or more authors, include the first author's name and *et al.*

3. **In formal writing, it is not appropriate to refer to authors simply by their first names:**

    Incorrect: Jose, Patricia, Lindy, Casey

4. **It is not appropriate to use a title before the author's name:**

    Incorrect: Mr. Vargas, Prof. Rickford, Ms. Shields, Dr. Campo

5. **The first time you refer to a reading or another text, provide its full title, including any subtitles:**

    Incorrect: In his essay, Casey discusses how common sports stereotypes may cause people to judge others in harmful ways.

    Correct: In "Athletic Blacks vs. Smart Whites: Why Sports Stereotypes Are Wrong," Casey Gane-McCalla discusses how common sports stereotypes may cause people to judge others in harmful ways.

    For any later references to the text, you can often just give the author's last name or give the title without the subtitle.

6. **Make sure you have a subject and verb in this common sentence pattern: "In author's 'Title,' the author states . . ."**

    Incorrect: In Amy Tan's "Personal Errata," describes finding an alternative version of herself online.

    There is no subject for the verb *describes.*

    Correct: In Amy Tan's "Personal Errata," the author describes finding an alternative version of herself online.

    For a more polished, sophisticated version, eliminate the possessive and make the author the subject of the sentence:

    Better: In "Personal Errata," Amy Tan describes finding an alternative version of herself online.

7. **When referring to what authors say in their texts, use the present tense.**

    Incorrect: In "Personal Errata," Amy Tan described finding an alternative version of herself online.

    Correct: In "Personal Errata," Amy Tan describes finding an alternative version of herself online.

What to Do

1. **Review your draft, looking only for those instances where you refer to an author or a specific text.**

2. **Closely review this checklist:**

    a. For the first mention of the author, is his or her full name used?

    b. For all other mentions, is only the author's last name used?

    c. For the first mention of an article, is the full title included?

d. For each introduction to a quotation or summary of an author's point, is the wording grammatically correct (e.g., is there both a subject and verb, if needed)?

e. For each reference to what an author has written, is the present tense used?

Toolkit
5.9

Using Signal Phrases

This toolkit will help you use signal phrases to prevent "dropped quotations"—quotations that appear in a paper without introduction or explanation—and to incorporate quotations more smoothly into your paper.

Using Signal Phrases

Introducing authors in written texts is a little bit like introducing people in a conversation. Imagine you have invited some of the authors you read to be part of a panel discussion. As the moderator, you would be expected to introduce the speakers and indicate when it was time for each one to talk. For example: "Next, we'll hear from Jose Antonio Vargas on the problems faced by undocumented immigrants."

Similarly, when you summarize, paraphrase, or quote another author's ideas in writing, you should let readers know that you are introducing other people's ideas and words into your work. Signal phrases do just that—signal to your readers that you are now turning to someone else's ideas or words.

Common Signal Phrases

Basic signal phrases refer to the author and sometimes the title of the source. The rules for referring to authors and titles apply here, so if it is your first mention of the author and the text, you should include the full name and full title; for subsequent references, you can use the author's last name and may be able to leave out the reference to the title. (See Toolkit 5.8 for more on referring to authors and texts.)

It is a convention to use the present tense in signal phrases. So, use *Kennedy writes* instead of *Kennedy wrote*.

When relevant, the signal phrase can also briefly identify the author's credentials or relevant experience to establish credibility.

In "Why They Came," John F. Kennedy writes

As Vargas states

Sports journalist Bob Ryan writes

As sports media expert Mary Jo Kane writes

Tip: It is generally inaccurate to use a form of *quote* as the verb in your signal phrase ("Vargas quotes" is inaccurate). *Quote* means to repeat something from another source. When you include a quotation in your essay, it is you, not the original author, who is doing the quoting. In rare cases where you quote a passage in which the other author *is* using a quotation, *quote* would be appropriate. For example:

> In "Non-Spanish Fluent Latinas: 'Don't Judge Us,'" Tracy López quotes Andria Morales's explanation of problems she has faced: "Not speaking fluently has made me ineligible for opportunities that call for someone who is bilingual. It has made it difficult to communicate with fluent speakers" (183).

Here, what is being quoted is not López's words but the words of one of her sources, Andria Morales. This is a rare situation of quoting an indirect source; in such cases, it may be that the signal phrase refers to someone other than the author (e.g., "As Andria Morales explains").

Better Signal Phrases

Signal phrases that use verbs like *writes, says*, and *states* can be vague. It is better to use more precise verbs to help your readers better understand the material and the other writer's position on it. Most writing handbooks include a list of verbs that can be used in signal phrases; here are just a few:

describes	*illustrates*
argues	*claims*
contends	*emphasizes*
disproves	*points out*
proves	*reports*

Even Better Signal Phrases

Signal phrases can be even more helpful in guiding your readers if you provide more information about the source you are summarizing or quoting from. For example, if you are writing an essay about the challenges immigrants face and want to quote Kennedy to illustrate a challenge, you could introduce the quotation like this:

> In "Why They Came," John F. Kennedy imagines the difficulties many immigrants to the United States faced on their journeys: "They huddled in their hard, cramped bunks, freezing when the hatches were open, stifling when they were closed. The only light came from a dim, swaying lantern. Night and day were indistinguishable. But they were ever aware of the treacherous winds and waves, the scampering of rats and the splash of burials" (237).

What to Do

1. **Look through your draft for places where you use a quotation, summary, or paraphrase.**

2. For each quotation, summary, or paraphrase, ask the following question:

- Have you introduced it with a signal phrase?
  - If not, add one. Make sure to use the present tense.
  - If you have one, work to make it into a better signal phrase.

Toolkit
5.10 Quotation Format Guidelines

This toolkit will help you properly format quotations using MLA guidelines.

Standard Quotation Formatting Guidelines

- Make sure to copy the source's words exactly.
- Do not add or delete any words without indicating these changes with an ellipsis or brackets. (See Toolkit 5.11 for more on using the ellipsis and brackets.)
- Use the same font as in the rest of your document.
- Do not italicize the entire quotation unless this is how it appears in the source.
- Keep the same spacing throughout your essay; do not space quotations differently.

Additional Formatting Guidelines for Short Quotations

Short quotations take up no more than four full lines in your paper.

- Put quotation marks at the beginning and end of the quoted material.
- Do not separate a short quotation from the rest of the paragraph.
- When using an MLA-style parenthetical reference, delete any punctuation at the end of the quoted material except for a question mark (?) or an exclamation point (!). (See Toolkit 5.13 for more on MLA style.)
- Put your punctuation after the MLA-style parenthetical reference.

Here are some examples of correctly formatted quotations:

> In considering whether certain words are offensive even if used in a friendly way, Rose Bridges explains, "[P]art of the problem, and the reason I'm not comfortable completely dismissing the importance of language, is that you can't always control the context. You can't always know who else is listening besides your friends" (424).

> Perceptions of whether words are offensive may vary by generation: "Yet, for many teenagers, these slurs may not be as serious as they are to the adults behind these

campaigns. An Associated Press / MTV survey found that a majority of American young people are not bothered by the use of offensive slurs by their peers" (Bridges 422).

Reflecting on recent campaigns against slurs, Rose Bridges asks, "But are slurs really such a big deal, or are there bigger issues we need to fix first before going after the language?" (422).

If any of the short quotations include quotation marks, change the internal double quotation marks to single quotation marks, as in the following example.

Source: Avoiding personal offense is both ridiculous and ridiculously hard and everyone knows it. If you're on Tumblr you've heard of "social justice warriors," people who enter a space or conversation which is meant to be fun and "take offense" where none was meant.

Integrated and formatted quotation: Anna Munsey-Kano discusses the challenges of interpreting comments: "Avoiding personal offense is both ridiculous and ridiculously hard and everyone knows it. If you're on Tumblr you've heard of 'social justice warriors,' people who enter a space or conversation which is meant to be fun and 'take offense' where none was meant" (427).

Additional Formatting Guidelines for Long Quotations

Long quotations take up more than four full lines in your paper.

- Use block format for long quotations:
  - Separate the quotation from your paragraph.
  - Indent the whole quotation one-half inch on the left side of the page (do not center).

- Do not put quotation marks around the quoted material.

- Double-space the quotation, but do not add any additional space before or after it.

- Put the MLA-style parenthetical reference *after* the end punctuation (the reverse of short-quotation format).

- If the original source includes quotation marks, keep those.

- Override any automatic indenting when you continue your paragraph after the quoted material.

Here are a few examples of long quotations (note that we have not included the full paragraphs here):

Obesity has become a serious health crisis in the United States. While there are many reasons for this change, it has also led to an increase in discrimination, especially against women. As Abigail Saguy explains:

Multiple studies have documented weight bias in employment, healthcare, education and public spaces—unequal treatment based on stereotyping fat people as lazy, unmotivated, sloppy, and lacking in self-discipline and competence. Heavier women are not only less likely to be hired and less likely to earn a higher salary compared with their similarly qualified thinner peers, but they are also less likely to marry or to marry a high-earning spouse. Unlike thinner women, who can more easily climb the social and economic ladder, heavy women face the prospect of downward social mobility. (211)

These stereotypes and discrimination are an underrecognized effect of the increase in obesity. They increase the stress faced by those who are overweight and probably make it even harder to lose weight.

* * *

Obesity has become a serious health crisis in the United States. While there are many reasons for this change, some are personal. Alice Randall recalls how special her grandmother (Dear) made her feel as a child:

There were twin beds in my grandmother's bedroom by the time I was born. When a child was lucky she got to sleep in the twin bed opposite Dear's. I loved those nights. We would "hold hands" by holding on to opposite ends of a rope Dear made from the sashes of her large flowery dresses. Between the beds hung a brown cross I had made in vacation Bible school. One night, while snuggling into my bed on the right wall, I heard Dear whisper from the left wall a pure home truth: "Never do nothing that make the angels cry. When you can, make the angels smile." (207)

Randall wanted to be exactly like her grandmother, and she was a size 26.

Side notes:
- Note: no opening quotation mark
- Note: no closing quotation mark
- Do not start a new paragraph (indent) after the block quotation.
- Keep the original quotation marks.

What to Do

1. Identify all short quotations you are using, and review against the standard formatting guidelines as well as the additional guidelines for short quotations.

2. Identify all long (block) quotations, and review against the standard formatting guidelines as well as the additional guidelines for long quotations.

Toolkit 5.11 **Using Ellipses and Brackets**

This toolkit will help you edit quotations so that they fit smoothly into your paper.

Sometimes a quotation that you want to include in your paper just doesn't fit smoothly. In some cases, the quotation is too long or has some information that is not needed. In these cases, it is useful to excerpt the quotation, marking the missing words by using an **ellipsis** (. . .). In other cases, the wording of the quotation makes it fit awkwardly into your prose or its meaning is unclear when taken out of its original context. In such cases, it is appropriate to edit the quotation by adding your own words to give context using **square brackets** [ ].

Note: Any editing or excerpting must not change or distort the original author's meaning and must be clearly indicated to your readers.

Excerpting with the Ellipsis Mark

Imagine that you want to include the following passage from Jose Antonio Vargas's "My Life as an Undocumented Immigrant" in your essay, but the data he provides about deportation is not relevant to your topic. You can cut that portion, using an ellipsis to indicate where you have left material out. As you may have noticed, in *Intersections* we frequently use ellipses to shorten the texts we chose for this book.

> **Source:** Last year I read about four students who walked from Miami to Washington to lobby for the Dream Act, a nearly decade-old immigration bill that would provide a path to legal permanent residency for young people who have been educated in this country. At the risk of deportation — the Obama administration has deported almost 800,000 people in the last two years — they are speaking out. Their courage has inspired me.

> **Quoted:** Vargas explains how other undocumented immigrants' actions encouraged him: "Last year I read about four students who walked from Miami to Washington to lobby for the Dream Act, a nearly decade-old immigration bill that would provide a path to legal permanent residency for young people who have been educated in this country. At the risk of deportation . . . they are speaking out" (263).

Use three spaced periods to form the ellipsis mark; use four spaced periods if you have deleted a full sentence or more, with no space between the last word and the first period.

> **Quoted:** Vargas explains how other undocumented immigrants' actions encouraged him: "Last year I read about four students who walked from Miami to Washington to lobby for the Dream Act, a nearly decade-old immigration bill that would provide a path to legal permanent residency for young people who have been educated in this country. . . . Their courage has inspired me" (263).

Editing with Square Brackets

Use brackets to indicate changes or additions you have made so that the quotation is clearer or fits more smoothly into your sentence. Following are the most common situations in which you might need to edit a quotation.

- To insert words that identify what the original source's pronoun refers to:

  > **Source:** They are much likelier to graduate high school and score better on standardized tests, no matter their socioeconomic level, and less likely to smoke cigarettes or use drugs.

Quoted version: "[Girls who play sports] are much likelier to graduate high school and score better on standardized tests, no matter their socioeconomic level, and less likely to smoke cigarettes or use drugs" (Beard 348).

- To change a capital letter to a lowercase letter (or vice versa) so that the quotation fits into your sentence:

  Source: They are much likelier to graduate high school and score better on standardized tests, no matter their socioeconomic level, and less likely to smoke cigarettes or use drugs.

  Quoted version: On the topic of girls who play sports, Hilary Beard explains that "[t]hey are much likelier to graduate high school and score better on standardized tests, no matter their socioeconomic level, and less likely to smoke cigarettes or use drugs" (348).

- To change a word (often a verb form or a pronoun) so that the quotation fits into your sentence smoothly:

  Source: I was immediately overcome with self-consciousness about my appearance. I started sucking in my stomach around other people, and have continued to do so every single day of the 30 years since.

  Quoted version: After overhearing two fifth-grade classmates say he was fat, Kevin Fanning "was immediately overcome with self-consciousness about [his] appearance. [He] started sucking in [his] stomach around other people, and ha[s] continued to do so every single day of the 30 years since" (217).

Toolkit 5.12 Quotation Integration Checklist

This toolkit will help you check your quotations for proper formatting and appropriate and smooth integration into your paper.

What to Do

Look at your draft for places where you have used quotations, and review each against the following checklist. Make notes to yourself about any changes needed.

1. **Check your typing: Proofread the quotation to make sure you have copied the author's words exactly.**

2. **Check the length of the quotation.** If it takes up no more than four full lines in your paper, use the short-quotation format; if it is longer, use the long (block) format. (For more on quotation format, see Toolkit 5.10.)

a. For **short quotations**, make sure you have placed double quotation marks at the beginning and end of the quoted material. Include the quotation in your paragraph; do not separate it out.

b. For **long quotations**, separate the quoted material from your paragraph by using block format. Indent the quotation one-half inch on the left side. Do not place quotation marks around the quotation.

3. **Check to make sure that you have introduced the quotation with a signal phrase.** If not, add one. (For more on signal phrases, see Toolkit 5.9.)

4. **Check to make sure that you have indicated any changes you made to the quotation.**

   a. Use square brackets for changes or additions.

   b. Use an ellipsis (. . .) for deletions.

   c. Make sure you have not changed the author's meaning with any edits. (See Toolkit 5.11 for more on editing quotations.)

5. **Check to make sure the sentences that use quotations are grammatically correct.** Check especially for run-ons. Run-ons with quotations often occur when your part of the sentence and the quotation could each stand alone as a sentence. Make any corrections needed.

Toolkit 5.13 Basic MLA Rules

> This toolkit will help you use MLA documentation style in your papers.

When you use a direct quotation, paraphrase, or summary of part of a text, you must give credit to the author by supplying information about the source. This involves providing appropriate documentation.

MLA (Modern Language Association) is one of many documentation styles (others include APA and *Chicago* or CMS). Different disciplines use different styles; MLA is most commonly used in the humanities. If you are using another style, consult and follow its guidelines.

Key Steps in Documenting Sources

● **Have access to a style guide (a handbook or an online resource).** Citation involves providing information about your specific source, following guidelines.

● **Figure out whether your source has a *container*.** Is it part of a larger source or "container," such as an article from an online newspaper, a film from a DVD collection, or a selection from an anthology like *Intersections*? Or is the source a standalone like an entire book? Figuring out whether your source has a container will help you determine what information you need to provide.

- **Collect information about your source.** An MLA Works Cited entry typically provides the following elements (note the order and the punctuation between elements): **Author. Title of work. Title of container, other contributors, version or edition, publisher, date, location**. If needed, add a second container. Not every source will have all of these elements—or even a container.

An Overview of MLA Citation Style

MLA citation style has two components: an *in-text parenthetical reference* and a *Works Cited page*. Components of the in-text citation and Works Cited page are linked. That is, the in-text citation directs readers to a particular entry on the Works Cited page. The Works Cited page provides full bibliographic information about the source, while the in-text citation provides the minimum amount of information necessary for readers to find the appropriate entry on the Works Cited page.

In-Text Parenthetical References

- **For most print sources, the typical in-text citation will include the author's last name and page number:**

  (Showfety 321).

  Note that there is no comma, "p.," "pg.," or "page" between the name and the number. In the following example, the in-text citation links to a Works Cited entry that begins with "Showfety."

  > In "Field Guide to the Tomboy: High Heels and Pink? No Way," tomboys are described as women whose preferences cross gender lines: "As young girls, tomboys shun Barbie dolls in favor of games that emphasize physicality and competition. They resist conventional feminine standards—avoiding pink clothes, lipstick, and nail polish—and often excel in sports" (Showfety 321).

- **If the author's last name is clear from context (used in a signal phrase, for example), the parenthetical reference will provide just the page number:**

  > In "Field Guide to the Tomboy: High Heels and Pink? No Way," Sarah Showfety describes tomboys as women whose preferences cross gender lines: "As young girls, tomboys shun Barbie dolls in favor of games that emphasize physicality and competition. They resist conventional feminine standards—avoiding pink clothes, lipstick, and nail polish—and often excel in sports" (321).

- **For two authors, give both names in the parenthetical reference:**

  (Gewirtz and Kern 399)

- **For three or more authors, give the first author's name and *et al.* before the page number.**

- **For online sources without pagination, the in-text citation includes the author's last name only:**

  (Greenblatt)

  Note that if the author is indicated in a signal phrase, no parenthetical reference is needed in these cases.

- **For sources from "time-based media" such as audio, video, and film, the in-text citation includes the relevant time or range of time in hours, minutes, and seconds, separated by colons, in place of a page number:**

  As Temple Grandin notes in her interview "The Autistic Brain," "There's no black-and-white dividing line between autism and not autism" (00:03:05-08).

Formatting Works Cited Entries

The Works Cited page is an alphabetized list of all the sources that you refer to, quote, and summarize in your paper. For samples, consult the papers by Selena Alvarez (p. 440), Miryam Abraham (p. 445), Mariia Cosmi (p. 450), and Nooron Eewshah (p. 455) in the Appendix.

What to Do

1. Begin with this centered title: *Works Cited.*

2. Place entries in alphabetical order.

3. Provide the information relevant to your source. This toolkit shows you how to format some common sources.

4. Format entries using a hanging indent (the first line is flush with the left margin; all other lines are indented one-half inch).

5. Double-space entries. Do not add extra space between entries.

Common Types of Sources

This information is inverted because the list is in alphabetical order.

Do not invert the first and last names of the editor(s).

- **A short work from a print anthology.** *Intersections* is an anthology, a collection of work written by a variety of authors. Therefore, individual selections are treated as short works from a print anthology.

  ———— Last name of author of selection, First name (and middle name or initial, if used). "Full Title of Selection." *Full Title of Anthology*, edited by First and Last names of editor(s), edition information (if other than a first edition), name of publisher, date of publication of the anthology, page range of the complete selection.

  Showfety, Sarah. "Field Guide to the Tomboy: High Heels and Pink? No Way." *Intersections: A Thematic Reader for Writers*, edited by Emily Isaacs and Catherine Keohane, Bedford/St. Martin's, 2017, pp. 321-323.

- **A short work from a website with an author:**

  Last name of author of short work, First name (and middle name or initial, if used). "Full Title of Short Work." *Title of Website*, website sponsor, date of last update of source, URL.

  Greenblatt, Alan. "Job Seekers Still Have to Hide Tattoos (from the Neck Up)." *NPR*, 21 Feb. 2014, www.npr.org/2014/02/21/280213268/ job-seekers-still-have-to-hide-tattoos-from-the-neck-up.

Sometimes this is the same as the title of the website. If so, omit the sponsor.

Use day, month, year order, abbreviating months with more than four letters. If the site gives no date, add your date of access at the end of the entry instead.

- **An entry from an online reference work (such as a dictionary) with no author:**

  "Name of Entry." *Title of Website*, website sponsor, date of last update, URL.

  "Stereotype." *Merriam-Webster*, 2015, www.merriam-webster.com/ dictionary/stereotype.

- **A work from an online database:**

  Author's last name, First name (and middle name or initial, if used). "Full Title of Article." *Full Title of Journal, Magazine, or Newspaper*, volume and issue numbers (for journal), date or year of publication, page range of article (if known). *Name of Database*, URL.

  Gill, Emmett L., Jr. "The Prevalence of Black Females in College Sports: It's Just an Illusion." *Diverse: Issues in Higher Education*, vol. 24, no. 8, 31 May 2007, p. 65. *EBSCOhost Connection*, connection.ebscohost.com/ c/editorials/25625615/prevalence-black-females-college-sports-just -illusion.

URLs do not include *http://*.

Use day, month, year order, abbreviating months with more than four letters. If there is no publication date, use your date of access at the end of the entry instead.

- **A single-author book:**

  Author's last name, First name (and middle name or initial, if used). *Full Title of Book*. Name of publisher, date of publication.

  Thompson, Clive. *Smarter Than You Think: How Technology Is Changing Our Minds for the Better*. Penguin, 2013.

Note: For sources with two authors, begin the entry like this, and then follow the rest of the pattern appropriate for the source (e.g., short work from an anthology or work from a database):

  Last name of first listed author, First name, and First and Last names of second author.

  Gewirtz, Julian B., and Adam B. Kern.

For other sources, like government documents, see your handbook or other documentation guide.

Here's an example of a Works Cited page:

Works Cited

Gill, Emmett L., Jr. "The Prevalence of Black Females in College Sports: It's Just an
Illusion." *Diverse: Issues in Higher Education*, vol. 24, no. 8, 31 May 2007,
p. 65. *EBSCOhost Connection*, connection.ebscohost.com/c/editorials/25625615/
prevalence-black-females-college-sports-just-illusion.

Greenblatt, Alan. "Job Seekers Still Have to Hide Tattoos (from the Neck Up)." *NPR*,
21 Feb. 2014, www.npr.org/2014/02/21/280213268/job-seekers-still-have-to-hide
-tattoos-from-the-neck-up.

Showfety, Sarah. "Field Guide to the Tomboy: High Heels and Pink? No Way."
Intersections: A Reader for College Writers, edited by Emily Isaacs and Catherine
Keohane, Bedford / St. Martin's, 2017, pp. 321-323.

"Stereotype." *Merriam-Webster*, 2015, www.merriam-webster.com/dictionary/
stereotype.

Thompson, Clive. *Smarter Than You Think: How Technology Is Changing Our Minds
for the Better*. Penguin, 2013.

Toolkit
5.14 Creating a Personal Editing Checklist

> This toolkit will help you identify and ultimately correct pattern (repeated)
> errors.

Writers often tend to make the same grammar and mechanics mistakes repeatedly.
That is, a draft that appears to have twelve different errors may actually have just
two types of errors, repeated.

By creating your own personal editing checklist, you will become aware of
those grammar, usage, and mechanical errors that you tend to repeat (pattern
errors). This will help you understand what concepts to review and what issues to
make time to proofread closely for.

What to Do

1. **To start creating your checklist, review a writing assignment that an instructor has marked up or graded.** On a separate sheet of paper, make a list of the
errors the instructor has marked, as well as any that you see on your own.
(Instructors will often mark only select errors.)

2. **When you are finished with your error list, go back over it and see if you can label the issues (e.g., "fragment" or "possessives").**

3. **Once you have labeled your errors, see if there are any that appear more than once (pattern errors).** Make a new list of the types that are repeated; this will be your personal editing checklist.

4. **Look at your checklist of pattern errors and make some notes about strategies for correcting these problems.** Other toolkits in sections 5 and 6 and your grammar handbook can help you with this.

5. **Review your list and corrections with a peer, a tutor, or your instructor.**

Format for Your Personal Editing Checklist

Your checklist should have four columns with the following information:

Type of Error	Example of Error	Strategies for Correcting Error	Example of Correction

Toolkit 5.15

Basic Proofreading Checklist

This toolkit breaks down the grade-saving skill of basic proofreading.

One of the most common mistakes made by student writers is skipping proofreading. Writers are often in a rush, and they don't save time for it. Yet it's the single easiest thing to do to improve your draft. All it takes is concentration and self-discipline.

What to Do

1. **Finish revising your draft.** Proofreading works best when you have finished working on the content of your draft and are ready to work on your sentences.

2. **Proofreading requires rereading.** *You need to read each and every sentence* to make sure you have not made careless errors. Careless errors are more common than you might imagine.

3. **Start at the end of your draft and read one sentence at a time, all the way to the beginning.** This is the most effective way to proofread. Use blank pieces

of paper to guide your reading, hiding the lines ahead of and behind the one you are focusing on to make sure you read just one sentence at a time.

4. **Read aloud to ensure that you catch more mistakes.**

5. **To catch the most errors, reread and proofread two ways: on the computer and with a printed draft.**

Checklist for Basic Proofreading

1. **Look for pattern errors.** Pattern errors are those errors that writers tend to make repeatedly. Look for the types of mistakes that are frequently pointed out to you by reviewers or teachers. Draw on your personal editing checklist, if you have one. (See Toolkit 5.14.)

2. **Include a good title.** A successful title suggests the issue you are addressing and sparks readers' interest. "Introduction" is not a great title, nor is using the name of the unit or text. (See Toolkits 5.2 and 5.3 for more on what makes a good title.) A title should always be centered but not underlined, put in quotation marks, or otherwise highlighted. The first letter of each major word, and of the first and last words, should be capitalized.

   Incorrect: "My best year in high school"

   Correct: My Best Year in High School

3. **Properly identify the author and title of any sources you use.** Make sure to spell names correctly. (See Toolkit 5.8.)

4. **Replace numerals (e.g., "57") with spelled-out numbers ("fifty-seven").** Spell out numbers below 100 or those that begin a sentence—for example, *I have twelve cards* rather than *I have 12 cards*; *One hundred fifty kids got on the bus* as opposed to *150 kids got on the bus*. Use numerals for addresses, dates, and time of day (except with *o'clock*).

5. **Remove talking words:** *a lot, really, so, like, then*, and *well*. Sometimes these words are necessary because they are being used to move action along, but most of the time they are just filler, as in the following: *So, my family has always been proud to be Italian American.* Here is a trick: If the sentence makes sense without the word, remove it. (See Toolkit 6.8.)

6. **Remove extra words.** Look to cut any phrases or words that are filler. Here are some examples:

   In my opinion

   I think that/It seems that

   I feel

In most cases, it is more effective not to use any version of *I feel* or *I think* as a way to express an opinion. For example, *Requiring school uniforms is unfair* is better than *I feel that requiring school uniforms is unfair.*

7. **Correct for common errors involving homonyms and frequently confused words.** If you know you have a problem with homonyms (words that sound alike but have different meanings) or other commonly confused words, search for one word at a time.

    There/their/they're

    Its/it's

    To/too/two

    You're/your

    Except/accept

    Whose/who's

Toolkit
6.1 Sentence Variety

This toolkit will help you identify whether you need more variety in your sentences and offers suggestions for how to revise your sentences to create stronger, more impressive writing.

In drafting, students often fall into the habit of using the same sentence formation again and again. Readers can become bored when the pattern seldom changes. To add more variety, you need to pay attention to length, word choice, and sentence structure.

What to Do

1. **Before turning to a draft of your own writing, read this list of common sentence variety problems.**

   a. **Length monotony.** Sentences should not all be the same length. If you see three sentences in a row that are the same length, mark the third as needing to be changed. It is often easy to combine very short sentences with transitions or to break up long sentences into shorter ones.

   b. **Word repetition.** Watch for the same word(s) being used to begin a series of sentences. Look especially for *It*, *This*, *There*, or *I* as the first word of a sentence. In each paragraph, mark the second time in a row that you see one of these words. To address this problem, move words from the middle or end of the sentence forward or otherwise reword the sentence. Here are some examples:

      Original

      <u>The commercial</u> starts off with two kids sitting at a table. <u>The commercial</u> has a little humor in it because one of the kids is trying to open a cereal box from the wrong side. <u>The commercial</u> captures our attention by focusing on the crazy things kids are capable of doing.

   Possible revisions of the third sentence:

      By focusing on the crazy things kids are capable of doing, the commercial captures our attention.

      Humor is effective at capturing our attention, and focusing on the kid doing this crazy thing is an example of this strategy.

LaunchPad Solo

142   Visit **LaunchPad Solo for Readers and Writers** for more practice on the skills covered in this section.

As viewers, we are immediately entertained by the crazy things kids are capable of doing, and so we pay attention, focusing on the commercial.

c. **Sentence-structure repetition.** First, some definitions:

- An **independent clause** has a subject and a verb, and can stand alone as a sentence.
- A **dependent or subordinate clause** has a subject and a verb, but cannot stand alone as a sentence.

There are four basic sentence types in English: **simple**, **compound**, **complex**, and **compound-complex**. In the following examples, independent clauses are underlined, and dependent clauses are double underlined.

- **A simple sentence contains just one independent clause:**

    Readers appreciate sentence variety.

- **A compound sentence contains at least two independent clauses:**

    Readers appreciate sentence variety, so writers should work to include some.

- **A complex sentence contains an independent clause and one or more dependent clauses:**

    Because readers appreciate sentence variety, writers should work to include some.

- **A compound-complex sentence contains two or more independent clauses and one or more dependent clauses:**

    Because readers appreciate sentence variety, writers should work to include some, and they should spend some time revising for this issue.

Evaluate your sentences to see what structures you use. If you find yourself using several simple or compound sentences in a row, try to revise to add more variety. Here is an example:

Original

In "Autism and Visual Thought," Temple Grandin describes the process of thinking in pictures. She writes that it is like having a library of video images in her mind. This thought process has been beneficial in her work designing equipment for handling cattle. Thinking in pictures also has its drawbacks.

Revised

In "Autism and Visual Thought," Temple Grandin describes the process of thinking in pictures as involving a library of video images in her mind. While this thought process has been beneficial in her work designing equipment for handling cattle, thinking in pictures also has its drawbacks.

2. **With a better understanding of how to vary your sentences, work through your draft twice.** The first time, highlight or underline sentences that are monotonous or repetitive, as described in this toolkit. Then, go back and revise, following the suggestions here or using your own techniques to make a more engaging, lively essay for your readers.

   The second time, read through the draft looking at sentence structure, marking any places where you use two or more simple or compound sentences in a row. Then, go back and revise to include some complex sentences.

Toolkit
6.2 **Coordination and Subordination**

> This toolkit will help you express connections between your ideas more clearly.

When you are presenting more than one idea, detail, or example, it is helpful to indicate to your readers how those ideas are related. A good way to establish relationships between ideas is through **coordination** and **subordination**.

Equally Weighted Ideas (Coordination)

Writers use coordination to indicate that ideas are equally important. In the following example of coordination, ideas are presented using similarly structured sentences or phrases.

First idea ——————— Arthur Chu believes that being proficient in English will have value in his life, and
Second idea ——————— he takes steps to develop his skills.

Unequally Weighted Ideas (Subordination)

Writers indicate that one idea is less important than another by using subordination. If the less important idea is presented in a subordinate clause (a **subordinate clause** has a subject and a verb but cannot stand alone as a sentence), the more important one can be emphasized as the main (independent) clause.

In the following examples, see how the idea in the dependent (subordinate) clause, which is double underlined, comes across as less important than the idea in the independent clause, which is single underlined.

> Although Arthur Chu argues that proficiency in English is essential to his identity as a Chinese American, he also believes that it is possible to be too good.

> Although Arthur Chu believes that it is possible to be too good in English, he argues that proficiency in English is essential to his identity as a Chinese American.

While both Sharon Haywood and Lauren Shields <u>change their appearances in order to feel more comfortable with themselves</u>, Shields makes changes that are less permanent than the ones Haywood makes.

What to Do

Look through your draft to see how you might combine or revise sentences so that you clearly communicate the relationship between ideas.

Good words to use to begin subordinate clauses include *although*, *because*, *since*, *unless*, *until*, *whether*, and *while*. You can find a more complete list of subordinate clause markers and relative pronouns in a writing handbook.

1. **Reviewing your draft, identify (highlight or italicize) all your subordinate clauses.** To do so, look for parts of your sentences that begin with subordinate clause markers. Then ask the following of each one:

   • Does the marked subordinate clause contain the less important idea in the sentence?

   • Is the most important point part of the unmarked main, independent clause?

   • If you identify a problem, rewrite the sentence to make sure that the most important point is also the main, independent clause.

2. **If you have not used any subordinate clauses, see if you can improve the clarity of your ideas by adding subordination to some sentences to indicate greater and lesser importance.**

Toolkit 6.3 Fragments

> This toolkit will help you identify and correct fragments.

Sentences are complete thoughts that can grammatically stand on their own. In technical terms, they are independent or main clauses. In contrast, **sentence fragments** are incomplete sentences that cannot stand on their own. Fragments can negatively affect clarity.

Fragments either lack a subject, a verb, or possibly both, or are subordinate clauses. Following are just a few types.

Phrase Fragments

This type of fragment consists solely of a phrase or phrases, often beginning with an -*ing* word. A phrase fragment typically needs to be attached to the beginning or end of a nearby sentence.

Beyond race, other barriers to participation in sports have existed historically and continue to exist today. <u>Including those created by stereotypes and prejudices about gender, religion, class, and ability.</u>

In this example, the second "sentence" is a fragment that should be connected to the previous sentence.

Possible revision: Beyond race, other barriers to participation in sports have existed historically and continue to exist today, including those created by stereotypes and prejudices about gender, religion, class, and ability.

Dependent Clause Fragments

These fragments consist solely of dependent or subordinate clause(s). Some common subordinate clause markers (words that begin dependent clauses) are *although*, *because*, *since*, *unless*, *until*, *whether*, and *while*.

Incorrect: Although Internet tools are valuable for enabling business growth, providing pleasure and personal utility, and allowing for social and political community.

Incorrect: Because teens believe terms like *fag* no longer have negative meanings.

One revision method is to connect the fragment to a nearby sentence.

Possible revision: While Internet tools are valuable for enabling business growth, providing pleasure and personal utility, and allowing for social and political community, they can also be abused or misused.

Another method is to rewrite the fragment so that the dependent clause becomes an independent clause.

Possible revision: Internet tools are valuable for enabling business growth, providing pleasure and personal utility, and allowing for social and political community, but they can also be abused or misused.

Possible revision: Teens believe terms like *fag* no longer have negative meanings.

Lists

Lists by themselves cannot stand as sentences.

Incorrect: It is very possible to spend your whole day checking out the multiplying social media sites. Facebook, Twitter, Tumblr, Instagram, Reddit, and many more.

Either a colon or a phrase like *such as* or *including* would fix this type of fragment:

Possible revision: It is very possible to spend your whole day checking out the multiplying social media sites: Facebook, Twitter, Tumblr, Instagram, Reddit, and many more.

Possible revision: It is very possible to spend your whole day checking out the multiplying social media sites, such as Facebook, Twitter, Tumblr, Instagram, Reddit, and many more.

Examples

This type of fragment presents examples that are not part of an independent clause.

> **Incorrect:** In "Breaking Out the Broken English," Arthur Chu reflects on the various forms of English he uses. For example, using broken English for certain voice-over roles.

As with other fragments, these can be revised by connecting the fragment to another sentence or by rewriting the fragment so that it is an independent clause.

> **Possible revision:** In "Breaking Out the Broken English," Arthur Chu reflects on the various forms of English he uses, including using broken English for certain voice-over roles.

> **Possible revision:** In "Breaking Out the Broken English," Arthur Chu reflects on the various forms of English he uses. For example, he uses broken English for certain voice-over roles.

What to Do

1. **Read your draft aloud, sentence by sentence, exaggerating the pauses at periods.** Note any places where you have sentences that seem incomplete.

2. **Check to see that each sentence includes at least one independent clause (with a subject, verb, and complete thought).**

3. **Return to the places you have marked and revise as needed, using the methods discussed in this toolkit.**

Toolkit 6.4 Run-ons

> This toolkit will help you identify and correct run-ons and comma splices.

Run-ons contain two or more independent clauses (independent clauses have a subject and verb, and can stand alone as a sentence). In run-ons, two or more of a writer's ideas bleed or blur into each other, confusing readers.

There are two main types of run-ons: **fused sentences** and **comma splices**.

A **fused sentence** contains two or more independent clauses that are not separated by appropriate punctuation:

> Properly punctuating sentences helps readers process your ideas more clearly faulty punctuation can lead to confusion.

In this example, there are two independent clauses:

a. Properly punctuating sentences helps readers process your ideas more clearly

b. Faulty punctuation can lead to confusion

A **comma splice** describes the run-on problem in which two independent clauses are connected with the wrong punctuation—a comma:

> Properly punctuating sentences helps readers process your ideas more clearly, faulty punctuation can lead to confusion.

Ways to Correct Run-on Sentences

The easiest method is to divide the run-on into two or more sentences.

> **Possible revision:** Properly punctuating sentences helps readers process your ideas more clearly. Faulty punctuation can lead to confusion.

A method that conveys a slightly closer relationship between the clauses is to use a semicolon or colon.

> **Possible revision:** Properly punctuating sentences helps readers process your ideas more clearly; faulty punctuation can lead to confusion.

Other methods can do an even better job of conveying the relationship between the two clauses.

- Use a comma and a coordinating conjunction (a quick fix for a comma splice). Coordinating conjunctions are *and*, *but*, *for*, *nor*, *or*, *so*, and *yet*.

  > **Possible revision:** Properly punctuating sentences helps readers process your ideas more clearly, but faulty punctuation can lead to confusion.

- Use a semicolon and a conjunctive adverb (conjunctive adverbs include *accordingly*, *consequently*, *for example*, *however*, *in addition*, *on the contrary*, *similarly*, and *therefore*; check a writing handbook for more examples).

  > **Possible revision:** Properly punctuating sentences helps readers process your ideas more clearly; in contrast, faulty punctuation can lead to confusion.

- Make one clause subordinate.

  > **Possible revision:** Whereas faulty punctuation can lead to confusion, properly punctuating sentences helps readers process your ideas more clearly.

What to Do

1. **Read your draft aloud, sentence by sentence; you may find that you naturally and logically pause where a run-on needs to be divided.**

2. **Look for any places that are hard to read because the division between ideas is unclear.**

3. **Look for places where you use coordinating conjunctions (*and, but, for, nor, or, so,* or *yet*).** If you are using any between two independent clauses, make sure to put a comma at the end of the first independent clause, before the conjunction.

Many immigrants come to the United States in search of job opportunities, so some Americans fear immigrants will take all the jobs and leave them with none.

Keep in mind that run-ons are not always overly long sentences.

Toolkit 6.5 Subject-Verb Agreement

This toolkit will help you identify and fix subject-verb agreement problems.

The subject-verb agreement rule is straightforward: **Singular** subjects need **singular** verbs, and **plural** subjects need **plural** verbs.

Subject-verb agreement problems come from four primary sources:

1. **Proofreading incorrectly.** The writer understands the rule but has not noticed the mistake.

2. **Misidentifying the subject that the verb is supposed to agree with.** Misidentifying the subject frequently happens when the subject and verb are not close together (keep in mind that the noun closest to the verb is not always its subject).

   SUBJECT   NOUN   VERB
   The <u>law</u> of <u>averages</u> <u>are</u> unreliable.

In this example, there are two nouns, but the subject of the sentence is *law*. (The law is unreliable, not the averages.) Because *law* is singular, it needs the singular form *is* instead.

   SUBJECT   NOUN   VERB
   The <u>woman</u> as well as many other <u>Italians</u> <u>wish</u> she could return to Italy.

Here the subject is singular (*woman*) and the verb needed is *wishes*. Alternatively, you could revise to emphasize that more than one person wishes to return to Italy: *The woman and many other Italians wish they could return to Italy.*

Note: For subjects joined with *or* or *nor*, make the verb agree with the closest subject.

                            CLOSEST
            SUBJECT   SUBJECT   VERB
   Neither the <u>students</u> nor the <u>teacher</u> <u>was</u> on time for class because of the storm.

                            CLOSEST
            SUBJECT   SUBJECT   VERB
   Neither the <u>teacher</u> nor the <u>students</u> <u>were</u> on time for class because of the storm.

3. **Misidentifying a pronoun's case (singular or plural).**

   - Singular subject pronouns: *anyone, everybody, everyone, nobody, no one, someone*

- Plural subject pronouns: *both, few, several*
- Indefinite subject pronouns that can be singular or plural depending on how they are used: *all, most, none, some*

SUBJECT   VERB
<u>All</u> of the students <u>use</u> the library's databases for research.

The pronoun *all* is plural in this sentence because it refers to "students," which is plural.

SUBJECT   VERB
<u>All</u> of the cake <u>is</u> gone.

All is singular in this sentence because it refers to "cake," which is singular.

Problem sentence: Sara is the only one of the authors who write too much.

In this sentence, the writer has incorrectly matched the verb *write* with the noun, *authors; who write* actually refers to *Sara*, as in *Sara is the only one who writes.*

Revision: Sara is the only one of the authors who writes too much.

4. **Following the rules for a vernacular form of English rather than formal English.** *Lopez write* rather than *Lopez writes*, for example, may be acceptable in some vernacular forms of English but not in formal English. One tip to remember is that for most regular English verbs, it is only the present tense, third-person singular form that changes.

	Singular	Plural
First Person	I write	We write
Second Person	You write	You write
Third Person	She write**s**	They write

What to Do

1. **Using a highlighter and a pencil, mark the subject-and-verb pairs in each sentence of a paragraph.** (If you're feeling ambitious, you can do the whole draft.) Note that some sentences may have more than one pair. Go all the way through, identifying subject-and-verb pairs by highlighting the subjects and underlining the verbs.

In a positive light, words can nurture a sense of confidence as a person grows within a society. They, along with hope and hard work, provides a person with great strength. Through words, individuals have the power to inspire others, provide hope, and shows care for one another. Throughout the generations, we can list many people who have been praised for their use of speech and specifically how they, amazingly and impressively, uses their words to inspire and encourage others to act on their ideas. We can traces the great speakers from biblical times, such as Moses, to early American history with Lincoln, transitioning to contemporary speakers, such as Dr. Martin Luther King Jr., Malcolm X, Gandhi, and even President Obama. These people have chosen to use their words to provoke action; they have driven their peoples to attack hate, racism, discrimination, and, ultimately, to promote peace.

2. **With the subjects and verbs isolated, look closely:** Have you chosen the correct verb form to match each subject? In the sample text from step 1, see if you can find and correct the four errors that are present. Reading each subject-verb pair aloud and isolated from any intervening words (e.g., "They provides") will help you hear and identify errors.

Toolkit
6.6 **Commonly Misused Words**

This toolkit will help you identify and correct frequently confused words.

What follows is a list of commonly misused words that many students have trouble with in their writing. These are problems that spell-checker won't catch because they involve words that are spelled correctly but used in the wrong situation. To learn about even more words that are misused with some frequency, consult a handbook.

Becoming more aware of your own set of problem words will help you edit for clarity, accuracy, and polish. Note that spell-checker programs can sometimes cause these problems if writers don't pay close attention to what change the program suggests.

1. **Defiantly vs. definitely.** Although you may wish to say that you **definitely** agree with another writer's argument, it is quite another thing to say that you **defiantly** agree with her ideas.

2. **Accept vs. except.** If you write that you **accept** another writer's arguments, you are saying that you agree with them; if you write that you **except** them, however, you are saying quite the opposite—that you exclude them.

3. **Dominate vs. dominant.** These closely related words sound very similar, but they are different parts of speech and thus are used in different ways. **Dominate** is a verb, whereas **dominant** is an adjective.

   In the debate, the senator clearly **dominated** her opponent, who had trouble stating his positions effectively.

   The senator was **dominant** in the debate because her opponent had trouble stating his positions effectively.

4. **Bias vs. biased** and **prejudice vs. prejudiced.** These two pairs of words are often confused in writing, most likely because the *d* in **biased** and **prejudiced** may not always be clearly pronounced in speech. **Bias** and **prejudice** are nouns, whereas **biased** and **prejudiced** are adjectives; thus, they are used in different ways.

The writer showed **bias** in describing the situation.

The **bias** of the writer was clear in his description of the problem.

The writer presented a **biased** description of the situation.

5. **Use to vs. used to** and **suppose to vs. supposed to.** Although we may not clearly pronounce the *d* at the end of **used to** or **supposed to**, those are the only correct forms. When you say someone **used to** do something, you are referring to something that happened in the past, so the past tense of the verb — **used** — is called for. In the case of "is / was / were / had been supposed to," the past participle — **supposed** — is required.

6. **Posses vs. possess.** Spell-check programs typically won't object to **posses** because it is the plural of the word *posse*, a noun that means "a group"; however, in most cases, writers probably intend to use the verb **possess**, which means "to have."

7. **Would of vs. would've.** **Would of** is a typo for the contraction **would've**, most likely originating from the way **would've** sounds when it is spoken. **Would have** is an even better choice.

8. **Apart vs. a part.** These words are different parts of speech. **Apart** can serve as an adjective or adverb, whereas **part** is a noun (preceded in this case by the article **a**).

Although the transfer student desperately wanted to be **a part** of the in crowd, he was forced to sit **apart** from them in the dining hall.

One trick: If you can substitute **part** without distorting meaning, then you know you need **a part**.

9. **Than vs. then.** Although close in spelling, the meanings of these two words are different. One trick is to remember that **than** is the comparative form — the word you use when you are contrasting — whereas **then** typically refers to time or sequence.

When we were younger, my sister was much shorter **than** I am, but **then** she had a growth spurt in high school and now towers over me.

10. **Their vs. there vs. they're.** These homophones (words that have different meanings and spellings but the same pronunciation) often trip up writers. **Their** is a possessive pronoun, whereas **there** can either refer to a location or serve to introduce a sentence or clause, among other things. **They're** is a contraction for **they are**, so if you can substitute that wording instead, you know you need **they're**.

Their house is on the corner.

You can see the new building over **there**.

They're doing a lot of construction in **their** neighborhood.

11. **Woman vs. women.** Unlike the similar words **man** and **men**, we find many students using the plural **women** when they intend to use the singular **woman**, in phrases such as **a women**.

12. **Quote vs. state.** To **quote** means "to repeat something from another source"; to **state** means "to express or announce something." Thus, it is typically incorrect to use **quotes** as part of a phrase introducing something you are quoting from another source. Here is an incorrect example:

> Patricia Rice **quotes**, "Some companies instruct their phone clerks to brush aside any chance of a face-to-face appointment to view a sales property or interview for a job based on the sound of a caller's voice."

A more accurate way to introduce this quote would be to write that "Patricia Rice **states**" or "Patricia Rice **reports**." This makes it clear that you are quoting what Rice states in her essay rather than repeating a quotation that Rice uses in her piece.

13. **Day in age vs. day and age.** **Day and age** is the correct form here; **day in age** is most likely a result of the "and" being slurred when speaking. Note that the phrase is a cliché; thus, it would be best to avoid it altogether, substituting something like "these days" or "today."

14. **Been vs. being.** Technically speaking, **been** is the past participle of the verb "be," whereas **being** is the present participle. Practically speaking, **been** is sometimes confused for **being**. Here's one example of a misused **been**:

> Texting allows us to stay connected with each other without actually **been** together.

This should be:

> Texting allows us to stay connected with each other without actually **being** together.

Here's a sentence that uses both words correctly:

> Although it is true that many students have **been** late to class recently, several missed the shuttle because they did not know the schedule was **being** revised.

What to Do

1. **Review one or two pieces of your own writing, looking for words or phrases that you tend to confuse or mistype.** Some may be among the preceding list, but others may be different.

2. **Based on what you noticed in step 1, make a list of words and phrases that you should especially look for when proofreading.**

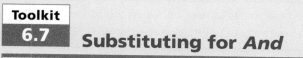

Toolkit 6.7 **Substituting for *And***

> This toolkit will help you present your ideas more clearly by eliminating overreliance on the word *and*.

And, one of the coordinating conjunctions, is a useful word that implies addition or connection. However, many writers overuse it when they could choose words that more precisely express the relationship between their ideas.

> **And-excessive sentence:** I needed to start writing my essay **and** I read the articles **and** I made some notes **and** I had lunch **and** then I went to class **and** then I finally worked on my draft.

Reworking this sentence by substituting other words for *and* in a few places conveys a sharper sense of the sequence of events.

> **Revised sentence:** I needed to start writing my essay, so I read the articles and made some notes. But I could not work on my draft until after I ate lunch and went to class.

In the next example, *and* is necessary where it forms a pair, but the other instances could be replaced or removed with some editing.

> **And-excessive sentence:** Writers quickly fall into the habit of over-relying on common adjectives **and** adverbs, **and** often it is the case that the most frequently used adjectives **and** adverbs are also imprecise, **and** using more specific words will better express your intentions.

> **Revised sentence:** Writers quickly fall into the habit of over-relying on common adjectives and adverbs, many of which are also imprecise, so using more specific words will better express your intentions.

What to Do

Look at your draft for places where you use *and* to connect clauses. You might simply conduct a word search in your word processor, so that all occurrences of the word *and* are highlighted, making them easy to see and examine. Consider whether you might be able to substitute some other words for greater precision and clarity. It is hard to write without *and*, so don't worry about replacing them all. (Definitely keep those that form lists or pairs.)

Toolkit
6.8 Editing for Wordiness

> This toolkit will help you in the final stages of revision, when the content of your draft is in good shape and you are ready to polish your sentences.

Wordiness—using more words than you need to make a point—clogs up written communication, distracting readers from your ideas. Following are some common forms of wordiness to watch for.

What to Do

1. Unnecessary repetition:

- Review your draft, looking for places where you use similar words in the same sentence.

- Try to reword these sentences to eliminate the repetition.

    Wordy sentence: When <u>applying</u> for jobs, <u>applicants</u> should fill out the forms carefully.

    Revised sentence: Job applicants should fill out the forms carefully.

    Wordy sentence: In <u>Amy Tan's</u> "Personal Errata," <u>she</u> writes about her experiences searching for information about herself online.

    Revised sentence: In "Personal Errata," Amy Tan writes about her experiences searching for information about herself online.

    Wordy sentence: In "Personal Errata" by <u>Amy Tan</u>, <u>Tan</u> writes about her experiences searching for information about herself online.

    Revised sentence: In "Personal Errata," Amy Tan writes about her experiences searching for information about herself online.

2. Unnecessary words or phrases to cut or replace:

Problem Word or Phrase	Example
There is/there are/it is	**It is** the case that linguistic profiling, and the harm it causes, is worth our attention. **Revision:** Linguistic profiling, and the harm it causes, is worth our attention.
I feel that/I feel/I think/ I believe	**I feel that** requiring school uniforms is unfair. **Revision:** Requiring school uniforms is unfair.
Like	It's **like** very unreasonable for the author to make this statement. **Revision:** It's very unreasonable for the author to make this statement.
So	**So** I have to write a thesis and make sure the ideas I discuss in my essay fit. **Revision:** I have to write a thesis and make sure the ideas I discuss in my essay fit.
Then/and then	**And then** the writer makes a ridiculous statement about how social media should be used in school. **Revision:** The writer makes a ridiculous statement about how social media should be used in school.

(Continued)

(Continued)

Problem Word or Phrase	Example
In my opinion	**In my opinion,** marijuana should not be legalized. **Revision:** Marijuana should not be legalized.
Well/really	**Well,** Ann Smith has some good points, but she does not like political correctness very much. **Revision:** Ann Smith has some good points, but she does not like political correctness very much.
In a way/kind of/sort of	**In a way,** the writer **sort of** describes the problem so that it seems **kind of** unclear. **Revision:** The writer describes the problem unclearly.
Basically	Stereotyping is **basically** an excuse for stupidity. **Revision:** Stereotyping is an excuse for stupidity.
The fact that	She writes about **the fact that** women are judged on their appearance when they apply for jobs. **Revision:** She writes about how women are judged on their appearance when they apply for jobs.
Pretty much	I would **pretty much** say that body image continues to put stress on many people. **Revision:** I would say that body image continues to put stress on many people.

- Review your draft, searching for and highlighting or circling these words and phrases.

- Read each sentence you've marked aloud, omitting the highlighted or circled word or phrase. Does the sentence still make sense? If it does, cut the word or phrase, or otherwise reword.

3. **Words or phrases to replace:**

Problem Word or Phrase	Exchange Word or Phrase
In today's society	Today
Being that	Because
The reason why is because	The reason is
Due to the fact that	Because
Back in the day	In the past; in 2004

- Review your draft, searching for and highlighting or circling these problem phrases — and others that are similar to them.

- Go back through the draft, trying out the suggested exchange word or phrase. Does it sound less wordy? Is the meaning unchanged? If so, use the exchange word or phrase.

4. **Self-editing — putting it all together:**

   - Alone or with a friend — or even with the whole class — expand on these lists of Words and Phrases to Cut and Words or Phrases to Replace.
   - Search your own draft for these additional words and phrases, removing or replacing them as you do so.

Note: Some instructors discourage the use of the first person (*I*) in academic writing, especially in cases like "I think," "I believe," or similar phrases. In these situations, it is usually easy to cut the phrase and leave just the statement of what you think or believe. For example, *I would pretty much say that body image continues to put stress on many people* can be edited down to *Body image continues to put stress on many people.* It is a good idea to ask your instructor if using the first person is appropriate.

**Toolkit
6.9** **Overused Verbs**

> This toolkit will help you raise the clarity and sophistication of your prose by varying your verbs and using the *to be* verbs less often.

Writers commonly fall into the habit of overusing certain verbs, particularly forms of the verb *to be*. When we draft, we focus on ideas and not on selecting specific words. This is a good approach for drafting, but because repeated use of the same word can become boring, it is important to identify and change these words during the editing stage, substituting more specific and precise verbs where possible.

To Be

The helping verb *to be* comes in many forms: *am, is, are, be, was, were, been,* and *being.* Revising sentences containing *to be* forms often makes the writing stronger and more active.

Verb-weak sentence: Issues of diversity are of interest to me.

Revised sentence: Issues of diversity interest me.

Verb-weak sentence: Temple Grandin was treated badly by her peers.

Revised sentence: Temple Grandin's peers treated her badly.

Verb-weak sentence: My paper is a study of how one person overcame her disability.

Revised sentence: My paper examines how one person overcame her disability.

Dull and Imprecise Verbs

Verbs other than *to be* can also be used in a dull or vague fashion.

Verb-weak sentence: Immigrants <u>had</u> an extremely hard time during World War II.

Revised sentence: During World War II, immigrants <u>endured</u> an extremely hard time.

Verb-weak sentence: Linguist John Baugh has found that speaking with an accent can <u>affect</u> someone's job prospects.

Revised sentence: Linguist John Baugh has found that speaking with an accent can <u>undermine</u> someone's job prospects.

Verb-weak sentence: Gewirtz and Kern <u>speak</u> about the need to rethink how we judge digital histories.

Revised sentence: Gewirtz and Kern <u>argue</u> for the need to rethink how we judge digital histories.

Incorrect or Overly Informal Verb Choices

In academic writing, you want to be accurate: Authors don't *speak*; they *write*. They don't *talk* about a topic; they *discuss* a topic. Elevate your prose by replacing informal and incorrect verbs with more precise verbs, such as *write*, *report*, *explain*, *discuss*, *suggest*, *argue*, *observe*, *state*, or *propose*. (For more on verbs used to discuss authors, see Toolkit 5.8.)

What to Do

1. **Review the following list of fifteen overused, imprecise verbs.**

   affect, affects / affected / affecting

   am, are, is / was, were / been / being

   come, comes / came / coming

   do, does / did / doing

   get, gets / got / getting

   go, goes / went / going

   have, has / had / having

   know, knows / knew / knowing

   look, looks / looked / looking

   make, makes / made / making

   relate, relates / related / relating

   say, says / said / saying

see, sees / saw / seeing

talk, talks / talked / talking

think, thinks / thought / thinking

2. **Using a highlighter, mark every time you use one of these overused verbs.**

3. **Go through your draft and make substitutions, selecting more precise verbs unless you are sure that the original word is the best choice.** When you are done, some of these overused verbs will necessarily remain in your essay, but you will have reduced their number and punched up the power of your prose as well.

Toolkit 6.10 Adjective and Adverb Variety

This toolkit will help you choose more precise and clear adjectives and adverbs.

Writers quickly fall into the habit of over-relying on common adjectives and adverbs, many of which are also imprecise. Using more specific words will allow for better expression.

Some reminders:

- **Adjectives** modify nouns; that is, they give more information about a person, place, or thing that is being described: the *black* cat; the *beautiful* sunset.

- **Adverbs** modify verbs, adjectives, or other adverbs: The woman walked *cautiously* on the ice; the *very* heavy book; the student *very confidently* spoke up in class.

Here are some adjectives and adverbs that are frequently overused. Often you can substitute a better word, and sometimes you should simply cut the word out entirely.

Overused adjectives	Overused adverbs
awesome	*actually*
bad	*basically*
different	*continually*
good	*differently*
great	*just*
important	*probably*
interesting	*really*
nice	*totally*
unique	*very*

What to Do

1. **Review the list of overused adjectives, and identify those words that you use frequently.** If you aren't sure, read one of your drafts, looking for frequently used adjectives. If there are other adjectives that you use frequently, add them to this list.

2. **Look up your commonly used adjectives in a thesaurus (you can use the one installed in your word processing program, an online thesaurus, or a printed version).** Write down the synonyms that you could imagine using *and that make sense in context*. Many words have similar meanings but are used in different situations. For example, for *bad*, you might feel comfortable using *cruel* or *corrupt* but not *debauched*.

3. **Highlight any overused adjectives in your draft.**

4. **Replace each of the overused adjectives with one from the list of options you have created, or consider whether you can use a more precise word (for example, instead of *different*, use a word that indicates the difference).**

5. **Repeat steps 1–4, this time paying attention to adverbs.**

Toolkit
6.11 Keeping Pronouns Consistent

> This toolkit addresses the common pronoun-antecedent agreement problem of switching between singular and plural in a sentence.

Consistency is an important principle in clear, academic writing. The consistency rule that seems to especially trip up students is sticking with either the singular or plural case and not switching between them in a sentence.

Pronouns are words that stand in for nouns (for example, *he*, *she*, *it*, or *they*, or the possessive forms *his*, *hers*, *its*, or *theirs*). The noun that is referenced by a pronoun later in the sentence or paragraph is called an **antecedent**. Problems arise when antecedents do not agree with their pronouns.

The most common agreement problems involve switches between singular antecedents and plural pronouns. In these cases, a writer starts presenting a singular case and then switches to plural. While "singular *they*" (or *their*) is increasingly common in speech, it is generally not accepted in formal writing. For example, few would object if a classroom teacher declared, in speech, "Everyone should clean up their tables before leaving!" Yet this sentence is grammatically incorrect because *everyone* is a singular antecedent and *their* is a plural pronoun.

Inconsistent pronoun: The author [*singular antecedent*] wrote a thought-provoking article, and they [*plural pronoun*] also made readers laugh out loud.

Possible revision: The author [*singular antecedent*] wrote a thought-provoking article, and he [*singular pronoun*] also made readers laugh out loud.

Possible revision: Kevin Fanning [*singular antecedent*] wrote a thought-provoking article, and he [*singular pronoun*] also made readers laugh out loud.

Because a specific article is being referred to here, another revision option is to identify the author, something that will help you see which pronoun form to use.

Inconsistent pronoun: Each student was supposed to submit their paper on Tuesday.

The writer began with singular (*each student*) and then switched to plural mid-sentence (*their*). In cases where it is clear that more than one person is meant, switching the first noun to plural works well most of the time.

Possible revision: Students were supposed to submit their papers on Tuesday.

Possible revision: Each student was supposed to submit her or his paper on Tuesday.

Inconsistent pronoun: When a teacher [*singular*] is insulting to their [*plural pronoun*] students, the superintendent has to refer them [*plural pronoun*] to the board of education.

Possible revision (change the antecedent): When teachers [*plural*] are insulting to their [*plural pronoun*] students, the superintendent has to refer them [*plural pronoun*] to the board of education.

Possible revision (eliminate the pronoun): When a teacher [*singular*] is insulting to students, the superintendent has to report the teacher to the board of education.

What to Do

1. **Read your draft, searching for plural pronouns that might be incorrectly matched up with singular pronouns or nouns.**

2. **Using the search function in your word processor or reading through a paper copy, highlight the plural pronouns that most frequently cause consistency problems:** *they, them, their,* **and** *theirs.*

3. **Check each sentence that contains a plural pronoun as well as the ones that precede and follow it:** Is the plural pronoun referencing a singular noun or pronoun? If so, rewrite the sentence or sentences to be consistently plural or consistently singular.

4. **Using the search function in your word processor or reading through a paper copy, look for the singular pronouns that are often frequently associated with pronoun inconsistency.** These words (indefinite pronouns) are often assumed to be plural, but they are singular:

anyone	*everyone*	*no one*	*someone*	*each*
anybody	*everybody*	*nobody*	*somebody*	*either*
anything	*everything*	*nothing*	*something*	*neither*

You probably have some favorites that you use frequently—for example, *everyone* or *everybody*. If you like, you can just search for those words, checking to see if you have referenced a singular or plural noun elsewhere in the sentence, and then correcting the sentence if necessary.

Toolkit
6.12 Vague Pronouns

This toolkit will help you replace vague pronouns—words that stand in for or take the place of nouns—with clearer language.

Pronouns can be useful words, standing in for nouns that have already been referred to (antecedents). Sometimes, however, the antecedent is unclear, making the pronoun vague. Any pronoun can create confusion or vagueness, but the pronouns that are most frequently associated with this problem are *this*, *they*, *it*, *that*, *one*, *which*, and *what*.

Vague pronoun sentence: After the politicians and immigration advocates debated policy, <u>they</u> left the meeting with some hope of compromise.

The use of *they* is confusing because we don't know who *they* refers to here: the politicians? the immigration advocates? both groups?

Possible revision: After the politicians and immigration advocates debated policy, <u>both groups</u> left the meeting with some hope of compromise.

Possible revision: After debating policy with the politicians, <u>the immigration advocates</u> left the meeting with some hope of compromise.

Vague pronoun sentence: People who suffer from obesity are often depressed and don't want to exercise as much as they should. <u>This</u> is a problem that I have seen many times.

The use of *this*—a singular pronoun—is confusing. Does *this* refer to the observation that those who suffer from obesity are often depressed? Or does it refer to the comment that those who suffer from obesity don't want to exercise as much as they should? Does the author mean that she has seen both of these problems, or just one in particular?

Possible revision: <u>Depression among the obese</u> is a problem I have seen many times.

Vague pronoun sentence: In Jose Antonio Vargas's "My Life as an Undocumented Immigrant," <u>it</u> says that <u>he</u> came to the United States as a young child.

In this example, the *it* and the *he* are not especially vague, but they are clunky: While the *it* means the article and the *he* means Vargas, there is the possibility that these terms could refer to something else. Perhaps in the article Vargas refers to another male who came to the United States as a child, and the writer of the sentence is referring to that person rather than Vargas.

Possible revision: In "My Life as an Undocumented Immigrant," <u>Jose Antonio Vargas</u> explains that <u>he</u> came to the United States as a young child.

Vague pronoun sentence: <u>The commercial</u> starts off with two kids sitting at a table, one of whom is trying to open a cereal box from the wrong side. <u>It</u> captures our attention by focusing on the crazy things kids are capable of doing.

What *it* is here is not clear. Does *it* mean the entire commercial? Or does *it* mean just the image of the kid trying to open the box from the wrong side?

Possible revision: The commercial starts off with two kids sitting at a table, one of whom is trying to open a cereal box from the wrong side. <u>This action</u> captures our attention by focusing on the crazy things kids are capable of doing.

What to Do

1. **Using a highlighter or the highlighter function in your word processing program, mark all the places in your draft where you use a pronoun.**

2. **Reviewing each highlighted sentence, identify what each pronoun is supposed to refer to, checking to see if this information is in your draft and clear to readers.** When in doubt, replace the pronoun with the specific noun that the pronoun is standing in for. To clarify your meaning, you may need to reword your sentence beyond changing one word.

3. **If you are having trouble finding pronouns, do a document search for just those pronouns that cause you trouble.** If you don't know which ones those are, search for the most common: *this, it, that, which,* and *what.*

Toolkit
6.13

Shifts in Point of View

This toolkit will help you maintain a consistent point of view.

The main points of view are first person (*I, we*), second person (*you*), and third person (*she, he, one, it, they*). Sometimes writers switch or shift between points of view as they write, leading to confusion.

Consider these shifts:

Confusing point of view: <u>Immigrants</u> from different countries may have trouble communicating in English when <u>they</u> first come to the United States. <u>You</u> may have trouble getting a job if <u>you</u> aren't fluent in English. As John Baugh has discovered, <u>they</u> may also have trouble getting an apartment.

The first and last sentences refer to the immigrants in the third person plural (*they*), but the middle sentence shifts to second person (*you*), even though the *you* still refers to immigrants.

Revision: <u>Immigrants</u> from different countries may have trouble communicating in English when <u>they</u> first come to the United States. <u>They</u> may have trouble getting a job if <u>they</u> aren't fluent in English. As John Baugh has discovered, <u>people with accents</u> may also have trouble getting an apartment.

What to Do

Look at your draft, checking to see if you move between points of view, and editing to maintain a consistent point of view where necessary.

Toolkit
6.14   # Reading Aloud

> This toolkit will show you how to edit your draft by reading aloud.

Reading your draft aloud can help you identify the places that need some attention.

What to Do

1. **Begin by reading your draft aloud from the beginning.** Make sure you read exactly what you have written and not what you think you have written. Listen for and mark where phrases or sentences

    - are hard to read (tongue twisters) — this may be a sign that the wording is jumbled
    - sound wrong
    - have too many words (are wordy)
    - are missing words
    - have wrong words written (*loose* for *lose*, for example)
    - express incomplete ideas (fragments)
    - express mixed-up or confusing ideas (run-ons or punctuation problems)

2. **Read your draft aloud again, sentence by sentence, *starting from the end*.** Starting from the end of your draft will help you see whether individual sentences work or don't work. Pay attention to sentence structure and word choice, marking places where you see potential problems.

3. **Returning to the places you have marked, look more closely at them to determine any problems, and revise where needed.**

Toolkit 6.15 Ten Common Sentence-Level Mistakes

> This toolkit will help you focus on the most common sentence-level errors.

This toolkit asks you to look for common errors that many writers make when they simply forget to apply a familiar grammar rule. If the problem is not forgetting a grammar rule but not knowing it, you will need to learn more about the rule and practice it, using a writing handbook or an online source.

1. **Carefully proofread after you have used spell-check, looking for any wrong words.** Use spell-check, but proofread again afterwards. Spell-check will ignore many words that are spelled correctly but are wrong for your sentences, such as *it's / its*, and *they're / their / there*. It will also change *apter* to *alter* when you meant *after*, for example. It may also suggest *too* at the end of a sentence when you really need *to*.

2. **Add a comma after an introductory clause or phrase.** Writers often forget to place a comma after an introductory clause or phrase — a set of words that begin a sentence but cannot stand alone as a complete sentence.

   > Although at first I found Smith's argument compelling, I became convinced that Smith was missing the point after I read the critique by Jones.

   > On social media platforms, users must be careful to adjust their privacy settings to take some control over their digital histories.

3. **Add a comma before conjunctions in compound sentences.** Another very common error is leaving out commas in compound sentences (sentences with independent clauses on either side of *and*, *but*, *for*, *nor*, *or*, *so*, or *yet*).

   > Online interactions may be immediate and in real time, but they leave a footprint.

4. **Use a pair of commas with a nonrestrictive element** — that is, around any phrases that are not essential to a sentence's grammatical sense and meaning.

   > Anna Quindlen, a columnist for *Newsweek*, writes compellingly on the subject of same-sex parenting.

5. **Break up sentences that are run-ons or comma splices.** A run-on combines two or more independent clauses within one sentence without appropriate punctuation. A comma splice combines two independent clauses with just a comma. Comma splices are corrected by substituting the comma with a semicolon or period, adding a conjunction after the comma, or rewriting the sentence.

   > **Comma splice:** Many social media sites have privacy settings that users can adjust to control who sees their information, these need to be managed very carefully to prevent future problems.

Possible revision: Many social media sites have privacy settings that users can adjust to control who sees their information; these need to be managed very carefully to prevent future problems.

Possible revision: Many social media sites have privacy settings that users can adjust to control who sees their information, but these need to be managed very carefully to prevent future problems.

Possible revision: Although many social media sites have privacy settings that users can adjust to control who sees their information, users need to manage these very carefully to prevent future problems.

6. **Finish or connect sentence fragments.** A fragment lacks a subject, a verb, or possibly both. It may also be a subordinate clause. The best way to spot a sentence fragment is to read each sentence by itself, without reading the ones that precede or follow it. The fragments in the following examples are double underlined. Read each double-lined section first, by itself, and it will be clear that it isn't a complete sentence.

   Fragment: Coach ridiculed students who did not fit the macho image that he believed in. Like Josh, my friend, who was one of the best players on the team.

   Possible revision: Coach ridiculed students who did not fit the macho image that he believed in, like Josh, my friend, who was one of the best players on the team.

   Fragment: The government may be trying hard to reduce obesity among Americans, but it's not working. Because every year kids are getting heavier and heavier.

   Possible revision: The government may be trying hard to reduce obesity among Americans, but it's not working because every year kids are getting heavier and heavier.

7. **Correct accidental tense shifts.** Without realizing it, writers will often switch tenses, as from the present to the past, in the middle of a sentence or paragraph.

   Tense problem: Sports occupy [*present tense*] an important place in American culture. Sports contribute [*present tense*] to individual, community, and national identity as athletes wore [*past tense*] their team jerseys and fans wore [*past tense*] the jerseys of their favorite players and teams.

   Possible revision: Sports occupy [*present tense*] an important place in American culture. Sports contribute [*present tense*] to individual, community, and national identity as athletes wear [*present tense*] their team jerseys and fans wear [*present tense*] the jerseys of their favorite players and teams.

8. **Correct missing or misplaced apostrophes (').** To make a noun possessive, use an apostrophe or *'s*. (Possessive personal pronouns [*hers, his, its, theirs, ours,* or *yours*] do not take apostrophes.) The trick with proofreading for absent or incorrect apostrophes is to remember that an apostrophe means something or someone owns or has possession of something else. Ask yourself this question: Does something or someone "own" or have something here?

Apostrophe problem: The <u>cars</u> backseat was boiling hot.

Apostrophe problem: The <u>cars'</u> backseat was boiling hot.

Apostrophe solution: The <u>car's</u> backseat was boiling hot.

Alternatively: The <u>cars'</u> backseats were boiling hot. ───────── If there are several cars with boiling-hot backseats

Apostrophe problem: <u>Societies</u> views of gender are changing gradually.

Apostrophe solution: <u>Society's</u> views of gender are changing gradually.

9. **Correct subject-verb agreement problems.** Make sure that singular nouns have singular verbs and plural nouns have plural verbs. Watch especially for subject-verb pairs that are interrupted by other words.

> **Subject-verb problem:** High <u>levels</u> [*plural subject*] of noise <u>distracts</u> [*singular verb*] students from their work.

> **Possible revision:** High <u>levels</u> [*plural subject*] of noise <u>distract</u> [*plural verb*] students from their work.

> **Subject-verb problem:** Tomorrow, this <u>group</u> [*singular subject*] of students <u>plan</u> [*plural verb*] to protest cuts to the student activities budget.

> **Possible revision:** Tomorrow, this <u>group</u> [*singular subject*] of students <u>plans</u> [*singular verb*] to protest cuts to the student activities budget.

> **Possible revision:** Tomorrow, these students [*plural subject*] <u>plan</u> [*plural verb*] to protest cuts to the student activities budget.

10. **Correct pronoun-antecedent agreement problems.** Check that pronouns and the nouns they refer to match—that is, that singular pronouns go with singular nouns, and plural pronouns go with plural nouns.

> **Agreement problem:** When <u>a writer</u> [*singular*] is not aware of the writing process, <u>they</u> [*plural*] can make the mistake of trying to write beautiful prose for the first draft instead of just trying to get the ideas out.

> **Possible revision:** When <u>writers</u> [*plural*] are not aware of the writing process, <u>they</u> [*plural*] can make the mistake of trying to write beautiful prose for the first draft instead of just trying to get the ideas out.

> **Possible revision:** When <u>a writer</u> [*singular*] is not aware of the writing process, <u>he or she</u> [*singular*] can make the mistake of trying to write beautiful prose for the first draft instead of just trying to get the ideas out.

CHAPTER 4

Language and Identity

Are We Made with Words?

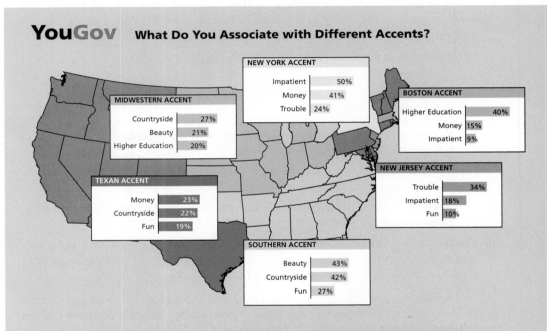

YouGov   **What Do You Associate with Different Accents?**

NEW YORK ACCENT
Impatient	50%
Money	41%
Trouble	24%

MIDWESTERN ACCENT
Countryside	27%
Beauty	21%
Higher Education	20%

BOSTON ACCENT
Higher Education	40%
Money	15%
Impatient	9%

TEXAN ACCENT
Money	23%
Countryside	22%
Fun	19%

NEW JERSEY ACCENT
Trouble	34%
Impatient	18%
Fun	10%

SOUTHERN ACCENT
Beauty	43%
Countryside	42%
Fun	27%

YouGov Omnibus Survey | Sample size was 964 adults | Fieldwork was undertaken between 12th–14th March 2013. The survey was carried out online. The figures have been weighted and are representative of all US adults (aged 18+).

Courtesy of YouGov America Inc.

Image Response: This map records responses from 964 adults who were asked to identify the qualities they associate with different American accents: Texan, Midwestern, New York, Boston, New Jersey, and Southern. Taking advantage of the **insider perspective**, select the accent with which you are most familiar and reflect on the following: Do these associations strike you as valid or invalid? positive or negative? advantageous or disadvantageous? Then, select an accent from an area in which you have not spent much time and reflect similarly on it, this time from the **outsider perspective**.

In This Chapter

Introduction

How Language Makes Us

In an ideal world, what we say and write would be interpreted only based on the meanings of the words and what they express. But as the authors collected here and many others have observed, we are judged not simply by the content of what we say but also by how we say it. Word choices, accents, and speech patterns reveal individuals' origins, as well as their socioeconomic, racial, ethnic, and gender identities. Sometimes language reveals even more about us, such as the neighborhood we live in, our friends, or our professional field. Language reveals so much about people because dialects, or variations on languages, develop and change through social interactions within communities. Thus, adolescent girls who spend a lot of time together begin to speak the same way, just as defense lawyers who work long hours together adopt a similar style of speech. Vocabulary, speech patterns, and other features of dialect are also passed down from parent to child. Language bonds individuals to "their people," whether defined by neighborhood, social circle, or socioeconomic group. This group bond, however, can lead outsiders to make assumptions about people based on *how* they speak rather than *what* they say. Ultimately, by shaping both who we are and others' perceptions of us, the language or languages we speak reveal us — or a particular version of us.

To begin to explore this topic more closely, let's consider the issue of regional differences in language. If a friend invites you to join her in grabbing some lunch at the deli, do you order a sub, a hoagie, a hero, a grinder, or a po'boy? Your answer likely depends not so much on your food preferences as on where you live because these different names for sandwiches reflect regional identity: *Sub* is more widely used across the United States, *hoagie* in Philadelphia, *hero* in New York, *grinder* in Boston, and *po'boy* in New Orleans (Katz). Although the subject is relatively insignificant, this example suggests the strong connection between language and identity — that is, the language we use may provide clues to where we are from as well as to other identity factors, such as our ethnicity and educational background. Our accents and our word choices can mark us as members of particular communities or groups, which themselves can be defined by things like region, age, or ethnicity.

We may be unaware of the way our membership in such groups shapes the language we use. For example, regional differences, such as the type of sandwich we order at the deli — or the sandwich shop — may seem natural to us, and we use these words without much, if any, thought. Yet the relationship between language and identity can be complex and conflicted, especially for individuals who must choose between different languages (like Chinese and English) or between "standard" and "nonstandard" dialects (variations on languages, like formal English and Black or African American Vernacular English), or for those who choose to blend the languages together (such as Spanglish, an informal mix of Spanish and English). Even people who are not multilingual face choices — about which tone or register to use, perhaps talking more informally to their friends than to their employer. Much of the time people are unaware that they are making choices because language patterns are memorized and internalized, quickly becoming automatic and unconscious.

Because it contains apparent clues, the language we use contributes — both correctly and incorrectly — to how others perceive our identity. Indeed, as the language scholar Dennis Baron observes, "Aside from a person's physical appearance, the first thing someone will be judged by is how he or she talks" (qtd. in MacNeil 10). These judgments go beyond ethnic or regional identification to judgments about personality and intelligence. Reporting on a study done by Katherine Kinzler and Jasmine DeJesus of the University of Chicago, R. Douglas Fields relates that by age ten, children judge people with northern accents as "smarter" and "in charge," while they view people with southern accents as "nicer." These judgments, often based on stereotypes, can be mistaken and lead to discrimination, as the writers in this chapter explore. Moreover, observed language can conflict with expectations: As Fields reports, "Americans can be taken [a]back when hearing a black person speak with a proper British accent, for example, or be just as perplexed when they discover that a rapper singing with a 'black' accent is Caucasian."

Though people may be judged and misjudged because of their language, the connection between language and identity is not unchangeable. On the one hand, we can cultivate different views of ourselves by speaking in a way intended to create a more positive impression, for example, or by tailoring the language we use to particular situations (or "code-switching"—a familiar concept to multilingual speakers who switch between languages). On the other hand, by becoming aware of the stereotypes we are tempted to use in order to judge others, we can train ourselves not to make potentially false conclusions.

Our connection to language is both personal and public, shaped by our families and displayed in our interactions with others, raising the question of how language determines who we are—or who we are seen to be. In this chapter, we invite you to explore how our accents, our speech patterns, and even our word choices can be connected to identity; to consider how individuals negotiate that relationship; and to examine how language shapes the impressions we inspire in others. Do our words make us, or do we use language to make (or remake) ourselves?

Works Cited

Fields, R. Douglas. "Why Does a Southern Drawl Sound Uneducated to Some?" *Scientific American*, 7 Dec. 2012, blogs.scientificamerican.com/guest-blog/why-does-a-southern -drawl-sound-uneducated-to-some/.

Katz, Joshua. "Beyond 'Soda, Pop, or Coke': Regional Dialect Variation in the Continental US." *North Carolina State U*, www4.ncsu.edu/~jakatz2/project-dialect.html. Accessed 30 July 2014.

MacNeil, Robert, and William Cran. *Do You Speak American?* Nan A. Talese/Doubleday, 2005.

Language and Identity

Before You Read: Recall your childhood view of your family's customs, habits, or language, and write briefly about a time when you felt embarrassed by those customs, habits, or language. Then reflect on how your views have changed as you have gotten older.

RAFAEL CAMPO

Born in New Jersey, Rafael Campo is a physician and a poet. In addition to practicing medicine at Beth Israel Hospital and teaching at Harvard, he writes about health and identity, as well as racial, class, and gender equality. Campo believes that both reading and writing poetry serve as tools for healing and understanding. He has won several prestigious awards, including the 2013 Hippocrates Open International Prize for Poetry and Medicine. "The Way of the Dinosaurs" was included in *How I Learned English: 55 Accomplished Latinos Recall Lessons in Language and Life* (2007).

As You Read: In the following narrative, Rafael Campo says that his childhood fascination with dinosaurs differed from that of a typical six-year-old. As you read, look for and mark passages where the author refers to dinosaurs and explains why they are important to him.

The Way of the Dinosaurs

pendejo: impolite Spanish word for *idiot* or *jerk*

coño: impolite Spanish word for *wimp*

¡*Pendejo!* I shouted the word at the top of my lungs, knowing exactly what kind of reaction it would elicit. ¡*Coño!* I added that one for good measure.

My father glowered at me from over his shoulder, taking his eyes off the congested highway just long enough to silence me. We were in the old family Ford LTD, with its textured beige upholstery, rust-red paint job, and brown vinyl hardtop. My younger brothers tried to suppress their giggles, sitting on either side of me in matching pastel-colored polyester miniature leisure suits, their black hair combed back neatly, shiny and hard from a liberal application of my mother's Aquanet hairspray. Around us, the highway stretched toward a horizon crowded with huge scaffolds and water towers and angled cranes, which reminded me of the fossilized dinosaur skeletons I had seen in museums. I was fascinated with dinosaurs, but not for the reasons most six-year-old boys were. To me, they were like my family, which was not yet extinct the way tyrannosaurus and triceratops were, but still on the verge of being lost forever. We were on our way to **Elizabeth, New Jersey**, to visit my *abuelos*. I was trying my hardest not to have to speak Spanish.

Elizabeth, New Jersey: large, primarily Hispanic/Latino city

abuelos: Spanish for *grandparents*

"Don't you talk that way," my father snapped. "We don't use that kind of language in this family!"

I loved being forbidden to speak Spanish. I tried to think of some more choice cusswords, but then thought better of getting my father too angry, noticing the speed with which the trash scattered amidst the tall roadside weeds streaked by. I wanted to speak English, and only English, like all my friends in school did. We lived in a house that my parents had hired some workers to paint a rich shade of gold, with a redwood deck off the back that looked out over a small lake, and neat little black shutters and our own basketball hoop at the end of the sloping driveway. Some of my mother's new friends even drove Cadillacs. Going back to Elizabeth was like going back into prehistory, with its grimy sidewalks, menacing streetwise teenagers, and small, crowded apartments in ugly brick buildings — "tenements," I said quietly to myself, recalling a particularly **mellifluent** word from the *Merriam-Webster's Dictionary* I was reading cover to cover. I had to admit I liked those words the best.

> **mellifluent:** richly or sweetly flowing

"What did you say?" My father asked pointedly into the windshield. I was glad he was still angry, and thus still speaking in English. I was grateful not to have to "practice" my Spanish anymore. English, cold, corrective, and formal, was employed whenever anyone in the family got in trouble. With any luck, we would stay in English mode for the rest of the journey.

My family had survived the savage world of Elizabeth, progressing into the secure white suburbs, with its sunny, tree-lined streets. That first winter, I noticed that even the snow stayed whiter longer in our new home; in the city, it was always spoiled within a few

> ❝ In fact, I believed that only by unlearning Spanish could I finally leave Cuba behind and become truly American. ❞

hours of falling, streaked with stray dogs' urine and soiled by the soot drifting down from the nearby smokestacks. Even the fire hydrants in **Ramsey** looked clean, standing at attention like bright red soldiers of the public good. And the trees! Full and healthy — not stunted, or half-dead and ghost-like in places, or missing whole big chunks of branches where **errant** trucks had plowed past them or black power lines cut through. "Birch," I whispered to myself. "Elm. Linden. Sycamore." I was trying especially hard to memorize the names of trees as I came across them in the dictionary, hoping they would take root in my mind and push out the Spanish. I didn't even know the Spanish names of most of them — *flamboyanes* and *palmeros* like those my **Tía** Yoya painted did not grow at all in America, at least in the places we had lived. Spanish, I had decided, was the language of the receding jungle, the language of the distant past, the language of certain extinction.

> **Ramsey:** suburb in northern New Jersey
>
> **errant:** wandering; inaccurate (here, not staying on the road)
>
> *flamboyanes* and *palmeros*: Spanish for *royal poinciana* and *palm trees* (typically found in tropical or subtropical climates)
>
> **Tía:** Spanish for *aunt*

By learning English, I hoped I would someday forget Spanish completely. In fact, I believed that only by *unlearning* Spanish could I finally leave Cuba behind and become truly American. Though I had never actually been to

primitive: seeming to come from an ancient time; not very evolved

inadvertently: unintentionally; unplanned

flora: plant life; **fauna:** animal life

entrepreneur: someone who starts a business and assumes the risks of doing so

Guantánamo province: region located in the easternmost part of Cuba

cabaña: beach or pool shelter

Cuba, I imagined it was a terribly **primitive** place. On the maps I had seen, it looked like something unpleasant the United States had **inadvertently** stepped on. I populated its uncharted mountainous terrain with naked, dark-skinned Indians and all manner of exotic **flora** and **fauna** — I even imagined it might be a last refuge for the dinosaurs.

Among the few stories my father told us about Cuba, one of my favorites was about the time he and my *abuelo* discovered gigantic bones at the far end of their property, where some men had come to dig sand, which my *abuelo*, ever the **entrepreneur**, had started to sell. I wasn't sure why anyone would want to buy sand, but that really wasn't the point of the story. I had surprised my father when I used vocabulary words like "entrepreneur" — sometimes I acquired English words he hadn't yet learned himself. Like my *abuelo*, he was first and foremost a good businessman. Whether those great bones belonged to a dinosaur or not, he couldn't say. In his new life, which involved manufacturing aluminum cans and plastic tubes for soda and toothpaste, there wasn't much time for wondering about dinosaurs — or even for telling us more stories about Cuba.

We were lucky to lose the family ranch in **Guantánamo province**, I told myself, likewise the small *cabaña* that stood on a nearby cliff overlooking an endless beach, because here in America six-year-old boys were not preyed on by stray velociraptors. It wasn't a good idea to try to get my father to talk about Cuba anyway, because he would usually lapse into Spanish; my mother, who was Italian-American, her skin white enough that in summertime she would freckle instead of tan, would then frown a little if we were all at the dinner table. She had met my father taking a Spanish literature course in college. She was beautiful and very popular, so when my father first called her to ask her out on a date, she didn't really remember who he was. Lots of young men called her asking for dates. I imagined him talking to her on the telephone with his thick accent, trying to persuade her to go to a movie. It's true my father was very handsome, but on the telephone, since she couldn't see his face, all she had was this heavy accent to go by. She almost said no. Therefore, because of Spanish, I might not ever have come into existence.

In my evolutionary view of the world, English had to overcome Spanish in my consciousness. Even though I didn't like girls, I was sure I would need English to survive in other ways. I thought of my *abuelo*, who was forced to work in a factory that made cheap preformed yellow plastic tables because he couldn't speak English. My *abuela* didn't have a job at all — not like my mother, who was a substitute teacher at my new school in Ramsey, New Jersey — so she stayed in their apartment all day long, crying a lot over all that they had been forced to leave behind in Cuba. That's why they were poor and had to stay in Elizabeth.

It was my mother who cared most about our intellectual and social advancement in the world. When she packed us into the car, instead of heading south on these same highways, it was northeast to New York City and its magical sites and endless museums. Besides being a teacher, she was an artist. Dominating our living room was her dramatic painting of a bullfight, with its blood-red background and glittering golds and silvers in the matador's costume. She took us to the Metropolitan Museum of Art, where I copied her **pensive** staring at the large canvases depicting places all over the world except, it seemed, Cuba. Even the dry, dusty expanses of Spain appeared; the Spaniards themselves, however, as painted by **El Greco** and **Goya**, and even **Velázquez**, seemed malformed, brutish, and backward.

Even better than the art museums was the Museum of Natural History. I savored one particular memory of my first visit there. I'd run shouting into the cavernous room where the massive dinosaur fossils were exhibited, calling out the name of each specimen and describing its habitat, range, and feeding preferences (***Carnivorous! Herbivorous! Omnivorous!***). The polished floors and the towering columns only emphasized the distance we had traveled, and from cold-blooded reptiles with brains the size of a pea to human beings with the capacity for self-awareness, from the overgrown jungles of Cuba to the **epitome** of culture and learning that was New York. I remembered the proud look on my mother's face as one of the museum's staff — surely an expert on dinosaurs himself — commended me for my clear pronunciation of so many difficult names and my mastery of scientific terminology. We all celebrated afterwards with ice cream sundaes, a delicacy far more decadent than the shaved ice in a paper cone doused in fruit syrup that was my father's treat years ago on visits to Havana with his family.

Soon I recognized the huge green sign for Elizabeth (and not the George Washington Bridge) as it flashed above us, and then heard the tinny clinking of the LTD's blinker as my father signaled to exit the highway. I tried to resist the surprising slight anticipation I began to feel as we neared the Cuban neighborhood. My father called back to us to lock the car doors as more and more buildings, old decrepit warehouses and boarded-up strip malls, began to enclose us. We were almost there.

My *abuela* had probably prepared the usual elaborate feast of *pernil*, *congrí*, and *yuca con mojo*. It always amazed me how she could produce such a sumptuous meal from the tiny kitchen at the back of their apartment. They would be playing old Cuban LPs, and in the middle of dinner, my *abuelo* would stand and then sweep her up into his arms, and they would dance for a few moments alongside the table that stretched into the living room, as they didn't have a big dining room with a proper dining room table like ours.

There would be Spanish newspapers lying about, drooping over the edges of those small plastic yellow tables brought home from the factory. My *abuelo* was always reading, though I still disbelieved my father's boast that he had a fancy library filled with books in their old ranch house in Cuba. Then, my

pensive: thoughtful; potentially sad

El Greco, Goya, and **Velázquez:** master Spanish painters

carnivorous: eating meat; ***herbivorous:*** eating plants; ***omnivorous:*** eating meat and plants

epitome: ideal example

pernil, congrí, and ***yuca con mojo:*** Spanish for *roasted pork, black (or red) beans,* and *yucca with garlic sauce*

abuela would cry a little, smiling through her tears at all of us kids as she settled back down in her chair.

Later, my *abuelo* would want to walk down the block to the Cuban bakery with us. The street they lived on was still relatively safe, and we would pass beneath windows with blinking colored Christmas lights framing them from the inside, even when it wasn't wintertime. Behind the tall glass of the bakery's display cases, countless varieties of **pastelitos** were arranged, gleaming like the fancy porcelain figurines my mother collected, each variety a different geometric shape: *carne*, *jamon y queso*, *chorizo*, *pollo*, and my Tía Marta's favorite, guava. Though we couldn't eat another bite, my brothers and I would still **clamor** to pick out our favorites, which were then neatly boxed and tied up with a red-and-white string for us to take home. While we would be making our choices, jostling each other for the best position in front of the glass, my grandfather would argue in Spanish about politics with the owner of the bakery, drinking coffee out of a tiny Dixie cup and smoking a cigarette. On the way back I clutched his hand, which felt as hard and strange-shaped as one of my toy dinosaurs.

Of course, the hardest part of these visits was when my *abuelos* would speak to me in Spanish, and I would have to pretend I didn't understand them. If truly mastering English meant truly unlearning Spanish, then I could make no exceptions. I knew this meant I would get to hear even fewer stories about Cuba, but even then I understood we were never going back there. My *abuela* would try for a while, telling me how much she loved me, asking me about what I was learning in school, but I would go on helping her wash the dishes with a perplexed look on my face. Sometimes I would just ignore her, drawing and coloring dinosaurs fierce reds and yellows and greens in a small corner of the kitchen table she'd clear off for me. Or I would interrupt her to inquire, standing on my tiptoes and looking out the window over the sink, "Isn't that a maple tree, Grandma?" knowing perfectly well she couldn't understand me.

I liked being in the kitchen with her, enveloped in the strong fragrances of garlic and cumin and olive oil, and the singsong lilt of her voice, but I reminded myself that I was helping her really because it was the least I could do, especially if I wasn't going to speak Spanish with her. Plus she had already suffered so much. Spanish was the language of her suffering, it was the language of betrayal. Spanish was the history that didn't really exist, vanished forever like "the **missing link**," or like other fossils of whole species of dinosaurs that the world would never know. It was best to unlearn this **primal** tongue, the deliberate loss of which became the **genesis** of how I learned English.

Now, almost forty years later, when I try to remember an intentionally forgotten Spanish word, what I first recall is the heartbroken expression on my *abuela*'s kind face.

---

pastelitos: Cuban pastries

carne, jamon y queso, chorizo, pollo: Spanish for *beef, ham and cheese, sausage, chicken*

clamor: ask for loudly; demand

missing link: term for the undiscovered fossil that would help explain evolution

primal: relating to an early evolutionary stage

genesis: origin

After You Read

Mapping the Reading

1. In this personal narrative, Campo describes a trip to his grandparents' home in Elizabeth, New Jersey. What does he most dislike about visiting his *abuelos*? What does he most like?

2. As his family is driving to Elizabeth, what does the young Campo do so that his father will speak to him in English? Why does he want his father to speak in English?

3. What jobs do Campo's family members have? How do these jobs help shape the young Campo's perception of English and Spanish?

4. Review the passages about dinosaurs you identified in "As You Read" or note these now. If, as Campo says, his was not the typical young child's interest in dinosaurs, what exactly was his interest in them? What connections or parallels does the six-year-old Campo see between dinosaurs and his family?

5. What does the six-year-old Campo believe he will gain by *"unlearning* Spanish"?

Discussing and Thinking Critically about the Reading

1. Campo draws contrasts throughout his essay, including the following:

    > Elizabeth (city) versus Ramsey (suburb)
    > His family's life in Cuba versus his family's life in America
    > Cuba versus New York City

    Choose one of these contrasts, or another you may notice, and list the details Campo provides about them. Then consider the effect of these contrasts. For example, what points do they allow Campo to make? How do they help Campo illustrate the perspective of his six-year-old self?

2. Why do you think Campo, the adult writer, uses several Spanish words in his personal narrative, even while writing of a time in his life when he was not only pretending he didn't understand Spanish but also consciously trying to "unlearn" the language?

3. At the end of the essay, Campo writes, "Now, almost forty years later, when I try to remember an intentionally forgotten Spanish word, what I first recall is the heartbroken expression on my *abuela*'s kind face." Interpret that sentence closely, brainstorming to identify all the meanings and feelings that the author is expressing.

4. Campo writes, "My family had survived the savage world of Elizabeth, progressing into the secure white suburbs, with its sunny, tree-lined streets." What is the effect of such a description? How does it help convey the young Campo's attitude?

Navigating the Intersections

1. Talk to family members or friends who speak more than one language (or think about yourself, if relevant). How might their (or your) experiences and attitudes toward English compare to Rafael Campo's?

2. In "The Way of the Dinosaurs," Campo is retelling his experiences as a child. Research the availability of bilingual education programs in the late 1960s. (Hint: "Bilingual education," "English as a Second Language," and "English Language Learner" may be useful terms to search.) How does this information help shed light on Campo's childhood perceptions of Spanish?

Before You Read: Use the following questions to think and write briefly about the way you speak: What kind of accent do you have? How does your speech compare to that of others in your community or family and to what you consider a "normal American accent"?

ARTHUR CHU

Voice-over artist, comedian, and blogger Arthur Chu is perhaps best known as a *Jeopardy!* contestant, winning $398,200 on the popular game show in 2014. Building on his game-show fame, Chu writes about issues such as racism and sexism in "nerd culture," and has had his work published in the *Daily Beast* and *Salon*. A graduate of Swarthmore College, Chu now lives with his wife in Cleveland, Ohio. He has acted in *Cleanland* and the short film *In-Towners*. This article was published by NPR as part of its *Code Switch* series in 2014.

As You Read: Mark passages where Chu discusses how language is connected to power.

Breaking Out the Broken English

cringes: feels and shows embarrassment or disgust

A little part of me **cringes** every time I do it, but at this point it's second nature.

It's hard to describe in words, but it involves a lot of leveling, a lot of smoothing. The tongue stays closer to the center of the mouth rather than doing the pronounced, defined highs and lows that shape the *l* and *r* sounds. The vocal cords vibrate in smooth, singing tones rather than doing the little hop up and down that makes for a normal American English syllable.

And after a few practice sentences, it slips effortlessly from my mouth. "Herro, and wercome to Beijing. Zhis is yoah guide to an ancient culchah . . ."

Lo and behold, I'm speaking English in a "Chinese accent."

I shouldn't complain—no actor can really get upset about a source of steady work. As I've pointed out, when Asian characters don't have accents it just means that white voice artists end up playing them. . . .

blatantly: obviously

Nor is there ever anything **blatantly** offensive in the content that makes me not want to take the role. I get uncomfortable with a narration having a "Chinese accent" just to give "color," so to speak, to a video set in China, but it's no different in spirit than having a Southern-accented narrator for a video set in Texas.

Most of my discomfort, I have to admit, is personal.

Because here's the thing. Nearly every Chinese immigrant I've met does, in fact, "talk like that," because it's almost impossible not to have a thick accent when your first language is as fundamentally **phonetically** different from English as **Mandarin** or **Cantonese** is.

> ❝ *And how terrifying it is to have that awesome feeling of privilege and safety in speaking the 'right' language be attacked.* ❞

But it's equally true that every single Chinese-American kid born here I've met emphatically does *not* "talk like that." In fact, there isn't a Chinese-American accent the way there's a distinct **cadence** to how black Americans or Latino Americans talk. Most Chinese-Americans have a pitch-perfect "invisible" accent for wherever they live.

If anything, the thing that made me weird as a kid was that my English was *too* perfect. My grammar was too **meticulously** correct, my words too carefully **enunciated**—I was the kid who sounded like "Professor Robot." In order to avoid being a social **pariah** in high school I had to learn to use a carefully **calibrated** proportion of slurred syllables and street slang in my speech—just enough to sound "normal," not enough to sound like I was "trying too hard." I would actually sit at home, talking to myself, practicing sounding like a normal teenager.

I don't think I'm alone in this, though of my Chinese-American colleagues I'm one of the few who's taken the quest to develop a perfectly "neutral" voice so far that I now market said voice to produce corporate videos and voice-mail greetings.

The "Asian accent" tells the story of Chinese-American **assimilation** in a nutshell. Our parents have the accent that white Americans perceive as the *most* foreign out of all the possible alternatives, so our choice is to have no accent at all. The accent of our parents is the accent of the grimy streets of Chinatown with its **mahjong** parlors and fried food stalls and counterfeit jewelry, so we work to wipe away all traces of that world from our speech so we can settle comfortably into our roles as respectable middle-class doctors, lawyers, engineers, hundreds of miles from Chinatown.

No wonder we react so **viscerally** to the "ching-chong, ching-chong" schoolyard taunt. To attack our language, our ability to sound "normal," is to attack our ability to *be* normal. It's to attack everything we've worked for.

And make no mistake about it—to sound like a "normal" American is to **wield** privilege.

I remember translating for my parents at customer service desks or in restaurants, where despite my youth my ability to carefully round my *r*'s and use perfectly grammatical sentences made my complaints more credible. Taking my mother's scattered notes in "broken English" and crafting perfectly

phonetically: related to speech sounds

Mandarin and **Cantonese:** Mandarin is the official language of China; Cantonese is another major Chinese language

cadence: rhythmic pattern in speech

meticulously: taking care to be accurate

enunciated: clearly pronounced

pariah: someone hated and rejected

calibrated: carefully measured

assimilation: integration into dominant, mainstream culture

mahjong: Chinese game

viscerally: emotionally rather than logically

wield: have and be able to use

> **“** *The 'Asian accent' tells the story of Chinese-American assimilation in a nutshell. Our parents have the accent that white Americans perceive as the most foreign out of all the possible alternatives, so our choice is to have no accent at all.* **”**

bemusedly: in an amusedly confused manner

dialect: regional variation of a language, usually with some of its own rules

dour: serious and unfriendly

pass: be accepted as something one is not

respectable job applications and cover letters out of them, all the while in the back of my mind wondering, "What are they going to think when she actually shows up for work and I can't translate for her?"

Most vividly I remember being on vacation at the Waterton-Glacier International Peace Park that straddles the U.S.-Canadian border, **bemusedly** translating between my dad and a park ranger, both of whom were speaking English. One of them would say something. The other would blink in confusion. Only when I repeated it did they understand. And suddenly I realized my dad's Chinese accent and the ranger's Canadian accent were too far apart from each other to be mutually intelligible.

I had the magic power, the royal privilege, of speaking the "correct" kind of English, the kind broadcast on the radio and TV. When I said something, people understood. My dad, who'd spoken English most of his life, and the ranger, who'd spoken English all his life, both depended on me to understand each other.

How strange, to be so important, to wield so much power, just because your version of the English language is the "right" one. How strange to be in a profession where people will pay you money to read words they wrote because their own, real, personal accent and **dialect** is "wrong."

And how terrifying it is to have that awesome feeling of privilege and safety in speaking the "right" language be attacked. When I was a contestant on *Jeopardy!* one of my quirks was that, having studied using books and flashcards, a lot of my pronunciations of words were unusual.

An enterprising YouTuber put together a supercut of all my pronunciation flubs — like saying "obstretrics" for "obstetrics" in the heat of the moment — and capped it with a clip from *Pulp Fiction*, Samuel L. Jackson screaming, "ENGLISH, MOTHER******! DO YOU SPEAK IT?!"

Of all the people making fun of me online for my weight, my appearance, my **dour** expression, or my general unlikeability, the attacks on my ability to speak English cut deepest. More than all the other YouTube videos made of me, that one made me want to jump in the comments yelling, "Yeah, well, my wife until last year said 'rheTORic' instead of 'RHEtoric,' but you wouldn't question her fluency in the English language over that because she's white, and she was born here, and that's racist!"

Luckily I restrained myself. But this weird fear of somehow losing my American-ness still haunts me.

So those embarrassing "Chinese accent" voice-over jobs? I don't think it's just the money; I think I go after them as a weird form of self-therapy, facing what you fear in order to master it.

I spent my entire childhood learning how to **pass** for "normal" in the way I spoke, to grasp for the privilege that came with assimilation. But as any

linguist will tell you, the idea of "perfect" speech is an illusion. No one actually has a "perfect" accent; the definition of "proper" English is **arbitrary** and **fluctuates** wildly over time.

Indeed, the single biggest barrier I have to getting voice-over jobs now is that my voice is *too* perfect, that the most common note you see from producers on spec sheets is "Not too announcer-y, must sound like a real person." The "proper" English that was on TV when I was a kid isn't "proper" anymore; the definition of proper English keeps updating itself, keeps readjusting to match what people think of as "real."

Well, the English I grew up with as "real" isn't the English I painstakingly forced on myself from listening to TV and my peers at school. It's the English of my parents, complete with underpronounced *l*'s and *r*'s, dropped "and"s and "the"s, singsongy and "broken" and embarrassing.

That accent is real, but my use of it can never be, not after so many years of **renouncing** it and avoiding it and **exterminating** any trace of it from my day-to-day speech. After a lifetime of rehearsals and training, the "announcer voice" *is* my voice, and the only reliable way to sound "less announcer-y" is to put on an accent that isn't mine, be it Brooklyn, Biloxi, or Beijing.

What a **paradox**. When I sound real, I'm fake, and when I sound fake, I'm real. I can only wonder how many of my fellow hyphenated Americans can say the same.

linguist: person who studies how languages work

arbitrary: not planned or based on reason

fluctuates: changes

renouncing: formally giving something up

exterminating: eliminating; getting rid of

paradox: a statement or idea that seems contradictory or impossible but perhaps is true

After You Read

Mapping the Reading

1. What is Chu's accent (that is, the one he uses normally and not when acting, for example)? Find and quote the passage in which you see him most clearly describing this accent.

2. Why is Chu uncomfortable performing roles that involve speaking in a "Chinese accent"?

3. As a child, how did Chu use his English skills to help his parents?

4. What was the problem with the way Chu spoke in high school, and what did he do to correct it?

5. In what ways does Chu's neutral accent hurt him? In what ways does it help him?

Discussing and Thinking Critically about the Reading

1. At the end of his article, Chu asserts, "When I sound real, I'm fake, and when I sound fake, I'm real." Explain what Chu means by this.

2. Chu writes: "The 'Asian accent' tells the story of Chinese-American assimilation in a nutshell." What does Chu mean by this? Explain why you agree or disagree with this claim.

3. Returning to your "As You Read" notations, summarize Chu's points about language and power, and then reflect on them. In what ways are his claims valid or not valid?

4. What privilege does Chu identify as being connected to speaking the "'correct' kind of English"?

5. Share your language "story." Describe both the way you speak English and how you think people perceive your use of English. What assumptions might people make about you because of the way you speak? In what ways are these assumptions right or wrong?

Navigating the Intersections

1. Compare and contrast Rafael Campo's and Arthur Chu's views on the connection between English and success in the United States.

2. Chu discusses "announcer voice," suggesting that there is just one accent that announcers are expected to use. Is this accurate? Compare the voice of a national network newscaster with that of a nearby city's local newscaster. How are their accents similar or different? What impressions do each of these accents give to listeners?

Before You Read: Brainstorm a response to the following: How important is language to cultural heritage? For example, how essential is speaking Korean to being Korean American?

TRACY LÓPEZ

A self-described "gringa" (white girl), Tracy López is a bilingual freelance writer and novelist with a "love of all things Latin American." Her work has appeared online and in print in various publications, including *Ser Padres* magazine, *Café* magazine, and *Plaza Familia*. She lives near Washington, D.C., with her Salvadoran husband and their sons. The following article (2012) was published in *New Latina*, an online publication whose mission is to "offer content that inspires, informs, and guides Latinas to live more centered and confident lives."

As You Read: Make a list of the different people López refers to in her article, and include a brief note about their experiences as Latinas who don't speak Spanish well.

Non-Spanish-Fluent Latinas: "Don't Judge Us"

fluent: able to speak a language easily and very well

By 2050, the United States will be home to the most Spanish speakers in the world, according to the general secretary of the Association of Spanish Language Academies. Even so, there are many Latinos born and raised in the U.S. who are either not **fluent**, or don't speak Spanish at all.

Historical Reasons for Lack of Fluency in Spanish

A common reason for the lack of fluency is simply due to parents not speaking Spanish to their children. There are various reasons why parents consciously choose not to pass their language on to the next generation. Those raised during the 1930s and '40s recall being forbidden from speaking Spanish at school, and being punished if they did. Due to racism during that time, even speaking Spanish in public was cause for being told to leave the area in some cases. Many who experienced this kind of discrimination didn't teach Spanish to their children. In turn, these second-generation Latino Americans were unable to teach it to their own children, even if they wanted to.

Some Latinos born and raised in the United States just never picked it up fluently, despite their parents' best efforts to teach them, and so being insecure in their own skills, don't speak it to their own children.

Another common reason given? Concerns about English fluency. To many immigrants coming to the United States, English is the priority. English, in their eyes, is what will open doors of opportunity to their children, which were not open to them. It is the nature of most immigrants to look towards the future, but sometimes a piece of the past is lost in the process.

According to one study, "The grandchildren of immigrants are likely to speak only English. By the third generation, only 17% of Hispanics speak Spanish fluently, and by the fourth generation, it drops to 5%."[1]

Feelings of Insecurity and Judgment from Others

For U.S. Latinos, not speaking Spanish is often a source of insecurity or even shame. Lacking Spanish fluency brings with it judgment from other Latinos in the community as well as a loss of opportunity.

"I wish I was fluent [but] I am only **proficient**," said Andria Morales (Puerto Rican descent). "Not speaking fluently has made me ineligible for opportunities that call for someone who is bilingual. It has made it difficult to communicate with fluent speakers. . . . I never really fit in well with the Latina crowd because of my language issue. I was once invited for a holiday party to a Rican family's house. . . . [A woman there] made me feel like I wasn't really Latina by insisting on unwrapping a ***pastele*** for me because she didn't think I would know how, even though I told her I grew up eating them. I remarked at how I was so grateful for the food which I don't get to eat all the time and she asked me why I didn't know how to cook. I told her my grandmother died when I was little and my mom was always working and she said 'or you didn't have any interest.'"

proficient: skilled; having knowledge

> ❝ *[A woman there] made me feel like I wasn't really Latina by insisting on unwrapping a* pastele *for me because she didn't think I would know how, even though I told her I grew up eating them.* ❞

pastele: traditional Puerto Rican dish, similar to a tamale

[1] Hispanic7.com

"I have had other Latinos refer to me as being 'fake' and . . . deliberately speak in Spanish to leave me out of conversations," says Gabrielle (Puerto Rican descent).

Laura Esquer, a graphic designer from Los Angeles and U.S.-born Latina of Mexican descent, says that to this day, even though her mother speaks to her in Spanish, she answers in English. "I am very proud of my heritage and I make that known. Even though I cannot speak Spanish fluently, I am able to read and understand it fluently. . . . I have sometimes been teased as being 'white washed' and 'white Mexican.' It didn't offend me. Other people's opinions have little effect on me. I know who I am."

Even Celebrities Are Not Immune to Judgment

Many Latina celebrities in the United States struggle with not being fluent in Spanish and even the famous are not immune to judgment from the Latino community.

Tejano: Tex-Mex popular music

Mexican-American **Tejano** singer Selena Quintanilla started out singing in both Spanish and English, while not fully understanding the words of the Spanish songs. As her popularity grew beyond Texas and into Latin America, she decided she needed to be able to speak Spanish. It was only after several years that she became fluent enough to handle the press by herself.

Boricua: person born in Puerto Rico or of Puerto Rican descent

Boricua Jennifer Lopez, who played the part of "Selena" in the movie about her life, has also faced criticism for her lack of Spanish skills. In an interview with Henri Béhar, she's quoted as saying, "Another controversy came up in the Latin press about the fact that I didn't speak very good Spanish — which Selena didn't either! So I felt some of that pressure at the beginning."

Another Selena, Disney sweetheart Selena Gomez, who is of Mexican descent, has never claimed to be fluent and has always been very honest about her Spanish-speaking skills. In an interview with Lee Hernandez of *Latina* magazine, Gomez said, "I practice it, but I can understand it better than I can speak it. . . . In a lot of my interviews that I did recently, they would speak to me in Spanish and I would answer back in English. They were like 'You pick it up so easily,' but I don't want to say it in Spanish because I'd be embarrassed if I mess something up."

Rosetta Stone: popular language-learning software

Selena Gomez also expressed the desire to become fluent, saying, "I really want to get **Rosetta Stone**, because I really need to learn my language."

Speaking Spanish Is Not a Requirement to Be "Latina"

Some Latinas are a little more defiant when their lack of fluency is brought up. Actress Jessica Alba's father is second-generation Mexican-American but she was never taught to speak Spanish. When *Latina* magazine's Monica Herrera asked Alba how she felt about critics who judged her for not speaking the language, Alba responded, "No one gives Cameron Diaz a hard time for not speaking Spanish. Her dad's Cuban, and I was telling her I feel so bad because everyone is so nasty to me for not speaking Spanish." Diaz reportedly told Alba, "I don't speak Spanish! I barely speak English!"

Alba also shared a conversation with *Latina* magazine that she had with actress Rosario Dawson, an actress of Puerto Rican and Cuban descent. Dawson told Alba that she doesn't speak Spanish either.

In the end, the voices of those I spoke to and the quotes from famous Latinas I picked up in interviews seemed to be saying the same thing: *I am proud of my Latino heritage and I have a desire to learn Spanish, but in the meantime, don't judge me.*

[As Andria Morales, who is of Puerto Rican descent, says,] "I think being Latina is about having pride in your heritage. Although I am not a fluent Spanish speaker and I can't make every dish without a recipe, I am 100 percent Boricua and I am proud of that. I know my family history and I have learned the important traditions. . . . I just think people need to stop judging one another, especially within our own community. I have grown up not feeling accepted by the Latina community for not speaking Spanish, but also for being into hard rock and heavy metal, for not dressing ultra feminine, for not following certain trends . . . basically not 'looking' or 'sounding' the part. . . . We are not all the same — Latinos vary greatly depending on their class, level of **assimilation**, and country or countries of origin. I think progress for us lies in our ability to express how varied we are and accept one another for our differences instead of holding each other to certain standards which basically reinforce the concept that we should all look and sound the same way."[2]

> **assimilation:** integration into dominant, mainstream culture

After You Read

Mapping the Reading

1. What problem does López identify in this article?

2. What are some reasons why Latinos in the United States may not be fluent in Spanish?

3. According to López and her sources, what are some of the consequences of U.S. Latinas not being fluent in Spanish?

4. What common feeling is shared by many of the non-Spanish-fluent Latinas López cites?

5. How is López's report organized? How does she indicate that organization to her readers?

[2] Hispanic-Culture-Online.com, Latino.FoxNews.com, FilmScouts.com, Latina.com, Hispanic7.com, and ImDiversity.com; special thanks to Andria, Laura, and Gabrielle.

Discussing and Thinking Critically about the Reading

1. Rather than writing an opinion-driven piece, López structures her article like a report. Return to your "As You Read" notes, or make a quick list now of the examples she uses and their content. How might her selection of examples give a sense of her own stance on this issue?

2. How does fluency (or lack of fluency) in Spanish affect Latinas' (and Latinos') sense of identity?

3. This report was published on a website aimed at Latina women that has a goal of "offer[ing] content that inspires, informs and guides Latinas to live more centered and confident lives." In what ways does López tailor her article to fit that audience? If she were writing for a broader audience (e.g., *Time* magazine or CNN.com), what might she have changed?

4. Take the opposite view: Why might a fluent Spanish speaker be angry or annoyed at Latinas who have assimilated and do not speak Spanish?

5. How essential is language fluency to someone's cultural identity? For example, how important is it for German Americans to speak German to be considered fully German American? for Korean Americans? for any other group? (Feel free to return to and develop your "Before You Read" response.)

Navigating the Intersections

1. Tracy López's sources and the young Rafael Campo seem to have opposing attitudes: While López's sources say they don't know Spanish but would like to learn it, Campo is eager to "unlearn" Spanish in favor of English. Reflect on possible reasons for these different attitudes toward learning Spanish.

2. Research trends and ideas about immigrants to the United States learning English. Is there a pattern of later generations (children and grandchildren of immigrants) failing to learn their cultural languages? If using an online search engine, you might start by choosing a specific language or national group, and typing in that term (e.g., *German* or *Italian*) along with the words *immigrant*, *learn English*, and *generations*.

Linguistic Profiling

Before You Read: Write briefly about how language affects the way you perceive other people. Have you ever guessed someone's ethnic or linguistic background based on how they speak? If so, how did that judgment affect your impression of the person?

PATRICIA RICE

A freelance writer based in St. Louis, Missouri, Patricia Rice often writes about cultural issues, contributing stories to the *St. Louis Beacon* and St. Louis Public Radio, among other media outlets. In this article, Rice profiles the work of Dr. John Baugh, a professor at Washington University in St. Louis, who is an expert in sociolinguistics — the study of the influences of language and society on each other. This article (2006) appeared in the *Record*, a digital publication of Washington University in St. Louis.

As You Read: Mark those passages where Rice indicates that she is summarizing Baugh's ideas, as opposed to offering her own (these might include the use of phrases such as "Baugh says").

Linguistic Profiling
The Sound of Your Voice May Determine
If You Get That Apartment or Not

Many Americans can guess a caller's ethnic background from their first hello on the telephone. However, the inventor of the term "linguistic profiling" has found . . . that when a voice sounds African-American or Mexican-American, racial discrimination may follow.

In studying this phenomenon through hundreds of test phone calls, John Baugh, PhD, the Margaret Bush Wilson Professor and director of African and African American Studies in Arts & Sciences at Washington University in St. Louis, has found that many people made racist, snap judgments about callers with diverse **dialects**.

> **dialects:** regional variations of a language, usually with some of their own rules

Some potential employers, real estate agents, loan officers, and service providers did it repeatedly, says Baugh. Long before they could evaluate callers' abilities, accomplishments, credit rating, work ethic, or good works, they blocked callers based solely on linguistics.

Such racist reactions frequently break federal and state fair housing and equal employment opportunity laws. In the first two years of his linguistic profiling study, Baugh has found that this kind of profiling is a skill that too often is used to discriminate and diminish the caller's chance at the American dream of a house or equal opportunity in the job market. . . .

Racist Telephone Tactics

While Baugh **coined** the term "linguistic profiling," many who suffer from twisted stereotypes about dialect have known for decades about the racist tactic. His mother knew and took protective action. When he was a youngster in Philadelphia, he could tell if she [was] talking to a white person or a black person on the telephone.

> **coined:** created

His study shows that some companies screen calls on answering machines and don't return calls of those whose voices seem to identify them as black or Latino. Some companies instruct their phone clerks to brush aside any chance of a face-to-face appointment to view a sales property or interview for a job based on the sound of a caller's voice. Other employees routinely write their guess about a caller's race on company phone message slips.

Such discrimination occurs across America, says Baugh, who is also a professor of psychology and holds appointments in the departments of Anthropology, Education, and English, all in Arts & Sciences.

If the availability of an advertised job or an apartment is denied at a face-to-face meeting with a person of color, employers and renters know that they can be accused of racism. However, when accused of racist and unfair tactics over the phone, many companies have played dumb about racial linguistic profiling.

> **❝** *In studying this phenomenon through hundreds of test phone calls, John Baugh . . . has found that many people made racist, snap judgments about callers with diverse dialects.* **❞**

Had You from "Hello"

Baugh has found racist responses in hundreds of calls. He tests ads with a series of three calls. First, someone speaking with an African-American dialect responds to an ad. Then, a researcher with a Mexican-style Spanish-English dialect calls. Finally, a third caller uses what most people regard as Standard English.

Many times researchers found that the person using the ethnic dialect got no return calls. If they did reach the company, frequently they were told that what was advertised was no longer available, though it was still available to the Standard English speaker.

In no test calls did researchers offer company employees information about the callers' credit rating, educational background, job history, or other qualifications.

"Those who sound white get the appointment," Baugh says.

Lack of response or refusal to offer face-to-face appointments was higher for Latinos than for African-Americans, Baugh adds.

When challenged in lawsuits, many businesses deny that they can determine race or ethnicity over the phone. However, Baugh's ongoing study shows that over the phone many Americans are able to accurately guess the age, race, sex, ethnicity, region of heritage, and other social **demographics** based on a few sentences, even just a hello.

demographics:
a specific group's characteristics (e.g., age, ethnicity, and income)

Baugh has prepared to be an expert witness in several court cases but so far all have been settled out of court.

Celebrating All Dialects

Recognizing heritage in a voice does not make a person a racist, Baugh says. . . . Such recognition is often made by many intelligent listeners. Millions of Americans speak with the **lilting cadences** of their ancestors.

lilting: pleasantly rising and falling in speech or music; **cadences:** rhythmic patterns in speech

"I celebrate all dialects," Baugh says.

So do musicians, playwrights, storytellers, historians, and actors. He and many other academic linguists have coached actors and actresses in preparing for roles that require the special tang of non-standard English accents.

Many professional speakers, especially those in broadcast, who learned to speak in South Boston, the Louisiana **bayous**, Minnesota's Scandinavian-American crossroads, Los Angeles **barrios**, Native American reservations, or Scotch-Irish Appalachian towns, have stripped their family's cadences from their pronunciation. They scrub down colorful, historic expressions that some-times are **shards** of a second language their family once spoke, says Baugh. Instead, these public speakers aim to speak General American English — what most Americans consider Standard American English.

Baugh's research shows that not all accents get a neutral or negative reaction from the American public. He has found that many Americans consider people with a British upper-class accent to be more cultured or intelligent than those who used General American. Listeners' snap judgments about the culture behind the British accent may reflect Americans' insecurity about their own English, he says.

Speakers with German accents — even if they stumble into grammatical errors — are considered brilliant, his research has shown. The listeners may not even be able to name the accent as German-American. Baugh expects that the brainy stereotype comes from comics and cartoons mimicking Albert Einstein's German-American accent and from a duck — Walt Disney's Germanic scientist Ludwig Von Drake.

Tapping a Vein

While Baugh coined the term "linguistic profiling," there is nothing new about the prejudice, as observing his mother's phone conversations taught him. Even now it still is only a sideline in his scholarship as the nation's foremost expert on varied African-American English, also called Ebonics.

It was not until he was about thirty-eight, with a **doctoral** degree, before he ever considered researching linguistic profiling. After being appointed to the Center for Advanced Studies in Behavior at Stanford University, he went shopping for a house for his family, then living in Los Angeles.

He telephoned agents advertising houses. When he made those calls he used what he calls his "professional" English. Even George Bernard Shaw's fictitious linguist **Henry Higgins** would not conclude that he is African-American using that voice.

All agents seemed eager to show him houses for sale. When he showed up, most welcomed him warmly, but four, surprised by his race, told him the properties were no longer available.

"I could do a comedy routine about reactions and what they didn't say."

No one ever told him, "Oh, we didn't know you were black on the phone," but their eyes popped and the unsaid remarks would be the core of his stand-up comic monologue, he says. Beyond the comedy, he recognized a serious racist problem.

Instead of just wondering what would have happened if he telephoned using an African-American dialect, he did an experiment. He made a series of three

bayous: areas of slow-moving water in the southern United States

barrios: neighborhoods in the United States where many residents speak Spanish

shards: sharp pieces

doctoral: highest degree awarded by a university

Henry Higgins: fictional character in Shaw's 1912 play *Pygmalion*, who gave speech lessons to a working-class woman to make her seem to have a higher status

telephone calls using both styles of English and then a Mexican-American accent. The Standard English voice got better treatment. He set out to do wider research.

"I **tapped a vein**," he says.

tapped a vein: opened up a source of concern

In a survey of his own accents, he had hundreds score his **disembodied** voices and try to identify his background. In those tests, 93 percent identified his "professional English voice" as a white person; 86 percent thought the black dialect [w]as a black person; and 89 percent identified his Latino voice as a Mexican.

disembodied: from a person who cannot be seen

He laughed about getting the least convincing score as a black person. His vocal differences in those tests were only in **intonation**, not in grammar.

intonation: tone

empathy: sharing someone's feelings

Extending Empathy

Americans tempted to use their ear for linguistic profiling in racist ways should remember two things, he says.

- They should realize that by an accident of birth they have the privilege to speak Standard English.

- Standard English speakers, descended from non-English immigrants, should show respect for their own ancestors who were challenged to become fluent in English as their second language. They should extend empathy with patience and tolerance to those whose linguistic styles differ from their own use of the English language.

Descendants of African slaves were especially challenged, Baugh notes. Their slave ancestors often were deprived of their family's language from the time of their capture in Africa.

Slave traders systematically separated captives — in holding pens, in ships, and on these shores at auctions — from others who shared the same language. Once sold, slaves were often isolated from anyone who shared their language.

The varied linguistic traditions of black English — Ebonics — evolved over generations when it was illegal to teach African slaves to read or write and when many had limited opportunities to hear native Standard English speakers.

After You Read

Mapping the Reading

1. What is linguistic profiling?

2. According to Baugh, how does linguistic profiling allow employers and businesses to get around antidiscrimination laws?

3. According to Baugh's studies, how are different accents judged, and what are the consequences of these judgments?

4. Who are some of the people Baugh identifies as having changed their dialect?

5. What were the personal experiences that influenced Baugh's choice to study linguistic profiling?

Discussing and Thinking Critically about the Reading

1. What is your reaction to Baugh's findings? From your own experiences and observations, is this research surprising or expected? Explain.

2. Rather than presenting her own opinion on the topic, Rice writes a report about John Baugh's research. Return to your "As You Read" notes or reread the article now, marking those passages where Rice indicates she is summarizing Baugh's ideas. How successful is Rice at making clear when she is presenting someone else's ideas?

3. Rice wrote this piece for a publication produced by the Office of Public Affairs at Washington University in St. Louis. What audience do you think she is envisioning? Where do you see her making choices that are designed for this expected audience?

4. Toward the end of the article, Rice summarizes Baugh's advice for eliminating or overcoming linguistic profiling: extending empathy. How effective do you think this strategy is? In what situations can you imagine empathy being extended? What other suggestions for combating linguistic profiling would you add?

Navigating the Intersections

1. How might John Baugh's concept of linguistic profiling be applied to some of the individuals or groups discussed in other selections in this chapter, or to individuals or groups that this chapter's authors have not discussed?

2. Patricia Rice's report focuses on consequences related to housing and employment. What are some *other* instances in which we might see linguistic profiling having negative consequences?

Before You Read: Write briefly about what you know about Black English. Where have you used it or heard it spoken? If you can't think of an example, read the dialogue exchange in the first paragraph of the reading that follows.

JOHN RUSSELL RICKFORD and RUSSELL JOHN RICKFORD

John Russell Rickford is the J.E. Wallace Sterling Professor of Linguistics and the Humanities at Stanford University. In studying language variation, he focuses on African American Vernacular English and Creole languages. Russell John Rickford — his son and coauthor — is an assistant professor of history at Cornell University and is considered an expert in the black radical tradition. Previously, Russell Rickford worked for the *Philadelphia Inquirer* and in public relations. Together the Rickfords wrote *Spoken Soul: The Story of Black English*, which won the American Book Award in 2000. This selection is excerpted from the last chapter of that book.

As You Read: Mark those passages where the authors offer reasons for using Black English (Spoken Soul) and Standard English.

Spoken Soul and Standard English

Here is a conversation as ordinary in its context as breathing. It took place recently in the office of a California elementary school, between three black people: a second-grade student, or eight-year-old; Miss P., the school secretary, in her forties; and a parent in his thirties who happened to be in the office at the time.

> **STUDENT:** Miss P., my teacher sen' me to the office.
>
> **MISS P.:** What she sen' you here fuh?
>
> **STUDENT:** She say I got a rash.
>
> **MISS P.:** A rash? Where the rash at?
>
> **STUDENT:** Right here on my chin . . .
>
> **MISS P.:** Come over here an' lemme see. [*The child walks over to her, and she examines his chin.*] So what you want me to do? [*No answer.*] I'ma call yo' dad, boy. [*She phones his father, learns that he can't come for his son right then, and hangs up.*] You know yo' dad got to go to school, boy, he can't come an' get you. . . .
>
> **STUDENT:** Where Miss G. at? [*Miss G. is a staff member the student likes.*]
>
> **MISS P.:** Miss G. in the room nex' to the library. [*The child leaves to look for Miss G.*]
>
> **PARENT:** [*To Miss P.*] That boy sound jus' like me. He remind me of me. He remind me of me. Don' seem like that long ago. Seem like jus' yesterday . . .

These speakers, youth and adults alike, used Spoken Soul [Black English] because it is the language in which comfortable informal conversation takes place daily for them — as is true within vast segments of the African American community. They drew on it . . . because it came naturally; because it was authentic; because it **resonated** for them, touching some **timbre** within and capturing a vital core of experience that had to be expressed *just so*; because it reached the heart and mind and soul of the addressee or audience in a way no other variety quite did; because to have used Standard English might have marked the relationships between the participants as more formal or distant than the speaker wanted. For these individuals, not to have used Spoken Soul might have meant they were not who or what or where they were and wanted to be.

resonated: struck a chord; had special meaning

timbre: quality or overtone of sound (usually relates to music)

The question remains about why Spoken Soul persists despite the negative attitudes toward it, and its speakers, that have been expressed for centuries. The primary answer is its role as a symbol of identity. . . . For many African Americans, the identity function of Spoken Soul is **paramount**, and very old. The repressive slave codes enacted in America between the late seventeenth century and the early eighteenth century (including whipping, maiming, branding, ear-nailing and -severing, and castration for various "offenses")

paramount: very important

may have helped forge an oppositional identity among blacks **vis-à-vis** whites, expressed in part through a distinctive **vernacular**. Continued hardships of the nineteenth and twentieth centuries (including lynchings, the denial of equal access to education and employment, segregation, poverty, police persecution, and criminal injustice) not only would have **facilitated** the development and/or maintenance of distinctive black ways of talking, dressing, dancing, making music, and behaving, but also would have made black Americans reluctant to mimic white ways of talking and behaving. . . .

vis-à-vis: in comparison to

vernacular: a nonstandard dialect

facilitated: enabled; made easier

As hip-hop culture and the language, body movements, dress, and music that embody it spread among young Americans of virtually every ethnicity and are adopted by teenagers in countries as distant as Russia and Japan, the status of black language and culture at the popular level is rising, and young African Americans of every class proudly claim it as originally and most authentically theirs. We shouldn't let this mention of teenagers delude us into thinking, as many do, that Spoken Soul figures in the identities of young people only. Black adults of all ages talk the vernacular, and it functions to express their black identity, too. While it is true that African Americans with less education and earning power use the grammatical features of Spoken Soul more extensively than do those with more education and earning power, the vernacular is often wrongly associated with ignorance. The use, enjoyment, and **endorsement** of the vernacular by blacks who are well educated and hold good jobs reveal that much more is going on. . . .

> ❝ *The question remains about why Spoken Soul persists despite the negative attitudes toward it, and its speakers, that have been expressed for centuries. The primary answer is its role as a symbol of identity.* ❞

endorsement: publicly offered support or approval

The most recent study of attitudes toward black vernacular and Standard English is an ongoing one being conducted by Jacquelyn Rahman, a linguistics graduate student at Stanford University. She asked black undergraduates and graduate students there what they thought of the two varieties of English, and found that even among these upwardly bound black academics and pre-professionals, the value of both varieties was endorsed. . . . On the one hand, Standard English was defended as the variety needed "in a white-dominated world . . . to gain respect and get good jobs," "in formal settings (work, school reports)," and "when I am around the white majority . . . because that is what my audience understands and it's socially more appropriate." On the other hand, Black English was praised for its "spirit, creativity, resilience and soul," for its "character and history," for "being more expressive and vibrant," and because "it keeps me close to my family and friends, as well as serving as a living reminder of my history as a member of a distinctive ethnic group in this country." Virtually all the students said that they were **bidialectal**, some becoming so after initial school experiences in which they were derided by black classmates for talking white. They draw on one variety or the other as audience and situation demand.

bidialectal: speaking two dialects or forms of a language

repertoires: all the things people know and can do

wrested: taken away, usually with force or effort

lineage: ancestry

template: pattern or example to follow

Malcolm X (1925–65): African American speaker, Muslim minister, and advocate for black rights

rhetorical: related to using language to persuade

intonation: tone

mean feat: small achievement

Because we have celebrated Spoken Soul throughout this book, one might be tempted to group us with those who argue that Standard English is unnecessary, and who insist that vernacular speakers need not extend their **repertoires**. On the contrary, we feel that shunning Standard English too easily lets the power structure and our own would-be spokespeople off the hook, allowing the former more wantonly to disregard the raw voice of protest, and the latter to have one less weapon hopelessly mute in affairs of business and the state.

That mainstream English is essential to our self-preservation is indisputable. Without it, how could we have **wrested** judgeships and congressional seats and penthouse offices from those who have long enjoyed such privileges almost unchallenged? We have come this far thanks, in part, to a distinguished **lineage** of race men and women who used elegant Standard English as a **template** for their struggle against the very oppressor responsible for imposing the language on them. **Malcolm X**'s speeches show his command of Standard English, especially a black Standard English that . . . is non-vernacular in grammar but soulful in its **rhetorical** style and pronunciation, including **intonation** and emphasis. . . . But in making the transition from the street to the podium, brother Malcolm also had to develop his expertise in speaking and writing Standard English, and his initial discouragement is described in his *Autobiography*:

> I became increasingly frustrated at not being able to express what I wanted to convey in letters that I wrote, especially those to Mr. Elijah Muhammad. In the street, I had been the most articulate hustler out there — I had commanded attention when I said something. But now, trying to write simple English, I not only wasn't articulate, I wasn't even functional. How would I sound writing in slang, the way I would say it, something such as "Look, daddy, let me pull your coat about a cat, Elijah Muhammad."

Before we even fix our mouths to snub the speech of the marketplace, we must remember Malcolm. . . . For in the academies and courthouses and legislatures and business places where policies are made and implemented, [Standard English] is as graceful a weapon as can be found against injustice, poverty, and discrimination. . . . We must learn to use it, too, for enjoyment and mastery of literature, philosophy, science, math, and the wide variety of subjects that are conducted and taught in Standard English, in the United States, and, increasingly, in the world. We must teach our children to do so as well. This, as you know, is no **mean feat**. It requires time, money and other resources, patience, discipline, and understanding, all of which tend to be in tragically short supply in schools with large black populations. But treating Spoken Soul like a disease is no way to add Standard English to their repertoire. On the contrary, building on Spoken Soul, through contrast and comparison with Standard English, is likely to meet with less resistance from students who are hostile to "acting white." . . .

True, the vernacular has been abused. . . . But we must reclaim it. We must stop importing this shame that is manufactured beyond our communities for something as **cellular** and spiritual as our language. We must refuse to allow Spoken Soul to remain a stepchild in the family of tongues. We must begin to do for language what we have done historically (in some cases only very recently) for our hair, our clothes, our art, our education, and our religion: that is, to determine for ourselves what's good and what's bad, and even what's *baaad*. The crucial thing is that we hold the yardstick, and finally become **sovereign** guardians and **arbitrators** and **purveyors** of our culture. . . . As the African American proverb — cast in Spoken Soul — cautions us, "Every shut eye ain't asleep, every goodbye ain't gone."

cellular: related to cells or basic parts

sovereign: the highest, with unlimited authority or power

arbitrators: those who make decisions or settle disputes

purveyors: providers; suppliers

After You Read

Mapping the Reading

1. What is Rickford and Rickford's view of Black English, or "Spoken Soul"? Where do you see their clearest expression of this view?

2. What is Rickford and Rickford's view of Standard English? Where do you see their clearest expression of this view?

3. The authors begin this chapter by presenting a dialogue featuring three people. How does this example introduce their topic?

4. According to the Rickfords, who uses Black English, and in what contexts?

5. Reread the section where the authors refer to and quote Malcolm X. What point does his example help them prove?

Discussing and Thinking Critically about the Reading

1. Rickford and Rickford have chosen to use the term *Spoken Soul* to refer to what others call Black English or African American Vernacular English. What does that choice suggest about their view of the language?

2. In your own words, what is the thesis of this essay? How successful are Rickford and Rickford in supporting this thesis?

3. In two moments in the essay, Rickford and Rickford call Standard English a "weapon." What do they mean by this? What is the effect of this label?

4. The essay cites a study conducted by the researcher Jacquelyn Rahman. What has she discovered, and why is her discovery important to Rickford and Rickford's point?

5. Toward the end of the essay, Rickford and Rickford offer a challenge to their readers. Reread the last paragraph, and summarize this challenge. Then reflect on it: Do you believe that their challenge can be met? Do you think progress has been made in changing attitudes toward Black English since the publication of this book in 2000?

Navigating the Intersections

1. Compare John Russell Rickford and Russell John Rickford's ideas about the connections among language, identity, and success to those presented by Rafael Campo, Arthur Chu, or Tracy López's sources.

2. Research debates about Black English's status as either a separate language or a dialect. What are the arguments for treating it as a separate language? What are the arguments for treating it as a dialect or vernacular of English? What might these arguments mean for how Black English is valued in society?

Before You Read: Brainstorm a list of the qualities that you think make someone an effective speaker.

ELLEN WELTY

In her twenty-plus-year writing career, Ellen Welty has written for many publications — including *GQ*, *Redbook*, *Good Housekeeping*, and *Mademoiselle* — and, more recently, for the tablet magazine *deliberateLIFE* and for *DailyWorth*. She has written advice columns for three magazines, covering such topics as managing money, parenting, and being assertive, and has also worked as an editor for *Mademoiselle*. This article appeared in *Redbook* in 2007.

As You Read: Make a list of the sources Welty uses in her article.

Are Your Words Holding You Back?

Um, sorry to bother you, but I was wondering if you'd want to read about this thing we women tend to do when we talk. It's this way we have of speaking where we kind of, like, put ourselves down, I think, without realizing it? Do you know what I mean? Oh, listen, this was probably a really stupid idea. It was just a thought, but jeez, I'm rambling. You must be so ready to, I don't know, turn the page, right?

Do yourself a favor and read on. Because if you're like most women, you regularly use some of the self-defeating speech habits illustrated above. That means you've been known, for instance, to tell others you have an idea, but that it's probably really lame — then you apologize for your really lame idea. You also may "kind of" give your needs **short shrift** (as in, "Gee, I was kind of hoping for an apology from you"). Sound familiar?

"Run my picture with this article," my friend Marion said. "Because I do all those things. I could make an 'L' for 'loser' on my forehead with my fingers while you take the picture."

No, Marion, we won't do that. But the fact is, using **self-deprecating** words does lead people to think — and treat you as if — you're less capable than you really are, says psychiatrist Anna Fels, MD, author of *Necessary Dreams:*

short shrift: little or no time or consideration

self-deprecating: presenting yourself or your ideas as unimportant

Ambition in Women's Changing Lives. And then you start to think, *Hey, maybe I'm not really that smart or that good at stuff.* It's a pretty lousy chain reaction.

So let's break that chain, shall we? Read on and learn how to ditch the wimpy-sounding words and phrases that may be holding you back so you can say your piece with confidence and show the world — and, really, your-self — how strong and **self-possessed** you truly are.

self-possessed: showing control of your emotions

"This is probably a stupid idea, but . . ."

File this mega-negative phrase alongside "I don't know if this is worth men-tioning, but . . ." and "I have a feeling this won't work, but . . ." Why do we predict such doom for our ideas before they even leave our lips? "When girls are growing up, they learn that other girls won't like them if they act as if they're better than other people or as if their ideas are better than anyone else's," explains linguist Deborah Tannen, author of *I Only Say This Because I Love You.* "They learn that there's a social value to downplaying their ideas."

Fast-forward to adulthood: You sit down at a table with a group of peo-ple, you want them to like you, and so you unconsciously **soft-pedal** your suggestion for, say, improving the way the neighbor-hood block-association meetings run. Your intro: "I'm no expert, and it's probably obvious to everyone but me, but what if we . . . ?" Trouble is, while you may suc-ceed in getting people to like you because you're so nonthreatening, you've also made it far less likely that they'll really listen to anything you say because you've devalued your comments, explains Fels: "Then a man offers the same idea in a non-self-deprecating way, and suddenly everybody hears it and says, 'Whoa! That's a great idea!'"

soft-pedal: downplay; deemphasize

> *But the fact is, using self-deprecating words does lead people to think — and treat you as if — you're less capable than you really are.*

Instead of trampling on your ideas, give them a simple, neutral intro such as "I have an idea," "Here's my thought," or "What if we . . . ?" You don't have to "sell" your idea if that's not your style — but you don't have to handicap it, either.

"Like"

You can thank the **Beat generation** of half a century ago for launching the popularity of this little word (as in, "Like, wow!"). These days it's used as a substitute for "said" ("I was like, 'Get out of here!'"), to soften what you say ("I make, like, a decent salary"), and as a filler ("I went, like, to the mall, and it was, like, so crowded").

Beat generation: group of American writers and artists who rejected traditional values and formats during the 1950s and 1960s

With its hipster image, "like" tries to pass itself off as cool, but it's a non-word, like "um" and "uh." Plus, "using 'like' makes you sound inarticulate and young — in a bad way," says Diane DiResta, author of *Knockout Presentations.* So ditch it — you'll sound less **tentative** (read: way cooler) without it.

tentative: hesitant

"Sorry!" "Oops, sorry." "Sorry, my bad!"

Women always seem to be on hyperalert for reasons to apologize: We beg someone's pardon when we're not sure we heard them correctly or when we lose our train of thought. We ask forgiveness for our messy house when someone drops by unannounced (as if we should have had it spotless, waiting for them). Heck, if we "inconvenience" another woman by reaching for a shirt on a store rack at the same moment that we think she's reaching for it, we say, "Sorry!"

Enough with politely assuming we're always in the wrong or that we haven't measured up to others' expectations, says Judith Selee McClure, a communications expert and author of *Civilized Assertiveness for Women*. She advises women who attend her assertiveness workshops to replace "I'm sorry, I didn't catch that" with "Could you please repeat that?" She also urges them to abandon "Sorry, the house is really such a mess" for the far less **neurotic** "Please come in!" Adds McClure: "Even 'I apologize' is better than 'Sorry.' 'I apologize' is at least active; 'sorry' is a passive little word."

neurotic: having a tendency to overthink or worry in an unhealthy way

McClure says that it takes most women in her workshops a while to become convinced that they say the word *sorry* much too much, but that sooner or later, they all do. It clicked for one woman the day she dropped a zucchini at the supermarket and heard herself exclaim, "Oh, I'm sorry!"—to the zucchini.

"I think"

"I think I can handle this project." "I think I might be able to help you." "I think I'm a pretty good cook." Linguistics experts call this phrasing "a **hedge**." Knowingly or not, you're likely counting on those "I thinks" to help you hedge your bets and play it safe. After all, you've just implied that you might not be up to the task (of completing the project, helping, or supplying a tasty dinner). The result: Some people will get fed up with you for never committing yourself wholeheartedly. And others may tune you out because "I think" is a needless addition to the sentence (well, of course you think the thought—you're the one saying it).

hedge: qualification or limitation

"It's easy to say, 'I think,' especially if you feel intimidated," says Paulette Dale, author of *"Did You Say Something, Susan?" How Any Woman Can Gain Confidence with Assertive Communication*. But remember, you're not expected to be an expert on everything. And you have the right to ask questions or make comments unapologetically—even if only to say, "I need more information" as opposed to the timid "I think I need more information."

Amy Huber, an executive coach in the Houston area, helped a female exec conquer her "I think" habit. "Her bosses wouldn't send her on client meetings because she didn't seem confident," says Huber. After observing this woman at work, says Huber, "I realized she always said, 'I think so'—even in answer to simple yes-or-no questions such as, 'Are we on schedule?'" With practice, she changed her ways—and started meeting with clients regularly.

"Kind of," "Sort of"

These gems also fall into the hedge category, as in, "I was kind of expecting the advertised discount" or "I was sort of disappointed you forgot my birthday." Sure, these modifiers protect you from confrontation, but the more you **water down** your convictions this way, the more you start to lose your sense of self (not to mention that advertised discount). Avoid them and you're **apt** to discover that (1) the much-feared confrontation isn't so unbearably stressful after all, and (2) it's a relief to stop hiding where you really stand on an issue.

water down: weaken; dilute

apt: likely

Believe it or not, even the experts occasionally catch themselves using these noncommittal words. "Sometimes I hear myself hedging," admits linguistics professor Deborah Tannen. "I might start to say, 'It's sort of . . .' Then I'll stop myself, laugh, and say, 'Not sort of. It is.'"

"Just"

You call up a friend and announce, "Hi, it's just me." If someone at a party asks you what you do for a living, you answer, "Oh, I'm just a stay-at-home mom" (or "just an office manager," or whatever). "I hate when I do that!" screams forty-two-year-old Maria Iriondo, of Key Biscayne, Florida, mother of a five-year-old. "As if being a mother isn't a huge, important job!" Iriondo "justed" herself back in her career days, too. "Someone would ask, 'Oh, are you a doctor like your husband?' and I'd answer, 'No, I'm just a journalist.'"

Here's a solution: Stop using "just" to describe yourself and your life. Say, "Hi, it's me," instead of "it's just me." Tell friends you're "up for the usual" instead of "just the usual." And — you guessed it — when someone asks you what you do with your days, reply with just "I'm a stay-at-home mom" (or whatever).

Added benefit: Because you haven't minimized your role or importance with that **insidious** little adverb, the person talking to you will likely ask you more questions about your life — and treat what you do as if it's, ahem, just as important as what they do. Which, of course, it is.

insidious: sneaky; treacherous

"Hi, it's me? I can do lunch on Friday?" (and any other statement you make sound like a question)

When you let your voice rise at the end of a sentence that's not a question, you're "uptalking." Do it too much and you can start to sound like a ditz. (Need proof? Fill in the blanks and listen to yourself as you say the following out loud: "Hi, my name is _____? I live in _____?")

Some experts theorize that women may be drawn to uptalk because it fits in with the common female desire for others' approval. You call out to your family, "I'm making burgers? We'll eat at six?" That question-type style of speaking "conveys tentativeness and is a way of hesitating or asking others for their permission," says Fels; it's another way of saying, "If that's okay with you."

You may not mind appearing so accommodating to your nearest and dearest, but beware of slipping into uptalk when you're making arrangements with others. Example: Tell a babysitter, "I need you at five?" and she may decide you're a pushover who won't **balk** if she shows up late. When a guy at your yard sale asks how much you want for your lawn chairs and you answer with "Twenty-five dollars?" he'll figure he can bargain you down. And at your next job interview, when your prospective boss asks, "How much do you think you're worth?" do not say, "X dollars?" Instead, state firmly, "X dollars"—as if there's no question you know what you're worth.

balk: suddenly be unaccepting of

Bye-Bye, Wimpy Words

Quit waffling and downplaying your worth. Follow this plan to banish self-defeating talk and put more me-power behind your words.

1. **Pick one word,** phrase, or other negative speech habit to focus on at a time.

2. **Spend several days noticing when, and around whom, you use it.** Maybe you get rattled around salespeople or competitive coworkers. If you know who sets you off, you can prepare yourself beforehand for what you're not going to say—and what you'll say instead.

3. **Share your goal with a friend or two.** You may well discover that she has the same problem; then it becomes something you two can conquer together.

4. **Ask one of those pals to give you a signal** (say, a raised eyebrow) every time you use a self-deprecating phrase to increase your awareness of that habit and eventually short-circuit it.

5. **Leave yourself some reminders of the shift in phrasing you want to make.** Example: Put a Post-it on your day planner that says, "Here's my idea . . ." so you'll say that instead of "I'm sure this is a dumb idea, but . . ."

6. **Record yourself** (1) using the word or phrase in all its awfulness and (2) restating the same thought in the desired way. You'll train your ear and speed up the process of learning the new speech habit.

7. **Remind yourself**—aloud, to reinforce the message to your brain—"I want to stop saying X because I want people I meet to stop dismissing my thoughts."

8. **Be patient.** It takes about a month to change a behavior, so don't let slipups deter you.

After You Read

Mapping the Reading

1. According to Welty, why is it important for people to be aware of the speech habits they adopt when they are presenting their ideas to others?

2. List all of the speech habits that Welty cautions women against using. Why is each "self-deprecating"?

3. What evidence does Welty offer in support of her claim that self-deprecating language negatively influences how women's ideas are received?

4. Advice pieces typically identify a problem, explain why it is worth attention, and offer a solution. How and where do you see Welty taking these steps?

Discussing and Thinking Critically about the Reading

1. Welty focuses on women who use self-deprecating language in speech. Consider whether this idea can be extended by choosing one of these options: (a) take a stand for or against the position that this problem affects only women, or (b) take a stand for or against the position that this problem can also be found in writing.

2. Return to your "As You Read" notes, or quickly make a list now of Welty's sources. Welty cites a number of experts in her article, including a psychiatrist, a linguist, and an executive coach. What is the value of including these sources in her article?

3. Welty wrote this advice article for a women's magazine. How are her style and examples tailored to that audience?

4. What is your reaction to Welty's point that certain words can lead to negative judgments of the speakers and their ideas? How do you react to these so-called wimpy words?

5. Brainstorm a list of other words that might be considered "wimpy," and explain how they could be self-deprecating.

Navigating the Intersections

1. John Baugh's research, as summarized by Patricia Rice in the article "Linguistic Profiling," focuses on racial and ethnic discrimination in linguistic profiling. Make a case for or against extending the concept of linguistic profiling to include biased judgments based on the gender of the speaker.

2. Choose one of the following activities:

    a. Go to a popular gathering place (like a dining hall) and eavesdrop on the conversations you hear. Make notes about what "wimpy words" get used and who uses them. Do you hear them being used by men or women? What is the reaction to these words?

    OR

    b. Regardless of your gender, research yourself: Look at a piece of your writing or listen to yourself speaking. Giving specific examples, analyze how your words might work to undercut your point or make it stronger.

CHAPTER 5

Appearance

Who Should Decide What We Look Like?

Corbis/Tim Tadder

Image Response: Look at this image and write two fifty-word paragraphs describing each man's personality, basing your description on what is suggested by the image alone. Then consider the following: How are the two profiles different? What do the two profiles suggest about the types of assumptions people make based on appearance?

In This Chapter

Troubles with Body Image

"My Soul to Keep, My Weight to Lose" — Alice Randall describes the place of family, work, and weight in her life.

"Why We Diet" — Abigail Saguy argues for body acceptance.

"Body-Image Pressure Increasingly Affects Boys" — Jamie Santa Cruz reports on the new, unrealistic body images that confront boys.

Appearance Choices

"One Man Explains Why He Swears by Wearing Spanx" — Kevin Fanning writes of the benefits of looking good to feel good.

"How Body Modification Ended the War against My Body" — Sharon Haywood defends piercing and body tattooing.

"My Year of Modesty" — Lauren Shields discovers that appearance matters.

Introduction

Appearance: A Personal Issue

With few exceptions, humans are concerned about what they look like to others. Whether we are simply mildly attentive or deeply obsessed and anxious, interest in appearance is fundamental to the human experience. On the one hand, our appearance is a reflection of our genetic inheritance; on the other hand, it is the result of our personal efforts to make a desired impression. Few among us can truthfully claim not to care at all about how we are seen. This is for good reason because appearances matter. Despite the old expression "Don't judge a book by its cover," that's exactly what most of us do, seemingly instinctively, the minute we meet a new person. Sometimes we don't even need to meet a person to make a judgment: Walking down the street or sitting in class, don't you find yourself observing people and making quick guesses about who they are based on what they look like?

Knowing that we are judged by how we look, most of us shape our appearance for the public (or private) eye. Humans differ from other species in that we can control some aspects of how we appear through what we wear, how we speak and behave, and how we decorate and style our skin and hair. This effort to influence how people judge us begins early. At age two, according to psychologists, children express emotions such as embarrassment or pride in their appearance for the first time (Rochat). Self-consciousness grows as children become teenagers. Teenagers shift their appearance, sometimes several times, to fit in socially, to attract others, or to announce that they have changed their identity and have become someone new. If asked, most teenagers deny any of these motives, claiming their appearance changes are *personal choices* reflecting whim, comfort, or simply personal preference, as in "This is just what I like!" Teenagers may be the most obvious in their efforts to manipulate the way people see and judge them, but people of all ages shape their appearance: to fit in by appearing as they believe is expected, or to stand out by presenting an atypical or unusual appearance. More dramatically, some people choose radical external transformation — consider transgender people, for example — to match, or change, how they feel internally.

Not all aspects of how we appear are under our control. Height, for example, can't be changed. Time and the aging process march on for all of us. Surgery is often considered as an answer, but realistically, surgery is limited in its effectiveness and availability. Once seen as an issue primarily for women, the search for ideal beauty today also traps men, as they are also subjected to the intense marketing that was previously reserved for women. Men are the targets of commercials for machines that promise six-pack abs and of billboards that advertise surgical pec implants. Increasingly, boys and men are subject to eating disorders, steroid addiction, muscle-building scams, and other psychological distresses as they, too, attempt to fit into a mass-marketed and unattainable concept of beauty. Thus, for both men and women, the quest for beauty is as difficult to attain as it is common.

However, some aspects of our appearance *seem* to be in our control — for example, body weight. Yet two-thirds of Americans are overweight or obese. We are overweight for many reasons: the genes we inherit, jobs and other responsibilities that don't allow much time for physical activity, and an abundance of appealing and unhealthy food options, to name just a few. Thus, although body weight is theoretically under our control, keeping our caloric intake at a level low enough to be thin is extremely difficult. And yet we keep trying. In 2015, marketing company Marketdata Enterprises valued the U.S. weight loss market at $59.8 billion ("U.S. Weight"). Still, most people who go on a diet either quit or gain back the weight. Does this mean that weight is really, effectively, out of our control?

Appearance: A Social Issue

In that appearance is also a societal issue, policies are debated and developed to protect people from bias and to support and promote public health. Interestingly, while there are specific laws banning discrimination against people with disabilities (the Rehabilitation Act of 1973, the Americans with Disabilities Act of 1990) and on the basis of race, color, religion, sex, and national origin (the Civil Rights Act of 1964), only a few local governments have laws that protect people specifically from discrimination based on appearance. Overwhelmingly, employment lawsuits claiming discrimination because of weight, tattoos, or body piercings are unsuccessful, with courts siding with employers as having the right to make personnel decisions based on employees' appearance. From a legal perspective, the law doesn't currently protect people based on their appearance. Should it?

Along with bias and discrimination are issues of health, including those relating to obesity, eating disorders, and steroid abuse. Obesity is an issue that receives a lot of attention in the public health realm, perhaps because of the staggering statistics. For example, in 2014, the Centers for Disease Control and Prevention reported that 69 percent of U.S. adults were overweight, with just over half that group (35.1 percent) falling into the category of obese ("Overweight"). Overweight adults, and especially children, face a troubling future in terms of basic health, to say nothing of practical limitations and psychological distress. Still, pressure to be thin and fit remains high. Not only are the overweight discriminated against on the job market, but reports of anorexia and bulimia — eating disorders caused by obsession with food and a desperate craving to be thin — are as common as they were in the 1970s and 1980s, when obesity rates were much lower. Thus, as a society, we need to help people manage their weight so that they — and society as a whole — can be healthy, while also protecting people who are overweight and obese from bullying and discrimination.

Appearance can be looked at from two perspectives: how we feel, think, and behave about our *own* appearance, and how we feel, think, and behave in response to *other* people's appearance. In this chapter, we invite you to consider both of these perspectives by looking at what a range of writers have to say about dieting and body image, body modification, and the role that clothing plays in affecting our appearance.

Works Cited

"Overweight and Obesity." *Centers for Disease Control and Prevention*, 2 June 2015, www.cdc.gov/obesity/.

Rochat, Philippe. "Five Levels of Self-Awareness as They Unfold Early in Life." *Consciousness and Cognition*, vol. 12, no. 4, Dec. 2003, pp. 717–31.

"The U.S. Weight Loss Market: 2015 Status Report." *Marketdata Enterprises*, Jan. 2015, www.marketdataenterprises.com/wp-content/uploads/2014/01/Diet-Mkt-2015-Status-Report-TOC.pdf.

Troubles with Body Image

Before You Read: Food and eating serve physical, social, and emotional needs. Think back on the last twenty-four hours, writing down what you ate, when you ate it, and why. Then reflect on your list: What needs (physical, social, emotional, or other) does food serve for you?

ALICE RANDALL

Alice Randall, born in Detroit, Michigan, is a country music songwriter, novelist, and writer-in-residence at Vanderbilt University. Her novels include *The Wind Done Gone* (2001) — a *New York Times* best seller and parody of *Gone with the Wind*, told from the perspective of a slave — and *Ada's Rules: A Sexy, Skinny Novel* (2012), referred to in this essay. She recently coauthored *Soul Food Love: Healthy Recipes Inspired by One Hundred Years of Cooking in a Black Family* (2015) with Caroline Randall Williams, her daughter. This essay is from *Essence* magazine (2012).

As You Read: Randall's essay is a personal narrative; as you read, underline the passages where Randall steps back from relating her narrative to make a point that is applicable to others.

My Soul to Keep, My Weight to Lose

A few years back I found myself in Tuskegee, Alabama, standing before a roomful of undergraduate English students immersed in a lively discussion of *Up from Slavery*. That's when it happened. We were talking about **Booker T. Washington's angst** over not knowing some basic facts about his life, such as the year, let alone the day, of his birth. We quickly progressed to a discussion of the power of Booker T. telling his story. I had engaged in this theme before, and so was surprised when I became aware of a growing sense of discomfort. It's not that the bright young faces were giving me the **stink eye**; my sense of unease was not coming from without, but from within: I didn't know one of the basic facts of my own life — how much I weighed. How far up was I from my own slavery if I didn't get down from my obesity? Part of me thought the question was too trivial. Part of me was too afraid to know.

I'd always thought that weight was a White girl problem, or a less-serious-woman-than-me problem. This was a mind-set I accepted without truly examining where it had **originated**.

When I was about four years old, Will Randall, my Alabama-born grandfather, crouched down in front of me on a Detroit sidewalk. Looking straight into my eyes, he thumped my brown forehead with two of his fingers

Booker T. Washington (1856–1915): famous American educator, writer, and leader born into slavery, and author of the autobiography *Up from Slavery*

angst: anxiety

stink eye: facial expression conveying dislike or disgust

originated: came from

and said, "That's the only thing they can't take away from you — what you got in your head." I was barely in nursery school but he made himself clear. There was a part of me, my mind and my spirit, that couldn't be touched or stolen, and these were the things I should treasure. My body was something less.

As a child I had been skinny, and as a teen I had a little meat on my five-foot, two-inch frame, but I typically tipped the scales at 118 pounds. It wasn't until after I had a baby at twenty-eight and began working eighteen-hour days as a writer and film producer that way too many pounds began to hold on way too tight for me to dislodge. By the time I turned forty in 1999, I weighed 200 pounds. Before I knew it, I was up to 225. And so were a lot of my sisters.

How did that come to be? Stress, overwork, super-size portions; advertising aimed at keeping us eating; parks and streets not safe for exercise; and the expense of high-quality food coupled with lower wages. The list goes on, and most of the items on it are beyond my control.

> ❝ With one in four Black women over fifty-five having diabetes, four in five Black women overweight, and obesity in danger of overtaking smoking as the number one cause of preventable cancer death, not taking care of myself and taking care of others first wasn't a lifestyle; it was a death style. ❞

About three years ago I decided to focus on what was in my immediate control. What was it inside me that was making it hard for me to lose weight? To figure this out took journaling, prayer, doodling pictures of my body, looking at a lot of family photographs, and therapy.

Reason one was I idolized my grandmother, Dear. There were twin beds in my grandmother's bedroom by the time I was born. When a child was lucky she got to sleep in the twin bed opposite Dear's. I loved those nights. We would "hold hands" by holding on to opposite ends of a rope Dear made from the sashes of her large, flowery dresses. Between the beds hung a brown cross I had made in vacation Bible school. One night, while snuggling into my bed on the right wall, I heard Dear whisper from the left wall a pure home truth: "Never do nothing that make the angels cry. When you can, make the angels smile."

I modeled myself after Dear. She paid so much attention to the people she loved and stayed so connected to us that I wanted to be just like her — down to her size-26 dresses large enough so that the belt of her dress could reach across a room and comfort someone she loved, and the way she was adored by a man as strong and handsome as Paw.

Other reasons for my love of largeness did not have their roots in honeyed admiration. Some of it is deeply rooted in defiance. Being large said "loud and proud" that I do not accept majority culture beauty **aesthetics**. I love kinky-curly hair, dark eyes, facial features sculpted by Africa, and great, big curves that cannot be contained or restrained in a narrow, majority-controlled life.

aesthetics: principles or ideas about beauty

But the most tangled part, and this is the part that it took me the writing of an entire novel, *Ada's Rules*, to fully explore, is I was secretly proud of spending so much time taking care of other people that I didn't take time to take care of myself. Having inherited a history of Black women's labor being **appropriated** for other people's use, I didn't want to be the **mule of the world**, but I got drunk and stayed drunk for years on the joyful privilege of being the mule of my family.

The year I turned thirty-one, I started working 360 days a year. My days began at 7:00 a.m., with making my daughter breakfast, usually French toast or eggs in a hat or peanut butter on a spoon if I was rushing, and ended at 2:00 a.m., when I turned the computer off for my five hours of sleep. I did this seven days most weeks. That's how I raised a daughter and sent her to Harvard, wrote four books — and how I got to weigh a **deuce and a quarter**.

We've all been on a plane and heard the flight attendant instruct us that in case of cabin pressure loss to put on our own oxygen masks first then put on our child's. I have never heard that and not thought, Yeah, right. This Black woman is putting on her child's mask first every day of the week. I've always prided myself on that. I thought self-sacrifice was the central part of being grown.

Now I know differently. With one in four Black women over fifty-five having diabetes, four in five Black women overweight, and obesity in danger of overtaking smoking as the number one cause of preventable cancer death, not taking care of myself and taking care of others first wasn't a lifestyle; it was a death style. For me, shifting the shape of my body has been a matter of confronting hard truths about myself, such as realizing that working all the time was killing my unborn grandchildren's grandmother.

I've come to understand, after fits and starts and bouts of willful ignorance, that the journey to being fit and healthy can be a sacred one: A walk can be a prayer; eight hours of sleep every night, which science tells us is essential for weight loss, celebrates the importance of Sabbath; jumping rope can be a form of worship — if we do it as thanks for the sacred gift of our bodies. And for some of us, it means stopping our mass march to a premature grave. It means stop giving angels reasons to cry.

On March 3, 2013, I will be walking across the bridge in **Selma, Alabama**. I will be walking to honor an earlier generation of civil rights leaders who risked their bodies so that the descendants of enslaved Africans might be free. I will be walking to celebrate getting under and staying under two hundred pounds as an act of self-love and community love. Come walk with me.

This is my new defiance. Claiming the nurturing of my body as prayer. **Acclaiming** my 10 percent body weight loss as **tithe**.

---

appropriated: taken without permission

mule of the world: a phrase used by Zora Neale Hurston and others to refer to the idea that African American women, through sexism and racism, take on the burdens that others refuse to carry

deuce and a quarter: a deuce is the number 2 playing card; here, combined with "quarter," Randall is indicating that her weight was 225 pounds

Selma, Alabama: best known for the 1965 Selma Voting Rights Movement and civil rights marches

acclaiming: cheering; praising; celebrating

tithe: payment; from the religious practice of tithing, or giving 10 percent of one's earnings to support one's religious order or as charity

After You Read

Mapping the Reading

1. What personal insight did Randall discover during her classroom discussion of *Up from Slavery*?

2. Randall mentions several reasons for her weight gain. Which reasons does she believe are out of her control? in her control?

3. Randall has decided to change her life and take better care of herself, even if this means taking care of other people a little less. Find a quote that best expresses Randall's decision to change her life.

4. Explain Randall's point about the connection between obesity and her identity as an African American woman.

5. How does Randall connect the civil rights journey and her journey to a healthier lifestyle?

Discussing and Thinking Critically about the Reading

1. What parts of Randall's personal narrative do you find the most effective in helping readers become convinced of her point of view? Why?

2. Return to your "As You Read" notes indicating the passages where Randall steps back from her narrative to make points applicable to others, or look for them now. Summarize these points, and then evaluate them: How widely can they be applied?

3. Randall recalls that when she was a child, her grandfather taught her to value her mind and spirit over her body. What do you consider to be the strengths and weaknesses of this lesson? Why?

4. Respond to Randall's belief that her poor health is, in part, the result of too much self-sacrifice and not enough self-care. Describe someone you know well who has an unhealthy lifestyle because of being too busy caring for others. What does that person do for others? for him- or herself?

Navigating the Intersections

1. Alice Randall writes about the great personal sacrifices that mothers (and grand-mothers) often make, suggesting that there is a physical and personal cost to motherhood. Talk to a mother or grandmother you know well, and get her per-spective on what the health cost of motherhood might be. Compare this response with Randall's.

2. Are there particular health challenges that members of your demographic group—those who share your gender, race, ethnicity, age, or some other characteristic—could face? Do some research and report on your findings.

Before You Read: Think back to the last time you went on a diet, and list all the reasons you chose to do so. What was your primary reason—health? beauty? appearance? social pressure? (If you have never gone on a diet, think about someone close to you who has and answer these questions about that person.)

ABIGAIL SAGUY

As a sociologist and college professor, Abigail Saguy studies gender, culture, and public health. The author of many articles and two books—*What's Wrong with Fat?* (2013) and *What Is Sexual Harassment? From Capitol Hill to the Sorbonne* (2003)—Saguy analyzes antiobesity campaigns, observing that fatness did not become unacceptable until the twentieth century, whereas for many centuries larger bodies had been not only acceptable but also desirable. This article was published in the *Los Angeles Times* in 2013.

As You Read: Using two different-colored highlighters or pens, identify all the fact statements in one color and all the opinion statements or claims in the other.

Why We Diet

pledge: promise

If your resolutions for the New Year are typical, they probably include a **pledge** to lose weight. But if you are like most Americans, any success you have shedding pounds will be short-lived, and you'll end the year weighing more than you do right now.

So why are Americans obsessed with weight loss? Many people say they want to lose weight to improve their health, but this may not actually be their primary motivation. In one of the more interesting polls I've seen, more than three-fourths of the 231 dieters surveyed said that they would take a pill that would guarantee they would achieve or maintain their desired weight even if it would lower their life expectancy. On average, they were willing to give up 5.7 years. Moreover, 91 percent said that they would not take a pill that would lengthen their life by five years if it guaranteed that they would also remain overweight. This was a small sample, but it is consistent with other research. For instance, a book published just last year showed that the desire to fit in or be "normal"—rather than improving health—is the primary motivation for many people who undergo weight-loss surgery.

These findings may seem puzzling, but they are not so surprising when you consider weight-loss attempts for what they really are: efforts to protect against weight-based discrimination. The fact is, fear and loathing of fat are real, and American attitudes about fat may be more dangerous to public health than obesity itself.

Yale researchers have shown that weight discrimination in the United States has increased dramatically in the last decade and is now comparable in **prevalence** to rates of reported racial discrimination, especially among women. Multiple studies have documented weight bias in employment, healthcare, education, and public spaces — unequal treatment based on stereotyping fat people as lazy, unmotivated, sloppy, and lacking in self-discipline and competence. Heavier women are not only less likely to be hired and less likely to earn a higher salary compared with their similarly qualified thinner peers, but they are also less likely to marry or to marry a high-earning spouse. Unlike thinner women, who can more easily climb the social and economic ladder, heavy women face the prospect of downward social mobility.

> ❝ *The fact is, fear and loathing of fat are real, and American attitudes about fat may be more dangerous to public health than obesity itself.* ❞

prevalence: commonness; how common something is

When I was doing research for a book on the social understanding of fat, several heavy women told me they were often **reproached** for eating in public. Some tearfully shared stories of having had people actually throw food at them. Other researchers have documented a practice called "hogging," in which young men sexually prey on fat women and then, during the sex act, have their male friends jump out of hiding and humiliate them. Heavy women are routinely ridiculed in advertisements, television, and film. Even children express negative attitudes about their heavier peers, a tendency that has gotten worse in the past forty years.

reproached: criticized; disapproved of

Of course, there are genuine health risks associated with higher body mass. The clearest case is that of Type 2 diabetes, which becomes more likely as weight goes up. Yet as many medical researchers have pointed out, this association may not be causal. That is, it's not clear whether obesity **per se** causes diabetes, whether diabetes causes obesity, or whether both conditions are caused by a third factor, such as poor nutrition, stress, or genetic factors.

per se: in itself

It has become increasingly clear that the link between weight and health is complicated. In some cases, higher body mass seems to protect against **mortality**. For instance, there is growing evidence documenting an "obesity **paradox**," in which elevated body mass is associated with lower mortality among people with heart disease and among those with Type 2 diabetes. And a recent report in the *Journal of the American Medical Association* concluded, after analyzing almost one hundred studies, that people with body mass indexes in the overweight category were at less risk of dying in a given year. In fact, they found that even those in the moderately obese category — in which the greatest number of Americans classified as obese fall — were at no greater risk of dying than those in the normal weight category.

mortality: death

paradox: a statement or idea that seems contradictory or impossible but perhaps is true

So it's not as simple as many assume, and we have much to learn about what these observations mean. But it is clear that anti-fat bias in and of itself takes a toll on public health in ways many may not suspect. Fear of ridicule leads many heavier women to avoid exercising in public or even—when they are very heavy—to avoid leaving their homes, depriving themselves of social interaction. Because many heavier women experience the doctor's office as a hostile environment, they are less likely to get Pap smears, which leads to higher rates of cervical cancer among women categorized as obese. And the fear of becoming fat can lead women of all sizes to develop eating disorders and body image problems that can diminish their lives and be dangerous to their health.

What Should Be Done about Weight-Based Discrimination?

The answer is to call for increasing tolerance and appreciation of diverse body types. This year, before embarking on yet another diet, ask yourself why you want to lose weight. If it is to improve your health, perhaps you should focus on health-enhancing behaviors that are more directly linked to health: pledge, for example, to get more sleep, eat more fruits and vegetables, get regular physical activity, or spend more time with friends.

But if you are trying to change your body to shield against discrimination and stigma, consider making a different kind of New Year's resolution: to stand up to intolerance and bigotry in all its various forms, whether racism, sexism, or fatphobia.

After You Read

Mapping the Reading

1. According to Saguy, what is the difference between why we *say* we diet and why we *actually* diet?

2. What is Saguy's message to those of us who are overweight? What is her message to those of us who are not overweight but who judge those who are?

3. What are some of the consequences of weight bias that Saguy cites?

4. What evidence does Saguy present for her claim that weight-based discrimination occurs?

5. What evidence does Saguy present for the position that being overweight may not be unhealthy and that being obese is less unhealthy than many people think?

Discussing and Thinking Critically about the Reading

1. How does Saguy answer the question of why we diet? Summarize and then evaluate her ideas. How convinced are you by her arguments? Why?

2. Look at the fact and opinion statements you identified in the "As You Read" exercise, or look for them now. What is the balance between facts (evidence) and opinions? How effective (or ineffective) is the evidence in supporting the opinions?

3. How do you relate and react to Saguy's essay? How do you feel about her giving us permission to give up the "I will lose weight" pledge that so many of us make at the beginning of every year?

4. Saguy refers to a variety of research articles. What evidence does she present that is especially surprising to you? Why is it surprising? What, if any, effect does this surprising evidence have on your thinking about dieting and weight?

5. Imagine that you are arguing against Saguy. What arguments could you make to suggest that she is wrong and that overweight people *should* go on diets?

Navigating the Intersections

1. In what ways do Abigail Saguy and Alice Randall agree on the issue of weight loss? In what ways do the two authors disagree?

2. Saguy refers briefly to many large research studies. Use a search engine to read one of these or to find other, recent studies, and then summarize the research and its findings.

Before You Read: Spend five minutes writing in response to the following questions: What kinds of body image pressures do you observe young men in your community experiencing? How much pressure is there to bulk up or develop six-pack abs, for example? To what lengths will young men go in trying to reach the male beauty standards set by models, athletes, and celebrities?

JAMIE SANTA CRUZ

A freelance writer from Colorado, Jamie Santa Cruz writes on health and biomedical issues for a variety of publications, including *Today's Geriatric Medicine*, *Vibrant Life*, and the *Atlantic*. Santa Cruz is also an editor, a writing teacher, and a writing tutor. Her article was published in the *Atlantic* in 2014.

As You Read: In a report such as this one, an author relies on outside sources. Pay special attention to the quoted passages in this article, and make a list of the sources Santa Cruz uses.

Body-Image Pressure Increasingly Affects Boys

Culturally, we're becoming well attuned to the pressure girls are under to achieve an idealized figure. But researchers say that lately, boys are increasingly feeling the heat. A new study of a national sample of adolescent boys, published in the

> **❝** *'The media has become more of an equal opportunity discriminator,' says Lemberg. 'Men's bodies are not good enough anymore either.'* **❞**

physique: form or shape of the body

January issue of *JAMA Pediatrics*, reveals that nearly 18 percent of boys are highly concerned about their weight and **physique**. They are also at increased risk for a variety of negative outcomes: Boys in the study who were extremely concerned about weight were more likely to be depressed, and more likely to engage in high-risk behaviors such as binge drinking and drug use.

The trend toward weight obsession among boys is cause for worry, says Dr. Alison Field, an associate professor of pediatrics at Boston Children's Hospital and the lead author of the study. "You want people to be concerned enough about their weight to make healthy decisions," she says, "but not so concerned that they're willing to take whatever means it takes — healthy or unhealthy — to achieve their desired physique."

muscularity: being muscular

Of the boys who were highly concerned with their weight, about half were worried only about gaining more muscle, and approximately a third were concerned with both thinness and **muscularity** simultaneously. Meanwhile, less than 15 percent were concerned only with thinness. Those statistics reflect a major difference between boys and girls when it comes to weight concerns: Whereas girls typically want to be thinner, boys are as likely to feel pressure to *gain* weight as to *lose* it.

"There are some males who do want to be thinner and are focused on thinness," Field says, "but many more are focused on wanting bigger or at least more toned and defined muscles. That's a very different physique."

If boys are increasingly concerned about weight, changing representations of the male form in the media over the last decade or two are at least partly to blame. "We used to really discriminate — and we still do — against women" in terms of media portrayals, says Dr. Raymond Lemberg, a Prescott, Arizona–based clinical psychologist and an expert on male eating disorders. "If you look at the Miss America pageant winners or the *Playboy* centerfolds or the runway models over the years, there's been more and more focus on thinness."

abated: lessened; weakened

But while the media pressure on women hasn't **abated**, the playing field has nevertheless leveled in the last fifteen years, as movies and magazines increasingly display bare-chested men with impossibly chiseled physiques and six-pack abs. "The media has become more of an equal opportunity discriminator," says Lemberg. "Men's bodies are not good enough anymore either."

Even toys contribute to the distorted messages youngsters receive about the ideal male form. Take action figures, for example, which Lemberg suggests are the male equivalent of Barbie dolls in terms of the unrealistic body images they set up for young boys. In the last decade or two, action figures have lost a tremendous proportion of fat and added a substantial proportion of muscle. "Only 1 or 2 percent of [males] actually have that body type," says Lemberg. "We're presenting men in a way that is unnatural."

In the face of the ideals they're bombarded with, it's no surprise that adolescent boys, like waves of girls before them, are **falling prey** to a distorted image of themselves and their physical inadequacies: Previous research suggests that up to 25 percent of normal-weight males nevertheless perceive themselves to be underweight.

And given their perception of themselves as too small, it's also no surprise that boys are searching out means to bring their bodies into **conformity** with the muscular ideal. A 2012 study of adolescents revealed that muscle-enhancing behaviors are **pervasive** among both middle school– and high school–age males: More than a third reported downing protein powders or shakes in an effort to boost their muscularity; in addition, almost 6 percent admitted to using steroids and 10.5 percent acknowledged using some other muscle-enhancing substance.

Pharmaceutical-grade injectable steroids are a definite concern, says Dr. Rebecka Peebles, codirector of the Eating Disorder Assessment and Treatment Program at the Children's Hospital of Philadelphia, but they're not the biggest worry, given that they're difficult to obtain. Of more concern are the "natural" powders or shakes that teens can pick up at their local GNC. The problem, Peebles says, is that "natural" in this case simply means unregulated. "They actually can include all kinds of things in them," says Peebles. In some cases powder or shake supplements "are actually **anabolic androgens** and just packaged as a natural supplement."

The consequences can be severe: Long-term use of steroids is associated with depression, rage attacks, suicidal tendencies, and **cardiomyopathies**. And the negative effects can be particularly significant for adolescents, since their bodies are going through a period of major growth and development.

In many cases, of course, weight concerns among young males remain at relatively **benign** levels, and when teens attempt to control their weight, they often do so in comparatively **innocuous** ways. But when adolescents demonstrate an extreme focus on physique and begin to engage in potentially dangerous behaviors, it can be a signal of an eating or weight-related disorder — in males just as much as in females.

"The misunderstanding has been the generalization that eating disorders are a woman's issue," says Lemberg. "What studies have shown is that, in the last 15 years or so, more men have eating disorders than ever before." The oft-cited figure is that only about one in ten eating disorders occur in males,[1] but according to Lemberg, newer research[2] suggests that the real ratio is probably closer to one in four.

Although awareness of the risk of weight disorders among males is growing, there is still a problem with under-recognition, Field says, primarily because of the assumption that the disorders look the same in males as they do in females. Current assessments for eating disorders focus on the classical presentation typical

falling prey: becoming a victim

conformity: behaving within societal rules or expectations

pervasive: very common; widespread

anabolic androgens: steroid drugs that increase protein within cells, especially muscles

cardiomyopathies: heart diseases that make it difficult for the heart to pump blood

benign: harmless

innocuous: not harmful or offensive

[1] www.nationaleatingdisorders.org/research-males-and-eating-disorders
[2] www.ncbi.nlm.nih.gov/pmc/articles/PMC1892232/?report=reader

of females, but since young men are often more concerned with gaining muscle than becoming thin, they typically don't present as underweight, as girls often do. They're also not as likely to starve themselves, use laxatives, or induce vomiting; instead, they're much more likely to engage in excessive amounts of exercise and steroid abuse. "Instead of wanting to do something unhealthy to get smaller, they're using unhealthy means to become larger," Field says.

But though the presentation might be different, excessive worries about weight, especially in combination with high-risk behaviors, are no less concerning in males than in females. According to Field, it's time to sit up and take note of the boys. "Pediatricians and adolescent medicine docs and parents [need] to become aware that they should be listening as much to their sons' conversations about weight as their daughters'."

After You Read

Mapping the Reading

1. Identify three points of evidence that Santa Cruz presents to support the position that eating and body image disorders are on the rise in boys.

2. Why is the increase in eating and body image disorders in boys a source of concern?

3. What body image do boys want to achieve? Where do they see these images?

4. What are the dangers associated with the use of steroids and even "natural" supplements designed to increase muscle mass?

5. Why do body image problems in boys often go unrecognized?

Discussing and Thinking Critically about the Reading

1. In general, how are boys' and girls' experiences with body image disorders different? Draw on Santa Cruz's article as part of your answer.

2. Look back at your "As You Read" notes, or mark Santa Cruz's sources now. How does Santa Cruz introduce the individuals she quotes? What function do the quoted passages serve?

3. Why do you think the incidence of body image disorders has increased for boys?

4. What actions might schools take to help prevent body image disorders in boys?

Navigating the Intersections

1. Abigail Saguy presents evidence that overweight and obese people, especially women, experience discrimination. Drawing in part on Jamie Santa Cruz's article, consider whether boys and men experience discrimination based on their appearance. If so, how is this discrimination both similar to and different from the discrimination Saguy discusses?

2. Jean ad analysis: Using a search engine, find a selection of blue jeans ads directed at males from today and twenty-five years ago. Compare the pictures. How has the idealized body represented in these ads changed?

Appearance Choices

Before You Read: Write briefly about how much you value being comfortable in what you wear versus looking good in what you wear. How uncomfortable are you willing to be to look good? For example, would you wear clothes that feel too tight? shoes that hurt? Do you buy clothes for comfort or for fashion and appearance?

KEVIN FANNING

Kevin Fanning is a Boston-based freelance writer who writes about celebrities, technology, relationships, and culture. He is best known as a writer of fan fiction—stories that are based on characters created by others. Fanning has written *Kim Kardashian: Trapped in Her Own Game*, a serial novel, and *Through the Dark*. Fanning writes for many magazines, and his work is found all over the web. This personal narrative appeared in *Racked* in 2015.

As You Read: As you read, take note of where Fanning uses self-deprecating humor—that is, where he makes fun of himself to amuse, entertain, and inform his readers.

One Man Explains Why He Swears by Wearing Spanx

I have been at war with my body since the fifth grade, when I overheard two girls in my class talking about how fat I was. I was like: *Wait, I'm fat???* It had never occurred to me before that, but okay, yes, maybe I was. I was immediately overcome with self-consciousness about my appearance. I started sucking in my stomach around other people, and have continued to do so every single day of the thirty years since.

My weight has fluctuated wildly since then, and there've been times when it was really bad and times when objectively I might have looked okay. But mentally I have never come to a place of acceptance. No matter what I weigh, how strict my diet is, or whether I'm going to the gym or not, I look in the mirror and think: *I'm so, so sorry, world.*

I understand that how I feel about my body is not rational. I don't like it. But I've gotten used to it. You can diet and exercise to address physical things to varying degrees, but how do you fix the mental thing? That was the problem.

Spanx: a brand of figure-enhancing bodywear, originally developed for women

Spanx has grown very quickly over the last few years to become a standard component of women's fashion. When I first heard about this fashion-accessory-slash-torture-device that somehow magically smooths and shapes the unshape-able, I experienced the same *That sounds horrifying, I really want to experience it* emotional roller coaster that accompanies every new Nic Cage movie.

But it was just for women. While my wife and many of the women I know online mention their Spanx all the time—no big deal, just a part of the uniform—I have never met or even heard of a man wearing Spanx. I've never seen them for sale at Target or Kohl's or Macy's or any of the typical stores where men in my **demographic** buy clothes. Spanx for Men exist, so someone must be buying them, but it isn't something men talk about. I felt no small amount of shame for how desperately I **coveted** them.

demographic: social group, as defined by demographic information—age, gender, region, social class, and so on

coveted: deeply wanted to possess

And price is a major factor. Spanx are not cheap and I hate spending money on myself. I would check the prices on Amazon and add them to my cart and then shut my browser, sighing wistfully at the email reminder that I had unpurchased items sitting in my shopping cart.

Then one day I got an Amazon gift card for my birthday and I sprinted to my laptop and put one medium black Spanx T-shirt in my cart and hit Purchase before I could second guess myself for the millionth time. I felt wild and **wanton**, leaping recklessly into uncharted men's fashion territory. When my Spanx arrived I was immediately taken with the fabric—stretchy, with a resolute, sinewy tension. It feels oddly synthetic, the material covered in some kind of space-age layer of science that presumably solves all your problems.

wanton: shameless; immodest

> **❝** The Spanx transformation is as much mental as it is physical. I was definitely still me. But it was like those bumper stickers that say 'Let go and let God.' With Spanx I could let go of my worries about my body. **❞**

Getting the shirt physically onto your body is a multi-step process. First you screw your head through the neck hole. Then you think: *Literally how is this going to get on my body?* Without the give of a regular T-shirt your limbs have to do significantly more contorting to fit within its confines.

You fold one arm up through and then just kind of stand there and breathe for a few minutes, committed now, realizing that the only way out is through. You bend your other arm back and up behind your head and then the shirt is around your shoulders. Then it's a slow process of wriggling and tugging it over your torso, an operation that feels like pulling a condom down over a cupcake. And then suddenly it's done. The Spanx is on. It is a part of you. And it feels AMAZING.

law of conservation of mass: the principle that mass—weight or some other measure of mass—cannot become smaller or greater, though its form may change

corporeal: bodily

Everything is tucked in and bound fast. Wearing Spanx didn't magically turn me skinny; the **law of conservation of mass** still applied to my **corporeal** form. I definitely was in no danger of wolf-whistling myself in a mirror. But when I finished getting dressed, my clothes magically fit for the first time ever.

I felt transformed into a newer, slightly less blobby version of myself. I felt confident about how I looked, in a way that was more like stepping into a new skin than merely cinching up the old.

It was as though I had been grasped firmly but gently in the soft hands of a loving giant and transported to a vivid new landscape. The shirt held me, had **dominion** over me, and I loved it. I felt myself beginning to understand the appeal of **corsets**, and **thunder shirts**, and maybe even kinbaku, the Japanese art of rope binding.

As I left for work I wondered if I should pack a backup T-shirt in case I felt myself suffocating around lunch. I could breathe, but for how long? But I forced myself to commit. Women do much more in the name of fashion every day. I could do this. And I was glad I did, because as confident as I felt all morning, lunchtime, it turns out, is the Spanx Magic Hour, when the beauty and majesty of Spanx truly unfolds and you learn how transformative it truly is.

Normally after lunch I feel gross. I can feel my salad or my gigantic sandwich distending my stomach and ruining the lines of my look for all those unfortunate enough to cast their gaze upon me. But nestled firmly inside my Spanx, my stomach stayed as tucked away as ever. I felt just as amazing after lunch as I had when I first put it on. This was the waterfall moment, when I went over the cliff, falling deep into a serious, long-term relationship with Spanx.

I spent the rest of the day learning to appreciate the new me, who stood tall and smiled at strangers. I felt like the type of person who could possibly be fun at parties. I was already starting to forget the old me, the lumpy and misshapen me who never stood up straight and whose shirt buttons continually puckered, and who prayed daily the castle wall of his jeans could withstand the attack of his **encroaching** waistline.

But by the time I got home that night, I was like: Okay, this thing has to come off. My body felt tired and longed for release. I said to my wife: "I get it now! When you get home and immediately have to take your bra off! I understand!" She rolled her eyes. "No, you do not," she said.

Getting the shirt off was even trickier than getting it on. I've never done yoga but I imagine I have a basic sense of it now. The stretching and bending and controlled breathing, the use of muscles you didn't know you had. I shimmied the shirt up over my chest and nearly dislocated my shoulder getting my arms to the necessary angles. But at last I pulled it up off my head and was free. Free to contemplate the horror of my old body. As I changed into a regular T-shirt, I wondered if you miss prison, on your first day back in the real world.

The Spanx transformation is as much mental as it is physical. I was definitely still me. But it was like those bumper stickers that say "Let go and let God." With Spanx I could let go of my worries about my body. I didn't have to suck in my stomach because it was being done for me. All the mental energy I spent each day worrying what people thought of me was freed up. I used it

dominion: control

corsets: tight women's undergarments designed to make waists look smaller; **thunder shirts:** tight shirts thought to calm dogs during thunderstorms

encroaching: intruding or crossing into another's space

to wonder if people noticed anything different about me, if they thought my outfit was cute or not.

I still only own the one Spanx, which is a problem. When I'm wearing regular T-shirts all I can think about is how much I would rather be wearing my Spanx. Having only the one shirt guarantees that I always have something to look forward to, a day when I'll feel slightly better about myself than I do every other day. If I wore Spanx every day, would my self-confidence become permanent? Would I become too confident? **Insufferable**, even? I think I could live with that. More easily than I could learn to accept my body, anyway.

insufferable:
unpleasant to deal with

After You Read

Mapping the Reading

1. How would you describe Fanning's body image both before and while wearing Spanx? Identify the passages that reveal to you how he feels about his body.

2. Why does Fanning put off buying Spanx?

3. According to Fanning, what problems can diet and exercise help with? What issues can't they address?

4. Why does Fanning think that his experience wearing Spanx makes him know what it is like to be a woman, and what is his wife's response?

5. According to Fanning, what does wearing Spanx all day do for him?

Discussing and Thinking Critically about the Reading

1. Fanning uses self-deprecating humor (humor that makes fun of himself). Look back at your "As You Read" notes, or find two examples of self-deprecating humor now. From these examples, explain how self-deprecating humor works. How effective is the humor? How does it help Fanning express his point of view?

2. Why does Fanning spend so much time explaining the process of putting on and taking off his Spanx T-shirt? What purpose do these descriptions serve?

3. Although written humorously, Fanning's essay raises the following question: Can what you wear actually change how you feel about your body and yourself? What does Fanning think? What do you think?

4. The author discusses body image issues and the potential power of shapewear to make people feel better about themselves from his perspective as a man. Argue for how much (or how little) gender is relevant to his point.

5. At the end of his essay, Fanning asks, "If I wore Spanx every day, would my self-confidence become permanent? Would I become too confident? Insufferable, even?" Answer Fanning's questions, which ultimately ask you to consider whether changing our external appearance can lead to changes in how we feel on the inside.

Navigating the Intersections

1. Select one of the other authors from this chapter, and write a response to Kevin Fanning in the voice of that person. What would that writer say to Fanning about his decision to attempt to resolve his body image problems by wearing painful clothing?

2. Fanning is not the only writer to document his experience wearing Spanx. Using a search engine, type in "my experience with Spanx" and read another story; then compare and contrast this writer's perspective with Fanning's.

Before You Read: Write briefly about your opinion on body modification. If you have tattoos or body piercings, why did you decide to get them? If you do not have tattoos or body piercings, why did you decide not to? For what reasons do you think others choose to get tattoos or body piercings?

SHARON HAYWOOD

A freelancer from Toronto, Canada, Haywood writes about medicine, web design, the American justice system, wind technology, anthropology, psychology, and language. From 2009 to 2014, Haywood was coeditor of AdiosBarbie.com—a website that promotes healthy body image—and now serves as an adviser to the team. In addition, she is a member of the global advisory board for the Dove Self-Esteem Project. This article was published in *Herizons* (2012), a Canadian feminist magazine.

As You Read: Haywood makes many points about why people choose body modification. Focus your underlining or note taking on identifying all the passages in which she offers explanations.

How Body Modification Ended the War against My Body

"You took out your ring?" my husband asked, eyebrows raised. He had never seen my belly button without a piercing.

I glided my thumb over the partially closed hole. "It was time to come out," I said, smiling down at my naked navel.

The small scar where my navel ring used to be doesn't bother me. Instead, it reminds me of a decision I made years ago when I chose to be kinder to myself and subsequently was transformed because of it. Yes, I forced a hole through my body in an act of self-love.

After years of battling **anorexia** and **bulimia**, I needed to make peace with my belly, the part of my body I loathed the most. I needed to befriend the

anorexia: a psychiatric eating disorder that results in self-starvation; primary causes are fear of weight gain and a distorted view of one's body size and shape; **bulimia:** a psychiatric eating disorder characterized by bingeing and/or purging; like anorexia, primary causes are fear of weight gain and a distorted view of one's own body size and shape

> *Part of my choice to be pierced and tattooed was to define my body—on my terms and mine alone. Not as defined by the media, nor by my partner, nor by the men who violated me.*

rotund: chubby or fat; round

cessation: stopping

depiction: picture or other representation

kaleidoscope: a constantly changing pattern of light and color

deviant: nonstandard; irregular; diverging from the social standard

periphery: edge; margin; fringe

core of my physical self as a way of creating a bridge with my emotional self. Prettifying my navel seemed like an appropriate symbolic gesture, a peace offering to the part of me upon which I had inflicted the most pain.

Beyond my **rotund** toddler years, I grew into a lean and muscular frame, but by the age of ten I began to battle my body. I would slap my dense calves (composed of solid muscle) and watch in revulsion as they wiggled. My childhood best friend and I had regular body-hating sessions on my front lawn, where we would examine our respective "gigantic" thighs. But it was always my belly rolls—or what I perceived as rolls—that were the primary target of my disdain and disgust. It was the core of myself that I raged against.

As I entered puberty, extreme food restriction and excessive exercising took hold, causing my weight to plummet to about twenty pounds less than what was healthy for me. These actions also triggered a **cessation** of my periods. About a year later, when my body screamed starvation and I could no longer continue sustaining myself on carrots and lettuce, I gained over fifty pounds.

I detested myself even more. Looking in the mirror was torturous and would provoke anxiety and despair. I continually sucked in my stomach. It still frightens me that I didn't realize that there was not one single thing wrong with me.

Throughout my adolescence and into my early twenties, I experienced a few more cycles of extreme highs and lows in my weight. By age twenty-six, I was deeply depressed. I had hit bottom. I sought help and was fortunate to find the right professionals to lead me out of the hell I was living.

I drew a lot during my eating disorder recovery. What I consider my most powerful sketch was a **depiction** of how I perceived my spirit at that point in time: a gray, shapeless, cartoon-like, two-dimensional flattened blob that allowed my beauty and power and gifts to escape through my navel in a **kaleidoscope** of vibrant, pulsing colors. Shortly after creating that image, I realized that I needed to connect with my body in a concrete way; I then began to think about piercing my navel.

Even though piercings and tattoos are no longer associated with the **deviant periphery** of society, some would argue that in piercing and tattooing my body, my primary motive was to harm myself. In 1999, the American Academy of Child and Adolescent Psychiatry classified tattooing and excessive piercing as self-injurious behaviors. A 2009 article in *Psychology Today* by Lawrence Rubin and Michael Brody reported, "Tattooing and body piercing have been associated with dangerous and sometimes lethal risk-taking behavior, eating disorders, self-loathing, substance abuse, depression and social alienation."[1]

From what I've seen of the data, however, the associations are far from overwhelming. For example, a 2006 study in the *Journal of Psychosomatic Research* explored the body modification–**masochism** connection and concluded that tattooing and piercing were more about exploring one's self-identity than they were indicative of self-harming behaviors. Based on my own experience, I agree.

masochism: enjoyment of pain

Even though I suffered through anorexia and bulimia (and made it out the other side), my choice to permanently accessorize my body wasn't about self-hatred or feeding a **pathology** — just the opposite. I purposely pierced my belly button with the intention of ending an eighteen-year war with my body.

pathology: something abnormal, diseased

"Is that a lotus?"

It's a question I'm familiar with. Since tattooing a **rendition** of a lotus on the nape of my neck three years ago, friends, acquaintances, and the occasional stranger have been curious as to why I chose that particular flower to etch into my body. Common to eastern religions, the lotus represents rebirth and regeneration and the beauty that can emerge from overcoming obstacles. It was a symbol that called my name. I had overcome what I thought was impossible, what I thought would actually cripple me forever. The only obstacle more challenging than recovering from almost two decades of eating disorders was learning how to move from being a victim to being a survivor.

rendition: interpretation or version

Although I had never considered when I got my tattoos to be relevant, I think my subconscious would disagree. I entered into the world of tattooing only a couple of months after I was sexually assaulted by my first boyfriend. Over a decade later, after a second sexual assault, I committed to my second tattoo after completing an intense nine-month period of weekly therapy, when I finally confronted and began the healing process from being sexually assaulted. And even though my third and most recent tattoo, the lotus, did not follow a traumatic event, it has a direct connection to the assaults and to my **fortitude** in being able to move past them.

fortitude: courage or mental strength

While I am a survivor of both eating disorders and sexual violence, I didn't accessorize my navel and commit to a few tattoos to reclaim my body — at least not on a conscious level. A recurring theme among body modification **aficionados** is the desire to be more in control of their bodies. In the 1996 fall issue of *Ms. Magazine*, Deborah Shouse wrote the essay "Mark Her Words" illustrating how her daughter Hilee used tattoos and piercings to re-inhabit her

aficionados: knowledgeable enthusiasts

[1] Lawrence Rubin, "Tattoos and Body Piercing: Adolescent Self-Expression or Self-Mutilation?" *Psychology Today*, July 2, 2009.

body and heal her spirit from sexual abuse: "Hilee is undoing her hurt. She is stepping out and embracing her body."[2]

Part of my choice to be pierced and tattooed was to define my body — on my terms and mine alone. Not as defined by the media, nor by my partner, nor by the men who violated me. My personal experience reflects current body modification research, which reveals that some tattooees and piercees who have been marginalized, live with a disability or long-standing illness, or have experienced trauma have chosen body modification as a vehicle for healing.

In the November 2000 issue of the journal *Feminism & Psychology*, University of Melbourne political science professor Sheila Jeffreys cites a sexual assault survivor's motivations for piercing: "I'm getting pierced to reclaim my body. I've been used and abused. My body was taken by another without my consent. Now, by this ritual of piercing, I claim my body back as my own. I heal my wounds."[3]

Body modification was one tool I used to heal. I recognize that some of my eating disorder history is intricately linked with being a rape survivor; but much of my motivation to pierce and tattoo simply focused on viewing my body through a compassionate lens, exploring my body in a loving way. As Silja J. A. Talvi wrote in *Body Outlaws*, "By getting tattooed, I consciously took a small step away from my emotional suffering and toward a radical new self-definition."[4]

When I got tattooed at nineteen, thirty-two, and forty, I was redefining myself via carefully chosen symbols, **infused** with deep personal meaning, that I placed purposefully (and more or less **inconspicuously**) on my body.

infused: filled or flavored with

inconspicuously: unnoticeably

They remind me that I am brave with the world and myself.

They remind me that I am not a victim.

They remind me of my strength that carried me through periods in my life that I thought were too dark to move beyond.

They remind me to keep growing.

Will I get another? At this point, I would say no, but I also know that as I age and **evolve** I might change my mind.

evolve: change; grow

As for my navel ring, I hadn't planned on removing it, but something inside me had said to take it out. I calculated how long it had been. I was twenty-seven when I got it, and that day, at forty years old, it felt like a cycle had completed. My belly no longer needed a sparkly accessory to remind me to be kind to it, to myself.

I finally had learned how.

---

[2] Deborah Shouse, "Mark Her Words: Daughter Attempts to Cope with History of Sexual Abuse through Tattooing and Body Piercing," *Ms.*, vol. 7, no. 2, Sept.–Oct. 1996, p. 96.
[3] Sheila Jeffreys, "'Body Art' and Social Status: Cutting, Tattooing, and Piercing from a Feminist Perspective," *Feminism & Psychology*, vol. 10, no. 4, Nov. 2000, pp. 409–27.
[4] Silja J. A. Talvi, "Marked for Life: Tattoos and the Redefinition of Self," *Body Outlaws: Rewriting the Rules of Beauty and Body Image*, edited by Ophira Edut, Seal Press, 2003, pp. 211–18.

After You Read

Mapping the Reading

1. Why does Haywood decide to remove her belly ring?

2. How would you describe the author's body image? Identify the passages that reveal how she feels about her body.

3. How does Haywood use body modification — tattooing and body piercing — to help her, in her words, end her "war with [her] body"?

4. For Haywood, what is the connection between body modification and eating disorders? between body modification and sexual assault?

5. Explain the symbolic meaning that body modification holds for the author by discussing two specific examples of body modification that Haywood undertakes.

Discussing and Thinking Critically about the Reading

1. Reflect on Haywood's claim that body modification helped in her personal transformation as she worked to overcome her eating disorders and trauma from sexual assault. How convincing (or not) do you find her explanations, and why?

2. Return to your "As You Read" notes, or look now at the explanations Haywood offers for body modification (these can be her own explanations or those from her secondary sources). Choose the explanations you find most and least convincing, and explain why you feel this way.

3. Haywood uses secondary sources (research articles by social scientists and quotations from others who have experiences with body modification) to support her analysis of her own experiences with body modification. Give an example of an especially effective use of a secondary source, as well as an example of a secondary source that is ineffectively used. Explain what makes these sources effective or ineffective.

4. In what ways, if any, has Haywood altered your view of people who have tattoos, piercings, and other body modifications?

5. Besides those offered by Haywood, what reasons might others have for deciding to modify their bodies?

Navigating the Intersections

1. Compare the personal satisfaction Sharon Haywood gets from body modification to that achieved by Kevin Fanning when he wears Spanx. What are the most surprising similarities and differences between their respective experiences of (fairly) permanent and temporary body modifications? Why are they surprising?

2. How common are tattoos? Investigate this question by searching online or through the library for professional organizations' polling and research reports (the Harris Poll, major newspapers, and so on), and summarize your findings. How can these findings be interpreted or analyzed?

3. People who are overweight and obese, and those with visible tattoos and body piercings, are often victims of stereotyping, typically born out of assumptions made by people without these characteristics about the personality or character of those with these characteristics. Create a public service announcement—for print, audio, or video—to break down one of these stereotypes.

Before You Read: Write two descriptive paragraphs: one about the beauty or grooming rituals you go through to prepare for work or school, and one about the beauty or grooming rituals you go through to prepare for going out socially. How are these rituals similar or different? What exactly do you do? How long does it take? What expenses do these preparations require?

LAUREN SHIELDS

Lauren Shields is a freelance writer based in the Atlanta, Georgia, area. A graduate of seminary school as well as a writer, Shields writes for her blog, *The Modesty Experiment*, and for a variety of publications. Shields is interested in feminism, antiracism, and social justice. This article was published in *Salon* in 2013.

As You Read: In personal narratives like this one, writers often make statements about the "epiphanies"—sudden realizations or insights—they experienced during the time they are writing about. Make note of Shields's epiphanies—those moments in the narrative where the writer announces a discovery or a realization about herself or the world in which she lives.

My Year of Modesty

The idea for my modesty experiment began when I worked in New York City as a receptionist for a company at Fifth Avenue and Fifty-Second Street, while I edited short films on the side. Every morning I would shoehorn myself onto the train with thousands of expensive-smelling, **coiffed** women who somehow managed to keep their hair looking great under wool caps in winter and despite hot, stinky gusts of subway backdrafts in the summer. It was an army of ladies sporting fitted waistlines, toned arms, blown-out hair, full faces of makeup and heels (which was incredible, considering all the walking we all had to do). Everyone looked good, no one was phoning it in, and we were all stylish.

I hated every second of it. It felt like putting on a costume. In fact, that was what I called it: my "Grown-Up Suit." Still, given where I worked, I had to look like that. Every. Damn. Day.

coiffed: having highly stylized hair

By contrast, on my way home to the warehouse I inhabited in Williamsburg, I would look at **Hasidic** women in their headscarves and long skirts with something akin to envy. Gawd, I thought. How nice would it be not to have to think about stupid crap like the latest accessories and whether my hair had gone limp?

Mind you, these Hasidic women were stylish: They looked good. They just didn't look like everyone else. These women were not "fashionable" first, like most of the women I saw everywhere else — they seemed to be focused on something else, something more important than what was trendy. They had a very good reason for not dressing like the train-squishing crowd of Fifth Avenue, and I wanted a reason too.

Out of curiosity, while I sat behind my desk answering phones or prepping conference rooms I began to research Quaker, Jewish, and Muslim belief systems, which allowed **adherents** of both sexes to dress modestly for spiritual reasons. I briefly considered beginning to dress like a Quaker, but I thought to myself, "What's my excuse? I can't just magically dress like a Quaker or a Muslim because I'm tired of dressing like an American."

Eventually I scrapped the idea: I had no excuse to buck the trend. Plus, it would be a little ridiculous: "No, I dress like this because I'm pretty sure the beauty industry is a ploy to keep us from thinking about how to break into the boys' club of corporate America, and obsession with your appearance is frivolous and time-consuming! Would you like some more coffee, expensively dressed and perfectly nice female co-worker?" No, thanks.

Two years later, I was a first-year student at Candler Theological **Seminary** in Atlanta. (Don't ask how I went from wanting to be a filmmaker in New York City to applying to seminary. It's as long and weird a tale as you might think.) One day, a woman came to my "Women in Church History" class. She had spent some time in the Middle East with her husband (who is Middle Eastern) and children, and while there she had been required to cover her hair and adhere to particular clothing requirements.

She was there to talk specifically about hijab, the modesty requirements for many Muslims, and its effect on women. To a classroom full of vocal, educated feminists who were eager to prove themselves, this lecture might have been your typical Islam-slamming discussion on whose fault it is that men desire women (it's men's, in case you're wondering). I was ready to go to battle.

Instead, it was a shock to all of us. The speaker explained very clearly how much she had enjoyed (and admittedly, sometimes hated) dressing in accordance with modesty rules. She talked about her daughter who, being half-Muslim, had decided to wear a headscarf at age eight soon after returning to the States from overseas. The speaker didn't advocate for hijab, but

Hasidic: of the Hasidic sect of Judaism; Hasidic laws require a modest appearance, with legs, arms, and hair covered

adherents: followers of a set of beliefs or ideals

seminary: school dedicated to training religious leaders

acrimonious:
bitterly
argumentative

hypocrisy:
contradiction in
belief

**Western
Imperialism:**
cultural as well
as economic
and military
domination by the
West (Europe and
the United States)

she certainly wasn't opposed to it. This was not the podium-pounding, **acrimonious** discussion I had prepared for. Instead of feeling self-righteous and angry, I felt inspired — and profoundly unsettled. I didn't know it then, but what I had learned about modest dress was teaching me about my own **hypocrisy**.

After class I retreated to my favorite couch — the one on the fifth floor the faculty didn't usually catch me napping on — and buried my nose in that week's reading assignment, "Muslim Women in America." It's not possible, I thought, that women would feel freer dressed modestly, that women would choose to be ashamed of their bodies. But it wasn't shame, I soon learned. In fact, for many women, it was pride. It was a desire to be considered for things other than what their hairstyle communicated, or whether their butts were shaped right — a desire that many people, not just women, share today.

In America, Islamic dress is often a choice, and the women who make this choice are declining to endorse **Western Imperialism** and the sexualization of their bodies. It's a way of expressing modesty and resisting the pressure to be scrutinized against Western standards of beauty.

And then, as I sat on the couch at one of the best seminars in the States, tummy sucked in so I looked thinner, makeup on my face to hide my blemishes, wearing uncomfortable shoes because they matched my outfit even though I had to walk three miles in them, hair with enough fifteen-dollar product so it laid just so, and my whole "look" completed with a scarf that was always in my way and skirt arranged to look natural but that was actually perfectly placed to cover my knee socks — pinched, pulled, painted, and still not good enough, I thought, "Is this really any better?"

> ❝ *It's not possible, I thought, that women would feel freer dressed modestly, that women would choose to be ashamed of their bodies. But it wasn't shame, I soon learned. In fact, for many women, it was pride. It was a desire to be considered for things other than what their hairstyle communicated, or whether their butts were shaped right — a desire that many people, not just women, share today.* ❞

Up until that moment, I had considered myself the kind of person who was "above" thinking too much about my appearance (remember, the Grown-Up Suit was just a costume — deep down I disdained all that "frivolous" stuff), but that day on the couch I was uncomfortably aware of how much I did care about how I looked. One day I had noticed **cellulite** where it had never been before, and it really upset me. My neck was saggier than it was when I was twenty, and I found myself awake at night wondering if I was just fat, or get-

cellulite: dimpled
skin caused by
shifting fat cells

ting older, and whether I was still beautiful.

Why should I care? Why, if beauty didn't matter to me, did I have more than six hundred dollars' worth of makeup in my closet (and I never left the house without at least some of it on) and more shoes than any sane individual needs? Why was I convinced that if I didn't look "sexy" or at least attractive no one would listen to what I had to say?

The fact that I was so afraid to let go of all those security blankets told me that I should try it. So I did.

With the support of my seminary community and my then-boyfriend, I designed the Modesty Experiment, in which I took my cues from Jewish, Muslim, and some Christian modesty practices in order to loosen my death grip on the idea that youth and beauty were **prerequisites** to relevance. I started a blog and a journal to stay accountable, and I gave away more than a third of my clothes. The clothes I couldn't wear during the Experiment because they had no sleeves or were too short or tight, I gave to a friend, along with all of my makeup. It was hard — I actually cried on the way home from the clothing drop box.

prerequisites: requirements

And for nine months, I covered all of my hair, wore nothing that was so fitted that I felt like I had to sit or stand funny to look good, and never exposed my knees or my shoulders, except at home. With rare exceptions, I wore no makeup or nail polish. It was kind of brutal, and really liberating.

It's easy to say that age and appearance don't matter when you're young and beautiful. Facing evidence of my own aging, I had found (to my disgust) that I was just as panicked about my looks as other women. I wasn't liberated. In fact, I had been telling myself I was beyond superficiality when in fact I had bought the whole thing **hook, line, and sinker**. But in nine months, I learned that, yes, you do get more done when you're not obsessed with your shoes, but you do still need to look put-together for your own self-confidence. I learned that looking good isn't necessarily a bad thing, but when it becomes the cornerstone of your identity — like the advertising industry tries to convince us it is — then you're doing nothing but damage to yourself.

hook, line, and sinker: completely deceived; an old expression that draws on the image of a fish being so fully tricked by bait dangling from a fishing rod that it swallows the entire thing — hook, line, and sinker

I learned that if you put down the Beauty Suit you will be ignored by people who think you have to look a certain way to be worth their time (men and women included), and that that is a small price to pay for not having to put on a costume every time you think you'll need to impress them. I learned that you will feel invisible until you open your mouth, and then people will be amazed at what you have chosen to do in protest of the Western beauty ideal. And then those people probably won't date you because you're kind of outspoken. Or whatever.

I learned that, to the people who matter, you do not become invisible when you stop trying so hard to look available. I became visible to the one guy I had been looking for, and his proposal three weeks ago rocked my world. I became visible to a community of women who began to have conversations about just how trapped they felt by the beauty ideal because it demands so much expensive upkeep and such a constant stream of internal criticism. I even heard from a lot of guys who swore that the more made-up and "rich" a woman looked (think the Kardashians), the less inclined they felt to take her seriously, either as a co-worker or a dating prospect.

More than anything else, I learned how to see my appearance for what it is: a "Lauren Suit," which does nothing more than provide a necessary exterior for an inner life that will never be available in stores. Also, you would be amazed at how much money you save not trying to buy the latest Grown-Up Suit.

After You Read

Mapping the Reading

1. What reasons does Shields give for deciding to conduct her modesty experiment?

2. How does Shields compare and contrast the women she observes around Fifth Avenue, Manhattan, with those she observes in Williamsburg, Brooklyn?

3. What is the "Beauty Suit"?

4. Returning to your "As You Read" notes or making some now, what epiphanies (or sudden insights) does Shields's experiment inspire? What lessons does she learn from her experiment?

5. How differently is Shields treated when she wears modest clothes than when she wears her "Grown-Up Suit"?

Discussing and Thinking Critically about the Reading

1. At several points in the essay, Shields refers to her "regular" work clothes as a "costume"; reflect on her word choice. What point is she trying to make with the word *costume*? How effective is this word in helping you understand her point?

2. Why do you think Shields and other women who dress modestly are treated differently than those who dress immodestly? That is, what about them changes? What do friends, onlookers, and passersby assume about a woman who is dressed modestly versus a woman who is dressed immodestly or fashionably?

3. What would an equivalent modesty experiment look like for a man? Could such an experiment even work for a man? Why or why not?

4. Would you be willing to try a modesty experiment of your own? If yes, why would you find such an experiment appealing? If no, why wouldn't you want to try such an experiment?

5. For what reasons might a person who follows modesty requirements for religious reasons — as opposed to personal reasons, like Shields — be offended or annoyed by Shields's decision to mimic the religious laws of certain Muslim, Jewish, and Christian religions?

Navigating the Intersections

1. Compare and contrast Lauren Shields's views about the personal transformations achieved through clothing choices with Kevin Fanning's. How are they similar? How are they different?

2. Many bloggers have responded, both positively and negatively, to Shields's modesty experiment. Using a search engine, seek out these responses, select one, and then summarize the response. What is the respondent's perspective, and how does (or doesn't) this perspective change your own response to Shields, and why?

CHAPTER 6

Immigration

America's Great Story

Library of Congress LC-USZC2-1255

Image Response: This illustration (from *Frank Leslie's Illustrated Newspaper*, July 2, 1887) depicts immigrants on the steerage deck of an ocean steamer passing the Statue of Liberty. How does the illustrator portray immigrants? Choose two or three figures to study more closely: Describe each figure, and then discuss the illustrator's possible intentions in presenting the figures in this way. What feelings do you think viewers are being encouraged to have?

In This Chapter

Introduction

Dreams and Anxieties

Immigrants come to America in search of a better life, bringing their hopes and dreams along with their talents, customs, and beliefs. With each new immigrant group's arrival, American culture changes as new food, music, and languages are introduced. The United States is known as a country of immigrants, as expressed in the words of Emma Lazarus's poem "The New Colossus," inscribed at the base of the Statue of Liberty, itself a symbol of America's welcoming of immigrants: "Give me your tired, your poor, / Your huddled masses yearning to breathe free, / The wretched refuse of your teeming shore."

Whereas Lazarus's words capture Americans' hopeful, positive attitude toward immigration, immigrants have not always felt welcome; in fact, many populations have been subject to suspicion and even prejudice and restrictions over the years. These two stances toward immigrants — welcoming and suspicious — have persisted throughout American history. In keeping with celebratory views of immigrants, politicians often point to their contributions to society. In one example from 1998, President Bill Clinton recognized the "renewal" immigrants represent:

> More than any other nation on Earth, America has constantly drawn strength and spirit from wave after wave of immigrants. In each generation, they have proved to be the

233

most restless, the most adventurous, the most innovative, the most industrious of people. Bearing different memories, honoring different heritages, they have strengthened
our economy, enriched our culture, renewed our promise of freedom and opportunity
for all. (United States)

While many presidents have praised immigrants, they have also stressed that there
are certain things immigrants must do to enjoy the rights and benefits of living in
the United States. For example, in 1874 President Ulysses S. Grant stated, "The
United States wisely, freely, and liberally offers its citizenship to all who may come
in good faith to reside within its limits on their complying with certain prescribed
reasonable and simple formalities and conditions" (United States).

Over the years, the question of what exactly an immigrant must do has been
the subject of vigorous discussion around governmental policies, often framed in
terms of assimilation (taking on American culture fully) and acculturation (merging
the immigrant's culture with American culture). Access to benefits has also been
hotly debated, as politicians and the public question, for example, whether undocumented immigrants — immigrants who have come to the United States without following legal procedures — and their children should be allowed access to public
education and health care.

Immigration Policies

Policies to control immigration to the United States have been in effect since the late
1800s. Two of the earliest federal laws on immigration were the Chinese Exclusion
Act of 1882, which barred entry to Chinese laborers and also made it impossible
for Chinese immigrants to apply for citizenship, and the Immigration Act of 1882,
which barred entry to those who appeared likely to cost taxpayers money (such as
people convicted of crimes or people suffering from mental illnesses). Immigration
was further restricted in 1924 with the passage of the National Origins Act, which
set limits on the numbers of immigrants who could come to the United States from
specific countries. The act used a quota system, a method of setting limits typically
based on a ratio or percentage of the whole.

More recently, the terrorist attacks of September 11, 2001, produced new anxieties that resulted in a policy requiring men from certain countries (primarily Muslim ones) to register with, and be fingerprinted and questioned by, the Immigration
and Naturalization Service. When this policy ended in 2003, the United States Vis-
itor and Immigrant Status Indicator Technology (US-VISIT) system went into effect
as a replacement. Under this system, biometric data (fingerprints and photographs)
are collected on most visitors to the United States — both travelers and immigrants.
While some see this law as a useful measure against terrorism, others see it as a
reflection of hostility toward "outsiders."

In addition to contributing to legal restrictions on immigrants, anxieties and
fears have been expressed through various forms of discrimination. Immigrants
who appear different superficially — in dress, skin color, or accent, for example — or

who appear to threaten majority values because of their religion or customs have often been singled out for discriminatory treatment in many areas of daily life, such as housing and employment. Germans in the 1700s and 1800s, Irish in the 1800s, Chinese in the 1800s and early 1900s, and Hispanics and Muslims in our own times have all faced discrimination of this kind.

Americans' connection to immigration is often very personal. Sociologist Charles Hirschman observes that "almost 60 million people—more than one fifth of the total population of the United States—are immigrants or the children of immigrants." Many others can trace their ancestry to a more distant immigrant. In this chapter, we invite you to think about immigration from multiple perspectives and to consider the tensions between the grand vision of America as welcoming of immigrants and a long national history of anxiety over immigration.

Works Cited

Hirschman, Charles. "The Impact of Immigration on American Society: Looking Backward to the Future." *Border Battles: The U.S. Immigration Debates*, SSRC, 28 July 2006, borderbattles.ssrc.org/Hirschman/printable.html.

United States, Department of Homeland Security, U.S. Citizenship and Immigration Services, Office of Citizenship. *The Citizen's Almanac: Fundamental Documents, Symbols, and Anthems of the United States*. Sept. 2014, www.uscis.gov/sites/default/files/USCIS/Office%20of%20Citizenship/Citizenship%20Resource%20Center%20Site/Publications/M-76.pdf.

The Immigrants: A Historical Perspective

Before You Read: Imagine that a first-grade child asks you to explain why people come to the United States. What would you tell that child? Write a letter to this child, telling him or her some of the main reasons people have come to the United States over the years.

JOHN F. KENNEDY

John F. Kennedy (JFK) was the thirty-fifth president of the United States (1960–63). An Irish American, Kennedy was the grandson of American immigrants who arrived in Massachusetts in the nineteenth century, when this country was not welcoming to the Irish. As president, Kennedy advocated for legislation that would replace the "national quota" system, which privileged people from Western Europe, with a fairer system. Kennedy's book *A Nation of Immigrants* (1958), from which this selection was excerpted, was written at the urging of Jewish leaders, who believed that many fewer people would have died in the Holocaust if America's immigration laws had been fairer and who saw in Kennedy a natural leader for their cause.

As You Read: Underline or otherwise mark the passages where Kennedy expresses his view of immigrants, noting the attitude he conveys.

Why They Came

migrate: move from one area or country to another

accumulation: gradual increase

compel: force

forebears: ancestors or family members from the past

proportions: relative importance compared to something else

emigrant: a person who leaves his or her home country for another

circumscribed: limited and predictable

Little is more extraordinary than the decision to **migrate**, little more extraordinary than the **accumulation** of emotions and thoughts which finally leads a family to say farewell to a community where it has lived for centuries, to abandon old ties and familiar landmarks, and to sail across dark seas to a strange land. Today, when mass communications tell one part of the world all about another, it is relatively easy to understand how poverty or tyranny might **compel** people to exchange an old nation for a new one. But centuries ago migration was a leap into the unknown. It was an enormous intellectual and emotional commitment. The forces that moved our **forebears** to their great decision — the decision to leave their homes and begin an adventure filled with incalculable uncertainty, risk, and hardship — must have been of overpowering **proportions**. Oscar Handlin, in his book *The Uprooted*, describes the experience of the immigrants:

> The crossing immediately subjected the **emigrant** to a succession of shattering shocks and decisively conditioned the life of every man that survived it. This was the initial contact with life as it was to be. For many peasants it was the first time away from home, away from the safety of the **circumscribed** little

villages in which they had passed all their years. Now they would learn to have dealings with people essentially different from themselves. Now they would collide with unaccustomed problems, learn to understand **alien** ways and alien languages, manage to survive in a grossly foreign environment.

alien: foreign, strange

Initially, they had to save up money for **passage**. Then they had to say good-bye to cherished relatives and friends, whom they could expect never to see again. They started their journey by traveling from their villages to the **ports of embarkation**. Some walked; the luckier trundled their few possessions into carts, which they sold before boarding ship. Some paused along the road to work in the fields in order to eat. Before they even reached the ports of embarkation, they were subject to illness, accidents, storm, and snow, even to attacks by outlaws.

passage: travel or a trip; here, on a ship

ports of embarkation: places where passengers board a ship

After arriving at the ports, they often had to wait days, weeks, sometimes months, while they bargained with captains or agents for passage. Meanwhile, they crowded into cheap lodging houses near the **quays**, sleeping on straw in small, dark rooms, sometimes as many as forty in a room twelve by fifteen feet.

quays: docks or wharfs

Until the middle of the nineteenth century the immigrants traveled in sailing vessels. The average trip from **Liverpool** to New York took forty days; but any estimate of time was hazardous, for the ship was subject to winds, tides, primitive navigation, unskilled seamanship, and the **whim** of the captain. A good size for the tiny craft of those days was three hundred tons, and each one was crowded with anywhere from four hundred to a thousand passengers.

Liverpool: port city in England

whim: sudden wish

For the immigrants, their shipboard world was the **steerage**, that confined space below deck, usually about seventy-five feet long and twenty-five feet wide. In many vessels no one over five and a half feet tall could stand upright. Here they lived their days and nights, receiving their daily ration of vinegar-flavored water and trying to **eke out sustenance** from whatever provisions they had brought along. When their food ran out, they were often at the mercy of **extortionate** captains.

steerage: section on a ship for passengers holding the least expensive tickets

eke out: to get with difficulty

sustenance: nourishment

extortionate: cruelly getting money by force

They huddled in their hard, cramped bunks, freezing when the hatches were open, stifling when they were closed. The only light came from a dim, swaying lantern. Night and day were indistinguishable. But they were ever aware of the treacherous winds and waves, the scampering of rats and the splash of burials. Diseases—cholera, yellow fever, smallpox, and dysentery—took their toll. One in ten failed to survive the crossing.

Eventually the journey came to an end. The travelers saw the coast of America with mixed feelings of relief, excitement, **trepidation**, and anxiety. For now, uprooted from old patterns of life, they found themselves, in Handlin's phrase, "in a prolonged state of crisis—crisis in the sense that they were, and remained, unsettled." They reached the new land exhausted by lack of rest, bad food, confinement, and the strain of adjustment to new conditions. But they could not pause to recover their strength. They had no reserves of food

trepidation: fear

or money; they had to keep moving until they found work. This meant new strains at a time when capacity to cope with new problems had already been over-burdened.

There were probably as many reasons for coming to America as there were people who came. It was a highly individual decision. Yet it can be said that three large forces—religious **persecution**, political oppression, and economic hardship—provided the chief motives for the mass migrations to our shores. They were responding, in their own way, to the pledge of the Declaration of Independence: the promise of "life, liberty, and the pursuit of happiness."

The search for freedom of worship has brought people to America from the days of the Pilgrims to modern times. In our own day, for example, **anti-Semitic** and anti-Christian persecution in Hitler's Germany and the **Communist empire** have driven people from their homes to seek refuge in America. Not all found what they sought immediately. The Puritans of the **Massachusetts Bay Colony**, who drove Roger Williams and Anne Hutchinson into the wilderness, showed as little tolerance for **dissenting** beliefs as the **Anglicans of England** had shown to them. Minority religious **sects**, from the Quakers and Shakers through the Catholics and Jews to the Mormons and Jehovah's Witnesses, have at various times suffered both discrimination and hostility in the United States.

But the very diversity of religious belief has made for religious toleration. In demanding freedom for itself, each sect had increasingly to permit freedom for others. The insistence of each successive wave of immigrants upon its right to practice its religion helped make freedom of worship a central part of the American **creed**. People who gambled their lives on the right to believe in their own God would not lightly surrender that right in a new society.

The second great force behind immigration has been political oppression. America has always been a refuge from tyranny. As a nation conceived in liberty, it has held out to the world the promise of respect for the rights of man. Every time a revolution has failed in Europe, every time a nation has **succumbed** to tyranny, men and women who love freedom have assembled their families and their belongings and set sail across the seas. Nor has this process come to an end in our own day. The Russian Revolution, the terrors of Hitler's Germany and Mussolini's Italy, the Communist suppression of the Hungarian Revolution of 1956, and the cruel measures of the Castro regime in Cuba—all have brought new thousands seeking sanctuary in the United States.

The economic factor has been more complex than the religious and political factors. From the very beginning, some have come to America in search of riches, some in flight from poverty, and some because they were bought and sold and had no choice. And the various reasons have intertwined. Thus some early arrivals were lured to these shores by dreams of amassing great wealth, like the Spanish conquistadors in Mexico and Peru. These adventurers, expecting quick profits in gold, soon found that real wealth lay in

persecution: poor and unfair treatment

anti-Semitic: anti-Jewish

Communist empire: Soviet Union (Russia) and its allies, then enemies of the United States

Massachusetts Bay Colony: English settlement community, 1628–84

dissenting: publicly disagreeing with religious beliefs

Anglicans of England: members of the Church of England

sects: religious groups

creed: set of beliefs

succumbed: given in; stopped resisting

such crops as tobacco and cotton. As they built up the plantation economy in states like Virginia and the Carolinas, they needed cheap labor. So they began to import indentured servants from England, men and women who agreed to labor a term of years in exchange for eventual freedom, and slaves from Africa.

The process of **industrialization** in America increased the demand for cheap labor, and chaotic economic conditions in Europe increased the supply. If some immigrants continued to believe that the streets of New York were paved with gold, more were driven by the hunger and hardship of their native lands. The Irish potato famine of 1845 brought almost a million people to America in five years. American manufacturers advertised in European newspapers, offering to pay the passage of any man willing to come to America to work for them.

industrialization: movement from an agricultural to a manufacturing economy

The immigrants who came for economic reasons contributed to the strength of the new society in several ways. Those who came from countries with advanced political and economic institutions brought with them faith in those institutions and experience in making them work. They also brought technical and managerial skills, which contributed greatly to economic growth in the new land. Above all, they helped give America the extraordinary **social mobility** which is the essence of an open society.

❝ *There were probably as many reasons for coming to America as there were people who came. It was a highly individual decision. Yet it can be said that three large forces — religious persecution, political oppression, and economic hardship — provided the chief motives for the mass migrations to our shores.* ❞

social mobility: the possibility of changing one's class

In the community he had left, the immigrant usually had a fixed place. He would carry on his father's craft or trade; he would farm his father's land, or that small portion of it that was left to him after it was divided with his brothers. Only with the most exceptional talent and **enterprise** could he break out of the mold in which life had cast him. There was no such mold for him in the New World. Once having broken with the past, except for sentimental ties and cultural inheritance, he had to rely on his own abilities. It was the future and not the past to which he was compelled to address himself. Except for the Negro slave, he could go anywhere and do anything his talents permitted. A sprawling continent lay before him, and he had only to **weld** it together by canals, by railroads, and by roads. If he failed to achieve the dream for himself, he could still retain it for his children.

enterprise: in this context, capacity to take on a difficult project

weld: bind or attach together

This has been the foundation of American inventiveness and **ingenuity**, of the multiplicity of new enterprise, and of the success in achieving the highest standard of living anywhere in the world.

ingenuity: cleverness; inventiveness

These were the major forces that triggered this massive migration. Every immigrant served to reinforce and strengthen those elements in American society that had attracted him in the first place. The motives of some were commonplace. The motives of others were noble. Taken together they add up to the strengths and weaknesses of America.

The wisest Americans have always understood the significance of the immigrant.

After You Read

Mapping the Reading

1. According to Kennedy, what are the three main reasons immigrants come to the United States?

2. What were the physical challenges and hardships that nineteenth-century immigrants experienced to travel to the United States?

3. Once immigrants arrived, what challenges and difficulties did they commonly face, according to Kennedy?

4. Kennedy mentions many specific groups; list the nationalities that are represented. What continent or region of the world do most of these people come from?

5. What is Kennedy's attitude toward immigrants? Identify two or three passages where he most clearly shows his attitude. (You may wish to consult your "As You Read" notes.)

Discussing and Thinking Critically about the Reading

1. Kennedy offers a fairly detailed description of immigrants' journeys (the decision to leave, getting to the port, being on the ship). What purpose does this attention to detail serve? What is Kennedy trying to inspire in readers with these details?

2. Who is Kennedy's audience? That is, whom do you imagine him to be writing this essay for? What does he want readers to understand about immigrants?

3. Return to your "Before You Read" response, and reflect on how you packaged your response for the first grader. What did you emphasize, and why? What did you leave out, and why? What were you attempting to teach the first grader? What, if anything, would you change if you were answering the same question posed by a college student?

4. This essay describes some of the physical, cultural, and emotional difficulties of immigration in the nineteenth century. How do you think the nineteenth-century experience compares to the twenty-first-century experience? In what ways do you suspect immigration today is similar and different?

Navigating the Intersections

1. Who are today's immigrants compared to those of the nineteenth century? That is, from what countries are people coming? Research the question by looking at the United States Department of Homeland Security website. (Hint: Searching for "mapping immigration" will bring you to a variety of graphs and maps that will help you explore this question.)

2. This essay was written by a politician who supported immigrants and wished to make U.S. policy on immigration more open to a greater diversity of people and to make the country a more welcoming place for new immigrants. Find a speech or other text about immigration by another politician, from the past or from today, and summarize the speech, focusing on what the politician calls for.

Before You Read: Brainstorm a list of stereotypes that you've heard or seen being used to describe or label immigrants.

JOE DeGUZMAN

Joe DeGuzman is a first-generation American whose parents emigrated from the Philippines to New York in the mid-1980s. With a BA in English and Media Studies from Rutgers University, and an MA in English from Montclair State University, DeGuzman has worked as an editorial intern in the music department at W.W. Norton, and looks forward to a career in publishing or academia.

As You Read: Mark any passages where DeGuzman provides reasons for why "nativists" — or certain native-born Americans — may have been fearful or hostile toward the Irish.

Targets of Caricature*
Irish Immigrants
in Nineteenth-Century America

The dream of living in the United States, the land where "life, liberty, and the pursuit of happiness" is a founding principle, became a reality for millions of people who migrated to the United States in the nineteenth century. However, the transition into American society was challenging for many immigrants, especially those who arrived without money or resources, finding themselves without plans for either housing or employment. The newcomers often had to settle for low-paying jobs that **nativists** wouldn't take. Because many employers cut costs by hiring immigrants, nativists grew frustrated with their new neighbors, who tended to work even for the lowest of wages. By 1890, when as much as 15 percent of the country's population was foreign-born — compared to 12 percent today ("Historical") — many nativists blamed the country's problems on the immigrant population, a sentiment echoed by political cartoons.

*****caricature:** an image designed to exaggerate characteristics to make a point

nativists: not to be confused with *Native Americans* or *American Indians*, native-born Americans who held anti-immigrant views

Library of Congress cai 2a14386

Imported, duty free, by Trust, Monopoly & Co. to compete with American Labor

marginalized:
made powerless

In the late nineteenth century, the two largest immigrant populations were from Germany and Ireland. Whereas German immigrants came to the United States for a variety of reasons, including religious persecution, most Irish people immigrated to the United States to escape the Great Famine, a national crisis of disease, starvation, and death that occurred between the years 1845 and 1852. During this period, roughly one million Irish people died, and another million emigrated, many to the United States. Upon their arrival, however, the Irish were frequently **marginalized** as tensions between nativists and immigrants grew. The media, reflecting and perhaps encouraging nativists' anxiety, published stereotypical caricatures of the Irish. Many artists suggested that the Irish threatened the status quo by portraying them as apelike beasts with small heads, extended jaws, and upturned noses (Soper 263). These depictions, which were similar to caricatures of blacks in the eighteenth, nineteenth, and twentieth centuries, promoted the idea that white, Protestant Americans were superior beings. Subject to prejudice and also frequently lacking the skills required for high-wage employment, Irish workers encountered limited job offerings.

"No Irish need apply" was a disclaimer commonly found in advertisements for employment throughout the country during this time period. Low wages and a high demand for cheap housing were major causes of the crowded and unsanitary living conditions portrayed in T. De Thulstrup's "Homes of the Poor," which was published in *Harper's Weekly*.

Profit-driven landlords, who crammed families into as many tight spaces as they possibly could, cared little about their tenants' health. As seen in "Homes of the Poor" (p. 243), single rooms often served as kitchen, dining area, workspace, living room, and bedroom.

In addition to its use of generic ethnic stereotypes, the media capitalized on the Irish-Catholic identity by drawing stark contrasts between Catholicism and Protestantism. In this way, religious difference became another reason for Protestant employers to limit the primarily Catholic Irish to unskilled urban jobs, ranging from construction to domestic service.

> ❝ The media, reflecting and perhaps encouraging nativists' anxiety, published stereotypical caricatures of the Irish. Many artists suggested that the Irish threatened the status quo by portraying them as apelike beasts with small heads, extended jaws, and upturned noses. ❞

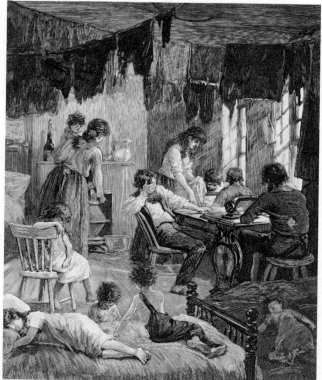

Photo courtesy of HarpWeek

"Homes of the Poor"

Library of Congress LC-USZ62-118126

THE BALANCE OF TRADE WITH GREAT BRITAIN SEEMS TO BE STILL AGAINST US.
650 Paupers arrived at Boston in the Steamship *Nestoria*, April 15th, from Galway, Ireland, shipped by the British Government.

"The Balance of Trade with Great Britain Seems to Be Still against Us"

650 Paupers arrived at Boston in the Steamship Nestoria, April 15th, from Galway, Ireland, shipped by the British Government

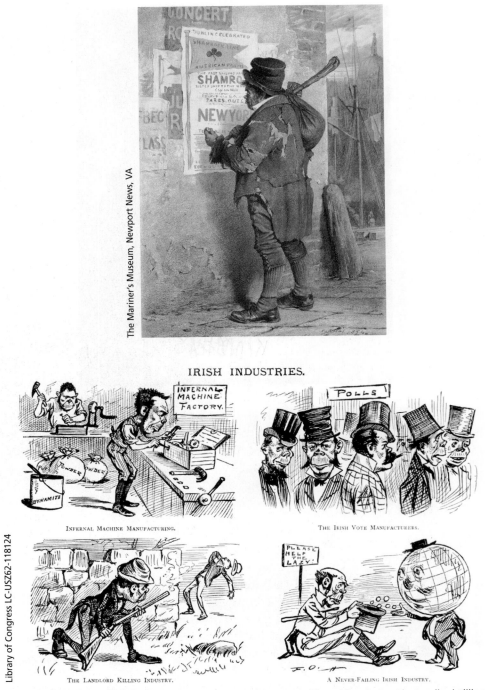

The Mariner's Museum, Newport News, VA

Library of Congress LC-USZ62-118124

(Clockwise from top right) *The Irish Vote Manufacturers; A Never-Failing Irish Industry; The Landlord Killing Industry; Infernal Machine Manufacturing*

Library of Congress LC-USZ62-57340

The ignorant vote

To the nativists, the Irish Catholics lacked the Protestant work ethic required to survive in the United States. Scholar and cartoonist Kerry Soper writes:

> Scapegoating the Irish gave the dominant "white" culture an opportunity to define itself in positive contrast to a laughable minority on the margins. Specifically, the Irish were held in contempt because they were Catholic (thus lacking the essential Protestant work ethic needed to survive in America); because they spoke English in a manner that seemed unschooled to Anglo ears; because they tended to resist full assimilation, sticking to their traditions and ethnic circles; and because they only seemed qualified to engage in blue-collar work. (265)

As the Irish fought for their right to jobs, they confronted the challenge of distinguishing themselves from blacks, who were also marginalized and **relegated** to the same low-paying employment opportunities by the white ruling class.

As the Catholic Church established new parish communities, charities, and **parochial schools** in the United States, a Thomas Nast cartoon from February 19, 1870, captured the anxiety that nativists felt about Catholics, who were seen as threatening the separation of church and state, a principle protected by the United States Constitution.

relegated: put in a lower position

parochial schools: private religious schools connected to a church or congregation

Photo courtesy of HarpWeek

monarchs: rulers (kings or queens)

The image depicts European **monarchs** tearing a banner marked "church" and "state," while American Catholics attempt to stitch the banner together. Nativists also considered the Irish immigrants as a nuisance because they were unwilling to assimilate into American culture, instead retaining the traditions and religion of their homeland (Soper 265). C. J. Taylor's "The Mortar of Assimilation" (p. 247), which was printed in the humor magazine *Puck* in 1889, represents this resistance dramatically, portraying a knife-wielding Irishman on the rim of the melting pot, embodying "the one element that won't mix."

propensity: strong, often natural tendency

Taylor's cartoon also plays on the nativist view of the Irish as drunkards with a **propensity** for violence.

This belief is captured more fully by Nast's "The Day We Celebrate" (p. 248), which depicts the Irish as bloodthirsty, rum-induced primates who commemorate St. Patrick's Day not through solemn prayer, but by attacking the police.

Concerned that Irish and other Catholic immigrants would have too great a say in politics, the nativist push for immigrant exclusion from politics and elected office culminated in the mid-1800s with the founding of the Order of the Star Spangled Banner, a secret society that lobbied for restrictions on immigrant rights, and support for the "Know Nothing" political party, which operated on a pro-Protestant, anti-immigrant platform.

At the city and state levels, Know Nothing politicians passed laws that disbanded Irish **militia** companies, delayed the citizenship process, and limited the Catholic Church's political influence (Cortés 1299).

THE MORTAR OF ASSIMILATION — AND THE ONE ELEMENT THAT WON'T MIX.

The mortar of assimilation — and the one element that won't mix

The Newberry Library, Chicago, Call #A57634, Vol. 25, P. 304

militia: group of citizens with some military training, to be called upon in an emergency

Some protests inspired by the Order of the Star Spangled Banner and the Know Nothings were deadly. During the Philadelphia nativist riots in 1844, for example, Catholic churches were set ablaze against the backdrop of a clash between Catholics and Protestants over which version of the Bible should be read in public schools (Dionne).

Catholic-Protestant tensions in the United States have greatly decreased since the mid-1800s, with Irish American assimilation symbolized for many

TAKING A "SMILE"

Library of Congress

Archive Photos/Getty Images

Photo courtesy of HarpWeek

"The Day We Celebrate"

Photo courtesy of HarpWeek

Orange head-quarters, corner Twenty-Ninth Street and Eighth Avenue

Library of Congress LC-USZ62-121400

when John F. Kennedy, an Irish American from Boston, became president of the United States in 1961. Yet nativism continues to be present in American politics, today directed at new immigrant groups whom some perceive as threats. And whereas stereotypical depictions of immigrants in the nineteenth-century media were often limited to cartoons, opportunities to use the media for propaganda today are virtually limitless. Now, in the early twenty-first century, it's fair to wonder whether the country will learn from history or be doomed to repeat its mistakes.

Works Cited

Cortés, Carlos E. *Multicultural America: A Multimedia Encyclopedia.* SAGE Reference, 2013.

Dionne, E. J., Jr. "Why the Culture War Is the Wrong War." *The Atlantic,* The Atlantic Monthly Group, Jan./Feb. 2006, www.theatlantic.com/magazine/archive/2006/01/why-the-culture-war-is-the-wrong-war/304502/.

"Historical Census Statistics on the Foreign-Born Population." *Random Samplings,* U.S. Census Bureau, 4 Jan. 2011, blogs.census.gov/2011/01/04/historical-census-statistics-on-the-foreign-born-population/.

Soper, Kerry. "From Swarthy Ape to Sympathetic Everyman and Subversive Trickster: The Development of Irish Caricature in American Comic Strips between 1890 and 1920." *Journal of American Studies,* vol. 39, no. 2, Aug. 2005, pp. 257–96.

After You Read

Mapping the Reading

1. According to DeGuzman, who were nativists? What fears did they have about the Irish immigrants? (You may wish to consult your "As You Read" notes.)

2. What stereotypes did Irish immigrants face in the 1800s?

3. What was the Know Nothing party, and what did it stand for?

4. According to DeGuzman, how is the contemporary American response to immigrants similar to nineteenth-century American responses?

5. Closely study one of the cartoons that DeGuzman includes in his article. What do you find most striking about it, and why?

Discussing and Thinking Critically about the Reading

1. Respond to this reading: How aware were you of the troubles that nineteenth-century Irish immigrants faced when they came to the United States? In your opinion, have Irish immigrants and their descendants overcome the stereotypes and prejudices they faced? Why or why not?

2. How do the stereotypes about Irish immigrants compare to the stereotypes you brainstormed in your "Before You Read" list? How have stereotypes about immigrants stayed the same? How have they changed?

3. In the nineteenth century, most native-born Americans were Protestant, and most Irish immigrants were Catholic. Why do you think this difference created tension between the two groups?

4. Select one of the reproduced images and analyze it closely, imagining that you are a nineteenth-century Irish immigrant viewing the image after a twelve-hour day working in construction or domestic service. Write a response to the image from that perspective.

5. Now take on the opposite perspective: Write a response to the selected image, this time imagining yourself as a nativist.

Navigating the Intersections

1. The histories of immigration that Joe DeGuzman and John F. Kennedy present are very different. Briefly characterize how each author describes the immigrant experience, and then consider why the two have such different points of view.

2. For this exercise, choose one of the following activities:

   a. If you have an immigrant in your family or in your circle of friends, interview that person about her or his immigrant experience. Before sitting down to have the conversation, draft five questions to ask your interviewee. The best questions are open ended, which is to say they cannot be answered with a yes, a no, or another short answer.

   OR

   b. Select an immigrant population you are interested in, such as Indian, Italian, or Japanese, and type the name of the group and "immigrant stereotypical cartoons" into a search engine to see what images come up. Select a few of these cartoons and compare them to the images in this article. How are they both similar and different? What do your findings suggest about the experiences of different immigrant groups or about the experiences of immigrants from different periods?

Before You Read: Take five or ten minutes to write briefly in response to these two questions: Why do people immigrate? What kinds of challenges do immigrants face?

ISABEL WILKERSON

Isabel Wilkerson won a Pulitzer Prize in Journalism in 1994 for her coverage in the *New York Times* of a Midwestern flood and her profile of a fourth grader from Chicago's South Side; she was the first African American woman to win a Pulitzer Prize and the first African American to win for individual reporting. Wilkerson has taught journalism and narrative nonfiction at many colleges and universities, and is an active speaker. The following excerpt is from her book *The Warmth of Other Suns: The Epic Story of America's Great Migration*, which has received several awards, including the 2010 National Book Critics Circle Award and the 2011 NAACP Image Award for best literary debut.

As You Read: Make note of the hardships that the migrants experienced because of prejudice and discrimination.

The Epic Story of America's Great Migration*

*Great Migration: movement of six million African Americans from the South to the North

The Great Migration, 1915–70

They fled as if under a spell or a high fever. "They left as though they were fleeing some curse," wrote the scholar Emmett J. Scott. "They were willing to make almost any sacrifice to obtain a railroad ticket, and they left with the intention of staying."

From the early years of the twentieth century to well past its middle age, nearly every black family in the American South, which meant nearly every black family in America, had a decision to make. There were **sharecroppers** losing at settlement. Typists wanting to work in an office. Yard boys scared that a single gesture near the planter's wife could leave them hanging from an oak tree. They were all stuck in a **caste system** as hard and unyielding as the red Georgia clay, and they each had a decision before them. In this, they were not unlike anyone who ever longed to cross the Atlantic or the **Rio Grande**.

It was during the **First World War** that a silent **pilgrimage** took its first steps within the borders of this country. The fever rose without warning or notice or much in the way of understanding by those outside its reach. It would not end until the 1970s and would set into motion changes in the North and South that no one, not even the people doing the leaving, could have imagined at the start of it or dreamed would take nearly a lifetime to play out.

Historians would call it the Great Migration. It would become perhaps the biggest underreported story of the twentieth century. It was vast. It was leaderless. It crept along so many thousands of currents over so long a stretch of time as to be difficult for the press truly to capture while it was under way.

Over the course of six decades, some six million black southerners left the land of their forefathers and fanned out across the country for an uncertain existence in nearly every other corner of America. The Great Migration would become a turning point in history. It would transform urban America and recast the social and political order of every city it touched. It would force the South to search its soul and finally to lay aside a **feudal** caste system. It grew out of the unmet promises made after the **Civil War** and, through the sheer weight of it, helped push the country toward the civil rights revolutions of the 1960s. . . .

The people did not cross the turnstiles of **customs** at Ellis Island. They were already citizens. But where they came from, they were not treated as such. Their every step was controlled by **meticulous** laws of **Jim Crow**, a nineteenth-century minstrel figure that would become shorthand for the violently enforced codes of the southern caste system. The Jim Crow regime persisted from the 1880s to the 1960s, some eighty years, the average life span of

sharecroppers: farmers who pay much of the value of their crops to a landlord

caste system: a rigid social system that defines people by wealth, occupation, or hereditary status

Rio Grande: a river that marks the border between the United States and Mexico

First World War: 1914–18

pilgrimage: long journey, often religious in purpose

feudal: from the Middle Ages; a very unequal social system

Civil War: 1861–65

customs: immigration processing center

meticulous: precise

Jim Crow: racist laws enforcing racial segregation; for example, Jim Crow prevented blacks from eating in "white" restaurants

> **❝** *The Great Migration was the final break from an abusive union with the South. It was a step in freeing not just the people who fled, but the country whose mountains they crossed.* **❞**

afflicted: caused suffering or trouble

Great Depression: severe, worldwide economic depression, 1930 to mid-1940s

menial: unskilled

Works Progress Administration: government agency created in 1935; employed millions of Americans to work on such projects as building roads and bridges

foremen: supervisors

finite: limited, with an end time or date

anthropologist: a person who studies the science of humanity and human culture

a fairly healthy man. It **afflicted** the lives of at least four generations and would not die without bloodshed, as the people who left the South foresaw. . . .

Chicago, Early 1939: [George and] Ida Mae Gladney

George and Ida Mae had been in the North for close to two years. They had three little ones to feed and were still having trouble finding work. They had arrived in the depths of the **Great Depression** with the fewest skills any migrant could have but with the most modest of expectations and the strongest of backs. They had taken their chances and found even the most **menial** jobs hard to come by.

Anything with the least amount of status or job security seemed reserved for people who did not look like them and often spoke with an accent from a small eastern European country they had never heard of. They were running into the same sentiment, albeit on a humbler level, that a colored man in Philadelphia faced when he answered an ad for a position as a store clerk. "What do you suppose we'd want of a Negro?" the storekeeper asked the applicant.

George had been struggling since he arrived. He had worked on a coal truck, dug ditches for the **Works Progress Administration**, delivered ice to the tenements on the South Side, and been turned away from places that said they weren't hiring or just had nothing for him. He would just keep looking until he found something.

Finally, he landed a job that suited his temperament on the soup-making line at the Campbell Soup plant, a place so big there was bound to be some work for him if the people were open to hiring him, which, fortunately for him, they were. The plant was on the twenty-two acres at Thirty-Fifth and Western by the panhandle tracks, where they mixed several thousand tomatoes and oxtails at a time to make soup for customers west of the Mississippi. He had been working all his life, but this was the first indoor job he had ever had.

His days would now turn on the directions of **foremen** and the spinning of machinery, the orderly and **finite** ticking of the company punch clock instead of the rhythms of the field, where he and Ida Mae used to work according to what an **anthropologist** once called "the great clocks of the sky." The plant turned out six thousand cans of soup a minute along three miles of tracks and switches. He was entering the world of assembly-line factory culture, the final destination of many unskilled black southerners once they got established in the North. Whatever reception he got, good or bad, he kept it to himself, as was his way, and he carried out whatever duties he was to perform without complaint, whatever kind of soup was coming down the vats in his direction.

Like so many others, he had gone from the mind-numbing sameness of picking cotton to the mind-numbing sameness of turning a lever or twisting a widget or stroking a flame for one tiny piece of a much larger thing he had no control over. He had moved to a different part of the country but was on the same **rung of the ladder**. It was, in some ways, not all that different from picking cotton. The raw boils went off to some mill in Atlanta or Massachusetts to be made into something refined and unrecognizable from what he saw of it, from the poorly **remunerated** kernel of the thing that represented George's and other sharecropper's contribution to the final product intended for someone far better off than he. Except now, in Chicago, he would get paid.

Just by being able to keep his job, which he would for many years, George would be spared the **contentious** relations at so many plants in the North, where the migrants were scorned if they were hired at all, or outright turned away. Most migrants like George were hired into either menial labor — janitors or window cleaners or assembly-line workers — or hard labor — longshoremen, coal miners, strikers of foundries, and diggers of ditches, which is what he had done before landing the assembly-line job at Campbell Soup.

Many companies simply didn't hire colored workers at all but for altogether different reasons from the South. It wasn't because of an explicit **Berlin Wall** of exclusion, written into law and so engrained as to not need to be spelled out for people on either side, as in the South. Instead, in the North, companies and unions said that, however much they might want to hire colored people, their white workers just wouldn't stand for it. And, for the sake of morale, the companies and unions weren't going to force the issue. . . .

By the time George managed to find steady work, he was joining the 40 percent of black men doing unskilled or semiskilled work in Chicago in the 1940s. Another 34 percent of black men were working as servants, meaning that, for three out of four black men, the only work they could get was work that nobody else wanted — lowly and menial or hard, dangerous, and dirty. Nearly the **inverse** was true for white men, the majority of whom — some 60 percent — were doing skilled, clerical, business, or professional work, clean indoor jobs.

The ceiling was even lower and the options fewer for colored women, a situation that was making it even harder for Ida Mae to find work. By 1940, two out of every three colored women in Chicago were servants, as against 17 percent of white women (most of those newly arrived immigrants). Only a fraction of colored women — a mere 7 percent — were hired to do clerical work — a common and upstanding position for women of the day — compared to 43 percent of white women.

Under these conditions, Ida Mae and George found themselves at the bottom looking up at the layers of immigrants, native-born white people, and even northern-born black people who were stacked above them in the economic **hierarchy** of the North. . . .

rung of the ladder: expression that refers to social class as a ladder with rungs to climb

remunerated: paid

contentious: controversial, with much disagreement

Berlin Wall: wall separating East (communist) and West (capitalist) Germany from 1961 to 1989

inverse: opposite

hierarchy: system in which people or groups are ranked by status

A central argument of [mine] has been that the Great Migration was an unrecognized immigration within this country. The participants bore the marks of immigrant behavior. They plotted a course to places in the North and West that had some connection to their homes of origin. They created colonies of the villages they came from, imported the food and folkways of the Old Country, and built their lives around the people and churches they knew from back home. They took work the people already there considered beneath them. They doubled up and took in roomers to make ends meet. They tried to instill in their children the values of the Old Country while pressing them to succeed by the standards of the New World they were in.

As with immigrant parents, a generational divide arose between the migrants and their children. The migrants couldn't understand their impatient, northern-bred sons and daughters — why the children who had been spared the heartache of a racial caste system were not more grateful to have been delivered from the South. The children couldn't relate to the stories of southern **persecution** when they were facing gangs and drive-by shootings, or, in the more elite circles, the embarrassment of southern parents with accents and peasant food when the children were trying to fit into the middle-class **enclave** of the North.

And though this immigration theory may be structurally sound, with sociologists even calling them immigrants in the early years of the Migration, nearly every black migrant I interviewed **vehemently** resisted the immigrant label. They did not see themselves as immigrants under any circumstances, their behavior notwithstanding. The idea **conjured** up the deepest pains of centuries of rejection by their own country. They had been forced to become immigrants in their own land just to secure their freedom. But they were not immigrants and had never been actual immigrants. The South may have acted like a different country and been proud of it, but it was a part of the United States, and anyone born there was born an American.

The black people who left were citizens, and many of their forebears had been in this land before the country was founded. They were among the first nonnative people to set foot in the New World, brought by the Europeans to build it from wilderness and doing so without pay and by force from the time of the first arrivals in 1619 to their **emancipation** 246 years later. For twelve generations, their ancestors had worked the land and helped build the country. Into the twentieth century, their fourth century in America, they still had had to step aside and fall further down the economic ladder with each new wave of immigrants from all over the world, after generations as burden bearers.

It is one of those circular facts of history that, in the three great receiving cities to which southern blacks fled . . . , blacks had been among the first nonnatives to set foot on the soil and to establish settlements centuries before. Black **mestizos** were among the forty-four Mexican settlers arriving in 1781 at the **pueblo** that would become Los Angeles. Jean Baptiste Point DuSable, a fur

---

persecution: poor treatment because of race, religion, or political beliefs

enclave: community in which the people are somehow different from those in the nearby areas

vehemently: strongly; angrily

conjured: brought to mind as if by a magic spell

emancipation: freeing from slavery

mestizos: people of mixed race, especially of mixed American Indian and Spanish

pueblo: an American Indian settlement in the Southwest

trader born of an African slave woman in Haiti, built, in 1779, the first perma-nent settlement in what is now known as Chicago. Jan Rodrigues, a sailor of African descent working for and later abandoned by Dutch merchants on an untamed island in the New World, created the first trading post on what is now known as Manhattan, in 1613.

And so when blacks who had migrated north and west showed resentment at being considered immigrants, it was perhaps because they knew in their bones that their ancestors had been here before there was a United States of America and that it took their leaving the South to achieve the citizenship they deserved by their ancestry and labors alone. That freedom and those rights had not come automatically as they should have, but centuries late and of the migrants' own accord.

With the benefit of hindsight, the century between **Reconstruction** and the end of the Great Migration perhaps may be seen as a necessary stage of upheaval. It was a transition from an era when one race owned another; to an era when the dominant class gave up ownership but kept control over the people it had once owned, at all costs, using violence even; to the eventual acceptance of the servant caste into the mainstream.

Reconstruction: the twelve-year period after the U.S. Civil War when new rights for African Americans were introduced

The Great Migration was the final break from an abusive union with the South. It was a step in freeing not just the people who fled, but the country whose mountains they crossed. Their **exodus** left a still imperfect but far dif-ferent landscape than before the Migration began.

exodus: exit of many people from the same place at the same time

It was, if nothing else, an affirmation of the power of an individual deci-sion, however powerless the individual might appear on the surface. "In the simple process of walking away one by one," wrote the scholar Lawrence R. Rodgers, "millions of African-American southerners have altered the course of their own, and all of America's history."

Over the decades, perhaps the wrong questions have been asked about the Great Migration. Perhaps it is not a question of whether the migrants brought good or ill to the cities they fled to or were pushed or pulled to their destinations, but a question of how they summoned the courage to leave in the first place or how they found the will to press beyond the forces against them and the faith in a country that had rejected them for so long. By their actions, they did not dream the Ameri-can Dream, they willed it into being by a definition of their own choosing. They did not ask to be accepted but declared themselves the Americans that perhaps few others recognized but that they had always been deep within their hearts.

After You Read

Mapping the Reading

1. According to Wilkerson, what is the Great Migration? When, where, and why did it occur?

2. What opportunities did migrants have in the North that they did not have in the South?

3. What hardships did migrants face in first journeying to the North and then living there? (You may wish to consult your "As You Read" notes.)

4. According to Wilkerson, how was the experience of *migration* from South to North by African Americans similar to the experience of *immigration* by people from outside the United States? How was it different?

5. How were George and Ida Mae Gladney's experiences in the North both similar to and different from their experiences in the South?

Discussing and Thinking Critically about the Reading

1. If you already knew about the Great Migration, what did you know and how did you know it? If you had never heard about the Great Migration, why do you think you didn't know about this part of American history?

2. In this excerpt, Wilkerson offers the example of two migrants, George and Ida Mae Gladney. What do their experiences illustrate about the Great Migration? That is, what does Wilkerson want readers to learn from their story?

3. Wilkerson argues that the Great Migration is an "unrecognized immigration." How effectively has she made the case that it is appropriate and reasonable to consider "internal immigrants" when discussing immigration? What are her strongest points and weakest points, and why?

4. Wilkerson notes that many of the participants in the Great Migration that she interviewed objected to being seen as immigrants. Why? How does their perspective affect your view of the Great Migration?

Navigating the Intersections

1. How do the experiences of George and Ida Mae Gladney compare to the experiences of immigrants described by John F. Kennedy or Joe DeGuzman?

2. Interview someone you know who has family who experienced the Great Migration. When did they migrate? from where? for what reason? Where did they move to, and what kinds of experiences awaited them in their new city or town?

3. Select an immigrant group whose stories of immigration are familiar to you from readings in this book, your own family history, or from other reading, and compare and contrast what you know about that group's experience with what you've learned from Isabel Wilkerson about the experience of the people who migrated from the South to the North as part of the Great Migration.

   a. Why did they immigrate?

   b. How did they travel?

   c. Where did they go?

   d. What challenges did they face when they arrived at their destination?

   e. How did their arrival change the place they settled in?

Today's Immigrant Voices

Before You Read: Choose one of the following questions, and then write briefly for a few minutes about names:

a. Have you or someone you know ever wanted to change his or her name? If so, why?

b. Do you know anyone who has an "American name" that he or she uses instead of his or her given name? Who gave the person the American name? Why and when does the person use it?

c. What do you like most about your name, and why? What do you dislike about it, and why?

FIROOZEH DUMAS

Writer Firoozeh Dumas was born in Iran and moved to the United States permanently in 1974, when she was nine. She has written two books: the international best seller *Funny in Farsi: A Memoir of Growing Up Iranian in America* (2003) and *Laughing without an Accent: Adventures of a Global Citizen* (2008). Dumas's essays have appeared in the *New York Times*, the *Los Angeles Times*, *Good Housekeeping*, and *Gourmet*, among other publications. This selection is from *Funny in Farsi*.

As You Read: Underline, highlight, or otherwise mark those passages where Dumas discusses how people treat her because of her name.

The "F Word"

My cousin's name, Farbod, means "Greatness." When he moved to America, all the kids called him "Farthead." My brother Farshid ("He Who Enlightens") became "Fartshit." The name of my friend Neggar means "Beloved," although it can be more accurately translated as "She Whose Name Also Incites Riots." Her brother Arash ("Giver") initially couldn't understand why every time he'd say his name, people would laugh and ask him if it itched.

All of us immigrants knew that moving to America would be **fraught** with challenges, but none of us thought that our names would be such an obstacle. How could our parents have ever imagined that someday we would end up in a country where **monosyllabic** names reign supreme, a land where "William" is shortened to "Bill," where "Susan" becomes "Sue," and where "Richard" somehow evolves into "Dick"? America is a great country, but nobody without a mask and a cape has a *z* in his name. And have Americans ever realized the great scope of the **guttural** sounds they're missing? Okay, so it has to do with

fraught: filled with (something dangerous); causing stress or anxiety

monosyllabic: having just one syllable

guttural: formed in the throat (e.g., the sound "kh")

> " *When I was twelve, I decided to simplify my life by adding an American middle name. This decision serves as proof that sometimes simplifying one's life in the short run only complicates it in the long run.* "

linguistic roots, but I do believe this would be a richer country if all Americans could do a little tongue aerobics and learn to pronounce "kh," a sound more commonly associated in this culture with phlegm, or "gh," the sound usually made by actors in the final moments of a choking scene. It's like adding a few nice spices to the kitchen pantry. Move over, cinnamon and nutmeg, make way for cardamom and sumac.

Exotic analogies aside, having a foreign name in this land of Joes and Marys is a pain in the spice cabinet. When I was twelve, I decided to simplify my life by adding an American middle name. This decision serves as proof that sometimes simplifying one's life in the short run only complicates it in the long run.

My name, Firoozeh, chosen by my mother, means "Turquoise" in Persian. In America, it means "Unpronounceable" or "I'm Not Going to Talk to You Because I Cannot Possibly Learn Your Name and I Just Don't Want to Have to Ask You Again and Again Because You'll Think I'm Dumb or You Might Get Upset or Something." My father, incidentally, had wanted to name me Sara. I do wish he had won that argument.

To strengthen my decision to add an American name, I had just finished fifth grade in Whittier, where all the kids incessantly called me "Ferocious." That summer, my family moved to Newport Beach, where I looked forward to starting a new life. I wanted to be a kid with a name that didn't draw so much attention, a name that didn't come with a built-in **inquisition** as to when and why I had moved to America and how was it that I spoke English without an accent and was I planning on going back and what did I think of America?

inquisition: harsh, unfair questioning

My last name didn't help any. I can't mention my maiden name, because: "Dad, I'm writing a memoir."

"Great. Just don't mention our name."

suffice it to say: more information could be given, but what follows is enough

Suffice it to say that, with eight letters, including a *z*, and four syllables, my last name is as difficult and foreign as my first. My first and last name together generally served the same purpose as a high brick wall. There was one exception to this rule. In Berkeley, and only in Berkeley, my name drew people like flies to **baklava**. These were usually people named Amaryllis or Chrysanthemum, types who vacationed in Costa Rica and to whom lentils described a type of burger. These folks were probably not the pride of **Poughkeepsie**, but they were refreshingly nonjudgmental.

baklava: a Middle Eastern pastry of nuts and honey

Poughkeepsie: a small industrial city north of New York City

When I announced to my family that I wanted to add an American name, they reacted with their usual laughter. Never one to let mockery or good judgment stand in my way, I proceeded to ask for suggestions. My father suggested, "Fifi." Had I had a special **affinity** for French poodles or been considering a career in prostitution, I would've gone with that one. My mom suggested

affinity: connection or closeness with

"Farah," a name easier than "Firoozeh" yet still Iranian. Her reasoning made sense, except that **Farrah Fawcett** was at the height of her popularity and I didn't want to be associated with somebody whose poster hung in every **post-pubescent** boy's bedroom. We couldn't think of any American names beginning with *F*, so we moved on to *J*, the first letter of our last name. I don't know why we limited ourselves to names beginning with my initials, but it made sense at that moment, perhaps by the logic employed moments before bungee jumping. I finally chose the name "Julie" mainly for its simplicity. My brothers, Farid and Farshid, thought that adding an American name was totally stupid. They later became Fred and Sean.

That same afternoon, our doorbell rang. It was our new next-door neighbor, a friendly girl my age named Julie. She asked me my name and after a moment of hesitation, I introduced myself as Julie. "What a coincidence!" she said. I didn't mention that I had been Julie for only half an hour.

Thus I started sixth grade with my new, easy name and life became infinitely simpler. People actually remembered my name, which was an entirely refreshing new sensation. All was well until the **Iranian Revolution**, when I found myself with a new set of problems. Because I spoke English without an accent and was known as Julie, people assumed I was American. This meant that I was often **privy** to their real feelings about those "damn I-raynians." It was like having those X-ray glasses that let you see people naked, except that what I was seeing was far uglier than people's underwear. It dawned on me that these people would have probably never invited me to their houses had they known me as Firoozeh. I felt like a fake.

When I went to college, I eventually went back to using my real name. All was well until I graduated and started looking for a job. Even though I had graduated with honors from UC-Berkeley, I couldn't get a single interview. I was guilty of being a humanities major, but I began to suspect there was more to my problems. After three months of rejections I added "Julie" to my resume. Call it coincidence, but the job offers starting coming in. Perhaps it's the same kind of coincidence that keeps African Americans from getting cabs in New York.

Once I got married, my name became Julie Dumas. I went from having an identifiable "ethnic" name to having **ancestors who wore clogs**. My family and non-American friends continued calling me Firoozeh, while my coworkers and American friends called me Julie. My life become one big knot, especially when friends who knew me as Julie met friends who knew me as Firoozeh. I felt like those characters in soap operas who have an evil twin. The two, of course, can never be in the same room since they're played by the same person, a struggling actress who wears a wig to play one of the twins and dreams of moving on to bigger and better roles. I couldn't blame my mess on a screenwriter; it was my own doing.

Farrah Fawcett: American actress who rose to stardom in the 1970s by starring in *Charlie's Angels*; her bathing suit poster sold twenty million copies

postpubescent: after reaching puberty, early to mid-teens

Iranian Revolution: 1978–79

privy: in the know about

ancestors who wore clogs: Pierre Dumas was a maker of shoes

I decided to untangle the knot once and for all by going back to my real name. By then, I was a stay-at-home mom, so I really didn't care whether people remembered my name or gave me job interviews. Besides, most of the people I dealt with were in diapers and were in no position to judge. I was also living in **Silicon Valley**, an area filled with people named Rajeev, Avishai, and Insook.

Every once in a while, though, somebody comes up with a new **permutation** and I am once again reminded that I am an immigrant with a foreign name. I recently went to have blood drawn for a physical exam. The waiting room for blood work at our local medical clinic is in the basement of the building, and no matter how early one arrives for an appointment, forty coughing, wheezing people have gotten there first. Apart from reading *Golf Digest* and *Popular Mechanics*, there isn't much to do except guess the number of contagious diseases represented in the windowless room. Every ten minutes, a name is called and everyone looks to see which cough matches the name. As I waited patiently, the receptionist called out, "Fritzy, Fritzy!" Everyone looked around, but no one stood up. Usually, if I'm waiting to be called by someone who doesn't know me, I will respond to just about any name starting with an *F*. Having been called Froozy, Frizzy, Fiorucci, and Frooz and just plain "Uhhhh . . . ," I am highly accommodating. I did not, however, respond to "Fritzy" because there is, as far as I know, no *t* in my name. The receptionist tried again, "Fritzy, Fritzy DumbAss." As I stood up to this most **linguistically** original version of my name, I could feel all eyes upon me. The room was momentarily silent as all of these sick people sat united in a moment of gratitude for their own names.

Despite a few exceptions, I have found that Americans are now far more willing to learn new names, just as they're far more willing to try new ethnic foods. Of course, some people just don't like to learn. One mom at my children's school **adamantly** refused to learn my "impossible" name and instead settled on calling me "F Word." She was recently transferred to New York where, from what I've heard, she might meet an immigrant or two and, who knows, she just might have to make some room in her spice cabinet.

Silicon Valley: area near San Francisco, California, that is home to many technology companies

permutation: version or arrangement

linguistically: related to languages or their study

adamantly: firmly; unwilling to change one's mind

After You Read

Mapping the Reading

1. Why does Dumas change her name from Firoozeh to Julie?

2. Why does she change her name back to Firoozeh?

3. In what ways do the author's names—both Firoozeh and Julie—create a barrier in her interactions with other people?

4.   What are two of the funniest experiences that Dumas has because of her name? (Refer to your "As You Read" notes to help you answer.)

5.   What are two of the saddest or most maddening experiences that Dumas has because of her name? (Refer to your "As You Read" notes to help you answer.)

Discussing and Thinking Critically about the Reading

1.   Write your own name biography, as Dumas has. Tell the story of your name, describing your own feeling about it as well as how people have responded to it as you have grown up. Consider especially whether your name was ever a source for teasing, whether it reveals your ethnic or national background, and whether people respond to it differently depending on the region or situation you are in.

2.   Dumas tells her story with humor. How does the humor affect the message of her personal narrative? Does it make it stronger or weaker? How so?

3.   Dumas makes a few references to spices and to spice cabinets in this personal narrative. What is she comparing spices to in these moments?

4.   If you had been in Dumas's position as a child, do you think you would have changed your name? Why or why not?

5.   Beyond entertaining her audience, what does Dumas want readers to learn from her experiences? What questions does her essay raise about the degree to which society asks its citizens to conform to mainstream American culture?

Navigating the Intersections

1.   Early in her narrative, Firoozeh Dumas observes: "All of us immigrants knew that moving to America would be fraught with challenges, but none of us thought that our names would be such an obstacle." Review the other readings in this chapter discussing immigrants' experiences, and describe what unexpected obstacles they faced. How are these obstacles similar or different to the obstacles Dumas describes?

2.   For this exercise, choose one of the following activities:

    a.   Research your own family's history with name changes. Has anyone changed his or her first or last name for reasons other than marriage? Or has anyone had his or her name changed by someone else? See if you can find a name-change story in your family history, and tell that story, being sure to include the reason the name was changed. If you cannot find any evidence of a name change in your family history, reflect on why that is the case—in other words, what about your family's names make them resistant to change?

    OR

    b.   Go to a search engine and research "changing immigrant names" to find an article explaining this phenomenon. Be sure to find an article that is published by a legitimate news outlet or governmental organization.

Before You Read: In your own words, without doing any research, explain the difference between a documented and an undocumented immigrant.

JOSE ANTONIO VARGAS

Jose Antonio Vargas is an award-winning journalist, filmmaker, and immigration activist. Born in the Philippines, he moved to California when he was twelve to be raised by his grandparents. In 2008, Vargas, who was a reporter for the *Washington Post*, received a Pulitzer Prize for his part in reporting on the Virginia Tech shootings. As a filmmaker, Vargas was the writer and coproducer of a documentary about AIDS in Washington, D.C., called *The Other City* (2010), and also the writer and producer of the autobiographical film *Documented: A Film by an Undocumented American* (2013). This essay was published in the *New York Times* in 2011.

As You Read: Mark those passages where Vargas describes his feelings about being an undocumented immigrant.

My Life as an Undocumented Immigrant

One August morning nearly two decades ago, my mother woke me and put me in a cab. She handed me a jacket. *"Baka malamig doon"* were among the few words she said. ("It might be cold there.") When I arrived at the Philippines' Ninoy Aquino International Airport with her, my aunt, and a family friend, I was introduced to a man I'd never seen. They told me he was my uncle. He held my hand as I boarded an airplane for the first time. It was 1993, and I was twelve.

My mother wanted to give me a better life, so she sent me thousands of miles away to live with her parents in America — my grandfather (*Lolo* in **Tagalog**) and grandmother (*Lola*). After I arrived in Mountain View, California, in the San Francisco Bay Area, I entered sixth grade and quickly grew to love my new home, family, and culture. I discovered a passion for language, though it was hard to learn the difference between formal English and American slang. One of my early memories is of a freckled kid in middle school asking me, "What's up?" I replied, "The sky," and he and a couple of other kids laughed. I won the eighth-grade spelling bee by memorizing words I couldn't properly pronounce. (The winning word was *indefatigable*.)

One day when I was sixteen, I rode my bike to the nearby DMV office to get my driver's permit. Some of my friends already had their licenses, so I figured it was time. But when I handed the clerk my green card as proof of U.S. residency, she flipped it around, examining it. "This is fake," she whispered. "Don't come back here again."

Tagalog: one of the languages spoken in the Philippines

Confused and scared, I pedaled home and confronted Lolo. I remember him sitting in the garage, cutting coupons. I dropped my bike and ran over to him, showing him the green card. *"Peke ba ito?"* I asked in Tagalog. ("Is this fake?") My grandparents were **naturalized American citizens** — he worked as a security guard, she as a food server — and they had begun supporting my mother and me financially when I was three, after my father's **wandering eye** and inability to properly provide for us led to my parents' separation. Lolo was a proud man, and I saw the shame on his face as he told me he purchased the card, along with other fake documents, for me. "Don't show it to other people," he warned.

I decided then that I could never give anyone reason to doubt I was an American. I convinced myself that if I worked enough, if I achieved enough, I would be rewarded with citizenship. I felt I could earn it.

I've tried. Over the past fourteen years, I've graduated from high school and college and built a career as a journalist, interviewing some of the most famous people in the country. On the surface, I've created a good life. I've lived the American dream.

But I am still an undocumented immigrant. And that means living a different kind of reality. It means going about my day in fear of being found out. It means rarely trusting people, even those closest to me, with who I really am. It means keeping my family photos in a shoebox rather than displaying them on shelves in my home, so friends don't ask about them. It means reluctantly, even painfully, doing things I know are wrong and unlawful. And it has meant relying on a sort of twenty-first-century **underground railroad** of supporters, people who took an interest in my future and took risks for me.

Last year I read about four students who walked from Miami to Washington to lobby for the DREAM Act, a nearly decade-old immigration bill that would provide a path to legal **permanent residency** for young people who have been educated in this country. At the risk of **deportation** — the Obama administration has deported almost eight hundred thousand people in the last two years — they are speaking out. Their courage has inspired me.

There are believed to be eleven million undocumented immigrants in the United States. We're not always who you think we are. Some pick your strawberries or care for your children. Some are in high school or college. And some, it turns out, write news articles you might read. I grew up here. This is my home. Yet even though I think of myself as an American and consider America my country, my country doesn't think of me as one of its own.

My first challenge was the language. Though I learned English in the Philippines, I wanted to lose my accent. During high school, I spent hours at a time watching television (especially *Frasier*, *Home Improvement*, and reruns of *The Golden Girls*) and movies (from *Goodfellas* to *Anne of Green Gables*), pausing

naturalized American citizens: citizens born in another country who have gone through the legal procedures to gain U.S. citizenship

wandering eye: expression that means someone is unfaithful

underground railroad: abolitionists' network of safe houses that nineteenth-century African American slaves used to escape from the South to free states in the North and Canada

permanent residency: legal status given to U.S. noncitizens, allowing for permanent stay but not the rights of citizenship

deportation: a legal process of sending noncitizens to the country where they have citizenship

the **VHS** to try to copy how various characters **enunciated** their words. At the local library, I read magazines, books, and newspapers — anything to learn how to write better. Kathy Dewar, my high-school English teacher, introduced me to journalism. From the moment I wrote my first article for the student paper, I convinced myself that having my name in print — writing in English, interviewing Americans — **validated** my presence here.

The debates over "illegal aliens" intensified my anxieties. In 1994, only a year after my flight from the Philippines, Governor **Pete Wilson** was reelected in part because of his support for Proposition 187, which prohibited undocumented immigrants from attending public school and accessing other services. (A federal court later found the law unconstitutional.) After my encounter at the DMV in 1997, I grew more aware of anti-immigrant sentiments and stereotypes: *They don't want to assimilate, they are a drain on society.* They're not talking about me, I would tell myself. I have something to contribute.

To do that, I had to work — and for that, I needed a Social Security number. Fortunately, my grandfather had already managed to get one for me. Lolo had always taken care of everyone in the family. . . . When I began looking for work, a short time after the DMV incident, my grandfather and I took the Social Security card to Kinko's, where he covered the "INS authorization" text with a sliver of white tape. We then made photocopies of the card. At a glance, at least, the copies would look like copies of a regular, unrestricted Social Security card.

Lolo always imagined I would work the kind of low-paying jobs that undocumented people often take. (Once I married an American, he said, I would get my real papers, and everything would be fine.) But even **menial** jobs require documents, so he and I hoped the doctored card would work for now. The more documents I had, he said, the better. . . .

For more than a decade of getting part-time and full-time jobs, employers have rarely asked to check my original Social Security card. When they did, I showed the photocopied version, which they accepted. Over time, I also began checking the citizenship box on my federal I-9 employment eligibility forms. (Claiming full citizenship was actually easier than declaring permanent resident "green card" status, which would have required me to provide an alien registration number.)

This **deceit** never got easier. The more I did it, the more I felt like an impostor, the more guilt I carried — and the more I worried that I would get caught. But I kept doing it. I needed to live and survive on my own, and I decided this was the way.

Mountain View High School became my second home. I was elected to represent my school at school-board meetings, which gave me the chance to meet and befriend Rich Fischer, the superintendent for our school district. I joined the speech and debate team, acted in school plays, and eventually

VHS: cassette-tape format for visual recordings

enunciated: pronounced

validated: confirmed; made valid or acceptable

Pete Wilson: California governor, 1991–99

menial: unskilled

deceit: deception; cheating or lying

became coeditor of the *Oracle*, the student newspaper. That drew the attention of my principal, Pat Hyland. "You're at school just as much as I am," she told me. Pat and Rich would soon become mentors, and over time, almost surrogate parents for me. . . .

Later that school year, my history class watched a documentary on Harvey Milk, the openly gay San Francisco city official who was assassinated. This was 1999, just six months after Matthew Shepard's body was found tied to a fence in Wyoming. During the discussion, I raised my hand and said something like "I'm sorry Harvey Milk got killed for being gay. . . . I've been meaning to say this. . . . I'm gay."

I hadn't planned on coming out that morning, though I had known that I was gay for several years. With that announcement, I became the only openly gay student at school, and it caused **turmoil** with my grandparents. Lolo kicked me out of the house for a few weeks. Though we eventually **reconciled**, I had disappointed him on two fronts. First, as a Catholic, he considered homosexuality a sin and was embarrassed about having *"ang apo na bakla"* ("a grandson who is gay"). Even worse, I was making matters more difficult for myself, he said. I needed to marry an American woman in order to gain a green card.

turmoil: confusion

reconciled: made up

Tough as it was, coming out about being gay seemed less daunting than coming out about my legal status. I kept my other secret mostly hidden.

While my classmates awaited their college acceptance letters, I hoped to get a full-time job at the *Mountain View Voice* after graduation. It's not that I didn't want to go to college, but I couldn't apply for state and federal financial aid. Without that, my family couldn't afford to send me.

But when I finally told Pat and Rich about my immigration "problem" — as we called it from then on — they helped me look for a solution. At first, they even wondered if one of them could adopt me and fix the situation that way, but a lawyer Rich consulted told him it wouldn't change my legal status because I was too old. Eventually they connected me to a new scholarship fund for high-potential students who were usually the first in their families to attend college. Most important, the fund was not concerned with immigration status. I was among the first recipients, with the scholarship covering tuition, lodging, books, and other expenses for my studies at San Francisco State University.

> ❝ But I am still an undocumented immigrant. And that means living a different kind of reality. It means going about my day in fear of being found out. It means rarely trusting people, even those closest to me, with who I really am. It means keeping my family photos in a shoebox rather than displaying them on shelves in my home, so friends don't ask about them. It means reluctantly, even painfully, doing things I know are wrong and unlawful. ❞

As a college freshman, I found a job working part-time at the *San Francisco Chronicle*, where I sorted mail and wrote some freelance articles. My ambition was to get a reporting job, so I embarked on a series of internships. First I landed at the *Philadelphia Daily News*, in the summer of 2001, where I covered a drive-by shooting and the wedding of the 76ers star Allen Iverson. Using those articles, I applied to the *Seattle Times* and got an internship for the following summer.

But then my lack of proper documents became a problem again. The *Times'* recruiter, Pat Foote, asked all incoming interns to bring certain paperwork on their first day: a birth certificate, or a passport, or a driver's license plus an original Social Security card. I panicked, thinking my documents wouldn't **pass muster**. So before starting the job, I called Pat and told her about my legal status. After consulting with management, she called me back with the answer I feared: I couldn't do the internship.

pass muster: be acceptable or good enough

This was devastating. What good was college if I couldn't then pursue the career I wanted? I decided then that if I was to succeed in a profession that is all about truth-telling, I couldn't tell the truth about myself. . . .

For the summer of 2003, I applied for internships across the country. Several newspapers, including the *Wall Street Journal*, the *Boston Globe*, and the *Chicago Tribune*, expressed interest. But when the *Washington Post* offered me a spot, I knew where I would go. And this time, I had no intention of acknowledging my "problem."

The *Post* internship posed a tricky obstacle: It required a driver's license. (After my close call at the California DMV, I'd never gotten one.) So I spent an afternoon at the Mountain View Public Library, studying various states' requirements. Oregon was among the most welcoming — and it was just a few hours' drive north.

Again, my support network came through. A friend's father lived in Portland, and he allowed me to use his address as proof of residency. Pat, Rich, and Rich's longtime assistant, Mary Moore, sent letters to me at that address. Rich taught me how to do **three-point turns** in a parking lot, and a friend accompanied me to Portland. . . .

three-point turns: series of maneuvers allowing a driver to reverse directions in just three turns

At the DMV in Portland, I arrived with my photocopied Social Security card, my college ID, a pay stub from the *San Francisco Chronicle*, and my proof of state residence — the letters to the Portland address that my support network had sent. It worked. My license, issued in 2003, was set to expire eight years later, on my thirtieth birthday, on February 3, 2011. I had eight years to succeed professionally, and to hope that some sort of immigration reform would pass in the meantime and allow me to stay.

It seemed like all the time in the world.

exhilarating: making one feel very excited and happy

My summer in Washington was **exhilarating**. I was intimidated to be in a major newsroom but was assigned a mentor — Peter Perl, a veteran magazine writer — to help me navigate it. A few weeks into the internship, he printed out one of my articles, about a guy who recovered a long-lost wallet, circled the first two paragraphs, and left it on my desk. "Great eye for details — awesome!"

he wrote. Though I didn't know it then, Peter would become one more member of my network. . . .

In the five years that followed, I did my best to "do enough." I was promoted to staff writer, reported on video-game culture, wrote a series on Washington's HIV/AIDS epidemic, and covered the role of technology and social media in the 2008 presidential race. I visited the White House, where I interviewed senior aides and covered a state dinner — and gave the Secret Service the Social Security number I obtained with false documents.

I did my best to steer clear of reporting on immigration policy but couldn't always avoid it. On two occasions, I wrote about Hillary Clinton's position on driver's licenses for undocumented immigrants. I also wrote an article about Senator Mel Martinez of Florida, then the chairman of the Republican National Committee, who was defending his party's stance toward Latinos after only one Republican presidential candidate — John McCain, the coauthor of a failed immigration bill — agreed to participate in a debate sponsored by Univision, the Spanish-language network.

It was an odd sort of dance: I was trying to stand out in a highly competitive newsroom, yet I was terrified that if I stood out too much, I'd invite unwanted **scrutiny**. I tried to compartmentalize my fears, distract myself by reporting on the lives of other people, but there was no escaping the central conflict in my life. Maintaining a deception for so long distorts your sense of self. You start wondering who you've become, and why.

scrutiny: critical observation

In April 2008, I was part of a *Post* team that won a Pulitzer Prize for the paper's coverage of the **Virginia Tech shootings** a year earlier. Lolo died a year earlier, so it was Lola who called me the day of the announcement. The first thing she said was, *"Anong mangyayari kung malaman ng mga tao?"*

Virginia Tech shootings: 2007 deadly shootings on the campus of Virginia Tech University

What will happen if people find out?

I couldn't say anything. After we got off the phone, I rushed to the bathroom on the fourth floor of the newsroom, sat down on the toilet, and cried. . . .

I'm done running. I'm exhausted. I don't want that life anymore.

So I've decided to come forward, own up to what I've done, and tell my story to the best of my recollection. I've reached out to former bosses and employers and apologized for misleading them — a mix of humiliation and **liberation** coming with each disclosure. All the people mentioned in this article gave me permission to use their names. I've also talked to family and friends about my situation and am working with legal counsel to review my options. I don't know what the consequences will be of telling my story.[1]

liberation: being freed from control

I do know that I am grateful to my grandparents, my Lolo and Lola, for giving me the chance for a better life. I'm also grateful to my other family — the support network I found here in America — for encouraging me to pursue my dreams.

---

[1] As of 2016, Vargas has not yet faced serious negative consequence for his decision to come forward, though he was arrested once, in 2014.

After You Read

Mapping the Reading

1. How did Vargas learn that he was an undocumented immigrant?

2. Why did Vargas's grandfather—or Lolo—think that his grandson would be able to manage his undocumented status? That is, what was his plan to keep Vargas out of trouble, and how did he think Vargas would eventually gain citizenship?

3. After he learns about his status as an undocumented immigrant, how does Vargas believe he will be able to earn citizenship?

4. In what specific ways has Vargas's life been affected by his status as an undocumented immigrant?

5. What are some examples of the support network that helped Vargas succeed?

6. Describe the illegal or deceitful actions that Vargas reveals, and how he feels about being deceitful.

Discussing and Thinking Critically about the Reading

1. Throughout the narrative, Vargas expresses unhappiness and discomfort with being a "hidden" undocumented worker. What made him finally decide to come out and admit his status? Why did he feel as though he should be honest? (Your "As You Read" notes might be useful here.)

2. How does Vargas's perspective help you understand the experiences of undocumented immigrants? What did you find most surprising about his opinions and experiences? least surprising?

3. Does Vargas's personal story make a compelling case for changing the law to more easily allow people like him to become legal residents? Why or why not?

4. Vargas writes, "Tough as it was, coming out about being gay seemed less daunting than coming out about my legal status." Why do you think it was harder for Vargas to "come out" about his immigration status than about his being gay? How is coming out as gay and as an undocumented worker similar and different?

5. In what ways does Vargas see his life as an example of the American Dream? In what ways is it not?

Navigating the Intersections

1. Go to a search engine to find "undocumented worker cartoons," select three, and then compare these cartoons with those of the Irish American immigrants in Joe DeGuzman's article by identifying similarities and differences.

2. For this exercise, choose one of the following activities:

   a. What is Jose Antonio Vargas doing today? Do some research to find out if he has faced legal action or if his legal status has changed. Is he still a writer and filmmaker? Is he still writing and speaking about undocumented workers? If so, what has he been working on?

OR

b. Research the status of efforts to reform immigration, specifically the DREAM Act and other efforts to offer a path to citizenship for undocumented immigrants like Vargas who have lived in the United States for many years.

Before You Read: What, if anything, do you think are the special challenges for Asian American immigrants and their children? Consider your own experiences and observations, if relevant.

NADIA MUSTAFA and JEFF CHU[1]

Nadia Mustafa is a writer, editor, copyeditor, and yoga instructor who has worked for *Time* and in communications and social media. Jeff Chu is a writer and editor who has worked at *Time*, *Conde Naste Portfolio*, and most recently *Fast Company*. A freelance writer, his work has appeared in the *New York Times Magazine* and the *Wall Street Journal*, among other publications. He is the author of *Does Jesus Really Love Me?* (2014). This article is from *Time* magazine (2006).

As You Read: Mustafa and Chu include many people's perspectives in their article. To help you keep track, make a list of the people they spoke with, including their names, who they are, and a brief note about the information they offer.

Between Two Worlds
Born in the USA to Asian Parents, a Generation of Immigrants' Kids Forges a New Identity

They are strangers, but they already know one another's stories. So when Mona Rahman, twenty-four, tells the other five people at a New York City dinner table about how her super-strict parents never let her sleep over at friends' houses, there are chuckles of recognition. There are equally **empathetic**, if more sober, nods when Grace Chang Lucarelli, thirty-two, speaking in a soft Texan drawl, recalls "people making fun of me" because she was one of the few Asian Americans in her town. The people around the table grew up in rural Texas, suburban New Jersey, upstate New York, small-town Virginia, and the real **O.C.** But they are the children of parents who immigrated to the US from India, the Philippines, Korea, Bangladesh, and Taiwan. What they share, says Korean American Suzette Won Haas, thirty-one, is the sense of "feeling like the hyphen in between" the Asian and the American in *Asian-American*.

empathetic: sharing another's feelings

O.C.: Orange County, California

[1] With reporting by Kristin Kloberdanz and Amanda Bower.

Immigration and Nationality Act: law abolishing the National Origins Formula, which restricted immigration based on quotas to maintain the country's ethnic composition

quotas: official limits

Manila: capital of the Philippines

brain drain: a social crisis that occurs in a country or region when a large percentage of the professional class moves away

physiognomy: a person's facial features

enclaves: communities in which the people are somehow different from those in the nearby areas

model minority: a myth about a minority group (ethnic, racial, or religious) being academically and socioeconomically more successful than average, and a model for other minorities

acculturation: process of taking on the culture of another group

mores: customs and moral attitudes

That particular identity was made possible forty years ago, in 1965, when President Lyndon B. Johnson signed the **Immigration and Nationality Act**. Exclusion laws passed in the early 1900s had reduced Asian immigration to a trickle. In 1965, the year the Civil Rights Act came into effect, says New York University sociologist Guillermina Jasso, "the racist elements of immigration law were abolished." Annual per-country **quotas** shot from 100 — yes, 100 — for most Asian nations to 20,000, with preferences for close relatives of US citizens and those skilled in fields with labor shortages, like medicine. The new law unleashed a wave of immigrants who came to the US to further their education or get a better job. By 1980 more than 190,000 Indians — some 90 percent of them college educated — had arrived. About 13,000 Korean doctors, pharmacists, and nurses got green cards. The Filipino population in the US nearly quintupled, to 500,000; so many medical professionals emigrated that politicians in **Manila** warned of **brain drain**.

The American story is, of course, made up of successive influxes of immigrants who arrive in the US, struggle to find a place in its society, and eventually assimilate. But the group of post-1965 Asians was different from the Jews, Irish, and Italians who had landed earlier. The Asian immigrants' distinctive **physiognomy** may have made it more difficult for them to blend in, but at the same time, their high education and skill levels allowed them quicker entrée into the middle class. Instead of clustering tightly in urban ethnic **enclaves**, they spread out into suburbia, where they were often isolated. And it was there that their kids, now twenty to forty years old, grew up, straddling two worlds — the traditional domain their recently arrived parents sought to maintain at home and the fast-changing Western culture of the society outside the front door. The six people at the New York City dinner are members of that second generation and — full disclosure — so are we, the authors of this article.

"The post-1965 generation really is different," says David Reimers, a historian of immigration at New York University. "The process of assimilation has been much faster." The inspiration for the notion of the "**model minority**," the generation's members have been most recognized for their high academic achievements, a reflection of their parents' drive for a certain kind of success. But that is only part of their story. Shuttling between two worlds — and seeming to fit into neither — many felt as if "they had no community," says Chang-rae Lee, a Korean-American novelist who has written about this generation's journey. "They had to create themselves." In doing so, they have updated the old immigrant story and forged a new Asian-American identity, not wholly recognizable in any of their parents' native lands but, in its hybrid nature, vibrantly American.

If you were to draw a diagram of **acculturation**, with the **mores** of immigrant parents on one side and society's on the other, the classic model might show a steady drift over time, depicting a slow-burn Americanization, taking as long as two or three generations. The more recent Asian-American curve, however, looks almost like the path of a boomerang: early isolation, rapid immersion and assimilation, and then a reappreciation of ethnic roots.

"Forever Foreigners"

As a child growing up in Pennington, New Jersey, Fareha Ahmed watched **Bollywood** videos and enthusiastically attended the annual Pakistan Independence Day Parade in New York City. By middle school, though, her parents' Pakistani culture had become uncool. "I wanted to fit in so bad," Ahmed says. For her, that meant trying to be white. She dyed her hair blond, got hazel contact lenses, and complained, "I'm going to smell," when her mom served fragrant dishes like lamb biryani for dinner. But at Villanova University in Philadelphia, Ahmed found friends from all different backgrounds who welcomed diversity and helped her, she says, become "a good balance of East meets West." Now twenty-three, she and her non-Asian roommates threw a party to mark the Islamic holiday Eid al-Fitr in November, then threw another for Christmas — which her family never celebrated. "I chose to embrace both holidays instead of segregating myself to one," she says.

Asian Americans say part of the reason it is so hard to reach an **equilibrium** is that they are seen as what sociologists call "forever foreigners." Their looks lead to a lifetime of questions like "No, where are you really from?" As a teenager in the affluent and overwhelmingly white Chicago suburb of Riverwoods, Illinois, Vanessa DeGuia, now twenty-six, endured incident after incident that made her aware that others regarded her as foreign, despite how her birth certificate read. One classmate told her, "You're my brown friend. You're so exotic." Another came over for dinner, took a bite of a Filipino egg roll made by Vanessa's mom, spat it out, and asked if it was made of dog. "I never felt like I belonged," DeGuia says. "Though I was born in this country and English was my first language, I was always seen as a foreigner."

For kids — who by nature desperately want to belong — the feeling of **alienation** can be so painful that they will do almost anything to make it go away, to fit in. For years, Mark Hong, thirty-one, shunned the only other Asian kid he knew in Davenport, Iowa, and hung out with the popular — and other than him, entirely white — crowd at school: the jocks. "I **repelled** anything that was Asian because it represented everything that was not cool at the time. Asians did kung fu and worked at Asian restaurants," he explains. That his Korean-born dad was actually an engineer at Caterpillar had no effect on Hong's teenage mind, which was focused on one goal: "I wanted to be cool."

> **❝** *One classmate told [Vanessa DeGuia], 'You're my brown friend. You're so exotic.' Another came over for dinner, took a bite of a Filipino egg roll made by Vanessa's mom, spat it out, and asked if it was made of dog. 'I never felt like I belonged,' DeGuia says. 'Though I was born in this country and English was my first language, I was always seen as a foreigner.'* **❞**

Bollywood: India's movie industry

equilibrium: balance

alienation: made to feel one is not part of a group

repelled: pushed away forcefully

Racial alienation and ethnic mockery are commonplace in the immigrant-kid experience, and the stories these Asian Americans tell of their childhood are "the same kind of talk about social exclusion that you might have found among Italians and Jews in the 1930s," says Harvard sociologist Mary Waters. But previous generations of immigrants' kids, including those Italians and Jews, lived in neighborhoods with built-in social support structures — people who looked like them, ate like them, prayed like them. They had what Marissa Dagdagan, twenty-eight, a daughter of Filipino-born doctors, who grew up in Burr Ridge, Illinois, says she did not — "people like me that I could **corroborate** with."

corroborate: confirm; verify by providing information

Cultural Awakenings

Many children of the Asian immigrants who came over in the 1960s and 1970s say they didn't find that kind of self-affirmation until, like Fareha Ahmed, they got to college. . . .

kindles: sparks; starts

The social awakening often **kindles** a cultural one. Once in the return part of the curve, many Asian Americans go from downplaying their differences to highlighting them. In fourth grade, Akira Heshiki, who grew up in Anchorage, Alaska, dropped out of the Japanese-language school she attended each Saturday because she didn't feel Japanese. Instead she treasured the moments when her high school classmates told her, "I always forget you're Japanese." But once at Oregon's Reed College, where more than 10 percent of the students were Asian American, she began to embrace her heritage. She started the Asian student union with two classmates. Its members discussed what it meant to be Asian American, organized **anti-sweatshop protests**, and supplied books on diversity issues, which they felt were lacking from Reed's library. Heshiki even dropped the English name her parents had given her — May — in favor of her middle name, which is Japanese for "bright." "I started using it because I wanted people meeting me to have to — for one minute — struggle or acknowledge I was a little different," says Heshiki, thirty-one, now a lawyer in Portland, Oregon.

anti-sweatshop protests: campaigns against places of low wages, poor working conditions, and often child labor

renaissance: rebirth

parses: explores closely

Grayce Liu's cultural **renaissance** began when she read Amy Tan's *The Joy Luck Club*, a novel that **parses** the complex relationships of Chinese mothers and daughters. Growing up in Rancho Palos Verdes, California, Liu dated only white boys. She hated speaking Mandarin, the language her parents used at home. She added a *y* to her name and changed the pronunciation to "Gray-cee" to distinguish herself from two other Asians at school named Grace. "I didn't want to be like other Asians," she recalls. But *The Joy Luck Club* turned her into a "born-again Asian." It gave her new insights into why her mom was so hard on her and why the ways she showed love — say, through food — were different from those of the families Liu saw on TV, who seemed to say "I love you" all day long. Liu even signed up for Mandarin and Chinese history courses at the University of California at Santa Cruz. Today she is an actor and producer, and her latest project is a kids' TV show called *Bakaboo*. Its goal: to teach Mandarin to American-born Chinese.

Seeing their children embrace their heritage is gratifying for the parents who withstood years of youthful rebellion and implied shame. "I was very moved by Grace's efforts," says Grayce Liu's mother, Sue, who still calls her daughter by her given name. "She was finally appreciative of all the things I tried to do for her." The hardship these parents and kids have in reaching that kind of understanding reflects more than just the usual generational divide. There is also a cultural **crevasse** larger than that faced by immigrants' kids whose families at least share a Western civilization that makes American customs a little less alien. Sam Chang's Korean parents were horrified when he got involved in student government at his high school in Phoenix, Arizona. They viewed his extracurricular activities as **frivolous** diversions from the main goal of his getting into a top college. "When I came home freshman year as president, they had no idea what that meant," says Chang, now twenty-six and a law student at the University of Arizona. It took congratulations from other parents for them to appreciate their son's coronation as homecoming king his senior year. "They just wanted me to finish school and go to Harvard," Chang says. . . .

crevasse: a deep crack, as in the earth

frivolous: silly; foolish

Jhumpa Lahiri, author of *The Namesake*, a novel about Indian immigrants and their US-born son, has observed the struggles of Asian Americans like Chang up close. "Asian kids are not just choosing a different way of doing things," she says. "They're choosing an entirely different [cultural] vocabulary. They're dealing with oil and water." Nowhere is that incompatibility more deeply felt than in romance. Most Asian-immigrant parents encourage their children to find partners of the same ethnicity, and many of the kids see the advantages of doing so. As June Kim, a Korean-American copywriter in Philadelphia who is engaged to another Korean American, Shane Kim, sees it, "there are certain things you don't have to explain — cultural nuances, how our families work, our roles within our families." Yet 40 percent of Asian Americans ages twenty-five to thirty-four marry people of other ethnicities, compared with 12 percent of African Americans in the same age group. Both Grace Chang Lucarelli and her sister married white men. Although their Taiwanese parents weren't pleased at first, Lucarelli says they understood the odds. "They took us to Texas," she says, of her upbringing in the small town of Terrell. "What did they expect?"

Nidhi Khurana, twenty-five, has dated Indian Americans, but for the past three years, she has been seeing an African-American man. "It definitely caused a rift with my parents," she says. "They were very confused." Her father Sunil, a gastroenterologist who came to the US in 1977, admits that accepting the interracial romance "was hard. We are very active in the Indian community,

[and] everybody watches you. Also, you grow up in a certain culture, and you expect that to continue."

Of course, such tension is common to generations of immigrants. But Jack Tchen, director of Asian/Pacific/American Studies at **NYU**, says these second-generation immigrants are beginning to find a middle ground and to "define a new modern form of Asian modernity, not necessarily the same as American modernity." That is what sociologists call identity building, and for the second generation, it is based not on a common ethnicity, faith, or language (except English) but on shared experience.

NYU: New York University

Which is what the six around the New York City table are discovering. For nearly three hours, they tell stories about their families, their work, their heartaches, their joys. They discuss their Asian identities and American habits. And they confess how hard it has been to walk an often lonely path. Says Mohip Joarder, twenty-seven, an Indian-American computer programmer from Spring Valley, New York, "I've never felt like there were people I could talk freely to about this stuff."

The talk about themselves provides some insights about their parents too. Rob Ragasa, thirty-one, a Filipino-American high school teacher raised in New Jersey, reflects on how his parents — conservative as they always seemed to him — had to be pretty daring to immigrate. "They had to come here and struggle. They had to be the first," he says, then pauses for a moment. "Maybe we are like our parents," he adds finally. "We are going to be pioneers too." And maybe they already are.

After You Read

Mapping the Reading

1. Explain how first-generation Asian Americans are "between two worlds."

2. According to Mustafa and Chu, why are first-generation Asian Americans considered "forever foreigners"?

3. Review the article to find examples of how the people interviewed took steps to assimilate in order to fit in better in the non-Asian communities they grew up in. Summarize two of the examples.

4. What are some of the actions that these interviewees took once they came to a "re-appreciation of [their] ethnic roots"?

5. According to the article, what advantages and disadvantages do post-1965 Asian immigrants and their children have compared to earlier immigrant groups, such as the Italians, the Jews, and the Irish?

Discussing and Thinking Critically about the Reading

1. Mustafa and Chu characterize first-generation Asian Americans as being "between two worlds" — that of their home culture and that of mainstream American culture. How successful are the authors in presenting a persuasive portrait of this sense of being in between? Which of their examples are most persuasive? least persuasive? Why?

2. What did you find most surprising and least surprising about each person's opinions and experiences as children of Asian American immigrants? (Your "As You Read" notes may be helpful here.) What, if anything, can you add from your own experiences or your observations of children of immigrants?

3. Mustafa and Chu refer to two models of acculturation: a traditional one and one they compare to a boomerang. Summarize these two models, and then discuss why first-generation Asian Americans seem to follow the boomerang model.

4. What does the term *model minority* mean, and how does the idea of a model minority affect both those who are members of that minority and those who are members of a group that is negatively compared to that minority?

5. Although Mustafa and Chu's main focus is on their Asian American interviewees, they also include information from experts, including sociologists and a historian. What purpose do these sources have for Mustafa and Chu? What value do these sources bring to the article? (Your "As You Read" notes may be helpful here.)

Navigating the Intersections

1. Nadia Mustafa and Jeff Chu suggest that the experiences of Asian immigrants and their children are different from that of other immigrant groups. Test their claim by comparing and contrasting Asian Americans' experiences to those of another group you have learned about in this chapter. How different and similar are the groups' experiences?

2. Select a social group (defined by nationality, ethnicity, or religion) that you belong to or are closely aligned with, and explore how well that group is represented in your hometown or city. Work from your own memories and perspective, but also use a search engine to find out basic demographic information about your home community: What percentage of the people in the community are from this social group? What is the dominant social group? How do local businesses and organizations reflect the different social groups in the community?

CHAPTER 7

Abilities and Disabilities

Are They Linked?

Michael Svoboda/Getty Images

Image Response: What message does this image convey? What is your first reaction? What does the angle of the image emphasize? In what ways might the image inspire viewers to rethink ideas about people with disabilities?

In This Chapter

Introduction

Abilities and Disabilities: Are They Linked?

In this chapter, we focus on the experiences of people with disabilities, asking questions about what it means to be disabled, how our society responds and supports the disabled, and ultimately whether or not disability — focus here on *dis* — is an accurate or helpful way to see people who have unusual or remarkable features or characteristics. Many people who have lived with disability — or who have loved ones with disabilities — recognize that unique abilities and special strengths often come with disability. In fact, observing the extraordinary talents of many *differently* abled people makes us ask whether disability actually encourages and enables extraordinary ability to blossom alongside disability.

Changing Views about Disability

Today much of America is open and accessible for people with disabilities, or at least it appears to be so. In city streets, classrooms, and many workplaces, people with visible and invisible disabilities are able to get around, learn, and work. However, just one generation ago, before the passage of laws to protect them, people with disabilities were largely kept outside mainstream society. For the wealthy, this meant educating and housing people with disabilities in private, specialized

277

schools and homes for the sick. For the rest of the population, this meant a life at home, cared for by family members, with few opportunities for help in overcoming their disabilities. When we read the famous story of Helen Keller—a woman who overcame blindness and deafness—we have to remember that her success was possible because of the wealth of her family: It was not the government or society that paid for her tutor, Anne Sullivan, but Helen's family. If she had been born today, Helen Keller (1880–1968) would receive assistance from the state; she would work with publicly provided special education teachers. In another example, before the disability laws, people in wheelchairs had no access to many public buildings because wheelchair ramps were not required. Today they are. Possibilities for Americans with disabilities have changed dramatically.

The Rehabilitation Act of 1973 and the Americans with Disabilities Act (ADA) of 1990 are the two principal legislative actions that have changed the prospects for people who have disabilities today. The Rehabilitation Act of 1973 states, "No otherwise qualified individual with a disability in the United States shall . . . solely by reason of her or his disability, be excluded from the participation in, be denied benefits of, or be subjected to discrimination" by the government (United States). The ADA extended these protections to the private sector; thus, for example, discrimination against people with disabilities is illegal both in the public schools and in the hiring practices of private companies. Additional pieces of legislation have offered other protections. These laws are responsible for dramatic changes: wheelchair ramps, alternative keyboards for the mobility impaired, audio books for the blind, interpreters for the deaf, and voice translators for the speech impaired, among others. Yet access to accommodations remains an ongoing concern for people with disabilities.

Stigma and Ignorance

People with disabilities have long faced stigma and discrimination. America's thirty-second president, Franklin Delano Roosevelt (FDR), who became paralyzed by polio at age thirty-nine, felt so stigmatized by his disability that he made sure he was not photographed while in a wheelchair. The stigma against his disability was so great that it was not until 2001 that a statue of Roosevelt clearly showing him sitting in a wheelchair was erected at his memorial in Washington, D.C. It is different today, of course, but are people with disabilities fully accepted without stigma? The relatively few examples of politicians, celebrities, and other famous people with openly acknowledged disabilities suggest that stigma still exists.

For those among us who see ourselves as able—or without a known disability—people with disabilities may seem sad and unfortunate, deserving of compassion and perhaps even pity. Yet for those of us who have disabilities or who know people who do, pity is unwelcome. Attempts to revise the terms used to label the disabled reflect this attitude. For many people with disabilities and their supporters, the term *disabled* is itself unwelcome. A proposed substitute, *differently abled*, was intended to get at the idea that the human body is always varied and that life with prosthetic legs, for example, is not a *disabled* life but a *differently abled* life—and in the case of the person pictured in the chapter-opening image, a life of very fast running. Yet this term has also faced some criticism for focusing on *difference*. For many, "people first" terminology is preferred over "disability first" language for its attempts to suggest that the disability does not define the person (Umstead). For example, this method would use *person with autism* in place of *autistic person*.

Jennifer Bartlett, a poet and teacher with cerebral palsy, writes of exiting subways in New York City: "It is not the physical strain of steps and crowds that is my main source of anxiety. It is the naïve, inappropriate, and sometimes downright mean comments that people make." She expands: "People who would otherwise mind their manners feel they have carte blanche when it comes to commenting on my condition. Bus riders have referred to me as mentally backward (while I was reading James Joyce), and waitresses routinely ask my companion what I want to order. In a club, once, an older man asked me to dance. Upon hearing my voice, he commented to his friend, 'She's some kind of retard,' and walked off." For Bartlett, and many others, her challenges in life are less about living with her disability than with living with others' assumptions about, and responses to, her disability.

Works Cited

Bartlett, Jennifer. "Complaint Box: Assumptions." *The New York Times*, 4 June 2010, p. 7.

Umstead, Alex. "An Introductory Guide to Disability Language and Empowerment." *Syracuse University Disability Cultural Center*, Syracuse University, 2012, sudcc.syr.edu/LanguageGuide/.

United States, Department of Labor, Office of the Assistant Secretary for Administration and Management. *Section 504, Rehabilitation Act of 1973.* www.dol.gov/oasam/regs/statutes/sec504.htm. Accessed 14 July 2015.

Beyond Disability: Stories of Ability

Before You Read: In your thinking process, how important is being able to visualize something? Write about an instance in which visualizing or not being able to visualize something affected your understanding.

TEMPLE GRANDIN

Temple Grandin is an expert in animal science, a professor at Colorado State University, and an animal rights activist. Grandin has designed equipment for handling animals safely and ethically, focusing on the cattle industry and slaughterhouses. The author of *Animals in Translation: Using the Mysteries of Autism to Decode Animal Behavior* (2005) and many articles, Grandin has shown the world both how her autism works and how she has used it to be successful in her career. In this excerpt from *Thinking in Pictures* (2006), Grandin tells her story of living with autism.

As You Read: Using underlining or another method, identify passages where Grandin writes directly about the disadvantages and advantages of her autism.

Autism* and Visual Thought

*autism: general term for a group of brain development disorders, characterized by difficulty communicating and interacting

I think in pictures. Words are like a second language to me. I translate both spoken and written words into full-color movies, complete with sound, which run like a **VCR** tape in my head. When somebody speaks to me, his words are instantly translated into pictures. Language-based thinkers often find this phenomenon difficult to understand, but in my job as an equipment designer for the livestock industry, visual thinking is a tremendous advantage.

VCR: videocassette recorder

Visual thinking has enabled me to build entire systems in my imagination. During my career I have designed all kinds of equipment, ranging from **corrals** for handling cattle on ranches to systems for handling cattle and hogs during veterinary procedures and slaughter. I have worked for many major livestock companies. In fact, one third of the cattle and hogs in the United States are handled in equipment I have designed. Some of the people I've worked for don't even know that their systems were designed by someone with autism. I value my ability to think visually, and I would never want to lose it.

corrals: cages, pens, or enclosures for livestock

spatial: space-related

One of the most profound mysteries of autism has been the remarkable ability of most autistic people to excel at visual **spatial** skills while performing so poorly at verbal skills. When I was a child and a teenager, I thought everybody thought in pictures. I had no idea that my thought processes were different. . . .

I credit my visualization abilities with helping me understand the animals I work with. Early in my career I used a camera to help give me the animals' perspective as they walked through a **chute** for their veterinary treatment. I would kneel down and take pictures through the chute from the cow's eye level. Using the photos, I was able to figure out which things scared the cattle, such as shadows and bright spots of sunlight. . . .

I create new images all the time by taking many little parts of images I have in the video library in my imagination and piecing them together. I have video memories of every item I've ever worked with — steel gates, fences, latches, concrete walls, and so forth. To create new designs, I retrieve bits and pieces from my memory and combine them into a new whole. . . .

Being autistic, I don't naturally **assimilate** information that most people take for granted. Instead, I store information in my head as if it were on a CD-ROM disc. When I recall something I have learned, I replay the video in my imagination. The videos in my memory are always specific; for example, I remember handling cattle at the veterinary chute at Producer's Feedlot or McElhaney Cattle Company. I remember exactly how the animals behaved in that specific situation and how the chutes and other equipment were built. The exact construction of steel fence posts and pipe rails in each case is also part of my visual memory. I can run these images over and over and study them to solve design problems.

If I let my mind wander, the video jumps in a kind of **free association** from fence construction to a particular welding shop where I've seen posts being cut and Old John, the welder, making gates. If I continue thinking about Old John welding a gate, the video image changes to a series of short scenes of building gates on several projects I've worked on. Each video memory triggers another in this associative fashion, and my daydreams may wander far from the design problem. The next image may be of having a good time listening to John and the construction crew tell war stories, such as the time the **backhoe** dug into a nest of rattlesnakes and the machine was abandoned for two weeks because everybody was afraid to go near it.

> *Growing up, I learned to convert abstract ideas into pictures as a way to understand them. . . . I thought of peace as a dove, an Indian peace pipe, or TV or newsreel footage of the signing of a peace agreement. Honesty was represented by an image of placing one's hand on the Bible in court.*

This process of association is a good example of how my mind can wander off the subject. People with more severe autism have difficulty stopping endless associations. . . . Charles Hart, the author of *Without Reason*, a book about his autistic son and brother, sums up his son's thinking in one sentence: "Ted's thought processes aren't logical, they're associational." This explains Ted's statement "I'm not afraid of planes. That's why they fly so high." In his

chute: a tube or slide

assimilate: take in and fully understand

free association: a kind of thinking that is based on visual, memory-based, or other connections rather than logic

backhoe: large machine that uses a scoop to dig into the earth

mind, planes fly high because he is not afraid of them; he combines two pieces of information, that planes fly high and that he is not afraid of heights. . . .

Different Ways of Thinking

It wasn't until I went to college that I realized some people are completely verbal and think only in words. I first suspected this when I read an article in a science magazine about the development of tool use in prehistoric humans.

speculated: made an educated guess

Some renowned scientist **speculated** that humans had to develop language before they could develop tools. I thought this was ridiculous, and this article gave me the first **inkling** that my thought processes were truly different from those of many other people. When I invent things, I do not use language. Some other people think in vividly detailed pictures, but most think in a combination of words and vague, generalized pictures. . . .

inkling: start of an idea

Unlike those of most people, my thoughts move from video-like, specific images to generalization and concepts. For example, my concept of dogs is **inextricably** linked to every dog I've ever known. It's as if I have a **card catalog** of dogs I have seen, complete with pictures, which continually grows as I add more examples to my video library. If I think about Great Danes, the first memory that pops into my head is Dansk, the Great Dane owned by the headmaster at my high school. The next Great Dane I visualize is Helga, who was Dansk's replacement. The next is my aunt's dog in Arizona, and my final image comes from an advertisement for Fitwell seat covers that featured that kind of dog. My memories usually appear in my imagination in strict **chronological** order, and the images I visualize are always specific. There is no generic, generalized Great Dane. . . .

inextricably: impossibly entangled

card catalog: file of cards that is the predecessor of electronic library catalogs

chronological: ordered by time

Processing Nonvisual Information

Autistics have problems learning things that cannot be thought about in pictures. The easiest words for an autistic child to learn are nouns, because they directly relate to pictures. Highly verbal autistic children like I was can sometimes learn how to read with phonics. Written words were too **abstract** for me to remember, but I could **laboriously** remember the approximately fifty phonetic sounds and a few rules. Lower-functioning children often learn better by association, with the aid of word labels attached to objects in their environment. Some very impaired autistic children learn more easily if words are spelled out with plastic letters they can feel.

abstract: theoretical or conceptual

laboriously: with a lot of effort and time

Spatial words such as "over" and "under" had no meaning for me until I had a visual image to fix them in my memory. Even now, when I hear the word "under" by itself, I automatically picture myself getting under the cafeteria tables at school during an air-raid drill, a common occurrence on the East Coast during the early fifties. The first memory that any single word triggers is almost always a childhood memory. I can remember the teacher telling us to be quiet and walking single-file into the cafeteria, where six or eight children huddled under each table. If I continue on the same train of thought, more and more associative memories of elementary school emerge. I can remember the teacher scolding me after I hit Alfred for putting dirt on my shoe. All of these memories play like videotapes in the VCR in my imagination. If I allow my mind to keep associating, it will wander a million miles away from the word "under," to submarines under the Antarctic and the Beatles song "Yellow Submarine." If I let my mind pause on the picture of the yellow submarine, I then hear the song. As I start humming the song and get to the part about people coming on board, my association switches to the **gangway** of a ship I saw in Australia. . . .

> **gangway:** walkway used to board a ship

When I am unable to convert text to pictures, it is usually because the text has no concrete meaning. Some philosophy books and articles about the cattle futures market are simply incomprehensible. It is much easier for me to understand written text that describes something that can be easily translated into pictures. The following sentence from a story in the February 21, 1994, issue of *Time* magazine, describing the Winter Olympics figure-skating championships, is a good example: "All the elements are in place—the spotlights, the swelling waltzes and jazz tunes, the sequined sprites taking to the air." In my imagination I see the skating rink and skaters. However, if I ponder too long on the word "elements," I will make the inappropriate association of a periodic table on the wall of my high school chemistry classroom. Pausing on the word "sprite" triggers an image of a Sprite can in my refrigerator instead of a pretty young skater.

Teachers who work with autistic children need to understand associative thought patterns. An autistic child will often use a word in an inappropriate manner. Sometimes these uses have a logical associative meaning and other times they don't. For example, an autistic child might say the word "dog" when he wants to go outside. The word "dog" is associated with going outside. In my own case, I can remember both logical and illogical use of inappropriate words. When I was six, I learned to say "prosecution." I had absolutely no idea what it meant, but it sounded nice when I said it, so I used it as an exclamation every time my kite hit the ground. I must have baffled more than a few people who heard me exclaim "Prosecution!" to my downward-spiraling kite. . . .

Abstract Thought

Growing up, I learned to convert abstract ideas into pictures as a way to understand them. I visualized concepts such as peace or honesty with symbolic images. I thought of peace as a dove, an Indian peace pipe, or TV or newsreel footage of the signing of a peace agreement. Honesty was represented by an image of placing one's hand on the Bible in court. A news report describing a person returning a wallet with all the money in it provided a picture of honest behavior. . . .

As a teenager and young adult I had to use concrete symbols to understand abstract concepts such as getting along with people and moving on to the next steps of my life, both of which were always difficult. I knew I did not fit in with my high school peers, and I was unable to figure out what I was doing wrong. No matter how hard I tried, they made fun of me. They called me "workhorse," "tape recorder," and "bones" because I was skinny. At the time I was able to figure out why they called me "workhorse" and "bones," but "tape recorder" puzzled me. Now I realize that I must have sounded like a tape recorder when I repeated things **verbatim** over and over. But back then I just could not figure out why I was such a social dud. I sought refuge in doing things I was good at, such as working on reroofing the barn or practicing my riding prior to a horse show. Personal relationships made absolutely no sense to me until I developed visual symbols of doors and windows. It was then that I started to understand concepts such as learning the give-and-take of a relationship. I still wonder what would have happened to me if I had not been able to visualize my way in the world.

verbatim: word for word

The really big challenge for me was making the transition from high school to college. People with autism have tremendous difficulty with change. In order to deal with a major change such as leaving high school, I needed a way to rehearse it, acting out each phase in my life by walking through an actual door, window, or gate. When I was graduating from high school, I would go and sit on the roof of my dormitory and look up at the stars and think about how I would cope with leaving. It was there I discovered a little door that led to a bigger roof while my dormitory was being remodeled. While I was still living in this old New England house, a much larger building was being constructed over it. One day the carpenters tore out a section of the old roof next to my room. When I walked out, I was now able to look up into the partially finished new building. High on one side was a small wooden door that led to the new roof. The building was changing and it was now time for me to change too. I could relate to that. I had found the symbolic key.

When I was in college, I found another door to symbolize getting ready for graduation. It was a small metal trap door that went out onto the flat roof of the dormitory. I had to actually practice going through this door many times. When I finally graduated from Franklin Pierce, I walked through a third, very important door, on the library roof.

I no longer use actual physical doors or gates to symbolize each transition in my life. When I reread years of diary entries while writing this book, a clear pattern emerged. Each door or gate enabled me to move on to the next level. . . . During my life I have been faced with five or six major doors or gates to go through. [After college, I confronted my difficulty with the] "social arena," largely because I didn't have a concrete visual **corollary** for the abstraction known as "getting along with people." An image finally presented itself to me while I was washing a bay window [that] consisted of three glass sliding doors enclosed by storm windows. To wash the inside of the bay window, I had to crawl through the sliding door. The door jammed while I was washing the inside panes, and I was imprisoned between the two windows. In order to get out without shattering the door, I had to ease it back very carefully. It struck me that relationships operate the same way. They also shatter easily and have to be approached carefully. I then made a further association about how the careful opening of doors was related to establishing relationships in the first place. While I was trapped between the windows, it was almost impossible to communicate through the glass. Being autistic is like being trapped like this. The windows symbolized my feelings of disconnection from other people and helped me cope with the isolation. Throughout my life, door and window symbols have enabled me to make progress and connections that are unheard of for some people with autism.

corollary: something that logically follows from something else

After You Read

Mapping the Reading

1. What does Grandin mean by "think in pictures"? How is this process useful in her work with animals?

2. For Grandin, what are the advantages of being autistic? (Draw on any "As You Read" notes you may have.)

3. For Grandin, what are the disadvantages of being autistic? (Draw on any "As You Read" notes you may have.)

4. In addition to visual thinking, Grandin mentions other types of thinking, including associational, abstract, and verbal. Give a brief definition of these methods based on Grandin's descriptions.

5. At different points in her life, how did Grandin use door and window symbols?

Discussing and Thinking Critically about the Reading

1. How does Grandin feel about being autistic? Look at the text for specific clues about her feelings.

2. How does Grandin use the writing technique of offering specific examples to help readers understand her ideas? Identify some specific examples from the text, and consider how they are or are not useful.

3. What advice does Grandin have for educators working with autistic children? Summarize and then reflect on her suggestions. What value do they have for students with autism? for other students?

4. Grandin describes different ways of thinking: visual, associational, verbal, and abstract. Most of the time, people think without labeling the process. Reflect now on your own thought process; what label would you give it? What are its benefits and drawbacks?

5. In what ways might Grandin be either downplaying or idealizing her disability?

Navigating the Intersections

1. Temple Grandin's perspective on autism has relevance for many people, but of course other people with autism have had different kinds of experiences. Use a search engine to find other first-person accounts by people with autism or by those with family members who have autism. Try such terms as "living with autism" or "my autistic story." Note the URL, the source (magazine, organization, blog), and the author's name, and summarize the author's perspective.

2. Is autism in your life? Reflect on whether there are people with autism in your family, among your friends or their families, among coworkers, or in your community. Try to think broadly about how visible or invisible autism is to you.

Before You Read: What devices, machines, or tools have you used today to make living your life possible or easier? List these items along with a brief explanation: for example, elevator — to get downstairs faster.

BRIAN EULE

Brian Eule is a journalist and freelance writer. In 2009, he published *Match Day*, about a single important day in medical students' careers, the day they receive their residency program placement. Eule writes frequently for *Stanford* magazine, which is where this article profiling the inventor Henry Evans appeared in 2014.

As You Read: This article relies on description. In your underlining or note taking, identify descriptive passages, and rate the effectiveness of each passage by considering how well you can picture what Eule is describing.

---

fanfare: attention or celebration

Silicon Valley: area near San Francisco, California, home to many technology companies

I Was Trapped in My Own Body

Atop long and winding Page Mill Road, where the miles turn over without **fanfare**, a driveway stretches, removed from **Silicon Valley** below. At its end, a house, and inside, Henry Evans lies in bed. It's where he spends between eighteen and twenty-four hours of each day. Occasionally, he is taken to the bathroom or put in a wheelchair. A few times each week, he is placed outside by the garden. Most of the time, though, he is here, head propped up, the rest of his body motionless beneath the covers.

It's been like this for more than eleven years. Though Henry can turn his head and has limited use of one finger on his left hand, the rest of his body is paralyzed. And though he can let out a deep laugh and cry, he cannot speak. But Henry can feel everything — every itch he cannot scratch, every pain he cannot ease, and every pressure he cannot relieve.

Then there are his eyes. They smile and roll when he teases. They narrow and focus, connecting the distant world with the bright and passionate mind still fully functioning inside his head. They speak.

And for someone who is mute, Henry Evans has a very strong voice.

> ❝ All humans are limited by nature in many ways. . . . I may have lost a few of the natural adaptations which evolution afforded me, but I have adapted to these limitations, often in a way similar to how you have adapted to nature's limitations. For example, I use a wheelchair to increase my mobility. You use a bike. You use a keyboard and mouse; I use a headtracker and a clicker to operate a computer. ❞

Nearly three thousand miles away, a capacity crowd in Sidney Harman Hall in Washington, D.C., applauds as Henry is introduced to give a **TED talk**. A robot rolls onto the stage. A monitor on top shows Henry, back in California. The audience grows quiet.

TED talk: one of a series of talks focusing on technology, entertainment, and design

When Henry lost the ability to move most of his body and to speak, the disabled world gained a strong advocate, and those who study robotics got a tireless and passionate thinker. A few years into his new life, Henry recognized the potential of robots to level the playing field for severely disabled individuals. Like Henry, many people are dependent on caregivers for their "activities of daily living," as they are called: eating, showering, moving around, shaving, even scratching an itch. But robotics has the potential to help by serving as extensions or **surrogates** for body parts. Living with **quadriplegia** had given Henry a grasp of what ideas would actually be helpful in practice. So he began reaching out to others. He has become an idea generator and a test pilot, using robots to open drawers and even to shave. He has helped create and test user **interfaces** and programs, providing feedback for his collaborators at more than half a dozen universities and labs across the country.

surrogates: substitutes or replacements

quadriplegia: loss of ability to move arms and legs

interfaces: devices or systems that allow a person to communicate with a computer

There are a few ways in which Henry speaks. A wink of his left eye is a request to scratch an itch. Two blinks means "thank you." Rolling his eyes toward the ceiling means Henry is requesting the letter board.

The board is rectangular and translucent, with sets of letters in various places: *ABC* in the top left; *DEF* in the top middle; *GHI* in the top right. The whole alphabet is there, and as Henry's wife, Jane, holds up the board, she follows his eyes and calls out the letters he focuses on, spelling words as he goes. Often, she finishes them for him, much like an autocomplete feature.

"I, P, O — I posted — A, N — and — T, W — two people . . . ," Henry begins telling me through Jane one evening, describing a note he posted to a website. With Jane's help, Henry's words come fast. But the real magic occurs when Jane puts the board down. She leans in, and Henry moves his eyes to where the letters would be, like a touch typist who has memorized the keyboard. Jane, too, has these memorized and reads as they go, spelling out his sentences.

Henry's story is as much about Jane as it is about him. "We are one person," Henry jokes. "We just can't decide if we are a boy or a girl."

Jane radiates warmth and positivity. She's quick to laugh, and Henry says she has greatly prolonged his life. The two grew close in high school and were married in their early twenties. "It was like magic," Jane says of their first dance. "I felt like I was home." Although she's more than a foot shorter than Henry, Jane manages to lift him out of the bed and into a wheelchair. She adjusts him to ease pressure, feeds him, and helps him communicate. Sometimes, when they long for an embrace, she maneuvers his arms to wrap around her, squeezes him, and feels the pressure of him leaning in.

There's another way Henry speaks, and particularly to the outside world. A small reflective circle dots his glasses, and a laptop sits in front of him, allowing him to type emails, post messages online, and stay in touch with the people who work on robotics.

"I use a headtracker, which converts tiny head movements into cursor movements. Using an onscreen keyboard, I can type up to fifteen wpm," he explains, using the abbreviation for *words per minute*. His emails read as if he had no disability, with the exception of a small signature at the bottom that, much like an apology for typos made via smartphone, asks the recipient to please pardon the message's brevity because it was typed with Henry's head.

"There are a lot of disadvantages to using email to talk, but it is better than being a complete vegetable," he noted on a blog. "Often people don't answer, but there is something about being able to ask that is better than the alternative."

And so Henry begins his TED talk. A speaking device reads what he has typed, and he controls a robot from the other side of the country with his headtracker. All of which seemed unimaginable eleven years ago, when Henry was inches from death.

In 2002, Henry's life was full. He was physically fit and a towering presence. The chief financial officer at a **start-up**, he and Jane had four young children.

start-up: short for *start-up company*—a newly created business that is in a developmental stage

Eight months earlier, they had bought their first house on a beautiful piece of land in Los Altos Hills. Henry, good with his hands, looked forward to renovating it. He was forty, and life was just beginning.

One August morning, despite a headache that had begun the night before, Henry was driving his children to school on the way to work. His vision narrowed and his speech began to slur. He focused on the road and dropped his children off, and then he turned around. Six miles back up the hill, Henry stumbled into the house. He braced against the walls and told Jane that he just wanted to lie down. She said they were going to the doctor. Henry had to crawl to get back to the car.

In the emergency room, Henry's right arm went limp. "I'm so scared," he told Jane. And then he fell into a coma.

Doctors initially thought Henry might have meningitis. It turned out that a birth defect had **precipitated** the stroke-like symptoms. The inner lining of his **basilar artery** had become detached and was blocking the blood flow. He was on life support, and when he finally emerged from the coma, he was unable to speak or move. Jane noticed he tracked her with his eyes.

precipitated: caused

basilar artery: important blood vessel at the base of the brain

"I soon realized they were all I could move," Henry writes. "My dad explained that I had no motor control, and I got it—I was trapped in my own body."

At first, Henry was unable to breathe on his own. He had a **tracheostomy** and a feeding tube, and he was on about twenty-five medications. Two blinks became "yes," and one, "no." He was barely alive, but his mind and his senses were perfectly intact.

tracheostomy: a hole created in the neck for breathing

"Minutes were hours, and hours were days," Henry writes. At the same time, his wife wasn't getting encouraging news. "They took Jane into a room full of doctors and told her that, in their professional opinion, I would never move and her best bet was to pump me full of antidepressants and stick me in an institution, and soon. Well, that was the wrong thing to say to Jane."

Four months later, Jane and Henry returned home. And though Henry had developed use of a finger and better control of his neck, he had a hard time thinking about living. For the next three years, Henry talked to Jane about helping him with suicide. Jane would try to get him laughing, saying that with his six-foot, four-inch body, she could never pull it off. She also let him know she understood.

"I know how normal you are by asking me to do that," she would tell him. But she also told him something else.

"There is a reason God left you with your mind and you have life," Jane said. "Those are two incredible gifts that we take for granted every day. And the hardest thing you have to do is figure out why you're left here on Earth. It wasn't your time. Why? You have a purpose here."

It started with an idea. Henry envisioned a head-mounted laser pointer that he could use to activate electrical switches. He made a sketch on the computer and sent it to a friend who was mentoring a robotics team at Palo Alto High School. The students designed a working prototype called the LaserFinger, which later won a grant from **MIT**. Though it was yet to be used in Henry's daily life, it got him thinking.

A few years later, while watching CNN, Henry saw an interview with Georgia Tech professor Charlie Kemp. Kemp was discussing his collaboration with Willow Garage, a robotics research lab in **Menlo Park**, and its robot, the PR2. Henry fired off emails to Steve Cousins at Willow and to Kemp. Thus began a long collaboration between Henry and Jane, Willow Garage, and the Healthcare Robotics Lab at Georgia Tech to use robots to function as body parts for the severely disabled. Henry called it Robots for Humanity, describing his work as "using technology to extend our capabilities, fill in our weaknesses, and let people perform at their best."

"From a distance, all humans are disabled," Henry notes. "As humans, we adapted to our environment through evolution. We developed sight and hearing and speech. Yet these adaptations are quite limited. We can't run faster than about twenty-five miles per hour. We can't fly. We can't stay underwater forever and we can't be in more than one place at the same time. All humans are limited by nature in many ways.

"Now, I may have lost a few of the natural adaptations which evolution afforded me, but I have adapted to these limitations, often in a way similar to how you have adapted to nature's limitations. For example, I use a wheelchair to increase my mobility. You use a bike. You use a keyboard and mouse; I use a headtracker and a clicker to operate a computer."

One of the first things Kemp and Cousins did with Henry and Jane was ask them to identify tasks that would be the most helpful for a robot to perform. Scratching and shaving ranked high on their lists.

"Henry provided a mock-up of an interface design that he thought would be a good system for him," says Kemp. "We used that as a basis. That was a great way to start."

Using his headtracker and a computer, Henry manipulated the PR2 to scratch an itch on his face. It was the first time he had been able to do so in ten years. Shaving, they felt, would take a little more practice.

Thanks to software developed by Chad Jenkins, an associate professor of computer science at Brown University, Henry could operate the robot remotely on his own computer. So Kemp sat very still in his lab at Georgia Tech as a robot controlled by Henry in California moved closer to his face. In the robot's arm was an electric razor. Tight in the professor's hand, a small control with a red **kill switch** button. . . .

MIT:
Massachusetts
Institute of
Technology

Menlo Park: city
near San Francisco

kill switch:
means to disable
machinery in an
emergency

The implications of the trial were significant. It provided further evidence that people with motor impairments could operate robots to perform physical labor from remote sites, perhaps for compensation. And, Kemp said, he could imagine people with impairments also helping one another remotely.

Not long after his practice run, Henry shaved his own face.

Occasionally, Henry plays soccer with Jenkins at Brown. After placing a soccer ball between two robots in the lab, Jenkins controls one while Henry controls the other from California.

Like other collaborators, Jenkins recognizes the value in having Henry test out his work. "Every time, you learn something new," he says. "If you don't get robots out of the lab and into the world, you're usually working with assumptions that aren't true."

So, earlier this year, Jenkins and Henry decided to take the robot out into the world for that TED talk. Not only did Henry speak—both beside Jenkins on the stage and at home beside Jane—but he also demonstrated how he could fly a drone remotely, onstage.

The next time you see a disabled person, Henry told the crowd, remind yourself that you use **assistive** devices at least as often as they do. But that doesn't **diminish** you as a person. "Your disability doesn't make you any less of a person, and neither does mine," he said.

They got a standing ovation.

assistive: providing aid or assistance

diminish: make or become less

After You Read

Mapping the Reading

1. Henry Evans's wife, Jane, tells him that he must figure out what his purpose is in life. What purpose does he find for himself?

2. Explain how Henry Evans communicates.

3. According to Henry Evans, who among us can reasonably be defined as disabled?

4. What are Henry Evans's contributions to creating assistive devices like the Laser-Finger and the remote-controlled shaver?

5. Write a three-sentence biography of Henry Evans. Who is Evans, and why is he important?

Discussing and Thinking Critically about the Reading

1. How does the author, Brian Eule, first describe Henry Evans? What is the effect of this description? How does the longer profile work to confirm or challenge this initial impression?

2. Select a quote from this reading and explain why it is inspirational in the context of disability, and why it is personally inspirational for you.

3. Eule uses Henry Evans's life story to make the case that *all* humans are disabled, and that *all* humans must adapt and develop "assistive devices" to overcome or compensate for their disabilities. Do you find that case persuasive? Why or why not?

4. Henry Evans clearly has remarkable personal qualities that helped him transform and rebuild his life. Besides his personal qualities, what things helped lead to his transformation? (Consider people as well as economic and social conditions.)

Navigating the Intersections

1. Compare the life story of Henry Evans to that of another person described in this chapter (e.g., Temple Grandin, Chuck Close, or Carol Greider). Identify similarities and differences, focusing particularly on *how* these people have positively transformed themselves, and the factors (people, events, or experiences) that helped them most with their transformations.

2. Henry Evans suggests that tools—assistive technologies—can be developed to overcome human disabilities. Review several readings in this chapter to consider whether or not tools are crucial to specific individuals as they overcome their disabilities.

Before You Read: Freewrite on the topic of creativity and its value to society. What is creativity? How do you value it personally? How is it valued in school? in business? in solving problems of the world?

SCOTT BARRY KAUFMAN

Psychologist Scott Barry Kaufman is the author or editor of several books, including *The Complexity of Greatness: Beyond Talent or Practice* (2013) and *Ungifted: Intelligence Redefined* (2013). Kaufman is scientific director of the Imagination Institute in the Positive Psychology Center at the University of Pennsylvania, and the recipient of many awards, including an Excellence in Research award from the Mensa Foundation. Kaufman's dual-process theory of human intelligence—a theory that argues for the importance of spontaneous thinking associated with creativity—recognizes the creative gifts of people classified with ADHD (attention deficit/hyperactivity disorder), as discussed in this 2014 post from *Beautiful Minds*, a blog published by *Scientific American*.

As You Read: Kaufman uses a lot of vocabulary from the field of psychology. As you read, pay special attention to the words and terms that are specific to his discipline, briefly translating his psychological language into more familiar, general language.

The Creative Gifts of ADHD

In his 2004 book *Creativity Is Forever*, Gary Davis reviewed the **creativity literature** from 1961 to 2003 and identified twenty-two reoccurring personality traits of creative people. This included sixteen "positive" **traits** (e.g., independent, risk-taking, high energy, curiosity, humor, artistic, emotional) and six "negative" traits (e.g., impulsive, hyperactive, argumentative). In her own review of the creativity literature, Bonnie Cramond found that many of these same traits overlap to a substantial degree with behavioral descriptions of Attention Deficit Hyperactive Disorder (ADHD) — including higher levels of **spontaneous** idea generation, mind wandering, daydreaming, sensation seeking, energy, and impulsivity.

Research since then has supported the notion that people with ADHD characteristics are *more likely* to reach higher levels of creative thought and achievement than people without these characteristics. Recent research by Darya Zabelina and colleagues have found that real-life creative achievement is associated with the ability to *broaden* attention and have a "leaky" **mental filter** — something in which people with ADHD excel.

Recent work in **cognitive neuroscience** also suggests a connection between ADHD and creativity. Both creative thinkers and people with ADHD show difficulty **suppressing** brain activity coming from the "Imagination Network."

Of course, whether this is a positive thing or a negative thing depends on the context. The ability to control your attention is most certainly a valuable asset; difficulty **inhibiting** your inner mind can get in the way of paying attention to a boring classroom lecture or concentrating on a challenging problem. But the ability to keep your inner stream of fantasies, imagination, and daydreams on call can be immensely **conducive** to creativity. By automatically treating ADHD characteristics as a disability — as we so often do in an educational context — we are unnecessarily letting too many competent and creative kids fall through the cracks.

Nine percent of children aged five to seventeen years old are labeled ADHD on average per year, and placed in special education programs. However, new data from the National Center for Learning Disabilities shows that only 1 percent of students who receive IDEA (Individuals with Disabilities Education Act) services are in gifted and talented programs, and only 2 percent are enrolled in an AP course. The report concludes that "students with learning and attention issues are shut out of gifted and AP programs, held back in grade level and suspended from school at higher rates than other students."

Why does this matter? Consider a new study conducted by C. Matthew Fugate and colleagues. They selected a population of students with ADHD characteristics who were part of a summer residential camp for gifted, creative, and talented students. The large majority of the students were selected for the

---

creativity literature: research articles and reports on the subject of creativity

traits: characteristics

spontaneous: occurring as a result of sudden inner impulse

mental filter: an automatic process a person goes through to evaluate positive or negative elements

cognitive neuroscience: study of how the brain produces certain psychological impulses

suppressing: putting an end to

inhibiting: restraining; discouraging

conducive: helpful; making possible

> " By automatically treating ADHD characteristics as a disability—as we so often do in an educational context—we are unnecessarily letting too many competent and creative kids fall through the cracks. "

infer: assume or conclude from evidence and reasoning

novel: new and interesting

creative cognition: the process of coming to understand or know

implications: consequences

attentional control skills: skills that help people pay attention

throw out the baby with the bathwater: an old saying that refers to not throwing out the good with the bad

non-sequential: not in any regular sequence or order

divergent: tending to develop in different directions

program because they either scored in the 90th percentile or above on a standardized test, or had a GPA of 3.5 or greater in specific areas (e.g., mathematics, chemistry).

The researchers then compared this ADHD group of students with a non-ADHD group of students who were participating in the same gifted program. They gave all the students tests of fluid reasoning, working memory, and creative cognition. *Fluid reasoning* involves the ability to **infer** relations and spot **novel** and complex patterns that draw on minimal prior knowledge and expertise. *Working memory* involves the ability to control attention and hold multiple streams of information in mind at once. They measured **creative cognition** by having the students come up with novel drawings that included one of the following elements: an oval shape, incomplete figures, and two straight lines.

The researchers found that students with ADHD characteristics (especially those who scored high in "inattention") had lower working memory scores than the non-ADHD students, *even though they did not differ in their fluid reasoning ability*. This is consistent with past research showing that people with ADHD tend to score lower on tests of working memory, but these findings also suggest that people with ADHD can still be quite smart despite their reduced ability to hold multiple pieces of information in memory. Also, despite their reduced working memory, 53 percent of the academically advanced students with ADHD characteristics scored at or above the 70th percentile on the creativity index. In fact, for both the ADHD and the non-ADHD group of students, the poorer the working memory, the *higher* the creativity!

This obviously has some important educational **implications**. To be sure, ADHD can make it difficult for students to pay attention in class and organize their lives. The importance of learning key **attentional control skills** should not be undervalued. But let's not **throw out the baby with the bathwater**. As the researchers note, "in the school setting, the challenge becomes how to create an environment in which creativity is emphasized as a *pathway* to learning as well as an outcome of learning."

One issue involves the identification of "twice exceptional" students and their appropriate educational programming. Assessments of creativity are notably absent from most gifted and talented programs in this country. Instead of automatically putting children with ADHD characteristics in special education, a broader assessment should be conducted. For one, IQ tests could be administered that focus less on working memory and memorization, and allow for a fairer assessment of fluid reasoning and **non-sequential** thought among this population of students.

A broader assessment could also allow students with ADHD characteristics to display their creative strengths, including **divergent** thinking, imagination, and **hyperfocus** (when interested). People with ADHD often are able to focus *better* than others when they are deeply engaged in an activity that is personally meaningful to them. Recent research suggests that the brain network that people with ADHD have difficulty suppressing (the "Imagination Network") is the same brain network that is conducive to flow and engagement among musicians, including jazz musicians and rappers!

hyperfocus: deep and intense concentration, common in people with ADHD

In terms of [school] programming, problem-based learning (PBL) approaches may enable ADHD students to engage more with the material, and become active learners, rather than passive observers. Additionally, learning can be assessed through project-based learning (PBL), in which students demonstrate their knowledge of the course material through the creation of different products (e.g., cartoons, role-playing, blogs, videos, newspaper articles), and the constant revision of these products.

Of course, these same possibilities should extend to all students in the classroom, academically advanced or not. Because we never really know whether an ADHD characteristic is a learning **impediment** or a creative gift.

impediment: obstacle or block

Consider the case of John, who in 1949 attended Eton College and dreamed of becoming a scientist. However, last in his class, he received the following comment on his report card:

> His work has been far from satisfactory . . . he will not listen, but will insist on doing his work in his own way . . . I believe he has ideas about becoming a Scientist; on his present showing this is quite ridiculous, if he can't learn simple Biological facts he would have no chance of doing the work of a Specialist, and it would be a sheer waste of time on his part, and of those who have to teach him.

This was Sir John B. Gurdon, winner of the 2012 Nobel Prize in Physiology or Medicine for his revolutionary research on **stem cells**. Like so many other highly creative, competent individuals, he might have been referred for testing and given the label "attention deficit hyperactive disorder."

stem cells: cells essential to medical research because they are unique in being able to develop into other kinds of cells

It's time to stop letting this happen.

After You Read

Mapping the Reading

1. Review the traits (characteristics) of creative people as defined by Kaufman and other psychologists, and select the five that best help you remember this definition of *creative*, which may be different from how you define the term.

2. According to researchers, what traits are possessed by both creative people and people with ADHD?

3. For what reasons does Kaufman think it may be unwise to label a child with ADHD?

4. Why is it significant that people with ADHD tend to score low on tests of *working memory*, while they score high on tests of *fluid reasoning ability*? (Make sure you review what these terms mean.)

5. What is Kaufman's argument, and what are his three best supporting points for making this argument?

Discussing and Thinking Critically about the Reading

1. From your observations and experiences in school, is creativity recognized, praised, and encouraged? Provide one or two examples to support your view.

2. Find the passage where Kaufman refers to a report from the National Center for Learning Disabilities. Summarize the report's findings in your own words, and then discuss or explain the significance of these findings.

3. Kaufman discusses the disadvantages of the ADHD label. Consider the other side: What are the advantages of the ADHD label? How might the label be helpful to individuals, teachers, and parents?

4. While many people talk about what people with ADHD lack, Kaufman discusses their strengths. According to this article, what are these strengths? Why is it important to have these strengths assessed and valued?

5. On its website, *Scientific American* calls itself "the leading source and authority for science, technology information and policy for a general audience." In what ways do you see Kaufman's article as being directed to this type of audience? For example, you could consider Kaufman's use of psychological terminology (drawing on your "As You Read" notes).

Navigating the Intersections

1. Scott Barry Kaufman suggests that traits associated with ADHD may indicate an extraordinary ability (creativity), not a disability. Compare his view on ability and disability with that of another author in this chapter. On what do they agree? disagree?

2. What are the special abilities of people with ADHD? Using the Internet, research the question by typing in "ADHD and successful people," "ADHD and famous people," or other phrases you think of on your own.

Rethinking Disability

Before You Read: Consider the world around you. How many people who live with you, live near you, or go to school with you have visible physical disabilities? In your community, do those who are blind, deaf, and physically impaired live, work, and go to school around those without visible physical disabilities? Or are community members with physical disabilities living, working, and learning separately from those without visible physical disabilities?

ROSEMARY MAHONEY

Rosemary Mahoney is the author of several nonfiction books on subjects ranging from teaching English in China to contemporary Irish life. Her most recent book is *For the Benefit of Those Who See: Dispatches from the World of the Blind* (2014). Mahoney also writes frequently for magazines (*O, The Oprah Magazine*; *Elle*; *National Geographic Traveler*; and the *New York Times Magazine*) and newspapers (the *New York Times*, the *Wall Street Journal*, and the *London Observer*). "Why Do We Fear the Blind?" appeared as an opinion column in the Sunday edition of the *New York Times* in 2014.

As You Read: Look for statements that reflect ignorance or fear of blindness, and underline or otherwise mark them.

Why Do We Fear the Blind?

A few years ago, when I mentioned to a woman I met at a party that I was teaching in a school for the blind, she seemed confused. "Can I just ask you one question?" she said. "How do you talk to your students?"

I explained that the students were blind, not deaf. Raising the palms of her hands at me, as if to **stem** further misunderstanding, she said: "Yes, I know they're not deaf. But what I really mean is, how do you actually talk to them?"

stem: stop

I knew, because I had been asked this question before by reasonably intelligent people, that the woman didn't know exactly what she meant. All she knew was that in her mind there existed a substantial intellectual barrier between the blind and the sighted. The blind could hear, yes. But could they properly understand?

Throughout history and across cultures the blind have been **traduced** by a **host** of mythologies such as this. They have variously been perceived as pitiable idiots incapable of learning, as artful masters of deception, or as mystics possessed of supernatural powers. One of the most persistent misconceptions about blindness is that it is a curse from God for misdeeds **perpetrated** in a past life, which cloaks the blind person in spiritual darkness and makes him not just dangerous but evil.

traduced: exposed to shame through inaccuracies

host: multitude

perpetrated: committed

A majority of my blind students at the International Institute for Social Entrepreneurs in Trivandrum, India, a branch of **Braille** Without Borders, came from the **developing world**: Madagascar, Colombia, Tibet, Liberia, Ghana, Kenya, Nepal, and India. One of my students, the twenty-seven-year-old Sahr, lost most of his eyesight to measles when he was a child. (Like many children in rural West Africa, Sahr had not been vaccinated.) The residents of Sahr's village were certain that his blindness — surely the result of witchcraft or immoral

Braille: a system of raised dots that allows blind people to read

developing world: countries with an underdeveloped industrial base, relative to other countries

actions on his family's part—would **adversely** affect the entire village. They surrounded his house and shouted threats and abuse. They **confiscated** a considerable portion of his parents' land. Eventually, the elders **decreed** that Sahr's father must take the child out to the **bush**, "where the demons live," and abandon him there. The parents refused and fled the village with their son.

> ❝ *We take our eyesight so much for granted, . . . and are so overwhelmed by its superficial data, that even the most brilliant sighted person can take a stupidly long time to recognize the obvious: There is usually a perfectly healthy, active, and normal human mind behind that pair of unseeing eyes.* ❞

Many of my students had similar experiences. Marco's parents, devout Colombian Catholics, begged a priest to say a Mass so that their blind infant son would die before his existence brought shame and hardship on their household. The villagers in Kyile's remote Tibetan village insisted that she, her two blind brothers, and their blind father should all just commit suicide because they were nothing but a burden to the sighted members of the family. When, as a child in Sierra Leone, James began to see objects upside down because of an **ocular** disease, the villagers were certain that he was possessed by demons.

In these places, schools for blind children were deemed a **preposterous** waste of resources and effort. Teachers in regular schools refused to educate them. Sighted children ridiculed them, tricked them, spat at them, and threw stones at them. And when they reached working age, no one would hire them. During a visit to the Braille Without Borders training center in Tibet, I met blind children who had been beaten, told they were idiots, locked in rooms for years on end, and abandoned by their parents. These stories, which would have been commonplace in the **Dark Ages**, took place in the 1980s, 1990s, and 2000s. They are taking place now. Nine out of ten blind children in the developing world still have no access to education, many for no other reason than that they are blind.

The United States has one of the lowest rates of visual impairment in the world, and yet blindness is still among the most feared physical afflictions. Even in this country, the blind are perceived as a people apart.

Aversion toward the blind exists for the same reason that most prejudices exist: lack of knowledge. Ignorance is a powerful generator of fear. And fear slides easily into aggression and contempt. Anyone who has not spent more than five minutes with a blind person might be forgiven for believing—like the woman I met at the party—that there is an unbridgeable gap between us and them.

For most of us, sight is the primary way we interpret the world. How can we even begin to conceive of a meaningful connection with a person who cannot see? Before I began living and working among blind people, I, too, wondered this. Whenever I saw a blind person on the street I would stare, transfixed, hoping, out of a vague and **visceral** discomfort, that I wouldn't

adversely: negatively

confiscated: took away as punishment

decreed: officially decided or declared

bush: areas of rural wilderness

ocular: related to the eye

preposterous: unreasonable or ridiculous

Dark Ages: approximately 500–1500; considered a barbaric period of little scientific advancement

aversion: strong dislike

visceral: emotional rather than logical

have to engage with him. In his 1930 book *The World of the Blind,* Pierre Villey, a blind French professor of literature, summarized the **lurid** carnival of prejudices and superstitions about the blind that were passed down the centuries. "The sighted person judges the blind not for what they are but by the fear blindness inspires. . . . The revolt of his sensibility in the face of 'the most atrocious of maladies' fills a sighted person with prejudice and gives rise to a thousand legends." The blind author Georgina Kleege, a lecturer at the University of California at Berkeley, more **tersely** wrote, "The blind are either supernatural or subhuman, alien or animal."

lurid: vivid or shocking; sensational

tersely: bluntly

We take our eyesight so much for granted, cling to it so slavishly, and are so overwhelmed by its superficial data, that even the most brilliant sighted person can take a stupidly long time to recognize the obvious: There is usually a perfectly healthy, active, and normal human mind behind that pair of unseeing eyes.

Christopher Hitchens called blindness "one of the oldest and most tragic disorders known to man." How horribly excluded and bereft we would feel to lose the world and the way of life that sight brings us. Blindness can happen to any one of us. Myself, I used to be certain I'd rather die than be blind; I could not imagine how I would have the strength to go on in the face of such a loss.

And yet people do. . . .

I've learned from my blind friends and colleagues that blindness doesn't have to remain tragic. For those who can adapt to it, blindness becomes a path to an alternative and equally rich way of living.

One of the many misconceptions about the blind is that they have greater hearing, sense of smell, and sense of touch than sighted people. This is not strictly true. Their blindness simply forces them to recognize gifts they always had but had heretofore largely ignored.

A few years ago, I allowed myself to be blindfolded and led through the streets of Lhasa by two blind Tibetan teenage girls, students at Braille Without Borders. The girls had not grown up in the city, and yet they **traversed** it with ease, without stumbling or getting lost. They had a specific destination in mind, and each time they announced, "Now we turn left" or "Now we turn right," I was compelled to ask them how they knew this. Their answers startled me, chiefly because the clues they were following—the sound of many televisions in an electronics shop, the smell of leather in a shoe shop, the feel of cobblestones suddenly underfoot—though out in the open for anyone to perceive, were virtually hidden from me.

traversed: traveled across

For the first time in my life, I realized how little notice I paid to sounds, to smells, indeed to the entire world that lay beyond my ability to see.

The French writer Jacques Lusseyran, who lost his sight at the age of eight, understood that those of us who have sight are, in some ways, **deprived** by it.

deprived: lacking something necessary or essential

"In return for all the benefits that sight brings we are forced to give up others whose existence we don't even suspect."

I do not intend to suggest there is something wonderful about blindness. There is only something wonderful about human **resilience**, adaptability, and daring. The blind are no more or less otherworldly, stupid, evil, gloomy, pitiable, or deceitful than the rest of us. It is only our ignorance that has cloaked them in these ridiculous garments. When Helen Keller wrote, "It is more difficult to teach ignorance to think than to teach an intelligent blind man to see the grandeur of Niagara," she was speaking, obviously, of the uplifting and equalizing value of knowledge.

resilience: the capacity to recover quickly from difficulties

After You Read

Mapping the Reading

1. How does Mahoney answer the question posed in her title?

2. Mahoney describes many misconceptions—mistaken beliefs—that people around the world have about those who are blind. Describe three misconceptions that she identifies.

3. According to Mahoney, what perceptive abilities do sighted people lack?

4. How did Mahoney come to the personal realization that "blindness doesn't have to remain tragic"?

5. Map or outline the article to determine how it is organized. What kinds of examples does Mahoney present, and in what order?

Discussing and Thinking Critically about the Reading

1. The article opens with the story of a woman who wonders how Mahoney is able to communicate with her blind students. Describe how this example is effective or ineffective in introducing Mahoney's topic.

2. Reread the last two paragraphs of this article. What is Mahoney trying to get her readers to realize? Reflect on whether she has changed your understanding or view of blindness. Why or why not?

3. Think about media depictions of the blind—a character in a book, movie, or TV show, or a famous person—and write a paragraph describing how this person is presented. In light of Mahoney's essay, explain whether this example depicts blindness accurately. Does it offer a perspective that displays understanding, or one that indicates ignorance of the blind?

4. Christopher Hitchens, widely believed to be a great thinker, is quoted as holding ignorant beliefs about blindness. What is Mahoney's purpose in including Hitchens's views on the blind?

Navigating the Intersections

1. Rosemary Mahoney writes, "Aversion toward the blind exists for the same reason that most prejudices exist: lack of knowledge. Ignorance is a powerful generator of fear. And fear slides easily into aggression and contempt." Identify another group of people, from this chapter or from your own knowledge, who, like the blind, also face prejudice because of ignorance.

2. Select a "disability" or "ability" that you have heard of or are curious about, and find a blog in which a writer who has this disability or ability shares his or her perspective. Once you have found an interesting blogger, select and read one blog entry. Print the blog post, and come to class prepared to summarize the blogger's perspective and explain what is interesting about his or her perspective on ability/disability.

Before You Read: Describe someone you know who has extraordinary abilities — whether physical, emotional, or cognitive (intellectual). Then write some more: What disability does that person also have? Next, try the opposite: Describe someone you know who has a significant disability, and consider whether that person also has a striking ability.

JOANN ELLISON RODGERS

Journalist and science writer Joann Ellison Rodgers is the author of seven books, including *Psychosurgery: Damaging the Brain to Save the Mind* (1992), and hundreds of magazine articles. Rodgers writes about psychology, medicine, and public health, among other topics, and is published regularly in such newspapers and magazines as the *New York Times Magazine*, the *Los Angeles Times*, *Cosmopolitan*, *Ladies Home Journal*, *Parade*, and *Psychology Today*, where "Cognitive Outlaws" was published in 2011.

As You Read: Make a list of the researchers Rodgers refers to in her article, and make a brief note about their theories about learning disabilities and people who have them.

Cognitive* Outlaws

A growing gallery of triumphant entrepreneurs, lawyers, scientists, artists, and writers own up to a history of **dyslexia**, ADHD [attention deficit/hyperactivity disorder], and related miswirings of the **cerebral cortex**. Web sites abound with the usual suspects — Einstein and Edison, whose **dyscalculia throttled** their

*cognitive: concerning conscious thought processes like thinking, learning, and recalling

dyslexia: a term for various language-based disabilities associated with difficulty in learning to read and write, and in interpreting words, symbols, or letters

cerebral cortex: the part of the brain responsible for coordinating sensory and motor information

dyscalculia: difficulties understanding numbers and calculations

throttled: suppressed

decipher:
interpret

Moby-Dick:
Herman Melville's
1851 classic
American novel
about a whale

cognition:
thinking,
understanding, and
remembering

instantiate:
represent abstract
ideas with concrete
examples

> ❝ *[The] inability to decode letters on a page is often accompanied by 'a sea of strength' in analytic thinking, reasoning, and creativity.* ❞

make lemonade:
part of the cliché
"When life gives
you lemons,
make lemonade,"
meaning to make
the best of a bad
situation

compensatory:
counterbalancing;
making up for

stigma: a mark of
shame or disgrace

**sort through
chaff:** part of
the expression
"To separate the
wheat from the
chaff," meaning to
separate things of
high quality from
those of lower
quality

spatial:
space-related

intrepid:
adventurous or
fearless

efforts at arithmetic—and gush over the more newly revealed, from aviation's Richard Branson and fashion's Tommy Hilfiger to Wall Street's Charles Schwab, author John Irving, and actor/comedian Henry Winkler, who once joked that "we all know what being called 'special' in school really means."

What drives a man who couldn't pass algebra to master physics and change our view of the universe? What compels a novelist who failed to **decipher** *Moby-Dick* to put words on a page for a living? Do they achieve in spite of the disability or because of it? Do dyslexia and similar afflictions rob the left brain, dominated by "logical" **cognition** processes that manage reading and other learning skills favored in school, but pay the right hemisphere, in which neurons **instantiate** more inventive, ambitious, and creative processes?

It's not yet clear whether dyslexics **make lemonade** by figuring out ways around their reading problems or actually come pre-equipped with **compensatory** strengths. But the issue matters to many. An estimated one in ten children in the United States is dyslexic, and for most, their stories bog down in **stigma**.

"The pain begins the first day in school when kids realize they can't do what others do so easily," says Sally Shaywitz, a pediatric neurologist at Yale, cofounder of its Center for Dyslexia and Creativity, and researcher of the reading disability that accounts for 80 to 90 percent of all learning problems. She believes the learning disabled are an unmined treasure with great potential value to society.

Shaywitz has evidence that their inability to decode letters on a page is often accompanied by "a sea of strength" in analytic thinking, reasoning, and creativity. Perhaps because they are forced to concentrate harder on particular problems, find work-arounds, and seek alternate ways to **sort through chaff**, they solve problems more easily, less distracted by irrelevant details. "They learn to think outside the box," she insists, "because they never fit inside."

Schools, however, generally describe cognitive success only one way—fluid reading, calculating, **spatial** navigation, and linear reasoning. Nevertheless, when doors most students dance through close on them, some of the "weird kids" become **intrepid** seekers of paths with fewer boundaries.

Their brain makeup may force that. In anatomical imaging studies, neurologist Martha Denckla of Johns Hopkins University finds that language flows far less efficiently through dyslexic brains than through typical ones. "Maybe," she says, "when dyslexics confront the word 'cat' they instantly get a bigger network of meaning. They see, feel, and smell cats." In school, this "rich associative network" encounters only exercises designed to shove the other senses back in the box. But it's the detours that contribute to the rich landscape of creativity and dot-connecting that so often mark the entrepreneur, the innovator, and the creative.

Some of the most exciting clues to the nature and nurture of "cognitive outlaws" come from the most successful among them. All report having developed the "courage to fail" because they experienced failure from an early age. They embraced the "cognitive quirks" that made school and sometimes relationships tough, but also made them charming.

They are self-described "risk takers," "very hard workers," "solution-focused" to a fault, and early on adopt what one has called "the C-student mentality," dedicated to the strategy of "invest low and reap high" by putting energy into what makes them happiest and what their lack of inhibitions tells them they can master if they try. The rest they discard.

Cognitive outlaws describe themselves as anxious, even **hypervigilant** in compensating for their disabilities. They rely on explicit routines for getting things done, as they can't trust their own instincts. Their impatience with details makes them **dogged** at simplifying complexity.

There are those among the learning disabled who somehow manage to reject the **pedagogical orthodoxy** they meet every day in school and instead work to rearrange the world to their own liking. . . .

> ❝ *I'd get in a tub of water, put a board over the rim to hold a book, turn off the bathroom lights, shine a bright light on the textbook, and sit there and read every page out loud five times to hear it in my ear. All night long I'd do that, then hurl my body out of the tub looking like a prune and rush to the classroom where I could spit back enough to get a C-minus. If the test was postponed a week, I had to do that all over again.* ❞

hypervigilant: excessively alert

dogged: determined; unwilling to give up

pedagogical: related to the method and practice of teaching

orthodoxy: established doctrine or convention

Chuck Close: Artist

Only at the end of a long phone conversation did American hyperrealist and portraitist Chuck Close reveal his most peculiar learning disability. "Sure, feel free to stop by my gallery when you're in New York," he said cheerily, "but even though I have been talking to you for an hour and using your name, have your name written down, and have been told by my assistant who you were when you called, I will have no idea who 'Joann Rodgers' is when you introduce yourself."

Close, seventy and confined to a wheelchair since 1988 after a spinal stroke left him a partial **quadriplegic**, is not only dyslexic but agnosic, unable to recognize letters, objects, faces, words, scenes, or spaces with any of the five senses. Not remembering names is the least of it; he can't memorize dates or events or anything he reads — although he can recite conversations he had years ago word for word. But if someone who sits in front of him for an hour turns his head ten degrees, he becomes a mystery guest. Close can't recognize faces no matter how frequently or long he looks at them, even if he knows them well.

quadriplegic: paralyzed in both arms and both legs

Ironically, perhaps, this grand master of contemporary art achieved his fame mostly with monumental portraits of friends, family members, and everyday things. His meticulous method of filling a huge canvas with rings or dots

pointillist: a
method of painting
using dots that
blend together to
form an image
when viewed from
a distance

of paint, ink, or paper pulp in whole families of hues brings a **pointillist** look to outsize images that seem, even up close, like photographs.

By his own account, Close's innovative style grew directly out of childhood difficulties. "I'm very learning-disabled," he says. "Art was the first thing I could do slightly better than most of my friends." After "failing at virtually everything else," he "put all my eggs in the art basket."

Growing up in rural Monroe, Washington, in the 1940s and '50s, "no one ever heard of dyslexia. I didn't until my older daughter [now a physician] was diagnosed," he recalls. "I was considered a dumb, lazy **shirker**. My biggest problem was trying to show my teachers I cared about the material although I couldn't spit back names and dates."

shirker: a slacker,
or a person who
avoids duties

Art and music, he says, saved his life. "I was first-chair sax in the band, did the art for the yearbook and poetry magazine and the sets for plays, and I would do twenty-foot-long murals. I sat in the front row and raised my hand even when I knew I couldn't answer the question, just to show I was eager."

Afflicted with physical disabilities to match his learning problems, Close couldn't run, throw, catch, or hit a ball. "I decided I needed to keep people around me some other way," he says, so he became a magician, puppeteer, and storyteller.

But it was the face blindness that drove him to paint portraits. "While I have very little ability to recognize a face in 3-D," he says, "I can remember a face almost photographically if I flatten it out. So I paint portraits to remember people close to me, but I do the act of flattening out from photos, not life, so that I can translate to canvas."

Overwhelmed by the "whole" of anything visual, he says, he figured out how to make big complicated things manageable by breaking them into parts. His canvases are first penciled with a grid.

"It takes away the fear and dread," he says. "I'm anxious, a nervous wreck with a short attention span, and a slob. I can't get mired in **minutiae**. I'm valuable only because I see big pictures and can put pieces together."

minutiae: small,
unimportant details

Like most successful dyslexics, Close recalls particular champions, teachers, and family members who believed in him, although one high school adviser told him he'd never make it to college because he couldn't take algebra and physics.

In high school, he became something of a celebrity for the coping mechanisms he devised. "I developed a method of getting a certain amount of information into my brain. I would use my sensory deprivation tank," he explains.

"I'd get in a tub of water, put a board over the rim to hold a book, turn off the bathroom lights, shine a bright light on the textbook, and sit there and read every page out loud five times to hear it in my ear. All night long I'd do that, then hurl my body out of the tub looking like a prune and rush to the classroom where I could spit back enough to get a C-minus. If the test was postponed a week, I had to do that all over again."

In college, Close was able to pick and choose courses and hire typists to whom he dictated all of his papers. He graduated **magna cum laude** from the University of Washington and earned an **MFA** from Yale.

His studies completed, Close sent his former high school adviser an official transcript with a note: "Think about this." . . .

magna cum laude: with high honors

MFA: master of fine arts degree

Carol Greider: Nobel Prize in Medicine, 2009

. . . Severely dyslexic, [Carol Greider] scored poorly on the **Graduate Record Exams**, as she did on all standardized tests. Unfortunately, most good schools enforced strict GRE cutoff scores. Of the thirteen schools she applied to, only two were interested. "If UC Berkeley had not invited me for an interview, I would never have gotten into grad school, discovered telomerase, and won the **Nobel Prize**," she says. . . .

Graduate Record Exams: GRE, standardized tests to get into graduate school, similar to the SAT or ACT test to get into college

Nobel Prize: annual prize awarded in different categories for excellence in academic, cultural, and scientific advances

For nine months, for twelve hours a day in the lab, Greider ran experiments using mostly Tetrahymena thermophila, an organism others call pond scum that has forty thousand or so chromosomes per cell, compared to the mere twenty-three pairs humans have. The organism afforded her far more opportunities to study chromosome ends. Such a practical/logical approach is an attribute shared by many dyslexics.

"For a student to want to get involved in this project was almost unheard of," [Elizabeth] Blackburn [Greider's PhD supervisor] has said. "Students want to do safe things [to advance their careers] and this was not safe. It could have completely crashed and burned. But Carol had a sense of adventure."

Alone in the lab on Christmas Day 1984, Greider spotted evidence of what would be called telomerase—a discovery others have likened to figuring out how cells divide. Greider, a triathlete and long-distance runner, rushed home and "danced and danced" to Bruce Springsteen.

The risk taking, the dogged persistence, the enthusiasm, the sense of fun are counterparts to the dyslexia she long struggled to overcome. Greider first confronted her disability in elementary school, where she was unable to spell or sound out words. "It was terrifying to read in front of a class. I could see the word, but couldn't pronounce it. I felt like a stupid outsider, not as smart as the other kids." She was pulled out of her classes by a tutor for remedial work, making her even more self-conscious.

Eventually, she gave up trying to sound words out. Instead, she began memorizing "literally thousands of words" and how they were spelled. She describes her approach as "putting on blinders and just forging ahead." When her approach garnered her A's, she figured out she wasn't so stupid after all. It wasn't until college, at the University of California at Santa Barbara, that she realized there was a word for what **plagued** her.

plagued: troubled

Like many fellow dyslexics, Greider now speaks with charming rapidity, her thoughts tumbling out in passionate coherence. Unlike many other dyslexics, however, she "loves" to read.

Greider doesn't really know if she thinks differently than others, but "we dyslexics do compensate with memory," she says. "I practice memorization." Oh, yes. There's one other thing the Nobel **laureate** does. "I see the core of a problem quickly. I'm good at rapidly separating wheat from chaff. Others can't or don't do it easily." Learning problems, she adds, "don't have to be obstacles to getting what you want. There are ways to compensate. Persevere. Do what you love and you'll find ways to get it done."

laureate: winner

Why Dyslexics Think Differently

As psychologists, educators, and neuroscientists tease out the nature of dyslexia and other learning disabilities, they find that the conditions also **confer** certain talents. Yale's Sally Shaywitz defines dyslexia as an unexpected difficulty in reading relative to IQ, education, or professional status.

confer: grant; give

Typical readers figure out quickly how to link letters with a particular sound. "After some practice, all they have to do is see the letters and it's automatic, like breathing," she says. But in dyslexics the process remains manual; each time they see a word, it's brand-new. With enormous effort, they learn to read, but always slowly. "What's clear is that their brains process information a different way, perhaps due to lower levels of inhibition."

Dyslexics see big pictures, adds Shaywitz. "Their minds wander wider. And they can cut to the chase of a problem and make quick decisions — often to the point that others are annoyed with them."

Learning problems may have their source in cultural evolution. Reading, Shaywitz explains, is based on spoken language, and spoken language took hundreds of thousands of years to evolve. It's hardwired and naturally acquired.

Written language, on the other hand, is ten thousand years old at most, neither natural nor hardwired, although some symbols and **glyphs** might be. Individual letters must be connected to something with **inherent** meaning learned from spoken language. "That's why dyslexics may have a hard time learning *Cat in the Hat*; they may mispronounce simple words repeatedly even after they've heard them a lot."

glyphs: pictures representing words, syllables, or sounds

inherent: natural; essential

Research now also suggests why efforts to force dyslexics to learn like everybody else often only make things worse. Dyslexia and related reading, visual, and spatial disabilities have little to do with intellectual capacity and IQ. In fact, reading ability and IQ operate independently, Shaywitz reports. In a twelve-year study of cognitive and behavioral development in 445 Connecticut school kids, Shaywitz and her husband, Bennett, showed that in typical readers, IQ and reading ability align closely at all ages. But in children with dyslexia, they do not, explaining why a dyslexic can be bright but not read well.

It may be that in the chemical soup that bathes all brains, and which flavors personality, cognitive outlaws rely a bit more on **dopamine** than on **serotonin**. That neurochemistry may explain their **proclivity** for **brain plasticity**, exploration, and risk taking—without which the modern world wouldn't exist.

> **dopamine** and **serotonin:** neurotransmitters that regulate neurological functions
>
> **proclivity:** tendency
>
> **brain plasticity:** theory that the brain can change over a lifetime

After You Read

Mapping the Reading

1. What is a "cognitive outlaw"?

2. In the second paragraph of this essay, Rodgers gives her main thesis, but she does so in the form of a series of questions. Reread the paragraph, choose the question you feel best states the thesis, and rewrite it as a thesis statement.

3. In the third paragraph, Rodgers writes the following: "An estimated one in ten children in the United States is dyslexic, and for most, their stories bog down in stigma." What does she mean by "their stories bog down in stigma"? How might they "bog down," and what is "stigma"?

4. Select one of the people profiled—Chuck Close or Carol Greider—and describe that person's disability, the strategies he or she used to overcome it, and how the disability ultimately became an advantage.

5. According to the researchers Rodgers refers to, why do people with dyslexia think differently?

Discussing and Thinking Critically about the Reading

1. Review your "As You Read" annotations about researchers' theories about learning disabilities and people who have them, or make some notes now. What was the most surprising theory to you? Why was it surprising?

2. What common characteristics do Chuck Close and Carol Greider have? In what ways do they respond differently to their disabilities?

3. What are the factors that led Close and Greider to succeed? To what extent are these individuals responsible for their own success? To what extent do they identify others as critical to their achievements?

4. How important do you think parental resources—income, education, time—were to the success that Close and Greider ultimately achieved?

5. What particular challenges do "cognitive outlaws" face in school, and why? What steps might you propose to help ease these challenges?

Navigating the Intersections

1. In this chapter, writers have described both physical disabilities (blindness and paralysis) and cognitive or learning disabilities (autism, dyslexia, agnosia, and ADHD). Reviewing the articles you have read, identify the common themes that emerge about coping with and overcoming disability, and write up your discoveries.

2. Consider someone you know who has a disability. How has this person been shaped by his or her disability? How has it made his or her life more challenging? more rewarding?

Before You Read: Write briefly: Among your friends and family or in your community, is mental illness thought of differently than physical illness? Is it a cause for shame or embarrassment in a way that physical illness is not? Why or why not?

UDOKA OKAFOR

Udoka Okafor is a writer, blogger, and recent graduate of McMaster University in Canada. Born and raised in Nigeria, Okafor has written about social activism, racism, art, and mental illness in the *Huffington Post*, *Incite* magazine, and many other publications. She maintains a blog called *The Society Cynic*. Her *Huffington Post* profile says, "I am a nerd who spends her Friday nights, alone, in her onesie, eating junk food, reading books, and watching her favorite super heroes kick some serious ass on Netflix. Oh . . . and I write sometimes, too." The following article appeared in the *Huffington Post* in 2014.

As You Read: Observe Okafor's language and methods for expressing complex feelings, underlining or otherwise noting passages where you find her words to be very powerful.

On Living with Depression, and the Dangers of Our Culture of Silence

clinical depression: professionally diagnosed major (serious) depression

Five times. That is the number of times that I have seriously thought about or tried to end my life. I have been living with **clinical depression** since I was eleven years old, and I was formally diagnosed when I was sixteen years old. I could give so many reasons for why it took so long for me to be formally diagnosed. But the main and overriding reason is that the issue of mental illness is a taboo back home in Nigeria and even here in Canada as well.

I came to Canada when I was fifteen years old to continue both my high school and my university education. I was enrolled in a private high school (that will remain unnamed for the purposes of this article), where I was to study for a year before I moved on to study at McMaster University, where I am currently in my senior year. Coming to Canada and leaving my home when I was fifteen years old was one of the hardest things that I have ever had to do. The sense of loss that I felt was unanticipated, incomprehensible, and **irreparable:** unfixable

irreparable. That sense of loss went on to trigger one of the longest episodes of depression that I have ever had.

During this episode, my mind and my thoughts were fragmented. They were divided between a desire to cope and a desire to escape it all with the finality it seemed only suicide could provide. Depression is a black hole that sucks you in, faster and further, as the moments go by, until it seems as though your only means of escape — and, ironically, your only means of self-preservation, at least on a mental level — is suicide. I started to cope with my depression the only way that the fifteen-year-old me knew how: through psychological self-abuse, **cutting**, and painkillers. I figured that if I could make myself feel worthless to the point where my "self" ceased to exist in a substantial way, I could finally find the courage to end my life.

> ❝ *I realized, for the first time in my life, that I was not worthless, that I was not a liability.* ❞

My composure quickly **deescalated**, and my high school caught wind of this. In retrospect, I think that they were quite overwhelmed and did not know how to respond. I was sent for a psychiatric evaluation, and I was foolish enough to trust them to the point where I let one of my school mentors sit through the evaluation with me. I was quickly sent for more psychiatric evaluations, as a result of which I was ultimately diagnosed with depression and pegged as a danger to myself. I was then sent to a psychiatric ward where I spent the next two to three weeks.

After my time in the psychiatric ward, I returned to the overwhelming environment that is school with my depression still intact. I was finding it harder and harder to cope with everything, and my **resolve** was wearing very thin. The school was keeping a close, watchful eye on me, and to everyone, I became a spectacle. I was reduced to this "thing" that could explode at any moment. I still remember the day I was called into the office of one of the teachers at the school. I still remember everything, from how the office looked, to the **condescending** look in her eyes, to the harsh and unsympathetic tone in her voice when these words exploded from her mouth: "You have become a **liability**, and the school is thinking about sending you back home."

Take a moment to think about those words. Think about what it means to tell a sixteen-year-old kid — who is frustratingly and profoundly depressed — that she is a liability and that she is not worth fighting for. My sense of my own self-worth, which was not very high at the time, **dissipated** further. I truly did believe that I was a liability to everyone around me, that I was worthless. And, even today, when I look in the mirror, the reflection that stares back at me looks broken, fragmented, and worthless. Those words, that idea, are not something that you ever truly get over. There will always be a creeping whisper at the back of your mind that is ready to pounce on you and remind you that you are, and will always be, a liability to everyone around you, even to yourself.

When **Robin Williams** committed suicide, a whole discussion exploded about the issue of mental illness and the dangers of a **normalized** silence about it in society. However, it is not simply the case that society does not

cutting: a form of repetitive self-injury through cutting one's skin to cope with negative emotions

deescalated: decreased in intensity

resolve: determination

condescending: looking down on someone or something

liability: a problem or burden; state of being legally responsible

dissipated: scattered; vanished

Robin Williams (1951–2014): famous American actor

normalized: made normal or standard; here, suggesting it is the norm not to discuss suicide

want to talk about mental illness. Rather, it is the case that society goes even further to—in some circumstances—criminalize mental illness. By labeling me a liability because of the **erratic** nature of my depression and wanting to send me back home, my school at the time successfully **ostracized** me from myself, imposed a broken image on me, made me believe that the broken image was who I was, and then went on to criminalize that image. But this cannot be our response to mental illness; the actions of my high school cannot be a **microcosm** of how society responds to the issues of mental illness, and yet, they are.

My English teacher at the time, Mark, knew I was going through a very hard time. When others proceeded to label me as a liability, when even my own family and friends did not seem to understand my plight, he saw great potential in me—as a writer and as a person—and he tried to **cultivate** that potential. We would meet after school at least once every week, and he introduced me to the beauty of words and the insightfulness that can be found in books. He taught me about the power of poetry and the magnificence of **prose**. More importantly, every day he reminded me that I was someone, and my sense of worth, my "self," and my identity did not seem so insubstantial anymore. Because of him, I realized, for the first time in my life, that I was not worthless, that I was not a liability.

My high school and society in general need to take a lesson from his playbook because we cannot continue down this path when it comes to understanding and responding to mental illness, depression, and suicide. We have to do better for the sake of the people suffering from mental illnesses and for the sake of society as a whole.

Today, I still battle—constantly—with clinical depression. My sense of self and worth still wages on, and some days are simply or complexly better or worse than others. But I was only able to survive because I had someone who did not **trivialize** my pain through silence, ostracism, and criminalization. Persons suffering from mental illnesses today need their family, their friends, their immediate community, and society as a whole, to **emulate** my English teacher's response to me. And then, maybe, just maybe, we will give them all a fighting chance.

erratic: unpredictable

ostracized: excluded; rejected

microcosm: a reflection, in miniature, of something that occurs in society

cultivate: help grow and develop

prose: language in ordinary form (as opposed to poetic form, for example)

trivialize: make small or unimportant

emulate: imitate

After You Read

Mapping the Reading

1. What factors contributed to Okafor's development of a deep depression?

2. Describe Okafor's school's response to her clinical depression.

3. In your own words, explain how being described as a liability was damaging to Okafor as a depressed adolescent.

4. Okafor writes of mental illness being "criminalized"; what does she mean?

5. What does Mark do for Okafor? What does she believe we should take from his "playbook"?

Discussing and Thinking Critically about the Reading

1. Okafor reports that a teacher at her school described her as a "liability." What do you think the teacher meant to communicate beyond saying that the school was literally liable or responsible, or that Okafor herself was a problem? In other words, what was meant but left unsaid?

2. From your perspective, is Okafor breaking a taboo or standard of behavior by writing publicly and honestly about her experience with cutting, suicidal thoughts, and depression? In your community, is depression just another illness, or does its classification as a mental illness make people respond differently to those who have it?

3. What criticism does Okafor have of the way the clinically depressed are treated? What is her belief about how people in Nigeria, at her school in Canada, and in much of society respond to mental illness? How do these responses make mental illness worse for those who suffer from it?

4. Return to the "As You Read" exercise and choose one passage in which you find Okafor's expressions or choice of language to be especially powerful. Quote that passage, and then reflect on what makes it so powerful.

5. Okafor does not use the term *disability*, but mental illnesses like clinical depression are classified as disabilities. In the United States, there are laws that require schools and public places to accommodate Udoka. Following this principle of accommodation, how should Okafor and other children with depression be accommodated in school? How should they be protected?

Navigating the Intersections

1. Compare Udoka Okafor's narrative with Temple Grandin's in terms of the authors' own perspectives on their disabilities. Consider whether the authors see personal or social value or ability coming from their disability, or whether they only see pain and disability.

2. Research the resources for depression, mental illness, and suicide prevention on your campus or in your community. What do they suggest about how these topics are perceived and discussed? How do they compare to the type of responses Okafor calls for at the end of her article?

3. Clinical depression or bipolar disorder afflicts many artists. A number of them, including poet Sylvia Plath, singer Britney Spears, and writer Sherman Alexie, have struggled with sticking to pharmaceutical treatment. Despite the success that medications can have, artists report that they feel less capable when their mental illness is in treatment. Do you think there is truth to the claim that mental illness gives birth to creativity? Why or why not?

CHAPTER 8

Twenty-First-Century Gender

When It Matters and When It Doesn't

Barnaby Chambers/Shutterstock

Image Response: What does this image suggest about men's roles as child-care givers? What stereotypes does the image play on? How accurate is its portrayal of gender roles today?

In This Chapter

Introduction

Gender in the Twenty-First Century

Given the Supreme Court's legalization of gay marriage and reports that young people today are radically more accepting of differences when it comes to issues of gender and sexuality than any other generation, gender remains a topic that engages discussion everywhere, from classrooms to talk shows to politics. People are wondering when and in what ways gender still matters—personally, socially, and politically.

Recent polls show evidence of changing understandings of gender, as more young women (66 percent) than young men (59 percent) rank having a successful, high-paying career as "very important," a noted reversal of past attitudes (Patten and Parker). Yet polls also show that gender inequality persists despite these changing attitudes. For example, a 2013 Pew Research Center poll found that 51 percent of women compared to 16 percent of men believed that being a working parent negatively affected career advancement (Parker).

Gender versus Sex

It is important to take a moment to define terms. Although the words *gender* and *sex* are frequently used interchangeably, these terms are, in fact, quite different:

Sex: *Sex* refers to a person's *biological* and *anatomical* identity.

Gender: *Gender* refers to social and psychological identities, or what are frequently referred to as people's "socially constructed" identities.

People might think that a person whose *sex* is male is automatically male in *gender* as well, but this is not necessarily the case. As the organization Gender Diversity clarifies, "Unlike biological sex — which is assigned at birth and based on physical characteristics — **gender identity** refers to a person's innate, deeply felt sense of being male or female (sometimes even both or neither)" ("Terminology," emphasis added). Moreover, while many activities appear to be predominantly participated in by one gender over the other, people of both sexes can and do participate in everything from the profession of cosmetology to the hobby of deer hunting.

Evolving understandings of gender are apparent in the growing number of terms available to describe it. While *male* and *female* are traditional labels, today many other terms are used, including *androgynous*, *gender nonconforming*, *transgender* (a person whose self-identity does not correspond to conventional notions of male or female gender), and *cisgender* (those whose gender identity corresponds with their biological sex). In fact, Facebook now offers users more than fifty labels for gender identity, along with custom options. These developments underscore what has always been true, even if not discussed openly: Individuals' sex and gender identities do not necessarily conform to each other.

Pink Is for Boys?

Society's ideas about gender are encoded in **gender roles**, or ideas about what is considered appropriate behavior for people based on their sex — that is, the anatomy they were born with. We all face some gender stereotypes, some of which we may find uncomfortable and rebel against, and others of which we may accept without much, if any, question. Wearing dresses and makeup, working as a preschool teacher, and crying openly in public are all activities that many people — but not all — think of as *gendered* female. Similarly, wearing a gun holster or jockstrap, shaving your face, working as a Marine Corps sniper, and playing football are all activities that many people — again, not all — think of as *gendered* male. Of course, both men and women *can* and *do* participate in all these activities.

Pressure to conform to the gender expectations or stereotypes associated with one's sex affects everyone. While many gender lines have disappeared or faded, others remain in place. For example, although today women are as likely as men to be doctors or lawyers, these professions were once gendered as male only.

Nursing—a high-wage, low-unemployment profession—remains female gendered today. According to the Department of Labor, just 9.9 percent of registered nurses are male, even though the average salary for registered nurses is $1,099 a week, well over the national average (United States). Thus, the pressure for gender conformity remains strong against men becoming nurses even as the pressure against women becoming doctors has decreased.

While gender stereotypes attempt to shape people's behavior and choices, they are not unchangeable. Consider, for example, attitudes toward gender-appropriate colors. Although the children's clothing section in any department store seemingly proves the "rule" that pink is for girls and blue is for boys, this color divide is not natural but learned. In "When Did Girls Start Wearing Pink?" Jeanne Maglaty reports that gender association of colors began in the 1910s—notably, at that time, pink was often assigned to *boys*, and blue was assigned to *girls*! A 1918 publication explains: "The generally accepted rule is pink for the boys, and blue for the girls. The reason is that pink, being a more decided and stronger color, is more suitable for the boy, while blue, which is more delicate and dainty, is prettier for the girl" (qtd. in Maglaty). It was not until the 1940s that pink really began to become a "girl color" as manufacturers and retailers became more organized and determined that the buying public preferred pink for girls and blue for boys (Maglaty). Certainly, since then there has been some loosening of color assignments, and girls wearing blue has become generally unremarkable. Pink for boys, however, remains less acceptable.

Gender Issues Are Everyone's Issues

In the 1960s, "second wave" feminism focused on women's rights, media objectification of women, violence against women, discrimination at work and at home, and women's health care rights. While many of these conversations continue, more recent attention to gender has expanded to include men's issues and other issues of gender identity: those involving transgender people and all who feel uncomfortable when asked to identify with, and conform to, traditional masculine or feminine behaviors, attitudes, and activities. Questions about gender ultimately address who we are, who we can be, and to what extent our biological and social identities should and do dictate our personal possibilities.

Gender ≠ Sexual Orientation

Sometimes discussions of gender and gender identity become confused with issues of sexual identification. A person's gender identity is *not* the same as that person's sexual identification or orientation. A gay man or a lesbian can be just as likely to conform to the social rules and customs of gender as a straight (heterosexual) person can. Thus, while some gays and lesbians may also be transgender, this is not typically the case, and transgender people are not necessarily gay or lesbian.

Works Cited

Maglaty, Jeanne. "When Did Girls Start Wearing Pink?" *Smithsonian.com*, 8 Apr. 2011, www
.smithsonianmag.com/arts-culture/when-did-girls-start-wearing-pink-1370097/?no-ist.

Parker, Kim. "Despite Progress, Women Still Bear Heavier Load Than Men in Balancing Work
and Family." *Pewresearch.org*, 10 Mar. 2015, www.pewresearch.org/fact-tank/2015/03/
10/women-still-bear-heavier-load-than-men-balancing-work-family/.

Patten, Eileen, and Kim Parker. "A Gender Reversal on Career Aspirations: Young Women
Now Top Young Men in Valuing a High-Paying Career." *Pewresearch.org*, 19 Apr. 2012,
www.pewsocialtrends.org/2012/04/19/a-gender-reversal-on-career-aspirations/.

"Terminology." *GenderDiversity.org*, 2015, www.genderdiversity.org/resources/terminology/.

United States, Department of Labor. *Women in the Labor Force: A Databook. Bureau of Labor
Statistics*, Dec. 2014, www.bls.gov/opub/reports/womens-databook/archive/women-in
-the-labor-force-a-databook-2014.pdf.

Rethinking Gender Identity

Before You Read: Brainstorm five words to describe masculinity and five words to describe femininity. Then reflect on your two lists: Which, if any, of the words can apply to both men and women?

MATT DURON

A police officer and former firefighter from Orange County, California, Matt Duron is a self-described "guy's guy." Matt and his wife, Lori, author of the memoir *Raising My Rainbow: Adventures in Raising a Fabulous, Gender Creative Son* (2013), have two sons. On her blog, Lori describes her husband as "an Irishman with a heart of gold hidden underneath his tough-guy façade and ever-present scowl." This essay is from the *Atlantic* (2013).

As You Read: Using different-colored highlighters or pens, or another method, mark those passages in which Duron describes (1) his interests and (2) his son C.J.'s interests.

My Son Wears Dresses; Get Over It

I've been a police officer for more than fifteen years. I've been a detective and now I'm a senior officer who trains the new recruits out on the street. Before that I was a firefighter. Before that I played football in college after playing baseball and football in high school, and **lettering** my sophomore year. I like beer, classic trucks, punk music, riding my motorcycle, and catching the game with my buddies. I'm a stereotypical "guy's guy" and hyper-masculine to a lot of people, I guess. Which may be why it surprises them when they find out that my son wears dresses. And heels, and makeup. It surprises them even more when they learn that I'm cool with it. And at this point, I wouldn't want him to change. Because, if my son liked boy stuff and dressed like a boy, he wouldn't be my boy, he'd be like a stranger.

> **lettering:** to earn a school letter for playing a sport

I grew up in a sports-oriented family. My father was a high school football and baseball coach and my mother was a professional surfer. I had one brother. Growing up, I don't remember homosexuality or gender being discussed in my house. No negative talk. No positive talk. No talk about it at all. My brother and I are straight. It appeared that all of my extended family and my parents' friends were straight. I thought that that's how it went. Then, at eighteen, I met my future wife and she introduced me to her brother. He was the first openly gay person I had ever met. He was cool, and who he chose to love or get physical with was none of my concern. That didn't matter to me. All that mattered was that I thought his sister was hot. I focused on that.

homophobic:
fear or hatred of, or discrimination against, gay people or homosexuality

degrade:
disrespect or treat badly

effeminate:
marked by having qualities that are *perceived* to be feminine

But, being an athlete, a firefighter, and a cop, I have spent a lot of time in locker rooms and around guys who dish out **homophobic** slurs like turkey on Thanksgiving. Faggot. Queer. Gay. Homo. Cocksucker. I started to notice the slurs more after I met my future brother-in-law. Then, I had a son who — as he describes himself — only likes girl stuff and wants to be treated like a girl, and those insults started to get under my skin in a new way.

Sometimes I'll call people out when they use them.

"Bro, I was just joking. You know I was kidding. What's your problem?"

Those are the responses I get.

Here's the thing. When you use those words as a way to **degrade** or get the upper hand on someone, you are implying that to be a man who is gay or **effeminate** is to be "lesser than." Now, when I hear those words, I feel like you are calling my son and people like him "lesser than." I won't stand for that. Get a dictionary. Learn some new words.

> ❝ My wife also gets a load of e-mails from people asking where our son's father is, as though I couldn't possibly be around and still allow a male son to display female behavior. To those people I say, I'm right here fathering my son. I want to love him, not change him. ❞

I don't tell most of the guys who I work with at the police department about my son. It's none of their business and I don't trust them with the information. I don't trust what they might think or say behind my back when they should just say it to my face. I don't trust them with a kid as kick-ass and special as mine.

My close friends know. And I know that they are my close friends because they don't give a shit. They don't care what toys my son likes or how he chooses to dress. They just care that he is happy and healthy and that I'm being a good dad.

I've slipped at times and told some of the other guys in my life.

"Man, how do you deal with that? I couldn't do it. Not in my house," they've said.

What does all of that mean? You couldn't parent a kid like mine? You'd be his first bully and "make him a man?" To me, that makes you less of a man. Much of the time when I confront such people they immediately begin to backpedal and try to move on. I'm not afraid of this discussion and many don't choose to argue with me or defend their position.

To me, loving a child who is different, a target, and seen as vulnerable is my role as a father and decent human being. He's just as special to me and loved by me as my oldest son, whose most prized possession is a pocketknife, who plays football, likes fart jokes, and is starting to notice girls.

caveats: warnings about conditions, limitations, or stipulations

I'm a father. I signed on for the job with no strings attached, no **caveats**, no conditions. I can name every Disney Princess and her movie of origin. I've painted my son's nails and rushed to remove it when he was afraid that he would get teased for wearing it. I didn't want to remove it, I wanted to follow him around and stare down anybody who even thought about teasing him. I only removed it because he started to have a panic attack. It was his decision and if he wants to edit himself to feel safer, I'll do it. Every time. No questions asked.

My wife started a blog about raising our son who is a girl at heart. At first, I didn't really think anybody would read it. They did, and she started to get e-mails from parents who are raising a son like ours. My wife calls C.J. "gender creative." Most people choose the more negative **connotation** and call him gender non-conforming or gender **dysphoric**.

Some of the e-mails she gets come from dads who are struggling. I feel bad for every single one of them. I've been there. I've struggled. A lot. But I've also evolved. A lot.

She's gotten e-mails from more moms than I can count who are now raising an effeminate boy alone because the dad couldn't deal. It pisses me off, but I know that it's the reality. A lot of marriages don't survive raising a gender-creative son who is, statistically speaking, most likely going to be gay or transgender as an adult. I wish I could talk to those men. I wish I could be there for their kids.

My wife also gets a load of e-mails from people asking where our son's father is, as though I couldn't possibly be around and still allow a male son to display female behavior. To those people I say, I'm right here fathering my son. I want to love him, not change him. My son skipping and twirling in a dress isn't a sign that a strong male figure is missing from his life; to me it's a sign that a strong male figure is fully vested in his life and committed to protecting him and allowing him to grow into the person who he was created to be.

I may be a "guy's guy," but that doesn't mean that my son has to be.

connotation: suggested or implied meaning

dysphoric: the American Psychological Association's diagnostic term to refer to someone with a strong and persistent cross-gender identification

After You Read

Mapping the Reading

1. How would you describe Matt Duron? What kind of a person is he? As part of your answer, choose two of the sentences from the essay that you feel best illustrate his personality.

2. What does "gender creative" mean?

3. What is Duron's reaction to negative comments made about his son C.J.?

4. Duron begins his essay by telling his readers a little about himself—his gender identity as a child, his parents and family, his wife's gay brother—before he discusses parenting his gender-creative child. How do these details help him make his point?

5. Summarize Duron's argument about what makes a good parent.

Discussing and Thinking Critically about the Reading

1. Compare and contrast Duron and his son C.J. by listing the activities that each of them likes to participate in. (Look at your "As You Read" notes, or make a list now.) What gender stereotypes do they conform to? Which ones do they break?

2. Duron has written a personal narrative that has the goal of changing readers' behavior and thinking. How effective do you find his essay? Has it changed your opinion? Why or why not?

3. The essay argues for loving and supporting one's child regardless of what choices the child makes about following society's "rules" about gender. What are the strongest arguments that Duron makes, and what makes them strong? What are the weakest arguments that Duron makes, and what makes them weak?

4. Duron uses a lot of informal language (slang, curses) and humor. What is the effect of this language on readers (including yourself)?

5. Write a response to this essay by taking on one of the following roles: someone who agrees with Duron or someone who disagrees with Duron. In your response, offer specific points and reasons.

Navigating the Intersections

1. Research the phrase "gender creative" to find out what other writers have to say about the gender-creative experience. Choose two of the sources, and write brief summaries of their views on gender creativity.

2. Matt Duron refers very briefly to a conflict about terms. His wife uses the term *gender creative* to describe their son, whereas others with more negative views use the terms *gender non-conforming* or *gender dysphoric*. Using a search engine, find a list of gender terms and their definitions. Read through the list carefully, identifying related terms that cast gender in slightly different ways. How might these terms change the way we see people individually? How might they change the way we understand gender more broadly?

Before You Read: How would you describe a tomboy (a female who likes things usually reserved for males)?

SARAH SHOWFETY

Sarah Showfety is a life coach, author, and speaker. Showfety volunteered with the Peace Corps in Guinea, West Africa, and has worked in documentary film production, database marketing, and finance. She wrote *Dating by the Books: One Blundering Singleton's Search for Love in the Self-Help Aisle* (2012), and her work has been featured in *Psychology Today*, the *New York Post*, and *Metro*. She created the blog *Dear Baby XO*, a forum for parents. This article was published in *Psychology Today* in 2008.

As You Read: Mark those passages in which Showfety describes the characteristics of a tomboy.

Field Guide to the Tomboy
High Heels and Pink? No Way

Tomboys embrace their masculine side, often coming late — or never — to traditional femininity.

Once a week, Maryellen White can be found at a local bar, watching *Monday Night Football* with her brothers. The thirty-one-year-old accountant is also not **averse** to an evening at **Hooters**, drinking beer with her guy friends, watching sports, and playing a game of "real or fake" — that is, assessing the endowments of passing waitresses.

When White was growing up, her mother tried to force "girlish things" on her, like pink bedroom walls and flowery bedspreads, but she wanted no part of them. And in high school when she announced she was trying out for boys' football, her mother forbade it — and shipped her off to an all-girls school. "I liked the feeling I got from winning," White says. "That made me want to do more guy-type things." One day, she even beat up a male classmate who was picking on her brother. Though she became more "girly" in college, buying new outfits to attract guys, she still rarely wears makeup, jewelry, or skirts — and can't remember the last time she shopped for clothes.

White is a classic tomboy, a female who engages in activities long considered primarily the **domain** of males. As young girls, tomboys **shun** Barbie dolls in favor of games that emphasize physicality and competition. They resist conventional feminine standards — avoiding pink clothes, lipstick, and nail polish — and often excel in sports. While "tomboy" is largely a term applied to **prepubescent** girls who prefer Tonka trucks to tea parties, some women retain tomboy characteristics into adulthood, gamely coaching the company softball team and downing brews with the guys.

How are tomboys made? On the simplest level, some girls are naturally predisposed to more active, "rough and tumble" pursuits. For others, tomboyism may reflect a desire to identify with the world of men. Many tomboys perceive their fathers as being "smart, strong, capable, and involved in interesting and valuable things," while they see their mothers as having "boring lives" they do not want to **emulate**, according to Seton Hall sociologist C. Lynn Carr. "Tomboys' statements that 'boy things' are 'more fun' are often cover for their desires for access to the more highly valued masculine realm," explains Carr. "This is upheld by tomboys' disappointment with female role models and their belief that women are 'weaker' than men."

In a society that still often expects men to be tough and rugged, and women to be gentle and pretty, embracing their inner tomboy allows females to stand out and be rewarded for activities, rather than appearance or **demeanor**.

"Many tomboys have competitive personalities. They may be born with a natural drive to win, or taught by parents that second best doesn't count," says Andrew

averse: having a strong dislike

Hooters: restaurant chain that uses the term *hooters* to refer to owls and human breasts (slang)

domain: region; province; area

shun: persistently ignore, avoid, or reject

prepubescent: preteen; before adolescence or puberty

emulate: imitate or follow

demeanor: outward or public behavior or appearance

> ❝ *Tomboys' statements that 'boy things' are 'more fun' are often cover for their desires for access to the more highly valued masculine realm. . . . This is upheld by tomboys' disappointment with female role models and their belief that women are 'weaker' than men.* ❞

prenatal: before birth

stigma: a mark of shame or disgrace

Smiler, a psychologist at SUNY Oswego. "They strive for success in many different domains, including sports and academics, and are drawn to risk-taking behavior."

There's reason to believe tomboys are more assertive and stand up for themselves more than other girls. They want to differentiate themselves — to not be a "typical girl" or get otherwise pigeonholed into one category — and they tend to be outspoken. White admits that she's known as "Blunt Maryellen" among her friends. "If you ask my opinion," she explains, "you better be prepared for the truth."

Prenatal hormones may also play a role. Female babies exposed to higher levels of prenatal testosterone exhibit more "masculine-typical" behaviors, playing more with male-typical toys like trucks, race cars, and guns, and choosing boys as friends, according to a study led by Melissa Hines, a psychologist at City University, London.

Because hormones influence basic processes of brain development, they exert permanent influences on behavior. On the flip side, mothers with low testosterone in pregnancy tend to have more feminine daughters, whose play often involves dolls, tea sets, and makeup.

Tomboys also enjoy social benefits. Athletic success can bring status and popularity, and female athletes, Smiler notes, tend to score among the highest GPAs, perhaps feeling the need to "offset" their sportiness by excelling in school, which is increasingly perceived as feminine. Masculinity — as measured by such traits as aggression, leadership, individualism, and self-reliance — also correlates with higher self-esteem in both boys and girls. Tomboys may reap payoffs in confidence, too, as well as feeling more in charge of their lives.

Most likely, tomboyism is the result of a complex interplay of genetics, prenatal hormonal influences, socialization, unconscious choice, and family structure. Hines also showed that tomboys are more likely to have brothers and parents who exhibit highly masculine behavior.

Being a tomboy may sometimes lead to being called a lesbian, a label that can carry a **stigma** among adolescents. Whether there is any real link to homosexuality depends on how you define tomboyism, says Carr. Tomboys who see their stance as a "rejection of femininity" are more likely to be lesbians. Those who conceive of it as "choosing masculinity" — in dress, activity, and identification with male figures and heroes — are no more likely to be gay than straight. Though lesbians are more likely to recall childhood gender nonconformity, almost half of women report having been tomboys as children, says Carr.

Though many girls leave tomboyism behind in their teens, Maryellen White has carried many of her boyish traits into adulthood. She still plays on co-ed sports teams, hates matching bridesmaid dresses, and enjoys male friendships. White attributes her strong cross-gender bonds to mutual interests and "a deep appreciation for beer and wings." That is not to say she lacks close female pals who listen, lend advice, and empathize, White says. "But they can't talk to me about who got traded yesterday."

After You Read

Mapping the Reading

1. What genre (type) of reading is this: an argumentative essay, a persuasive piece, a personal narrative, or an informative piece? Identify a genre, and explain your choice. (Consult Toolkit 1.6 on p. 42 for more about genres.)
2. What are the characteristics of a tomboy? (Draw on your "As You Read" notes, if you have any.)
3. What details about Maryellen White does Showfety share to illustrate that she is still a tomboy as an adult?
4. According to the experts Showfety cites, what are three reasons females become tomboys?
5. According to Showfety, what advantages and challenges exist for tomboys?

Discussing and Thinking Critically about the Reading

1. Why does Showfety describe White as a tomboy rather than just a person who likes sports and male friendships and isn't interested in dresses and high heels? What is useful about the label *tomboy*? What isn't?
2. Describe how women and femininity are portrayed in this article. Then respond: Do you agree with Showfety's portrayal of what is typical of women? of how femininity is defined? Why or why not?
3. Showfety cites C. Lynn Carr's findings that nearly half of women identify themselves as having been tomboys. Did you (or your sister or a friend) identify as a tomboy as a child? If so, what, if anything, makes you (or her) feel less like a tomboy as an adult?
4. Describe the male equivalent to a tomboy if you think there is one. If you don't, explain why you think there is no male equivalent.

Navigating the Intersections

1. Compare and contrast Sarah Showfety's article with Matt Duron's. Specifically, compare how Duron's son is viewed for being interested in stereotypically female activities and appearance with how Maryellen White is viewed for being interested in stereotypically male activities and appearance. How are their situations similar and different?
2. Showfety cites several experts and their research on tomboys. Research one of the experts mentioned in the article to find out more about his or her findings. Using a search engine, type in the expert's name and the name of the school he or she is affiliated with to find articles and presentation information. Write a summary of your findings.

Before You Read: Think about your day thus far, and write briefly, reflecting: How did gender shape your experiences? How did your gender affect something that happened to you or that you did today? (Think harder if your first response is that gender had no effect.)

JENNIFER FINNEY BOYLAN

Jennifer Finney Boylan is a college teacher and writer, well known for her 2003 memoir, *She's Not There: A Life in Two Genders*, one of the first best sellers by a transgender author. Born James Boylan, the author felt uncomfortable being a boy from an early age and, as an adult, transitioned genders and underwent sex reassignment surgery. The author of thirteen books (including the young adult Falcon Quinn series), Boylan is also a columnist with various media outlets, and often writes and speaks on issues related to the transgender community. Boylan is the Anna Quindlen Writer-in-Residence at Barnard College. She is married and has two sons. The following essay is an excerpt from *She's Not There*.

As You Read: This excerpt from Boylan's memoir has three parts: (1) Boylan's childhood memories of feeling uncomfortable in a male body; (2) Boylan's experiences during the period of transition from male to female; and (3) Boylan's reflections on being a transgender woman. Mark the sentences that most surprise you in each section.

A Life in Two Genders

Childhood (1968)

One day when I was about three, I was sitting in a pool of sunlight cast onto the wooden floor beneath my mother's ironing board. She was watching ***Art Linkletter's House Party*** on TV. I saw her ironing my father's white shirt—a sprinkle of water from her blue plastic bottle, a short spurt of steam as it sizzled beneath the iron. "Someday you'll wear shirts like this, [James,]" said Mom.

Art Linkletter's House Party: a popular daytime variety show (1952–69)

I just listened to her strange words, as if they were a language other than English. I didn't understand what she was getting at. *She* never wore shirts like that. Why would I ever be wearing shirts like my *father's*?

Since then, the awareness that I was in the wrong body, living the wrong life, was never out of my conscious mind—never, although my understanding of what it meant to be a boy, or a girl, was something that changed over time. Still, this conviction was present during my piano lesson with Mr. Hockenberry, and it was there when my father and I shot off model rockets, and it was there years later when I took the SAT, and it was there in the middle of the night when I woke in my dormitory at **Wesleyan**. And at every moment as I lived

Wesleyan: university in Connecticut

my life, I countered this awareness with an **exasperated** companion thought, namely, don't be an *idiot*. You're *not* a girl. Get over it.

But I never got over it. . . .

Although my understanding of exactly how much trouble I was in grew more specific over time, as I child I surely understood enough about my condition to know it was something I'd better keep private. By **intuition** I was certain that the thing I knew to be true was something others would find both impossible and hilarious. My conviction, by the way, had nothing to do with a desire to *be feminine*, but it had everything to do with being *female*. Which is an odd belief for a person born male. It certainly had nothing to do with whether I was attracted to girls or boys. This last point was the one that, years later, would most frequently **elude** people, including the overeducated smarty-pants who constituted much of my inner circle. But being gay or lesbian is about sexual orientation. Being **transgender** is about identity. . . . In the end, what it is, more than anything else, is a *fact*. It is the dilemma of the **transsexual**, though, that it is a fact that cannot possibly be understood without imagination. . . .

Boygirl (Winter 2000–2001)

I was aware, during the time of **boygirl** [when I was in the process of transforming physically from male to female], that I had been given a rare and precious gift, to see into the worlds of both men and women for a time and to be able to travel almost effortlessly between them. I taught my classes at **Colby** with my baggy, button-down shirts hiding my figure, I wore a tweed coat and my hair tied back in a ponytail. In the parking lot, after class, I would take off the coat and the shirt (leaving on my undershirt), slip in a pair of earrings, and shake my hair loose, and I would then be seen as female, at least by people who did not know me. It was like being Clark Kent and Superman, in a way. I really did have that sense of "Into a nearby phone booth . . ." and could move from one world to another with an ease I found **uncanny**.

I undertook, during this period, the writing of a supposedly amusing magazine piece making use of my superpowers. What I had in mind was to perform certain **gender-pungent** rituals in society, several weeks apart, first as James and then as Jenny, and to then compare the experiences. I wanted to apply for a job, for instance, first as [a] man and then as a woman, and see which one of me would get the offer and whether the starting salary would be different. I thought of spending an evening sitting at a bar with **Russo** and going in the following night as Jenny with **Grace**. I considered going to a formal shop, getting fitted for a bridal gown, then a week later being measured for a tux. I was full of ideas.

I actually got as far as three of these exercises — buying a car, shopping for a handgun, and purchasing a pair of blue jeans at the Gap. . . . My experiences in

---

exasperated: very irritated; annoyed

intuition: unconscious, immediate understanding

elude: escape; fail to be grasped by

transgender: an individual who does not identify with the gender assigned at birth

transsexual: an individual whose gender identity does not match his or her biological sex at birth; the term is often used to refer to someone like Boylan who medically changes his or her sex or anatomy

boygirl: Boylan's son's word for Boylan's period of transition from male to female

Colby: college in Maine where Boylan taught creative writing

uncanny: strange or mysterious

gender-pungent: strongly associated with a specific gender

Russo: Richard Russo, Boylan's friend, and also a famous fiction writer

Grace: Boylan's wife

> ❝ *Whether I 'really' am a woman, or whether I 'had a choice' or not, or whether* anything, *no longer matters. Having an opinion about transsexuality is about as useful as having an opinion on blindness. You can think whatever you like about it, but in the end, your friend is still blind and surely deserves to see. Whether one thinks transsexuals are heroes or lunatics will not help to bring these people solace.* ❞

writing the piece were perhaps predictable, but I found them amazing, at least I did at the time. For instance, when I went to the Nissan dealer as Jenny, the salesman showed me the most expensive car on the lot, the Maxima, and talked up the cup holders and the illuminated speedometer. A week later, he tried to sell James a midrange car, the Altima, and his focus now was on the platinum-tipped spark plugs. The punch line, although inevitable, was still remarkable, I thought: The deal they offered me as a man was a thousand dollars better than the one they'd offered Jenny.

The gun shop part of the article didn't really work, since I didn't know anything about guns and couldn't bring myself to go back there a second time as a man. . . .

Buying the jeans at the Gap was more sobering to me as a soon-to-be former man than it was to my female editors. What I found in the Gap was what most women know already — that buying clothes is complicated. As a man, of course, you simply made the choice between regular or relaxed fit, told the salesman the measure of your inseam and waist, and were then led to a huge wall of pants in your size, all of which you knew would fit just fine, even if you never tried them on. As a woman, I found that there were six different styles of jean, from "boot cut" to "reverse," and that the sizes bore no relation to any known system of measure.

The jeans that fit me best at the Gap were the "reverse," which I thought was appropriate. I was right between a ten and a twelve and spent some time neurotically trying to tell myself I could get by in the tens. They're perfectly comfortable if I don't sit down, I thought. How much time do I actually spend sitting, anyway? If I buy the tens, it will be an incentive to lose weight.

I recognized the insanity of this kind of talk, recognized it from the lives of the women I knew, and as I moved into this territory I realized, not for the first time, that all of the cruel expectations that society puts upon women — and that so many women put upon themselves — were now falling on my shoulders. . . .

No issue was as hard to resolve as the issues around food. My weight was stable, and at five feet eleven, I was healthy, tall, and slender. Yet whenever I went out for lunch, I would hear myself ordering diet soda or asking for the spinach salad. I bought a scale and started weighing myself constantly. I'd say, *If only I could lose five pounds.* I bought Slim-Fast and had thick, gloopy milkshakes for lunch instead of food.

internalized: adopted and believed ideas from others, often unconsciously

It was madness, and it was exactly the kind of madness that I found least appealing in the lives of the women I knew. Yet the culture had its hooks in me, like it or not. In no time at all I'd **internalized** many of the things I'd spent years imploring my students to fight against. I worried that I was too fat.

I apologized when someone else stepped on my foot, as if it were my fault. My sentences often ended with a question, as if I were unsure of myself. All of these changes transpired without any conscious thought, and if I became aware of them, I felt ashamed.

Partially, I think what I wanted was to *belong.* If being female — to others, at any rate — seemed to include self-doubt, insecurity, and anorexia, then some part of me felt, *Okay, well, let's do all that, then.*

Later when I tried to let some of this go, there were some who saw me as "less female" — like when I ordered the barbecued baby back ribs for lunch instead of a salad and a diet soda. Why shouldn't a woman eat real food for lunch, I wondered, instead of the pretend kind?

I realized, as **Jimmy Durante** used to say, that "**them's the conditions what prevails**," but it didn't sit well with me. There were times when it was as if I were trying to prove I was truly female by oppressing *myself.*

Reflections

. . . For many people, transgendered or not, womanhood is thought, wrongly, to be **synonymous** with femininity — with makeup and stretchy T-shirts and an obsession with Brad Pitt. None of this has a damn thing to do with it, of course, and in the long run, a transsexual who hopes to build a life around high heels and sponge cake is in for something of a disappointment.

I moved forward into transition not in order to be **Dolly Parton** (or, for that matter, **Janet Reno**), but in order to be Jenny Boylan. There are aspects of me that are feminine now, but I was feminine when I was a man, for that matter. I still retain a number of masculine **affects** that I am not ashamed of, and which many other women possess as well. I like to drink beer on a hot summer afternoon; I like to watch baseball, at least late in the season; and I still like to hike in the Maine woods and go camping. I prefer music to be loud; I like to tell jokes; and I have been known to swear like a Barbary pirate. Had I been born female, no one would remark upon these things — but since I was not, any masculine affect is considered a **vestigial** link to a previous life; conversely, any feminine affect that seems excessive can be hauled out as evidence that I . . . have arrived at middle age just in time to be fourteen years old.

As time has gone by, I have become more mellow about the whole damn business, content to let the primary concerns of my life — children, teaching, music, my relationship with Grace, friendships with Russo and Zero and others — take up my attention. Whether these things are masculine or feminine is not particularly important to me anymore.

They are simply what I do.

Most of all, perhaps, I have let go of constantly trying to explain what this is all about. Early in transition, it was essential to me that everyone understand the condition of transsexuality — that they grasp the horror of the dilemma,

Jimmy Durante: American entertainer from the 1920s to the 1970s

them's the conditions what prevails: the situation is what it is and cannot be changed

synonymous: equivalent to

Dolly Parton: country singer famous for her large chest

Janet Reno: President Bill Clinton's attorney general (1993–2001), made fun of for her alleged unfeminine appearance

affects: term from psychology referring to outward expressions of someone's emotions

vestigial: remaining as a trace of something lost

that they understand its medical components, that they know I had done all I could to remain the person they had known and loved, and so on. I had an answer ready for every objection.

What I have come to realize is that no matter how much light one attempts to throw on this condition, it remains a mystery. . . .

Quite frankly, there are times when I think about transsexuality and I just have to shrug. I'm sorry I can't make it make more sense to you, I told Zero. But it is what it is. Whether I "really" am a woman, or whether I "had a choice" or not, or whether *anything*, no longer matters. Having an opinion about transsexuality is about as useful as having an opinion on blindness. You can think whatever you like about it, but in the end, your friend is still blind and surely deserves to see. Whether one thinks transsexuals are heroes or lunatics will not help to bring these people **solace**. All we can do in the face of this enormous, infinite anguish is to have compassion.

solace: comfort

After You Read

Mapping the Reading

1. What does the opening story about ironing illustrate?

2. Where does Boylan offer the strongest, clearest message about what is important for her as a transgender person, and what support she thinks transgender people need from others? Find a quotation to support your answer.

3. What surprises Boylan about her experiences shopping at the Gap while presenting as a man and as a woman?

4. The author writes, "There were times when it was as if I were trying to prove I was truly female by oppressing *myself*." What does she mean?

5. In the final section, Boylan writes that she has become "more mellow." Explain what she means. What perspective on gender and the transgender experience does she express in this section?

Discussing and Thinking Critically about the Reading

1. What do you find most surprising about this essay? (Look at your "As You Read" notes, or pick out the most surprising things now.) Why do these things surprise you?

2. For Boylan, what is the difference between being female and being feminine? What do *you* think is the difference? Compare your ideas to Boylan's: Do you agree with her distinction? Why or why not?

3. Boylan writes about being responded to differently when she shops as a male and as a female at the Gap and at a car dealership. How has gender affected your experiences as a shopper? (Refer to your "Before You Read" notes, if relevant.) If you aren't sure, speculate and make a guess.

4. The author writes that she began her experiences as a woman by being obsessed with food, dieting, and weight. Why might food and dieting have been one of her first ways to "be" female? Why was she able to finally move beyond this phase?

Navigating the Intersections

1. Compare and contrast the experiences of two or three of the main examples in this cluster (C.J. Duron, Maryellen White, and Jennifer Finney Boylan). What might their experiences tell us about the rigidity and flexibility of gender roles? What have they taught you about gender, gender stereotypes, and the possible blurring of gender roles?

2. In this excerpt, we see Boylan's maturing vision of gender. As she grows from child to middle age, her feelings about her gender and being a transgender woman change. Investigate what Boylan is writing about now by going to her website or looking for recent articles she has published (such as in the *New York Times*).

Masculinity: What Does It Mean to Be Masculine?

Before You Read: Drawing on your opinion, experiences, and observations, describe what makes a man "macho" or masculine. As part of your response, consider whether men can be macho and still do housework and take care of children. Why or why not?

ANDREW ROMANO

Journalist Andrew Romano covers politics, national issues, cultural issues, and a wide variety of other topics, from the making of the TV series *Breaking Bad* to profiles of prominent conservative politicians. Romano covered presidential campaigns for *Newsweek* before moving to *Yahoo News*, where he reports on national affairs. His 2008 blog about the presidential campaign, *Stumper*, won a national award and generated an average of two million views per month. This article appeared in *Newsweek* in 2010.

As You Read: Underline or highlight those passages in which Romano makes statements about the need to reimagine and redefine masculinity.

Why We Need to Reimagine Masculinity

What's the matter with men? For years, the media have delivered the direst of **prognoses**. Men are "in decline." Guys are getting "stiffed." The "war on boys" has begun. And so on. The *Atlantic*'s Hanna Rosin went so far as to declare that "The End of Men" is upon us.

prognoses: predictions about the future

brawn: physical strength

Great Recession: economic downturn (2007–9)

decimated: severely damaged or destroyed

deadline anthropologists: journalists who report dramatic cultural or social change based on little or poor evidence (slang)

trend pieces: informal term for articles about popular topics

off the rails: an expression that comes from the railroad; if a train goes off the rails or track, it's out of control

mores: customs or social conventions

perpetuates: makes something continue indefinitely

Marlboro Manliness: featured in an ad campaign (1954–99) for Marlboro cigarettes, the Marlboro Man symbolizes a traditional, ultramasculine man

nigh: near; approaching

Mr. T: a character actor from the 1980s, known for playing the ultimate muscle-bound tough guy on shows such as *The A-Team*

There's certainly some substance to these claims. As the U.S. economy has transitioned from **brawn** to brain over the past three decades, a growing number of women have gone off to work. Men's share of the labor force has declined from 70 percent in 1945 to less than 50 percent today, and in the country's biggest cities, young, single, childless women — that is, the next generation — earn 8 percent more than their male peers. Women have matched or overtaken men as a percentage of students in college and graduate school, while men have retained their lead in alcoholism, suicide, homelessness, violence, and criminality. Factor in the **Great Recession**, which has **decimated** male-heavy industries like construction and manufacturing, and it's no wonder so many **deadline anthropologists** are down on men. But while the state of American manhood has inspired plenty of anxious **trend pieces**, few observers have bothered to address the obvious question: If men are going **off the rails**, how do they get back on track?

Without an answer, some men have turned to old models and **mores** of manhood for salvation. . . . But suggesting that men should stick to some musty script of masculinity only **perpetuates** the problem. For starters, it encourages them to confront new challenges the same way they dealt with earlier upheavals: by blaming women, retreating into the woods, or burying their anxieties beneath machismo. And it does nothing to help them succeed in school, secure sustainable jobs, or be better fathers in an economy that's rapidly outgrowing **Marlboro Manliness**. . . .

Since the 1950s, the image of the American woman has gone through numerous makeovers. But masculine expectations remain the same — even as there are fewer opportunities to fulfill them. As a result, says Joan C. Williams, author of *Reshaping the Work-Family Debate: Why Men and Class Matter*, "men have a choice: either feel inadequate or get a lot more creative." What's required, then, is not a reconnection with the past but a liberation from it; not a revival of the old role but an expansion of it. The End of Men isn't **nigh**, nor is macho dead. But its definition should be broadened to include both **Mr. T** and Mr. Mom. It's time, in other words, for a New Macho: a reimagining of what men should be expected to do in the two realms, home and work, that have always determined their worth. . . .

Parenting and Parental Leave

The home is a natural place to start. As the novelist Michael Chabon discovered on a trip to the grocery store with his son, society still expects very little from fathers. "You are such a good dad," a woman told him as he waited in line to pay. "I can tell."

Exactly what she could tell was a mystery to Chabon, who recounts the story in his 2009 essay collection *Manhood for Amateurs*. But clearly no woman would earn kudos for toting her kids around the frozen-foods aisle. "The handy thing about being a father," he later concludes, "is that the historic standard is so pitifully low."

The modern standards aren't much better. Despite apparent progress — young couples believe in co-parenting and sharing the household chores — very little has actually changed. The average wife still does roughly double the housework of the average husband: the equivalent of two full workdays of additional chores each week. Even when the man is unemployed, the woman handles a majority of the domestic workload, and it's the same story with child care. If both parents are working, women spend 400 percent more time with the kids. Meanwhile, the number of fatherless kids in America has nearly tripled since 1960, and the percentage of men who call themselves stay-at-home dads has stalled below 3 percent. The old roles, say sociologists, are hard to shake.

> ❝ *[Masculinity's] definition should be broadened to include both Mr. T and Mr. Mom. It's time, in other words, for a New Macho: a reimagining of what men should be expected to do in the two realms, home and work, that have always determined their worth.* ❞

There's growing evidence, however, that they can be expanded. Consider contemporary family life in Sweden. In the past, new parents split 390 days of paid leave however they liked — monthly, weekly, daily, and even hourly. Women used far more of it than men. But today, new fathers no longer rush back to work, leaving the mother to raise little Sven all by herself. The reason for the change? Smart public policy.

In 1995, Sweden passed a simple but revolutionary law: Couples would lose one month of leave unless the father was the one who took it. A second use-it-or-lose-it month was added in 2002, and now more than 80 percent of Swedish fathers take four months off for the birth of a new child, up from 4 percent a decade ago. And a full 41 percent of companies now formally encourage fathers to go on parental leave, up from only 2 percent in 1993. Simply put, men are expected to work less and father more.

By altering the roles of the Swedish father and the Swedish worker, Sweden's paternity-leave legislation has, in turn, rewritten the rules for Swedish men (and, by extension, women). "Swedish dads of my generation and younger have been raised to feel competent at child-rearing," writes *Slate*'s Nathan Hegedus, an American who experienced the system firsthand. "They simply expect to do it, just as their wives and partners expect it of them." If a man refuses time at home with the kids, he faces questions from friends, family, and, yes, other guys. Policy changes produced personal changes — and then, slowly but surely, society changed as well.

Around the world, similar shifts are already underway. . . . The U.S. is now the only wealthy country that doesn't **bankroll** a bonding period for either parent. This could change sooner than you think. Recent polls show that majorities of Republicans (62 percent), Democrats (92 percent), and independents (71 percent) now support the idea of paid paternity leave. Big companies — especially those with lots of male workers, such as Texas Instruments, Sun Microsystems, and Ernst & Young — are beginning to offer at least

bankroll: pay for (slang)

two weeks of paid leave. New Jersey, Washington, and California have already launched programs that offer partially paid leave, and more than twenty other states are currently considering legislation — a bloc that covers almost half the working population. . . .

Of course, policy changes will be pointless unless attitudes change as well. In California, the first U.S. state to fund leave (six weeks of it) for both parents, only 26 percent of men seize the opportunity, compared with 73 percent of women. All told, most new fathers take off two weeks or less for a new child, no matter what. Baby time is simply not seen as masculine. The only way that perception will fade is if men who are already living double lives as dedicated professionals and parents "come out" and start writing their senators and petitioning their HR departments. The motivation is certainly there; over the last thirty-five years, the number of employed fathers in dual-earner families who say they suffer work-family conflict has risen from 35 percent to 59 percent, according to Joan Williams. Now it's up to "twenty-first century dads," as Jeremy Adam Smith argues in his recent book, *The Daddy Shift*, "to go on the offensive."

The Workplace

The campaign for a New Macho shouldn't end when men leave the house. . . . Of the 15.3 million new jobs projected to sprout up over the next decade, the vast majority will come in fields that currently attract far more women than men. In fact, men dominate only two of the twelve job titles expected to grow the most between 2008 and 2018: construction worker and accountant. The rest, including teachers (501,000 new positions), registered nurses (582,000), home health aides (461,000), and customer-service reps (400,000), remain heavily female. All told, the social sector of the economy will gain 6.9 million jobs by 2018. But unless the complexion of the workforce changes, according to a recent study by Northeastern University, a whopping 2.5 million of them will go unfilled.

The coming employment gap represents a huge opportunity for working-class guys — and for the families they're struggling to support. The problem is that men, unlike many women, still feel limited to a narrow range of acceptable roles — a range that hasn't kept pace with the changing employment landscape. As manufacturing continues to migrate overseas and underpaid immigrants continue to provide cheap manual labor, they continue to lose ground. . . .

It's possible to imagine **protectionist trade** and immigration **policies** boosting blue-collar employment at the margins. But the U.S. can't stop globalization. If male morale — and the American economy — are ever going to recover, the truth is that the next generation of Homer Simpsons will have to stop searching for **outsourced** manufacturing jobs and start working toward teaching, nursing, or social-service positions instead. To **hasten** this transition, schools that train "nurturing professionals" should launch aggressive, male-oriented advertising campaigns and male-to-male recruiting drives that stress technical expertise, career-advancement potential, and beyond-the-bedside opportunities.

protectionist trade . . . policies: policies that make overseas labor more expensive, thereby pressuring American companies to manufacture in the United States

outsourced: moved from the United States to countries where labor is cheaper

hasten: speed up

Community colleges ought to focus on preparing students for the social-sector jobs of the future. Certain institutions might even consider raising their admissions requirements, a tactic that has helped the University of Pittsburgh School of Nursing increase its male-applicant pool by 34 percent over the past five years. And the government should fund or incentivize as many of these initiatives as it possibly can. . . .

Skeptics will argue that men are "designed" for some gigs and not for others. But while no one would claim that men and women don't have their differences, women long ago proved that **gender essentialism** doesn't determine what kind of work they can do. Today women still serve as teachers, nurses, and social workers. But they're also CEOs, soldiers, and secretaries of state. The time has come for a similar expansion of what men can do for a living. The raw numbers show that a change is already underway; the percentage of nurses who are men has doubled over the past twenty-five years (to about 6 percent of the field), and there are more guys teaching elementary school than ever before. But it's not nearly enough. Mining and machinist jobs will still be available in the future — just not as many. Why wouldn't men look elsewhere for work? . . . .

The New Macho

It's clear that we've arrived at another crossroads — only today the prevailing codes of manhood have yet to adjust to the changing demands on men. We're not advocating a genderless society, a world in which men are "just like women." We're not even **averse** to decorative manhood, or the kind of escapism that men have turned to again and again — think Paul Bunyan, Tarzan, and bomber jackets — when the actual substance of their lives felt light. If today's men want to be hunters, or **metrosexuals**, or metrosexuals dressed in hunting clothes, they should feel free.

But they need to be more than that, too. On the surface, the New Macho is a **paradox**, a path to masculinity paved with girly jobs and dirty diapers. Dig a little deeper, however, and it begins to make a lot of sense — not just for men but for everyone. If men embraced parental leave, women would be spared the **stigma** of the "mommy track" — and the professional penalties (like lower pay) that come along with it. If men were involved fathers, more kids might stay in school, steer clear of crime, and avoid poverty as adults. And if the country achieved gender **parity** in the workplace — an optimal balance of fully employed men and women — the **gross domestic product** would grow by as much as 9 percent, according to a recent study by the World Economic Forum.

Ultimately, the New Macho boils down to a simple principle: In a changing world, men should do whatever it takes to contribute their fair share at home and at work, and schools, policymakers, and employers should do whatever they can to help them. After all, what's more masculine: being a strong, silent, unemployed absentee father, or actually fulfilling your half of the bargain as a breadwinner and a dad?

gender essentialism: the belief that men and women are innately different in ways beyond biological differences

averse: having a strong dislike

metrosexuals: young, urban, straight males interested in fashion (slang)

paradox: a statement or idea that seems contradictory or impossible but perhaps is true

stigma: a mark of shame or disgrace

parity: equality, especially regarding status or pay

gross domestic product: total value of all goods and services produced by a country; indicator of a country's economy

After You Read

Mapping the Reading

1. Summarize Romano's concept of the "New Macho." How does he envision the New Macho with respect to men's roles at home and at work?

2. As his title reveals, Romano is making an argument that we need to revise our ideas about masculinity. Quote one or two sentences in which you see him most clearly stating his claim. (You may draw on your "As You Read" notes, if you have them.)

3. Romano presents many statistics and facts to support the claim that men today are having a hard time economically and otherwise. What three statistics or facts do you find especially persuasive in supporting this claim?

4. What does the example of Michael Chabon's experience at the grocery store help Romano to illustrate?

5. Reread and summarize Romano's explanation of Sweden's laws governing parental leave. Explain how Romano sees these laws changing Swedish culture and ideas about masculinity.

Discussing and Thinking Critically about the Reading

1. How do women and children stand to benefit under the "New Macho" that Romano proposes? How would men benefit?

2. What is your reaction to the author's position that traditional masculinity needs to be reimagined and expanded to allow and encourage men to take on a wider variety of roles, responsibilities, and occupations?

3. Why does Romano see traditional masculinity as ineffective in helping men face the challenges of today? What do you think? What value, if any, might there be in traditional ideas about masculinity?

4. How do people in your community respond when men take on traditionally female roles, such as child-rearing and other domestic activities? How do their reactions compare to those experienced by Michael Chabon? How common is it to find men taking an active part in child-rearing in your family or community?

Navigating the Intersections

1. Select two readings from this chapter, and compare and contrast how the authors describe masculinity or femininity. How do they differ in their definition of what it is to be male or female? How are their definitions similar?

2. Andrew Romano refers to attempts to pass parental leave legislation in the United States and to companies' leave policies. Research whether your state has any form of parental or family leave, and report back on the issue. Alternatively, research and report on parental leave policies at big companies (such as Facebook or Google).

3. Research current attitudes toward gender and gender roles by studying recent polls by organizations such as the Pew Research Center. Write a summary of your findings.

Before You Read: Write for five minutes: Do you hold the door open for someone else? If so, when, for whom, and why? Do people ever hold the door open for you? If so, how does it make you feel?

THEODORE R. JOHNSON III

Theodore R. Johnson III has been writing in the public sphere since high school. His work has been featured in the *Huffington Post*, the *San Francisco Chronicle*, the *Hill*, and the *Wall Street Journal*, among other publications. Johnson often discusses issues related to race, energy, and public policy. He has also served in the U.S. Navy for over fifteen years, attaining the rank of commander and serving in many countries on security and humanitarian missions. In June 2011, Johnson was honored with a White House Fellowship, recognizing his roles in both leadership and public service. This article appeared in the *Grio* in 2013.

As You Read: Make note of those passages in which Johnson includes examples of positive or negative attitudes toward chivalry.

Chivalry, Feminism, and the Black Community

I recently watched a woman put gas in her car on a 100-degree summer day — while her boyfriend sat in the driver's seat of the air-conditioned car texting on his phone. I shook my head in disgust and wondered what kind of man lets his lady pump gas and what kind of woman would find this behavior acceptable.

From the outside looking in on this scene, it would seem to confirm the growing sense that **chivalry** is dead. The word is out that men are decreasingly making gentlemanly gestures such as opening doors for women, offering their coats when there is a chill in the air, giving up their seats on public transportation, or bringing the car around in inclement weather.

chivalry: polite, respectful behavior, usually from men toward women

Moreover, expressions of modern feminism have led some to believe that not only are many women no longer welcoming these gestures, but that they are also insulted by them.

Chivalry: A Code of Knights

Speaking from experience, I have never expected that my holding a door open for a woman would result in her frustration and a curt, "I am more than capable of opening the door myself" retort. As it turns out, this is not an **anomaly**. Many men have received similar responses to their small chivalrous acts, I have been told.

anomaly: atypical, or very unusual, occurrence or condition

Much has changed.

Chivalry originated as the code of conduct associated with knights in the medieval era. It governed their actions in battle, mandated dedicated training

attributes: good
qualities

and personal excellence, and required a deep commitment to the service and protection of others. These **attributes** and the prestige of the knight's rank in society made chivalry a desirable and definitive masculine quality.

This remained true even as chivalry evolved to mean courtesies with deep gender associations that played on the physical differences between men and women. In other words, because the average man was physically stronger than the average woman, chivalry was an expression of protection and strength.

Sign of Respect or Subordination?

infer: assume or
conclude

In many ways, acts of chivalry do **infer** a woman's weakness, or desire for help. This can play on the stereotypes that men are supposed to be gallant knights and women are distressed damsels in need of rescue.

Of course, this type of outdated thinking imposes traditional gender roles on men and women alike, and is particularly out of place in modern-day social interaction.

subordinate:
treat as of lesser
importance or rank

What remains true, however, is that there are many who choose to adhere to traditional roles — not necessarily as a sign of weakness or a desire to **subordinate** women to men, but as a sign of respect and an expression of personal preference. The nation's attitude towards chivalry also seems conflicted.

Gender Messages Clashing

In a recent Harris Poll, eight out of ten people said women are treated with less chivalry than in the past.

Yet in another study on who pays for dates — one of the most definitive gestures of chivalry — researchers found that 84 percent of men were paying for nearly all the dating expenses well into a relationship, and even more pay for first dates. Only 60 percent of women said they would pull out their wallets and offer to help, but 40 percent of those women expected their offer to be declined.

Even more said they'd be upset if men actually expected them to split the bill.

As a result of all this, men are simultaneously accused of being lacking in chivalry, while also insulting women with chivalry. Some women also feel pulled between rejecting chivalry out of allegiance with feminism, and embracing it because it makes some men feel more comfortable.

The New Gender Normal

Men and women around the country are learning to adjust to the new normal. For African-Americans, this change is especially pronounced.

The major problem most have with chivalry is that it assumes traditional gender roles. At the same time, feminism has legitimized the concept of women's independence from men for protection and provision. As economic empowerment has replaced physical strength as the means of generating security, women's academic achievements coupled with anti-discriminatory employment policies has led them to becoming more self-sufficient, and often household breadwinners.

This is especially true for black women, who in 2010 attained 66 percent of the bachelor's degrees and 71 percent of the master's degrees conferred on black graduates. Additionally, as of 2011, 68 percent of black women that had given birth over the past year were unmarried, meaning they are more and more responsible for being the sole or primary provider.

So any notion that perpetuates their supposed weakness, however symbolic, is rejected.

Black Chivalry: What It Can Mean

Despite all this, black men are accused of exerting male privilege in expecting women to conform to our notion of gender roles. Black women are accused of being unappreciative of a social privilege that affords them special treatment because of their gender in everyday interactions, or when danger approaches.

Black women are constantly **harangued** as "hard," "bossy," and not feminine enough when it comes to accepting protection, assistance, and **subtle** guidance from black men. Black men are accused of not being supportive enough by black women. What we need to understand is that gender roles are evolving. There is no longer a standard, society-wide acceptable set of gender-based norms for how men and women are supposed to act.

harangued: criticized; lectured at harshly

subtle: hard to perceive or see

But common courtesy and thinking of others should remain alive and well.

Courtesy: The New Chivalry?

Courtesy has no gender baggage associated with it.

Opening the door for the person behind you, man or woman, is courteous, not chivalrous. Giving up your seat to someone, man or woman, is courteous. And yes, even pumping gas while your significant other, man or woman, sits in the car texting is courteous, too. As is replying with a civil "thank you" when someone extends a courtesy to you.

> *What we need to understand is that gender roles are evolving. There is no longer a standard, society-wide acceptable set of gender-based norms for how men and women are supposed to act.*

For me, I will always open the door for my lady and wouldn't be caught dead sitting in the car while she puts gas in it — and, most importantly, she appreciates, and expects, the courtesy.

When it comes to relationships though, the people involved should determine what is right for them. The traditional code of chivalry is indeed dead.

After You Read

Mapping the Reading

1. What makes Johnson believe that chivalry is in decline today?

2. How is chivalry related to traditional gender roles?

3. According to Johnson, why are changing attitudes toward chivalry especially apparent in the African American community?

4. How do ideas about who should pay for dates reflect conflicted ideas about chivalry?

5. What is the difference between chivalry and courtesy, according to Johnson?

Discussing and Thinking Critically about the Reading

1. In the opening paragraph, Johnson gives an example of a woman pumping gas while her boyfriend sits in the car. How do you react to this example?

2. Think further about the author's distinction between chivalry and courtesy: If both involve the same actions, how does courtesy differ from chivalry? Do you think Johnson has made a valid distinction between the terms? Why or why not?

3. What is your take on the value or relevance of chivalry? More specifically, do you believe society can both expect and promote chivalry and also expect and have equality between women and men?

4. Johnson claims that many people "choose to adhere to traditional roles—not necessarily as a sign of weakness or a desire to subordinate women to men, but as a sign of respect and an expression of personal preference." Explain and then reflect on what he means by this statement.

5. Argue both sides: Write a list of reasons for why giving up chivalry is a bad idea and another list of reasons for why giving up chivalry is a good idea. (Refer to your "As You Read" notes, if relevant.)

Navigating the Intersections

1. Theodore R. Johnson III observes changing gender roles, and in light of this evolution, he proposes courtesy as a replacement for chivalry. Choose one other author from this chapter, and argue for how she or he is proposing a replacement or an updating of gender roles.

2. Conduct your own poll: Ask at least ten people who they think should offer to pay for dinner on a first date. Observe and record differences in responses between men and women; older and younger people; and perhaps members of different races, ethnicities, or other category. Report and reflect on your results.

Before You Read: Think back to a recent movie or TV show you watched. How were the women presented? How did they dress? What did they do? What was their role in the story line? What message about women was conveyed?

HAILEY YOOK

Hailey Yook was first published as a teenager, when she won a *Huffington Post* writing contest. She is a college student who served as managing editor for the *Berkeley Undergraduate Journal* and wrote the Social Double-Take column on contemporary social issues for the *Daily Californian*, a student newspaper at the University of California, Berkeley, where this article was published in 2014.

As You Read: Mark those passages where you see Yook expressing her view about chivalry.

Chivalry Isn't Dead, but It Should Be

According to the traditional conception of women, we women aren't so womanly anymore. Thankfully, [dominant] ideas of femininity—being delicate (honestly, just a **euphemism** for "weak"), submissive, and **servile** to men, as well as pretty and attractive at all times—are constantly being challenged. Things are looking much better for women today. But many notions of sexism—chivalry being one of the worst offenders—are still embedded in our society today.

Compared to the formerly oppressive **status quo**, the progress of gender equality in the United States is undeniable. Today, women possess the right to vote and can walk down the street with their ankles showing in broad daylight without anyone gasping in horror.

Besides the obvious stuff, we're beginning to notice the **subtle**, underlying gender stereotypes in previously disregarded aspects of everyday life, such as the media. There are compelling arguments about the effects of gendered colors and toys on the development of children's identities and hidden gender discrimination in the almighty Walt Disney Company's movies and fairy tales—all things that most people used to see as completely harmless and pure. But this makes it easy for some people, frustrated at the nitpicky feminist for pointing out every minor form of perceived sexism, to say that those brutish, modern "**feminazis**" are just overreacting.

But noticing **covert** sexism matters. Recognizing subtle forms of gender discrimination allows us to see just how systemic sexism truly is and helps us get that much closer to achieving gender equality. When a boy acts slightly too feminine, it's totally routine to say, "Come on, be a man. Stop acting like a girl." Although it is increasingly frequent, rarely will anyone notice the unyielding societal expectations and burdens imposed on that little boy. Some of the **highest-grossing** children's movies (*Shrek, Aladdin, Tarzan, Beauty and the Beast*, etc.) depict a woman falling in love with a chivalrous man . . . who is a complete stranger. For her, their first kiss is magical and, in many cases, **literally** and **figuratively** transformative.

euphemism: a substitute, indirect word used in place of a direct, offensive word

servile: too willing to serve or please others

status quo: the way things are

subtle: hard to perceive or see

feminazis: a put-down term that mocks the aims of feminism (equality between the sexes) by suggesting that what feminists want is unreasonable and militant

covert: secret; not openly acknowledged

highest-grossing: most profitable

literally: actually

figuratively: indicating something beyond the basic meaning

> *Some of the highest-grossing children's movies (Shrek, Aladdin, Tarzan, Beauty and the Beast, etc.) depict a woman falling in love with a chivalrous man . . . who is a complete stranger. For her, their first kiss is magical and, in many cases, literally and figuratively transformative.* ”

No matter how ordinary or traditional these incidents may seem, their messages reinforce gender stereotypes. Now, with my friends' mushy, picturesque, tear-jerking Valentine's Day stories still fresh on my mind, I want to talk about an instance of this subtle sexism, and one that I've noticed is regarded by most of my girlfriends as "more than OK" and "not sexist at all" — chivalry.

Let's be clear about the definition of chivalry here. The term *chivalry* derives from a system of values, such as loyalty and honor, that knights were expected to follow during the Middle Ages. The *Merriam-Webster Dictionary* defines the term as "an honorable and polite way of behaving especially toward women."

So here's the simple question with no simple answer: Is chivalry sexist? Well, what do you think? He pays for her dinner, he gives up his bus seat for her, he carries her bag and books while walking to class, he pushes in her chair for her once she sits down. Is this discrimination? It can definitely get confusing, and my own friends found they were contradicting themselves. One of my female friends said, "It's probably sexist since it's implying we shouldn't do things on our own . . . but I still like when a guy does those things for me." Then one of my male friends chimed in, "I don't see it as sexism at all. It's just politeness and courtesy."

He's right. Doing all of those things is merely polite and can definitely be seen as a means of affection or kindness toward another. There can never be enough kindness in the world, and it seems counterproductive to question people who are simply being nice. But let's take a look at the rigid gender construction at play here. One hardly expects women to ever do those things for men. (Ladies, have you ever taken a boy's stack of books from his hands? And fellas, try telling me you've had or wanted your car door opened by your girlfriend.) Because of this lack of **reciprocity**, I can't help but wonder if these aren't mere acts of kindness and affection but acts rooted in protection and power as well as displays of masculine strength and resourcefulness.

reciprocity:
the practice of exchanging things or actions with others for mutual benefit

OK, whatever, maybe men just like doing nice things for women, regardless of whether they think women are weak or not. So what? It's about the implications: If a girl shouldn't carry her own books, does this promote an image of fragility, perhaps even in other aspects of her life, such as her career? I mean, do you want your CEO, someone who is leading you, to be a person who appears weak? If the man should always pay for dinner, does the woman even need an equal salary? In such scenarios, chivalry is certainly discriminatory.

I'm sure most chivalrous men are well-intending. But to me, chivalry still seems like a rather contradictory representation of kindness, maybe better off left in the dark ages.

After You Read

Mapping the Reading

1. Yook begins by acknowledging changing understandings of women and their roles. What purpose does this opening serve?

2. What is "covert sexism"? Why is it important to recognize?

3. What is Yook's argument against chivalry? What is her clearest expression of her view? (Draw on any "As You Read" notes you have to help you answer this question.)

4. How does the article critique the chivalrous act of a man carrying a woman's books?

5. Yook calls chivalry "a rather contradictory representation of kindness." What does she mean?

Discussing and Thinking Critically about the Reading

1. The author asks, "If the man should always pay for dinner, does the woman even need an equal salary?" She appears to be saying that when women expect men to pay for dinner, they are also, indirectly, giving up their claim to an equal salary. Take a position on the suggestion that inequality in paying for dinner leads to inequality in salary. Why do you agree or disagree?

2. Looking at your own beliefs, what kindness or courteous behavior would you feel comfortable doing for the opposite sex? Why? What kindness or courteous behavior would you feel *un*comfortable doing for the opposite sex? Why? (Consult your "Before You Read" response, if relevant.)

3. Yook identifies some Disney children's movies as examples of "covert sexism." Explain your stance on these or similar movies or books aimed at children. What messages about gender do you see them sending?

Navigating the Intersections

1. On the most obvious level, Theodore R. Johnson III and Hailey Yook have opposing views about chivalry. Compare and contrast their views, thinking about not just the ways they disagree but also the ways in which they might agree.

2. Research five popular recent movies targeted at children. Read their summaries, and try to determine whether the plot involves a young woman falling in love "with a chivalrous man . . . who is a complete stranger," to quote Yook. In other words, how do or don't these movies reflect the culture of chivalry that Yook and Johnson write about?

CHAPTER 9

More Than Just a Game
What Sports Say about American Society

Dustin used with the permission of Steve Kelley and Jeff Parker, King Features Syndicate, and the Cartoonist Group. All rights reserved.

Image Response: In this cartoon from the *Dustin* comic strip, the title character expresses concern that his sister, Meg, is going to coach a youth baseball team. How do you interpret the twentysomething Dustin's question? How do you interpret his young friend Hayden's response? What generational shift might the artist, Stephen Kelley, be trying to capture? What does each character's response say about perceptions of girls, women, and their athletic skills? Do you agree? Explain your answer.

In This Chapter

Introduction

Sports in American Society

From the billion-dollar industry of professional sports to Little League to shooting hoops after school, sports occupy an important place in American culture. Sports contribute to individual, community, and national identity as athletes wear their team uniforms and fans wear the jerseys of their favorite players and teams. Even if someone is not an athlete or a fan, sports are hard to escape. The feel-good story of the victorious underdog is familiar from countless movies. Sports lingo has slipped into everyday language as we talk of "a whole new ballgame," "striking out," "Monday morning quarterbacks," "slam dunks," and "sucker punches." In addition, claims about the benefits of playing sports are widely shared and accepted: Playing sports can build teamwork skills and contribute to health, calculating players' stats can help students learn math, and mastering a sport can be excellent training for life's challenges.

Woven into the fabric of our culture, sports are also the subject of hot debates among friends, academic researchers, and those of us who hope and strive to change our society for the better. More than just fun activities to participate in or observe, sports force us to engage in discussions on significant issues in our country — about equality, racism, sexism, and opportunity. These debates play out in many forms, from trash talk in the stands to talk radio to blogs to scholarly articles. In this chapter, we present writers who focus on two of these issues: the personal and societal value of sports, and concerns about stereotypes and bias.

The Value of Sports

Excelling in sports has long been considered a path to success — whether on the field or off. The aspiring high school athlete dreams of being offered a scholarship to college or of making it on the field professionally. Of course, professional opportunities are limited, and there are many contenders. Yet while some, like business journalist Jim Edwards, argue that throwing a ball is not a valuable skill in the business world, many former athletes claim that participating in sports provides transferable life skills, such as leadership, teamwork, discipline, and confidence. A Cornell University study confirms that former student athletes are recognized for their leadership skills and self-confidence as they pursue careers outside sports (Segelken). Another study found that many women in leadership roles played sports (Smith). The results of these and other studies echo the familiar argument that sports participation and competition prepare student athletes for career achievement.

The highly touted benefits of sports for future success, as well as for health and fitness, inspire many parents to sign their children up to play, often starting at a very early age. Thus, questions related to sports intersect with parenting concerns: Are some sports more dangerous than others? Should children be required to play a sport? Should they specialize in one sport or play several? At what age should children start playing sports? Should all kids — winners and losers — win a prize? Should kids' sports be structured, or should children be allowed free play?

Sports and Culture

Sports provide a window on American cultural conversations around stereotypes and bias, as well as race and gender relations. Who gets to play sports has long been a question at the heart of American sporting life. Racial segregation with all-white and all-black teams persisted well into the twentieth century. Although some baseball teams had both white and black players before the 1890s, it was not until Jackie Robinson and Larry Doby broke the color barrier in 1947 that baseball, the so-called national pastime, moved toward integration (professional football was integrated the previous year, and professional basketball was integrated in 1950). Although a quick look at the highlight videos from last night's games suggests racial integration, questions remain as to how well and fully each sport has been integrated, and what, if any, lingering biases and prejudices exist both on and off the playing field. Scholar Emmett L. Gill Jr., for instance, contends that the high number of African American women on college basketball and track teams disguises their limited participation in other sports, such as soccer and rowing. His research raises the question of whether athletes of particular backgrounds are being directed into certain sports.

That said, many point to sports for improvements in relations among America's racial and ethnic populations; a 2013 Rasmussen Report survey found that 53 percent of Americans credit sports as helping race relations ("53%"). Beyond race, barriers to participation in sports have existed historically and continue to exist today, including those created by stereotypes and prejudices about gender, religion, class, sexuality, and ability.

Stereotypes and Bias on the Field and in the Media

Athletes face "dumb jock" stereotypes and questions about sexual orientation. These stereotypes — and the related jokes and assumptions — are so common that many people are not aware that they are based on generalizations and prejudices. Limiting, generalizing assumptions about the abilities of women, gays and lesbians, and of people from specific racial and ethnic backgrounds are often held and thoughtlessly expressed by teammates, fans, and sports reporters. For example, while women athletes were once routinely labeled lesbians for entering a "men's arena," they may now face a different type of judgment than male athletes, critiqued not just for their athletic achievements but also for their looks. As *New York Times* reporter Ben Rothenberg explains, female athletes may have body image concerns as they try to balance the strength and fitness needed to succeed in their sports with cultural pressures to look traditionally feminine.

Male athletes also face gendered, "macho" stereotypes, especially concerning sexual orientation (Wolf). Historically, most gay athletes stayed in the closet, coming out, if ever, only after they retired (Pearlman). Basketball player Jason Collins is considered the first active American male athlete in a prominent sport to come out, doing so in 2013. Homophobic comments remain part of the trash talk players and fans use, creating a hostile atmosphere for gay athletes (Taylor). Sports, then, remain an arena in which ideas about gender and race are illustrated and tested.

This chapter invites you to think more deeply about what sports say about America. Step up to the plate, and join in the conversation about the issues that extend beyond the playing field.

Works Cited

Edwards, Jim. "Let's Stop Pretending That People Who Are Good at Sports Make Great Business Leaders." *Business Insider*, 20 Mar. 2015, www.businessinsider.com/stop-pretending-people-who-are-good-at-sports-make-great-business-leaders-2015-3?r = UK&IR = T.

"53% Say Pro Sports Have Helped Race Relations in U.S." *Rasmussen Reports*, 19 Apr. 2013, www.rasmussenreports.com/public_content/lifestyle/general_lifestyle/april_2013/53_say_pro_sports_have_helped_race_relations_in_u_s.

Gill, Emmett L., Jr. "The Prevalence of Black Females in College Sports: It's Just an Illusion." *Diverse: Issues in Higher Education*, 31 May 2007, diverseeducation.com/article/7384/.

Pearlman, Jeff. "Coming Out in the Big Leagues." *Advocate*, 2008, www.advocate.com/news/2007/12/14/coming-out-big-leagues.

Rothenberg, Ben. "Tennis's Top Women Balance Body Image with Ambition." *The New York Times*, 10 July 2015, nyti.ms/1JYK4Eq.

Segelken, H. Roger. "Youth Sports 'Spill Over' to Career Success." *Cornell Chronicle*, Cornell U, 17 June 2014, news.cornell.edu/stories/2014/06/youth-sports-spill-over-career-success.

Smith, Jacquelyn. "Playing Sports May Be the Secret to Women's Career Success." *Business Insider*, 9 Oct. 2014, www.businessinsider.com/playing-sports-is-secret-to-womens-success-2014-10.

Taylor, Phil. "Mixed Messages." *Sports Illustrated*, 6 June 2011, www.si.com/vault/2011/06/06/106075848/mixed-messages.

Wolf, Sherry. "America's Deepest Closet." *The Nation*, 27 July 2011, www.thenation.com/article/americas-deepest-closet/.

Do Sports Have Value?

Before You Read: Brainstorm a list of the benefits you think that participating in sports offers. You can draw on experience, observations, or what you've heard others say.

HILARY BEARD

An Ohio native, Hilary Beard turned to writing mid-career, having previously worked for Fortune 500 companies. As writer, editor, public speaker, and life and career coach, Beard focuses on health, wellness, spirituality, and psychology. She has coauthored eight books, including *Mo'ne Davis: Remember My Name: My Story from First Pitch to Game Changer* (2015) and *Promises Kept: Raising Black Boys to Succeed in School and in Life* (2014), which won an NAACP award. She has served as the editor in chief of both *Real Health* and *HealthQuest* magazines. This article was published on the online news site *The Root* in 2015.

As You Read: Underline, highlight, or otherwise note the benefits that Beard claims sports offer participants.

What I Learned from Mo'ne Davis about Girls, Sports, and Success

When I worked with **Mo'ne Davis** to write her new book, *Mo'ne Davis: Remember My Name: My Story from First Pitch to Game Changer*, I met a thirteen-year-old who **epitomizes** the benefits of girls' involvement in sports.

Of course, I already knew about Mo'ne's women's-history-making Little League pitching performances, when she struck out **scores** of boys and gave a whole new meaning to the phrase "You throw like a girl." But it wasn't until I started working with her that I began to learn about her grit and resilience off the field (she's an honor roll student) that she carries with the same comfort with which she wears her baseball glove.

And I saw how much she embodies the growth mind-set, the understanding that working hard and engaging in difficult tasks (think: rigorous academics, playing up an age group in sports, and competing against older boys and men) make you smarter and more capable. . . . She also has close relationships with girls at school and on her basketball and soccer teams in an era when same-gender friendships sometimes seem **tenuous**.

Indeed, sports have not only protected this low-income girl. They've also totally transformed her life.

Studies have shown that girls who play sports are healthier for the short term and long run; they have lower rates of obesity well into their thirties

Mo'ne Davis: the first African American girl to play in the Little League World Series, and the first girl to pitch a shutout and earn a win

epitomizes: is the perfect example of

scores: large numbers of

tenuous: weak; shaky

and forties.[1] They are much likelier to graduate high school and score better on standardized tests, no matter their socioeconomic level, and less likely to smoke cigarettes or use drugs. Black adolescent girls who are athletes are less than half as likely to have unplanned pregnancies.

Female business executives who were formerly athletes believe that sports improves their leadership potential and makes it easier for them to find a job.[2] More than half of the female chief executive officers, chief financial officers, and chief information officers surveyed in a recent global research study used to play sports.

And Mo'ne is experiencing the **pinnacle** of sports' benefits that most black girls are missing out on. Fewer than one-third of black girls and Latinas play sports, compared with three-fourths of white girls. The drop-off in their physical activity is **precipitous**: One study showed that black girls demonstrate a 100 percent decline in such activities between kindergarten and high school.

"By high school, black girls were doing no physical activity at all, versus a 50 percent decline among white girls," exercise-science expert and **epidemiologist** Melicia Whitt-Glover has previously explained.

There are many reasons for this difference, and as **their village**, we must fight them.

In 2010 the National Women's Law Center filed suit against twelve cities — including New York, Chicago, and Houston — for denying girls the right to play ball.[3] And just in February, the U.S. Department of Education found that New York City had failed to provide girls the same opportunities to play sports as boys.[4]

pinnacle: height of success

precipitous: sudden and steep

epidemiologist: scientist who studies how diseases spread

their village: reference to the African proverb "It takes a village [community] to raise a child"

> ❝ We must also oppose rigid gender roles that have led to some girls being engaged in child care and household tasks while their brothers play video games and ball, as well as challenge the idea that sports are not feminine that exists in too many communities of color. ❞

Fortunately, groups like Black Girls Run, Black Women Do Workout, and GirlTrek are encouraging African-American girls and women — who have historically preferred rest over exercise during their downtime — to learn to enjoy physical activity. But we must advocate for safe and attractive places to exercise in our communities.

We must also oppose rigid gender roles that have led to some girls being engaged in child care and household tasks while their brothers play video games and ball, as well as challenge the idea that sports are not feminine that exists in too many communities of color.[5]

[1] http://www.ncwge.org/PDF/TitleIXat40.pdf

[2] http://www.ey.com/GL/en/Newsroom/News-releases/news-female-executives-say-participation-in-sport-helps-accelerate—leadership-and-career-potential

[3] http://www.nytimes.com/2010/11/11/sports/11titleIX.html?_r=1

[4] http://www.nwlc.org/press-release/us-department-education-finds-nyc-public-school-system-violation-title-ix-thousands-gi

[5] http://www.apadivisions.org/division-35/news-events/news/physical-activity.aspx

And let's not overlook the concerns many of us have about sweating out our hair or worrying about makeup or how we will appear to boys and men. Mo'ne works with her hairdresser to identify chemical-free styles that support her heavy workout schedule. But she says that a girl's character is more important than her appearance: Mo'ne is free from the insecurity about looks that has many grown women stuck.

Back in my day, I was no Mo'ne Davis. But as an early beneficiary of Title IX — the law that bars sexual discrimination in schools — I experienced adolescence feeling confident and loving my body's appearance, strength, and performance long before any "mean girls" or boys had either noticed me or chipped away at my self-esteem.

At a time when black girls' lives and looks are under assault, our daughters deserve no less than to grow up with the same life-affirming benefits that sports have provided our sons and that have propelled Mo'ne into the **stratosphere**. If her example encourages other black girls and women to get in the game, that could be her greatest accomplishment of all.

stratosphere: in this usage, high position

After You Read

Mapping the Reading

1. What characteristics and qualities does Beard admire in Mo'ne Davis?

2. According to Beard, what short- and long-term benefits do girls receive from playing sports? (You may consult your "As You Read" notes.)

3. Summarize the statistics Beard provides about the racial and ethnic backgrounds of girls who play sports. Were these surprising to you, or were they what you expected, and why?

4. Beard cites several reasons girls, particularly African American girls, do not participate or stay involved in sports. Identify three of them.

5. As the title of her article asserts, Beard believes Mo'ne Davis can help us understand something important about girls, sports, and success. Find and quote a sentence or two in which Beard expresses what she hopes people will learn from Davis's example.

Discussing and Thinking Critically about the Reading

1. Beard clearly believes that playing sports offers many important benefits for African American girls. How important are these benefits? Which benefits do you think would also apply to boys or to girls of different backgrounds? Feel free to focus on one or two benefits, and explain both Beard's and your own view on them. (You may refer to your "Before You Read" and "As You Read" notes to get started.)

2. Beard cites several reasons for why girls, particularly African American girls, do not participate in sports. From your experiences and observations, what are the primary reasons girls (of any background) do not participate more in sports? What could be done to encourage girls to participate more?

3. Beard argues, "We must also oppose rigid gender roles that have led to some girls being engaged in child care and household tasks while their brothers play video games and ball, as well as challenge the idea that sports are not feminine that exists in too many communities of color." How strong are gender stereotypes concerning girls and sports in your community? In what, if any, ways might they work to prevent or discourage girls from participating in sports?

4. Beard proposes steps that can be taken to encourage more girls to participate in sports. What are they? What additional steps would you propose?

5. Of Mo'ne Davis, Beard asserts that "sports have not only protected this low-income girl. They've also totally transformed her life." Why might low-income girls especially benefit from sports? Why is it that low-income girls might find it more difficult to participate in sports?

Navigating the Intersections

1. Write a profile (a description, often told as a story) of an athlete—a friend, a class-mate, a professional athlete you are familiar with, or perhaps even yourself. In your description, pay some attention to both the benefits and the drawbacks of sports for this person.

2. Hilary Beard briefly mentions Title IX, a law that aims to protect gender equity across all areas of education, including sports. Research some Title IX success stories, and then choose one and write a brief summary of it. (If you are using a search engine, try searching for "my Title IX success story" or "Title IX success stories.")

Before You Read: Imagine that you were being asked to manage or coach a youth team (it could be a sports team or any other kind of team). Write a letter to this imagined team, telling them what they should hope to get out of the experience and how they should approach it.

MIKE MATHENY

A former major-league catcher, Mike Matheny became the manager of the St. Louis Cardinals baseball team in 2012. In his book, *The Matheny Manifesto: A Young Manager's Old-School Views on Success in Sports and Life* (2015), written with Jerry B. Jenkins, Matheny shares his belief that sports teaches eight skills that are transferable off the field: leadership, confidence, teamwork, faith, class, character, toughness, and humility. After retiring as a player due to post-concussion symptoms, Matheny was asked to manage his ten-year-old son's youth baseball team. Matheny wrote this letter to the parents of the team's players, later including it in his book.

As You Read: Note or mark passages in which Matheny expresses strong opinions about how a youth sports team should be run.

The Letter That Went Viral

Dear Fellow Parents:

I've always said I would coach only a team of orphans. Why? Because the biggest problem in youth sports is the parents.

But here we are, so it's best I nip this in the bud. If I'm going to do this, I'm asking you to grab the concept that this is going to be ALL about the boys. If anything in this is about you, we need a change of plans.

My main goals are to:

1. teach these boys how to play the game of baseball the right way
2. make a positive impact on them as young men
3. do all this with class

We may not win every game, but we will be the classiest coaches, players, and parents at every game we play. The boys are going to show respect for their teammates, for the opposition, and for the umpires — no matter what.

That being said, you need to know where I stand. I have no hidden agenda, no ulterior motives. My priorities in life will **permeate** how I coach and what I expect from the boys. My Christian faith guides my life, and while I have never been one to force it down someone's throat, I also think it's cowardly and hypocritical to shy away from what I believe. You parents need to know that when the opportunity presents itself, I will be honest about what I believe. That may make some uncomfortable, but I did that as a player, and I want it out in the open from the beginning that I plan to continue it now.

permeate: spread through

I believe that the biggest role a parent can play is to be a silent source of encouragement. If you ask most boys what they want their parents to do during a game, they'll say, "Nothing." Again, this is ALL about the boys. I know youth league parents feel they must cheer and shout, "Come on, let's go, you can do it!" but even that just adds more pressure.

I will be putting plenty of pressure on these boys to play the game the right way — with class and respect — and they will put too much pressure on themselves and each other as it is. You need to be the silent, constant, source of support. . . .

Really, I'm doing you a favor you probably don't realize at this point. I have eliminated a lot of work for you. All you have to do is get your son there on time, and enjoy. And all they need to hear from you is that you enjoyed watching them and that you hope they had fun.

I know it's going to be very hard not to coach from the stands and yell encouraging things, but trust me on this: Coaching and yelling (even encouraging) works against their development and enjoyment. I'm not saying you can't clap for them when they do well. I'm saying that if you entrust your child to me to coach him, then let me do that job.

That doesn't change the fact that a large part of how much your child improves *is* your responsibility. What makes a difference for kids at this level is how much repetition they get, and that goes for pitching, hitting, and fielding. You can help out tremendously by playing catch, throwing batting practice, hitting ground balls, or finding an instructor who will do this in your place. The more of this your child can get, the better. The one constant I've found with major leaguers is that someone spent a lot of time with them between games.

I am completely fine with your son getting lessons from whomever you see fit. The only problem I will have is if you or your instructor counters what I'm teaching the team. I won't teach a lot of mechanics at first, but I will teach a mental approach, and I'll expect the boys to comply. If I see your son doing something drastically wrong mechanically, I will talk with you or his instructor and clear it up.

The same will hold true with pitching coaches. We will have a pitching philosophy, and will teach the pitchers and catchers how to call a game and why we choose the pitches we choose. There'll be no guessing; we'll have reasons for the pitches we throw. A pitching coach will be helpful for the boys to get their arms in shape and be ready to throw when spring arrives. . . .

I will be throwing so much info at these boys that they will suffer from overload for a while, but eventually they'll get it. I'm a **stickler** about the thought process of the game. I'll talk nonstop about situational hitting, situational pitching, and defensive preparation. The question they'll hear the most is "What were you thinking?"

stickler: someone who believes certain rules are important and should be followed at all times

What were you thinking when you threw that pitch?

What were you thinking during that at bat?

What were you thinking before the pitch was thrown; what were you anticipating?

I am a firm believer that this game is more mental than physical, and though the mental may be more difficult, it can be learned by ten- and eleven-year-olds.

If it sounds like I'm going to be demanding, you're exactly right. I'm definitely going to demand their attention, and I'm going to require effort.

Attitude, concentration, and effort are three things they can control. If they give me those three things every time they show up, they will have a great experience.

It works best for all of us if you would plan on turning your kid over to me and the assistant coaches when you drop him off, and entrust him to us for the two hours or so that we have scheduled for a game or practice. I want him to take responsibility for his own water, not have you running to the concession stand or standing behind the dugout asking if he's thirsty or hungry or hot—and I'd appreciate if you would share this information with other guests, like grandparents. . . .

As I'm writing this I realize I sound like a kids-baseball dictator, but I really believe this will make things easier for everyone involved. . . .

I believe this team will eventually be competitive. When we get to where we are focusing on winning, like in a tournament, for example, we are going to put the boys in the positions that will give us the best opportunity. Meanwhile, as the season progresses, there's a chance your son may be playing a position he doesn't like. That's when I most need your support about his role on the team.

I know times have changed, but one of the greatest lessons my father taught me was that my coach was always right—even when he was wrong. That principle is a great life lesson about how things really work. Our culture has lost respect for authority, because kids hear their parents complain about teachers and coaches. That said, I'm determined to exhibit enough humility to come to your son and apologize if I've treated him wrong. Meanwhile, give me the benefit of the doubt that I have his best interests in mind, even if you're convinced I'm wrong.

I need you to know that we are most likely going to lose many games this year. The main reason is that we need to find out how we measure up against the local talent pool, and the only way to know that is to play against some of the best teams. I'm convinced that if the boys put their work in at home and give me their best effort, we'll be able to play with just about any team. Time will tell. . . .

The boys will be required to show up ready to play every time they come to the field. That means shirts tucked in, hats on straight, and no pants drooping to their knees.

There is never an excuse for lack of hustle on a baseball field. From the first step outside the dugout they will hustle. They will quickly jog to their positions, to the plate, and back to the bench after an out. We will run out every hit harder than any team we will play, and we will learn to always back up our teammates. Every single play, every player will be required to move to a spot. Players who don't hustle and run out balls will not play. The boys will catch on to this quickly.

> " I know times have changed, but one of the greatest lessons my father taught me was that my coach was always right—even when he was wrong. That principle is a great life lesson about how things really work. Our culture has lost respect for authority, because kids hear their parents complain about teachers and coaches. "

Baseball becomes very boring when players are not thinking about the next play and what they could possibly do to help the team. **Players on the bench** will not be messing around. I will constantly talk with them about situations and what they would do in a specific position or if they were the batter. There is as much to learn on the bench as there is on the field.

players on the bench: players who are not currently on the field

All this will take some time for the boys to conform to. They are kids, and I am not trying to take away from that, but I believe they can bear down and concentrate during the games and practices.

I know this works because it was how I was taught the game and how our parents acted in the stands. We started our Little League team when I was ten years old in a little suburb of Columbus, Ohio. We had a very disciplined coach who expected the same from us. We committed eight summers to this man, and we were rewarded for our efforts. I went to Michigan, one teammate went to Miami of Florida, one to Ohio State, two to North Carolina, one to Central Florida, two to Kent State, and most of the others played smaller Division 1 or Division 2 baseball. Five of us went on to play professionally—not a bad showing from a small-town team.

I'm not guaranteeing this is what's going to happen to our boys, but I want you to see that this system works. I know that by now you're asking if this is what you want to get yourself into, and I understand that for some it may not be the right fit. But I also think that there's a great opportunity here for these boys to grow together and learn lessons that will last far beyond their baseball experience.

Let me know as soon as possible whether or not this is a commitment that you and your son want to make.

Thanks,

Mike

After You Read

Mapping the Reading

1. How does Matheny want the parents of his team's players to behave, and why?

2. What does Matheny expect of his players? What does he expect of himself?

3. What are some of Matheny's beliefs concerning how a youth sports team should be run? (You may consult your "As You Read" notes to help you answer.)

4. What is the "mental" aspect of baseball, and what is Matheny's stance on it?

5. What does Matheny believe the players on his team can control?

Discussing and Thinking Critically about the Reading

1. What most surprises you about Matheny's expectations for parents and for players, and why?

2. Matheny believes that the players will "learn lessons that will last far beyond their baseball experience." Although he does not specify these lessons, what lessons can you infer—figure out—from the points he makes in the letter?

3. In the introduction to his book, Matheny states that although this letter specifically refers to a boys' baseball team, his larger ideas also apply to girls and women. Do you think his advice applies equally to girls and women as it does to boys and men? Why or why not? What other advice might parents of daughters benefit from hearing?

4. Matheny writes, "I know times have changed, but one of the greatest lessons my father taught me was that my coach was always right—even when he was wrong. That principle is a great life lesson about how things really work. Our culture has lost

respect for authority, because kids hear their parents complain about teachers and coaches." What do you think about this idea? Respond to Matheny's claim.

5. Matheny chooses to express his ideas in a letter addressed to parents. In what ways does he tailor his letter to fit that audience? If he were writing for a different audience (e.g., the players on the team, fellow coaches, or a broader audience), what might he have changed?

Navigating the Intersections

1. Hilary Beard and Mike Matheny are clear supporters of youth sports. Compare and contrast their ideas about the value of sports for children.

2. Do an Internet search for a commentator who critiques the practice of youth sports, arguing that it is damaging or unhealthy for children. Summarize the commentator's viewpoint, and then include your response. (Try searching with the terms "youth sports" and "dangerous," "damaging," "problems with," "exclusive," or any other negative term that you suspect will bring up a critical point of view.)

Before You Read: Write briefly about why it is that so many people love to watch sports. What are some of the many reasons that sports are so entertaining — in both good and bad ways — for spectators? To answer, feel free to draw on your own ideas or observations of others.

BOB RYAN

A retired sportswriter for the *Boston Globe*, Bob Ryan began his journalism career by covering the Celtics and later became a sports columnist, writing about more than basketball. He has also been a TV and radio commentator, and regularly appears on ESPN's *The Sports Reporters*. Ryan's awards include National Sportswriter of the Year (four times) and a 2015 PEN/ESPN Lifetime Achievement Award for Literary Sports Writing. He is the author of numerous books, including *The Pro Game: The World of Professional Basketball* (1975), *The Road to the Super Bowl* (1997), and *Scribe: My Life in Sports* (2014), from which this selection is excerpted.

As You Read: Note or mark those passages where Ryan expresses his concerns about football.

I Can Hardly Believe It's Legal

If they stopped playing football in the next five minutes it wouldn't bother me at all.

I mean, what if someone came to you with the proposal for a new game called "football"? It's a territorial game, you'd be told. The object is to advance an oblong leather ball down a one-hundred-yard-long field into an expanse of land called the "end zone." Well, you'd say, I've heard of worse **premises**. Tell me more.

premises: ideas accepted as true and used to build an argument

Okay, there are eleven men on a side. A whole bunch of big people, and I'm talking about participants who might weigh as much as 350 pounds, smash into each other at a place called the "**line of scrimmage**." The object of the team not in possession of the ball is to find the person on the other team who has possession of it and bring him to the ground in as violent a manner as possible. The object of the team with the ball, of course, is to prevent that from happening. Now, the offensive team can throw the ball to someone, but the man who catches it had better be ready to **sustain** a very hard blow designed to make him drop the ball.

line of scrimmage: imaginary line that separates teams at the beginning of a play

sustain: deal with; withstand

Wow, you'd say. Sounds pretty rough.

> **"** *How do we as a nation reconcile having chosen football as our new national game? Is the trade-off in body carnage worth the type of entertainment the game provides?* **"**

Oh, you don't know the half of it, you'd be told. Injury is not only possible, it is expected. You cannot play this game without the understanding that, sooner or later, you will sustain an injury to your knee, ankle, arm, shoulder, neck, back, or, worst of all, head. The injuries are often not short-term issues. Countless people who have played this game, especially at the highest level, suffer debilitating injuries that will last their entire lives. Oh, and their life expectancy falls somewhat short of the norm for American males.

Wait a minute, you'd say. This is legal? It not only is legal, you'd be told, it is America's sport of choice. Autumn Saturdays, Sundays, and Monday nights are given over to this. The climactic game each season is called the "Super Bowl" and is the highest-rated television program of the year, every year. America comes to a stop for that game.

This can't be, you'd say. Has the country gone mad? Apparently.

barbaric: extremely brutal; cruel

genteel: polite

sanctioning: officially approving

Perhaps you don't think of football that way. But you should. Football is a **barbaric** game. In a more civilized, more **genteel** society, no one would even think of **sanctioning** such an activity. Yet as the twentieth century came to a close, I found myself out of step with frightening numbers of my fellow Americans: Football was not my favorite sport.

That said, I wouldn't dream of missing the Super Bowl or the National Championship football game. I never said I don't enjoy watching football. I've been watching it for more than sixty years. But I'm talking philosophy. How do we as a nation reconcile having chosen football as our new national game? Is the trade-off in body **carnage** worth the type of entertainment the game provides? For most people the answer seems to be yes, and that includes some of the aforementioned participants who have been **maimed**—there is no other word—by this brutal game.

carnage: slaughter, as in battle (used metaphorically here)

maimed: badly injured

subtleties: small but important details that are often overlooked

In the end, I'm torn. I can roll up my mental sleeves and talk collegiate and professional football history with just about anyone. I have enjoyed many a football game. I think I understand its **subtleties** and nuances. But the older I get the more mystified I have become with the easy acceptance of football's

inherent brutality and viciousness by so many who love it above all other sporting endeavors. How can people justify the very existence of this game? Why did it take so long for people to arrive at the conclusion that using the head as a **battering ram** was not such a good thing?

I addressed this issue as far back as 1989 in the aftermath of an incident where San Francisco 49er defensive back Jeff Fuller **speared** New England Patriots running back John Stephens, launching headfirst into Stephens's helmet. He was not the tackler who first met up with Stephens; that was 49er linebacker Jim Fahnhorst. Fuller decided he would finish off Stephens, who was about to go down. The twist here was that Fuller got the worst of it. When they took him off the field he had no use of or feeling in his right arm. Initial fears were that Fuller had sustained a broken neck; nonetheless, he sustained spinal damage. That was the last hit of his career. Jeff Fuller never did regain use of his right arm.

Bill Walsh, the former great 49ers coach, was working on TV that day. Walsh was supposed to be a thoroughly **erudite** individual, a man whose approach to the game was almost professorial. Surely, he would **decry** Fuller's actions. Here, however, was Walsh's take: "Fuller is one of the really devastating hitters in football. . . . And he's probably as big a hitter as they've had, and he has the reputation, not only of being fast, explosive, play the ball well, but his run support has been the best in football."

His broadcast partner that day was Dick Enberg. He, too, had a reputation as a thoughtful, sensitive man, but he was also working a football game. As an ambulance arrived, Enberg observed, "This is one positive out of how we've progressed in terms of how we handle injuries on the field. In the old days, just dragging a player off and tending to him, and here they're not going to take any chances, and how carefully they'll move Fuller to the stretcher and then to the emergency vehicle."

Yup, we were all so darn happy they weren't going to just drag Fuller off the field. Bill Walsh had a further positive spin on the proceedings: "Sports medicine," he said, "has been a real science in recent years . . . there's a real career for 'em now, for many doctors."

After Fuller had been tended to, and both an IV bag and oxygen mask had been produced, Walsh summed it all up for his viewers: "And let's hope Jeff's okay and can return to action, most likely not in this game, but in the near future."

I was **appalled** at the general casual nature of the public response and pored over the game tape extensively to verify what I had seen and heard. How could people so badly miss the point? Jeff Fuller had been spearing. And he paid a terrible price. But football life just went on, with minimal commentary about the reckless and vicious nature of what Fuller had done. Few saw this as a cautionary tale. There was no crusade launched to **denounce** spearing.

I wrote a column in the *Globe* **lamenting** this but got very little response. It was a journalistic tree falling in an enormous forest. I was messing with football, and perhaps worse than being **vilified**, I was being ignored.

---

inherent: part of the basic nature of something

battering ram: piece of metal or wood used to break down doors

speared: football tackling move to block an opponent by ramming with a helmet (now against the rules)

erudite: intelligent; learned

decry: strongly and publicly say something is wrong

appalled: shocked and disgusted

denounce: publicly say something is wrong

lamenting: expressing unhappiness or sorrow

vilified: harshly criticized

In recent years public consciousness has been raised on the subject of head injuries. The NFL has learned to address neurological concerns. Of course, it's way too late to help many former players, whose innumerable "dings" were actually concussions, the effects of which would surface in later life.

Football's most ardent proponents have decried many of the attempts in recent years to lessen the violence in the game. They call it "girly ball" or "glorified **flag football**," with much of their **ire** directed at the measures that have been instituted to protect the quarterback. They fear the game they have come to know and love is being defanged. The game continues to appeal to people with a thirst for violence I just don't share. I get far more enjoyment from seeing an acrobatic catch along the sideline or a successful **double reverse** than seeing someone hit hard enough to leave the game. To this, many will say I just don't get it. Oh, I get it, all right. I just don't accept it.

flag football: version of American football that does not involve tackling

ire: intense anger

double reverse: a trick offensive play in football involving teammates going in opposite directions

After You Read

Mapping the Reading

1. What are Ryan's concerns about football? (Return to your "As You Read" notes, if you have them, to help you start your answer.)

2. According to Ryan, what should football players expect to experience as a result of playing the sport?

3. Summarize the comments and reactions to the 49ers-Patriots play involving Stephens and Fuller that bother Ryan, and note his concerns about them.

4. How does Ryan compare himself to other fans?

5. Ryan notes that when he wrote an article criticizing spearing, a tackling method, as dangerous, he got little response, and he suspects he knows why: "I was messing with football, and perhaps worse than being vilified, I was being ignored." What does he mean by this?

Discussing and Thinking Critically about the Reading

1. Reread Ryan's opening description of football in the first five paragraphs. What is the purpose of this description? What most surprises you about it?

2. Ryan admits that although football is not his favorite sport, he enjoys watching it and talking about it. How do these admissions affect his credibility?

3. Ryan challenges readers, asking, "How do we as a nation reconcile having chosen football as our new national game? Is the trade-off in body carnage worth the type of entertainment the game provides?" What do you think? How would you answer these questions? Explain your response. (Feel free to consult any "Before You Read" ideas you jotted down.)

4. Ryan notes that those who oppose attempts to reduce the injury risks in football "call it 'girly ball' or 'glorified flag football.'" How much do you see gender stereotypes,

especially stereotypes about masculinity, influencing ideas about football (or another sport)?

5. Ryan focuses his critique on football. From your experience, is football exceptionally dangerous, or might some other sports be similarly characterized? Support your response with details.

Navigating the Intersections

1. Whereas Hilary Beard and Mike Matheny believe in the larger benefits of playing sports, Bob Ryan focuses on the negatives. Comparing their ideas, explain whether you think the benefits outweigh the negatives, or vice versa. Consider if and how we can and should reconcile the risks and rewards.

2. Research current views about football players and injuries or, if you prefer, about another sport's players and their injuries. What, if any, steps are being taken to prevent injuries? What are the arguments for and against making such changes?

Stereotypes and Biases

Before You Read: Brainstorm a list of descriptive words that come to mind when you think about athletes. You can have a specific athlete in mind as you do so, or you can think about athletes more generally.

CASEY GANE-McCALLA

Casey Gane-McCalla is the assistant editor for *NewsOne*, a website devoted to news and information for Black America. He writes about politics, fatherhood, sports, and entertainment, and his work has been featured in the *Huffington Post*, the *Grio*, and *Urban Daily*. Gane-McCalla formerly worked in the South Bronx in New York City as a community organizer and teacher. He is also a rapper and actor, appearing in the 2004 movie *White Chicks*. This 2009 blog post is from *NewsOne*.

As You Read: Mark those places where the author mentions specific sports stereotypes.

Athletic Blacks vs. Smart Whites
Why Sports Stereotypes Are Wrong

Before playing the Stanford team in the **Final Four**, UConn women's coach, Geno Auriemma, said people underestimated Stanford because they think white players are soft.[1] More pointedly, [Auriemma] pointed out that his players, who

Final Four: final rounds of the National Collegiate Athletic Association (NCAA) annual basketball tournament; the height of "March Madness"

[1] See Gane-McCalla's *NewsOne* blog post titled "UConn Coach Says White Kids Are Always Looked Upon as Being Soft," April 6, 2009.

> " *Biological factors do not compel people from certain races to excel in certain sports. Cultural factors do.* "

read defenses: recognize the defensive strategies being used by opponents

Rush Limbaugh: popular conservative radio talk show host

Jimmy the Greek (1918–96): American sports commentator and bookie

flack: criticism

blatant: obvious; clear

insinuating: indirectly introducing an insulting or negative idea

NFL MVP: National Football League Most Valuable Player, awarded annually

Steve McNair (1973–2009): starting quarterback for the Tennessee Titans, 1997–2005

caliber: level of excellence or quality

NBA: National Basketball Association

are predominantly African-American, should be given the same respect for their discipline for which Stanford's team was praised. The coach was simply exposing stereotypes that have been around for a long time.

Black athletes are usually given credit for their "natural athleticism," while whites are credited for their "hard work," "discipline," and "knowledge of the game"; as if Black athletes are naturally given the gift of great athleticism, and white people become great athletes through hard work, discipline, and intelligence.

Every Black athlete who is successful has worked very hard and is knowledgeable of their sport. Every white athlete who is successful has natural athletic ability.

The problem with stereotypes in sports is that they often lead to general stereotypes. If you say "white men can't jump," why not "Black men can't **read defenses**"? And if Black men can't read defenses, maybe they can't read books either?

Sports stereotypes have a real effect in the real world. Most employers are not concerned with employees' natural athletic abilities, so stereotypes of African-Americans being athletically superior for the most part do not help Blacks in the real world. However, the stereotypes of whites being hardworking, disciplined, and smart are helpful to them in finding employment.

One of the most prevalent stereotypes in sports is that of the Black quarterback. Both **Rush Limbaugh** and former sports commentator **Jimmy the Greek** have caught **flack** for their philosophies on African-American quarterbacks. Jimmy's explanation of how blacks were bred for physical skill but whites were bred for intelligence was **blatant** racism, but there have been many more subtle ways at **insinuating** the same point.

Former **NFL MVP Steve McNair** played for a small Black college because every major college recruited him to play defensive back rather than quarterback, his natural position. Many African-Americans are discouraged from playing quarterback and asked to play other positions in high school, college, and the professional ranks. How many other black MVP-**caliber** quarterbacks were forced to play other positions because coaches didn't feel Blacks made good quarterbacks?

Biological factors do not compel people from certain races to excel in certain sports. Cultural factors do. China produces a lot of good ping-pong players because ping-pong is part of Chinese culture. Kenya produces a lot of marathon winners because long-distance running is part of their culture. Jamaica produces sprinters because track and field has become a strong part of their culture and national identity. Baseball has become a big part of Latin American culture and subsequently several of baseball's top players come from Latin America. Basketball is a big part of African-American culture, so a good deal of players in the **NBA** are African-American.

Sports stereotypes are made to be broken. Athletic basketball players are popping up all over the world from all different backgrounds, from Argentina to Turkey, from Kenya to China. Boxing, once a sport dominated by African-Americans, is now being dominated by boxers of other ethnicities from all around the world. Russians are dominating the heavyweight division, and a Filipino, Manny Pacquiao, will fight an Englishman, Ricky Hatton, for the title of best fighter, pound for pound (at least while Floyd Mayweather is retired).

While no Black quarterback has won a Super Bowl since Doug Williams proved Jimmy the Greek wrong in 1988, two of the last three Super Bowl winning coaches have been African-American.[2] This goes even further to disprove Jimmy the Greek's theory, given that African-Americans have excelled at coach, the most **cerebral** position of all.

> **cerebral:** intellectual

Despite all the stereotypes of Black athletes not being intelligent or caring about their education, an African-American, **Myron Rolle**, has become the first major U.S. athlete to win the Rhodes Scholarship since **Bill Bradley**. He bypassed a career in the NFL to get an education from Oxford University, one of the world's most prestigious schools.

> **Myron Rolle** (1986–): after finishing his degree, Rolle played professional football

When stereotypes begin to insinuate that certain races have certain characteristics, whether they be positive or negative, they fall into the same racist generalizations that are at the root of racism and race-based discrimination.

> **Bill Bradley** (1943–): former professional basketball player and U.S. senator

After You Read

Mapping the Reading

1. List the sports stereotypes Gane-McCalla mentions in his article. (Review any "As You Read" notes you may have.)

2. According to Gane-McCalla, how do sports stereotypes actually affect athletes?

3. Gane-McCalla offers examples of stereotyping of sports events and athletes' experiences to support his points. Choose one, and then summarize the example and the point it supports.

4. According to Gane-McCalla, how might culture positively or negatively affect someone's skill in sports? Use examples (your own and from the article) to support your answer.

Discussing and Thinking Critically about the Reading

1. Gane-McCalla mentions several sports stereotypes in his article. Do you think many people believe these stereotypes? Why or why not? What sports stereotypes have you observed that he has not mentioned?

2. According to this article, why are sports stereotypes wrong? Since the word *wrong* has several meanings, look up its definitions and argue for how many Gane-McCalla may be invoking in this article.

---

[2] *Editors' Note:* In 2014, Russell Wilson became the second African American quarterback to win the Super Bowl. Through 2016, four other black quarterbacks have played in the Super Bowl.

3. The author concludes with this observation: "When stereotypes begin to insinuate that certain races have certain characteristics, whether they be positive or negative, they fall into the same racist generalizations that are at the root of racism and race-based discrimination." What is your opinion? Are *positive* and *negative* stereotypes equally a problem? Explain your answer.

4. What sports are popular in your community? Explain whether there are cultural ties to those particular sports in your community.

5. Returning to your "Before You Read" response, how many items on your list reflect sports stereotypes like the ones Gane-McCalla discusses? If any of them do, why do you think this happened?

Navigating the Intersections

1. Casey Gane-McCalla focuses on male athletes in his argument against sports stereotypes. In what ways might female African American athletes face race-based stereotypes? For help with this question, consult Hilary Beard's article.

2. Choose two or three professional athletes from different backgrounds. Research how each is described, referred to, and more generally reported on in the media. Choosing a few articles, look carefully at the words used to describe the athletes and their actions and behaviors. What evidence of any sports stereotypes do you see? What descriptions or references seem to be based on race or ethnicity? Report on your findings.

Before You Read: Write briefly, offering your view on which of the two pictures of Olympian skier Lindsey Vonn reproduced on page 365 would be more effective in sparking interest in attending a women's sporting event, and why.

MARY JO KANE

A professor of sports sociology at the University of Minnesota, Mary Jo Kane is an expert on media coverage of women's sports. Kane is also the director of the Tucker Center for Research on Girls & Women in Sport at the University of Minnesota. The author of numerous scholarly articles and books, she has consulted with ESPN about its coverage of women's sports. Among her many awards, she was named one of the 100 Most Influential Sports Educators by the Institute for International Sport in 2013. This article was published in the *Nation* in 2011.

As You Read: Mark each of the supporting points and examples that the author uses to argue her main idea, noting those that are especially effective.

Sex Sells Sex, Not Women's Sports

The newest kid on the women's sports block is finding that the old formula for attention-getting is as robust as ever. "Sex sells," says Atlanta Beat defender Nancy Augustyniak, who was astonished to learn she finished third in a *Playboy.com* poll of the sexiest female soccer players.

— Wendy Parker, *Atlanta Journal-Constitution*

Champion alpine skier Lindsey Vonn won the downhill gold medal at the Vancouver Winter Olympics, the first American woman to achieve gold in this prestigious event. From 2008 to 2010, Vonn also won three consecutive World Cup championships, the first U.S. woman and second woman ever to accomplish such a **feat**. For her unprecedented achievements, Vonn was named Sportswoman of the Year by the U.S. Olympic Committee.

feat: achievement

Even *Sports Illustrated* [*SI*] — notorious for its lack of coverage of women's sports — couldn't ignore this historic moment and devoted its cover to Vonn. *SI*'s cover, however, blatantly portrayed Vonn as a sex object and spoke volumes about the **rampant** sexual depictions of women athletes. Rather than emphasize her **singular** athletic talent, the magazine depicted Vonn in a posed photograph, smiling at the camera in her ski regalia [see Image A on page 365]. What was most noticeable — and controversial — about the pose was its **phallic** nature: Vonn's backside was arched at a forty-five-degree angle while superimposed over a mountain peak.

rampant: widespread

singular: exceptional

phallic: resembling a phallus, or penis

Offensive as this portrayal may have been, it came as no surprise to sports-media scholars. Over the past three decades we have amassed a large body of **empirical** evidence demonstrating that sportswomen are significantly more likely to be portrayed in ways that emphasize their femininity and heterosexuality rather than their athletic **prowess**. Study after study has revealed that newspaper and TV coverage around the globe routinely and systematically focuses on the athletic **exploits** of male athletes while offering **hypersexualized** images of their female counterparts.

empirical: based on experience or testing

prowess: exceptional ability

exploits: brave or heroic actions

hypersexualized: excessively focused on sexual activity

These findings are no trivial matter. Scholars have long argued that a major consequence of the media's tendency to sexualize women's athletic accomplishments is the reinforcement of their status as second-class citizens in one of the most powerful economic, social, and political institutions on the planet. In doing so, media images that emphasize femininity/sexuality actually **suppress** interest in, not to mention respect for, women's sports.

suppress: slow the development

Many of those charged with covering and promoting women's sports take an entirely different view. As the quote beginning this article makes clear, the "sex sells" strategy remains deeply **embedded** among sports journalists and marketers, who also believe that reaffirming traditional notions of femininity and heterosexuality is a critical sales strategy. This approach, or so the argument goes, reassures (especially male) fans, corporate sponsors, and TV

embedded: placed within

audiences that females can engage in highly competitive sports while retaining a nonthreatening femininity.

The widely held assumption that sexualizing female athletes is the most effective way to promote women's sports creates **cognitive dissonance**. To begin with, marketing campaigns for leagues like the **WNBA** also emphasize the wholesome nature of women's sports, highlighting the connection between fathers and daughters. The underlying message is that women's sports embrace traditional "family values" and that their appeal cuts across generational lines. Given this message, a "sex sells" strategy is counterproductive. How many fathers would accept the notion that support for their daughters' sports participation would be increased by having them pose nude in *Playboy*? And should we buy the argument that what generates fan interest is how pretty athletes are versus how well they perform when a championship is on the line?

cognitive dissonance: confusion from holding incompatible or contradictory ideas

WNBA: Women's National Basketball Association, professional league, 1997–present

> ❝ *Scholars have long argued that a major consequence of the media's tendency to sexualize women's athletic accomplishments is the reinforcement of their status as second-class citizens in one of the most powerful economic, social, and political institutions on the planet.* ❞

I don't disagree that when *SI* publishes its swimsuit issue males are quite interested in buying that particular issue of the magazine. It does not automatically follow, however, that their interest in women's sports has increased. On the contrary, I would argue that what males are interested in consuming is not a women's athletic event but sportswomen's bodies as objects of sexual desire.

To investigate empirically whether sex truly sells women's sports, I conducted a series of focus groups based on gender and age (18–34; 35–55) with a colleague at the University of Minnesota. Study participants were shown photographs of female athletes ranging from on-court athletic competence to wholesome "girls next door" to soft pornography and asked to indicate which images increased their interest in reading about, watching on TV, and attending a women's sporting event.

Our findings revealed that in the vast majority of cases, a "sex sells" approach offended the core fan base of women's sports — women and older men. These two groups rated the image that portrayed athletic prowess as the one most likely to influence their interest in women's sports. Said one younger female: "This image [of a WNBA player driving toward the basket] really sucked me in. I want to be there. I want to be part of that feeling." In contrast, younger and older females, as well as older males, were offended by the hypersexualized images. One older male said: "If she [Serena Williams in a sexually provocative pose] were my sister I'd come in, slap the photographer, grab her, and leave." Even when younger males, a prime target audience, indicated that sexually provocative images were "hot," they also stated that such images did not fundamentally increase their interest in women's sports, particularly when it came to attending a sporting event. The key takeaway? Sex sells sex, not women's sports.

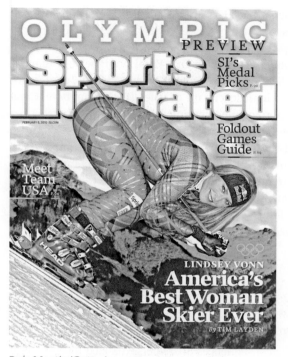

Bob Martin/Getty Images

Image A
Lindsey Vonn on the cover of Sports Illustrated.

Image B
Lindsey Vonn competing in the 2015 FIS Alpine Skiing World Cup Finals Giant Slalom race.

Jeff Pachoud/Getty Images

**NCAA's March
Madness:**
term referring
to the period
of the National
Collegiate Athletic
Association's
basketball
tournament finals

garner: earn or
acquire

Final Four:
four teams that
qualify for the
championship
round of the NCAA
tournament

caricature: an
image that makes
someone look
foolish through
exaggeration

So what *does* sell women's sports? The answer lies with women's college basketball and the coverage it receives on ESPN. Each year during the **NCAA's March Madness** tournament, women's hoops **garner** record attendance and TV ratings. Coverage of the women's **Final Four** bears a remarkable resemblance to that of the men's — a focus on great traditions, conference rivalries (Duke vs. North Carolina), legendary coaches (Pat Summitt vs. Geno Auriemma) — and, most important, showcasing sportswomen as physically gifted, mentally tough, grace-under-pressure athletes.

Millions of fans around the globe . . . witnessed such media images and narratives during coverage of the Women's World Cup in Germany. Perhaps such coverage will start a trend whereby those who cover women's sports will simply turn on the camera and let us see the reality — not the sexualized **caricature** — of today's female athletes. If and when that happens, sportswomen will receive the respect and admiration they so richly deserve.

After You Read

Mapping the Reading

1. According to Kane, how are male and female athletes typically portrayed in the media?

2. Why does Kane find the *Sports Illustrated* cover of skier Lindsey Vonn so offensive?

3. What does Kane argue are the consequences of "hypersexualized images" of female athletes?

4. Kane observes that the belief that "sex sells" "creates cognitive dissonance." What does she mean?

5. Kane reports on an empirical study she conducted to test the belief that sex sells women's sports. Summarize her method and findings.

Discussing and Thinking Critically about the Reading

1. Respond to Kane's argument: Were you aware of the "sex sells" strategy? Do you agree with her critique? Do you agree that men and women athletes are used by marketers differently? Why or why not? Explain your answers.

2. According to Kane, what rationale do sportswriters and marketers have for using a "sex sells" strategy? How credible is that rationale? How does it compare to the strategy, as described by Kane, behind a WNBA marketing campaign?

3. Toward the end of her article, Kane claims that the NCAA finals offer a model for marketing women's sports that doesn't rely on the "sex sells" approach. What is this alternative strategy? Do you think it would be effective? Why or why not? What other marketing plans might you propose?

4. Return to your "Before You Read" response. The question presented a small-scale version of Kane's research. How did your response compare to those of her study's participants?

5. Writing about supporters of the "sex sells" approach, Kane summarizes their counterargument: "This approach, or so the argument goes, reassures (especially male) fans, corporate sponsors, and TV audiences that females can engage in highly competitive sports while retaining a nonthreatening femininity." How do you respond to this argument? What is your view of women athletes? your community's view?

Navigating the Intersections

1. Mary Jo Kane concentrates on gender stereotypes about women athletes. How do her concerns about the larger effects of these stereotypes compare to Casey Gane-McCalla's concerns about stereotypes about male athletes?

2. Look at a selection of *Sports Illustrated* covers from a set period of time — for example, May–July of a particular year — or compare covers from two periods of time — such as August–October 2006 and August–October 2016. First, note how many of the covers feature female athletes and how many feature male athletes. Then, note how many covers feature female and male athletes actually playing their sports and how many use posed pictures of male and female athletes. Looking again at any posed pictures of men and women, how would you describe the content or style? Compare the results to determine whether your particular selection of covers portrays male and female athletes differently.

3. Choose one or two professional female athletes to research. Look for stories about them in the news, online, or in magazines. Evaluate how they are portrayed to see if any of the stories use the stereotypes that Kane identifies.

Before You Read: Make a list of the images, names, and ideas that come to mind when you think about male athletes. Or select a specific male athlete that you know, and list all the words that come to your mind as you think about him. (This athlete does not have to be famous.)

CYD ZEIGLER

An expert on LGBT (lesbian, gay, bisexual, and transgender) sports issues, Cyd Zeigler is cofounder of *Outsports.com*. His writing has appeared in the *Huffington Post*, *Out*, *Playboy*, *Time*, and the *Advocate*. He has appeared on CNN, CBS Sports Radio, and ESPN. The recipient of an Excellence in Journalism Award from the Association of LGBT Journalists, Zeigler has covered homophobia in sports as well as athletes' coming-out stories. This 2014 article is excerpted from *Outsports.com*.

As You Read: Identify one sentence that you find meaningful in each section of Zeigler's article.

Derrick Gordon Finds His Freedom

*After a year of isolation, gay UMass basketball player Derrick Gordon discovered the strength to share his truth with family and teammates. He becomes the first active male **NCAA Division 1** basketball player to come out publicly.*

NCAA Division 1:
National Collegiate Athletic Association Division 1, the highest level

redshirt: a college athlete who doesn't play games so that he can improve his skills and extend his playing eligibility another year

Last Wednesday, at the request of **redshirt** sophomore shooting guard Derrick Gordon, University of Massachusetts men's basketball head coach Derek Kellogg called a team meeting. Two weeks after his team's upset loss to Tennessee in the NCAA tournament, Gordon had a secret he wanted to share with them, one that in a week's time he would share with the world: He's gay. No active male athlete in Division 1 college basketball, football, baseball, or hockey had ever said those words publicly. After years of waiting for someone else to break the barrier, Gordon wasn't going to wait any longer. . . .

For the last eight months [Gordon] had distanced himself from the team, struggling with teasing from teammates and internal torment that nearly drove him from basketball. Gordon had locked himself away, separate from the team and the rest of the campus, since September. But in the last month, spending time with other gay people in sports, something different had suddenly driven him to share his secret: Hope.

It Began with Rumors and Snickers

. . . Gordon's then-boyfriend last summer posted a photograph on Instagram of the two of them in front of a gay bar on the New Jersey coast. Gordon was wary of the post but figured there was little chance someone would stumble across the photo on a random Instagram account and identify him and said gay bar. Shortly after the post, almost as though he wanted to be discovered, Gordon "liked" the photograph online. Within hours, some of his teammates asked him if he were gay.

Gordon denied it repeatedly, but that didn't stop various members of the team from teasing him about it. The snickers and snide remarks carried on for weeks. Slowly, it consumed him.

"That was probably the lowest point I was ever at. I didn't want to play basketball anymore. I just wanted to run and hide somewhere. I used to go back to my room and I'd just cry. There were nights when I would cry myself to sleep.

"Nobody should ever feel that way."

When Gordon eventually confronted his team—again asserting he was straight and demanding they stop harassing him—the teasing slowed. Yet the damage was already done. Throughout the season—all the way into the NCAA tournament last month—some teammates continued to wait until Gordon was done in the locker room before they would venture into the showers. The "gay" label lingered. The treatment built distance between him and the rest of the team. Gordon responded by isolating himself, which in turn was met with more distance from various players.

"Most of the time when you see me on campus, I'm alone. I eat alone a lot. Since the school year started in September I haven't been to one party. I'm always working out or lifting or in my room. I do the same thing over and over every day. I feel like I can't be who I am or live my life." . . .

"It was torture. I was just going around faking my whole life, being someone I'm not. It's like wearing a mask because everyone else was wearing that mask. Now that I'm taking the mask off, people can finally see who I really am," [said Gordon.]

> *That was probably the lowest point I was ever at. I didn't want to play basketball anymore. I just wanted to run and hide somewhere. I used to go back to my room and I'd just cry. There were nights when I would cry myself to sleep.*
>
> *Nobody should ever feel that way.*

Cracks in the Facade

The first cracks in the straight **facade** came last year when a mutual friend introduced Gordon to Wade Davis, a gay former NFL player and You Can Play project executive director. Gordon was struggling with the isolation that drove him to the brink of quitting the sport he loved, and their mutual friend didn't want to see Gordon go that route.

facade: superficial appearance or front

"He seemed lost and confused," Davis said. "He was searching for family, searching for a space where he could be himself. I don't think he had that on his team, and he hadn't met other gay males whom he could connect with. He was trying to navigate his love of basketball with his need to be his authentic self. He was bordering on depression." . . .

It was the night of Friday, March 14, that changed the course of Gordon's life forever. UMass had just lost a heartbreaker to George Washington, 85–77, in the quarterfinals of the Atlantic-10 tournament in Brooklyn. Gordon had a fine game, shooting four-for-nine with three steals, but the loss stung.

Sitting courtside was Davis, who comforted Gordon with a night out on the town in Manhattan. Joining them were former ESPN radio host Jared Max and Saunders High School basketball coach Anthony Nicodemo, who had come out as gay himself a year earlier. Suddenly Gordon found himself surrounded by openly gay men in various corners of sports, all of whom were publicly out. . . .

While Gordon said he had read about gay athletes on *Outsports* for years, meeting these people—talking with them and laughing with them over the last month—has been a revelation. He had long felt he would come out to his family and friends after college, maybe a few seasons into his NBA career if he heads that direction. . . . [But now,] coming out and living his life authentically suddenly became urgent for him. He wasn't going to live in the closet another day. . . .

Coming Out

Last Wednesday, after Coach Kellogg broke the ice with the team, Gordon stood before them and revealed that he's gay. As he shared with them his story of isolation, there wasn't a dry eye in the room. While it had been easy for some of the young men to tease someone they thought was gay — and someone who denied it — the impact of their actions hit home when Gordon revealed the speculation was true, and that the teasing nearly drove him from the team.

"It was powerful for these players to see one of their brothers be so vulnerable," said Davis, who said he had to turn away from the group in the room lest they see him get emotional. "These are some inner-city kids, some rough, tough kids who Derrick wants to be friends with. They understand who he is a little bit better now."

The team responded well. Some of them **lamented** that Gordon had pulled away from them. It wasn't their intent: The teasing had hit home in a way that landed wrong with him. In the locker room, guys tease one another for everything from penis size to haircut. Even your mama is fair game. They didn't know how to talk with Gordon about their assumption that he was gay, so they relied on locker room teasing.

Of course, without that teasing, Gordon wouldn't have pulled away. But it wasn't just the teasing. So much of the conversation on the team was about girls. It's a conversation Gordon has never felt part of. While he acknowledged that all of the perspectives in the room have some truth to them, he's hopeful that now that he's out to them he'll be able to share his real dating experiences with them. It will be a true test for the team. . . .

"*Happy* is not even the word," Gordon said. "It's a great feeling. I haven't felt like this. Ever. It's a lot of weight lifted off my shoulders. I can finally breathe now and live life happily. I told all the people I need to tell."

Davis cut in with the word — Gordon had found "freedom." . . .

Confronting Stereotypes

Off the court, Gordon feels he now has a responsibility to other young gay athletes. . . .

"God put me in this situation for a reason, so I have to take advantage of it. Maybe he wants me to be the starter of something big. Maybe he doesn't want me to feel the way I felt anymore. Whatever he has in store for me, I'm ready."

One of the areas he is taking aim at is stereotypes often **saddled** on gay men. Gordon is no "pansy." From a rough-and-tumble neighborhood, he has added twenty-five pounds of muscle to his frame since high school. This isn't **gym-bunny** muscle, it's the hardened body of a warrior.

"People think gay men are soft," Gordon said. "I'm not. Especially my background growing up, I was never a soft kid and I'll never be a soft kid. People think gays are very delicate. That's not the case at all. I know **Michael Sam** and **Jason Collins** aren't delicate. My strength coach compares me to a pit bull. There's no softness in this body."

lamented: expressed sorrow or regret

saddled: put a burden on

gym-bunny: someone who works out to look muscular

Michael Sam: professional football player who came out before he was drafted

Jason Collins: first active, openly gay American professional basketball player

While Gordon will be laser-focused on basketball, he also understands his potential role in helping LGBT people avoid the depression and isolation he experienced. It's not something he is going to shy away from.

"When kids aren't able to come out, I know why. It's a scary thing. That's one of the reasons I'm doing this. I want to give kids some courage and someone they can look up to. If I can come out and play basketball, then why can't they do it? I want to be able to help those people."

After You Read

Mapping the Reading

1. What led Gordon's teammates to question whether he was gay?

2. How did Gordon respond to his teammates' "teasing" him about possibly being gay?

3. What inspired Gordon to come out to his teammates?

4. What stereotypes does Gordon want to challenge?

Discussing and Thinking Critically about the Reading

1. Return to your "As You Read" notes. Choose one of the sentences you marked, and explain why you found it meaningful.

2. Although much of society has become more accepting of LGBT individuals, athletics seem slower to change. Why do you think this is so?

3. Teasing is presented here as the "norm" in locker rooms. As Zeigler writes of Gordon's teammates, "They didn't know how to talk with Gordon about their assumption that he was gay, so they relied on locker room teasing." Why might bullying be accepted as the norm in the locker room?

4. Return to your "Before You Read" response. What about male athletes did you focus on when you were coming up with your list — performance? appearance? sexual orientation? something else? Do you see any evidence of stereotypes about male athletes in your list?

5. While being gay may be seen as a private, personal matter, why did Gordon feel it was important to come out publicly?

Navigating the Intersections

1. Compare the sports stereotypes discussed by Cyd Zeigler and another author from this chapter. Which seem to be the most deeply rooted and difficult to change?

2. Visit the website of the You Can Play project to explore its campaign to erase homophobia in sports. Report back on some of the strategies the project is using.

3. Research the connection between sports and bullying. How big a problem is it? What is being done to combat it?

CHAPTER 10

The Digital Age

Risks and Rewards

JGI/Jamie Grill/Getty Images

Image Response: Millennials are often represented as they are in this image: glued to their devices and seldom talking face-to-face. To what degree is this representation a stereotype, and to what degree is it accurate? How would you describe millennials' relationships with their devices?

(*Tip:* Millennials are typically considered to have been born between 1982 and 2004.)

In This Chapter

Introduction

The Digital Age

In this chapter, we explore important aspects of the digital age: social media's effect on personal relationships and on self-esteem, and digital histories' potential to preserve and promote inaccurate, possibly harmful versions of ourselves.

Consider the following news and magazine headlines:

"Is Social Media Ruining Your Relationship?" — CBS News
"Pope Urges Young People Not to Waste Time on Internet" — NBC News
"Is Texting Killing the English Language?" — *Time*
"Is Google Making Us Stupid?" — *Atlantic Monthly*
"Is Social Media Sabotaging Real Communication?" — *Forbes*
"Ever-Present Devices Can Push Our Crazy Buttons" — *USA Today*

Headlines such as these capture some of the concerns of the digital age. Social media, the Internet, and other forms of digital interaction are part of contemporary life, connecting family and friends who are separated geographically, offering fast and easy access to a wealth of information (both reliable and unreliable), and allowing people the ability to socialize or collaborate professionally from hundreds or even thousands of miles apart. While Internet tools are valuable for enabling business growth, providing pleasure and personal utility, and allowing for social and political community, they can also be abused or misused; many wonder if we have allowed social media and digital interaction to take over our lives.

Online Is a Fact of Life

A 2013 study found that Americans spend more than five hours a day online (Kleinman). These five hours include a variety of activities, one of which is social networking, whose use continues to grow. According to the Pew Research Center's Internet Project, in 2006, 16 percent of adults who spent time online used social media; by 2014, that number had grown to 74 percent, with young adults using social media at even higher rates. Time spent online on social media or surfing the Internet necessarily means that Americans have had to give up activities that they used to spend time on before the online world became available. A 2013 study documents these changes in how we spend our time, with Max Nisen reporting that "[o]n the more obvious side, we spend less time watching TV, socializing offline, relaxing, and thinking. But leisure time online also comes at the expense of work, sleep, and education." Does it matter that we are spending less time thinking? working? sleeping? doing homework? Is social media simply another invention — like the automobile, the telephone, or the radio — that is revolutionary in what it allows but not a cause for great worry or concern?

Social or Antisocial?

Without a doubt, the digital age has provided a new territory for long-existing antisocial behaviors, such as theft, fraud, and cruelty. Every age has struggled with these behaviors, yet lawmakers and even digital pioneer Bill Gates worry about the Internet's capacity for theft and fraud aided by digital tools and developments in artificial intelligence (Statt). Similarly, the capacity for cruelty online, through cyberbullying, impersonation, and Internet trolling, has prompted legal action, legislation, and heated conversation, both online and off. Stories of digital cruelty go viral because they are so shocking, perhaps most especially for parents, grand-parents, and people who are unfamiliar with the online world. The frequency with which we read about the cruelty of trolls and cyberbullies who go on the Internet to insult, harass, and argue with others certainly raises questions for many about the personal and social cost of our beloved online lives. Ultimately, is social media social or antisocial?

The image at the beginning of the chapter presents a familiar scenario: a group of people in a room, all looking at their devices rather than interacting with one another. It is what Sherry Turkle, an expert on technology's impact on relationships, calls being "alone together" in her book of the same name. While people are con-necting with those far away, they may be ignoring those who are right in front of them. Some have argued that this makes it harder, if not impossible, to have mean-ingful, in-person relationships. Of course, it is also possible that the people sitting in the room together are talking to one another through their devices: sending notes, images, and videos, and sharing links. Yet the idea that time online detracts from face-to-face interactions persists, as this cartoon by Isabella Bannerman illustrates:

© 2013 Margaret Shulock—Distributed by King Features Syndicate, Inc.

This cartoon questions the kinds of relationships we have online. Can we truly feel connected to someone on social media? What kinds of friends are our online friends? Does social media really connect us or merely present a pale imitation of genuine human relationships?

As these questions continue to be debated, it is important to recognize that the Internet is ever changing, and the lines between online and off-line socializing may be blurring. For example, some social media platforms are being used to help people get together in person, as is the case with dating apps and other "meetup" services. Nonetheless, the question remains: How have social media platforms changed human interactions, if at all?

Digital Footprints

Online interactions may be immediate and in real time, but they leave a footprint. What we post online—and what others may post about us—creates a digital version of ourselves, a digital history that others can use to form opinions about us. Researchers at Stanford and Cambridge have discovered that computers are better at predicting someone's personality than friends, coworkers, siblings, or parents, a development that raises some questions about privacy—namely, what will and should be done with this information ("Computers")? Digital histories can also be managed and manipulated by individuals. For instance, users can control a social networking site, giving some friends more access than others. This means that a teenager, for example, can include her father as a "friend" but make sure that this online friendship is limited, with the father thinking he is seeing everything while the daughter is making sure he isn't. Other sites, such as Snapchat, have developed "fade" functions so that a message or an image disappears once it is viewed. Managing toward different goals, some people may seek Internet fame by targeting their posts to attract interest in an attempt to get more "likes," friends, views, followers, reposts, and retweets. Others may seek to disguise who they are online by using initials or fake names. From sexy selfies to heat-of-the-moment posts to misinformation broadcast online, our digital histories form a permanent—and possibly misleading, if not downright inaccurate—picture of us. How we manage this wealth of information and misinformation—and how we *should* manage it—remains a challenge.

Works Cited

"Computers Using Digital Footprints Are Better Judges of Personality Than Friends and Family." *ScienceDaily*, 12 Jan. 2015, www.sciencedaily.com/releases/2015/01/150112154456 .htm.

Kleinman, Alexis. "Americans Will Spend More Time on Digital Devices Than Watching TV This Year." *Huffington Post*, 1 Aug. 2013, www.huffingtonpost.com/2013/08/01/tv-digital -devices_n_3691196.html.

Nisen, Max. "These Charts Show What We're Not Doing Because We're Online All the Time." *Business Insider*, 21 Oct. 2013, www.businessinsider.com/how-much-time-people -spend-online-2013-10.

Pew Research Center. "Social Networking Fact Sheet." *Pewinternet.org.* Accessed 10 Oct. 2014.

Statt, Nick. "Bill Gates Is Worried about Artificial Intelligence, Too." *CNET News.com*, CNET Networks, 28 Jan. 2015, www.cnet.com/news/bill-gates-is-worried-about-artificial-intelligence -too/.

Turkle, Sherry. *Alone Together: Why We Expect More from Technology and Less from Each Other*. Basic Books, 2012.

Connected or Disconnected?

Before You Read: Write briefly about your views on social media's impact on society: Do you think social media has a positive, a negative, or some other kind of impact on society? Offer a few reasons and examples to support your view.

JOSH ROSE

Josh Rose is a marketing expert, writer, public speaker, and — when time permits — photographer. Rose is known for developing strategies for marketing brands across several digital platforms. He has won many awards for marketing, including Clios, Beldings, Effies, Webbys, ADDYs, and the Yahoo! Creativity Award. Rose has written articles on social media and the digital age for the *Huffington Post*, *iMedia Connection*, *Contagious* magazine, and *Mashable*, which is where this article was published in 2011.

As You Read: In making an argument about the impact of social media, Rose offers an example from his own life as well as other examples. Make a list of these examples and of the points he supports with these examples.

How Social Media Is Having a Positive Impact on Our Culture

Two events today, although worlds apart, seem **inextricably** tied together. And the bond between them is as human as it is electronic.

First, on my way to go sit down and read the newspaper at my coffee shop, I got a message from my ten-year-old son, just saying good morning and letting me know he was going to a birthday party today. I don't get to see him all the time. He's growing up in two houses, as I did. But recently, as I handed down my old iPhone 3G to him to use basically as an iPod touch, we both installed an app called Yak, so we could communicate with each other when we're apart.

The amount of calming satisfaction it gives me to be able to communicate with him through technology is undeniably **palpable** and human. It's the other side of the "I don't care what you ate for breakfast this morning" argument against the **mundane** broadcasting of social media. In this case, I absolutely care about this. I'd listen to him describe a piece of bacon, and hang on every word. Is it better than a conversation with "real words"? No. But is it better than waiting two more days, when the mundane moment that I long to hear about so much is gone? Yes.

I guess one man's **TMI** is another man's treasure.

inextricably: closely related; cannot be separated

palpable: capable of being felt or touched

mundane: ordinary; common

TMI: too much information (abbreviation)

Moments later, I sat down and opened the paper. A headline immediately stood out: "In China, microblogs finding abducted kids" with the subhead, "A 6-year-old who was snatched when he was 3 is discovered with a family 800 miles away." Apparently, the occurrence of reclaimed children through the use of China's version of Twitter — and other online forums — has become triumphant news over there. I'm reading about the father's tears, the boy's own confusing set of emotions, the rapt attention of the town and country, and I'm again marveling at the human side of the Internet.

The Paradox* of Online Closeness

*paradox: a statement or idea that seems contradictory or impossible but perhaps is true

I recently asked the question to my Facebook friends: "Twitter, Facebook, Foursquare . . . is all this making you feel closer to people or farther away?" It sparked a lot of responses and seemed to touch one of our generation's exposed nerves. What is the effect of the Internet and social media on our humanity?

From the outside view, digital interactions appear to be cold and inhuman. There's no denying that. And without doubt, given the choice between hugging someone and "**poking**" someone, I think we can all agree which one feels better. The theme of the responses to my Facebook question seemed to be summed up by my friend Jason, who wrote: "Closer to people I'm far away from." Then, a minute later, wrote, "but maybe farther from the people I'm close enough to." And then added, "I just got confused."

poking: Facebook method of getting attention or saying hello

❝ *The Internet doesn't steal our humanity, it reflects it. The Internet doesn't get inside us, it shows what's inside us. And social media isn't cold, it's just complex and hard to define.* **❞**

It *is* confusing. We live in this paradox now, where two seemingly conflicting realities exist side-by-side. Social media simultaneously draws us nearer and distances us. But I think very often, we **lament** what we miss and forget to admire what we've become. And it's human nature to want to reject the machine at the moment we feel it becoming **ubiquitous**. We've seen it with the printing press, moving pictures, television, video games, and just about any other advanced technology that captures our attention. What romantic rituals of relationship and social interaction will die in the process? Our hearts want to know.

lament: express sorrow or regret

ubiquitous: seemingly everywhere

truism: accepted, common (often obvious) truth

slew: a large number of things

In the [February 14, 2011] *New Yorker . . .* , Adam Gopnik's article "How the Internet Gets Inside Us" explores this cultural **truism** in depth. It's a fantastic read and should be mandatory for anyone in an online industry. He breaks down a whole **slew** of new books on the subject and categorizes it all into three viewpoints: "the Never-Betters, the Better-Nevers, and the Ever-Wasers." In short, those who see the current movement as good, bad, or normal. I think we all know people from each camp. But ultimately, the last group is the one best equipped to handle it all.

Filling in the Space with Connections

Another observation from the coffee shop: In my immediate vicinity, four people are looking at screens and four people are reading something on paper. And I'm doing both. I see Facebook open on two screens, but I'm sure at some point, it's been open on all of them. The dynamic in this coffee shop is quite a bit more revealing than any article or book. Think about the varied **juxtapositions** of physical and digital going on. People aren't giving up **long-form reading**, **considered thinking**, or social interactions. They are just filling all the space between. And even that's not entirely true as I watch the occasional stare out the window or long glance around the room.

The way people engage with the Internet and social media isn't like any kind of interaction we've ever seen before. It's like an intertwining **sine wave** that touches in and out continuously. And the Internet itself is more complex and interesting than we often give it credit for. Consider peer-to-peer networking as just one example, where the tasks are distributed among the group to form a whole. It's practically a **metaphor** for the human mind. Or a township. Or a government. Or a family.

The Internet doesn't steal our humanity, it reflects it. The Internet doesn't get inside us, it shows what's inside us. And social media isn't cold, it's just complex and hard to define. I've always thought that you really see something's value when you try to destroy it. . . . The Internet has quickly become the **atom** of cultural media; intertwined with our familial and cultural bonds, and destroyed only at great risk. I think if we search our own souls and consider our own personal way of navigating, we know this is as true personally as it is globally. The machine does not control us. It is a tool. As advanced today as a sharpened stick was a couple million years ago. Looked at through this lens, perhaps we should re-frame our discussions about technology from how it is changing us to how we are using it.

juxtapositions: placements of different things together

long-form reading: extended or book-length, as opposed to the length of social media posts, tweets, and blogs

considered thinking: deep, thoughtful consideration

sine wave: a mathematical curve that describes predictable moving back and forth around a central line

metaphor: something that is representative or symbolic of something else, particularly an abstract idea; not literal

atom: smallest part of something

After You Read

Mapping the Reading

1. How does social media help Rose feel closer to his son?

2. Explain and describe the "human side of the Internet," according to Rose.

3. What is the "paradox of online closeness"?

4. According to Rose, how do social media and digital communication have a positive impact on culture? What examples does he provide to support his idea? (You may draw on your "As You Read" notes to answer.)

5. What suggestion does Rose offer for changing the way that we think about the Internet?

Discussing and Thinking Critically about the Reading

1. As part of his argument, Rose acknowledges *counterarguments* (other opposing view-points) about social media's impact on relationships. What counterarguments does he mention, and how does he critique them?

2. What does Rose mean when he says, "The Internet doesn't steal our humanity, it reflects it"? Do you agree? Why or why not?

3. Look at your response to question 4 under "Mapping the Reading"; how convincing are Rose's examples?

4. Rose indicates that he lives with his son only part-time. How much do you think that fact influences his view on the positive impact of social media? How much does physical distance between you and the people you care about factor into *your* view of social media?

5. Reflecting on your own experiences and observations, explain your view on whether social media draws people together or pulls them apart.

Navigating the Intersections

1. Track all your social media use and other digital interactions for a day by simply not-ing down the time, length, and type of digital interactions you engage in, using the following example to get you started:

   6:28 a.m. texted mom
   6:29 a.m. texted her back
   6:30 a.m. checked Instagram; made a few comments
   7:25 a.m. read e-mail from cousin

   When your notes are complete, examine them: What kinds of interactions are you having? How many, how frequently, and with whom? What kinds of information are you sharing? What kinds of information are others sharing with you? Why? How does this information affect your sense of closeness to these people?

2. What do other writers think about the question of whether social media brings people together or pulls them apart? To get more perspective on this question, find a relevant article in a newspaper, magazine, or blog by using a search term such as "does social media bring us closer." Read the article and summarize the author's argument.

Before You Read: Write briefly in response to the following: In your experience, how competitive can social media be, with individuals competing for best pic-ture, funniest post, most "likes," or most contacts? In what, if any, ways might time spent on social media have an effect on a person's self-esteem?

ANDREA SHEA

Andrea Shea is a radio reporter, having worked mostly for public radio as a producer and journalist, most recently reporting on arts and culture for WBUR in Boston, Massachusetts. She has received an Edward R. Murrow Award, an Associated Press award, and a PRNDI (Public Radio News Directors Incorporated) award. A version of this article was originally aired on WBUR in 2013 as part of a series titled *Digital Lives*.

As You Read: In the following article, journalist Andrea Shea reports on a problem; identify the problem and the positions that her sources put forward.

Facebook Envy
How the Social Network Affects Our Self-Esteem

Facebook has been growing at an explosive clip since it launched in 2004, and the number of users on the site topped one billion last year. Plenty of people have figured out how to use the vast social network in productive, positive ways — but for others it still feels like a challenging, new frontier.

Some of us **project** — and consume — idealized images through Facebook, and researchers have been trying to figure out how all this flawlessness affects us in the real world.

project: broadcast; show

Some of the freshest data on Facebook's impact on us comes out of two German universities. Researchers [have] released details from joint studies exploring how the mass **proliferation** of so-called "perfect lives" on Facebook can cause **rampant** envy and distress.

proliferation: rapid increase

rampant: uncontrolled; widespread

Daily Show host Jon Stewart couldn't resist ribbing a report about it on *NBC News*, delivered by Brian Williams:

> **WILLIAMS:** A lot of items in the news today about our health and well-being, including that Facebook can full on bum you out.
>
> **STEWART:** Whoa! Thank you, brah! . . . Pray tell, what about Facebook puts [us] at risk for the bumming?
>
> **WILLIAMS:** Researchers call it Facebook envy. It's the act of viewing all of your friends' fabulous vacations, lovely children, attractive friends, and great social lives. The research showed it can leave people feeling — you guessed it — lonely, frustrated, and angry.
>
> **STEWART:** I'm not a doctor, but if you get upset because other people are happy, it seems your problem might not be Facebook, but that you're an [expletive].

Not a Laughing Matter

Sure, it's easy to crack jokes about Facebook, but Belmont-based clinical psychologist Craig Malkin takes findings like this seriously. The studies showed that one in three respondents felt more dissatisfied with their own lives after spending time on the site. Viewing the number of birthday greetings and "likes" were big **culprits**. **Unprecedented** access to other people's photos also triggered emotional pain and resentment.

culprits: offenders

unprecedented: unheard of; new

"This is something that keeps showing up in the research," Malkin explained. "Some people out there wind up negatively comparing themselves to what's portrayed on Facebook by their friends."

> ❝ *Researchers [have] released details from joint studies exploring how the mass proliferation of so-called 'perfect lives' on Facebook can cause rampant envy and distress.* ❞

We all know how the definition of the word *friend* has been challenged by social media. Our circles have grown to include everyone from best buddies to co-workers, to kindergarten classmates and friends of friends of friends, to strangers. Connecting with this vast online community can upend our sense of self, according to Malkin. He says many twentysomethings are telling him and his colleagues that they actually "hate" Facebook—even though they're on it a lot.

Malkin grabs his laptop and launches his profile page. He's an instructor at Harvard Medical School and mainly uses Facebook as a platform for the books and articles he's written. Malkin said the social network's negative impact on our identity and self-esteem is playing out in therapy rooms everywhere.

"We're really just in the infancy when it comes to this research, but there are some themes that are emerging," he said. "And one of the clearest themes is when people go on to Facebook they're often crafting a **persona**—they're portraying themselves at their happiest. They're often choosing events that feel best to them and they're leaving out other things."

persona: a personality that one has created

These picture-perfect images can be especially difficult for teenagers to grapple with because they're often hyper-conscious of measuring up to their peers. It's a tender and critical stage in life—a time for forming an understanding of who you are.

Seventeen-year-old Hannah Musgrove is a senior at Milton High School. She agreed to meet me on Harvard's campus, where Facebook was born. Right now she's taking a break from the site—mainly because it's time-consuming—but she can relate to the research.

"When you go on Facebook it's kind of like you're going through everyone's pictures, and you get lost in it," Musgrove said. "And you're looking at everyone's life, like, 'Oh, that looks like so much fun, oh they're so cool, they're so pretty, they have all these cool pictures.' But really they've taken so much time just to make that image on their Facebook."

And Hannah admitted with a little laugh, "It can make you feel bad I guess, or like, you know, down about yourself."

Crafting an Image

It can be hard looking around Facebook, but it's also stressful presenting an image of yourself, Musgrove admitted. And not surprisingly, people go to lengths to perfect their profile.

"You can literally airbrush your pictures online for free. I know, I've done this," said sixteen-year-old Chloe Miller, a sophomore at Newton South High School. "You upload your picture and you can take out all your little pimples and stuff to make it look like your skin is perfect, your hair is perfect."

Miller and her real-world friend Paige Herer told me they log on to Facebook ten to twenty times a day, sometimes between classes. Each has about one thousand Facebook friends and they say profile pictures — or "pro pics," as they're called by their peers — are a huge deal. Some teens update them obsessively, vying for "likes" on Facebook. It's a photo-driven numbers game, Miller and Herer said, pointing to one Brookline High student's "pro pic" that attracted more than six hundred likes.

Posting pictures of high school parties is another preoccupation.

"There's definitely people that [in] all of their pictures from parties look like they're having such a great time and you wish you were there," Herer explained. "But then when you actually go to one of those parties everyone's just sitting around and not doing anything except for taking these pictures."

Keeping up a type of **facade** by only posting pretty pictures and fun experiences can be tough, Herer admitted, especially when things aren't going so well.

> **facade:** superficial appearance or front

"It just makes you feel worse about what's going on, and it makes you feel bad that you feel like you have to hide it from other people," she said.

Omitting Our Flaws

"The self is, to some extent, a story we tell," Malkin explained. "When people are choosing to leave out the normal chinks in human armor, the normal vulnerabilities, how can they again not feel like there's something wrong with that?"

Malkin also said he's been observing a common sentiment in his private practice. "People are leery of saying that they're struggling in some ways, and saying it openly." And not just on Facebook, Malkin clarified, "but even in their everyday relationships."

The psychologist said concealing the less desirable aspects of our lives over and over again "**forecloses** intimacy," meaning it can condition and prevent us from nurturing truly intimate connections with others. But what about our relationship to ourselves?

> **forecloses:** shuts out

"It affects it deeply," Malkin answered, "because part of the way we develop a strong sense of self and identity is by being known and known by others — appreciated. They see who we are, and they value who we are, including our flaws."

Cultivating Postures Is Nothing New

But Steven Cooper, a clinical psychologist in Cambridge, says being selective as we design and share our identity isn't anything new. We're constantly posturing in the real world, too.

"When deciding what shirt we're going to put on, or jacket, or dress, whether we're going to wear makeup, all these things, we're always cultivating postures," Cooper said. "It's an agreed upon human behavior that we all present ourselves, and cover up and cultivate these images and personas. So now it's broadened."

And it's broadcast to a much wider audience in ways that were unthinkable in the past. But even with all of this **curating**, Cooper believes the truth about us has a knack for revealing itself — in life, and online.

curating: taking care of

"Our thoughtfulness, our inhibitions, our expressiveness, our creativity, our humor, our sadness, our aggression. Those elements of our personality are probably going to shine through," he said.

Malkin says he looks forward to future research on the different ways we **disclose** ourselves and perceive others via social media, and how those experiences affect our sense of personal identity.

disclose: reveal; open up about

"I think the mistake is just assuming that we're just going to figure out how to use it in a way that makes us feel good," Malkin said, "because that's clearly not the case."

And of course there are as many ways to use Facebook as there are Facebook users. There's a growing body of research **extolling** the benefits we reap from social media. For now, though, Malkin believes we'll have to learn as we go because there are very few signposts telling us exactly how the largest social network ever will make us feel about ourselves.

extolling: enthusiastically praising

After You Read

Mapping the Reading

1. What is "Facebook envy"?

2. Summarize the research findings on how viewing "so-called 'perfect lives' on Facebook" affects self-esteem. (You may consult your "As You Read" notes.)

3. Explain psychologist Craig Malkin's theory that "concealing the less desirable aspects of our lives over and over again 'forecloses intimacy.'" For Malkin, what is the long-term personal effect of this concealment?

4. What is psychologist Steven Cooper's point of view on how social media affects self-esteem?

5. According to Cooper, how is "posturing" on Facebook both similar to and different from other forms of posturing as part of a strategy to impress others?

Discussing and Thinking Critically about the Reading

1. What are the ways that a person can cultivate a persona online that is deliberately different from the persona most of their off-line friends would recognize? In your experience or observations, how does social media make it easier to create a personality and persona that is new and different from what is presented in the off-line world?

2. Respond to the research findings identified in question 2 under "Mapping the Reading." Do these findings reflect your experiences or observations? Why or why not?

3. Analyze Shea's reporting. Who are her sources, and how credible are they? Has Shea favored one side of the argument about social media's capacity to lower self-esteem over the other? If so, in what ways?

4. Malkin observes that "many twentysomethings are telling him and his colleagues that they actually 'hate' Facebook — even though they're on it a lot." Based on your observations and experiences, do you agree or disagree with this observation? Why might people feel it is necessary to use certain social media platforms even if they don't like them? How relevant are factors like age and gender in how people consume social media?

5. Explain your point of view on whether social media might damage people's self-esteem. Which, if any, people might be more vulnerable than others? In what other ways might social media be psychologically damaging?

Navigating the Intersections

1. Compare the ideas of Andrea Shea's sources to those of Josh Rose. How are they similar? How are they different? How do the individuals' different interests shape their perspectives on social media use?

2. Evaluate a friend's or a family member's use of social media, reviewing everything that person posts on a platform you are familiar with. How does the individual self-present? What persona or personality is projected? How does it compare to that person's offline persona? Alternatively, you can evaluate your own use of social media, asking the same questions.

Before You Read: Write a brief summary of an example of Internet bullying that you have observed or experienced. What was your reaction? What was the reaction of others?

LINDY WEST

Writer, editor, and performer Lindy West covers popular culture, social justice, humor, and body image in her work. West has provided commentary for National Public Radio programs and has appeared on several television shows. She has written for *GQ*, *Slate*, the *New York Daily News*, *New York* magazine's culture blog *Vulture*, *Cosmopolitan*, and the *Guardian*, among other publications. She is the founder and editor of *I Believe You/It's Not Your Fault*, a blog that addresses young women's questions about mental illness, child abuse, and violence. Her book, *Shrill: Notes from a Loud Woman*, was published in 2016. This article appeared in the *Guardian* in 2015, and another version was also produced for the radio show *This American Life*.

As You Read: Note the passages where West uses humor and sarcasm as she relates her experiences.

What Happened When I Confronted My Cruelest Troll*

*troll: someone who posts comments online intended to cause disruption or argument

pithy: short and to the point

barrage: large quantity, quickly and continuously received

For the past three years or so, at least one stranger has sought me out pretty much every day to call me a fat bitch (or some **pithy** variation thereof). I'm a writer and a woman and a feminist, and I write about big, fat, bitchy things that make people uncomfortable. And because I choose to do that as a career, I'm told, a constant **barrage** of abuse is just part of my job. Shrug. Nothing we can do. I'm asking for it, apparently.

Being harassed on the Internet is such a normal, common part of my life that I'm always surprised when other people find it surprising. You're telling me you don't have hundreds of men popping into your cubicle in the accounting department of your mid-sized, regional dry-goods distributor to inform you that—hmm—you're too fat to rape, but perhaps they'll saw you up with an electric knife? No? Just me? People who don't spend much time on the Internet are invariably shocked to discover the barbarism—the eager abandonment of the **social contract**—that so many of us face simply for doing our jobs.

social contract: unofficial agreement within society concerning rules of behavior

Sometimes the hate trickles in slowly, just one or two messages a day. But other times, when I've written something particularly controversial (i.e., feminist)—like, say, my critique of men feeling entitled to women's time and attention,[1] or literally anything about rape—the harassment comes in a **deluge**. It floods my Twitter feed, my Facebook page, my e-mail, so fast that I can't even keep up (not that I want to).

deluge: severe flood

---

[1] Lindy West, "Attention, Men: Don't Be a Creepy Dude Who Pesters Women in Coffee Shops and on the Subway," *Guardian*, October 21, 2014.

It was in the middle of one of these deluges two summers ago when my dead father contacted me on Twitter.

At the time, I'd been writing a lot about the problem of **misogyny** (specifically jokes about rape) in the comedy world. My central point — which has been gleefully **misconstrued** as "pro-censorship" ever since — was that what we say affects the world we live in, that words are both a reflection of and a **catalyst** for the way our society operates. When you talk about rape, I said, you get to decide where you aim: Are you making fun of rapists? Or their victims? Are you making the world better? Or worse? It's not about censorship, it's not about obligation, it's not about forcibly limiting anyone's speech — it's about choice. Who are you? Choose.

> " *Trolling is recreational abuse — usually anonymous — intended to waste the subject's time or get a rise out of them or frustrate or frighten them into silence. . . . It's a silencing tactic. The message is: You are outnumbered. The message is: We'll stop when you're gone.* "

misogyny: hatred toward women as a group of people

misconstrued: misunderstood

catalyst: spark; stimulus

The backlash from comedy fans was immediate and intense: "That broad doesn't have to worry about rape." "She won't ever have to worry about rape." "No one would want to rape that fat, disgusting mess." "Holes like this make me want to commit rape out of anger." It went on and on, to the point that it was almost white noise. After a week or so, I was feeling weather-beaten but **fortified**. Nothing could touch me anymore.

fortified: strengthened

But then there was my dad's dear face twinkling out at me from my Twitter feed. Someone — bored, apparently, with the usual angles of harassment — had made a fake Twitter account purporting to be my dead dad, featuring a stolen, beloved photo of him, for no reason other than to hurt me. The name on the account was "PawWestDonezo," because my father's name was Paul West, and a difficult battle with prostate cancer had rendered him "donezo" (goofy slang for "done") just eighteen months earlier. "Embarrassed father of an idiot," the bio read. "Other two kids are fine, though." His location was "Dirt hole in Seattle." . . .

There's a term for this brand of **gratuitous** online cruelty: We call it Internet trolling. Trolling is recreational abuse — usually anonymous — intended to waste the subject's time or get a rise out of them or frustrate or frighten them into silence. Sometimes it's relatively **innocuous** (like asking **contrarian** questions just to start an argument) or juvenile (like making fun of my weight or my intelligence), but — particularly when the subject is a young woman — it frequently crosses the line into **bona fide** dangerous stalking and harassment.

gratuitous: unnecessary and inappropriate

innocuous: harmless

contrarian: deliberately oppositional

bona fide: genuine; real

And even "innocuous" harassment, when it's coming at you **en masse** from hundreds or even thousands of users a day, stops feeling innocuous very quickly. It's a silencing tactic. The message is: You are outnumbered. The message is: We'll stop when you're gone. The volume and intensity of harassment is vastly magnified for women of color and trans women and disabled women

en masse: in a group

and fat women and sex workers and other intersecting identities. Who gets trolled has a direct impact on who gets to talk; in my personal experience, the fiercest trolling has come from traditionally white, male-dominated communities (comedy, video games, atheism) whose members would like to keep it that way.

I feel the pull all the time: I should change careers; I should shut down my social media; maybe I can get a job in print somewhere; it's just too exhausting. I hear the same **refrains** from my colleagues. Sure, we've all built up significant armor at this point, but, you know, armor is heavy. Internet trolling might seem like an issue that only affects a certain subset of people, but that's only true if you believe that living in a world **devoid** of diverse voices — public discourse shaped primarily by white, heterosexual, able-bodied men — wouldn't profoundly affect your life.

Sitting at my computer, staring at PawWestDonezo, I had precious few options. All I could do, really, was ignore it: hit "block" and move on, knowing that that account was still out there, hidden behind a few **gossamer** lines of code, still putting words in my dad's mouth, still using his image to mock, abuse, and silence people. After all, it's not illegal to reach elbow-deep into someone's memories and touch them and twist them and weaponize them (to impress the ghost of **Lenny Bruce** or whatever). Nor should it be, of course. But that doesn't mean we have to tolerate it without dissent.

Over and over, those of us who work on the Internet are told, "Don't feed the trolls. Don't talk back. It's what they want." But is that true? Does ignoring trolls actually stop trolling? Can somebody show me concrete numbers on that? Anecdotally, I've ignored far more trolls than I've "fed," and my inbox hasn't become any quieter. When I speak my mind and receive a howling hurricane of abuse in return, it doesn't feel like a plea for my attention — it feels like a demand for my silence.

And some trolls are explicit about it. "If you can't handle it, get off the Internet." That's a persistent refrain my colleagues and I hear when we confront our harassers. But why? Why don't YOU get off the Internet? Why should I have to rearrange my life — and change careers, essentially — because you wet your pants every time a woman talks?

My friends say, "Just don't read the comments." But just the other day, for instance, I got a tweet that said, "May your bloodied head rest on the edge of an ISIS blade." Colleagues and friends of mine have had their phone numbers and addresses published online (a harassment tactic known as "doxing") and had trolls show up at their public events or threaten mass shootings. So if we don't keep an eye on what people are saying, how do we know when a line has been crossed and law enforcement should be involved? (Not that the police have any clue how to deal with online harassment anyway — or much interest in trying.)

refrains: repeated lines

devoid: free; empty

gossamer: light, cobweb-like substance

Lenny Bruce (1925–66): stand-up comedian

Social media companies say, "Just report any abuse and move on. We're handling it." So I do that. But reporting abuse is a tedious, labor-intensive process that can eat up half my working day. In any case, most of my reports are rejected. And once any troll is blocked (or even if they're suspended), they can just make a new account and start all over again. I'm aware that Twitter is well within its rights to let its platform be used as a vehicle for sexist and racist harassment. But, as a private company—just like a comedian mulling over a rape joke, or a troll looking for a target for his anger—it could choose not to. As a collective of human beings, it could choose to be better.

So, when it came to the case of PawWestDonezo, I went off script: I stopped obsessing over what *he* wanted and just did what felt best to me that day. I wrote about it publicly, online. I made myself vulnerable. I didn't hide the fact it hurt. The next morning, I woke up to an e-mail:

> Hey Lindy, I don't know why or even when I started trolling you. It wasn't because of your stance on rape jokes. I don't find them funny either.
>
> I think my anger towards you stems from your happiness with your own being. It offended me because it served to highlight my unhappiness with my own self.
>
> I have e-mailed you through 2 other gmail accounts just to send you idiotic insults.
>
> I apologize for that.
>
> I created the PaulWestDonezo@gmail.com account & Twitter account. (I have deleted both.)
>
> I can't say sorry enough.
>
> It was the lowest thing I had ever done. When you included it in your latest Jezebel article it finally hit me. There is a living, breathing human being who is reading this shit. I am attacking someone who never harmed me in any way. And for no reason whatsoever.
>
> I'm done being a troll.
>
> Again I apologize.
>
> I made donation in memory to your dad.
>
> I wish you the best.

He had donated fifty dollars to Seattle Cancer Care Alliance, where my dad was treated.

That e-mail still unhinges my jaw every time I read it. A reformed troll? An admission of weakness and self-loathing? An apology? I wrote back once, expressed my disbelief, and said thank you—and that was that. I returned to my regular routine of daily hate mail, scrolling through the same options over and over—Ignore? Block? Report? Engage?—but every time I faced that choice, I thought briefly of my remorseful troll.

Last summer, when a segment of video game fans began a massive harassment campaign against female critics and developers (if you want to know more, Google "GamerGate," then shut your laptop and throw it into the sea), my thoughts wandered back to him more and more. I wondered if I could learn anything from him. And then it struck me: Why not find out?

We only had made that one, brief exchange, in the summer of 2013, but I still had his e-mail address. I asked the popular U.S. radio program *This American Life* to help me reach out to him. They said yes. They e-mailed him. After a few months of grueling silence, he finally wrote back. "I'd be happy to help you out in any way possible," he said.

And then, there I was in a studio with a phone — and the troll on the other end. We talked for two-and-a-half hours. He was shockingly self-aware. He told me that he didn't hate me because of rape jokes — the timing was just a coincidence — he hated me because, to put it simply, I don't hate myself. Hearing him explain his choices in his own words, in his own voice, was heartbreaking and fascinating. He said that, at the time, he felt fat, unloved, "passionless," and purposeless. For some reason, he found it "easy" to take that out on women online.

I asked why. What made women easy targets? Why was it so satisfying to hurt us? Why didn't he automatically see us as human beings? For all his self-reflection, that's the one thing he never managed to articulate — how anger at one woman translated into hatred of women in general. Why, when men hate themselves, it's women who take the beatings.

But he did explain how he changed. He started taking care of his health, he found a new girlfriend, and, most importantly, he went back to school to become a teacher. He told me — in all seriousness — that, as a volunteer at a school, he just gets so many hugs now. "Seeing how their feelings get hurt by their peers," he said, "on purpose or not, it derails them for the rest of the day. They'll have their head on their desk and refuse to talk. As I'm watching this happen, I can't help but think about the feelings that I hurt." He was so sorry, he said.

I didn't mean to forgive him, but I did.

prescriptive:
instructional;
offering rules

This story isn't **prescriptive**. It doesn't mean that anyone is obliged to forgive people who abuse them, or even that I plan on being cordial and compassionate to every teenage boy who tells me I'm too fat to get raped

timbre: sound
quality

(sorry in advance, boys: I still bite). But, for me, it's changed the **timbre** of my online interactions — with, for instance, the guy who responded to my radio story by calling my dad a "faggot." It's hard to feel hurt or frightened when you're flooded with pity. And that, in turn, has made it easier for me to keep talking in the face of a mob roaring for my silence. Keep screaming, trolls. I see you.

After You Read

Mapping the Reading

1. What is an Internet troll?

2. According to West, when and why do Internet trolls harass her?

3. What did West's "cruelest troll" do, and what is his explanation for his actions?

4. How is West's response to this troll different from her response to other trolls? Why does she decide to respond to and then follow up with this particular troll?

5. After this experience, how has West changed her view of Internet trolls?

Discussing and Thinking Critically about the Reading

1. Why does West share the story of her experiences with her "cruelest troll"? What does she hope readers will learn from her story?

2. West writes, "People who don't spend much time on the Internet are invariably shocked to discover the barbarism . . . that so many of us face simply for doing our jobs." Are you shocked by the experiences that West reports that she and other women face? Why or why not?

3. Offer your take: Why do people who dislike West's *ideas* choose to make fun of and threaten her rather than argue their point of view?

4. Throughout this article, West uses humor and sarcasm. Identify one of those moments, and then analyze the effectiveness of that humor and whether it enhances or hurts her point. (You may refer to any "As You Read" notes you made.)

5. West mentions several options that she and other opinionated online writers have for responding to trolls. Summarize the options that she presents. Which option makes the most sense to you? Why? What alternatives would you propose?

Navigating the Intersections

1. Would Josh Rose see Lindy West's experiences as evidence that the Internet creates intimacy? Support your position with evidence from each article.

2. Return to the explanation Lindy West's troll offers for his behavior. How might it compare to the findings of Andrea Shea's sources about social media's impact on self-esteem?

3. Find a blog that is maintained by an individual or group that holds a controversial position, and then read through the comments section. Describe the blog and its mission, and then characterize the commentary: Explain whether the comments are supportive or critical, whether they involve hostile personal attacks, or whether they remain on topic and address the issues.

Digital Histories and Privacy

Before You Read: Write for five minutes in response to the following questions: How much do you worry that the information you have posted on social media is being used to judge you? Who might judge you based on this information? What impression of you might someone get just by looking at your social media presence?

JON RONSON

Jon Ronson is a journalist, humorist, and documentary filmmaker who is best known for writing *The Men Who Stare at Goats* (2004), a book about the military's investigations of the paranormal, which was made into a 2009 comic film starring George Clooney. Ronson writes about politics and science, and his work has appeared in such publications as the *Guardian*, *City Life*, and *Time Out*. He is a storyteller who has appeared on BBC Radio and National Public Radio's *This American Life*. His 2014 book, *So You've Been Publicly Shamed*, was the basis for this 2015 article, published in the *Guardian*.

As You Read: Make an outline of the key points in this article.

"Overnight, Everything I Loved Was Gone"
The Internet Shaming of Lindsey Stone

In October 2012 a group of adults with learning difficulties took an organized trip to Washington, DC. They visited the National Mall, the U.S. Holocaust Memorial Museum, the Smithsonian, Arlington National Cemetery, the U.S. Mint. At night they sang karaoke in the hotel bar. Their caregivers, Lindsey Stone and her friend Jamie, did a duet of "Total Eclipse of the Heart." "They had the greatest time on that trip," Lindsey told me. "They thought we were fun and cool."

Lindsey was telling me the story eighteen months later. We were sitting at her kitchen table, in a seaside town on the U.S. east coast. "I like to dance and I like to do karaoke," Lindsey said, "but for a long time after that trip, I didn't leave the house. During the day I'd just sit here. I didn't want to be seen by anybody."

"How long did that last?" I asked.

"Almost a year."

Lindsey and Jamie had been with LIFE (Living Independently Forever) for a year and a half before that trip. LIFE was a residence for "pretty high-functioning people with learning difficulties," Lindsey said. . . .

Off-duty, she and Jamie had a running joke: taking stupid photographs, "smoking in front of a no-smoking sign or posing in front of statues, mimicking the pose. We took dumb pictures all the time. And so at Arlington [the national cemetery] we saw the Silence and Respect sign . . . and inspiration struck."

Lindsey posed in front of it, pretending she was shouting and swearing — flipping the bird, and with her hand to her open mouth. "So," Lindsey said, "thinking we were funny, Jamie posted it on Facebook and tagged me on it with my consent, because I thought it was hilarious."

Nothing much happened after that. A few Facebook friends posted unenthusiastic comments. "One had served in the military and he wrote a message saying, 'This is kind of offensive. I know you girls, but it's tasteless.' Another said, 'I agree,' and another said, 'I agree.' Then I said, 'Whoa! It's just us being douchebags! Forget about it!'"

After that, Jamie said to Lindsey, "Do you think we should take it down?"

"No!" Lindsey replied, "What's the big deal? No one's ever going to think of it again."

Their Facebook settings were a mystery to them. Most of the privacy boxes were ticked. Some weren't. Sometimes they'd half-notice that boxes they'd thought they'd ticked weren't ticked. . . .

Jamie's mobile uploads weren't private. And four weeks after returning from Washington, DC, they were in a restaurant, celebrating their birthdays — "We're a week apart" — when they became aware that their phones were vibrating repeatedly. So they went online.

"Lindsey Stone hates the military and hates soldiers who have died in foreign wars," "You should rot in hell," "Just pure Evil," "Spoke with an employee from LIFE who has told me there are veterans on the board and that she will be fired. Awaiting info on her accomplice," "After they fire her, maybe she needs to sign up as a client. Woman needs help," "Send the dumb feminist to prison." There were death and rape threats.

"I wanted to scream: 'It was just about a sign,'" Lindsey said.

By the time she went to bed that night, at 4:00 a.m., a Fire Lindsey Stone Facebook page had been created. It attracted twelve thousand likes. Lindsey read every comment. "I really became obsessed with reading everything about myself."

The next day, camera crews had gathered outside her front door. Her father tried talking to them. He had a cigarette in his hand. The family dog had followed him out. As he tried to explain that Lindsey wasn't a terrible person, he noticed the cameras move from his face down to the cigarette and the dog, as if they were a family of hillbillies.

LIFE was **inundated** with e-mails demanding their jobs, so Lindsey was called into work. But she wasn't allowed inside the building. Her boss met

inundated:
flooded

insomniac: a person unable to sleep

her in the car park and told her to hand over her keys. "Literally overnight, everything I knew and loved was gone," Lindsey said. And that's when she fell into a depression, became an **insomniac**, and barely left home for a year.

That year, Lindsey scanned Craigslist for career work, but nobody replied to her applications. She was eventually offered a job caring for children with autism. "But I'm terrified," she said.

"That your bosses will find out?"

"Yeah."

iconic: widely recognized

rightwingers: people with strong conservative beliefs

This was a likely scenario. The photograph was everywhere. It had become so **iconic** among swaths of **rightwingers** that one man had even turned it into patriotic wallpaper, superimposing on to the wall behind Lindsey's shrieking face and upturned finger a picture of a military funeral, complete with a coffin draped in the American flag. Lindsey had wanted the job so much she'd been "nervous about even applying. I was conflicted on whether to say to them, 'Just so you know, I am this Lindsey Stone.' Because I knew it was just a mouse click away." She left it until the moment of the interview. And then the interview was over and she found that she hadn't mentioned it.

Now she'd been in the job four months, and she still hadn't told them. "And obviously, you can't ask them, 'Have you noticed it and decided it's not a problem?'" I said.

"Right," Lindsey said.

"So you feel trapped in a paranoid silence?" I said.

"I love this job so much," Lindsey said. "I love these kids. One of the parents paid me a really high compliment the other day. I've only been working with her son for a month and she was like, 'The moment I met you, seeing the way you are with my son, and the way you treat people, you were meant to work in this field.' But what if she found out? Would she feel the same way?"

Lindsey could never just be happy and relaxed. The terror was always there. "It really impacts the way you view the world. Since it happened, I haven't tried to date anybody. How much do you let a new person into your life? Do they already know?"

The Village Pub in Woodside, near Menlo Park, Silicon Valley, looks like no big deal from the outside, but when you get inside, you realize it's filled with tech billionaires. I had recently discovered the world of digital reputation management—companies that "game" Google to hide negative stories stored online. One of these companies is Reputation.com, launched by my dining companion, Michael Fertik. . . .

"I have no idea what you actually do," I had told Michael on the telephone before we met. "Maybe I could follow someone through the process?"

And so we planned it out. We'd just need to find a willing client.

• • •

"Are there any hobbies you're particularly passionate about right now? Marathons? Photography?"

Farukh Rashid was in San Francisco, talking down a conference line to Lindsey Stone. I was listening in from my sofa in New York. I'd met Farukh a few months earlier, when Michael's publicist, Leslie, gave me a tour of the Reputation.com offices: two **open-plan** floors with soundproofed booths for the sensitive calls to celebrity clients. She introduced me to Farukh and explained that he usually works on Michael's VIP customers — the CEOs and celebrities.

"It's nice that you're giving Lindsey the **bespoke** service," I said.

"She needs it," Leslie replied.

She really did. Michael's strategists had been researching Lindsey's online life and had discovered nothing about her besides that Silence and Respect incident.

"That five seconds of her life is her entire Internet presence?" I said.

Farukh nodded. "And it's not just this Lindsey Stone. Anyone who has that name has the same problem. There are sixty Lindsey Stones in the U.S. and they're all being defined by that one photograph."

"I'm sorry to have given you such a tricky one," I said, feeling a little proud of myself.

"Oh, no, we're excited," Farukh replied. "We're going to introduce the Internet to the real Lindsey Stone."

"Are cats important to you?" Farukh asked Lindsey, now down the conference line.

"Absolutely," said Lindsey.

I heard Farukh type. He was young and energetic, and just as upbeat and **buoyant** and lacking in cynicism and **malevolent** irony as he was hoping to make Lindsey seem. His Twitter profile says he enjoys "biking, hiking, and family time." His plan was to create Lindsey Stone Tumblrs and LinkedIn pages and WordPress blogs and Instagram accounts and YouTube accounts to overwhelm that terrible photograph, wash it away in a tidal wave of positivity, away to a place on Google where normal people don't look — a place like page two of the search results. According to Google's own research, 53 percent of us don't go beyond the first two search results, and 89 percent of us don't look past the first page.

"I'm passionate about music," Lindsey told Farukh.

"That's really good," Farukh said. "Let's work with that. Do you play an instrument?"

"I used to," Lindsey said. "I was kind of self-taught. It's just something I mess around with. It's not anything I . . ." Suddenly, she trailed off. She seemed self-conscious, as if the endeavor was giving her troubling **existential** thoughts: questions such as "Who am I?" and "What are we doing?"

> 'Literally overnight, everything I knew and loved was gone,' Lindsey said. And that's when she fell into a depression, became an insomniac, and barely left home for a year.

open-plan: designed without dividing walls

bespoke: custom-made; made to fit

buoyant: cheerful; optimistic

malevolent: mean, evil, or malicious

existential: concerning or affirming existence

"I'm having a hard time with this," she said. "As a normal person I don't really know how to brand myself online."

"Piano? Guitar? Drums?" said Farukh. "Or travel? Where do you go?"

"I don't know," Lindsey said. "I go to the beach. I get ice cream."

At Farukh's request, Lindsey had been e-mailing him photographs that didn't involve her flipping off at military cemeteries. She'd been providing biographical details, too. Her favorite TV show was *Parks and Recreation.* Her employment history included five years at Walmart, "which was kind of soul-suckingly awful."

"Are you sure you want to say that Walmart was soul-sucking?" Farukh said.

"Oh . . . What? Really?" Lindsey laughed, as if to say, "Come on! Everyone knows that about Walmart!" But then she hesitated. The conference call was proving an unexpectedly **melancholic** experience. It was nothing to do with Farukh. He really felt for Lindsey and wanted to do a good job for her. The sad thing was that Lindsey had **incurred** the Internet's wrath because she was **impudent** and playful and foolhardy and outspoken. And now here she was, working with Farukh to reduce herself to safe **banalities**—to cats and ice cream and top 40 chart music. We were creating a world where the smartest way to survive is to be bland. . . .

. . . Michael predicted that Lindsey's love of cats (or whatever) would achieve "initial strong impact," followed by "**fluctuation**," and, after fluctuation, "**reversion**."

Michael's clients dread reversion. There's nothing more dispiriting than seeing the nice new judgments disappear and the horrific old judgments bubble back up. But reversion is actually their friend, as Michael's strategist, Jered Higgins, told me. "Reversion shows that the **algorithm** is uncertain," he said. And during this uncertainty, Jered said, "We go in and blast it."

The blasting—the bombardment of the [Google search] algorithm with Tumblr pages about Lindsey's trips to the beach, the shock and awe of these pleasant banalities—has to be choreographed just right. Google knows if it's being manipulated (alarm bells go off) "so we have a strategic schedule for content creation and publication," Jered said. "We create a natural-looking activity online. That's a lot of accumulated intelligence."

In October 2014, I took a final drive to visit Lindsey Stone. Four months had passed since I'd last spoken to her or Farukh—and given that they'd only taken her on for my benefit, I'd half-wondered if maybe it had all been quietly wound down in my absence.

"Oh God, no," said Lindsey. We sat at her kitchen table. "They call me every week, week after week." She took out her phone and scrolled through her innumerable e-mails from Farukh. She read out loud some blogs his team

melancholic: very sad

incurred: brought on an undesirable experience for oneself

impudent: disrespectful

banalities: unoriginal or unimaginative ideas

fluctuation: variation or constant change

reversion: return to the original version

algorithm: set of steps to complete a computer process

had written in her voice, about how it's important when traveling to use the hotel safe — "Stay alert, travelers!" — and how, if you're in Spain, you should try the **tapas**.

tapas: small plates of food

Lindsey got to pre-approve everything, and she'd only told them no twice, she said — to a blog about how much she's looking forward to Lady Gaga's upcoming jazz album ("I like Lady Gaga, but I'm not really excited about her jazz album") and to her tribute to Disneyland on the occasion of its fiftieth birthday: "Happy Birthday Disneyland! The Happiest Place on Earth!" "Happy Birthday Disneyland!" Lindsey blushed. "I would never . . . I mean, I had a great time at Disneyland. But still . . ." She trailed off. "One of my friends from high school said, 'I hope it's still you. I want people to know how funny you are.' But it's scary. After all that's happened, what's funny to me . . . I don't want to go anywhere near the line, let alone cross it. So I'm constantly saying, 'I don't know, Farukh, what do you think?'" . . .

Lindsey hadn't typed her name into Google for eleven months. The last time had been a shock: It was Veterans' Day, and she found some ex-army people "wondering where I was, and not in a good way."

"They were thinking about tracking you down so they could re-destroy you?" I asked.

"Yeah," she said. She hadn't looked since. And now she swallowed and began to type: L . . . I . . . N . . .

Lindsey shook her head, stunned. "This is monumental," she said.

Two years ago, the photograph stretched to Google Images horizon — uninterrupted, mass-production shaming, "pages and pages and pages," Lindsey said, "repeating endlessly. It felt so huge. So oppressive." And now: nearly gone. There was still a scattering, and there would inevitably be some reversion, but for now there were lots of photographs of Lindsey doing nothing bad. Just smiling.

Even better, there were lots of photographs of other Lindsey Stones — people who weren't her at all. There was a Lindsey Stone volleyball player, a Lindsay Stone competitive swimmer. The swimmer had been captured mid-stroke, moments from winning the New York State 500-yard freestyle championship. It was captioned, "Lindsay Stone had the right plan in place and everything was going exactly to plan."

Here was a whole other person, doing something everyone could agree was lovely and **commendable**. There was no better result than that.

commendable: deserving praise

After You Read

Mapping the Reading

1. What exactly occurred during the "Silence and Respect" incident?

2. What role did privacy settings play in the "Silence and Respect" incident?

3. What were the responses to and the consequences of the publicly posted photo of Lindsey Stone at Arlington National Cemetery?

4. Compare Stone's personality *before* her Facebook posting and afterward. In what ways is she shown to be different?

5. What does Michael Fertik's business, Reputation.com, do? What, specifically, did it do for Stone?

Discussing and Thinking Critically about the Reading

1. List all the moments when Lindsey Stone might have acted differently and avoided the disaster that eventually occurred. In each of these moments, what might she have done differently?

2. Did Lindsey Stone deserve the public shaming she received? If so, why? If not, what, if any, type of scolding did she deserve, and why?

3. Lindsey Stone tells Ronson that a friend questioned whether her Reputation.com-managed online persona is really her. What concerns might this response suggest about the value of this solution?

4. Reflecting on Reputation.com's work on Lindsey Stone's case, Ronson observes, "We were creating a world where the smartest way to survive is to be bland." What does he mean by this? Do you agree with this observation about how best to exist in the online world? Why or why not?

5. What primary lesson do you take away from this article?

Navigating the Intersections

1. Compare and contrast the ways that Lindsey Stone and Lindy West responded to their Internet tormentors. How did they approach their problems differently?

2. Follow up on these stories:

    a. Profile Lindsey Stone. What is her Internet presence today? Is the "Silence and Respect" image easy or hard to find? What is her online persona? If she is active, is she a bland, cat-loving woman who likes music, eating ice cream, and going to the beach? Or does she come across as impudent, playful, and outspoken?

    b. Profile Reputation.com or a company offering a similar service. What does the business promise? What is its image? How does it market itself? What limitations does it admit to?

Before You Read: Write briefly about whether concern about digital privacy is influenced by age. Do millennials (born circa 1982–2004), baby boomers (1946–64), and generation Xers (1965–84) have different levels of concern? Compare yourself with individuals you know well from other generations, and consider whether age is a factor in dictating privacy worry.

JULIAN B. GEWIRTZ and ADAM B. KERN

Julian B. Gewirtz is a Rhodes Scholar who received his master's degree in history from Oxford University in 2014. He writes about U.S.-China relations and modern Chinese culture and politics, and has been published in the *Boston Globe*, the *Atlantic*, the *Washington Post*, and the *New Republic*, among other publications. Adam B. Kern, a college classmate of Gewirtz, completed advanced study in philosophy at Oxford University. This article was published in the *Cap Times* of Madison, Wisconsin, in 2013.

As You Read: Make note of the authors' concerns about digital records and the potential problems associated with them.

Escaping Digital Histories

We just graduated from college. We've got thousands of pictures on Instagram, conversations on Gchat, and status updates on Facebook to show for it—a digital record of that long week, seemingly each fragment of thought and every step of the day we graduated.

And we, like many people, often forget that so many less important moments of our lives are cataloged in the same way. Recently, Facebook launched a sophisticated tool called Graph Search, which helps reveal information from within your social network. Such tools make it dramatically easier to unearth data about the lives of everyone we know—and people we don't. They also underscore the urgent need to define the norms that govern how this information will be used.

Ours is the first generation to have grown up with the Internet. The first generation that got suspended from school because of a photo of underage drinking posted online. The first generation that could talk in chat rooms to anyone, anywhere, without our parents knowing. The first generation that has been "tracked" and "followed" and "shared" since childhood.

All this data will remain available forever—both to the big players (tech companies, governments) and to our friends, our sort-of friends, and the rest of civil society. This fact is not really new, but our generation will confront the **latter** on a scale beyond that experienced by previous generations.

This digital **longevity** raises new issues: One is that our former selves may live on beyond their real existence. It used to be that if a teenager went through "a phase," generally only their family, friends, and teachers would know or remember. Those days are gone. Another issue is that false versions of your identity, suggested by **disparate** pieces of data, might be **contrived** and proposed as the real you. Thanks to technology, someone can know more about you than you know about yourself—or, at least, think that they do.

latter: second of two things mentioned

longevity: long life

disparate: made up of different, even incompatible things

contrived: formed or made with difficulty or skill; unnatural

These misrepresentations matter because they can shape unfair opinions or even cause unnecessary harm. Say that as an opinionated sixteen-year-old, someone wrote **polemical** public posts about her opposition to abortion. Her views shifted during college, but she never posted an announcement of that. Then, ten years later, she applies to teach under a pro-choice principal. The principal checks Facebook, sees her history — and then glances to his five other equally qualified applicants.

polemical: aggressively attacking other views

Nearly the entire lives of our generation have been cataloged and stored in servers, with the most mature and carefully thought-through utterances indistinguishable, as data, from thoughtless preteen rants. We gave much of this information willingly, if **half-wittingly**. A fact of being a young person today is that our data are out there forever, and we must find ways to deal with that.

half-wittingly: only partially knowingly

Certainly there will be many uses for information, such as health data, that will wind up governed by law. But so many other uses cannot be predicted or legislated, and laws themselves have to be informed by values. It is therefore critical that people establish, with their actions and expectations, cultural norms that prevent their digital selves from imprisoning their real selves.

> ❝ It is therefore critical that people establish, with their actions and expectations, cultural norms that prevent their digital selves from imprisoning their real selves. ❞

We see three possible paths: One, people become increasingly restrained about what they share and do online. Two, people become increasingly restrained about what they do, period. Three, we learn to care less about what people did when they were younger, less mature, or otherwise different.

The first outcome seems unproductive. There is no longer much of an Internet without sharing, and one of the great benefits of the Internet has been its ability to nurture relationships and connections that previously had been impossible. Withdrawal is unacceptable. Fear of the digital future should not drive us apart.

John Locke (1632–1704): English philosopher

The second option seems more deeply unsettling. Childhood, adolescence, college — the whole process of growing up — is, as thinkers from **John Locke** to **Dr. Spock** have written, a necessarily experimental time. Everyone makes at least one mistake, and we'd like to think that process continues into adulthood. Creativity should not be overwhelmed by the fear of what people might one day find **unpalatable**.

Dr. Spock (1903–99): American pediatrician and author of *Baby and Child Care*

This leaves the third outcome: the idea that we must learn to care less about what people did when they were younger or otherwise different. In an area where regulations, privacy policies, and treaties may take decades to catch up to reality, our generation needs to take the lead in negotiating a "cultural **treaty**" endorsing a new value, related to privacy, that secures our ability to have a past captured in data that is not held to be the last word but seen in light of our having grown up in a way that no one ever has before.

unpalatable: unpleasant or unacceptable

treaty: formal agreement

Growing up, that is, on the record.

After You Read

Mapping the Reading

1. How do Gewirtz and Kern see their generation as different from previous ones? What potential problems does this difference create?

2. Summarize the potential problems that the authors see with the cataloging or preserving of our lives on social media. (Return to your "As You Read" notes to get started.)

3. What solutions do Gewirtz and Kern identify? How do they critique each?

4. What is the purpose of the "cultural treaty" the authors propose at the end of their article?

5. Gewirtz and Kern observe, "Another issue is that false versions of your identity, suggested by disparate pieces of data, might be contrived and proposed as the real you. Thanks to technology, someone can know more about you than you know about yourself—or, at least, think that they do." Explain what they mean by this statement.

Discussing and Thinking Critically about the Reading

1. Review Gewirtz and Kern's three proposed solutions, and look at your response to question 3 under "Mapping the Reading." Do you agree with their view about which solution seems best? Why or why not? What other solutions might you propose?

2. Gewirtz and Kern argue that people need to "care less" about what others did in the past. How do you think this would work in practice? What things do you think would be easy for people to "care less" about or excuse? What things do you think would be harder (or unwise) to "care less" about or excuse?

3. Develop a draft of a "cultural treaty" of the type Gewirtz and Kern propose. Consider the perspectives and needs of the different parties involved (e.g., not only the people who post on social media but also employers seeking information about potential new hires).

4. Take another perspective: What value is there in being able to look up another person's digital history? Have you ever done this? If so, when and why?

5. Gewirtz and Kern argue that millennials are represented online in many different ways. Summarize the ways that the authors identify. What would you add to their list?

Navigating the Intersections

1. Consider Lindsey Stone's experiences in light of Julian B. Gewirtz and Adam B. Kern's proposed solutions. How well does her situation fit their guidelines? Do her experiences confirm Gewirtz and Kern's views about the best solution? Why or why not?

2. What is your digital history? Research your online presence, analyze your online profiles, and read them as though you were a future employer. What does your digital

history say about you? How accurate is the impression it gives? Is there anything of importance missing? Is anything overemphasized? Alternatively, you can research a friend's or family member's digital history.

3. Consider what adolescents should do to protect their digital histories from possible misinterpretation. Write a social media guide for adolescents, explaining the dos and don'ts of social media.

Before You Read: Write briefly about the amount of trust you have in information that you find online.

AMY TAN

Acclaimed novelist Amy Tan studied English and linguistics in college and graduate school, and later served as a language development specialist in programs for children with developmental disabilities. She was a freelance business writer for such companies as AT&T, IBM, and Wells Fargo Bank before turning to fiction writing when she was thirty-three. Her first collection of stories, *The Joy Luck Club*, was published in 1989 and was adapted into a movie in 1993. This essay was excerpted from her 2004 collection *The Opposite of Fate: Memories of a Writing Life*.

As You Read: Tan catalogs the many errors she finds about herself on the Internet. Make two lists: one containing the errors she finds simply amusing, the other containing the errors she finds troubling.

Personal Errata*

*errata: a list of published errors and their corrections (from Latin for *errors*)

Big Bang: scientific theory that the universe began with an explosion

ubiquitous: seemingly everywhere

doctorate: the degree of doctor; a PhD is a type of doctorate

Between the time I wrote my first book and today, the Internet accomplished the equivalent of the **Big Bang**, and the World Wide Web expanded into the **Ubiquitous** Uncontrollable Universe. As a result, certain errors of fact about me began to circulate and became part of my unofficial biography now often used by students, interviewers, booksellers, and public relations staffs before I come to give talks.

At first, there were only minor mistakes, for example, that I had received my master's degree and a PhD from UC Berkeley, which is a fine school and one that I did attend while studying for my **doctorate**. But the only doctorates I have are honorary, and according to one university president who handed me a diploma, this entitles me to a free parking space in the faculty lot, though solely when I come to give a free talk. To set the record straight, I never finished my doctoral program, and my BA and MA degrees came from San Jose State University.

As the Internet became more widespread, so did the errors. They are not quite **urban-legend strength**, but they have definitely been magnified. I remember the day I saw announced before a live online interview that Amy Tan had won the Nobel Prize in Literature. It then occurred to me that one could actually conduct several lives of different realities, even better ones, certainly with more prestigious prizes. But as the online interview began, I typed in my greeting: "Hi, Amy Tan here, only I never did win that Nobel Prize. Wish I had. Thanks for the vote of confidence."

urban-legend strength: having the staying power of an untrue story that many believe

Most often I am aware of the mistakes when I am receiving other honors having to do with being Asian-American or a writer or Chinese or an alumna of one of the colleges I attended. Then I learn of all the other prizes I have supposedly won, among them the National Book Award, the *Los Angeles Times* Book Prize, and the **Pulitzer**. I was in fact nominated for the first two, so a little exaggeration there is understandable, but the Pulitzer reference is a fluke from the Web, and one that keeps **replicating** like a virus. It's embarrassing to start my acceptance speeches with a list of errata, which then seems to show only how truly unworthy I am to be standing on the podium or **festooned** stage, holding an engraved plaque or crystal bowl.

Pulitzer: short for Pulitzer Prize, a prestigious award

replicating: copying or reproducing

festooned: decorated

Some of the mistakes are maddening, like those in a *Los Angeles Times* piece published in 2000, which I did not read, but which a friend felt his duty to read aloud to me for my own **edification**; it described me as having a big smile that displayed teeth discolored by my nicotine habit. The reporter must have looked up that old *Salon* interview in which I was **surreptitiously** smoking on my terrace and asked the reporter to please not mention this. Whatever the source, I never realized my teeth looked that bad, and if they are indeed discolored enough to be worth mentioning, I must make it known that it is not due to cigarettes. I am proud of the fact that I gave up smoking for good in 1995, and since then I have actually brushed my teeth from time to time and have gone for routine professional teeth cleaning every six months.

edification: education or enlightenment

surreptitiously: secretly

> " *It then occurred to me that one could actually conduct several lives of different realities, even better ones, certainly with more prestigious prizes.* "

Inaccuracy, I fear, has become epidemic among publications whose writers rely on the Internet for research. For there, past interviews and articles survive and even thrive, as if they were fresh off the press, perpetually part of today's news. An interview dating from 1989 said, rightly, that I had been married for fifteen years. A reporter who evidently used this interview as background in 1996 stated that I had been married for fifteen years. Other reporters, perhaps wishing to differentiate between the first set of fifteen years and the second, have referred to Lou as my "current husband."

consternation: surprise or disappointment that results in confusion

Having a twenty-year-old photograph of me run with articles also causes me **consternation**. I have had PR people refuse to take me to the **greenroom**

greenroom: room where media guests can relax

before an event, only to have them later rush up to me and say, "Oh, I'm so sorry. I didn't know you were *the* Amy Tan. I was looking for *someone else*." Read between the lines.

I did some sleuthing the other day to see who exactly is this Amy Tan who looks forever the same as in 1989, has been married to multiple husbands for always the same number of years, and has won all the literary prizes on earth. I found her lurking in at least one den of **iniquity**. This website opened with the following come-on:

> *Do you need a quality paper on Amy Tan — today, tomorrow, next week, or next month?*
>
> Since 1997, our experts on Amy Tan have helped students worldwide by providing the best, lowest-priced writing service on the Internet. If you've waited too long to start your paper on Amy Tan, or have more writing than you can handle, we can help. Our staff of over two hundred professional writers located around the world has produced thousands of college term papers, essays, research papers, dissertations, theses, and book reports on all topics involving Amy Tan. These excellent papers are available to you instantly for only $25.99 each.

How **dismal** to think I can be instantly summed up for only $25.99. These papers could not possibly be correct. I've paid psychiatrists two hundred dollars for fifty minutes many times over, and I still don't understand who I am.

For years, I have felt **stymied** by my alternative reality. It has created a new kind of **existential angst**. Who was I really, if not what all these articles said I was? If the Internet and its share of misinformation went on in **perpetuity**, then I too would live on in immortal muddle. The real me would become lost to misstatements of fact.

Then I realized I could use the same methods by which the errata grew to quash them, all 48,291 hits. I decided to write this piece, the one right before your very eyes. It would become part of the Internet Archives Used by Reporters, and thus I would at least have recorded my **rebuttal** for posterity.

So herewith the facts, as put forth by the ultimate expert, Amy Tan, and you don't have to pay $25.99 to get the scoop on what in her life is only a mistake.

Erratum 1. Tan's works do not include *The Year of No Flood* (1995). That was a chapter in her novel *The Hundred Secret Senses*. At one time, Tan thought she might write a book with that title that would include the flood and then the drought that preceded the Boxer Uprising, but because she blabbed about that book so much before it was written, it ejected itself from her imagination. Apparently someone to whom she blabbed assumed she finished the novel and published it.

---

iniquity: immorality

dismal: sad; depressing

stymied: stopped by an obstacle

existential angst: anxiety or dread caused by the weight of experiencing human freedom and responsibility

perpetuity: forever

rebuttal: argument that disproves something

Erratum 2. Tan did not attend eight different colleges. It was five, she says, and that number proved excessive enough, particularly when the fund-raising season rolls around every year and she is asked to contribute to the **coffers** of her alma maters.

coffers: treasury; funds

Erratum 3. Tan did not teach poetry at a university in West Virginia. She has no idea where that came from, because she has never been to West Virginia and she has never taught. But the idea is rather flattering, and she has always wished she could write poetry, let alone teach it. Along those same lines, Tan has never been a workshop leader of a writers' group, and as to those who claim to her agent and editor that she led their group, that was Molly Giles who was the leader. She has red hair. Tan has red hair only when she performs in a literary garage band called The Rock Bottom Remainders. She has never worn the red wig while leading a writers' workshop.

Erratum 4. Tan never worked in a factory alongside a certain person who was your best friend, not in this life or in any past life that she can remember. Among Tan's early jobs, she was a switchboard operator at her high school, a carhop at an A&W drive-in, and a Round Table pizza slinger.

Erratum 5. Tan has never lived in a mansion in the multi-millionaired hills of Hillsborough, California. She went to a fund-raiser there once where guests were asked to shell out $25,000 to help a political candidate but she was somehow let in for free; the political candidate later lost. As to where Tan lives, that would be a more modest condominium in San Francisco, a town that has some pretty nice hills itself, and a mix of billionaires and poor, both of whom the political candidates **profess** to have in their camp.

profess: declare; say; claim

Erratum 6. Tan's condominium is not the top floor of a former mansion. Her building was constructed in 1916 as apartments. Her unit is on the third and fourth floors, the fourth being a former attic. Tan, no spring chicken, having been born in 1952 (to determine approximate age, take today's year and subtract 1952), now wishes she had an elevator.

Erratum 7. Tan has never had a fight with anyone from her publishers in a bookstore, nor did she scream and fling books around, causing store patrons to run for their lives. Tan claims that she and her publishers have always had an **amicable** relationship, and they fight only over bills at restaurants, and then only as an **ostentatious** show of politeness. Most times, Tan lets them win. They pay the bill.

amicable: friendly; polite

ostentatious: designed to grab attention

Erratum 8. With the exception of arguments over restaurant bills, Tan has never had a fight with her agent, Sandy Dijkstra, and switched to a new agent. Sandy was the one who encouraged her to write fiction early on. She is like a Jewish mother, badgering Tan week after week to keep writing. Tan owes her life to her agent for giving her the life of a writer. For that reason, Tan probably also owes her lunch, but Sandy usually pays anyway.

Erratum 9. Lou DeMattei is indeed Tan's first husband. He is also her current husband. In addition, he is her only husband. They have been together since 1970, married since 1974. To discover how many total years that is, take today's year and subtract from it 1970 for togetherness or 1974 for marriage.

Erratum 10. Tan does not have two children, unless you consider, as she does, that her dogs are her children. In articles about Tan after 1997, Tan's cat, Sagwa, should be referred to not as her pet but as her late and dearly beloved kitty. Tan acknowledges that she has included children in most of her books, except the one about the cat. Predictably, these children have grown older with each subsequent book. Although they are imaginary, she is terribly fond of them. But she has never done homework with them every night, taken them to soccer practice or swim meets, cried in an emergency room when it turned out they had merely stuck beans in their ears, or gone through the cycle of being angry, then worried, then hysterical when they drove off to a forbidden place and went missing for six hours. Thus Tan cannot say with real conviction that her dogs are her children.

Erratum 11. Tan does not have yellow skin as depicted in a cartoon version of her on *The Simpsons*. It is yellow-skin depictions like these that make Tan slightly uncomfortable in being called a Writer of Color. Also, Tan did not really **berate** Lisa Simpson and humiliate her mercilessly in front of a TV audience. Those words were put in Tan's mouth by another cartoon character, namely **Matt Groening**. Other than the skin-color thing, she thinks Matt Groening is a sweetheart and a pretty nice guy. She once argued with him in public over the lunch bill, but he pushed her credit card aside and paid.

berate: yell at; scold

Matt Groening: co-creator of the TV series *The Simpsons*

That's it for now. I will be adding to this regularly, as needed. Look for installments in 48,291 websites and growing listed by Google for "Amy Tan."

After You Read

Mapping the Reading

1. According to Tan, how does the availability of information online help create errors?

2. How does online misinformation about Tan affect the way people treat her in person?

3. In what situations has Tan had to correct errors about herself?

4. Identify a few ways in which the online Tan is different from the real Tan.

5. What made Tan decide to write this essay? What did she hope to accomplish?

Discussing and Thinking Critically about the Reading

1. Choose a few of the mistakes Tan writes about. How serious are they? Which mistakes matter more than others, and why? (You can consult your "As You Read" notes to get started.)

2. Choose a few passages in which Tan uses humor. Why do you think she made the choice to treat the subject of online errors with humor? How would her message have come across if she used a different tone — for example, anger? Why?

3. While the misrepresentation of celebrities and famous people like Tan may seem like a minor disadvantage of the rich, in what ways are regular people misrepresented — and damagingly so — through social and other media?

4. Tan begins her errata by writing, "Tan's works do not include *The Year of No Flood* (1995). That was a chapter in her novel *The Hundred Secret Senses*. At one time, Tan thought . . ." Why do you think she chooses to use the third person ("Tan's," "her," "Tan") instead of the first person ("My," "my," "I") in this section?

5. Thinking of the online version of herself, Tan reflects, "It has created a new kind of existential angst. Who was I really, if not what all these articles said I was?" What does she mean? How much power do you think online misinformation can have over an individual's view of him- or herself?

Navigating the Intersections

1. Compare Amy Tan's approach to digital history to that advocated by Julian B. Gewirtz and Adam B. Kern or by Reputation.com as described by Jon Ronson. How do Tan's experiences and approach differ from that of millennials or Lindsey Stone? What additional problems related to digital histories do Tan's experiences expose?

2. Research online articles about Amy Tan. What errors do you see being repeated? Where do you see evidence that writers have taken "Personal Errata" into account?

CHAPTER 11

Words: Sticks and Stones?

You Don't Say? Campaign/Shayan Asadi

Image Response: Review and reflect on the phrases depicted in this image, using one of the following options:

a. How often do you hear or use these phrases? Which, if any, are offensive to you? Which, if any, are acceptable? Explain your responses, thinking in part about how your opinion might be influenced by the situations in which these words are used.

b. What is the message of this image? How effective (or not) is the image (both the text and the visuals) in getting this message across? How, if at all, does it make you rethink your ideas about these phrases?

In This Chapter

Introduction

Word Choice and Perception

The old saying "Sticks and stones will break my bones but words will never hurt me" proclaims that any insults or name-calling directed our way cannot hurt us. Intended to help children cope with taunts, the very existence of this nursery rhyme suggests that words *can* insult and harm. Although insults most obviously display language's power to harm, words also have the power to shape our actions and our perceptions of people, ideas, and situations in more subtle and wide-ranging ways. As Lera Boroditsky, a professor of cognitive science, asserts, "Language is central to our experience of being human, and the languages we speak profoundly shape the way we think, the way we see the world, the way we live our lives." Focusing on politically charged and challenging words, this chapter invites you to explore the potential impacts—positive and negative, intended or unintended—that word choices may have.

Since Franz Boaz, an anthropologist who studied humans and human culture, first reported in 1911 that the Inuit (people from the Arctic regions of the United States, Canada, and Greenland) have multiple words for snow, people have repeated the story that Eskimos have at least a hundred words for snow (a recent study puts it at fifty; see Robson). Although this story has been challenged, not least because there is not one "Eskimo" language, it reminds us that the languages and words we use, see, hear, and read shape our focus, influencing our perceptions of people, groups, and issues. Word choice, as journalist Mitch Moxley asserts, "affect[s] not just how we describe [a problem], but also how we try to fix it." For example, one University of California, San Diego, study found that describing crime as "a beast" produced harsher responses among participants than did describing it as "a virus" (Moxley).

Slurs

Like other languages, English contains words that have been labeled **slurs** or **derogatory words** (words that convey insults and disrespect, often about some-one's race, ethnicity, gender, or sexual orientation), which many people feel are taboo and should never be used. Yet some people *do* use these words freely — some to insult but others to reclaim the word or to use it as a sign of friendship. One such controversial word is the "N-word," a word with roots in slavery. Its public use by celebrities, politicians, and other well-known figures often provokes outrage; yet at the same time, its use in music and movies, as well as on the playing fields and the streets, is common and seemingly accepted in certain contexts, particularly when it is used by African Americans. These mixed opinions raise further questions about the N-word and other slurs:

- Why do many people object to the word?
- Whom does it affect?
- How and when can the word be used, if at all?
- When is it inappropriate to use the word?
- Who can — and can't — use it?

That these questions do not have easy or obvious answers reminds us that any decisions society makes about taboo words are not final because language and ideas about language are ever changing.

In discussing or writing about these words, we find ourselves confronted with another question: Should we write out the slur word, or should we refer to it by its first letter, as we have done here — for example, by writing "the N-word"? In this book, we chose to follow the preferred practice of the individual writers we include, even though this means being inconsistent: writing out *bitch* and *fag* but not the N-word. Others, including you, might make different decisions. It is important to note that there is a difference between using a word and referring to it in discussion; using the word often causes offense, whereas referring to the word in an academic, reasoned discussion of the word should not.

Political Correctness

The potential bias contained in some words is highlighted by efforts to eliminate sexist language. Supporters of non-biased language argue that supposedly neutral terms like *mankind*, *chairman*, and *waitress* have a built-in bias, and they seek to replace these words with more inclusive terms, like *humanity, chairperson,* and *server.* Understanding the harm of bias is easy if you imagine children learning vocabulary and culture: Words that are gender specific (*policeman, congressman,* or *actress*) implicitly teach children — and all of us — that only males or only females are included in the discussion or should anticipate these careers.

Efforts to change sexist language are similar to those of the broader political correctness movement, which began in the 1970s. **Political correctness** is a term used to describe the belief that discriminatory or biased words should be eliminated in favor of more inclusive, bias-free vocabulary. Consider the following short list; how do the pairs differ?

Potentially Biased Term	Politically Correct Term
fireman	*firefighter*
meter maid	*parking officer*
retarded	*developmentally delayed*
Oriental	*Korean, Japanese, Pakistani, etc.*
crazy	*people with mental illness*
handicapped	*person with a disability*
freshman	*first-year student*
fat	*overweight*

Another effort to draw more attention to the potential harm of words is Duke University's "You Don't Say" campaign, which "aims to educate the community on reasons why certain words are offensive and hurtful to many" (Lawrence). The image reproduced at the beginning of this chapter is part of this campaign. Describing the reasoning behind this campaign, Duke's Christine Lawrence explains:

> "You Don't Say" is not an effort to diminish the freedom of speech that we are born with, but instead seeks to educate individuals on why certain words and phrases, particularly those related to the LGBTQ (Lesbian, Gay, Bisexual, Transgender, and Questioning) community and gender identities, diminish and invalidate many individuals. Many of these phrases and words carry years of history and negative implications that make them more powerful and hurtful than most language.

While supporters of more inclusive language have had some success in raising awareness and in changing vocabulary, the political correctness movement also has its critics. Some critics see political correctness as censorship by the "language police." Other critics argue that focusing attention on language may distract attention from the key issues. For example, speaker and author B. J. Gallagher argues the following:

> While the original intent of political correctness may have been good (to encourage tact and sensitivity to others' feelings around issues of gender, race, religion, sexual orientation, physical abilities, and such), the *effect* of political correctness has been to make everyone avoid these topics altogether — thereby hindering our ability to get comfortable in living and working with those who are different from us.

On both sides, politically correct language debates examine whether words can cause inaction, incorrect perceptions, or unclear thinking.

In this chapter, we invite you to consider the extent to which words have both the power to harm and the power to shape ideas — the power to serve as not only sticks and stones but so much more.

Works Cited

Boroditsky, Lera. "How Does Our Language Shape the Way We Think?" *Edge.org*, 11 June 2009, www.edge.org/conversation/how-does-our-language-shape-the-way-we-think/.

Gallagher, B. J. "The Problem with Political Correctness." *Huffington Post*, 25 Feb. 2013, www.huffingtonpost.com/bj-gallagher/the-problem-political-correctness_b_2746663 .html/.

Lawrence, Christine. "You Don't Say." *Duke Student Affairs*, Duke University, 27 Jan. 2014, studentaffairs.duke.edu/blog-entry/you-dont-say/.

Moxley, Mitch. "Can Language Influence Our Perception of Reality?" *Slate*, 2014, www.slate .com/articles/news_and_politics/uc/2014/06/can_language_influence_our_perception _of_reality.html/.

Robson, David. "There Really Are 50 Eskimo Words for 'Snow.'" *Washington Post*, 14 Jan. 2013, www.washingtonpost.com/national/health-science/there-really-are-50-eskimo-words -for-snow/2013/01/14/e0e3f4e0-59a0-11e2-beee-6e38f5215402_story.html/.

Debating Slurs

Before You Read: Under what, if any, circumstances is it acceptable to use slurs or derogatory words? Briefly set out your position and your reasoning.

SHANELLE MATTHEWS

Shanelle Matthews is an award-winning political communications strategist with a decade of experience in journalism, legislative, litigation, rapid-response, and campaign communications. She serves as the Director of Communications for the Black Lives Matter International Network, a network of more than forty chapters working to rebuild the Black liberation movement and affirm the lives of Black people. Previously, she served as the Deputy Communications Director for the Sierra Club, lead communications strategy for Beyond Coal, and worked as a strategist for the ACLU of Northern California. She serves on the boards of the National Network of Abortion Funds and Rewire, and graduated from the Manship School of Mass Communications at Louisiana State University. This article is from *Said It: Feminist News, Culture, & Politics* (2013).

As You Read: Underline or make note of those passages where Matthews expresses her feelings about the word *bitch*.

The B-Word

I hated my American Fiction class. The professor, who always came to class fifteen minutes late, was **blatantly** sexist. He liked to let all the women in the class know that women were still viewed as substandard in the elite world of literature. He would even make comments about how women should remain in traditional female roles as opposed to progressing in the professional world. And he led me to rethink hate language — through his use of it.

blatantly: obviously

One day in class, he was talking about the movie *Dracula*, and he saw fit to describe Wynona Ryder's character as a "bitch," not once, but again and again. The rest of the class laughed at this unusual outburst, but I found nothing funny about his use of this sexist word. I wondered: Is this appropriate, and do I have to listen to it? It seemed I was the only one in the class who was offended by the slur.

It was then that I realized this very nasty word was becoming more and more acceptable in society as a synonym for "woman." The fact that this fifty-plus-year-old "professional" felt perfectly comfortable expressing his **contempt** for a woman by repeatedly using the word "bitch" in class, and the fact that most of the students seemed to find it funny, confirmed my belief that gender-specific insults are a norm in contemporary society.

contempt: lack of respect

Obviously the word "bitch" is not only being used by young America but by people of all types. It is being freely used in television programs, on the radio, and in publications. Even though the Federal Communications Commission does have "decency" standards regulating what can be broadcast—indecent material must not be aired from 6:00 a.m. to 10:00 p.m. when it is likely that children may be watching, and obscene and **profane** material must never be aired—**derogatory** language that targets women isn't filtered out. The FCC has defined broadcast indecency as "language or material that, in context, depicts or describes, in terms **patently** offensive as measured by contemporary community standards for the broadcast medium, sexual or excretory organs or activities." But apparently, the B-word is not considered "offensive as measured by contemporary community standards."

profane: disrespectful, especially of religion or religious practices

derogatory: disrespectful; insulting

patently: obviously

Ironically, the more commonly a derogatory word is used, the more invisible it becomes. But since it is a word loaded with negative meaning, it is worth investigating what it truly means, where it came from, and why people are so hung up on using it.

According to *Merriam-Webster's Collegiate Dictionary*, the first definition of "bitch" is "the female of the dog or some other carnivorous mammals." The second is "a malicious, spiteful, or overbearing woman—sometimes used as a generalized term of abuse." And the third is "something that is extremely difficult, objectionable, or unpleasant."

> ❝ *Ironically, the more commonly a derogatory word is used, the more invisible it becomes.* ❞

Although these definitions seem familiar and unremarkable, one can find, with a little bit of analysis and breakdown, a much more menacing concept underneath. The basic idea is that if a woman is in any way disagreeable she is deemed a bitch, so I ask: Where does the association between a female canine animal and a woman cross paths?

According to dog breeders, it is very difficult to breed a female dog because they are only receptive to the male on specific occasions, whereas breeding a male is much simpler because he is always open to the breeding process.

If we apply this comparison to women and men it can be understood that women are more reluctant to the "breeding" process, i.e., sex.

Nowadays the music industry is in the forefront of encouraging this prostitution-like attitude toward the mothers and daughters of the world. For a long time now, the industry has used sex to sell records, while promoting the use of this derogatory and offensive word. They have marketed women as "bitches" and "**hoes**" in order to ensure themselves money, power, and respect. In this culture, objectification and **misogyny** is what sells. It is what attracts many listeners to the music.

hoes: whores (slang)

misogyny: hatred of women

Musician and producer O'Shea "Ice Cube" Jackson stated in the documentary *The N Word* directed by Todd Williams, "If someone calls me a 'nigga,'

I'm so used to the word that it won't faze me. I won't want to kill them or anything. But if somebody calls me a 'bitch,' then we have a serious problem." For Ice Cube and many other men, being called a "bitch" puts into question the validity of their manhood. If indeed men **rail against** the word when it is directed toward them, what does it mean to these men when they direct it toward women?

rail against: speak bitterly or very strongly against

We cannot overlook the women who call each other and themselves the B-word. These women fall into two categories: those who accept the misogynistic definition of the word, and those who attempt to redefine it.

Bitch magazine proclaims on its Web site: "When it's being used as an insult, 'bitch' is an **epithet** hurled at women who speak their minds, who have opinions and don't sit by and smile uncomfortably if they're bothered or offended. If being an outspoken woman means being a bitch, we'll take that as a compliment, thanks."

epithet: insulting label

Bitch magazine has taken up the challenge to redefine the meaning of the word as something powerful and strong. This is a complicated position because as often as women are eager to reclaim, embrace, and redistribute a word that is so often used to insult them, this often backfires and reinforces the initial intention of the expression.

Hip hop feminist Joan Morgan strikes a chord while discussing this concern in her latest book, *When Chicken Heads Come Home to Roost: My Life as a Hip Hop Feminist*. "There are **inherent** dangers in building an identity based on the prejudices of one's oppressor; eventually the line between myth and morality becomes dangerously irreversibly blurred," she writes.

inherent: natural; essential

On the one hand, the word "bitch," like other derogatory words used in pop culture, can express **camaraderie** and affection amongst those who use it. However, it's my belief that the meaning of the word can't be changed at its very root, and therefore, like other offensive phrases, [the word] should be eliminated. Society is creative when it chooses to be. Why not find altogether new ways to express camaraderie and affection?

camaraderie: friendliness among a group

Trying to use derogatory words in a positive way is risky because all too often playful slang turns into harmful **jargon** that sends a wounding message to the person on the receiving end.

jargon: vocabulary; typically, specialized language that outsiders find unclear (e.g., legal jargon)

So, what can be done to abolish this word and the offensive atmosphere it fosters? Women should start by evaluating the meaning of the B-word and assessing their personal feelings about it. Let's think about how we feel when men or other women call us a "bitch" in an act of rage or anger. Men and women can make a sincere effort to become more socially conscious, more aware that these words are damaging. Using the word "bitch" has become a tradition. Instantaneous and cutting, we should remember that this tradition has a history of exclusion, which compromises the atmosphere of freedom we should be striving for.

adamantly:
strongly sticking to
an opinion

I considered filing a grievance against my professor, but in the end, I decided against it. However, I did **adamantly** express to him my irritation with his thoughtless outburst. I let him know that, like his students, he has a right to express his opinions openly but he also needs to be aware that somewhere in his midst someone might be hurt by such language.

The word "bitch" is outdated and overrated. We can't keep flinging people into negative categories. We can't simply brand a person with a word, dismissing everything that's unique and worthy about them. It's time to be progressive.

After You Read

Mapping the Reading

1. What reasons does Matthews offer to support her position that the word *bitch* is offensive? (Consult your "As You Read" notes, if you have them.)

2. What does her professor's use of *bitch* in class lead Matthews to realize?

3. What point does Matthews try to prove by looking up the dictionary definitions of *bitch*?

4. According to Matthews, what are the different ways that women use the word? What is her response to these uses?

5. What type of message does Matthews believe is sent by using the word *bitch*?

Discussing and Thinking Critically about the Reading

1. Matthews strongly argues against using the word *bitch*, considering it very offensive. What is your opinion about this word and its use?

2. What does Matthews mean when she writes "the more commonly a derogatory word is used, the more invisible it becomes"? Summarize and then reflect on her point; do you agree or disagree? Why or why not?

3. Matthews is shocked by her professor's use of the word *bitch* in class. How important is the setting in which a word is used in determining whether it is offensive?

4. Matthews observes that though some "women are eager to reclaim, embrace, and redistribute a word that is so often used to insult them, this often backfires and reinforces the initial intention of the expression." Is it possible for groups to rehabilitate slurs? Consider the word *bitch* and others that people have tried to reclaim.

5. Track Matthews's use of the word *bitch* and its substitute, the "B-word." What patterns do you find in how and where she uses each term? How do her choices reflect her stance about using *bitch* over the B-word?

Navigating the Intersections

1. Shanelle Matthews suggests that the "B-word" is "becoming more and more acceptable in society as a synonym for 'woman.'" How acceptable is the use of *bitch* in

your community? In what places (if any) does the word seem to be appropriate or acceptable — or inappropriate or unacceptable? Who can and cannot use it?

2. There are opposing views about whether the word *bitch* is offensive. Find another writer who takes a position on this word, and compare that author's arguments to Matthews's. (Enter "using the word bitch" into a search engine to find articles.)

Before You Read: Early in his article, Steven A. Holmes asks, "Why does anyone have to use [the N-word] anymore? Why won't it just go away?" Before reading his view, write briefly in response to these questions.

STEVEN A. HOLMES

Steven A. Holmes is CNN's Executive Director for Standards and Practices, a department that oversees pieces that may be controversial. Formerly, he was a reporter and editor for the *Washington Post* and the *New York Times*. In his writing and editing, Holmes often focuses on race; he contributed to the Pulitzer Prize–winning *Times* series titled "How Race Is Lived in America." This article is from *CNN.com* (2015).

As You Read: Mark those passages in which Holmes identifies reasons that people continue to use the N-word.

Why the N-Word Doesn't Go Away

There's that word again, muscling its way into the public square, prompting sharp intakes of breath, embarrassed silences, **euphemisms**, and lots and lots of heated discussion. And this time, the speaker is the president of the United States, **unabashedly** using and forcing all of us to deal with that hateful (to some), endearing (to some), and confusing (to many) word: *nigger*.

"Racism, we are not cured of it," President Barack Obama said in an interview released Monday for the podcast "WTF with Marc Maron."

"And it's not just a matter of it not being polite to say *nigger* in public. That's not the measure of whether racism still exists or not. It's not just a matter of **overt** discrimination. Societies don't, overnight, completely erase everything that happened two hundred to three hundred years prior."

Whether or not his point is valid, there are, no doubt, millions of people saying, why did he have to use that word? Why does anyone have to use it anymore? Why won't it just go away?

Like those other words did.

euphemisms: substitute, indirect words used in place of offensive words

unabashedly: expressing strong opinions without shame or embarrassment

overt: obvious; not secret

Like the one in the headline Anthony Federico wrote two years ago, the one that cost him his job at ESPN.

Jeremy Lin, a Chinese-American point guard for the New York Knicks, had been lighting up NBA scoreboards with his play and generating a wave of rapturous excitement among fans. Finally, the player had an error-filled game, prompting Federico, twenty-eight, to note Lin's fall from grace with the headline, "Chink in the Armor: Jeremy Lin's 9 Turnovers Cost Knicks in Streak-Stopping Loss to Hornets."

The outcry over what many considered a racist headline was immediate. ESPN promptly fired Federico, who apologized and defended himself by saying that he had used the term in hundreds of headlines and that he had connected it in his mind to Lin's play, not his race. "This had nothing to do with me being cute or **punny**," he said.

punny: using humorous wordplay (informal)

If true, Federico can hardly be faulted for his failure to draw the link between the word and its history as a **pejorative** for Asian Americans.

pejorative: insulting word

Over the years, a curious phenomenon has taken place.

So many of the racial and ethnic pejoratives for a whole host of groups — Irish, Italians, Jews, Latinos, Poles, even, with the exception of a notable football team, Native Americans — thankfully have virtually disappeared from the **lexicon**.

lexicon: words of a language

Terms such as *spic* or *polack*, which used to be fighting words back in the day, now elicit blank stares and confusion when mentioned to teenagers, **millennials**, or **Gen Xers**. Blank stares or answers like I got from Justin Morton, a thirty-five-year-old grad student from New York, when I tossed some old-time **epithets** at him.

millennials: people born circa 1982–2004

Gen Xers: members of Generation X, or people born circa 1965–84

epithets: insulting labels

Wop.

"What?" asked Morgan, who is black.

Wop. W-o-p.

"I don't know. We used to chant 'wop, wop, wop' at concerts when we wanted to boo somebody off the stage."

Mick.

"Never heard of it."

Dago.

"No."

Kike.

"Is that for somebody who's gay?"

> ❝ *No one can argue that the reduction in the use of traditional racial and ethnic slurs means that American society has rid itself of all its prejudices. At the same time, it is undeniable that so many racial and ethnic slurs have been driven out of the public square by a general view that uttering such words is unacceptable. And that's a good thing.* ❞

No one can argue that the reduction in the use of traditional racial and ethnic slurs means that American society has rid itself of all its prejudices. At the same time, it is undeniable that so many racial and ethnic slurs have been driven out of the public square by a general view that uttering such words is unacceptable. And that's a good thing.

"These are hard, hard, bigoted words," says Abraham Foxman, national director of the Anti-Defamation League. "There are consequences for their use — social consequences, political consequences, commercial consequences."

To be sure, there are new terms generally targeting immigrants, just like the old pejoratives were directed at folks just off the boat from Europe. *Terrorist* has become a euphemism for Arabs and Muslims, whether or not they are law-abiding. *Illegal* is used for Latinos, no matter what their citizenship status. And as Seattle Seahawks star Richard Sherman has noted, black people, especially black men, have collectively become *thugs*. What binds these new terms is that they are **ambiguous**.

In today's supposedly more tolerant society, they serve a **dog-whistle** function that allows users to **denigrate** people without suffering social consequences.

"People can **evade** accusations of racism," says Paul Garrett, associate professor of linguistic anthropology at Temple University. "But everybody knows exactly who you are talking about."

There is, of course, one slur that has refused to be consigned to the **dustbin** of linguistic history and one whose target is clear: *nigger*.

The N-word's resiliency is probably because of two major factors.

It is evidence that bigotry against black people is more virulent than **animus** toward any other racial or ethnic group. Sure, it's been driven underground too. As Obama noted, it's no longer polite to use it in public — at least in its use among white people. But it seems to dwell there like subsurface magma rather than die out like other slurs. While white use of *nigger* may occasionally burst through to the surface, no one is going to produce a cell phone video of a bunch of frat boys singing, "There will never be a guinea in **SAE**."

But let's face it, another reason the N-word has a **half-life** that rivals plutonium is that black people keep it alive; and not just alive in the **code-switching** way where it is bandied about in private, but shunned in public.

"When I was growing up, black people would get together in a group, and we would use it," says Randall Kennedy, a Harvard law professor and author of *Nigger: The Strange Career of a Troublesome Word*. "But it was for in-group use only, and we would be watchful that other people didn't hear us.

"Today, you're on a bus or in the subway or in a mall, and people are just out-and-out using it. There's no self-consciousness, no embarrassment. It's normalized. That too has led to its singular prominence in the society."

The generational divide in the black community over the use of the word has been noted many times. But black baby boomers like myself have to acknowledge our role in keeping it alive. Go to any barbershop or beauty parlor with a black clientele on a Saturday afternoon, and you will hear phrases like the dismissive putdown "Nigger, please" uttered repeatedly in storytelling, followed by riotous **guffaws** from fifty-, sixty-, and seventy-year-old men and women.

ambiguous: having more than one meaning; unclear

dog-whistle: sending a message with two meanings, one for the general public and another for a subgroup

denigrate: slander or belittle

evade: avoid dealing with

dustbin: trash can

animus: intense hatred

SAE: Sigma Alpha Epsilon fraternity; University of Oklahoma's chapter was disbanded in 2015 after members posted a video chanting the N-word

half-life: time a substance takes to lose half of its effectiveness; time something remains popular

code-switching: using multiple languages or styles within a conversation

guffaws: loud laughs

Richard Pryor
(1940–2005):
American stand-up
comic and actor

Chris Rock
(1965–):
American
comedian and
actor

And it was members of my generation who, forty years ago, laughed uproariously at **Richard Pryor**'s brilliant albums like *That Nigger's Crazy*, and his N-word-infused comedy routines in front of mixed audiences that helped give the term its shaky public acceptability.

Who are we now to wag our fingers at rappers like Trinidad James? Can we ask whites and other blacks to not use the word and not give up our love of **Chris Rock**?

So, for better or worse, what the N-word has — and what other racial and ethnic slurs lack — is a constituency, a broad-based coalition whose component parts have embraced the word for their own reasons.

There are white racists who use it because they are, well, white racists.

decry:
strongly and
publicly say
something is
wrong

There are black baby boomers who may **decry** the term, but use it in private settings and are loath to fess up to the fact that it is they who let *nigger* out of the black closet.

There are black rappers and other entertainers who make millions of dollars exploiting a word associated with poor people in the ghetto.

There are younger black people who have embraced it as a hip term of endearment.

There are whites who are not racists but who want to sound cool and feel protected by black people's use of the term. And now there are analysts such as President Obama who will make use of the term apparently to get our attention as they seek to explain the country's still-volatile racial dynamic.

nettlesome:
producing troubles
or annoyance

In the face of this army of the N-word, do those who wish it would go the way of the ethnic slurs of yesteryear really have a chance? Or should we all resign ourselves to the idea that, despite the hand-wringing, this **nettlesome** word sadly isn't going away anytime soon?

After You Read

Mapping the Reading

1. Identify all the different ways that the N-word is viewed and used, according to Holmes.

2. What point does Holmes hope to prove by referring to ethnic slurs that are no longer widely used or known?

3. According to Holmes, what are some reasons "why the N-word doesn't go away"? (Draw on your "As You Read" notes, if you have them.)

4. What is Holmes's position on use of the N-word? Summarize his point of view and quote a passage in which he states his position most clearly.

5. Who are the members of what Holmes calls the "army of the N-word"?

Discussing and Thinking Critically about the Reading

1. Holmes concludes his article with these questions: "In the face of this army of the N-word, do those who wish it would go the way of the ethnic slurs of yesteryear really have a chance? Or should we all resign ourselves to the idea that, despite the hand-wringing, this nettlesome word sadly isn't going away anytime soon?" How do you respond? Do you think your age and race have any influence on your response? Why or why not?

2. Although Holmes is concerned about use of the N-word, he admits that his generation contributes to its continued use. How does this admission affect his argument?

3. Holmes claims that terms like *terrorist*, *illegal*, and *thug* allow users "to denigrate people without suffering social consequences." What do you think? Are these words hidden slurs? Why or why not?

4. Holmes mentions celebrities and public figures (President Obama, Richard Pryor, Trinidad James, and Chris Rock) who use the N-word. What place do public figures and celebrities have in shaping attitudes toward this word or any topic, and why? What place do you think they should have? If public figures stopped using the word, do you think the word would go away?

5. When publishing this article, CNN offered a warning to readers, saying "This article contains offensive language." Do you think this warning was necessary? Why or why not? What is the difference between using a word and discussing it? Which do you see Holmes doing?

Navigating the Intersections

1. Compare and contrast Shanelle Matthews's and Steven A. Holmes's arguments about the effects of using derogatory words, making sure to explore at least three points of comparison.

2. The use of the N-word is the subject of much debate. Use a search engine to find a few recent articles about its use, and then explain how the arguments compare to the ones made by Holmes.

Before You Read: The following reading begins by raising this question: "Does the use of words like *fag* and *dyke* and the phrase *so gay* contribute to homophobia?" Before reading any further, answer this question and explain your reasoning.

ROSE BRIDGES

A native of Detroit, Michigan, Rose Bridges studied musicology first in Boston and then at the University of Texas at Austin. She is also a staff writer at *Autostraddle* — a website for lesbian, bisexual, queer, and transgender women — where she writes about politics, news, and entertainment. Her blog, *The Brave Little Tumblr*, focuses on media analysis. Bridges has also written for *Bitch* magazine and *Anime News Network*. This 2011 article is from *Autostraddle*.

As You Read: Make a list or an outline of Bridges's sources, examples, and main points.

You Can Call Me "Fag"
American Teens Don't Find
Offensive Slurs Offensive

homophobia: fear or hatred of, or discrimination against, gay people or homosexuality

GLSEN: Gay, Lesbian & Straight Education Network, an organization that promotes acceptance in schools

LGBT: lesbian, gay, bisexual, and transgender

Jane Lynch: American comic actor

Lauren Potter: actor who has Down syndrome

Glee: a popular TV show

What's in a word? Does the use of words like "fag" and "dyke" and the phrase "so gay" contribute to **homophobia** among young people? It's pretty taken for granted that they do. But are slurs really such a big deal, or are there bigger issues we need to fix first before going after the language? **GLSEN** clearly believes the former, as they have a specific campaign, Think B4 You Speak,[1] dedicated to ending the use of the aforementioned words and phrases. . . . Whether it's working or not, people are taking notice, both inside and outside of the **LGBT** community. The Special Olympics has recently started its own "Spread the Word to End the Word"[2] campaign dedicated to ending the use of the word "retarded," and it uses a lot of the same tactics: Internet pledges and petitions, commercials featuring celebrity endorsements (including **Jane Lynch** and **Lauren Potter**, who plays Becky on *Glee*), and guides for students on how to start the discussion. Clearly, language is an issue that a lot of activists across the social justice spectrum think is important.

Yet, for many teenagers, these slurs may not be as serious as they are to the adults behind these campaigns. An Associated Press/MTV survey found that a majority of American young people are not bothered by the use of offensive slurs by their peers:[3]

> Fifty-one percent of those polled said they see slurs on Facebook or MySpace but most (57 percent) say these are due to people trying to be funny.
>
> Only around half that number believe people who use slurs hold hateful views.
>
> Just a third of young people saw words like "fag" and "slut" as seriously offensive.

That's quite a lot to tackle. Most people are automatically going to see this as a bad thing—that these kids are not getting the message that GLSEN and the

[1] See www.thinkb4youspeak.com/.

[2] See www.r-word.org/.

[3] "Poll: Young People See Online Anti-Gay or Racist Slurs as 'Just Joking,'" *Pink News*, September 20, 2011.

Special Olympics are trying to send, that language matters and can hurt people. Another possibility is that there's so much of it out there these days that kids have become **desensitized** to it. On the other hand, at least some of the kids telling us that they're not affected by the language are those who it's intended to hurt: "Of those who are gay, or have a gay friend, 36 percent find the word 'fag' offensive online, whereas just 23 percent of others did." While there is a significant difference there, it's still a minority of gay students and allies (though I have some issues with them lumping in allies with kids who are actually gay, and would like to know how the individual numbers differ) who are bothered by homophobic language. When so many kids are being bullied for their actual or perceived sexual orientation, but they aren't too bothered with homophobic language — maybe these kids are telling us that GLSEN is missing the mark. Maybe language isn't the problem.

desensitized: made less affected by

It reminds me of [a] **Dan Savage** video where he is asked to give his opinion on the subject of anti-gay slurs. When I heard him start to say that such language-policing is wrong because *he*, a gay person, likes to use "fag" and "so gay," I was all ready to disagree with him on this. But then he said this:

Dan Savage: American journalist and relationship blogger

> As adults we have a responsibility when kids use "That's gay" to put it in their heads that that's a little [expletive]. . . . But the occasional "That's so gay" in a high school that has a Gay-Straight Student Alliance and openly-gay kids who are not being tormented and bullied, is **pretty small beans**. But, a "That's so gay" in a school where gay kids are being brutalized, it becomes another kind of brutalization.

pretty small beans: inconsequential (slang)

It hit me because it reminded me of my own school days. I went to a high school that was like the first example Savage gives: Most of the kids were supportive of gay rights, and the minority was not a very vocal one. There were lots of openly gay kids (and at least one openly gay teacher) and even same-sex couples, who were able to be just as obnoxious in their hallway make-out sessions as the straight couples. We had a Gay-Straight Alliance, and it was respected — but it didn't have that many members, because many gay students *didn't see why we needed one.* (In fact, a large number of the members when I was there were bisexual or trans, two groups that were less understood and accepted — the exceptions that proved the rule.) Of course, even high schools like mine were still full of immature boys who loved shock value and who enjoyed slinging around homophobic words, *but in an environment where gay kids were accepted and empowered, we could just laugh in their faces.*

> ❝ But are slurs really such a big deal, or are there bigger issues we need to fix first before going after the language? ❞

Contrast that with my middle school experience, where hearing every single kid throw "gay" around as a synonym for "stupid" was *just one more reminder that being gay wasn't okay* on top of being surrounded by **fundamentalist Christian** classmates, their parents, and even teachers who loudly and explicitly

fundamentalist Christians: Christians who believe in a literal reading of the Bible opposed gay equality. All things considered, I'm going to have to say that I agree with Savage on this one, that offensive language is a problem when it's the **straw that breaks the camel's back,** when it's the cherry on top of a mountain of crap that gay kids are forced to endure. They're like **Dementors** — slurs need an environment full of hate and fear to be powerful. When gay kids are happy and accepted, those words shrivel and die, and aren't that difficult to defeat.

Another thing that Savage says that **resonates** with me is about context — knowing the difference between a bigot who really means the word and an ally or member of the group who is just joking around. That's something that the survey indicates kids understand: "The poll found that 54 percent of young people see the use of the words in their own social circles as acceptable because 'I know we don't mean it.' But when asked the question in a wider context, most said such language was always wrong." I know plenty of queer people who are fine with their straight friends calling them "fag" and "dyke" because they know their friend doesn't mean it and is poking fun at the stereotype rather than at them. I've even heard similar statements made about friends using racial slurs. But the same people would never hesitate to call out a true hater using those words to condemn those groups.

But part of the problem, and the reason I'm not comfortable completely dismissing the importance of language, is that you can't always control the context. You can't always know who else is listening besides your friends. *Others could hear it and think you* do *mean it as a slur and be offended. Still others might actually be bigots themselves and take your use of offensive words as evidence that people out there agree with them.* This is especially true online, the area where this study focuses. Who can tell whether YouTube comments full of slurs are being made by people who actually hold such despicable attitudes, or people merely mocking bigots? Nobody knows, least of all the bigots they may be trying to **parody**. It's **Poe's Law** at its worst.

And while gay kids may not have as much of a problem as adults think with anti-gay slurs, the survey found a bigger gap between African-American kids' perception of the N-word compared to all kids, which suggests this isn't universal:

> More young people (44 percent) said they would be "very" or "extremely" offended if they saw someone using the word "nigger" online but 35 percent said they wouldn't be too bothered and 25 percent said they wouldn't be bothered at all.
>
> However, 60 percent of African-American young people said they would be offended if they saw the word directed at someone else.

Overall, it's hard to tell for certain whether to see this study as a good or a bad sign. Maybe we should just let the kids tell us.

---

straw that breaks the camel's back: the seemingly minor action that causes an unpredictably large reaction (idiom)

Dementors: soul-sucking demons from J. K. Rowling's *Harry Potter* series who find their prey by sensing emotions

resonates: strikes a chord; has special meaning

parody: make fun of through imitation or exaggeration

Poe's Law: theory that if authors do not make their intentions clear online, it is impossible to tell whether they are being an extremist or making fun of extremists

After You Read

Mapping the Reading

1. According to Bridges, how do teens view the use of potentially homophobic slurs?

2. What is the goal of the campaigns by the Special Olympics and GLSEN?

3. Summarize the different environments Bridges experienced in her middle school and high school. What point(s) does this contrast help her make?

4. Bridges observes, "When so many kids are being bullied for their actual or perceived sexual orientation, but they aren't too bothered with homophobic language—maybe these kids are telling us that GLSEN is missing the mark. Maybe language isn't the problem." What does she mean?

5. What is Bridges's position on the use of slurs? As part of your answer, include a quotation of what you consider to be her clearest expression of her view.

Discussing and Thinking Critically about the Reading

1. Early in her article, Bridges raises this question: "But are slurs really such a big deal, or are there bigger issues we need to fix first before going after the language?" What answer does she offer? How would you answer her question?

2. List Bridges's sources and examples. What points does each allow her to make? (Refer to any "As You Read" notes you have to get started.)

3. Bridges refers to poll results that say "54 percent of young people see the use of the words in their own social circles as acceptable because 'I know we don't mean it.' But when asked the question in a wider context, most said such language was always wrong." Have you observed this difference? Give some examples.

4. Bridges ends her article with the line, "Maybe we should just let the kids tell us." Is that a good or an effective conclusion? Why or why not?

5. Bridges suggests that while words and phrases like "so gay" are used in a joking way among friends, they are also used to bully. How might these words and phrases be used in bullying?

Navigating the Intersections

1. Shanelle Matthews, Steven A. Holmes, and Rose Bridges all discuss the use of slurs. Compare and contrast their perspectives and arguments. What similarity do you find most interesting? What difference do you find most interesting? Explain your answers.

2. Go online to look at the campaigns Bridges mentions or to find similar ones. How do these language campaigns present the issues? What arguments do they raise about the importance of language? Who is their target audience?

Politically Correct Language Debates

Before You Read: Writing guides frequently advise writers to be careful to avoid words that offend others. Write a brief response: In your opinion, how important is it for people to avoid potentially offensive language when they speak or write?

ANNA MUNSEY-KANO

Anna Munsey-Kano is a writer and filmmaker from New Hampshire. While majoring in women's studies at Agnes Scott College in Atlanta, Georgia, Munsey-Kano became interested in the ways in which media shapes ideas about gender and sexuality. She created the blog *Queer Guess Code* with the goal of "encouraging critical thinking about the formation of Western culture, reveal[ing] its inherent male bias, and gradually unravel[ing] the social codes that make it so imbalanced." The following essay originally appeared on her blog in 2013. The formatting has been adapted for this text.

As You Read: Mark those passages where Munsey-Kano offers explanations in support of the claim she makes in her title.

Why You Shouldn't Be Politically Correct

It has become commonplace to hear the term "politically correct" tossed around in all sorts of circles. The way I see it, non-PC statements are only a problem because they are indicative of a deeper problem in the way people think. But staying politically correct does not solve this problem. By eliminating discussion and acknowledgment, it creates a bigger problem.

> POLITICALLY CORRECT: conforming to a belief that language and practices which could offend political sensibilities (as in matters of sex or race) should be eliminated. (*Merriam-Webster*)

Enforcing political correctness is censorship. If we believe certain racist, sexist, and otherwise insensitive or discriminatory *ideas* and *behaviors* are bad, it makes sense that we want to stop them. But by forcing people to use specific terminology or avoid certain conversation topics, we are going about it all wrong. Staying "politically correct" is not medicine for the problems that exist — it's a Band-Aid to cover up the wounds.

In addition, its goals are all wrong. Political correctness doesn't teach people to be mindful of problems in the way they think; it teaches them to avoid offending people.

What's wrong with this? Isn't that a noble goal? Perhaps in theory, but it will never work unless one understands the root of what is offensive. It is almost never a word, but rather an attitude or belief reflected by that word, which is indicative of prejudice and structures of power inequality. There is a moral transgression political correctness ought to be avoiding.

> OFFEND: to transgress the moral or divine law; to violate a law or rule: do wrong. (*Merriam-Webster*)

Instead, political correctness seeks to avoid interpersonal conflict and discomfort.

> OFFEND: to cause difficulty, discomfort, or injury; to cause dislike, anger, or vexation. (*Merriam-Webster*)

By focusing on hurt feelings or anger provoked in people instead of focusing on the moral **transgression** or underlying mistake, political correctness skips over the real problems, discrediting itself in the process. On the scale of societal importance, feelings are way lower than morals, so taking offense is deemed petty. As soon as we made political correctness a game of feelings, we allowed people to stop caring about it, and thus, to stop caring about the problems which inspired it.

transgression: the act of doing something that is not allowed

So there are two problems with political correctness: It is unattractive and therefore rarely upheld, and when it is upheld, it accomplishes the wrong goals.

> ❝ *So there are two problems with political correctness: It is unattractive and therefore rarely upheld, and when it is upheld, it accomplishes the wrong goals.* ❞

Avoiding personal offense is both ridiculous and ridiculously hard and everyone knows it. If you're on **Tumblr** you've heard of "social justice warriors," people who enter a space or conversation which is meant to be fun and "take offense" where none was meant. These "**white knights**" try to stick up for every marginalized group everywhere, potentially without full understanding of the issues they raise and potentially for reputation purposes or just to feel better about themselves for being sensitive and aware. Sometimes they appear more ignorant in trying not to be. They are often criticized for trying to "out-politically-correct" other people.

Tumblr: website used for short blogs and multimedia posts

white knights: heroes who come to someone's rescue (idiom)

Recently I've encountered several Facebook arguments vaguely about this concept, the **crux** of the problem being that some people want a fun space where they can feel free to post statements without being attacked for insensitivity and other people want a mindful space where they can feel free to respond negatively to a post without being attacked for over-sensitivity. (Hint: Don't attack people . . . for any reason!) This conflict is a result of frustration with political correctness.

crux: most important part

Political correctness is a bad term and a bad idea. We do not live in a "politically correct" world, where race, sex, religion, and gender issues don't exist, so we cannot live in a world where we don't mention or talk about them. Nor can we always avoid causing discomfort. That simply is not realistic or practical. There is always the possibility that a conversation will make somebody upset, but we cannot be responsible in advance for the feelings of everybody in the world. We can be accountable for our own attitudes and behaviors. The answer to solving problems is not to stop talking about them. It's exactly the opposite.

Instead of censoring your language to avoid sensitive words and discussion topics, be mindful of how your attitudes and behaviors are influenced by prejudices, privileges, and stereotypes, and also how your words actively influence the reinforcement and **embodiment** of those prejudices, privileges, and stereotypes.

embodiment:
perfect example of
an idea

If you catch you or someone you know using the term "politically (in)correct" for any reason, either to censor or to mock, stop yourselves and:

1. Consider why the subject at hand has been labeled "politically incorrect." Here's a tip: The answer is *not* because it will hurt someone's feelings. Think of the moral or divine law it transgresses, or the way it makes assumptions about, disrespects, or diminishes a person or group's identity.

2. Consider your own associations and beliefs surrounding this concept, where those beliefs came from, and how your current actions/words/thoughts both influence and are influenced by those beliefs.

3. Don't stress about it. Create a mental file folder for this issue and continue the conversation the next time something comes up.

admonishing:
expressing
disapproval

Please stop trying to be politically correct, and **admonishing** those who are not. Instead, consider earnestly the ways you think and act and have mindful, respectful conversations about it.

After You Read

Mapping the Reading

1. According to Munsey-Kano, what does it mean to be "politically correct"?

2. What point(s) does Munsey-Kano try to prove by looking at the dictionary definitions of *politically correct* and *offend*?

3. What are the problems Munsey-Kano sees in current ideas about political correctness?

4. What does Munsey-Kano mean by being "mindful" of how we think and act?

5. What are "social justice warriors," and what is Munsey-Kano's view of them?

Discussing and Thinking Critically about the Reading

1. According to Munsey-Kano, the concept of "political correctness" focuses on words and distracts attention from ideas. What explanations does she offer in support of this claim? (Refer to any "As You Read" notes you made.) Are you convinced? Why or why not?

2. Munsey-Kano believes that political correctness "focus[es] on hurt feelings or anger provoked in people instead of . . . on the moral transgression or underlying mistake." Do you agree? Why or why not?

3. Although Munsey-Kano argues against being politically correct, does she believe it is acceptable to freely use language that offends other people? Point to or quote specific sentences in her essay to support your answer.

4. Look at the advice Munsey-Kano offers at the end of her essay, and evaluate her suggestions. Do they address the problems she details in the essay? Do they seem practical? Which would you revise or cut? What other advice might you add?

Navigating the Intersections

1. Both Shanelle Matthews and Anna Munsey-Kano cite dictionary definitions. Compare their use of these definitions: What do they try to prove with them? How effective (or not) is their use of this type of evidence? What other method(s) might they have used to make the same points?

2. Visit the Global Language Monitor website to view its list of politically incorrect words. Choose one term to explore further, and search for articles on it elsewhere. What problems do opponents see in using these terms? What arguments are offered in support of these terms?

Before You Read: Write briefly about or list the images and ideas that come to mind when you hear the phrase *illegal immigrant* or *illegal alien*.

CHARLES GARCIA

Charles Garcia is the CEO of Garcia Trujillo, a nationally recognized consulting, banking, and investment firm that caters to the Hispanic market. *Hispanic Business* magazine named Garcia "one of the 100 most influential Hispanics in the United States." The book *Hispanics in the USA: Making History* (2004) recognized him as one of fourteen Hispanic role models for the nation. Garcia has published two books on leadership and success. President Obama appointed him chairman of the Board of Visitors of the U.S. Air Force Academy; Garcia also serves on many other advisory boards. This article was published on *CNN.com* in 2012.

As You Read: Underline, highlight, or otherwise mark those passages where Garcia discusses arguments made for and against using the phrase *illegal immigrant*.

Why "Illegal Immigrant" Is a Slur

The Supreme Court decision in the landmark **Arizona immigration case** was groundbreaking for what it **omitted**: the words "illegal immigrants" and "illegal aliens," except when quoting other sources. The court's nonjudgmental

Arizona immigration case: controversial 2012 ruling allowing police to ask about immigration status during routine traffic stops

omitted: left out

humanistic: related to a philosophy that believes that humans are basically good

language established a **humanistic** approach to our current restructuring of immigration policy.

When you label someone an "illegal alien" or "illegal immigrant" or just plain "illegal," you are effectively saying the individual, as opposed to the actions the person has taken, is unlawful. The terms imply [that] the very existence of an unauthorized migrant in America is criminal.

> ❝ *When you label someone an 'illegal alien' or 'illegal immigrant' or just plain 'illegal,' you are effectively saying the individual, as opposed to the actions the person has taken, is unlawful.* ❞

In this country, there is still a presumption of innocence that requires a jury to convict someone of a crime. If you don't pay your taxes, are you an illegal? What if you get a speeding ticket? A murder conviction? No. You're still not an illegal. Even alleged terrorists and child molesters aren't labeled illegals.

By becoming judge, jury, and executioner, you dehumanize the individual and generate **animosity** toward them. *New York Times* editorial writer Lawrence Downes says "illegal" is often "a code word for racial and ethnic hatred."[1]

animosity: strong hatred or dislike

The term "illegal immigrant" was first used in 1939 as a slur by the British toward Jews who were fleeing the Nazis and entering Palestine without authorization. Holocaust survivor and Nobel Peace Prize winner Elie Wiesel **aptly** said that "no human being is illegal."

aptly: appropriately

Migrant workers residing unlawfully in the U.S. are not — and never have been — criminals. They are subject to deportation, through a civil administrative procedure that differs from criminal prosecution, and where judges have wide **discretion** to allow certain foreign nationals to remain here.

discretion: power to choose what to do in a specific situation

Another misconception is that the vast majority of migrant workers currently out of status sneak across our southern border in the middle of the night. Actually, almost half enter the U.S. with a valid tourist or work visa and overstay their allotted time. Many go to school, find a job, get married, and start a family.[2] And some even join the Marine Corps, like Lance Cpl. Jose Gutierrez, who was the first combat veteran to die in the Iraq War. While he was granted American citizenship **posthumously**, there are another 38,000 non-citizens in uniform, including undocumented immigrants, defending our country.[3]

posthumously: after death

[Supreme Court] Justice Anthony Kennedy, writing for the majority, joined by Chief Justice John Roberts and three other justices, stated: "As a general rule, it is not a crime for a removable alien to remain present in the United

---

[1] Lawrence Downes, "What Part of 'Illegal' Don't You Understand?" *New York Times*, October 28, 2007.
[2] Aaron Sharockman, "Fla. Republican Rubio Says Close to Half of Illegal Immigrants Entered the U.S. Legally," *PolitiFact Florida*, January 18, 2010.
[3] Larry Banda, "Illegal Immigration and the U.S. Military: The Challenge of Reconciliation," *National Latina/o Law Student Association Blog*, February 2, 2011, nllsa.wordpress.com/?s = Illegal+Immigration+and+the+U.S.+Military.

States." The court also ruled that it was not a crime to seek or engage in unauthorized employment.

As Kennedy explained, removal of an unauthorized migrant is a civil matter where even if the person is out of status, federal officials have wide discretion to determine whether deportation makes sense. For example, if an unauthorized person is trying to support his family by working or has "children born in the United States, long ties to the community, or a record of distinguished military service," officials may let him stay. Also, if individuals or their families might be politically **persecuted** or harmed upon return to their country of origin, they may also remain in the United States.

While the Supreme Court has chosen language less likely to promote hatred and divisiveness, journalists continue using racially offensive language.[4]

University of Memphis journalism professor Thomas Hrach conducted a study of 122,000 news stories published between 2000 and 2010, to determine which terms are being used to describe foreign nationals in the U.S. who are out of status. He found that 89 percent of the time during this period, journalists used the biased terms "illegal immigrant" and "illegal alien."[5]

Hrach discovered that there was a substantial increase in the use of the term "illegal immigrant," which he **correlated** back to the *Associated Press Stylebook*'s[6] decision in 2004 to recommend "illegal immigrant" to its members. (It's the preferred term at CNN and the *New York Times* as well.) The *AP Stylebook* is the decisive authority on word use at virtually all mainstream daily newspapers, and it's used by editors at television, radio, and electronic news media. According to the AP, this term is "accurate and neutral."[7]

For the AP to claim that "illegal immigrant" is "accurate and neutral" is like **Moody's** giving **Bernie Madoff**'s hedge fund a triple-A rating for safety and creditworthiness.

It's almost as if the AP were following the script of pollster and Fox News contributor Frank Luntz, considered the foremost GOP expert on crafting the perfect conservative political message. In 2005, he produced a twenty-five-page secret memorandum[8] that would radically alter the immigration debate to distort public perception of the issue.

persecuted: treated poorly because of race, religion, or political beliefs

correlated: showed or identified a close connection

Moody's: company that evaluates financial creditworthiness

Bernie Madoff: investment manager who pled guilty to scamming investors in 2009

---

[4] Carolyn Salazar, "Almost Half of Latino Voters Find 'Illegal Immigrant' Offensive, Says Poll," *Fox News Latino*, March 8, 2012.

[5] George Daniels, "Study: 'Illegal Immigrant' Most Commonly Used Term in News Stories," *Who's News? Diversity Every Day* (blog), *Spjnetwork.org*, March 14, 2012, blogs.spjnetwork.org/diversity/2012/03/14/study-illegal-immigrant-most-commonly-used-term-in-news-stories/.

[6] *Editors' Note:* In 2013, the AP revised its stylebook to remove recommendation of the term *illegal immigrant*.

[7] Monica Novoa, "The Associated Press Updates Its Stylebook, Still Clings to I-Word," *ColorLines*, November 10, 2011.

[8] See images.dailykos.com/images/user/3/Luntz_frames_immigration.pdf.

conjures: brings to mind, almost as if by magic

specter: an image that is troubling and frightening

Nineteen Eighty-Four: 1949 novel depicting a futuristic society in which the government restricts citizens' thoughts

susceptible: easily influenced or harmed by

prefabricated: standardized; seemingly factory-made

doublespeak: language meant to deceive by appearing to mean one thing but actually saying something else

anaesthetizes: puts to sleep through anesthesia

dustbin: trash can

. . . For maximum impact, Luntz urges Republicans to offer fearful rhetoric: "This is about overcrowding of YOUR schools, emergency room chaos in YOUR hospitals, the increase in YOUR taxes, and the crime in YOUR communities." He also encourages them to talk about "border security," because after 9/11, this "argument does well among all voters — even hardcore Democrats," as it **conjures** up the **specter** of terrorism.

George Orwell's classic *Nineteen Eighty-Four* shows how even a free society is **susceptible** to manipulation by overdosing on worn-out **prefabricated** phrases that convert people into lifeless dummies, who become easy prey for the political class.

In *Nineteen Eighty-Four*, Orwell creates a character named Syme who I find eerily similar to Luntz. Syme is a fast-talking word genius in the research department of the Ministry of Truth. He invents **doublespeak** for Big Brother and edits the Newspeak Dictionary by destroying words that might lead to "thoughtcrimes." Section B contains the doublespeak words with political implications that will spread in speakers' minds like a poison.

In Luntz's book *Words That Work*, Appendix B lists "The 21 Political Words and Phrases You Should Never Say Again." For example, destroy "undocumented worker" and instead say "illegal immigrant," because "the label" you use "determines the attitudes people have toward them."

And the poison is effective. Surely it's no coincidence that in 2010, hate crimes against Latinos made up 66 percent of the violence based on ethnicity, up from 45 percent in 2009, according to the FBI.[9]

In his essay "Politics and the English Language," Orwell warned that one must be constantly on guard against a ready-made phrase that "**anaesthetizes** a portion of one's brain." But Orwell also wrote that "from time to time one can even, if one jeers loudly enough, send some worn-out and useless phrase . . . into the **dustbin**, where it belongs" — just like the U.S. Supreme Court did.

After You Read

Mapping the Reading

1. According to Garcia, why is it technically incorrect to use the term *illegal immigrant*?

2. What is Garcia's view of the Supreme Court's choice of terms in the ruling he mentions?

3. Why is it important to Garcia's argument that undocumented immigrants would face civil rather than criminal action?

4. Why was the Associated Press's 2004 judgment that the term *illegal immigrant* is "accurate and neutral" so important? (The Associated Press has since changed its policy on the use of this term.)

5. What point does Garcia make with the questions he raises in the third paragraph?

[9] Elizabeth Aguilera, "Documentary Kicks Off Anti-Hate Crimes Discussion in SD," *San Diego Union-Tribune*, February 6, 2012.

Discussing and Thinking Critically about the Reading

1. According to Garcia, what are the consequences of using the term *illegal immigrant*? What evidence does he offer in support? How convincing do you find it?

2. What is the effect of Garcia's use of the second person ("you," "you're") in the second, third, and fourth paragraphs?

3. Does Garcia prove the claim expressed in his article's title? Why or why not? (To get started, you may consult your "As You Read" notes.)

4. Garcia quotes Frank Luntz's assertion that "'the label' you use 'determines the attitudes people have toward them.'" What do you think? How much influence do words have in shaping attitudes toward people or ideas?

Navigating the Intersections

1. Toward the end of his article, Charles Garcia suggests there is a link between the use of the term *illegal immigrant* and an increase in hate crimes against Latinos. Compare his argument about the effect of words to that of another writer in this chapter.

2. Search a newspaper for recent stories about immigration. What terms do the stories use for immigrants who are out of status? How might the terminology influence your or other readers' view of the issue?

3. Since the publication of Garcia's article, the Associated Press (AP) revised its stylebook. *Illegal immigrant* is no longer a recommended term. Research the reasons the AP offered for this change as well as reactions to it. Write a summary of your findings.

Before You Read: List the first five words that come to mind when you think about the poor, and then list the first five words that come to mind when you think about the rich. Then reflect: How do these words differ?

ANAT SHENKER-OSORIO

Founder of ASO Communications, Anat Shenker-Osorio is a strategic communications consultant. In her work and writing, Shenker-Osorio examines the rhetoric and language used in discussions of clean energy, economic justice, and immigrants' and women's rights, among other issues. She is the author of the book *Don't Buy It: The Trouble with Talking Nonsense about the Economy* (2012). Her articles have appeared in the *Huffington Post*, *Salon*, the *Atlantic*, and the *Christian Science Monitor*, which published this article in 2011.

As You Read: Make two columns. In the first, list the terms that Shenker-Osorio says are commonly used to describe the rich, the poor, and wealth inequality. In the second, list the replacement words she offers. (Note: Your lists will not be equal in length.)

Do You Think the Poor Are Lazy?

Even if you said "No," the way we talk about wealth assigns moral superiority to the rich. Terms like "the wealth gap" obscure basic truths about inequality, casting it as a natural economic function. Inequality is really a barrier made to keep others out. We can **dismantle** it, starting with our words.

dismantle: take apart; strip of components

Americans are in deep denial about our wealth inequality. In the US, the richest fifth have 84 percent of the wealth—and most of us don't consider this to be a problem. In fact, we don't even guess at the distribution close to correctly. In a recent poll by Duke's Dan Ariely and Harvard's Michael Norton, respondents thought that lucky fifth has more like 59 percent of all US wealth and favor them owning just 32 percent of it.[1]

> *But our blindness to the amount of inequality and its effects on our society isn't pure ignorance or apathy. It's at least partly a function of how we talk about the issue.*

But our blindness to the amount of inequality and its effects on our society isn't pure ignorance or **apathy**. It's at least partly a function of how we talk about the issue. We say things like "the wealth gap" and "bridge the gulf"—phrases that obscure some basic truths about inequality.

apathy: indifference; lack of concern

It's automatic and necessary to explain the world in metaphors—to describe **abstractions** by comparing them to concrete things. In the case of inequality, we're characterizing the differences between the rich and the poor[2] as though they're objects **affixed** on opposite sides of a **chasm**. But viewing inequality as an economic canyon makes it hard to argue for policies that might actually diminish it. A canyon, after all, is a natural formation.

abstractions: general ideas, rather than actual things

affixed: attached

chasm: deep gap or division

"Gap" isn't a stirring call to action; it's a clothing store. It may provide a ready image of where we are, but it says nothing about how we got here. Studies of **cognition** and decades of experience tell us that when we don't provide an explanation, our audiences will fill one in themselves.

cognition: reasoning or thinking process

Poor Is "Bad," Wealthy Is "Good"

In this case, the cause-effect narrative for our "gap" seems to go like this: Those who are poor have chosen this condition. Whether it's character flaw (lazy bum), moral failure (welfare queen), **inherent** defect (the **bell curve**), or all of the above, this story tells us what have-nots have not is ambition or intelligence.

inherent: essential; natural

bell curve: normal distribution, graphed as a bell-shaped curve

It's no accident that we routinely refer to the wealthiest as the "top" and the rest as the "bottom."[3] In English, good is up and bad is down. That's why we say, "things are looking up" and "she's down in the dumps." No wonder we pull ourselves *up* (not forward or along) by our bootstraps. Calling certain folks upper class implies they are worth more not just materially but also morally.

---

[1] See www.people.hbs.edu/mnorton/norton%20ariely.pdf.
[2] Peter Grier, "Rich-Poor Gap Gaining Attention: A Remark by Greenspan Symbolizes Concern That Wealth Disparities May Destabilize the Economy," *CSmonitor.com*, June 14, 2005.
[3] "Ford Stock: CEO Mulally Gets $56.5 Million of It," *CSMonitor.com*, March 9, 2011.

Inequality Isn't an Individual Choice

If being rich or poor is understood as the result of **differential** effort, then we can conclude each category is simply a lifestyle choice. Inequality is then a sign that our economy is doing exactly what it should — rewarding the deserving and motivating the lazy. And the line of reasoning continues: Since there's nothing wrong with this, there's nothing anybody should do about it.

We use this "gap" language all the time. And then we wonder why the statistics we cite, the graphs we generate, and the examples we offer of widening inequality don't raise the eyebrows, let alone the **ire**, of many in our audiences.[4] Using this language **tacitly** degrades individuals and makes current conditions seem natural. By employing it, we blind the public to the fact that inequality isn't an individual choice. Rather, it's the direct result of the rules financial and political elites have crafted for their own enrichment.

In One Economy, Inequality Hurts All

A wealth *divide* further implies we have two separate economies, with the rich on one side of the gap and everyone else on the other.[5] If we believe the wealth of a few has absolutely no relationship to the **deprivation** of others, then there is no solution for inequality. Because there's no problem.

This is not just a false assumption but also a dangerous one. All of us engage with one another, producing, consuming, saving, and investing in our one economy. But the wealthy have managed to make off with the lion's share. When wealth **connotes** moral goodness, it's easy to believe that these riches are **just desserts**. As **Dan Quayle** argued against **progressive taxation**, "Why should the best people be punished?" Yet history shows that some people are **unfathomably** rich because others are inexcusably poor.

So how do we get the word out about economic inequality? Not just how much of it exists, but also where it comes from, and why it's destroying the long-term stability of American society and the proper functioning of our economy?

Make no mistake: Impoverishing certain populations is, in fact, derailing our entire economy.[6] As we **suppress** real wages for the majority, we shrink purchasing power and with it **consumption** and then available employment. Without money to maintain our homes and care for our families, we have less and less reason to follow the tacit agreements of civil society.[7]

differential: relating to a difference between similar groups

ire: intense anger

tacitly: expressed without a direct statement

deprivation: state of lacking something necessary

connotes: conveys; suggests

just desserts: reward or punishment that is deserved

Dan Quayle: forty-fourth vice president of the United States under President George H. W. Bush (1989–93)

progressive taxation: method under which people with higher incomes pay taxes at a higher rate than those with lower incomes

unfathomably: hard to understand

suppress: slow the growth of

consumption: buying things

[4] David R. Francis, "US Begins Crackdown on CEO Pay. Will It Work?" *CSmonitor.com*, September 10, 2009.

[5] David R. Francis, "Estate Tax Bills Take Aim at a Growing 'Aristocracy of Wealth,'" *CSmonitor.com*, August 2, 2010.

[6] David R. Francis, "Yawning Rich-Poor Gap Could Hobble Economy," *CSmonitor.com*, July 30, 2007.

[7] Dmitri Iglitzin and Steven Hill, "A Fair Way to Shrink the Wealth Gap," *CSmonitor.com*, January 24, 2007.

Not a "Gap," but a "Barrier"

Instead of a "gap between rich and poor," we're far better served calling it a "barrier."[8] A barrier connotes a big, imposing wall behind which a few can hoard the goodies, while those on the other side are left wanting. When you barricade yourself in, you keep others out. Instead of asking to "bridge the divide," let's insist on dismantling the obstacles that keep too many from the gains produced of their own hard work.

The metaphor of inequality as a barrier, wall, or other obstruction highlights several critical truths about our economy. It tells us these objects are man-made. This conveys that inequality is not some God-given, inevitable, natural wonder. We have built these barriers, and we can bring them down. In other words, there's another way our economy can be structured if we elect and work for it.[9]

Deconstructing Barriers

deconstructing: analyzing to reveal faults

prenatal care: health care for pregnant women

We can start by **deconstructing** the foundations of these barriers[10]—spotty **prenatal care**, no universal preschool, lead-painted walls, and cheap, accessible junk food. We can continue by combating overcrowded classrooms managed by a revolving cast of untrained teachers. We can improve the recreational and after-school choices for children. And we can work to eliminate the neighborhood violence, dirty air, and contaminated water that form the perfect blockade to adult success.

Crafting our inequality narrative from this metaphor, we would use phrases like this: Inequality holds people back from contributing to our nation. It sets in place obstacles not only to success, but survival. Trapping some Americans in poverty, policies that promote inequality exclude certain groups from making a living, no matter how much they work. The rules we've crafted block access to resources and opportunities, and prevent huge numbers of us from participating meaningfully in our economy.

Let's have our language lay the blame where it belongs—on the obstructions erected by decades of greed and concentrated wealth and power, not on the people who find themselves trapped on the wrong side of them.[11] This is America. Don't fence me in.

After You Read

Mapping the Reading

1. What do the statistics that Shenker-Osorio offers at the beginning of her article suggest?

---

[8] Grier, "Rich-Poor Gap Gaining Attention."

[9] David R. Francis, "How Long Will Politicians Look the Other Way on CEO Pay?" *CSmonitor.com*, August 25, 2008.

[10] David R. Francis, "Are CEOs 300 Times More Valuable Than Their Lowest-Paid Workers?" *CSmonitor.com*, March 15, 2011.

[11] Ibid.

2. What is the problem that the author sees in using phrases like *wealth divide* and *wealth gap* to describe the difference in wealth between the rich and the poor?

3. In Shenker-Osorio's view, how does the language of *up* and *down* and *top* and *bottom* influence our view of the morality of the rich and the poor?

4. In the author's view, why would calling wealth inequality a "barrier" be more productive than calling it a "gap between rich and poor"?

5. What does Shenker-Osorio think can happen as a result of changing the way we talk about the rich and the poor? As part of your response, include a statement that best expresses her view.

Discussing and Thinking Critically about the Reading

1. What is the effect of Shenker-Osorio's choice to use the first-person plural ("we," "us," "our") rather than the third-person plural ("they," "them," "their") throughout the article? For example, compare Shenker-Osorio's version (version *a* below) and a version written in the third person (*b*):

   a. "Americans are in deep denial about our wealth inequality. In the US, the richest fifth have 84 percent of the wealth—and most of us don't consider this to be a problem. In fact, we don't even guess at the distribution close to correctly."

   b. "Americans are in deep denial about their wealth inequality. In the US, the richest fifth have 84 percent of the wealth—and most Americans don't consider this to be a problem. In fact, they don't even guess at the distribution close to correctly."

2. Looking at the next-to-last paragraph, evaluate Shenker-Osorio's language. In her description of wealth inequality, has she effectively corrected the problems she finds with other ways of describing this issue? Why or why not?

3. Compare your "Before You Read" and "As You Read" lists. What might Shenker-Osorio say about the language you used? How might you revise your "Before You Read" lists to meet her recommendations?

4. Shenker-Osorio argues that we as a society mistakenly believe that the poor have chosen to be poor and that they lack ambition and intelligence. Respond to her argument: Do you agree or disagree with her assessment of American society? Why?

Navigating the Intersections

1. Charles Garcia, Anat Shenker-Osorio, and Anna Munsey-Kano discuss the potential power of words to shape opinions and to offend. Compare their arguments.

2. Search for other articles on wealth inequality or income distribution. What terms are being used to describe the rich, the poor, and the distribution of wealth? Do you see any examples of the type of language Shenker-Osorio criticizes? of the type of language she recommends? Give examples of the usage you see. What message(s) do these terms send about the possibility of eliminating wealth inequality?

Annotated Student Essays

In This Appendix

Analysis: Selena Alvarez, "Beauty according to Society"

Argument: Miryam Abraham, "Reforming Social Media"

Research Report: Mariia Cosmi, "'Linguistic Profiling' across the Country and Beyond"

Reflective Response: Nooron Eewshah, "Consumed by Social Media"

Reflective Narrative: Xiaomei Dong, "The Power of Language"

In this appendix, we present examples of student writing in four genres that are commonly assigned in college writing classes:

- Analytical
- Argumentative
- Informative (Research)
- Reflective

For more on these genres, see Chapter 2 (pp. 32–33).

We have annotated these essays to show how the writers make use of examples, sources, and discussion to support their points. We have also noted the writers' use of MLA style and other academic writing conventions (such as signal phrases and transitions).

For this **analytical essay**, Selena Alvarez responds to an assignment asking her to describe and analyze the standard of beauty in her society, drawing on personal observations and sources. She brainstormed ideas and decided to focus on the role of the media in creating restrictive models of beauty. She wrote three drafts, the final of which we present here. In this final draft, Alvarez analyzes, or breaks down, how standards of beauty are established within a society, focusing especially on the media's part in shaping people's ideas.

Alvarez 1

Heading includes writer's name, instructor's name, course title, and date of assignment, all double-spaced. (For more on document formatting, see Toolkit 5.1.)

Selena Alvarez

Professor Keohane

Introduction to College Writing

March 6, 2017

Centered title, indicating Alvarez's focus. (For more on titles, see Toolkits 5.2 and 5.3.)

Introductory paragraph begins with the broad topic of beauty standards and then narrows to the connection between beauty and weight. (For more on introductions, see Toolkit 2.7.)

Here, Alvarez first questions why thinness is valued and then proposes an answer.

Thesis statement, which Alvarez will support with examples. (For more on thesis statements, see Toolkit 2.4.)

First body paragraph, focusing on the Internet.

Beauty according to Society

For many generations, there has been a specific description of what beauty really is. This description defines the way beauty should look and be expressed. The mainstream representation of beauty in the media has to do with thinness. People others usually confirm as beautiful are those who appear thin. Little girls have grown up to believe that a Barbie doll is perfect. There was never a doll made to look a little overweight. As females grew older, they wanted to be like that Barbie doll they once had. In my household, everyone I live with is always telling me that they envy my flat stomach. They constantly tell me how lucky I am or how they envy my petite body shape. Why is it that they believe that being thin is something to envy or cherish? The fear of judgment may be the answer to this question. Society seems to constantly make fun of obesity as if it were horrible for a person to be overweight. The media creates and promotes the standards of beauty that lead to negative judgments that make it hard for those who look different.

Today we observe teenagers all over the world using the Internet on a daily basis. Not only do they use the Internet for communication and

Alvarez 2

entertainment; they also use it for inspiration. In the article "The Hunger Blogs: A Secret World of Teenage 'Thinspiration,'" Carolyn Gregoire introduces the hidden world of Tumblr, a social network based mainly on sharing pictures and updating blogs, in this case health and fitness blogs. Gregoire highlights some popular bloggers who show their opinions on how much they love being thin even if it means being unhealthy and losing weight in dangerous ways, such as through anorexia or bulimia. These thin bloggers aren't only damaging their figures; they are setting a bad example for their followers or fans. They give tips on how to lose weight as fast as possible, leading their followers to think it is normal to want to become thin and develop eating disorders. One of the popular bloggers in the article shares her opinion: "I like images that show skinny, happy girls. They look so confident and we can see their bones through their skin. It's the most beautiful thing ever. I also like the tips about food or how to ignore hunger" (qtd. in Gregoire). In this way, the media pressures women and young girls to believe that their bodies must look a certain way in order to be considered beautiful.

Media pressure also relates to men or even young boys. In the article "Muscular Body Image Lures Boys into Gym, and Obsession," Douglas Quenqua states that "many of these boys probably see themselves in Mike Sorrentino, 'The Situation' from the *Jersey Shore* series on MTV, or the Adam Sackler character, on the HBO series *Girls*, who rarely wears a shirt or takes a break from his crunches." Instead of boys having an obsession with video games, they have an obsession with wanting to fit in. Now more than ever, someone's image is more important than his or her personality. All those celebrities on reality television aren't the best role models for teenagers or anyone else when they act as if

Source introduction, which provides author and title along with a relevant summary. (For more on directed summaries, see Toolkit 2.5.)

Signal phrase introducing a quote. (For more on signal phrases, see Toolkit 5.9.)

MLA in-text citation for a web source; abbreviation "qtd. in" for "quoted in" indicates that it's an indirect source, not the author's own words.

Last sentence reinforces example's connection to the thesis.

Second body paragraph, introducing Alvarez's second example. Using "also" serves as a transition between paragraphs.

Second source introduced with a signal phrase that includes the article's title because it's a first reference. No parenthetical citation is necessary because the author's name is in the signal phrase and the source is an unpaginated website.

partying all day and drinking alcohol are the key to happiness. The media is constantly making boys believe that being thin and fit is the key to happiness and popularity.

Maybe this generation's idea about beauty is good, since it is a good thing to be healthy and fit. But does that mean everyone has to fit this image to be considered beautiful? Have you ever stopped to think about those who don't necessarily fit the thin or fit criteria? In the article "Why We Diet," Abigail Saguy goes more in depth as to why people actually try to lose weight. People expect that dieters exercise and eat less to improve their health. Saguy cites a source in her article about a survey of 231 dieters that asked if they would take a pill that would guarantee they would achieve or maintain their desired weight even if it would lower their life expectancy. Over seventy-five percent answered that they would (210). As Saguy explains, the true reason people diet is to protect themselves from being discriminated against because of their weight. On television, the media tends to show thin women having a happy ending with the man of their dreams, while overweight girls live miserably and get made fun of. The media is promoting that being thin is beautiful and will give you happiness in life. Saguy states that the solution to weight-based discrimination is to appreciate diverse body types. Her article helps explain that those who want to lose weight should have a better reason than just wanting to be "normal."

Beauty has a different meaning for everyone. No one should waste energy trying to fit in. Learn to love yourself for who you are. In the end, we will all end up in the same place no matter how "beautiful" we are. We shouldn't let the media control what the meaning of beauty is. No one really knows the true definition of beauty. While I see my family

Introduction of third source, a course reading.

Summary of one of Saguy's examples.

Conclusion paragraph. (For more on conclusions, see Toolkit 2.8.)

Alvarez 4

members as truly beautiful human beings, they see the exact opposite. I see the true beauty they think does not exist. If we didn't have society and the media judging body types and telling us what to think, maybe we would all understand what beauty really is. If we didn't have the media telling us what beauty is or should be, we wouldn't have to worry about people judging others for their appearance alone.

Alvarez ends her essay with a strong statement.

Alvarez 5

Works Cited list starts
on a new page with a
centered heading.

Sources listed in
alphabetical order,
double-spaced, and
formatted with a hang-
ing indent. (For more
on formatting entries
for common sources,
see Toolkit 5.13.)

Works Cited

Gregoire, Carolyn. "The Hunger Blogs: A Secret World of Teenage
    'Thinspiration.'" *Huffington Post*, 9 Feb. 2012, www.huffingtonpost
    .com/2012/02/08/thinspiration-blogs_n_1264459.html.

Quenqua, Douglas. "Muscular Body Image Lures Boys into Gym, and
    Obsession." *The New York Times*, 19 Nov. 2012, nyti.ms/1wTfWCh.

Saguy, Abigail. "Why We Diet." *Intersections: A Thematic Reader for
    Writers*, edited by Emily Isaacs and Catherine Keohane, Bedford/St.
    Martin's, 2017, pp. 210-12.

In this **argumentative essay**, Miryam Abraham explores the place of social media in people's lives, drawing on readings from this textbook. As she brainstormed and wrote multiple drafts of the essay, Abraham decided to focus on one particular aspect of social media—the oversharing of information—and its negative consequences. Narrowing the focus in this way allowed Abraham to construct a specific, arguable thesis and to offer a possible remedy to the problem she identified. In her body paragraphs, Abraham offers examples to support her thesis.

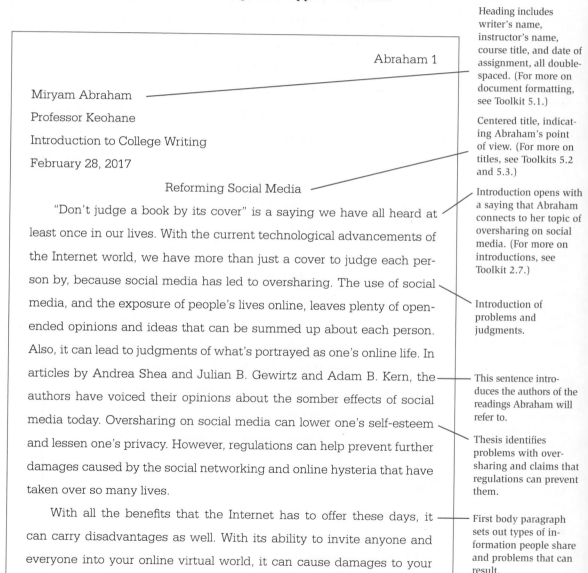

Abraham 1

Miryam Abraham

Professor Keohane

Introduction to College Writing

February 28, 2017

Reforming Social Media

"Don't judge a book by its cover" is a saying we have all heard at least once in our lives. With the current technological advancements of the Internet world, we have more than just a cover to judge each person by, because social media has led to oversharing. The use of social media, and the exposure of people's lives online, leaves plenty of open-ended opinions and ideas that can be summed up about each person. Also, it can lead to judgments of what's portrayed as one's online life. In articles by Andrea Shea and Julian B. Gewirtz and Adam B. Kern, the authors have voiced their opinions about the somber effects of social media today. Oversharing on social media can lower one's self-esteem and lessen one's privacy. However, regulations can help prevent further damages caused by the social networking and online hysteria that have taken over so many lives.

With all the benefits that the Internet has to offer these days, it can carry disadvantages as well. With its ability to invite anyone and everyone into your online virtual world, it can cause damages to your

Heading includes writer's name, instructor's name, course title, and date of assignment, all double-spaced. (For more on document formatting, see Toolkit 5.1.)

Centered title, indicating Abraham's point of view. (For more on titles, see Toolkits 5.2 and 5.3.)

Introduction opens with a saying that Abraham connects to her topic of oversharing on social media. (For more on introductions, see Toolkit 2.7.)

Introduction of problems and judgments.

This sentence introduces the authors of the readings Abraham will refer to.

Thesis identifies problems with oversharing and claims that regulations can prevent them.

First body paragraph sets out types of information people share and problems that can result.

Abraham 2

actual life. Marital infidelity, parental trust issues, and interference with employment are examples of what can be the result of social media destruction. Without any second thought about posting pictures or announcing one's whereabouts, it almost seems as if the whole world has to know everything about you. What was once taboo to talk about or discuss openly, such as one's sexual orientation or personal desires, can be easily seen on almost anyone's profile. The human desire to be known and to be categorized under a certain type of personality is driving people to this behavior. In "Facebook Envy: How the Social Network Affects Our Self-Esteem," Andrea Shea writes about psychologist Craig Malkin's research on how Facebook causes negative feelings after seeing others' so-called happy lives and comparing them to your own. The study "showed that one in three respondents felt more dissatisfied with their own lives after spending time on the site" (382). This study is important because it shows that people are perceived through the images they release about their lives online. These images may not completely reflect what is happening in their actual lives but the persona that they want to show other people. This is why social media is referred to as the virtual world. This study elaborates on how Facebook is linked to lowering viewers' self-esteem. The people who are living a so-called dream life can cause those who don't have the same luxuries of life to feel depressed about their own lives. Thus, oversharing on social media websites can cause those who don't have what others are showing off to feel negative about themselves.

In this age of modern technology, connections can be a fingertip away. With social media being so available to almost anyone, anywhere, it's almost impossible to be unidentified. With the ease of

---

Abraham offers a reason that people overshare and then uses a source (Shea's article) to support it.

Signal phrase provides the author and title of the source, as well as a brief summary of a study referenced by Shea, the findings of which are quoted. The parenthetical reference provides only the page number because the author's last name is in the signal phrase. (For more on signal phrases, see Toolkit 5.9.)

Example of the "Thinking with and against Other Writers" strategy discussed in Toolkit 2.11.

Paragraph ends by reinforcing the connection of its focus (lowered self-esteem) to oversharing.

This paragraph develops the thesis by identifying and discussing a second oversharing problem: easily accessible, outdated information online.

Abraham 3

locating anyone, there is a lack of privacy, and social media can be a disadvantage to those who may have outdated information online. In the article written by Julian B. Gewirtz and Adam B. Kern titled "Escaping Digital Histories," the authors bring up a point about the younger generations and the problems they will face with the social media epidemic. They argue that people may change their views, their beliefs, or their appearance as they age or mature and then forget to update these changes online. Therefore, the writers pinpoint that "[t]hese misrepresentations matter because they can shape unfair opinions or even cause unnecessary harm" (Gewirtz and Kern 400). This dilemma creates a need for encouraging new laws to help manage these websites and to help protect one's past from seeping into one's future. Preventive measures such as limiting how many posts each person can add each day would help resolve the issue of oversharing. They would help social media sites contain less information for viewers and protect people from losing out on employment opportunities. These new laws could also better shape the children of the future.

Social media is a part of our daily life. For some, it is part of their daily routine. We can't completely forsake the use of the Internet and abandon social media websites. However, we can limit the information that each post will contain. People post absurd things from the moment they open their eyes to right before they fall asleep. The unnecessary posts of the scrambled eggs that one has for breakfast or the scenic view from an intimate moment while on vacation shouldn't be what everyone views. Enforcement should not take away freedom of speech. Instead, it would contain the outbursts by limiting posts for each user. This means that one would think twice before posting anything online. Limiting

Example further developed using a brief summary and quote from source. (For more on discussion and analysis, see Toolkit 2.12.)

Statement of proposed solution.

Examples of types of posts that should be limited.

Clarification of the proposed solution and response to potential objection.

Abraham 4

posts would eliminate the profound tribulations that are caused by the negative effect of social media in one's life.

Finally, social media websites are windows that have been opened wide for anyone to peer into, enabling viewers to pry into others' personal affairs. When the world of technology came about, no one knew that social media was going to take over with the popularity and the push it did. However, while social media can be useful for connecting people, those connections can have horrible effects, especially in terms of lack of privacy and lowering self-esteem. Like with everything else in this world, too much of a good thing can easily turn bad. New regulation to lessen the vast and widening oversharing of information would be a benefit for all those who feel negative about their lives online. Privacy is a major concern, and the reduction of social media in each home that would result from regulation would benefit the entire family by exposing them to less negative attention. Because oversharing is a threat to privacy and self-esteem, preventive measures should be enforced.

Reference back to two supporting examples.

Conclusion ends with a direct and forceful restatement of the proposed solution and its value. (For more on conclusions, see Toolkit 2.8.)

Abraham 5

Works Cited

Gewirtz, Julian B., and Adam B. Kern. "Escaping Digital Histories." *Intersections: A Thematic Reader for Writers*, edited by Emily Isaacs and Catherine Keohane, Bedford/St. Martin's, 2017, pp. 399-400.

Shea, Andrea. "Facebook Envy: How the Social Network Affects Our Self-Esteem." *Intersections: A Thematic Reader for Writers*, edited by Emily Isaacs and Catherine Keohane, Bedford/St. Martin's, 2017, pp. 381-84.

Works Cited list starts on a new page with a centered heading.

Sources listed in alphabetical order, double-spaced, and formatted with a hanging indent. (For more on formatting entries for common sources, see Toolkit 5.13.)

In this **informative essay** or **research report**, Mariia Cosmi compares two articles about judgments based on accents. More specifically, she uses the report to make the point that John Baugh's concept of "linguistic profiling," detailed in one of the articles, sheds light on the prejudices about regional accents described in the second article. Cosmi brainstormed ideas and wrote multiple drafts. In comparing the articles, she discovered that the similarities extend beyond the idea of accent-based prejudices to include theories about the media's role in creating these judgments.

Heading includes writer's name, instructor's name, course title, and date of assignment, all double-spaced. (For more on document formatting, see Toolkit 5.1.)

Centered title. Quotation marks are used because "linguistic profiling" is from the Rice article. (For more on titles, see Toolkits 5.2 and 5.3.)

Introduction of John Baugh, and of Patricia Rice's article about his research.

Identification of second article's author, title, and relationship to first article.

Specifies the point of comparison between the two articles.

Focus of report: the similarities between Baugh's and Fields's points about accents. Though most reports don't have thesis statements, this one does.

First body paragraph summarizes Baugh's theory as presented in Rice's article. Quotations are followed by parenthetical references with author's name and page number. (For more on summarizing, see Toolkit 1.3.)

Cosmi 1

Mariia Cosmi

Professor Keohane

College Writing

February 25, 2017

"Linguistic Profiling" across the Country and Beyond

The term "linguistic profiling" was coined by John Baugh, PhD, a sociolinguist at Washington University in St. Louis. In the article "Linguistic Profiling: The Sound of Your Voice May Determine If You Get That Apartment or Not," Patricia Rice validates the argument made by Baugh and provides the examples of how exactly he reached the conclusion that certain common dialects get a specific treatment in the United States. A similar idea is expressed by R. Douglas Fields in the article "Why Do Southern Drawls Sound Uneducated to Some? Study Suggests Media Exposure Plays Role," in which Fields compares the northern, "smarter" sounding accent to the "dim-witted" southern "twang." Both articles share the notion that most Americans tend to categorize people on the basis of hearing their speech alone. Baugh and Fields condemn such practices and try to identify historical and media influences in order to shed light on the problem of "linguistic profiling."

As Rice reports, Baugh dives into meticulous research using his own diverse linguistic abilities in order to prove that Hispanic and African

Cosmi 2

American dialects, when heard over the phone, are being discriminated against. He points out that some companies don't return calls recorded by answering machines if the voices sound Black or Latino. He claims that some employers and renters, in order not to be accused of racism, prefer the over-the-phone rejection technique, which gives them the opportunity to pretend to be unaware of race in case the accusation of racism arises (Rice 188). Baugh concludes that a white-sounding person "get[s] the appointment" (Rice 188). He is certain of this because, due to his ability to imitate a variety of accents, including white, Hispanic, and African American, Baugh was able to personally conduct a significant portion of the study and experience the outcomes firsthand. In fact, he claims that "[h]is vocal differences in those tests were only in intonation, not in grammar" (Rice 190).

While Baugh shows the negative impact of linguistic profiling of ethnic groups, Fields fosters a debate on the perception of southern and northern dialects. On the basis of the evidence currently available, he suggests that dialects are categorized into cultural stereotypes, most likely affected by a combination of upbringing and media influence. Fields references a current study conducted by Katherine Kinzler and Jasmine DeJesus in the Psychology Department at the University of Chicago, which focuses on the attitudes of children toward accents. The study by Kinzler and DeJesus provided insight into how younger children from the South appeared to be less judgmental than the northerners of both younger and older age groups. Fields points out that the changes in attitudes can be attributed to the "learning and acculturation [that] are imposed on us by subtle indoctrination and experience."

Transition sentence connects two articles that are similar but focu on different accent-base judgments. (For more o transitions, see Toolkits 3.8 and 3.9.)

This quote has no parenthetical reference because Fields, the author, is identified in the quote's signal phrase and the source is an unpaginated website.

Cosmi 3

This paragraph sum-
marizes and compares
the authors' interest in
historical influences,
supporting the first
part of the report's
main idea.

Baugh and Fields share an important premise: they suggest that historical events can also be influencing the bigotry surrounding the accents. Fields mentions the Civil War briefly, from which we can assume that the linguistic bias can be seen as a remnant of past segregation and racism in the Southern slave states. The author redirects the topic by remarking on singer Adele's "Cockney accent," which he was surprised to hear (Fields). Fields includes both ideas in the same paragraph due to the meaning he is attempting to convey with their help, which has to do with historical and geographical differences and how they affect what we hear and think. Adele could have been calling about a job opening in London and not have gotten it because of her accent.

Transition to Baugh's
ideas and relationship
to Fields's idea.

Baugh is more direct in his reference to the history of slavery. To him it is obvious that "by an accident of birth [Americans] have the privilege to speak Standard English" (Rice 190), whereas for African slaves, it was extremely hard and at times even impossible to acquire the necessary linguistic abilities. He points out that frequently the slaves were separated from their families and "often isolated from anyone who shared their language" (Rice 190).

This paragraph
summarizes the
authors' interest in
media influences,
supporting the second
part of the main idea.

One of the common factors influencing our perception of different accents, as both authors suggest, may be the media's influence. Fields devotes a good portion of his argument to the idea that news anchors and celebrities do, in fact, play a major role in establishing the northern American accent as a superior one, whereas in the article by Rice it is only briefly suggested: "Many professional speakers, especially those in broadcast . . . have stripped their family's cadences from their pronunciation" (Rice 189). It can be inferred from the article by Rice that linguistic preference is affected by popular culture and the media. Baugh

Acknowledgment
that although the
media is not a focus
of Rice's article, it's
important. Draws a
conclusion (inference)
from Baugh's idea
about professional
speakers.

Cosmi 4

refers to his research on German accents, which are "considered brilliant" even if the speakers "stumble into grammatical errors" (Rice 189). Baugh suggests that comic books and cartoons might be responsible for the "brainy stereotype" associated with Albert Einstein's character (Rice 189). Both Fields and Baugh reference foreign accents to provide a broader outline for the reader and to support their argument on the media and cultural influence.

The idea of "linguistic profiling" lies at the heart of the discussion by both Rice and Fields. The articles are concerned with the issue of how people with various accents are being mistreated in the United States. Rice reports on Baugh's argument that people lack the opportunity to get a job or find housing if they sound African American or Hispanic, while Fields suggests that people who speak with southern dialects are prevented from making a good impression because of how they sound to most Americans. There is no doubt that Baugh and Fields condemn such practices and encourage the public to contemplate the issue.

Conclusion of report stresses the most important points of comparison between the two examples.

Cosmi 5

Works Cited

Fields, R. Douglas. "Why Do Southern Drawls Sound Uneducated to Some? Study Suggests Media Exposure Plays Role." *Scientific American*, 7 Dec. 2012, blogs.scientificamerican.com/guest-blog/why-does-a-southern-drawl-sound-uneducated-to-some/.

Rice, Patricia. "Linguistic Profiling: The Sound of Your Voice May Determine If You Get That Apartment or Not." *Intersections: A Thematic Reader for Writers*, edited by Emily Isaacs and Catherine Keohane, Bedford/St. Martin's, 2017, pp. 187-90.

Works Cited list starts on a new page with a centered heading.

Sources listed in alphabetical order, double-spaced, and formatted with a hanging indent. (For more on formatting entries for common sources, see Toolkit 5.13.)

In this **reflective response essay**, Nooron Eewshah offers a response to Josh Rose's "How Social Media Is Having a Positive Impact on Our Culture" (p. 377). The assignment was to choose an article to which students reacted strongly—whether in agreement, in disagreement, or perhaps in a mix of both—and to write an essay responding directly to the article using one's own point of view. Eewshah demonstrates critical reading of Rose's article, pointing to specific points of disagreement and offering support for an alternative point of view. In this essay, Eewshah uses "I think," "I feel," and "I believe"—phrases that should typically be avoided in academic writing. However, because this was a homework assignment rather than a formal essay, a more informal style was appropriate. Check with your instructor about whether it is appropriate to use such phrases for your assignments, or consult Toolkit 6.8 for advice on editing for wordiness.

Eewshah 1

Nooron Eewshah

Professor Keohane

Introduction to College Writing

March 13, 2017

Consumed by Social Media

Josh Rose's article "How Social Media Is Having a Positive Impact on Our Culture" is a self-explanatory writing piece. He discusses how texting someone and using apps like Facebook bring people closer together. Rose further extends his argument when he explains that China's version of Twitter helped to find a missing boy that was abducted far away from home. Rose explains that social media as a whole has positively affected the youths of today. He goes on to make a point that communication is kept alive due to texting and social media apps.

Though I do find social media to have some perks, I disagree with Rose's argument. I think social media has corrupted the minds of younger people. Social media is almost like an addiction to teenagers. The kids become so consumed with their phones and whatever may be happening on social media that they totally block out what surrounds

Annotations (right margin):

Heading includes writer's name, instructor's name, course title, and date of assignment, all double-spaced. (For more on document formatting, see Toolkit 5.1.)

Centered title, indicating Eewshah's focus. (For more on titles, see Toolkits 5.2 and 5.3.)

Introduction and summary of Rose's article, identifying both author and title. (For more on summarizing, see Toolkit 1.3.)

Eewshah acknowledges a point of agreement with Rose, and then takes an opposing stance. (For more on taking a position with respect to another writer, see Toolkit 2.11.)

Using specific examples, Eewshah expands on the viewpoint that social media can be too distracting.

Eewshah 2

them. Rose writes contrary to this point when he says, "The Internet doesn't get inside us, it shows what's inside us" (379). He describes how the Internet reflects who we are as people. However, while I feel that the Internet can reflect the kind of person someone may be, the Internet does get inside us. For example, I have witnessed it firsthand when I am asking someone a question and the person totally ignores what I am saying due to the fact that he or she is so hypnotized with scrolling through Twitter. It isn't until I say, "Are you even listening?" that the person decides to lift his or her head up and ask, "What did you say?"

The Internet also lives inside of people in the sense that it brainwashes them. Rose argues that "[the Internet] does not control us. It is a tool" (379). However, I disagree with this because I feel that it does control some people. It programs them to think that they must post a certain kind of picture because many other kids are doing it. Or a person may become obsessed with checking out certain people's Facebook pages, which controls them to want to constantly check pictures or statuses. I have seen this happen with certain girls that are interested in a guy, so they eventually begin to stalk his profile to find out what he is up to and what he likes to do. Social media also brainwashes people in the sense that they believe that what they post defines them. For example, one of my friends was so worried about a picture she posted of herself on Twitter because she thought her followers would unfollow her page and get annoyed by her tweet. This sounds like a silly instance, but it goes to show that people get so consumed by their social media that it begins to play a role in their everyday lives.

Margin annotations:

Quotation with page number in parenthetical reference, followed by a restatement of Rose's point.

Personal example to support the main point of the paragraph.

Second point of disagreement with article.

Observational examples as well as commentary.

Eewshah 3

At the end of his article, Rose notes that the technology is changing and so is how we are using it, which I totally agree with. However, the way we are using it is not completely positive. Rose believes that social media has an encouraging impact on people. However, I feel it plays a negative role within someone's everyday life. People become so consumed in uninformative tweets that they totally blank out what is truly around them.

Conclusion references Rose's final idea and connects it to the response's main point.

Eewshah 4

Work Cited

Rose, Josh. "How Social Media Is Having a Positive Impact on Our Culture." *Intersections: A Thematic Reader for Writers*, edited by Emily Isaacs and Catherine Keohane, Bedford/St. Martin's, 2017, pp. 377-79.

Work Cited list starts on a new page, with a centered heading. Because Eewshah has one source, the page is called "Work Cited" instead of "Works Cited."

In this **reflective narrative** inspired by readings about language and identity, Xiaomei Dong shares a personal experience in which being an English language learner created a potentially life-threatening situation. Importantly for the reflective genre, Dong does not just tell the story of the "EpiPen mistake" but reflects on what it meant to her personally and also questions what the incident may mean for society more broadly. Following the introduction, Dong begins in the middle of the story—its most dramatic point—and then returns to the beginning, relating the events that led up to that dramatic moment.

Dong 1

Xiaomei Dong

Professor Isaacs

College Writing

February 10, 2017

The Power of Language

Every culture is associated with a unique language. Language expresses the differences between races and defines the character of a country's civilization. It is the most basic and yet the most powerful tool in communication. Living in America and being an English second language learner, I found that language isn't just about being a better communicator or being connected with people. It also defines who you are. A person's accent, vocabulary, and way of speaking English can lead others to prejudiced and unfair treatment. An incident that happened to me recently has led me to rethink the power of language.

"... Can you go get someone who can speak better English?" came the nurse's voice over the phone, filled with sarcasm.

"It's nothing about speaking better English! You never told me I could only use the EpiPen when I needed it!" I cried out in a helpless voice.

The conversation was totally frustrating and unpleasant. I hung up the phone with anger and lay on the bed helplessly. My heart was

Heading includes writer's name, instructor's name, course title, and date of assignment, all double-spaced. (For more on document formatting, see Toolkit 5.1.)

Centered title. (For more on titles, see Toolkits 5.2 and 5.3.)

Introduces topics of language, culture, and communication.

Claims the thought-provoking nature of the personal example that will be the essay's focus.

The personal example begins in the middle of the story, using dialogue. The exchange catches readers' attention and introduces problems of communication and prejudice.

Summary of Dong's reaction to the conversation.

Dong 2

Identification of the problem resulting from the earlier miscommunication.

pounding like a hammer. It felt like it would jump right out of my chest, all because of the EpiPen mistake. The heartbeats were so loud that I couldn't think of anything. Before I fell asleep, I asked myself, "Has this been caused by my misunderstanding or the nurse's carelessness?"

Narrative returns to the beginning of the story, describing the events that led to the "EpiPen mistake."

It had been a typical Sunday evening. I had spent hours preparing dinner for my family, and we had enjoyed our weekly day together. At the dinner table, there were many dishes, including vegetables, meats, and seafood. Each dish was colorful and tasted even better than it looked. I was addicted to one of the dishes—a fish dish that I hadn't eaten in a while. It was cooked in a special Chinese style with a homemade red wine sauce. I ate one piece after the other. It was so delicious that I couldn't stop eating until my stomach was full.

After the meal, I went back to my room to watch my favorite drama. Everything seemed normal until I felt an itch that started on my back and expanded to my whole body. Within an hour, my body was covered in red spots. From my knowledge I could tell that it was an allergic reaction. I thought it was from the fish I ate, but I had been eating this type of fish for more than twenty years without an allergic reaction. I didn't pay too much attention to the itching, thinking it would go away the next day.

I couldn't sleep that night because the itchiness got worse. I started worrying that the problem might affect my ability to take an exam scheduled for the next day. I did not hesitate. Without waking up anyone in the house, I snuck quietly out the door and went to the emergency room. A nurse asked many simple questions and checked my temperature. She did not smile, which made me feel unwelcome. Then she asked me if I was Vietnamese. I told her that I am Chinese and tried

Dong 3

to be as friendly as I could, even though I wasn't feeling well. To show my respect, I continued the conversation with her and tried not to keep silent. I asked her if she was Vietnamese. Suddenly her face turned red, and she just looked at me without answering. From her expression, I felt I had said something wrong.

I didn't mean to irritate the nurse with my question. However, from her silence, I found that I had. I couldn't guess her race correctly, but it was obvious that she disliked being labeled Vietnamese in the same way that Koreans don't like to be called Japanese or Dominicans don't like to be called Mexican. There are many political, emotional, and cultural issues embedded within these simple words.

Speculation on the reasons for the nurse's curt treatment.

I did not stay at the hospital long. After the doctor diagnosed me with an allergic reaction, he dismissed me. Before I left the hospital, I took all the medications that the doctor had handed me, even though I was unsure of what they were. The words he spoke about the medications were all just vague medical terms, which were not easy for me to understand because I am from another country. I went home with the four medications inside me, and I fell asleep quickly because of the sleeping pill.

The next morning I woke up late, with dizziness and a headache. I wished I could stay home on that day and relax. However, I couldn't because I had an exam in the afternoon. As soon as I finished the test, I went to another class for an exam review. I left early because my skin was so itchy that I couldn't tolerate it anymore. On my way home, I stopped by the pharmacy to pick up my filled prescriptions. The pharmacist did not explain anything after she gave me the medicine. She was young, and I guessed she had just gotten out of school and did not have much experience. To assure my safety, I called her back to the counter so she

Dong 4

could tell me which medicines would make me sleepy or dizzy. As soon as I arrived home, I took out one of the medicines and started reading the directions, but I did not read the "Purpose" section. I thought that the medicines were for the itchiness and that nothing would be harmful, especially in this medically advanced country. As I followed the directions, I injected the EpiPen into my leg. A second after, I could feel the pain in my leg go through my body, and I could feel my heart beat abnormally. I didn't realize that the EpiPen caused my heart rate to increase until I called the pharmacy to ask if I could take all my prescribed medications together. The lady at the pharmacy was shocked. After a moment of silence, she replied in a gentle and concerned voice: "You took the EpiPen? Wow . . ." Her voice was shaking. "You only take it when you have difficulty breathing. When your throat is closed."

This section describes the "EpiPen mistake."

She realized that their careless mistake had caused trouble, and she recommended that I call the doctor, who could prescribe more medication to help me.

I called the emergency room where I was treated the night before. The same nurse who had dismissed me answered the phone. She pushed all the responsibility away from her, which was unfair, but it was not so important to me at that moment. I had already injected the pen, and I couldn't do anything to take it back. I was scared. All I wanted to know was what I could do going forward. So I asked the nurse what else I could do to fix the problem.

"If you want, you can come to the emergency room, and we will watch you for four hours," she said.

"Thank you."

Dong 5

I hung up the phone. I wouldn't go back. I didn't trust them any-more. They didn't provide me their best service, and they also let the mistake happen. Miscommunication was not the only problem. I felt that from their perspective, an immigrant probably doesn't deserve the best service that they supposedly give. It is a biased behavior that most Americans have against immigrants. Thinking back to my incident, if the nurse and the pharmacist had explained to me the purpose of the medication a little better, I wouldn't have ended up in bed. Lan-guage is the basis of communication. When communicating through language fails, I believe everyone should have respect and sympathy for the person who speaks the different language but still tries hard to explain her- or himself. However, because immigrants, and especially nonwhite immigrants, aren't originally from the United States, people have prejudices against them and make assumptions without respect. I can't prove that my experience was because of a racial bias or a race stereotype, but I'm sure that if a white man were in the same situation as I was, no such incident would have happened.

> Reflection on the experience, includ-ing speculation about the reasons for the incident.

Language can be powerful if it is used in the right way. However, language can also be so weak in front of racism and language biases. I didn't get the right service from both the nurse and the pharmacist because I couldn't express myself in the way they were accustomed to. Language problems are definitely a part of the reason for discrimination. But when we look thoroughly into this issue, was it my language that was the problem, or was it my ethnic and racial identity as a Chinese person?

> Conclusion of the narrative ends with a question designed to make readers think about the issue of bias raised by the essay.

Acknowledgments

Text Credits

Hilary Beard. "What I Learned from Mo'ne Davis about Girls, Sports, and Success." From TheRoot.com (March 20, 2015). Reprinted by permission of The Root and the author.

Jennifer Finney Boylan. "A Life in Two Genders." Excerpt(s) from *She's Not There: A Life in Two Genders*, by Jennifer Finney Boylan. Copyright © 2003 by Jennifer Finney Boylan. Used by permission of Broadway Books, an imprint of the Crown Publishing Group, a division of Penguin Random House LLC. All rights reserved.

Rose Bridges. "You Can Call Me 'Fag': American Teens Don't Find Offensive Slurs Offensive." From Autostraddle.com (September 25, 2012). Copyright © Rose Bridges. Reprinted by permission.

Rafael Campo. "The Way of the Dinosaurs." Copyright © 2007 by Rafael Campo. Originally appeared in *How I Learned English: 55 Accomplished Latinos Recall Lessons in Language and Life*, ed. Tom Miller, National Geographic Society. Reprinted by permission of Georges Borchardt, Inc., for the author.

Arthur Chu. "Breaking Out the Broken English." From NPR, *Code Switch: Frontiers of Race, Culture, and Ethnicity* (July 31, 2014). Copyright © Arthur Chu. Reprinted by permission of the author.

Joe DeGuzman. "Targets of Caricature: Irish Immigrants in Nineteenth-Century America." Courtesy of Joseph DeGuzman.

Firoozeh Dumas. "The 'F Word.'" From *Funny in Farsi: A Memoir of Growing Up Iranian in America*, by Firoozeh Dumas. Copyright © 2003 by Firoozeh Dumas. Used by permission of Villard Books, an imprint of Random House, a division of Penguin Random House LLC. All rights reserved.

Matt Duron. "My Son Wears Dresses; Get Over It." Copyright © 2014 The Atlantic Media Co., as first published in *The Atlantic Magazine*. All rights reserved. Distributed by Tribune Content Agency, LLC.

Brian Eule. "I Was Trapped in My Own Body." From *Stanford Alumni* magazine (January/February 2014). Copyright © *Stanford* magazine. Reprinted with permission from *Stanford* magazine, published by Stanford Alumni Association, Stanford University.

Kevin Fanning. "One Man Explains Why He Swears by Wearing Spanx." From Racked.com (April 8, 2015). Copyright © 2015. Reprinted by permission.

Casey Gane-McCalla. "Athletic Blacks vs. Smart Whites: Why Sports Stereotypes Are Wrong." Copyright © Casey Gane-McCalla. Reprinted by permission of the author.

Charles Garcia. "Why 'Illegal Immigrant' Is a Slur." From CNN.com (July 6, 2012). Copyright © 2012 Turner Broadcast Systems. All rights reserved. Used by permission and protected by the Copyright Laws of the United States. The printing, copying, redistribution, or retransmission of this Content without express written permission is prohibited.

Julian B. Gewirtz and Adam B. Kern. "Escaping Digital Histories." Reprinted by permission of the authors.

Temple Grandin. "Autism and Visual Thought." Excerpt(s) from *Thinking in Pictures*, by Temple Grandin. Copyright © 1995, 2006 by Temple Grandin. Used by permission of Doubleday, an imprint of the Knopf Doubleday Publishing Group, a division of Penguin Random House LLC. All rights reserved.

Sharon Haywood. "How Body Modification Ended the War against My Body." *Herizons* (Fall 2012): 24–29. Reprinted by permission of the author.

Steven A. Holmes. "Why the N-Word Doesn't Go Away." From CNN.com (June 22, 2015). Copyright © 2015 Turner Broadcast Systems. All rights reserved. Used by permission and protected by the Copyright Laws of the United States. The printing, copying, redistribution, or retransmission of this Content without express written permission is prohibited.

Theodore R. Johnson III. "Chivalry, Feminism, and the Black Community." Copyright © 2013. Reprinted by permission of the author.

Mary Jo Kane. "Sex Sells Sex, Not Women's Sports." From *The Nation* (July 8, 2011). Copyright © 2011 The Nation Company, LLC. All rights reserved. Used by permission and protected by the Copyright Laws of the United States. The printing, copying, redistribution, or retransmission of this Content without express written permission is prohibited.

Scott Barry Kaufman. "The Creative Gifts of ADHD." *Scientific American* Blog, *Beautiful Minds* (October 21, 2014). Copyright © 2014. Reprinted by permission.

John F. Kennedy. "Why They Came." From *A Nation of Immigrants*, by John F. Kennedy. Copyright © 1964, 2008 by Anti-Defamation League of B'nai B'rith. Reprinted with permission of HarperCollins Publishers.

Tracy López. "Non-Spanish-Fluent Latinas: 'Don't Judge Us.'" From NewLatina.net (March 9, 2012). Reprinted by permission of the author.

Rosemary Mahoney. "Why Do We Fear the Blind?" From *The New York Times* (January 4, 2014). Copyright © 2014 The New York Times Company. All rights reserved. Used by permission and protected by the Copyright Laws of the United States. The printing, copying, redistribution, or retransmission of this Content without express written permission is prohibited.

Mike Matheny. "The Letter That Went Viral." Excerpt(s) from *The Matheny Manifesto: A Young Manager's Old-School Views on Success in Sports and Life*, by Mike Matheny and Jerry B. Jenkins. Copyright © 2015 by Mike Matheny and Jerry B. Jenkins. Used by permission of Crown Archetype, an imprint of the Crown Publishing Group, a division of Penguin Random House LLC. All rights reserved.

Shanelle Matthews. "The B-Word." From *Said It: Feminist News Culture & Politics* 4.2 (2012). Reprinted by permission of the author.

Anna Munsey-Kano. "Why You Shouldn't Be Politically Correct." From queerguesscode .wordpress.com (October 29, 2013). Reprinted by permission of the author.

Nadia Mustafa and Jeff Chu. "Between Two Worlds." From *Time* 167(3). Copyright © 2006 Time Inc. All rights reserved. Reprinted from *Time* and published with the permission of Time, Inc. Reproduction in any manner in any language in part or in whole without written permission is prohibited.

Udoka Okafor. "On Living with Depression, and the Dangers of Our Culture of Silence." From Huffpost.com (October 16, 2014). Reprinted by permission of the author.

Alice Randall. "My Soul to Keep, My Weight to Lose." From the pages of *Essence* 43.5 (2012): 168–69. Copyright © 2012 Time Inc. All rights reserved. Reprinted from *Essence* and published with permission of Time Inc. Reproduction in any manner in any language in whole or in part without written permission is prohibited.

Patricia Rice. "Linguistic Profiling: The Sound of Your Voice May Determine If You Get That Apartment or Not." From *The Record*, Washington University in St. Louis (February 2, 2006). Copyright © Washington University in St. Louis. Reprinted by permission.

John Russell Rickford and Russell John Rickford. "Spoken Soul and Standard English." From *Spoken Soul: The Story of Black English*. Copyright © 2000 by John Russell Rickford and Russell John Rickford. Originally published by John Wiley, now Turner Publishing. All rights reserved. Reprinted by permission.

Joann Ellison Rodgers. "Cognitive Outlaws." *Psychology Today* 44.1 (2011): 70–77. Copyright © 2015 www.psychologytoday.com. Reprinted by permission.

Andrew Romano. "Why We Need to Reimagine Masculinity." From *Newsweek* (September 27, 2010). Copyright © 2012 IBT Media. All rights reserved. Used by permission and protected by the Copyright Laws of the United States. The printing, copying, redistribution, or retransmission of this Content without express written permission is prohibited.

Jon Ronson. "'Overnight, Everything I Loved Was Gone': The Internet Shaming of Lindsey Stone." From *The Guardian* (February 21, 2015). Adapted from *So You've Been Publicly Shamed* by Jon Ronson, copyright © 2015 by Jon Ronson Ltd. Used by permission of Riverhead, an imprint of Penguin Publishing Group, a division of Penguin Random House LLC.

Josh Rose. "How Social Media Is Having a Positive Impact on Our Culture." From Mashable .com (February 23, 2011). Copyright © 2011. Reprinted by permission.

Bob Ryan. "I Can Hardly Believe It's Legal." Excerpt from *Scribe: My Life in Sports* (pp. 226–29). Copyright © 2014 Bob Ryan. Bloomsbury Publishing Inc. Reprinted by permission.

Abigail Saguy. "Why We Diet." From *The Los Angeles Times* (January 4, 2013). Copyright © 2013. Reprinted by permission of the author.

Jamie Santa Cruz. "Body-Image Pressure Increasingly Affects Boys." Copyright © 2014 The Atlantic Media Co., as first published in *The Atlantic Magazine*. All rights reserved. Distributed by Tribune Content Agency, LLC.

Andrea Shea. "Facebook Envy: How the Social Network Affects Our Self-Esteem." From WBUR (February 20, 2013). wbur.org. Copyright © 2013. Reprinted by permission of the author.

Anat Shenker-Osorio. "Do You Think the Poor Are Lazy?" From CSMonitor.com (April 4, 2011). Reprinted by permission of the author.

Lauren Shields. "My Year of Modesty." This article first appeared on Salon.com, at http://www.Salon.com. An online version remains in the *Salon* archives. Reprinted with permission.

Sarah Showfety. "Field Guide to the Tomboy: High Heels and Pink? No Way." From *Psychology Today*. Copyright © 2015 www.psychologytoday.com. Reprinted by permission.

Amy Tan. "Personal Errata." From *The Opposite of Fate: A Book of Musings*. Copyright © 2003 by Amy Tan. Used by permission of G. P. Putnam's Sons, an imprint of Penguin Publishing Group, a division of Penguin Random House LLC.

Jose Antonio Vargas. "My Life as an Undocumented Immigrant." From *The New York Times* (February 12, 2013). Copyright © 2013 The New York Times Company. All rights reserved. Used by permission and protected by the Copyright Laws of the United States. The printing, copying, redistribution, or retransmission of this Content without express written permission is prohibited.

Ellen Welty. "Are Your Words Holding You Back?" From *Redbook* (September 24, 2012). Reprinted by permission of the author.

Lindy West. "What Happened When I Confronted My Cruelest Troll." From *The Guardian* (February 2, 2015). Copyright © 2015 Guardian News & Media Ltd. Reprinted with permission.

Isabel Wilkerson. "The Epic Story of America's Great Migration." Excerpt(s) from *The Warmth of Other Suns: The Epic Story of America's Great Migration*, by Isabel Wilkerson. Copyright © 2010 by Isabel Wilkerson. Used by permission of Random House, an imprint and division of Penguin Random House LLC. All rights reserved.

Hailey Yook. "Chivalry Isn't Dead, but It Should Be." From *The Daily Californian* (March 28, 2014). Copyright © 2014 The Daily Californian. Reprinted by permission.

Cyd Zeigler. "Derrick Gordon Finds His Freedom." Reprinted by permission of the author.

Index

Instructor's Manual

Intersections
A THEMATIC READER FOR WRITERS

Emily Isaacs ◆ Catherine Keohane

Cover art: Cove, painting by Julia Ricketts

Instructor's Manual for

Intersections

A Thematic Reader for Writers

Instructor's Manual for

Intersections

A Thematic Reader for Writers

Emily Isaacs

Montclair State University

Catherine Keohane

Montclair State University

bedford/st.martin's
Macmillan Learning

Boston | New York

Copyright © 2017 by Bedford/St. Martin's

All rights reserved. No part of this book may be reproduced, stored in a retrieval
system, or transmitted in any form or by any means, electronic, mechanical,
photocopying, recording, or otherwise, except as may be expressly permitted by
the applicable copyright statutes or in writing by the Publisher.

For information, write: Bedford/St. Martin's, 75 Arlington Street, Boston, MA
02116   (617-399-4000)

ISBN 978-1-319-04742-9

Contents

Teaching a Co-Requisite Writing Class   106

Course Design for Co-Requisite Sections   114

Instructor's Manual for

Intersections

A Thematic Reader for Writers

Introduction

We provide this teaching manual to support instructors as they develop their courses and teach writing with *Intersections*. Our approach to teaching writing is to engage students with high-level conversation about debatable ideas and important issues through readings and then to support students' reading and writing development through lots of coaching, mini-lessons, collaborative activities, and encouragement. We approach this *Instructor's Manual* similarly; in it, we provide useful coaching and mini-lessons to support teachers as they work with *Intersections* to teach writing. However, we anticipate that instructors will develop their own pathways through *Intersections*, and so the goal of this manual is to facilitate their design process.

Organization

Intersections is arranged as follows:

Chapter 1, "Getting Active: An Approach to Successful College Reading" — This chapter provides practical advice and strategies for successful active and critical college reading. Instructors may find it useful to begin the course with this chapter or to return to sections of the chapter when they observe students struggling with productive reading.

Chapter 2, "Breaking It Down: An Approach to Successful College Writing" — This chapter teaches students the logic and value of process writing — of breaking down the steps that successful writers take to get the job done. We work hard to persuade students to take on the strategies of process writers by defining writing terms and genres, the conventions of academic writing, and the importance of clarity, style, and editing. Instructors may find it valuable to have students read this chapter as they begin writing their first essay. The chapter closes with an overview of the essential elements of academic essays. On p. 33, you will find "Essential Elements of Academic Essays: Focus, Development, Discussion, Organization, and Clarity," which introduces terms that are used repeatedly in Chapter 3.

Chapter 3, "Toolkits for Reading and Writing" — This chapter provides mini-lessons, directed skill development, and support activities for process writing through more than eighty individual, targeted instructional toolkits. Each toolkit teaches students a specific concept through brief explanation and by providing more extended practice in using that skill. The toolkits, which are activity based, are designed to be used in support of a variety of reading and writing tasks. For example, instruction in summarizing can be applied to any reading; instruction in drafting an introduction can be applied to any writing assignment; and instruction in developing an editing checklist can be used by a student of any level.

Chapter 3 should not be assigned as a whole but rather assigned as needed to the whole class or to individual students. For example, in preparation for reading an argumentative essay, we assign Toolkit 1.10, "Decoding Arguments," to the whole class, and whenever we assign a peer review activity, we use a peer review toolkit (Toolkits 4.2 through 4.8). The key to successful use of Chapter 3 is to read through all the toolkits to become familiar with what is available and then dip in and preview them so you can select toolkits to assign as students engage in the reading and writing process. In addition, as you respond to drafts, you will find it very helpful to have the list of toolkits from the table of contents open nearby so that you can selectively send students to complete specific toolkits that will help them successfully revise and edit their drafts.

Chapters 4 through 11 are reading chapters, organized thematically. We selected the themes based on our many conversations with students and instructors. We wanted themes that are of interest to students and that provoke the kind of engagement and questioning that instructors find essential to good writing. Our chapters include topics that have always been successful with first-year and developing students — such as language and gender — and also issues that we do not often find in readers but in which students are interested — such as sports, disabilities, appearances, and immigration. Each reading chapter has two thematic clusters, which are useful if instructors find three readings appropriate but want them to be closely related. Instructors may also choose selections from different clusters and across chapters. (For example, Mary Jo Kane's piece on stereotypes of female athletes from Chapter 9, "More Than Just a Game," might also be used in a gender unit.)

Chapter 4, "Language and Identity: Are We Made with Words?" — In this chapter, we invite students to explore how our accents, our speech patterns, and even our word choices can be connected to identity; to consider how individuals negotiate the relationships between these factors; and to examine how language shapes the impressions we inspire in others. Do our words make us, or do we use language to make (or remake) ourselves?

Chapter 5, "Appearance: Who Should Decide What We Look Like?" — Appearance can be looked at from two perspectives: how we feel, think, and behave about our *own* appearance and how we feel, think, and behave in response to *other* people's appearance. In this chapter, we invite students to consider both of these perspectives by looking at what a range of writers have to say about dieting and body image, body modification, and the role that clothing plays in affecting our appearance and sense of ourselves.

Chapter 6, "Immigration: America's Great Story" — Americans' connection to immigration is often very personal, as so many of us have been told stories of our family's immigrant history. Immigration is also a public political issue that engages citizens and politicians in heated arguments. In this chapter, we invite students to think about immigration from multiple perspectives and to consider the tensions between the grand vision of America as welcoming of immigrants and a long national history of anxiety over immigration.

Chapter 7, "Abilities and Disabilities: Are They Linked?" — In this chapter, we focus on the experiences of people with disabilities. In it, we consider what it means to be disabled, how our society responds to and supports disabled individuals, and ultimately whether disability — focus here on *dis* — is an accurate or helpful way to see people who have unusual or remarkable features or characteristics. This chapter thus raises questions about whether disability actually encourages and enables extraordinary ability to blossom alongside disability.

Chapter 8, "Twenty-First-Century Gender: When It Matters and When It Doesn't" — In recent years, the culture at large has turned its attention to gender as it relates to men's issues and issues of gender identity involving transgender people and those who feel uncomfortable when asked to identify with, and conform to, traditional masculine or feminine behaviors, attitudes, and activities. This chapter raises questions about gender that address who we are, who we can be, and to what extent our biological and social identities should and do dictate our personal possibilities.

Chapter 9, "More Than Just a Game: What Sports Say about American Society" — From the billion-dollar professional sports industry to Little League to shooting hoops after school, sports occupy an important place in American culture. Even those who are not athletes or fans have difficulty escaping sports. This chapter invites students to think more deeply about what sports say about America, encouraging them to join in the conversation about the value of sports, sports culture, and stereotypes and bias on the field and in sports media.

Chapter 10, "The Digital Age: Risks and Rewards" — While social media and Internet tools are valuable for enabling business growth, providing pleasure and personal utility, and allowing for social and political community, they can also be abused or misused. In this chapter, we explore the impact of the digital age: the effect on personal relationships and on self-esteem, the capacity to create communities, and the potential to preserve and promote inaccurate, possibly harmful, versions of ourselves.

Chapter 11, "Words: Sticks and Stones?" — The old saying "Sticks and stones will break my bones, but words will never hurt me" proclaims that insults or name-calling cannot hurt us; however, the very existence of this nursery rhyme suggests that words *can* insult and harm. In this chapter, we invite students to consider the extent to which words have both the power to harm and the power to shape ideas.

Appendix, "Annotated Student Essays" — In the appendix, we provide several student papers to demonstrate and model common genres of student writing: analysis, argument, research report, and reflection. The student papers are annotated, providing explanations to students about the writing choices that the writers made.

Features of Thematic Chapters

Each thematic chapter includes significant scaffolding to support critical and active reading, to prepare for engaged class discussion, and to provide a variety of opportunities to write in response to reading and thinking.

Image Response. Each chapter opens with an image followed by a question that asks students to critically read the visual text as a way to prime the pump for engaged reading.

Chapter Introduction. A short essay, the introduction provides students with the context and background knowledge needed to follow and engage in the issues raised by the readings. The introductions also provide students with the kinds of facts and statistics they look for when they are writing a paper on a specific topic.

Before You Read. This pre-reading prompt supports reading comprehension, getting students thinking about the issues and engaging them with an idea through writing.

As You Read. This prompt, which appears at the beginning of each reading, directs students to complete a task such as marking the text or taking notes while reading. The task helps engage students in the reading and also directs preparation of annotations that will make discussion and answering questions after reading easier and more productive. Frequently students find post-reading questions that ask them to refer to the "As You Read" notes.

Headnotes. Brief notes about the author provide students with context, identifying the author's field if the author is well established or the author's interests if the author is a student or citizen author. Publication dates and sources are also provided.

Marginal Glossary Terms. We have found that students often misunderstand readings because they lack understanding of words, terms, or cultural references, and so we have provided marginal glossary terms to explain vocabulary or references that could be particularly difficult. Students who don't need them can easily ignore the glossary terms, and those who do need them will have no trouble locating these contextual explanations.

Mapping the Reading. A list of questions directly after each reading support student reading comprehension. Strong readers will speed through these questions, and weaker readers will be prompted to go back to the reading to find what they need to know to answer each question. These questions may also ask readers to pay attention to the structure of the reading.

Discussing and Thinking Critically about the Reading. These questions engage students personally and intellectually. The questions ask students to offer opinions about the ideas expressed by the authors, and they also ask students to draw on their own experiences.

Navigating the Intersections. These questions push students to a higher level of engagement by asking for either independent research or data gathering or comparisons between authors' ideas and points.

Teaching with Toolkits

Chapter 3 provides a collection of pedagogical materials that we developed to help college writers learn the skills essential in American academic reading and writing. These materials include both informational resources and activities that guide students through a series of questions or steps in the reading and writing process. The toolkits are grouped into six sections: "Getting the Most Out of Reading," "Generating Writing," "Organizing Writing," "Revising Writing," "Following Writing Rules and Conventions," and "Polishing Sentences." We envision instructors picking and choosing toolkits from among these six sections, using their selections in the order that is most appropriate for their class and for individual students.

While the toolkits help students develop as readers and writers, they were also designed to make course planning easier for instructors. We know writing instructors often have heavy teaching loads and students with diverse needs. It is difficult to create, copy, and distribute supplementary materials that meet all students' needs. After all, not every student needs the same lesson: One student may have trouble with introducing quotes while another may have trouble writing topic sentences. The toolkits allow instructors to assign the appropriate activity to each student. The toolkits are designed for flexibility and can be used with any of the reading and writing assignments in the text or with outside materials you have assigned. They are versatile in that they can be assigned as homework, as planned classwork, or as an on-the-spot classwork assignment in response to emerging student needs. It's worth repeating that the toolkits do not need to be completed in the order in which they appear, nor in their entirety; moreover, individual toolkits can be repeated at different points in the semester, as needed. This may be most obvious with the peer review toolkits in section 4, but it is true for the other toolkits as well.

Suggested Toolkit Teaching Methods

Early in the semester, we assign the first three reading toolkits (Toolkit 1.1, "Margin Notes," Toolkit 1.2, "Outlining," and Toolkit 1.3, "Summarizing") to the class to introduce active reading. Typically, we assign them in sequence over three classes, along with readings, and we do some follow-up work in class. When students are comfortable with basic summaries, we have them write one for homework and then use Toolkit 2.11, "Thinking with and against Other Writers," in class to introduce a way of effectively using a summary. When the students are in the drafting process, we use Toolkit 2.5, "Directed Summaries," to reinforce this idea.

In addition to serving as homework assignments, many of the toolkits can be addressed in class to introduce or reinforce concepts. For example, we typically look at Toolkit 5.8, "How to Refer to Authors and Texts," in class early in the semester as students are starting to write about readings. When students come in with their first written homework in response to readings, we use this toolkit in class and have them make quick edits on their homework. We can then direct them back to this toolkit in feedback on papers when needed—for example, when a student refers to authors by first name only.

Students often have trouble distinguishing sources' ideas from authors', so we use Toolkit 1.11, "Decoding Voices," with a reading that uses a lot of sources (e.g., Tracey López's "Non-Spanish-Fluent Latinas: 'Don't Judge Us'" on p. 182 or Nadia Mustafa and Jeff Chu's "Between Two Worlds" on p. 269). This toolkit not only helps students sort out the ideas within a reading but also helps them grasp that if they are quoting one of López's sources, for example, they can't use "López says" as the signal phrase. This toolkit can be used more than once for different readings over the course of the semester. We usually let the readings determine when to assign this toolkit rather than always using it at the same point in each semester. For example, in a semester when we use Chapter 4 as the basis of the first unit, we may assign Toolkit 1.11 in the first few weeks; when we use Chapter 4 later in the semester, we may not need Toolkit 1.11 until that point, depending on which readings we have assigned.

We have found that Toolkit 2.2, "Directed Brainstorming," helps students write their first drafts. We typically use it with the first essay as a homework assignment; then, for later essays, we can have students repeat it with a new assignment or point them to it as an option for their brainstorming work. This toolkit helps students think about the assignment prompt and start to develop possible ways of addressing it. Once students have a revised draft, we use Toolkit 4.11, "Revising Your Thesis," to help them revise their working thesis as well as review what makes a thesis strong.

Once students have developed some familiarity with the conventions of using sources (through work with Toolkit 5.8, "How to Refer to Authors and Texts," Toolkit 5.9, "Using Signal Phrases," and Toolkit 5.10, "Quotation Format Guidelines," for example), we use Toolkit 2.6, "Quote Sandwiches," on an essay draft. This toolkit helps students start to effectively use—rather than just have—quotations in their papers; it walks them through the process of adding the guidance and explanation needed to make meaning of the quoted material.

Students in our classes often have some shared mechanics problems, and so we use the relevant toolkits with the whole class. Often, however, different students have different problem areas, and it can be helpful to assign individual toolkits, as needed, to different students at different points in the semester or on a day devoted to work on mechanics. For example, if Ryan has trouble with fragments, he will work on Toolkit 6.3, "Fragments"; if Yasmine overuses the word *and*, she will work on Toolkit 6.7, "Substituting for *And*"; and if Micah and Sasha have trouble with pronoun-antecedent agreement, they will work on Toolkit 6.11, "Keeping Pronouns Consistent."

You will find more examples of how we use toolkits in the sample syllabi in this manual.

Sample Syllabi

Sample Basic Writing Syllabus

Basic Writing

[Individual instructor information: name, office location and hours, e-mail address, section number, and semester identifier]

Course Overview: The aim of Basic Writing is to provide students with instruction, opportunities for writing practice, and feedback that will enable them to become capable college writers. Basic Writing serves to initiate students into the writing processes that enable most students to produce clear, meaningful, and intellectually valuable prose. The course stresses the development of thinking and writing abilities through frequent writing assignments that engage freewriting, brainstorming, receiving and giving peer feedback, revising multiple drafts, and editing. The central goal of Basic Writing is to help students become effective writers.

Expected Outcomes: At the conclusion of the course, students should be able to demonstrate basic competence in:

- Generating writing through prewriting activities such as brainstorming, freewriting, and prompt writing
- Generating an arguable central claim
- Organizing ideas around a central claim with logic and clarity
- Integrating the ideas of others into essays through summary and quotation
- Understanding and correcting surface-level grammatical and mechanical problems such as sentence boundaries, punctuation, and word choice

Course Requirements (see below for exceptions)

Essay 1 (3 pages): 10%

Essay 2 (3–4 pages): 15%

Essay 3 (4 pages): 15%

Essay 4 (4–5 pages): 15%

Participation and Homework: 20%

Writing Portfolio: 25%

Course Expectations [Instructor: Add to and adjust as needed.]

- Students will complete all reading assignments and all short and long writing assignments.
- Students will attend class regularly and be active participants during class discussions and collaborative activities.
- Students will be academically honest, following the university's Academic Honesty Policy.

Schedule

The schedule lists the reading and writing assignments that are DUE FOR that class.

Unit 1	Language and Identity
Class 1	Introduction to course; introduce active reading (Toolkit 1.1, "Margin Notes")
Class 2	**Reading Assignment:** "Introduction: How Language Makes Us" Arthur Chu, "Breaking Out the Broken English" (follow the "Before You Read" and "As You Read" instructions) **Writing Assignment:** Complete Toolkit 1.3, "Summarizing," for the article by Chu. **In Class:** Introduce ways of using summaries actively as part of discussion (Toolkit 2.11, "Thinking with and against Other Writers").
Class 3	**Reading Assignment:** Chapter 1, "Getting Active" Rafael Campo, "The Way of the Dinosaurs" (follow the "Before You Read" and "As You Read" instructions)

continued >

	Tracy López, "Non-Spanish-Fluent Latinas: 'Don't Judge Us'" (follow the "Before You Read" and "As You Read" instructions) **Writing Assignment:** Complete Toolkit 1.7, "Decoding Narratives," for Campo's narrative and Toolkit 1.11, "Decoding Voices," for López's article. **In Class:** Toolkit 5.8, "How to Refer to Authors and Texts"
Class 4	**Reading Assignment:** John Russell Rickford and Russell John Rickford, "Spoken Soul and Standard English" (follow the "Before You Read" and "As You Read" instructions) Patricia Rice, "Linguistic Profiling: The Sound of Your Voice May Determine If You Get That Apartment or Not" (follow the "Before You Read" and "As You Read" instructions) **Writing Assignment:** Answer "Discussing and Thinking Critically about the Reading" questions 2 and 4 for Rice and question 5 for Rickford and Rickford. **In Class:** Toolkit 5.9, "Using Signal Phrases," and work on quotation selection
Class 5	**Writing Assignment:** Use Toolkit 2.2, "Directed Brainstorming," to create an **exploratory draft** (2 pages) of the Language Unit essay. [Essay assignment will be given out in advance.] **In Class:** Peer review
Class 6	**Writing Assignment:** Second draft of Essay 1 due (at least 2 pages) **In Class:** Central claim workshop (Toolkit 4.11, "Revising Your Thesis")
Class 7	**Reading Assignment:** Chapter 2 (especially "Process Writing 101: Writing in College," pp. 24–32) **In Class:** Toolkit 4.9, "Using Feedback to Revise"

Class 8	**Writing Assignment:** Final draft of Essay 1 due (4 pages) **In-Class Editing:** Use Toolkits 5.8, "How to Refer to Authors and Texts," 5.9, "Using Signal Phrases," and 5.10, "Quotation Format Guidelines," to edit your final draft before turning it in. Start Unit 2 (complete and then discuss the image response for Chapter 9).
Unit 2	**More Than Just a Game: What Sports Say about American Society**
Class 9	**Reading Assignment:** Chapter 9 Introduction: "Sports in American Society" Casey Gane-McCalla, "Athletic Blacks vs. Smart Whites: Why Sports Stereotypes Are Wrong" (follow the "Before You Read" and "As You Read" instructions) Mary Jo Kane, "Sex Sells Sex, Not Women's Sports" (follow the "Before You Read" and "As You Read" instructions) **Writing Assignment:** Complete Toolkit 1.10, "Decoding Arguments," for both Gane-McCalla's and Kane's articles.
Class 10	**Reading Assignment:** Hilary Beard, "What I Learned from Mo'ne Davis about Girls, Sports, and Success" (follow the "Before You Read" and "As You Read" instructions) Mike Matheny, "The Letter That Went Viral" (follow the "Before You Read" and "As You Read" instructions) Bob Ryan, "I Can Hardly Believe It's Legal" (follow the "Before You Read" and "As You Read" instructions) **Writing Assignment:** These writers have different perspectives on the value of sports. Write an integrated response of 1½–2 pages in which you consider their positions: What are the writers' perspectives on sports? What points are they trying to prove? Have the writers been realistic or unrealistic in their depictions? How so? What evidence or examples do they offer to support their claims? How convinced are you, and why?

continued >

Class 11	**Writing Assignment:** First draft of Essay 2 due (at least 2 pages) **In Class:** Toolkit 2.12, "Discussion and Analysis"
Class 12	**Writing Assignment:** Second draft of Essay 2 due (at least 3–4 pages) **In Class:** Toolkit 2.6, "Quote Sandwiches"; peer review
Class 13	**Writing Assignment:** Toolkit 4.11, "Revising Your Thesis" **In Class:** Toolkit 3.7, "Topic Sentences"
Unit 3	**Appearance**
Class 14	**Writing Assignment:** Final draft of Essay 2 due (4 pages) **In-Class Editing:** [Based on sentence-level issues instructor has noticed in prior drafts, assign one or more of the toolkits from sections 5 and 6 to the entire class or to individual students or groups of students.] Start Unit 3; complete and discuss Chapter 5 image response.
Class 15	**Reading Assignment:** Alice Randall, "My Soul to Keep, My Weight to Lose" (follow the "Before You Read" and "As You Read" instructions) Abigail Saguy, "Why We Diet" (follow the "Before You Read" and "As You Read" instructions) **Writing Assignment:** Answer "Discussing and Thinking Critically about the Reading" question 2 for Randall and question 1 for Saguy.
Class 16	**Reading Assignment:** Jamie Santa Cruz, "Body-Image Pressure Increasingly Affects Boys" (follow the "Before You Read" and "As You Read" instructions) Kevin Fanning, "One Man Explains Why He Swears by Wearing Spanx" (follow the "Before You Read" and "As You Read" instructions) **Writing Assignment:** In a 1½- to 2-page response, summarize and reflect on these writers' ideas about the pressure society places on men to look a certain way.

Class 17	**Reading Assignment:** Sharon Haywood, "How Body Modification Ended the War against My Body" (follow the "Before You Read" and "As You Read" instructions)
	Lauren Shields, "My Year of Modesty" (follow the "Before You Read" and "As You Read" instructions)
	Writing Assignment: Toolkit 2.9, "Comparing and Contrasting Ideas"
Class 18	**Writing Assignment:** Rough draft of Essay 3 due. If you are stuck, try Toolkit 2.2, "Directed Brainstorming."
	In Class: Peer review
Class 19	**Writing Assignment:** Second draft of Essay 3 due (at least 2 pages)
	In Class: Organization workshop (Toolkit 3.5, "Reverse Outline")
Class 20	**Writing Assignment:** Final draft of Essay 3 due
	In Class: Start Unit 4 (social media use self-assessment).
Unit 4	**Social Media**
Class 21	**Reading Assignment:** Josh Rose, "How Social Media Is Having a Positive Impact on Our Culture"
	Andrea Shea, "Facebook Envy: How the Social Network Affects Our Self-Esteem"
	Writing Assignment: Compare the ideas of Andrea Shea's sources to Josh Rose's ideas. How are they similar? How are they different? How do Rose's and Shea's sources' different interests and situations shape their perspectives on social media use?
Class 22	**Reading Assignment:** Jon Ronson, "'Overnight, Everything I Loved Was Gone': The Internet Shaming of Lindsey Stone"
	Lindy West, "What Happened When I Confronted My Cruelest Troll"

continued >

	Writing Assignment: Answer "Navigating the Intersections" question 1 for Ronson. **In Class:** Toolkit 2.10, "Making Connections between Texts"
Class 23	**Reading Assignment:** Julian B. Gewirtz and Adam B. Kern, "Escaping Digital Histories" Amy Tan, "Personal Errata" **Writing Assignment:** Answer "Navigating the Intersections" question 1 for Tan.
Class 24	**Writing Assignment:** Rough draft of Essay 4 due (2 pages) **In Class:** Peer review
Classes 25 and 26	**Writing Assignment:** Revised mid-process draft of Essay 4 due at your conference (3 pages)
Class 27	**Writing Assignment:** Final draft of Essay 4 due (4–5 pages) *Important:* Bring to class a copy of one of the essays you are planning to revise for your portfolio (one whose support and development you would like to improve). **In Class:** Portfolio revision workshop (support/discussion) Section 2 toolkits, as needed
Class 28	**Writing Assignment:** Continue to work on your portfolio. *Important:* Bring to class a copy of one of the essays you are planning to revise for your portfolio (one whose organization you would like to improve). **In Class:** Portfolio revision workshop (organization) Section 3 toolkits, as needed
Final exam period	Portfolio due

Sample ALP/Co-Requisite Model Course Schedule

[Individual instructor information: name, office location and hours, e-mail address, section number, and semester identifier]

Schedule

The schedule lists the reading and writing assignments that are DUE FOR that class.

	Credit-Level Comp	*Developmental Cohort Class or Studio (weekly workshop)*
Unit 1	**Twenty-First-Century Gender**	
Class 1	Course intro; introduction to active reading strategies **In-Class Writing:** Taking stock and plan for the semester: What do you see as your strengths and weaknesses as a writer and reader? What do you most want to work on with respect to your writing this semester? What steps do *you* think you will need to take to accomplish your goals? **Begin Unit 1:** Brainstorm ideas about masculinity and femininity.	**In Class:** Introduction to workshop component of course; practice active reading strategies (Tool-kits 1.1, "Margin Notes," 1.2, "Outlining," or 1.3, "Summarizing")
Class 2	**Reading Assignment:** Chapter 1 Sarah Showfety, "Field Guide to the Tom-boy: High Heels and Pink? No Way" Jennifer Finney Boylan, "A Life in Two Genders" **Writing Assignment:** Summarize and discuss these two authors' ideas about the cultural expectations people face with respect to how they should act, behave, dress, etc. What might the experiences of the individuals described in the articles tell us about the rigidity and flexibility of gender roles? What might they tell us about gender, gender stereotypes, and the possible blurring of gender roles? (1½ pages)	

continued >

	Credit-Level Comp	*Developmental Cohort Class or Studio (weekly workshop)*
	In Class: Review Toolkit 5.8, *"How to Refer to Authors and Texts."*	
Class 3	**Reading Assignment:** Chapter 8 Introduction: "Gender in the Twenty-First Century" Matt Duron, "My Son Wears Dresses; Get Over It" Andrew Romano, "Why We Need to Reimagine Masculinity" **Writing Assignment:** How do Duron and Romano define traditional masculinity? In what ways do they believe this definition needs to be revised, and why? How convincing are their arguments? What makes these arguments convincing, or not? (1½ pages)	**In Class:** Conventions of American academic writing; Toolkits 5.8, "How to Refer to Authors and Texts," and 5.9, "Using Signal Phrases"; Toolkit 1.3, "Summarizing," for summarizing practice, if needed
Class 4	**Reading Assignment:** Theodore R. Johnson III, "Chivalry, Feminism, and the Black Community" Hailey Yook, "Chivalry Isn't Dead, but It Should Be" **Writing Assignment:** Toolkit 2.9, "Comparing and Contrasting Ideas"	
Class 5	**Writing Assignment:** Rough draft of Essay 1 due **In Class:** Peer review for Essay 1	**In Class:** Making sense of first essay assignment, drafting steps (Toolkit 2.2, "Directed Brainstorming")
Class 6	**Writing Assignment:** Second draft of Essay 1 due (at least 2 pages) **In Class:** Central claim workshop (Toolkit 4.11, "Revising Your Thesis")	

	Credit-Level Comp	Developmental Cohort Class or Studio (weekly workshop)
Class 7	**Reading Assignment:** Chapter 2 (especially "Process Writing 101") **In Class:** Toolkit 5.13, "Basic MLA Rules"	**In Class:** Revision work, using peer feedback and instructor comments; Toolkit 4.9, "Using Feedback to Revise"
Class 8	**Writing Assignment:** Final draft of Essay 1 due (4 pages) **In-Class Editing:** Use Toolkits 5.8, "How to Refer to Authors and Texts," 5.9, "Using Signal Phrases," and 5.10, "Quotation Format Guidelines," to edit your final draft before turning it in. Start Unit 2 (watch Henry Evans TED talk).	
Unit 2	**Abilities and Disabilities**	
Class 9	**Reading Assignment:** Chapter 7 Joann Ellison Rodgers, "Cognitive Outlaws" Temple Grandin, "Autism and Visual Thought" Brian Eule, "I Was Trapped in My Own Body" **Writing Assignment:** What factors led Close, Greider, Evans, and Grandin to succeed? To what extent are they responsible for their own success? To what extent do they identify others as critical to their achievements? How important do you think that family resources — income, education, time — were to the success that Close, Greider, Evans, and Grandin ultimately achieved?	**In Class:** Reading critically practice: Use selected reading toolkits (1.7–1.10) for this week's readings.

continued >

	Credit-Level Comp	Developmental Cohort Class or Studio (weekly workshop)
Class 10	**Reading Assignment:** Rosemary Mahoney, "Why Do We Fear the Blind?" Udoka Okafor, "On Living with Depression, and the Dangers of Our Culture of Silence" Scott Barry Kaufman, "The Creative Gifts of ADHD" **Writing Assignment:** Although writing about different subjects, Mahoney, Okafor, and Kaufman express concerns about stereotypes attached to people with disabilities. Write a response in which you consider the authors' arguments, answering the following questions: What are the writers' main points? Why are the main points significant? (That is, why are these points worth making? Why are they important to the writers?) What are the two or three most compelling points of evidence or logic the authors offer in support? Are they successful in making the case that stereotypes about disabilities exist and are problematic? Why or why not? (1½–2 pages total; answer in paragraph form)	
Class 11	**Writing Assignment:** First draft of Essay 2 due (at least 2 pages) **In Class:** Discussion workshop (Toolkit 2.12, "Discussion and Analysis")	**In Class:** Responding to the Essay 2 prompt, drafting, and revising
Class 12	**Writing Assignment:** Second draft of Essay 2 due (at least 3–4 pages) **In Class:** Toolkit 2.6, "Quote Sandwiches"; peer review	

Sample ALP/Co-Requisite Model Course Schedule ◆ **19**

	Credit-Level Comp	*Developmental Cohort Class or Studio (weekly workshop)*
Class 13	**Writing Assignment:** Toolkit 4.11, "Revising Your Thesis" **In Class:** Toolkit 3.7, "Topic Sentences"	**In Class:** Create a personal editing checklist (Toolkit 5.14, "Creating a Personal Editing Checklist") based on teacher feedback on Essay 1; use as part of the revision of Essay 2.
Unit 3	**Immigration**	
Class 14	**Writing Assignment:** Final draft of Essay 2 due (4 pages) **In-Class Editing:** [Based on sentence-level issues instructor has noticed in prior drafts, assign one or more of the toolkits from sections 5 and 6 to the entire class or to individual students or groups of students.] Start Unit 3. (Complete and then discuss the "Before You Read" activity for John F. Kennedy, "Why They Came.")	
Class 15	**Reading Assignment:** Chapter 6 introduction: "Dreams and Anxieties" Firoozeh Dumas, "The 'F Word'" Nadia Mustafa and Jeff Chu, "Between Two Worlds" **Writing Assignment:** What do the individual perspectives of Dumas and the people Mustafa and Chu interview help us to understand about the experiences of immigrants? Drawing on the context provided by the Chapter 6 introduction, how do these narratives and examples reflect dreams and/or anxieties? (1½–2 pages total)	**In Class:** Toolkit 2.10, "Making Connections between Texts"

continued >

	Credit-Level Comp	*Developmental Cohort Class or Studio (weekly workshop)*
Class 16	**Reading Assignment:** John F. Kennedy, "Why They Came" Jose Antonio Vargas, "My Life as an Undocumented Immigrant" **Writing Assignment:** Kennedy and Vargas offer two narratives about immigration, one collective and the other personal, focused on different periods of time, and written with different motives. Consider the goals of each writer and how these shaped the way in which each presented immigration and the experience of immigrants. Reflect on the most surprising similarities and differences in their narratives. Taken together, what do they help us understand about immigration? (1½–2 pages total)	
Class 17	**Reading Assignment:** Joe DeGuzman, "Targets of Caricature: Irish Americans in Nineteenth-Century America" Isabel Wilkerson, "The Epic Story of America's Great Migration" **Writing Assignment:** Toolkit 2.9, "Comparing and Contrasting Ideas"	**In Class:** Continue working with making connections between articles in preparation for Essay 3 draft.
Class 18	**Writing Assignment:** Rough draft of Essay 3 due. If you are stuck, try Toolkit 2.2, "Directed Brainstorming." **In Class:** Peer review for Essay 3	
Class 19	**Writing Assignment:** Second draft of Essay 3 due (at least 2 pages) **In Class:** Organization workshop (Toolkit 3.6, "Purpose Outline")	**In Class:** Work on organization using Toolkit 3.2, "Clustering," 3.3, "Scissors and Tape," or 3.4, "Color-Coding," to get a better sense of your draft, what it does, and what it's missing at this stage.

	Credit-Level Comp	*Developmental Cohort Class or Studio (weekly workshop)*
Class 20	**Writing Assignment:** Final draft of Essay 3 due **In Class:** Start Unit 4 (social media presence self-assessment).	
Unit 4	**Social Media**	
Class 21	**Reading Assignment:** Josh Rose, "How Social Media Is Having a Positive Impact on Our Culture" Andrea Shea, "Facebook Envy: How the Social Network Affects Our Self-Esteem" **Writing Assignment:** Compare the ideas of Shea's sources to Rose's ideas. How are they similar? How are they different? How do Rose's and Shea's sources' different interests and situations shape their perspectives on social media use?	**In Class:** Continue to practice active reading strategies and work with assigned readings.
Class 22	**Reading Assignment:** Jon Ronson, "'Overnight, Everything I Loved Was Gone': The Internet Shaming of Lindsey Stone" Lindy West, "What Happened When I Confronted My Cruelest Troll" **Writing Assignment:** Choose one from the following options: 1. Would Josh Rose see West's experiences as evidence that the Internet creates intimacy? Support your position with evidence from each article. 2. Return to the explanation West's troll offers for his behavior. How might it compare to the findings of Andrea Shea's sources about the Internet and self-esteem? Support your position with evidence from each article.	

continued >

	Credit-Level Comp	Developmental Cohort Class or Studio (weekly workshop)
	3. Compare and contrast the ways that Lindsey Stone and Lindy West responded to their Internet tormentors. How did they approach their problems differently? What do their experiences and choices help us understand about the digital age? Explain and support your position with evidence from each article.	
Class 23	**Reading Assignment:** Julian B. Gewirtz and Adam B. Kern, "Escaping Digital Histories" Amy Tan, "Personal Errata" **Writing Assignment:** Answer "Navigating the Intersections" question 1 for Tan.	**In Class:** Mechanics week: Work on select toolkits from sections 5 and 6 that address common or individual sentence-level problems.
Class 24	**Writing Assignment:** Rough draft of Essay 4 due (2 pages) **In Class:** Peer review of Essay 4	
Classes 25 and 26	**Writing Assignment:** Revised, mid-process draft of Essay 4 due at your conference (3 pages)	**In Class:** Revision work: Toolkit 4.12, "Strengthening Evidence and Examples"
Class 27	**Writing Assignment:** Final draft of Essay 4 due (4–5 pages) *Important:* Bring to class a copy of one of the essays you are planning to revise for your portfolio (one whose support and development you would like to improve). **In Class:** Portfolio revision workshop (support/discussion) Section 2 toolkits as needed	

	Credit-Level Comp	Developmental Cohort Class or Studio (weekly workshop)
Class 28	**Writing Assignment:** Continue to work on your portfolio. *Important:* Bring to class a copy of one of the essays you are planning to revise for your portfolio (one whose organization you would like to improve). **In Class:** Portfolio revision workshop (organization) Section 3 toolkits as needed	
Final exam period	**Writing Assignment:** Portfolio due	

*For more information on teaching a co-requisite model course, please see pp. 106–25.

Sample Traditional Composition/College Writing Course Schedule

[Individual instructor information: name, office location and hours, e-mail address, section number, and semester identifier]

Course Description

A workshop course to develop reading and writing abilities through frequent writing assignments based on critical responses to diverse readings that address compelling contemporary questions. Emphasis is on the writing process — prewriting, drafting, revising, using peer and teacher critique, editing, and proofreading. Four essays are required, including a documented essay that requires research. Evaluation is partly based on a portfolio of revised writing.

Course Outcomes

By the end of the course students will:

- Gain rhetorical knowledge related to writing tasks, developing a sense of how to negotiate purpose, audience, context, and conventions as they compose a variety of texts for different situations.

- Develop critical thinking abilities in analyzing, synthesizing, interpreting, and evaluating ideas, information, situations, and texts.

- Experience and gain facility in writing as a process, with particular attention to drafting, revising and editing through a variety of methods, including those that are conducted alone and in collaboration with other writers.

- Develop competency in successful academic essay writing, with particular attention on the following elements: focus, development, discussion, organization, and clarity. Students will therefore be able to:

  o Generate a compelling thesis

  o Develop and support a thesis with appropriate evidence and discussion

  o Organize writing in a sequence that is rhetorically effective

  o Evaluate, analyze, and integrate secondary material appropriately

  o Understand and correct surface-level writing problems, including grammar, usage, and punctuation.

Course Expectations

- Students will complete all reading assignments and all short and long writing assignments.

- Students will attend class regularly and be active participants during class discussions and collaborative activities.
- Students will be academically honest, following the university's Academic Honesty Policy.

Evaluation

Reading Questions	10%
Writing Toolkits	10%
Essay 1	10%
Essay 2	15%
Essay 3	15%
Essay 4	15%
Writing Portfolio	25%

Schedule of Reading and Writing

Week 1: Introduction

Unit 1—Immigration: America's Great Story

Day 1:

Read: Chapter 1, "Getting Active: An Approach to Successful College Reading"

Read: Introduction to Chapter 6, "Dreams and Anxieties"

Write: Complete image response.

Day 2:

Read: John F. Kennedy, "Why They Came" (follow directions in "Before You Read" and "As You Read")

Write: Answer questions 1, 3, and 5 in "Mapping the Reading" and questions 1 and 3 in "Discussing and Thinking Critically about the Reading."

Read: Joe DeGuzman, "Targets of Caricature: Irish Americans in Nineteenth-Century America" (follow directions in "Before You Read" and "As You Read")

Write: Answer questions 1, 4, and 5 in "Discussing and Thinking Critically about the Reading," answer question 2 in "Navigating the Intersections," and complete Toolkit 1.8, "Decoding Reports," or 1.10, "Decoding Arguments," as appropriate, to analyze either Kennedy or DeGuzman.

Week 2:

Day 1:

Read: Isabel Wilkerson, "The Epic Story of America's Great Migration" (follow directions in "Before You Read" and "As You Read")

Write: Answer questions 1–5 in "Mapping the Reading," question 4 in "Discussing and Thinking Critically about the Reading," and one question of your choice in "Navigating the Intersections."

Read: Firoozeh Dumas, "The 'F Word'"

Write: Answer question 5 in "Discussing and Thinking Critically about the Reading" and complete Toolkit 1.3, "Summarizing," using Wilkerson.

Day 2:

Read: Jose Antonio Vargas, "My Life as an Undocumented Immigrant" (follow directions in "Before You Read" and "As You Read")

Write: Answer question 4 in "Mapping the Reading" and questions 1 and 4 in "Discussing and Thinking Critically about the Reading."

Read: Chapter 2, "Breaking It Down"

Write: Complete Toolkits 2.1, "Basic Brainstorming," and 2.2, "Directed Brainstorming," in response to this assignment: take one issue related to immigration and draw upon the readings to discuss how that issue is shaped by the past. *(Instructors: See p. 99 of the IM for full assignment.)*

Week 3:

Day 1:

Write: Exploratory draft (3–4 pages) of Essay 1

In Class: Toolkits 3.1, "Keys to Organization," and 3.3, "Scissors and Tape"

Day 2:

Write: Complete Toolkits 2.4, "Drafting a Thesis," and 2.7, "Drafting the Introduction"; then revise your essay for a mid-process draft of Essay 1.

In Class: Peer review (Toolkits 4.2, "Peer Review Guidelines," and 4.3, "'Basic Checklist' Peer Review")

Week 4:

Day 1:

In Class: Toolkits 6.14, "Reading Aloud," and 6.15, "Ten Common Sentence-Level Mistakes."

Write: Complete Toolkits 5.1, "Document Design Basics," and 5.2, "The Good Enough Title," in advance of revising your essay to complete a final draft of Essay 1.

Unit 2 — Words: Sticks and Stones?

Day 2:

Read: Introduction to Chapter 11, "Word Choice and Perception"

Write: Complete image response.

Read: Shanelle Matthews, "The B-Word" (follow directions in "Before You Read" and "As You Read")

Write: Answer questions 1 and 4 in "Mapping the Reading" and question 1 in "Navigating the Intersections."

Read: Steven A. Holmes, "Why the N-Word Doesn't Go Away" (follow directions in "Before You Read" and "As You Read")

Write: Answer questions 1–5 in "Discussing and Thinking Critically about the Reading" and question 1 in "Navigating the Intersections" and complete Toolkit 1.13, "Evaluating Arguments," with either Bridges or Holmes.

Week 5:

Day 1:

Read: Charles Garcia, "Why 'Illegal Immigrant' Is a Slur" (follow directions in "Before You Read" and "As You Read")

Write: Answer questions 1–4 in "Discussing and Thinking Critically about the Reading" and question 1 in "Navigation the Intersections."

Read: Anat Shenker-Osorio, "Do You Think the Poor Are Lazy?" (follow directions in "Before You Read" and "As You Read")

Write: Answer questions 3 and 4 in "Discussing and Thinking Critically about the Reading" and complete Toolkit 1.3, "Summarizing," to prepare a summary of Shenker-Osorio's essay.

Day 2:

Write: Complete an exploratory draft (3–4 pages) of Essay 2 in which you compare and analyze the arguments made by two or more of the authors in this chapter to determine whether language reform simply covers up a social problem or whether it helps solve a social problem. *(Instructors: See p. 105 of the IM for full essay assignment.)* Complete Toolkit 3.5, "Reverse Outline," after you have completed your draft.

Week 6:

Day 1:

Write: Mid-process draft of Essay 2 due

In Class: Peer review (Toolkit 4.6, "Conversational Peer Review"); Toolkit 3.8, "A Checklist for Transitional Expressions"

Write: Complete Toolkits 2.4, "Drafting a Thesis," and 2.7, "Drafting the Introduction," in advance of revising your essay to complete a mid-process draft of your essay.

In Class: Peer review (Toolkits 4.1, "Tackling Revision," and 4.4, "Peer Review for Essay Development"); Toolkit 4.9, "Using Feedback to Revise"

Day 2:

Write: Continue working on your draft.

In Class: Toolkit 4.8, "Peer Review for Clarity," and select two toolkits from sections 5 and 6 to strengthen your essay

Week 7:

Unit 3 — Twenty-First-Century Gender: When It Matters and When It Doesn't

Day 1:

Write: Final draft of Essay 2

Read: Introduction to Chapter 8, "Gender in the Twenty-First Century"

Read: Matt Duron, "My Son Wears Dresses; Get Over It" (follow directions in "Before You Read" and "As You Read")

Write: Answer questions 2 and 3 in "Discussing and Thinking Critically about the Reading" and question 1 or 2 in "Navigating the Intersections."

Day 2:

Read: Sarah Showfety, "Field Guide to the Tomboy: High Heels and Pink? No Way" (follow directions in "Before You Read" and "As You Read")

Write: Answer questions 1 and 2 in "Discussing and Thinking Critically about the Reading" and question 1 in "Navigating the Intersections."

Read: Jennifer Finney Boylan, "A Life in Two Genders" (follow directions in "Before You Read" and "As You Read")

Write: Answer questions 1 and 2 in "Discussing and Thinking Critically about the Reading" and question 1 or 2 in "Navigating the Intersections."

Week 8:

Day 1:

Read: Andrew Romano, "Why We Need to Reimagine Masculinity" (follow directions in "Before You Read" and "As You Read")

Write: Answer questions 1–5 in "Mapping the Reading."

Read: Theodore R. Johnson III, "Chivalry, Feminism, and the Black Community" (follow directions in "Before You Read" and "As You Read")

Write: Answer question 2 in "Navigating the Intersections."

Read: Hailey Yook, "Chivalry Isn't Dead, but It Should Be" (follow directions in "Before You Read" and "As You Read")

Write: Answer question 1 in "Navigating the Intersections."

Day 2:

Write: This chapter takes up the issue of whether gender roles are becoming blurred, revised, or replaced. While some people welcome these changes, others are upset by them. Write an essay in which you explore *how* and *why* some people feel uncomfortable with gender roles that are unclear or unfixed.

Toolkit 2.6, "Quote Sandwiches," using one of the essays you intend to use for your essay

Exploratory draft of Essay 3

In Class: Toolkit 3.5, "Reverse Outline," or Toolkit 3.6, "Purpose Outline"

Week 9:

Day 1:

Write: Toolkit 2.12, "Discussion and Analysis," and mid-process draft of Essay 3

In Class: Peer review and Toolkit 4.9, "Using Feedback to Revise"

Day 2:

Write: Final draft of Essay 3

Unit 4 — Abilities and Disabilities: Are They Linked?

Read: Introduction to Chapter 7, "Abilities and Disabilities: Are They Linked?"

Week 10:

Day 1:

Read: Temple Grandin, "Autism and Visual Thought" (follow directions in "Before You Read" and "As You Read")

Write: Answer question 2 in "Mapping the Reading" and question 1 in "Discussing and Thinking Critically about the Reading."

Read: Brian Eule, "I Was Trapped in My Own Body" (follow directions in "Before You Read" and "As You Read")

Write: Answer questions 2 and 3 in "Discussing and Thinking Critically about the Reading."

Read: Scott Barry Kaufman, "The Creative Gifts of ADHD" (follow directions in "Before You Read" and "As You Read")

Write: Answer question 5 in "Mapping the Reading," question 3 in "Discussing and Thinking Critically about the Reading," and question 1 in "Navigating the Intersections."

Day 2:

Read: Rosemary Mahoney, "Why Do We Fear the Blind?" (follow directions in "Before You Read" and "As You Read")

Write: Answer question 2 in "Discussing and Thinking Critically about the Reading" and question 2 in "Navigating the Intersections."

Read: Joann Ellison Rodgers, "Cognitive Outlaws" (follow directions in "Before You Read" and "As You Read")

Write: Answer question 1 in "Mapping the Reading" and question 1 in "Navigating the Intersections."

Read: Udoka Okafor, "On Living with Depression, and the Dangers of Our Culture of Silence" (follow directions in "Before You Read" and "As You Read")

Write: Answer question 4 in "Discussing and Thinking Critically about the Reading" and question 3 in "Navigating the Intersections."

Week 11:

Day 1:

Write: Exploratory draft of Essay 4

In Class: Peer review

Day 2:

Write: Mid-process draft of Essay 4

In Class: Editing (toolkits in sections 5 and 6)

Week 12:

Unit 5 — Portfolio of Revised Essays

Day 1:

Write: Final draft of Essay 4

In Class: Portfolio introduction and review of semester's work

Day 2:

In Class: Portfolio planning and revision workshop

Week 13:

Day 1:

In Class: Portfolio work and revision workshop

Day 2:

In Class: Portfolio work and revision workshop

Portfolio due at final exam day (in lieu of exam).

Portfolio Assignment

What Is the Portfolio?

A portfolio is a collection of a writer's work. For this class, the collection will consist of two essays and a shorter final essay, "Me as a Writer." This portfolio will reflect your very best work, and to achieve that aim, you will need to revise your essays using the comments made by your instructor and peers and from your own careful rereading of your essays. Finally, you will need to correct and proofread your essays for clarity of prose: grammar, usage, mechanics, and style. You should review toolkit sections 5 and 6, though you will also be directed to specific ones to work with. This is your final chance to demonstrate your achievement in expository writing and your readiness to move on.

1. **The Essays.** These revised essays are the most important part of your portfolio. You ought to add substantially to each of your essays. Successful essays will include *several* new paragraphs, a dozen new sentences, and, just as importantly, cutting of words. Selections from toolkit sections 3 and 4 will help you with revision!

2. **Prefaces for Essays.** With each essay you must include a paragraph explaining the changes you've made to your essay. In the portfolio you will include two versions of your essay: the old final draft and the new portfolio version. It might also be useful to put new sections in bold so that your instructor can see your changes.

   Here is an example of a preface:

   In essay four I wrote an entirely new introduction, removed the second example, and greatly expanded the third example. I also worked on the introduction to the quotes, adding content and signal phrases. Finally, I worked really hard to remove all my previous typos and to get rid of the fragments and run-ons. I also fixed my Works Cited page.

3. **Final Essay, "Me as a Writer."** This is a 2-page essay. Consider the following questions to brainstorm possibilities for your topic:

> Who are you as a writer?
>
> What are your strengths and weaknesses?
>
> What characterizes your writing?
>
> What do you like best about your writing?
>
> What is the point of writing?
>
> How has your writing changed over the semester? How has it not changed?
>
> Or, take a longer view: How has your writing changed, or not changed, over your many years of schooling?

In this essay you should demonstrate the skills you have developed. Do not attempt to answer all those brainstorming questions in your actual essay as then you will not have a central claim. Rather, choose your own way to focus your essay and develop it with examples and evidence, as you have learned to do this semester.

4. **Presentation.** Put your portfolio together neatly, in an organized and clear format.

Assessment

Your final portfolio will be assessed using the criteria articulated and discussed all semester. The final grade will be determined primarily based on the quality of the new final drafts you present and secondarily on the improvement you have made through the course of revising your portfolio drafts.

Chapter-by-Chapter Guide for Chapters 4–11

Chapter 4, "Language and Identity: Are We Made with Words?"

Image Response

Taking advantage of the insider perspective, select the accent with which you are most familiar and reflect on the following: Do these associations strike you as valid or invalid? positive or negative? advantageous or disadvantageous? Then, select an accent from an area in which you have not spent much time and reflect similarly on it, this time from the outsider perspective.

This map of regional accents of the United States and the accompanying character judgments reminds us that questions of language and identity are not limited to those with "foreign" accents. It provides a visual representation of how where we live shapes how we speak and how we are seen. The image and response are meant to get students to think about the ways accents are tied to judgments about people. The map also illustrates the chapter introduction's discussion of regional word choices.

Rafael Campo, "The Way of the Dinosaurs"

In this personal narrative, Campo, son of an Italian-American and a Cuban immigrant, describes his childhood desire to "unlearn" Spanish as a way of ensuring success in America. He shares his six-year-old self's elaborate comparison of his Cuban family members with dinosaurs, linking Spanish to prehistory and English with evolution. We have found it useful to discuss whether the young Campo is someone who is trying to remake himself with words.

Suggested Responses to "Mapping the Reading" Questions

1. In this personal narrative, Campo describes a trip to his grandparents' home in Elizabeth, New Jersey. What does he most dislike about visiting his *abuelos*? What does he most like?

   He dislikes the neighborhood with its tenements as well as the dirt and grime of the city of Elizabeth. He dislikes having to pretend not to understand his grandparents when they speak to him in Spanish because it hurts them and also because it means they will share fewer stories with him.

   He appreciates his grandmother's cooking because she always makes a feast for them. He likes the environment of his grandparents' apartment where they play Cuban music and dance and tell stories about Cuba. He likes visiting the Cuban bakery with his grandfather.

2. As his family is driving to Elizabeth, what does the young Campo do so that his father will speak to him in English? Why does he want his father to speak in English?

   Campo uses Spanish curse words or cusswords because he knows his father uses English "whenever anyone in the family got in trouble" (p. 173). Campo does not want to have to practice Spanish because he associates English with success.

3. What jobs do Campo's family members have? How do these jobs help shape the young Campo's perception of English and Spanish?

   His father, who attended college, works for a company that makes aluminum soda cans and plastic toothpaste tubes. His grandfather works in a factory that makes "cheap preformed yellow plastic tables." Campo believes that his grandfather was "forced" to take a factory job because he did not speak English. His grandmother does not work. His Italian-American mother, who seems to have been born in the United States and speaks English, is presented as more cultured and intellectual. His mother works as a substitute teacher in Ramsey and is also an artist.

4. Review the passages about dinosaurs you identified in "As You Read" or note these now. If, as Campo says, his was not the typical young child's interest in dinosaurs, what exactly was his interest in them? What connections or parallels does the six-year-old Campo see between dinosaurs and his family?

   Campo sees multiple connections between his family and dinosaurs. He explains his fascination with dinosaurs by saying "To me, they were like my family, which was not yet extinct the way tyrannosaurus and triceratops were, but still on the verge of being lost forever" (p. 172). He envisions Cuba, his paternal family's homeland, as a primitive space where a few dinosaurs might still remain. Elizabeth, where his grandparents now live, is also associated with "prehistory." Spanish also becomes associated with the primitive past, the "missing link" he has to move on from to evolve or succeed in the world.

5. What does the six-year-old Campo believe he will gain by "*unlearning* Spanish"?

    Although he was not born in Cuba, Campo believes "unlearning Spanish" will help him "leave Cuba behind and become truly American." He sees English as being essential to his success, to being able to fit into his new suburban community, to leaving the "primitive" behind, and to the praise of his knowledge he receives while at the Museum of Natural History.

Arthur Chu, "Breaking Out the Broken English"

The voice-over actor and *Jeopardy!* champion Arthur Chu writes about his experience speaking English without an accent and his work to cultivate a neutral "announcer voice." The son of immigrants who spoke with an accent, he, like most other "hyphenated Americans" (e.g., Mexican-American, Irish-American) born in the United States, does not. He reflects on the power that speaking English gives him and also the judgments that he is subjected to. Ironically, as an actor Chu is often required to speak in broken English to play a role. Like Campo, Chu is someone who chooses to perfect his English, seeing it as a way of reinforcing his identity as an American. Yet, because he looks Asian, people expect him to speak with a Chinese accent, raising questions of how essential speaking a family language or not is to identity, an issue that is addressed in López's article as well.

Suggested Responses to "Mapping the Reading" Questions

1. What is Chu's accent (that is, the one he uses normally and not when acting, for example)? Find and quote the passage in which you see him most clearly describing this accent.

    Chu describes his normal accent as "neutral." He claims that "[m]ost Chinese-Americans have a pitch-perfect 'invisible' accent for wherever they live" (p. 179), but he has taken this further, developing an announcer voice, free of any noticeable accent. He explains, "of my Chinese-American colleagues I'm one of the few who's taken the quest to develop a perfectly 'neutral' voice so far that I now market said voice to produce corporate videos and voice-mail greetings" (p. 179).

    Alternate response: He writes, "After a lifetime of rehearsals and training, the 'announcer voice' *is* my voice, and the only reliable way to sound 'less announcer-y' is to put on an accent that isn't mine, be it Brooklyn, Biloxi or Beijing" (p. 181).

2. Why is Chu uncomfortable performing roles that involve speaking in a "Chinese accent"?

    He finds them "embarrassing" because they stereotype people; the "Chinese accent" is related to schoolyard teasing or ridicule. Chu cites the "'ching-chong, ching-chong' schoolyard taunt" (p. 179). Although he believes that Chinese immigrants do have noticeable accents, he feels that Chinese-Americans do not.

3. As a child, how did Chu use his English skills to help his parents?

   He "translated" for them in various interactions with others, such as at customer service desks and in restaurants; he edited his mother's job applications. He was the intermediary in a conversation between his father and a Canadian park ranger, each of whom spoke English in a way incomprehensible to the other.

4. What was the problem with the way Chu spoke in high school, and what did he do to correct it?

   He spoke too perfectly, in both grammar and enunciation. As a remedy, he learned to slur some works and use some slang to sound like a "normal teenager."

5. In what ways does Chu's neutral accent hurt him? In what ways does it help him?

   His neutral accent has created an obstacle to getting some voice-over jobs because it is too perfect as well as being outdated (the proper English of the past). For people who judge him by appearance and expect him to have a Chinese accent, it does not sound "real." In terms of helping him, the neutral accent has given him the power to be understood and has helped him create his identity as an American.

Tracy López, "Non-Spanish-Fluent Latinas: 'Don't Judge Us'"

Tracy López discusses the stigma faced by Latinas who are not fluent in Spanish, placing this lack of fluency in the context of immigration and questioning whether language proficiency is essential to cultural identity. She compiles information from a variety of Latinas, including celebrities, who have faced questions regarding their Latina identity because of their lack of fluency in Spanish. López's article can be used to consider the question of whether speaking a particular language is essential to cultural identity.

Suggested Responses to "Mapping the Reading" Questions

1. What problem does López identify in this article?

   Some Latinas are criticized for not speaking Spanish (either well or at all) and are not considered real Latinas as a result.

2. What are some reasons why Latinas in the United States may not be fluent in Spanish?

   Parents may have decided not to speak Spanish to their children. Historically, some immigrants faced discrimination for not speaking English and therefore made certain that their children could speak English. Other immigrants believed that their children would have more opportunities to succeed if they were fluent in English.

3. According to López and her sources, what are some of the consequences of U.S. Latinas not being fluent in Spanish?

   They can feel insecure or ashamed. They may face criticism from others of Latino descent and may also miss out on opportunities.

4. What common feeling is shared by many of the non-Spanish-fluent Latinas López cites?

   "I am proud of my Latino heritage and I have a desire to learn Spanish, but in the meantime, don't judge me" (p. 185).

5. How is López's report organized? How does she indicate that organization to her readers?

   López's report is organized in sections with headings that convey their individual topics. She begins with historical background and then gives examples of judgment faced by individuals. She follows this with examples of celebrities facing similar criticism and ends with a section that discusses Latina identity and Spanish.

Patricia Rice, "Linguistic Profiling: The Sound of Your Voice May Determine If You Get That Apartment or Not"

Rice reports on a study by Washington University professor John Baugh, who found that many people were able to identify people's race from their voices. This "linguistic profiling" can lead to discrimination as some people whose language is judged unfavorably may lose out on job opportunities, for instance. The article concludes with suggestions for overcoming our tendency to profile in this way. This article introduces a valuable concept, linguistic profiling, that can be used to discuss other articles in the chapter: Does the young Rafael Campo engage in a form of linguistic profiling based on languages rather than accents when he decides English is better than Spanish? Does Arthur Chu face a variation on linguistic profiling when people see him and expect him to speak with a Chinese accent? Are the women Tracy López's reports on subject to a variation on linguistic profiling when they do not speak Spanish as expected? Do Ellen Welty's women who use "wimpy words" face discrimination and judgment because of their word choices?

Suggested Responses to "Mapping the Reading" Questions

1. What is linguistic profiling?

   Linguistic profiling is guessing someone's ethnicity or race based solely on the way he or she speaks.

2. According to Baugh, how does linguistic profiling allow employers and businesses to get around antidiscrimination laws?

   Baugh discovered that some companies screen calls, making guesses at callers' ethnicity and race, and then do not return the calls of those they assume to be of particular groups. This allows companies to get around antidiscrimination laws because they can say they have never met the individuals and therefore cannot be discriminating on race or ethnicity.

3. According to Baugh's studies, how are different accents judged, and what are the consequences of these judgments?

Those with Latino and African American accents received fewer call-backs in Baugh's study, leading to missed opportunities for housing and employment. Those using British upper-class accents were judged more intelligent than General (or Standard) American English speakers. Those with German accents were considered "brilliant."

4. Who are some of the people Baugh identifies as having changed their dialect?

For particular roles, actors may learn to use a particular group's dialect. Professional speakers, such as those involved in broadcasting, adopt General American English or Standard American English.

5. What were the personal experiences that influenced Baugh's choice to study linguistic profiling?

When he was a child, he was aware that his mother changed the way she spoke on the phone depending on whether she was talking to a white person or a black person. As an adult, when he went house hunting in Los Angeles, he realized that some agents were surprised to discover he was black when they met in person after having spoken on the phone. In some cases, at the face-to-face appointment, he was told the house was unavailable.

John Russell Rickford and Russell John Rickford, "Spoken Soul and Standard English"

In this excerpt from the conclusion to their study of Black English, or "Spoken Soul," John Russell Rickford and Russell John Rickford discuss the reasons African Americans continue to use and value Black English even when it may be viewed negatively by some people. In addition, the father-and-son writing team argues for the value and use of Standard English and suggests the need to find a balance between the language of home and community and the language of those in power. While Campo and Chu favor speaking one language (English) as a way of cultivating their identity, Rickford and Rickford point to a middle ground, arguing for *both personal and public language fluency*, discussing the ways that Black English is important to African Americans' identity, while at the same time contending that formal English also is valuable.

Suggested Responses to "Mapping the Reading" Questions

1. What is Rickford and Rickford's view of Black English, or "Spoken Soul"? Where do you see their clearest expression of this view?

"Spoken Soul" is important to African Americans' identity: Although its use is sometimes negatively judged, it connects them to the past and to each other. "The question remains about why Spoken Soul persists despite the negative attitudes toward it, and its speakers, that have been expressed for centuries. The primary answer is its role as a symbol of identity" (p. 192).

2. What is Rickford and Rickford's view of Standard English? Where do you see their clearest expression of this view?

Standard English is a valuable tool in areas such as business, education, state, law, and government. "That mainstream English is essential to our self-preservation is indisputable" (p. 194) or "For in the academies and courthouses and legislatures and business places where policies are made and implemented, [Standard English] is as graceful a weapon as can be found against injustice, poverty, and discrimination" (p. 194).

3. The authors begin this chapter by presenting a dialogue featuring three people. How does this example introduce their topic?

The example features three people using Spoken Soul in a casual, everyday conversation. It allows readers to "hear" Spoken Soul, and it also allows Rickford and Rickford to illustrate their points that Spoken Soul is spoken across generations and that it that allows its users to feel comfortable.

4. According to the Rickfords, who uses Black English, and in what contexts?

African American adults and children of all educational and economic backgrounds use Black English. As the opening example illustrates, they use it in informal conversations and with family members and peers. Researcher Jacquelyn Rahman discovered that some students tailor their language to their audience, speaking Black English to peers, for example. Hip-hop culture and its fans have adopted Black English.

5. Reread the section where the authors refer to and quote Malcolm X. What point does his example help them prove?

Rickford and Rickford praise Malcolm X as someone who was able to master Standard English in order to express himself forcefully and effectively to the larger public. They quote a passage from his *Autobiography,* in which he comes to the realization that he needs to speak Standard English in certain contexts where slang would be misunderstood or else his ideas will be ignored.

Ellen Welty, "Are Your Words Holding You Back?"

In this advice article, Welty asks women to consider what image their words convey, arguing that women often choose "wimpy words" or phrases that can make them less persuasive and less effective speakers. Welty presents examples of the phrases women may use that unintentionally serve to downplay their ideas, suggesting that people's word choice, regardless of accent, can be subject to prejudiced interpretation. This reading presents another angle on the ways people are judged based on their language — here word choice rather than accents or languages.

Suggested Responses to "Mapping the Reading" Questions

1. According to Welty, why is it important for people to be aware of the speech habits they adopt when they are presenting their ideas to others?

   Using self-deprecating speech habits or words can diminish the effectiveness and force of someone's ideas. These habits can lead people to consider and treat speakers as though they are less intelligent or capable.

2. List the speech habits that Welty cautions women against using. Why is each "self-deprecating"?

   Negative phrases ("This is probably a stupid idea but" [p. 197]): These phrases downplay ideas, creating a negative impression before the speaker even shares the idea.

   "Like": This word makes speakers sound "inarticulate and young" (p. 197).

   Apologizing in situations that do not require apologies ("sorry," "oops, sorry," "sorry, my bad" [p. 198]): This makes people seem less assertive.

   Hedges ("I think," "kind of," "sort of" [pp. 198–99]): These phrases downplay ideas, making both speaker and idea sound tentative and timid.

   "Just" (p. 199): This word works to diminish the speaker's role.

   Uptalking: Raising the voice at the ends of sentences, which makes them sound like questions, suggests lack of firmness.

3. What evidence does Welty offer in support of her claim that self-deprecating language negatively influences how women's ideas are received?

   Welty offers information from a psychiatrist, a linguist, a career coach, and other experts who believe self-deprecating language is a problem. She also offers examples of the speech habits in question as well as quotations from "regular" people who have found themselves using them.

4. Advice pieces typically identify a problem, explain why it is worth attention, and offer a solution. How and where do you see Welty taking these steps?

   The article is organized by example, using headings. The first section introduces the issue, with some examples and quotes from sources. In the sections that follow, she provides further examples of the problem and its consequences, along with expert sources, to further establish its importance. She concludes with a chart that offers advice for tackling the problem.

Chapter 5, "Appearance: Who Should Decide What We Look Like?"

Image Response

Look at this image and write two fifty-word paragraphs describing each man's personality, basing your description on what is suggested by the image alone. Then consider the following: How are the two profiles different? What do the two profiles suggest about the types of assumptions people make based on appearance?

Students' responses to this image will likely reveal how they perceive physical fitness. Do they see the very fit, muscular man in the left image as the ideal? Or do they see him as a kind of unattainable model of beauty? The image on the left presents a young man who has extremely large muscles, suggesting many things, including that he is a body builder, a gym-enthusiast, or perhaps a steroid user. Whether or not students see the image on the left as desirable or undesirable will be interesting and indicative of their own points of view.

Alice Randall, "My Soul to Keep, My Weight to Lose"

Novelist and college professor Alice Randall explores her own journey to obesity and her fight to get to a healthy weight. Weight comes on, she explains, from a complicated mix of family history, too much work, and often putting other people first. Although she isn't interested in blaming herself for her weight, or becoming overly obsessed with it, she also thinks Americans, and especially African Americans, can and should look at and address their challenges related to eating and weight. Randall's narrative is useful for opening up issues of weight for personal, familial, and cultural meanings.

Suggested Responses to "Mapping the Reading" Questions

1. What personal insight did Randall discover during her classroom discussion of *Up from Slavery?*

    Discussing Booker T. Washington's lack of knowledge of certain key facts about himself, like the year in which he was born, made Randall realize she didn't know something important about herself: how much she weighed.

2. Randall mentions several reasons for her weight gain. Which reasons does she believe are out of her control? in her control?

    Randall cites "[s]tress, overwork, supersize portions; advertising aimed at keeping us eating; parks and streets not safe for exercise; and the expense of high-quality food coupled with lower wages" (p. 207) as reasons out of her control. Reasons under her control include idolizing and modeling herself after her grandmother, Dear, who was overweight; defying societal standards of beauty that emphasize thinness; sacrificing care of herself to care for others; and working long hours.

3. Randall has decided to change her life and take better care of herself, even if this means taking care of other people a little less. Find a quote that best expresses Randall's decision to change her life.

    "With one in four Black women over 55 having diabetes, four in five Black women overweight, and obesity in danger of overtaking smoking as the number one cause of preventable cancer death, not taking care of myself and taking care of others first wasn't a lifestyle; it was a death style. For me, shifting the shape of my body has been a matter of confronting hard truths about myself, such as realizing that working all the time was killing my unborn grandchildren's grandmother" (p. 208).

    Alternate response: "I've come to understand, after fits and starts and bouts of willful ignorance, that the journey to being fit and healthy can be a sacred one" (p. 208).

4. Explain Randall's point about the connection between obesity and her identity as an African American woman.

    Randall describes African American women as being self-sacrificing; she gives the hypothetical example of a black woman putting the oxygen mask on her child first in an airplane emergency, going against the safety instructions. She writes that she took pride in being "the mule of her family" (p. 208).

5. How does Randall connect the civil rights journey and her journey to a healthier lifestyle?

    Near the end of her narrative, Randall explains that she will walk across the Selma, Alabama, bridge to commemorate the civil rights leaders who faced danger and bodily harm in their efforts to free others and also to commemorate her weight loss, which she presents as a mark of health and love for her community.

Abigail Saguy, "Why We Diet"

Written at the beginning of a new year, when many of us make New Year's resolutions to lose weight, Saguy argues that many of us diet not for health reasons but because we still live in a society that discriminates against overweight and obese people in employment, health care, use of public spaces, and the social sphere — and now more so than ever. Without dismissing many of the benefits of avoiding obesity, Saguy argues for body acceptance.

Suggested Responses to "Mapping the Reading" Questions

1. According to Saguy, what is the difference between why we *say* we diet and why we *actually* diet?

    People claim that they want to lose weight to become healthier, but they really diet to fit in and avoid weight-based discrimination.

2. What is Saguy's message to those of us who are overweight? What is her message to those of us who are not overweight but who judge those who are?

    Saguy asks those who are overweight to think carefully about their reasons before starting a diet. If they want to become healthier, they should take other steps, such as eating better, exercising, spending time with friends, and getting enough sleep. They should also "stand up to intolerance and bigotry in all its various forms, whether racism, sexism, or fatphobia" (p. 212), which is her implicit message to those who judge as well.

3. What are some of the consequences of weight bias that Saguy cites?

    Saguy focuses on the health consequences for heavier women: Being afraid of ridicule may lead them to not exercise publicly, to stay home, to skip regular health care, and to develop eating and body image disorders.

4. What evidence does Saguy present for her claim that weight-based discrimination occurs?

    Saguy cites studies by Yale researchers that indicate increased weight discrimination in the United States as well as studies that "have documented weight bias in employment, healthcare, education and public spaces" (p. 211). She also relates examples of "hogging" that she discovered in her own research and points to media ridicule of heavy women.

5. What evidence does Saguy present for the position that being overweight may not be unhealthy and that being obese is less unhealthy than many people think?

    Saguy cites research that suggests overweight people are less likely to die and that moderately obese people were no less likely to die in a given period.

Jamie Santa Cruz, "Body-Image Pressure Increasingly Affects Boys"

This report describes the increasing body-image pressures faced by boys and young men and presents research data and experts' ideas about the reasons boys are concerned about their weight. Santa Cruz covers not only the issue of eating disorders but also the use of steroids among boys. This reading helps expand students' understanding of appearance issues while also showing that these concerns are not limited to women and girls.

Suggested Responses to "Mapping the Reading" Questions

1. Identify three points of evidence that Santa Cruz presents to support the position that eating and body image disorders are on the rise in boys.

    *   A study published in *JAMA Pediatrics* that indicates boys' concern about being muscular
    *   Changing media depictions of the male body that now emphasize muscularity
    *   Changes in the muscularity represented in action figures marketed to boys

2. Why is the increase in eating and body image disorders in boys a source of concern?

Boys who are concerned about their weight face higher rates of depression and risky behavior such as drug use and binge drinking. In their efforts to achieve a more muscular body type, boys may make unhealthy choices, such as using steroids or other muscle-enhancing substances.

3. What body image do boys want to achieve? Where do they see these images?

Most want to be more muscular. They see these images in the media and in their toys.

4. What are the dangers associated with the use of steroids and even "natural" supplements designed to increase muscle mass?

Santa Cruz reports that "[l]ong-term use of steroids is associated with depression, rage attacks, suicidal tendencies, and cardiomyopathies. And the negative effects can be particularly significant for adolescents, since their bodies are going through a period of major growth and development" (p. 215). Because they are unregulated, natural supplements can have dangerous ingredients.

5. Why do body image problems in boys often go unrecognized?

Their symptoms or effects are different than those that girls present: Girls with body image problems want to be thin and can be identified as underweight, but boys want to gain weight, so they may not show any attention-grabbing symptoms.

Kevin Fanning, "One Man Explains Why He Swears by Wearing Spanx"

The author discusses his discovery of Spanx, the body-slimming shapewear that women and now also men turn to as a way to look and feel better about themselves. Fanning writes: "The Spanx transformation is as much mental as it is physical" (p. 219). His personal narrative raises the question of whether we can in fact change our appearances, our self-image, and how we feel about ourselves by what we wear. Fanning's narrative can be paired with Santa Cruz's article about boys' body image concerns. Although he does not use steroids or engage in other risky behaviors, Fanning is concerned enough about his appearance to take steps to change it.

Suggested Responses to "Mapping the Reading" Questions

1. How would you describe Fanning's body image both before and while wearing Spanx? Identify the passages that reveal to you how he feels about his body.

Before wearing Spanx, Fanning was anxious and embarrassed about his appearance. He writes, "My weight has fluctuated wildly since then, and there've been times when it was really bad and times when objectively I might have looked okay. But mentally I have never come to a place of acceptance. No matter what I weigh, how strict my diet is, or whether I'm going to the gym or not, I look in the mirror and think: *I'm so, so sorry, world*" (p. 217).

While wearing Spanx, he feels more confident: "I spent the rest of the day learning to appreciate the new me, who stood tall and smiled at strangers. I felt like the type of person who could possibly be fun at parties. I was already starting to forget the old me, the lumpy and misshapen me who never stood up straight and whose shirt buttons continually puckered, and who prayed daily the castle wall of his jeans could withstand the attack of his encroaching waistline" (p. 219).

2. Why does Fanning put off buying Spanx?

He is concerned about the expense and the fact that shapewear is not considered mainstream men's clothing.

3. According to Fanning, what problems can diet and exercise help with? What issues can't they address?

He believes diet and exercise can help with physical issues like weight, but they can't help with mental, self-image issues.

4. Why does Fanning think that his experience wearing Spanx makes him know what it is like to be a woman, and what is his wife's response?

He writes that he believes that the tightness and restrictiveness of the shirt helps him understand his wife's desire to take off her bra at the end of the day because it's so uncomfortable. From that connection he then tells her that he knows what it's like to be a woman, which his wife rejects for the obvious reason that there is a lot more to being a woman than wearing uncomfortable undergarments.

5. According to Fanning, what does wearing Spanx all day do for him?

While it makes him look thinner, it also transforms him mentally. He gains self-confidence because he does not worry about what people think of his body.

Sharon Haywood, "How Body Modification Ended the War against My Body"

The author explores why she values body modification, such as piercing and tattooing. In telling her story, she argues against popular beliefs that people turn to body piercings and other body modifications because they hate themselves or enjoy physical pain. Rather, it's a way for the author to create herself and take control of who she is. Haywood is concerned about her physical appearance (weight) and presents her body modifications as a method to find healing and make peace with her body.

Suggested Responses to "Mapping the Reading" Questions

1. Why does Haywood decide to remove her belly ring?

   The belly ring was a symbol of Haywood's desire to make peace with her belly, to prettify the part of her body that was the source of much concern. Haywood decides to remove her belly ring because she has accomplished her goal.

2. How would you describe the author's body image? Identify the passages that reveal how she feels about her body.

   Growing up, she hated her body: "Beyond my rotund toddler years, I grew into a lean and muscular frame, but by the age of ten I began to battle my body. I would slap my dense calves (composed of solid muscle) and watch in revulsion as they wiggled. My childhood best friend and I had regular body-hating sessions on my front lawn, where we would examine our respective 'gigantic' thighs. But it was always my belly rolls—or what I perceived as rolls—that were the primary target of my disdain and disgust. It was the core of myself that I raged against" (p. 222). "[During adolescence] I detested myself even more. Looking in the mirror was torturous and would provoke anxiety and despair. I continually sucked in my stomach" (p. 222).

3. How does Haywood use body modification—tattooing and body piercing—to help her, in her words, end her "war with [her] body"?

   Body modification for Haywood is a way to heal and to express self-love for her body. It helps her to look at her body, which had greatly troubled her during her eating disorders, with compassion rather than hatred.

4. For Haywood, what is the connection between body modification and eating disorders? between body modification and sexual assault?

   For Haywood, body modification is a method for dealing with emotional pain that is tied to her experiences and feelings about her body. An eating disorder is a physical problem caused by emotional pain, and sexual assault is a physical experience of violation that causes emotional pain. In both of these experiences, the physical pain of body modification, which Haywood chose on her own (rather than through coercion) helps her to emotionally heal from these damaging experiences.

5. Explain the symbolic meaning that body modification holds for the author by discussing two specific examples of body modification that Haywood undertakes.

   She sees the navel ring as a way to make peace with her belly, the focal point of her low body self-image and eating disorders. Her lotus tattoo is a symbol of rebirth following her battle with eating disorders.

Lauren Shields, "My Year of Modesty"

For nine months, Lauren Shields adopted a modest style of dress and adornment, drawing on Muslim, Jewish, and Christian modesty rules to develop her own "Lauren style." She discovered that rejecting contemporary expectations of wardrobe and makeup caused some people to treat her differently, but it was also liberating. Shields's narrative raises questions about the pressures to conform to a certain look and how those who fail to conform are treated. Like Fanning's article, it can be used to raise questions about the transformative power of clothes for their wearers.

Suggested Responses to "Mapping the Reading" Questions

1. What reasons does Shields give for deciding to conduct her modesty experiment?

   Working as a receptionist in New York City, Shields hates having to be fashionable every day. After hearing a woman discuss the hijab, she confronts how concerned she is with looking good and decides to try another method.

2. How does Shields compare and contrast the women she observes around Fifth Avenue, Manhattan, with those she observes in Williamsburg, Brooklyn?

   The women around Fifth Avenue are very fashion focused: fit, with highly styled hair, makeup, high heels, and stylish clothes. They are wearing a uniform of sorts. The Hasidic women, in their long skirts and headscarves, are stylish but individual. Shields believes they are focused on something more important than fashion trends.

3. What is the "Beauty Suit"?

   Also called the "Grown-Up Suit," the "Beauty Suit" is the fashionable uniform that Shields wears to her receptionist job. It is stylish, trendy, and well-put together rather than comfortable.

4. Returning to your "As You Read" notes or making some now, what epiphanies (or sudden insights) does Shields's experiment inspire? What lessons does she learn from her experiment?

   She learns that she had previously been overly focused on her looks. She gets more done without having to worry about putting on makeup, etc. She learned that some people will ignore her but that others will listen to her more intently. She learns that it's important not to make appearance the "cornerstone" of oneself.

5. How differently is Shields treated when she wears modest clothes than when she wears her "Grown-Up Suit"?

   Some people ignore her, but others listen to her more intently.

Chapter 6, "Immigration: America's Great Story"

Image Response

How does the illustrator portray immigrants? Choose two or three figures to study more closely: Describe each figure, and then discuss the illustrator's possible intentions in presenting the figures in this way. What feelings do you think viewers are being encouraged to have?

This image clearly shows new immigrants aboard a ship, gazing toward New York and the United States. They point and gesture, talking among themselves or simply looking hopefully toward the land. The immigrants are wearing different types of clothing, suggesting, perhaps, that they are not all from the same place. With the Statue of Liberty in the background, there can be no doubt that they are approaching Ellis Island, the most famous landing place for immigrants. The immigrants' faces are hopeful, wistful, or excited; no one looks angry, unhappy, or disappointed. Viewers are encouraged to see immigrants as calm but eager, appreciative, and very pleased to be coming to the United States. Overall, it is a positive image of immigrants and immigration.

John F. Kennedy, "Why They Came"

In this short reading, the thirty-fifth president of the United States, the son of Irish immigrants himself and a student of American history, describes the hopes and hardships of American immigrants, acknowledging challenges for both immigrants and the country as he urges Americans to embrace and celebrate their immigrant history and future. Kennedy provides a historical perspective on immigration and makes the argument that immigrants are great contributors to America.

Suggested Responses to "Mapping the Reading" Questions

1. According to Kennedy, what are the three main reasons immigrants come to the United States?

   Kennedy writes that most immigrants came to the United States to escape religious persecution, political oppression, or economic hardship.

2. What were the physical challenges and hardships that nineteenth-century immigrants experienced to travel to the United States?

   First, immigrants had to endure simply getting to the port where ships would take them to the United States. Before and during the trip, many immigrants suffered illnesses, accidents, storms, and even attacks by outlaws. The ships were crowded, subject to harsh weather and the often-poor navigation skills of their captains. Food and water were limited. One in ten died from malnourishment and diseases such as cholera, yellow fever, smallpox, and dysentery.

3. Once immigrants arrived, what challenges and difficulties did they commonly face, according to Kennedy?

Upon their arrival, immigrants typically had no reserves of food or money. Having no time to rest after the exhausting trip, they had to immediately start the hard job of finding employment so they could buy food and, eventually, pay for housing.

4. Kennedy mentions many specific groups; list the nationalities that are represented. What continent or region of the world do most of these people come from?

Most of the people Kennedy mentions came from Europe—England, Russia, Germany, Italy, Ireland, and Hungary. He also mentions immigrants coming from Cuba.

5. What is Kennedy's attitude toward immigrants? Identify two or three passages where he most clearly shows his attitude. (You may wish to consult your "As You Read" notes.)

Answers will vary but may include the following:

Kennedy admires the immigrants for their significant role in growing the American economy.

He writes, "Those who came from countries with advanced political and economic institutions brought with them faith in those institutions and experience in making them work. They also brought technical and managerial skills, which contributed greatly to economic growth in the new land. Above all, they helped give America the extraordinary social mobility which is the essence of an open society" (p. 239).

Later on he notes, "A sprawling continent lay before [the immigrant], and he had only to weld it together by canals, by railroads, and by roads. If he failed to achieve the dream for himself, he could still retain it for his children" (p. 239).

Joe DeGuzman, "Targets of Caricature: Irish Immigrants in Nineteenth-Century America"

Joe DeGuzman highlights images from nineteenth-century periodicals that reflect unfriendly, stereotypical views of the newly arrived Irish; in these cartoons and sketches, native-born Americans, who were typically Protestant, depict the Irish as uncivilized, unskilled, and impoverished. Although readers today may be offended by these stereotypes of the Irish, these images make clear that these ideas were held by many in the nineteenth century, raising questions about whether similar stereotypes are held about today's immigrants. This article and its collection of images can be used to explore the ways in which views of immigrants have been historically conflicted.

Suggested Responses to "Mapping the Reading" Questions

1. According to DeGuzman, who were nativists? What fears did they have about the Irish immigrants? (You may wish to consult your "As You Read" notes.)

    Nativists are Americans who were born in the country and hold anti-immigrant beliefs. Nativists believed that the Irish immigrants threatened their way of life, claiming that the Catholic Irish didn't have their Protestant work ethic, for example.

2. What stereotypes did Irish immigrants face in the 1800s?

    They were stereotyped as drinking excessively, being ape-like, and behaving violently. They were perceived to be less educated because they spoke English differently than Anglo Americans.

3. What was the Know Nothing party, and what did it stand for?

    The Know Nothing party was a nineteenth-century pro-Protestant (anti-Catholic) political party that was formed on an anti-immigrant platform. Its members proposed laws against Catholics and immigrants, and they inspired protests that were violent and even deadly.

4. According to DeGuzman, how is contemporary American response to immigrants similar to nineteenth-century American responses?

    Nativist, anti-immigrant beliefs exist today, just as they did in the nineteenth century. The difference is that today it is not the Irish who are subject to anti-immigrant prejudice and hostility but other new immigrant groups.

5. Closely study one of the cartoons that DeGuzman includes in his article. What do you find most striking about it, and why?

    Answers will vary.

Isabel Wilkerson, "The Epic Story of America's Great Migration"

Pulitzer Prize–winning journalist Isabel Wilkerson writes of the journey of almost six million African Americans from the American South to the North and West, seeking a better life. While this is an experience of "migration" rather than "immigration," the stories Wilkerson tells allow readers to see that much about African Americans' journey to the North is very similar to immigrants' journeys to America from other countries. How does our understanding of the African American experience change when we consider that this group of Americans has experienced both enslavement and also a kind of immigration? How do the experiences of immigrants and migrants inform each other?

Suggested Responses to "Mapping the Reading" Questions

1. According to Wilkerson, what is the Great Migration? When, where, and why did it occur?

   The Great Migration refers to the period between 1915 and 1970 when six million African Americans moved from the rural South to the industrial North. The movement was inspired by a desire to escape the Jim Crow laws in the South and to find better employment opportunities in urban environments, which the feudal caste system of the South couldn't provide.

2. What opportunities did migrants have in the North that they did not have in the South?

   The North offered more modern, higher-paying industrial and commercial jobs.

3. What hardships did migrants face in first journeying to the North and then living there? (You may wish to consult your "As You Read" notes.)

   Coming out of the feudal caste system that remained after the Civil War when slavery became illegal, African Americans had few resources or opportunities, and many migrants had few of the skills required for the jobs that they wanted in the North. Outside Jim Crow territory, the migrants continued to face racism in the North, making it difficult to find job opportunities from mostly white employers.

4. According to Wilkerson, how was the experience of *migration* from South to North by African Americans similar to the experience of *immigration* by people from outside the United States? How was it different?

   Like immigrants, African Americans built their lives around people and churches that were familiar to them from back home. Similarly, African Americans struggled with prejudice, poverty, and unexpected hardships once they were finally able to make it to the place they had dreamed of for many years. They passed on to their children the values of the Old Country, while challenging them to be successful in the New World. At the same time, Wilkerson notes that the migrants' experience differed from that of the immigrants because African Americans came from the South, which was already part of the United States, and so these migrants specifically rejected the label of immigrant. Most of the migrants were natural born citizens whose ancestors helped to build the country.

5. How were George and Ida Mae Gladney's experiences in the North both similar to and different from their experiences in the South?

   In the North, George and Ida Mae continued to experience racism, especially from prospective employers who didn't want to hire blacks. Although George's assembly line job at a Campbell Soup plant was the first indoor job he had ever had, his duties were just as mind numbing as when he was picking cotton in the South. The major difference was that George's new job allowed him to earn a living wage. Similarly, Ida Mae and other black women competed with immigrant women for servant and clerical work, which was difficult, but ultimately Ida Mae was able to find moderate financial success as well.

Firoozeh Dumas, "The 'F Word'"

Dumas reflects on her childhood decision to go by the name "Julie" instead of Firoozeh, arguing that "simplifying one's life in the short run only complicates it in the long run" (p. 258). While humorous, this essay raises questions about just how much American society asks its citizens to conform to Anglo cultures. It can also be used to explore changing attitudes toward so-called ethnic names.

Suggested Responses to "Mapping the Reading" Questions

1. Why does Dumas change her name from Firoozeh to Julie?

   Dumas wants to have a simple name that is easy for Americans to pronounce. She doesn't want to feel alienated by people simply because of her foreign name.

2. Why does she change her name back to Firoozeh?

   Dumas feels like her life became "one big knot" (p. 260), particularly when friends who knew her as Firoozeh started to meet those who knew her as Julie. She compares this experience to that of a soap opera character who has an "evil twin" (p. 260), noting that she no longer wanted to have a double identity.

3. In what ways do the author's names — both Firoozeh and Julie — create a barrier in her interactions with other people?

   The name has caused barriers at all stages of Dumas's life. Growing up, Firoozeh's schoolmates called her "Ferocious" because her name was difficult to pronounce. When she wanted to change her name to something simpler, Firoozeh's family laughed and suggested names that would only complicate matters. As Julie, the author felt like "a fake," often noting how much more welcomed she was by peers just because her name was simpler. Because she had a difficult time landing job interviews after college as Firoozeh, she started referring to herself as "Julie" on her resume, which resulted in more calls from prospective employers but also more mixed feelings. Returning to Firoozeh meant recurring problems with people mispronouncing or, worse, refusing to learn how to pronounce her name.

4. What are two of the funniest experiences that Dumas has because of her name? (Refer to your "As You Read" notes to help you answer.)

   Answers will vary.

5. What are two of the saddest or most maddening experiences that Dumas has because of her name? (Refer to your "As You Read" notes to help you answer.)

   Answers will vary.

Jose Antonio Vargas, "My Life as an Undocumented Immigrant"

In this article by a Pulitzer Prize–winning journalist, Jose Antonio Vargas exposes himself as an undocumented immigrant, telling the story of the secret that haunted him as he developed into a successful young journalist, working at many of America's most prestigious publications. Vargas's belief that if he worked hard enough he could prove his worth as an American raises questions about stereotypes of undocumented immigrants and also how immigrants' contributions are valued.

Suggested Responses to "Mapping the Reading" Questions

1. How did Vargas learn that he was an undocumented immigrant?

    Vargas found out he was an undocumented immigrant when he tried to apply for his driver's permit at age sixteen. When he handed the DMV clerk his green card as proof of U.S. residency, Vargas was told that his identification was fake.

2. Why did Vargas's grandfather — or Lolo — think that his grandson would be able to manage his undocumented status? That is, what was his plan to keep Vargas out of trouble, and how did he think Vargas would eventually gain citizenship?

    Lolo imagined that Vargas would take a low-paying job with an employer who would not closely scrutinize his social security card, which was not faked. Eventually, Lolo imagined that Vargas would marry an American, which would make it easier for Vargas to gain a path toward citizenship.

3. After he learns about his status as an undocumented immigrant, how does Vargas believe he will be able to earn citizenship?

    Vargas thinks that if he works hard and achieves enough that he'll be rewarded with citizenship. He also thinks the laws might change and that immigration reform will provide him with a path to citizenship.

4. In what specific ways has Vargas's life been affected by his status as an undocumented immigrant?

    Vargas's life has been greatly affected by being an undocumented worker. For example, in order to receive financial aid for his college education, Vargas has to find scholarships that don't require him to reveal his immigration status. As an undocumented immigrant, Vargas can't receive state or financial aid. It is also difficult for Vargas to apply for internships during college because most of the companies he wants to work for require proof of residency. He receives one excellent offer from the *Seattle Times,* but it is rescinded when he confesses that he is undocumented. As a reporter, it affects the kind of assignments he feels he can accept. Most of all what he has to do is lie and live in fear of getting caught, which is why he eventually "comes out" publicly as an undocumented immigrant.

5. What are some examples of the support network that help Vargas succeed?

Vargas's high school principal and the school district's superintendent helped him find a scholarship for college. A friend's father allowed Vargas to use his address as proof of residency so that Vargas could apply for a driver's license. Again and again, friends of friends helped Vargas hide or get around the problem of his undocumented status.

6. Describe the illegal or deceitful actions that Vargas reveals, and how he feels about being deceitful.

Vargas notes that he felt guilty about using a fake Social Security card and claiming full citizenship on federal employment eligibility forms. He writes, "Maintaining a deception for so long distorts your sense of self. You start wondering who you've become, and why" (p. 267).

Nadia Mustafa and Jeff Chu, "Between Two Worlds: Born in the USA to Asian Parents, a Generation of Immigrants' Kids Forges a New Identity"

Asian Americans from around the United States speak about their twenty-first-century immigrant experiences of "racial alienation and ethnic mockery" (p. 272) and of trying to be at once American and Asian. Born to Indian, Korean, Bangladeshi, Taiwanese, and Filipino immigrant parents, these young adults share stories that are similar to those that might have been told by Jewish, Irish, and Italian immigrant children in the nineteenth century. This article allows another set of perspectives on the immigrant experience today, here focusing particularly on the struggles of the children of immigrants.

Suggested Responses to "Mapping the Reading" Questions

1. Explain how first-generation Asian Americans are "between two worlds."

While their parents try to maintain their culture's traditions at home, Asian Americans must also adapt to the "fast-changing Western culture of the society outside the front door" (p. 270).

2. According to Mustafa and Chu, why are first-generation Asian Americans considered "forever foreigners"?

No matter how much Asian Americans adapt to Western culture, their physical appearances seem to invite non-Asians to question where they came from.

3. Review the article to find examples of how the people interviewed took steps to assimilate in order to fit in better in the non-Asian communities they grew up in. Summarize two of the examples.

Answers will vary but may include the following:

Grayce Liu dated only white boys while growing up and hated speaking Mandarin, the language her parents spoke at home. In order to distinguish herself from other Asians named Grace in school, Grayce changed the pronunciation of her name to "Gray-cee."

Fareha Ahmed dyed her hair blond, used hazel contact lenses, and worried about smelling like the ethnic dishes that her mother cooked at home.

4. What are some of the actions that these interviewees took once they came to a "re-appreciation of [their] ethnic roots"?

Answers will vary but may include the following:

After reading *The Joy Luck Club*, Liu began to have a newfound appreciation for her heritage. One of her projects, a TV show called *Bakaboo*, teaches Mandarin to American-born Chinese.

Ahmed learned to appreciate "a good balance of East meets West" (p. 271). Her embrace of multiple cultures began in college, when she met people of diverse backgrounds. Now she celebrates both Eastern and Western holidays.

5. According to the article, what advantages and disadvantages do post-1965 Asian immigrants and their children have compared to earlier immigrant groups, such as the Italians, the Jews, and the Irish?

Like earlier immigrant groups, Asian immigrants face alienation and mockery. However, Asians look different from Westerners and often don't share their cultural practices.

Chapter 7, "Abilities and Disabilities: Are They Linked?"

Image Response

What message does this image convey? What is your first reaction? What does the angle of the image emphasize? In what ways might the image inspire viewers to rethink ideas about people with disabilities?

This image conveys the message that despite challenges, the differently abled can still accomplish great feats. The angle has the viewer look up to the athlete, cementing the idea that disabled athletes are awe-inspiring.

Temple Grandin, "Autism and Visual Thought"

Temple Grandin, author, animal science expert, and designer of tools that enable humane treatment of animals, tells her story of living with autism. She describes her visual thinking process, detailing the special abilities she has, while also revealing her disabilities. Grandin demonstrates what is possible with support from family and an ideal education system and also proves that extraordinary ability can live alongside disability. Grandin offers a good example to discuss in terms of the connection between abilities and disabilities.

Suggested Responses to "Mapping the Reading" Questions

1. What does Grandin mean by "think in pictures"? How is this process useful in her work with animals?

    Grandin is able to think visually, meaning she can translate words into "full-color movies" (p. 280). This ability has allowed her to "build entire systems in [her] imagination" (p. 280). In her work with livestock companies, Grandin has designed corrals for handling cattle and hogs during veterinary treatment and for slaughter.

2. For Grandin, what are the advantages of being autistic? (Draw on any "As You Read" notes you may have.)

    One of the advantages that Grandin talks about in detail is her mind's ability to store a large amount of visual information about how things like steel gates, fences, and latches are constructed. This ability allows her not only to build these apparatuses but also to invent new ones. For Grandin, her autism is essential to her creativity and her professional accomplishments.

3. For Grandin, what are the disadvantages of being autistic? (Draw on any "As You Read" notes you may have.)

    Because autistic people have trouble learning things that cannot be thought of visually, they struggle with written words, phonetic sound, and philosophical ideas. Spatial words like "over" and "under" are difficult concepts for autistic people to comprehend because, unlike nouns, which can be easily pictured, spatial words are more abstract. In addition, because autistic people have trouble with change and abstractions, Grandin had to develop concrete symbols to help her prepare for and deal with changes in her life, such as graduating from high school. In addition, Grandin has had difficulty learning how to get along with other people and has therefore struggled with isolation.

4. In addition to visual thinking, Grandin mentions other types of thinking, including associational, abstract, and verbal. Give a brief definition of these methods based on Grandin's descriptions.

    Associational: When the mind moves from one series of images to another through a path of associations or connections.

    Abstract: A non-concrete thought or idea that needs to be associated with an image for an autistic person to comprehend.

    Verbal: A way of thinking with words and language, which autistic people struggle with because they think in terms of pictures.

5. At different points in her life, how did Grandin use door and window symbols?

During many transitional periods of her childhood and young adult life, Grandin needed to actually walk through physical doors to help her understand and prepare for the emotional reality of change—for example, from life at her high school to life in college. Doors and windows gave Grandin a better understanding of how her life would change. Later in life she learned to associate doors and windows with the importance of human connection and the fragility of human relationships, as they came to represent "the give-and-take" (p. 284) of relationships.

Brian Eule, "I Was Trapped in My Own Body"

Eule profiles Henry Evans, a man who became paralyzed after a stroke but who is also an inventor developing ideas and devices to make life easier for those who are severely disabled. Evans raises questions about the assistive devices everyone uses, helping to bridge the gap between people with disabilities and people considered able-bodied.

Suggested Responses to "Mapping the Reading" Questions

1. Henry Evans's wife, Jane, tells him that he must figure out what his purpose is in life. What purpose does he find for himself?

Evans realizes that through his disability and his natural talents for invention, he could have a new purpose in life. He devotes himself to designing robots that function as body parts for the disabled.

2. Explain how Henry Evans communicates.

Evans communicates either by winking or by rolling his eyes to spell out words on a board on which there are sets of letters. He can also type using a headtracker.

3. According to Henry Evans, who among us can reasonably be defined as disabled?

According to Evens, nature limits all humans in various ways. He says we all use assistive devices, regardless of whether we are classified as disabled.

4. What are Henry Evans's contributions to creating assistive devices like the Laser-Finger and the remote-controlled shaver?

First, Evans is the creator. Then, after robotics specialists design each system he creates, he becomes the product tester, helping identify strengths and weaknesses that the specialists can address as they further develop each tool.

5. Write a three-sentence biography of Henry Evans. Who is Evans, and why is he important?

One morning, while driving his four children to school on his way to work, Henry Evans, a chief financial officer for a startup tech company, suffered an attack that left him quadriplegic and mute. Eventually he learned how to communicate using devices such as a headtracker, which allows him to type. Today, Evans works with robotics teams that develop new ways for disabled people to regain physical functionalities. He is thus a developer but also a spokesperson for a campaign to see people with disabilities as no more disabled than anyone else.

Scott Barry Kaufman, "The Creative Gifts of ADHD"

Kaufman reports on research that has found a link between ADHD and creative thought and achievement. Researchers have found that many of the traits associated with ADHD — a diagnosis of a medical condition — are very similar to the traits associated with creativity — a desired label. Kaufman observes that these labels have consequences: Students with ADHD are in special education courses, while students considered creative are in gifted and talented programs, which provide many more opportunities and advantages.

Suggested Responses to "Mapping the Reading" Questions

1. Review the traits (characteristics) of creative people as defined by Kaufman and other psychologists, and select the five that best help you remember this definition of *creative*, which may be different from how you define the term.

   Answers will vary, but the traits identified by the author include two types, positive and negative. The sixteen positive traits include independent, risk-taking, high energy, curiosity, humor, artistic, emotional; the six negative traits include impulsive, hyperactive, argumentative.

2. According to researchers, what traits are possessed by both creative people and people with ADHD?

   Shared traits that are mentioned are high-level spontaneous idea generation, wandering, daydreaming, sensation seeking, energy, and impulsivity. Both creative people and people with ADHD also have a hard time suppressing brain activity from the "Imagination Network," which can either translate to having difficulty with focus or being very creative.

3. For what reasons does Kaufman think it may be unwise to label a child with ADHD?

   Kaufman quotes a study from the National Center for Learning Disabilities: "[S]tudents with learning and attention issues are shut out of gifted and AP programs, held back in grade level and suspended from school at higher rates than other students" (p. 293). Data from the study indicate that while 9 percent of children who are labeled with ADHD are placed in special education programs, only 1 percent are placed in gifted and talented programs, and only 2 percent are enrolled in an AP course. Thus the label can make educators see a child's limitations rather than his or her potential.

4. Why is it significant that people with ADHD tend to score low on tests of *working memory*, while they score high on tests of *fluid reasoning ability*? (Make sure you review what these terms mean.)

    Working memory is about being able to hold a lot of information in your mind at once. Fluid reasoning is about being able to figure out relationships and observe new and complex patterns that draw on prior knowledge and expertise. Although people with ADHD have low working memory scores, their high scores in fluid reasoning are indicative of potential for increased creativity and reasoning.

5. What is Kaufman's argument, and what are his three best supporting points for making this argument?

    Kaufman argues, "By automatically treating ADHD characteristics as a disability—as we so often do in an educational context—we are unnecessarily letting too many competent and creative kids fall through the cracks" (p. 293). Kaufman cites two scientific research studies and one real-life example to support his case. The first study, by the National Center for Learning Disabilities, indicates that students with ADHD are "held back in grade level and suspended from school at higher rates than other students" (p. 293). Second, Kaufman cites a study by C. Matthew Fugate, which shows that despite their low working memory capabilities, those with ADHD tend to score high on the creativity index. In addition to these studies, Kaufman writes about Sir John B. Gurdon, the 2012 winner of the Nobel Prize in Physiology or Medicine, who was told in college that his desire to be a scientist was a "waste of time" because of his ADHD.

Rosemary Mahoney, "Why Do We Fear the Blind?"

Mahoney explores the reasons people fear the blind, from general ignorance to cultural myths. She shows that a frequent question about how she communicates with blind students exposes a significant misunderstanding of the blind as other.

Suggested Responses to "Mapping the Reading" Questions

1. How does Mahoney answer the question posed in her title?

    Mahoney argues that we tend to think that the sighted and the blind can't understand or relate to one another. Throughout the essay, Mahoney notes that our fears stem from our ignorance about and aversion toward the blind. We think that to be blind would mean life would be terrible, when in fact those who are blind do not feel that way at all.

2. Mahoney describes misconceptions—mistaken beliefs—that people around the world have about those who are blind. Describe three misconceptions that she identifies.

    Two of the misconceptions come from cultural myths. The first misconception is that blind people are "perceived as pitiable idiots incapable of learning, as artful masters of deception, or as mystics possessed of supernatural powers" (p. 297). The second misconception is that blindness is a "curse from God" (p. 297) for sins in a past life. The third misconception is that the blind have increased senses of hearing, touch, and smell compared to sighted people. Mahoney says this isn't true; rather, blindness allows those who are blind to recognize gifts the sighted already have but have always ignored.

3. According to Mahoney, what perceptive abilities do sighted people lack?

Because most sighted people take their vision for granted, they can't quickly recognize that the blind are healthy, active, and normal human beings.

4. How did Mahoney come to the personal realization that "blindness doesn't have to remain tragic"?

Mahoney describes a time when she traveled through a city blindfolded with two blind people who seamlessly guided her by using their senses of smell, touch, and hearing. Mahoney writes: "For the first time in my life, I realized how little notice I paid to sounds, to smells, indeed to the entire world that lay beyond my ability to see" (p. 299).

5. Map or outline the article to determine how it is organized. What kinds of examples does Mahoney present, and in what order?

- Mahoney introduces her topic through an anecdote about being asked how she communicates with blind people, introducing the subject of communication between sighted and blind people.

- Mahoney summarizes the history of misunderstanding of people with blindness.

- Mahoney writes about the abuses that her blind students at a school in India have experienced.

- Mahoney introduces her thesis, that hostility and misunderstanding of the blind are both born of ignorance of the reality that "blindness becomes a path to an alternative and equally rich way of living" (p. 299).

- Mahoney tells her story of getting over her fear of blindness and coming to appreciate the rich life possible for people without sight, offering herself as an example of the path away from fear and pity.

Joann Ellison Rodgers, "Cognitive Outlaws"

Joann Ellison Rodgers profiles "cognitive outlaws," or individuals who became successful in their various fields despite—or perhaps because of—learning disabilities such as dyslexia and attention deficit/hyperactivity disorder. Without a doubt, these individuals have suffered from their disabilities, but they have also achieved amazing success due to their extraordinary abilities. The examples of Chuck Close and Carol Greider engage students and help them consider how apparent disabilities can be seen as great strengths.

Suggested Responses to "Mapping the Reading" Questions

1. What is a "cognitive outlaw"?

   Cognitive outlaws are learning disabled people who "rely on explicit routines for getting things done, as they can't trust their own instincts" (p. 303). Cognitive outlaws, according to Rodgers and others who use the term, are people who manage to overcome one or more learning disabilities and in fact use their disabilities and the coping mechanisms they have developed to make extraordinary achievements.

2. In the second paragraph of this essay, Rodgers gives her main thesis, but she does so in the form of a series of questions. Reread the paragraph, choose the question you feel best states the thesis, and rewrite it as a thesis statement.

   Answers will vary, but the following is an example:

   "Do dyslexia and similar afflictions rob the left brain, dominated by 'logical' cognition processes that manage reading and other learning skills favored in school, but pay the right hemisphere, in which neurons instantiate more inventive, ambitious, and creative processes?" (p. 302)

   While dyslexia and similar afflictions rob the left brain, dominated by "logical" cognition processes that manage reading and other learning skills favored in school, they favor and enrich the right hemisphere, in which neurons instantiate more inventive, ambitious, and creative processes.

3. In the third paragraph, Rodgers writes the following: "An estimated one in ten children in the United States is dyslexic, and for most, their stories bog down in stigma." What does she mean by "their stories bog down in stigma"? How might they "bog down," and what is "stigma"?

   Rodgers means that the stories of those with dyslexia are focused on the negative, on what they lack and how they are incapable. These stories of hardship and incapability leave little room for the positives and the great potential that people with dyslexia have.

4. Select one of the people profiled—Chuck Close or Carol Greider—and describe that person's disability, the strategies he or she used to overcome it, and how the disability ultimately became an advantage.

   Close is a partial quadriplegic who is dyslexic and also agnosic. As a child Close discovered that he was a gifted musician and artist, and these strengths helped him survive growing up. He became a storyteller and also developed methods for focusing so he could at least pass his college classes that required memorization. Close's agnosia is foundational to his highly successful career as an artist.

   For Greider, who is severely dyslexic, standardized tests were very difficult. However, she had a great memory, so she memorized everything to help her compensate for what she wasn't good at. In school she was braver than most and thus took on a research area—telomerase—that few others dared to investigate because it was so challenging.

5.   According to the researchers Rodgers refers to, why do people with dyslexia think differently?

They approach tasks differently because their brains process information more slowly. For example, non-dyslexics learn how to read automatically, whereas dyslexics read manually. Dyslexics also see more widely and are thus better able to see the big picture, "cut to the chase of a problem" and "make quick decisions" (p. 306). Researchers believe that the neurochemistry in dyslexics is probably the reason dyslexics and non-dyslexics think differently.

Udoka Okafor, "On Living with Depression, and the Dangers of Our Culture of Silence"

Okafor recounts her ongoing struggle with depression, a struggle made more difficult by her high school's stigmatizing of her and eased by one teacher's helping her see she was more than a "liability." Okafor's personal narrative is useful for raising questions about the ways in which disabilities and those who have them are judged.

Suggested Responses to "Mapping the Reading" Questions

1.   What factors contributed to Okafor's development of a deep depression?

Factors that contributed to Okafor's depression were her "sense of loss" after leaving Nigeria for Canada at fifteen years old, feeling like a "spectacle" at school, and being told by a teacher that she was becoming a "liability."

2.   Describe Okafor's school's response to her clinical depression.

Okafor says that the school felt "overwhelmed" by her condition and responded by sending her for psychiatric evaluations and ultimately to a psychiatric ward for two to three weeks.

3.   In your own words, explain how being described as a liability was damaging to Okafor as a depressed adolescent.

Okafor was already feeling low about her self-worth, and being told that she was a liability damaged her even further because it made her feel like a burden not only on herself but on everyone around her.

4.   Okafor writes of mental illness being "criminalized"; what does she mean?

According to Okafor, the general perception is that the mentally ill are like criminals who are ostracized for illegal action.

5. What does Mark do for Okafor? What does she think we should take from his "playbook"?

Realizing Okafor's potential as a writer, Mark taught her "about the power of poetry and the magnificence of prose" (p. 310) while helping Okafor realize that she was neither a liability nor worthless.

Chapter 8, "Twenty-First-Century Gender: When It Matters and When It Doesn't"

Image Response

What does this image suggest about men's roles as child-care givers? What stereotypes does the image play on? How accurate is its portrayal of gender roles today?

The picture of a man holding a crying baby and looking perplexed and uncomfortable raises questions about modern gender stereotypes. Is it still funny to see a man who does not know what to do with a baby? Is it an accurate stereotype? These and similar questions can get students thinking about how ideas about gender shape our understanding of people's roles and responsibilities in society. The image can be used to open discussion about gender conformity and nonconformity and also links to the chapter's cluster on masculinity.

Matt Duron, "My Son Wears Dresses; Get Over It"

Police officer and former firefighter Matt Duron offers perspective on raising a son who is "gender creative" and likes things typically reserved for girls. A self-described "man's man," Duron writes with compassion and honesty about the negative comments his son has been subjected to and reflects on what it means to be a good parent. This personal narrative offers one perspective on gender nonconformity from someone who himself conforms but has learned to value and love those who do not.

Suggested Responses to "Mapping the Reading" Questions

1. How would you describe Matt Duron? What kind of a person is he? As part of your answer, choose two of the sentences from the essay that you feel best illustrate his personality.

Duron is confident, tough, and self-assured. He is fiercely protective of his son C.J. and angry at those who make rude comments. Illustrative sentence answers may vary and may include: "I don't trust them with a kid as kick-ass and special as mine" (p. 318). "I didn't want to remove it, I wanted to follow him around and stare down anybody who even thought about teasing him" (p. 318).

2.   What does "gender creative" mean?

This is the term Duron's wife uses to describe their son C.J., who likes girl things and wants to be treated like a girl. Duron sees this term as more positive than some of the other terms people use, such as "gender non-conforming or gender dysphoric" (p. 319). For Duron, these have more negative overtones than "gender creative."

3.   What is Duron's reaction to negative comments made about his son C.J.?

Negative comments make Duron feel as though people consider his son "lesser than." He will sometimes challenge the commenter. He also is careful not to share information about his son with people he believes will be critical.

4.   Duron begins his essay by telling his readers a little about himself — his gender identity as a child, his parents and family, his wife's gay brother — before he discusses parenting his gender-creative child. How do these details help him make his point?

Duron uses these details to provide perspective. As someone who was raised to follow and accept standards for masculine behavior without question, he becomes an example of someone whose thinking has changed and who has become more accepting of those who do not follow gender stereotypes. This information also helps to establish his personality as a tough guy: In defending C.J., he is going against the ideas he was brought up believing. Yet, at the same time, he is fulfilling the macho, protective stereotype.

5.   Summarize Duron's argument about what makes a good parent.

For Duron, a good parent is someone who accepts and supports his or her child's decisions without question. He sees his role as not trying to change his child. He states that "loving a child who is different, a target and seen as vulnerable is my role as a father and decent human being. . . . I signed on for the job [of father] with no strings attached, no caveats, no conditions" (p. 318). He sees his role as a father as helping his son grow into the person he was meant to be.

Sarah Showfety, "Field Guide to the Tomboy: High Heels and Pink? No Way"

Combining information from experts and from a tomboy, Sarah Showfety reports on the psychology of tomboyism and, in doing so, raises question about it: Is it social? Are there biological roots? Although tomboys may face some negative comments by those who want them to conform to a more feminine gender role, Showfety explains that some tomboys gain social and professional advantages by being more assertive. Providing another example of gender non-conformity, Showfety's report raises questions about whether certain forms of gender bending are more acceptable than others. Does a woman who likes to do "masculine" things face less criticism than a man who likes to do "feminine" things, for example?

Suggested Responses to "Mapping the Reading" Questions

1. What genre (type) of reading is this: an argumentative essay, a persuasive piece, a personal narrative, or an informative piece? Identify a genre, and explain your choice. (Consult Toolkit 1.6 on p. 42 for more about genres.)

   This is a report. Showfety profiles Maryellen White as a tomboy. She interviews and quotes experts to help provide some explanation and interpretation of tomboyism. She does not set out to make a claim about tomboys but to explain them.

2. What are the characteristics of a tomboy? (Draw on your "As You Read" notes, if you have any.)

   The "classic tomboy" is "a female who engages in activities long considered primarily the domain of males" (p. 321). These individuals reject stereotypical toys for girls like Barbie dolls in favor of stereotypical toys for boys like trucks. For example, they are more interested in playing sports than in fashion.

3. What details about Maryellen White does Showfety share to illustrate that she is still a tomboy as an adult?

   Showfety describes White as enjoying activities that are typically associated with men: going to Hooters, drinking beer, watching sports, engaging in sports talk. She does not wear makeup and does not shop frequently.

4. According to the experts Showfety has interviewed, what are three reasons females become tomboys?

   - Tomboys may find the world of men more attractive. Carr believes that tomboys may wish to imitate fathers rather than mothers because they see their fathers' lives as more interesting and powerful.

   - Smiler believes that tomboys are competitive risk-takers, which makes it more likely that they will participate in activities associated with men, such as athletics.

   - Hines believes that exposure to higher testosterone levels in the womb may cause women to "exhibit more 'masculine-typical' behaviors" (p. 322).

5. According to Showfety, what advantages and challenges exist for tomboys?

   Advantages: Because they are more competitive and less interested in fitting feminine standards of beauty, tomboys are able to stand out from other women and be judged on their skills rather than their looks. They can gain status and popularity as athletes. They are more confident and have higher self-esteem. They do well in school.

   Challenges: They may be labeled incorrectly as lesbians. Others, like White's mother, may try to change them so that they fit into traditional feminine roles.

Jennifer Finney Boylan, "A Life in Two Genders"

A college English professor and de facto spokeswoman for the transgender community, Boylan recounts a story of transformation not only from male to female but also from self-loathing to self-acceptance. In this excerpt from her memoir, Boylan shares her childhood sense of having been born in the wrong body and describes her sometimes unexpected and uncomfortable encounters with gender stereotypes as she transitioned from male to female. Boylan's personal narrative links to themes of gender stereotypes in a few important ways. The opening anecdote about her mother's ironing illustrates the force of expectations tied to biological sex. Her experiences shopping while presenting as a man and as a female can be used to discuss how gender shapes the way that people are treated. In addition, her feelings of falling prey to negative feminine behaviors expose the pressure of gender stereotypes.

Suggested Responses to "Mapping the Reading" Questions

1. What does the opening story about ironing illustrate?

   Her mother's comments that she would grow up to wear shirts like her father's and Boylan shuddering at the thought provides an early example of Boylan's sense of distance from stereotypical masculine behaviors. At age three, Boylan did not identify as a boy but as a girl.

2. Where does Boylan offer the strongest, clearest message about what is important for her as a transgender person, and what support she thinks transgender people need from others? Find a quote to support your answer.

   In the final section, Boylan explains that she underwent transition in order to be herself. In the last paragraph, she expresses the belief that the world needs to offer support rather than judgment to transgender individuals. "Having an opinion about transsexuality is about as useful as having an opinion on blindness. You can think whatever you like about it, but in the end, your friend is still blind and surely deserves to see. Whether one thinks transsexuals are heroes or lunatics will not help to bring these people solace. All we can do in the face of this enormous, infinite anguish is to have compassion" (p. 328).

3. What surprises Boylan about her experiences shopping at the Gap while presenting as a man and as a woman?

   Presenting herself as a man, Boylan has an easy experience shopping: The style choices are limited, and the sizing (by inseam) is easy and logical. As a woman, there are many more choices, and the sizing system is unclear. When she finds herself thinking that she should buy a smaller size to inspire herself to lose weight, she recognizes the negative thought process she had observed and criticized in many women friends.

4. The author writes, "There were times when it was as if I were trying to prove I was truly female by oppressing *myself*." What does she mean?

   Boylan oppresses herself by feeling pressure to conform to feminine stereotypes. Even though she is not overweight, Boylan becomes concerned with her weight, specifically with becoming fat, and is more conscious of what she eats. She also finds herself talking in a way that makes her seem less confident (ending her sentences with a question [which, you'll remember from Chapter 4, Welty calls this "uptalking"]).

5. In the final section, Boylan writes that she has become "more mellow." Explain what she means. What perspective on gender and the transgender experience does she express in this section?

   She has become less concerned about whether people judge her behaviors as masculine or feminine; she is content to be herself and to focus on her family, friends, and work. She has also stopped trying to explain herself and what being a transgender person means.

Andrew Romano, "Why We Need to Reimagine Masculinity"

Surveying the ways in which current conceptions of men's roles in the family and the workplace have created an unproductive understanding of American manhood, Romano argues for the need to develop a "New Macho," a version of masculinity that allows men to be more active fathers and to expand their job prospects. He looks at the efforts to compel greater participation in child care by fathers through parental leave laws in Sweden, offering them as a model to inspire American men to rethink the balance of fatherhood and work. Romano's article confronts stereotypes of masculinity and how they may hold men back from success in today's economy. His argument about the value of men taking a greater role in parenting can be tied back to the chapter opening image. What would Romano think of the man depicted? What kind of macho does the image depict?

Suggested Responses to "Mapping the Reading" Questions

1. Summarize Romano's concept of the "New Macho." How does he envision the New Macho with respect to men's roles at home and at work?

   For Romano, the "New Macho" involves rethinking what men should be expected to do at home and at work. At home, they should become more involved in parenting and household work, doing their fair share. In terms of work, men should be willing to take jobs in what are considered women's fields (for example, nursing) because those fields are growing, leading to an increase in the number of available jobs.

2. As his title reveals, Romano is making an argument that we need to revise our ideas about masculinity. Quote one or two sentences in which you see him most clearly stating his claim. (You may draw on your "As You Read" notes, if you have them.)

   Answers will vary but may include the following:

   "It's time, in other words, for a New Macho: a reimagining of what men should be expected to do in the two realms, home and work, that have always determined their worth" (p. 330).

   "Ultimately, the New Macho boils down to a simple principle: In a changing world, men should do whatever it takes to contribute their fair share at home and at work, and schools, policymakers, and employers should do whatever they can to help them. After all, what's more masculine: being a strong, silent, unemployed absentee father, or actually fulfilling your half of the bargain as a breadwinner and a dad?" (p. 333).

3. Romano presents many statistics and facts to support the claim that men today are having a hard time economically and otherwise. What three statistics or facts do you find especially persuasive in supporting this claim?

   Answers will vary.

4. What does the example of Michael Chabon's experience at the grocery store help Romano to illustrate?

   Chabon reports being praised for being "a good dad" when he was waiting to check out at the grocery store. Chabon feels that this comment shows the low standards to which society holds fathers; taking his children to the grocery store should not provide the woman with enough evidence to make a true judgment of his parenting.

5. Reread and summarize Romano's explanation of Sweden's laws governing parental leave. Explain how Romano sees these laws changing Swedish culture and ideas about masculinity.

   Sweden passed a parental leave law in 1995 under which parents would lose a month of leave unless it was taken by the father. In 2002, they added a second "use-it-or-lose-it" month. Following implementation of these laws, there has been a significant increase in the number of fathers taking parental leave. Romano believes that these laws helped shape the impression that "men are expected to work less and father more" (p. 331). Men are expected to take parental leave and face questions when they do not.

Theodore R. Johnson III, "Chivalry, Feminism, and the Black Community"

Theodore Johnson discusses traditional gender roles and the history of chivalry, looking specifically at its practices and significance for African Americans, in light of changing gender roles. At first Johnson, a military officer, portrays chivalry as a wonderful tradition and laments its apparent disappearance from modern life. Ultimately, he decides that we can view courtesy as a modern, gender-neutral form of chivalry. Johnson suggests that some people appreciate conformity to gender stereotypes, while others find it insulting. He discusses challenges to traditional conceptions of masculinity and also the contradictory expectations (about who pays for dates, for example) that cloud criticism of conformity. His essay can be read alone or paired with the article that follows, by Hailey Yook, as a debate about chivalry.

Suggested Responses to "Mapping the Reading" Questions

1. What makes Johnson believe that chivalry is in decline today?

    Johnson believes that chivalry has gone out of style due to his observations, polls, and stories he's heard. He believes that some women reject chivalrous acts as insulting, which may discourage men from being chivalrous.

2. How is chivalry related to traditional gender roles?

    Growing out of the tradition of medieval knights, chivalry was associated with traditional masculine characteristics of strength and protection. Johnson recognizes that chivalrous acts suggest that women are weak and in need of men's help, playing into traditional gender stereotypes.

3. According to Johnson, why are changing attitudes toward chivalry especially apparent in the African American community?

    Black women earn a clear majority of degrees awarded to African Americans (66 percent of bachelor's degrees; 71 percent of master's degrees). Many black women are sole providers for their families, so chivalry, by suggesting women's weakness, has the potential to undermine or ignore women's important place in the family and community.

4. How do ideas about who should pay for dates reflect conflicted ideas about chivalry?

    There is a general sense that chivalry is in decline, but polls suggest that women expect men to pay for dates. Although polls show people believe there are fewer acts of chivalry, a study has found that 84 percent of men pay for dating expenses beyond the first date. Sixty percent of women said they would offer to pay, but 40 percent wanted these offers to be rejected; even more women would find splitting the bill upsetting. "As a result of all this, men are simultaneously accused of being lacking in chivalry, while also insulting women with chivalry. Some women also feel pulled between rejecting chivalry out of allegiance with feminism, and embracing it because it makes some men feel more comfortable" (p. 336).

5. What is the difference between chivalry and courtesy, according to Johnson?

   In the second paragraph, Johnson defines chivalry as offering "gentlemanly gestures such as opening doors for women, offering their coats when there is a chill in the air, giving up their seats on public transportation, or bringing the car around in inclement weather" (p. 335). Toward the end of his article, Johnson labels these acts as courtesy, saying courtesy does not have any "gender baggage" (p. 337). The key difference is that anyone, not just men, can engage in courtesy, while only men can practice chivalry.

Hailey Yook, "Chivalry Isn't Dead, but It Should Be"

Yook, a college student, takes on the issue of chivalry from a different angle than Johnson, arguing that its continued presence in modern life is sexist. She argues for the importance of recognizing subtle forms of sexism, even those hidden in seemingly kind gestures. For Yook, the main problem with chivalry is the lack of reciprocity. Her essay can be read alone or paired with the previous article, by Theodore Johnson, to form a debate about chivalry.

Suggested Responses to "Mapping the Reading" Questions

1. Yook begins by acknowledging changing understandings of women and their roles. What purpose does this opening serve?

   It shows that she is aware that progress has been made toward gender equality; she is not just a complainer. It allows her to make the argument that, while things are better, they are not perfect, and some forms of sexism remain.

2. What is "covert sexism"? Why is it important to recognize?

   Yook argues that covert sexism is hidden or overlooked in everyday aspects of life like toys and movies. She argues that "[r]ecognizing subtle forms of gender discrimination allows us to see just how systemic sexism truly is and helps us get that much closer to achieving gender equality" (p. 339).

3. What is Yook's argument against chivalry? What is her clearest expression of her view? (Draw on any "As You Read" notes you have to help you answer this question.)

   She believes that chivalry is sexist and a form of "covert sexism" that may go unrecognized. Her main concern about chivalry is that it is not reciprocal because it is something done for women by men only. This lack of reciprocity implies weakness and is discriminatory. In one of the clearest expressions of her view (*answers may vary here*), she writes: "Because of this lack of reciprocity, I can't help but wonder if these aren't mere acts of kindness and affection but acts rooted in protection and power as well as displays of masculine strength and resourcefulness" (p. 340).

4. How does the article critique the chivalrous act of a man carrying a woman's books?

   In the case of a man carrying a woman's books, the problem for Yook is that the action implies weakness and promotes stereotypes about women's capabilities. Yook writes: "It's about the implications: If a girl shouldn't carry her own books, does this promote an image of fragility, perhaps even in other aspects of her life, such as her career? I mean, do you want your CEO, someone who is leading you, to be a person who appears weak?" (p. 340).

5. Yook calls chivalry "a rather contradictory representation of kindness." What does she mean?

   Yook acknowledges that some people see chivalrous acts such as paying for dates as simple politeness. She does not object to politeness, only to its being extended in situations that reinforce gender stereotypes (and that are therefore not truly kind).

Chapter 9, "More Than Just a Game: What Sports Say about American Society"

Image Response

How do you interpret the twentysomething Dustin's question? How do you interpret his young friend Hayden's response? What generational shift might the artist, Stephen Kelley, be trying to capture? What does each character's response say about perceptions of girls, women, and their athletic skills? Do you agree? Explain your answer.

This *Dustin* cartoon strip and related questions are meant to get students thinking about sports stereotypes. The reference to "throwing like a girl" introduces one common stereotype. Instructors could use this cartoon to push students to think about whether that saying is still derogatory or whether now, with more girls and women participating in sports, "throwing like a girl" might be seen as a good thing.

Hilary Beard, "What I Learned from Mo'ne Davis about Girls, Sports, and Success"

Beard uses the example of Little League sensation Mo'ne Davis to discuss the multiple benefits sports participation offers girls in terms of health, academic, and career success. Beard discusses the various cultural and environmental obstacles that may prevent girls, particularly African American girls, from participating in sports. Beard's article helps to establish not only the value of sports but also the perhaps unexpected difficulties of access.

Suggested Responses to "Mapping the Reading" Questions

1. What characteristics and qualities does Beard admire in Mo'ne Davis?

   She admires Mo'ne's grit and resilience, her demonstration of the growth mindset, her academic success (honor roll), her ability to maintain friendships with girls, and her lack of insecurity about her looks.

2. According to Beard, what short- and long-term benefits do girls receive from playing sports? (You may consult your "As You Read" notes.)

   Girls who play sports are healthier than those who don't—in both the short term and the long term; sports-playing girls also have higher graduation rates and do better on standardized tests. Finally, girls who play sports are less likely to smoke, use drugs, or have unplanned pregnancies.

3. Summarize the statistics Beard provides about the racial and ethnic backgrounds of girls who play sports. Were these surprising to you, or were they what you expected, and why?

   More white girls (three-fourths) play sports than do African American and Latina girls (one-third). Black girls have a 100 percent decline in sports from kindergarten to high school, compared with 50 percent for white girls. (Answers concerning whether this data is surprising or expected will vary.)

4. Beard cites several reasons girls, particularly African American girls, do not participate or stay involved in sports. Identify three of them.

   Answers will vary but may include the following:

   Some cities have denied girls the right to play sports.

   Black women need to "learn to enjoy physical activity" (p. 348).

   Some people need safer places to exercise.

   Gender roles may lead to girls taking on household chores rather than playing sports.

   Some women are concerned about sweating and looking less attractive.

5. As the title of her article asserts, Beard believes Mo'ne Davis can help us understand something important about girls, sports, and success. Find and quote a sentence or two in which Beard expresses what she hopes people will learn from Davis's example.

   Answers may vary, but here is one possible answer:

   "At a time when black girls' lives and looks are under assault, our daughters deserve no less than to grow up with the same life-affirming benefits that sports have provided our sons and that have propelled Mo'ne into the stratosphere. If her example encourages other black girls and women to get in the game, that could be her greatest accomplishment of all" (p. 349).

Mike Matheny, "The Letter That Went Viral"

Mike Matheny, former professional baseball player and current manager of the St. Louis Cardinals, writes a letter to parents of his youth baseball team's players, outlining the demands of sports and the lessons and benefits that sports — and these demands — will bring. Matheny argues for sports as preparation for life. Matheny offers another perspective on the value of sports, and his article could be used to explore this often unquestioned belief.

Suggested Responses to "Mapping the Reading" Questions

1. How does Matheny want the parents of his team's players to behave, and why?

   He wants them to act as "a silent source of encouragement" (p. 351). They are not to coach from the stands or hover around the dugout offering water, for example. They are to be observers at games and practices. Off the field, they can help the players practice skills. Matheny believes that parents being too involved can put too much pressure on the players.

2. What does Matheny expect of his players? What does he expect of himself?

   Matheny expects his players to be serious in their efforts: They should show up on time, be prepared, and be respectful. They should take responsibility for themselves (having water, for example). They should pay attention, even if they are on the bench. They should think about what they are doing.

   Matheny sets three main goals for himself: teach the players how to play the right way, have a positive impact on them, and "do all this with class" (p. 351). He plans to help players learn the mental aspect of the game. He will help them learn multiple positions, and he will apologize to them if the situation warrants.

3. What are some of Matheny's beliefs concerning how a youth sports team should be run? (You may consult your "As You Read" notes to help you answer.)

   Answers will vary but may include the following:

   Parents should be "a silent source of encouragement" (p. 351).

   Players should show respect to their teammates, opponents, and umpires.

   Players should be asked questions about their decisions during the game.

   Players should take responsibility for their own water.

4. What is the "mental" aspect of baseball, and what is Matheny's stance on it?

   The "mental" side of baseball is the thought process behind what players do. Matheny believes that this is hard but crucial. He intends to talk to the players a lot about what they should do in certain game situations. They will have reasons for what they do during the game.

5. What does Matheny believe the players on his team can control?

Matheny believes players can control attitude, concentration, and effort.

Bob Ryan, "I Can Hardly Believe It's Legal"

Bob Ryan, a long-time sports writer, reflects on the increasingly violent nature of football and especially the increasingly bloodthirsty nature of fans, which has led him to question the value of the sport. Ryan challenges readers to take another look at football and, in doing so, provides another perspective on sports: Are sports valuable when they come with the expectation of serious injuries?

Suggested Responses to "Mapping the Reading" Questions

1. What are Ryan's concerns about football? (Return to your "As You Read" notes, if you have them, to help you start your answer.)

Ryan is concerned that the game is too violent and that players are suffering severe injuries. He is also concerned that fans and others overlook the consequences of this violence and, in fact, value the violence.

2. According to Ryan, what should football players expect to experience as a result of playing the sport?

Ryan believes that players should expect to be seriously injured, to suffer long-term effects, and to face shorter life expectancy.

3. Summarize the comments and reactions to the 49ers-Patriots play involving Stephens and Fuller that bother Ryan, and note his concerns about them.

Bill Walsh's comments focused on Fuller's skills and overlooked the unnecessary violence of the play. Dick Enberg talked about the progress in sports medicine, praising the fact that the medical staff was taking Fuller off the field and to the hospital, rather than just "dragging a player off and tending to him" (p. 357). Enberg also said that sports medicine is a good career opportunity. Ryan is troubled by two main things: first, that no one labels the tackle (spearing) as excessive and dangerous; second, that the seriousness of the injury is accepted as normal and expected.

4. How does Ryan compare himself to other fans?

He questions those who love and accept the violence and brutality of football. He sees some as having a "thirst for violence" (p. 358). He appreciates acrobatic catches, for example, and other plays that do not involve injury-inducing hits.

5. Ryan notes that when he wrote an article criticizing spearing, a tackling method, as dangerous, he got little response, and he suspects he knows why: "I was

messing with football, and perhaps worse than being vilified, I was being ignored." What does he mean by this?

Even though he was writing about a controversial topic that he expected would lead to criticism, his argument was ignored. This suggests that people did not feel it was an issue worth discussing.

Casey Gane-McCalla, "Athletic Blacks vs. Smart Whites: Why Sports Stereotypes Are Wrong"

Looking at some common sports stereotypes, Gane-McCalla argues that they not only impact players in terms of what position or even sport they play but also their lives outside sports. For example, Gane-McCalla notes that the stereotype about African Americans being athletic has a flip side: the belief that African Americans are not as valuable on the job market as their white counterparts, who are stereotyped as achieving in sports because of their strong work ethic rather than natural ability. Gane-McCalla thus offers perspective on how stereotypes shape the view of athletes and suggests how this perception impacts athletes not only on the field but also in the workforce and larger world.

Suggested Responses to "Mapping the Reading" Questions

1. List the sports stereotypes Gane-McCalla mentions in his article. (Review any "As You Read" notes you may have.)

   White players are soft.

   Black athletes are naturally athletic.

   White athletes work hard, have discipline, and know the game.

   "White men can't jump" (p. 360).

   "Black men can't read defenses" (p. 360).

   Blacks can't be quarterbacks.

2. According to Gane-McCalla, how do sports stereotypes actually affect athletes?

   Stereotypes about white athletes "being hard working, disciplined, and smart" (p. 360) are useful to them in finding jobs. In contrast, stereotypes about blacks being athletic do not suggest transferable job skills.

3. Gane-McCalla offers examples of stereotyping of sports events and athletes' experiences to support his points. Choose one, and then summarize the example and the point it supports.

   Answers will vary but may include the following:

   In the Final Four, UConn coach Geno Auriemma made comments that showed that sports stereotypes exist: People were underestimating Stanford, whose players were white, and failing to give his predominately African American players credit for being disciplined.

Major colleges did not recruit Steve McNair to play quarterback, so he went to a small black college, where he could. This supports the idea that there are stereotypes against blacks being quarterbacks.

Recent Super Bowl–winning coaches have been black, disproving stereotype that blacks can succeed in "cerebral" positions.

Myron Rolle won a Rhodes Scholarship; he disproves the stereotype that black athletes do not succeed academically.

4. According to Gane-McCalla, how might culture positively or negatively affect someone's skill in sports? Use examples (your own and from the article) to support your answer.

Although it may appear as though certain groups excel in certain sports, culture—not biology—is the reason. Certain sports are popular in certain cultures, and so people of those backgrounds are good at those sports. For example, he cites Chinese ping-pong players and Jamaican sprinters.

Mary Jo Kane, "Sex Sells Sex, Not Women's Sports"

Looking at stereotypes about female athletes, Kane focuses on their presentation as sex objects, women whose femininity and physical attractiveness take priority over their athletic prowess. Drawing on her research, Kane argues that such marketing strategies are not only demeaning but can also backfire. The accompanying images provide an opportunity for students to engage in a small-scale version of Kane's study. Like Gane-McCalla's piece, Kane's article allows for discussion of how stereotypes of athletes can be limited and demeaning.

Suggested Responses to "Mapping the Reading" Questions

1. According to Kane, how are male and female athletes typically portrayed in the media?

Rather than focus on women's athletic skills or success, the media often depicts female athletes in ways that highlight their femininity and appearance. Coverage of male athletes tends to focus on how they perform in competition.

2. Why does Kane find the *Sports Illustrated* cover of skier Lindsey Vonn so offensive?

Kane believes the way Vonn is posed in the photograph downplays her skiing talent. She also believes that the pose is phallic, an example of the hypersexualization of female athletes.

3. What does Kane argue are the consequences of "hypersexualized images" of female athletes?

   These images underline "their status as second-class citizens in one of the most powerful economic, social, and political institutions on the planet" (p. 363). They lead to a lack of interest in and respect for women's sports.

4. Kane observes that the belief that "sex sells" "creates cognitive dissonance." What does she mean?

   The "sex sells" strategy is not compatible with the WBNA campaign emphasizing family values. Family values and "sex sells" pull in opposite directions.

5. Kane reports on an empirical study she conducted to test the belief that sex sells women's sports. Summarize her method and findings.

   Kane and her colleague asked focus groups to look at photographs of female athletes; some were action shots, some were "soft pornography," and some were "wholesome." Participants indicated which pictures made them more interested in women's sports. The researchers found that "sex sells" was offensive to women and older men. They gave higher ratings to the pictures showing athletic skill. Younger males thought the soft porn images were "hot," but they did not make them more interested in women's sports. "The key takeaway? Sex sells sex, not women's sports" (p. 364).

Cyd Zeigler, "Derrick Gordon Finds His Freedom"

In this article, Zeigler tells the story of collegiate basketball player Derrick Gordon, who struggled with the decision to come out as gay publicly but ultimately found it too difficult to remain silent. Gordon confronts stereotypes about gay men not being athletic and also chronicles a harsh locker room culture in which teasing and bullying look very much alike.

Suggested Responses to "Mapping the Reading" Questions

1. What led Gordon's teammates to question whether he was gay?

   They saw some photographs online (on Instagram) that his then-boyfriend had posted, showing Gordon and his boyfriend outside a gay bar.

2. How did Gordon respond to his teammates' "teasing" him about possibly being gay?

   He denied that he was gay, and then he became depressed, withdrawing, staying in his room, crying, and even losing interest in basketball. He isolated himself from his teammates.

3. What inspired Gordon to come out to his teammates?

   After losing a tournament game in New York City, Gordon met other people involved with sports who were gay and who were out publicly. This led him to believe that he could and should come out publicly and not wait until later in his career.

4. What stereotypes does Gordon want to challenge?

   Gordon wants to disprove the stereotype that gay men are "soft" and "delicate."

Chapter 10, "The Digital Age: Risks and Rewards"

Image Response

Millennials are often represented as they are in this image: glued to their devices and seldom talking face-to-face. To what degree is this representation a stereotype, and to what degree is it accurate? How would you describe millennials' relationships with their devices?

The image will evoke a variety of responses. Some students will see this as highly representative of their experiences and observations, indicating that they perceive a lack of face-to-face interactions among their generation. Other students will likely acknowledge that millennials are regular users of electronic devices but refute the notion that this usage precludes important face-to-face conversations.

Josh Rose, "How Social Media Is Having a Positive Impact on Our Culture"

In this piece, Rose discusses how digital communication allows him to maintain a close relationship with his son, giving him access to mundane details of his son's day. He also acknowledges the debate over digitally based relationships, asking if perhaps we should "re-frame our discussions about technology from how it is changing us to how we are using it" (p. 379). Rose's article provides a useful introduction to the issues surrounding social media use.

Suggested Responses to "Mapping the Reading" Questions

1. How does social media help Rose feel closer to his son?

   It allows Rose to communicate with his son when they're apart. He gets to learn the mundane details of his son's day that he otherwise would not know.

2. Explain and describe the "human side of the Internet," according to Rose.

   He's referring to social media's ability to reconnect people who have been separated for a long time. Citing a Chinese news story about a six-year-old who was abducted and then reunited with his family through a social media site, Rose notes feeling touched by the father's emotional reaction and the son's response.

3. What is the "paradox of online closeness"?

    As social media draws people closer, it also keeps them apart. More specifically, it may allow people to feel closer to those at a distance but further apart from those nearby.

4. According to Rose, how do social media and digital communication have a positive impact on culture? What examples does he provide to support his idea? (You may draw on your "As You Read" notes to answer.)

    They have given us a new way to communicate with one another in addition to, not in spite of, long-form reading, considered thinking, and social interactions. His examples include communicating with his son while they are apart, reading about an emotional family reunion in China, and juxtaposing physical and digital interactions at a coffee shop.

5. What suggestion does Rose offer for changing the way that we think about the Internet?

    Rose suggests that we challenge the idea that the Internet is dehumanizing the way we communicate with one another. He suggests that we "re-frame our discussions about technology from how it is changing us to how we are using it" (p. 379).

Andrea Shea, "Facebook Envy: How the Social Network Affects Our Self-Esteem"

Research suggests that time on social media lowers our self-esteem, and this is especially the case for teenagers. Andrea Shea's reporting suggests that there are some psychological and social costs to social media beyond the "big" stories of violation and abuse through cyberbullying and stalking. She interviews teens and experts to look at how seeing others' possibly fake lives online can lead to lowered self-esteem. Shea's article offers a contrast to Rose's in that she focuses on the potential problems related to how we use social media.

Suggested Responses to "Mapping the Reading" Questions

1. What is "Facebook envy"?

    Facebook envy occurs when users view their friends' "fabulous vacations, lovely children, attractive friends and great social lives" (p. 381) and want these things for themselves.

2. Summarize the research findings on how viewing "so-called 'perfect lives' on Facebook" affects self-esteem. (You may consult your "As You Read" notes.)

    Viewing the "perfect lives" of others can make people feel more dissatisfied with their own lives the more time they spend on Facebook, ultimately causing emotional pain, resentment, and envy.

3. Explain psychologist Craig Malkin's theory that "concealing the less desirable aspects of our lives over and over again 'forecloses intimacy.'" For Malkin, what is the long-term personal effect of this concealment?

   This concealment can prevent us from making intimate connections with others, which negatively affects our self-worth.

4. What is psychologist Steven Cooper's point of view on how social media affects self-esteem?

   Because social media broadens the ways in which we create our public personas, Cooper is interested in how our identity is affected by our perceptions of others and ourselves through social media.

5. According to Cooper, how is "posturing" on Facebook both similar to and different from other forms of posturing as part of a strategy to impress others?

   We're constantly "posturing" in real life, and Facebook broadens our audience.

Lindy West, "What Happened When I Confronted My Cruelest Troll"

Lindy West, a blogger who thought she'd gotten used to mean comments and e-mails in response to her blogging, was almost undone by one especially cruel Internet troll. However, West chose to engage with her troll and gained surprising insights into his actions that led her to have sympathy for him. West's article can be used to discuss trolling, a form of bullying. It can also be compared to Shea's article: Is the troll's jealously of West an example of a form of Facebook-envy? And to Rose's: Is trolling a problem of the Internet or of how the Internet is used?

Suggested Responses to "Mapping the Reading" Questions

1. What is an Internet troll?

   Someone who engages in a form of "recreational abuse" (p. 387) that involves wasting the targets' time, inciting a reaction from them, or scaring them into silence.

2. According to West, when and why do Internet trolls harass her?

   West is trolled regularly, especially when she writes about controversial issues. Those who troll West take offense at her feminist views on issues like rape and misogyny in the comedy world.

3. What did West's "cruelest troll" do, and what is his explanation for his actions?

   Her "cruelest troll" pretended to be West's dead father on Twitter by creating the username "PawWestDonezo," and his bio stated that he was the "Embarrassed father of an idiot." In his e-mail explanation to West, the troll wrote: "I think my anger towards you stems from your happiness with your own being. It offended me because it served to highlight my unhappiness with my own self" (p. 389).

4. How is West's response to this troll different from her response to other trolls? Why does she decide to respond to and then follow up with this particular troll?

   Normally, West simply blocks her trolls and reports them to the relevant social media companies. In this instance, however, West "went off script" (p. 389) and wrote about the ordeal publicly because PawWestDonezo's attacks reached too far into her personal life to be ignored.

5. After this experience, how has West changed her view of Internet trolls?

   She isn't hurt by Internet trolls' attacks anymore because her past ordeal with PawWestDonezo allowed her to feel pity for her trolls.

Jon Ronson, "'Overnight, Everything I Loved Was Gone': The Internet Shaming of Lindsey Stone"

Ronson tells the story of a young woman whose spontaneous decision to take and post a "stupid photo" on Facebook spirals into a life-changing series of events. Ronson writes of her destruction and also of strategies that can be taken to recover a life ruined by becoming the center of a bad digital story. Ronson's article provides an example of how someone's digital history can have long-term negative effects.

Suggested Responses to "Mapping the Reading" Questions

1. What exactly occurred during the "Silence and Respect" incident?

   Lindsey posed in front of the "Silence and Respect" sign at Arlington National Cemetery while "pretending she was shouting and swearing—flipping the bird, and with her hand to her open mouth." With Lindsey's consent, her friend Jamie uploaded the photo onto Facebook.

2. What role did privacy settings play in the "Silence and Respect" incident?

   Because Jamie's Facebook uploads weren't set to private, the image ended up having a public audience and was posted and reposted throughout the world.

3. What were the responses to and the consequences of the publicly posted photo of Lindsey Stone at Arlington National Cemetery?

   The responses were mostly negative, with one user commenting, "You should rot in hell." A "Fire Lindsey Stone" page was created, which gained 12,000 likes. Ultimately, Lindsey was fired from her job.

4. Compare Stone's personality *before* her Facebook posting and afterward. In what ways is she shown to be different?

   The once fun and outgoing Lindsey "fell into a depression, became an insomniac and barely left home for a year" (p. 394).

5. What does Michael Fertik's business, Reputation.com, do? What, specifically, did it do for Stone?

    It's a company that manipulates Internet search results in order to hide clients' negative stories. Through this business, Lindsey was able to increase her online presence in a way that buried the photograph of her at Arlington by "wash[ing] it away in a tidal wave of positivity, away to a place on Google where normal people don't look" (p. 395).

Julian B. Gewirtz and Adam B. Kern, "Escaping Digital Histories"

Gewirtz and Kern, recent college graduates, reflect on being members of the first generation to grow up having their lives documented online. Realizing some of the dangers of having so much personal information available online, the authors consider the options of coping with these dangers — increased restraint online, increased restraint more generally, and not judging people by what they did in the past — and settle on the third option as the most workable. The writers help us explore whether we can become a society that is tolerant of individuals' digital histories.

Suggested Responses to "Mapping the Reading" Questions

1. How do Gewirtz and Kern see their generation as different from previous ones? What potential problems does this difference create?

    Their generation is the first to have digital histories, which can be problematic since online data remains on the web forever. This data is not only available to friends and family but also to future employers who might consider it as part of the hiring process.

2. Summarize the potential problems that the authors see with the cataloging or preserving of our lives on social media. (Return to your "As You Read" notes to get started.)

    Online data from the past doesn't reflect who an individual is presently, which is a misrepresentation that can lead others to think they know who somebody is based on what is posted online.

3. What solutions do Gewirtz and Kern identify? How do they critique each?

    First, people could be more restrained about what they post online. The authors note that this can be unproductive because so much of human relationships is now about making connections online.

    Second, people's behavior could be more restrained—both online and offline. They note that this would be problematic because it could limit one's potential as a human being.

    Third, people could care less about what others did when they were younger. They critique this idea by calling on their generation to be leaders in "negotiating a 'cultural treaty'" (p. 400), which would involve not allowing people's digital pasts to influence the way they are judged in the present.

4. What is the purpose of the "cultural treaty" the authors propose at the end of their article?

    It would help to create a new culture in which people would not be judged based on their digital histories.

5. Gewirtz and Kern observe, "Another issue is that false versions of your identity, suggested by disparate pieces of data, might be contrived and proposed as the real you. Thanks to technology, someone can know more about you than you know about yourself—or, at least, think that they do." Explain what they mean by this statement.

    Our past online data doesn't reflect who we are presently. As we grow older, we move past our younger selves, perhaps even forgetting what we did when we were young. But with searching technology, our past often becomes our present in the eyes of the searcher, leading to misrepresentation.

Amy Tan, "Personal Errata"

In this essay, acclaimed novelist Amy Tan takes on the task of discovering her digital history, finding that much of what is posted about her online is so incorrect that, in effect, there is an Internet "Amy Tan," who isn't much like the real Amy Tan at all. While the misrepresentation of celebrities may seem like a minor disadvantage of the rich and famous, in what ways are more regular people misrepresented, and damagingly so, through social and other media? Tan's essay offers another take on digital histories: not the history produced by someone's own posts but that made by others' posts.

Suggested Responses to "Mapping the Reading" Questions

1. According to Tan, how does the availability of information online help create errors?

    Because information online is so widespread, it's difficult to tell which bits of information are factual.

2. How does online misinformation about Tan affect the way people treat her in person?

    Those who get biographical information about Tan online often misattribute certain awards, degrees, and honorary titles to her. Sometimes people congratulate her on accomplishments that she has never achieved.

3. In what situations has Tan had to correct errors about herself?

    Tan had to correct errors about herself during online interviews, award acceptance speeches, and in this very article, as she writes a list of "errata."

4. Identify a few ways in which the online Tan is different from the real Tan.

   Answers will vary but may include the following:

   The online Amy Tan is more accomplished, having won a Nobel Prize and completed a doctoral program. The online Amy Tan has a different husband, different numbers of children, and lives in a different place.

5. What made Tan decide to write this essay? What did she hope to accomplish?

   She wanted to write about how one person could have multiple identities based on the erroneous information online. She also wanted to set her own record straight by separating facts and fictions in her biography.

Chapter 11, "Words: Sticks and Stones?"

Image Response

Review and reflect on the phrases depicted in this image, using one of the following options:

a. *How often do you hear or use these phrases? Which, if any, are offensive to you? Which, if any, are acceptable? Explain your responses, thinking in part about how your opinion might be influenced by the situations in which these words are used.*

b. *What is the message of this image? How effective (or not) is the image (both the text and the visuals) in getting this message across? How, if at all, does it make you rethink your ideas about these phrases?*

This image from Duke University's "We Don't Say" campaign introduces the issues of slurs and politically correct language. Instructors can ask students to share ideas about the phrases and offer examples of terms they find offensive.

Shanelle Matthews, "The B-Word"

Spurred by her professor's repeated use of the word *bitch*, Matthews investigates the history of the word, arguing that despite its increased acceptance today, *bitch* is still a powerfully damaging word. Matthews's article can be used to discuss when and how once-offensive words become more acceptable in mainstream use.

Suggested Responses to "Mapping the Reading" Questions

1. What reasons does Matthews offer to support her position that the word *bitch* is offensive? (Consult your "As You Read" notes, if you have them.)

   It is a gender-specific insult, "loaded with negative meaning" (p. 414). Its meaning includes a "menacing concept" (p. 414) that defines women by the sex act. It is part of a "prostitution-like attitude" (p. 414) toward women. It is outdated.

2. What does her professor's use of *bitch* in class lead Matthews to realize?

    Because her classmates laugh at his use of the word, Matthews realizes that its use to mean "woman" is becoming more common and accepted.

3. What point does Matthews try to prove by looking up the dictionary definitions of *bitch*?

    She finds three meanings (female dog, "malicious . . . woman," "something . . . difficult, objectionable, or unpleasant"). She explores the connection between women and dogs, coming to the conclusion that because dog breeders say that female dogs are hard to breed suggests that calling women *bitches* has to do with sex.

4. According to Matthews, what are the different ways that women use the word? What is her response to these uses?

    She identifies two ways women use *bitch*: using it with its misogynistic meaning and using it to try to reclaim it. She cites *Bitch* magazine's use of the word to mean "outspoken women." However, she feels that the word can never lose its derogatory meaning, and so any attempts to use it in a positive way don't really work.

5. What type of message does Matthews believe is sent by using the word *bitch*?

    She believes it sends a negative, sexist message that is demeaning to women. She sees it as a word that can "brand" people, ignoring their positive and individual qualities. She writes, "Instantaneous and cutting, we should remember that this tradition has a history of exclusion, which compromises the atmosphere of freedom we should be striving for" (p. 415).

Steven A. Holmes, "Why the N-Word Doesn't Go Away"

Holmes questions the continued use of the N-word by various groups, making the argument that other ethnic slurs have fallen out of use or earn their users heavy criticism. Acknowledging its continued troubling use as a racist slur, Holmes also recognizes that entertainers and youth have tried to reclaim the word. Ultimately he questions whether these seemingly positive uses will prevent the word's critics from making a successful case against it. Like Matthews, Holmes takes on a word that has been seen as a slur but that now sees more accepted use in particular communities. In pairing the readings, instructors could ask students to consider how and why slurs can become acceptable and the different degrees to which this is the case for these two words.

Suggested Responses to "Mapping the Reading" Questions

1. Identify all the different ways that the N-word is viewed and used, according to Holmes.

    In addition to racist uses, Holmes identifies the following uses: Entertainers and rappers use it to make money; younger black people use it as "a hip term of endearment" (p. 420); whites use it to sound cool; analysts use it to grab attention so they can talk about issues related to race.

2. What point does Holmes hope to prove by referring to ethnic slurs that are no longer widely used or known?

    These slurs have been recognized as bigoted and hurtful and so are no longer used; he wants to make the point that the N-word should follow that same path, but it hasn't.

3. According to Holmes, what are some reasons "why the N-word doesn't go away"? (Draw on your "As You Read" notes, if you have them.)

    He cites two primary reasons: evidence of continued prejudice against black people and black people's continued use of the word.

4. What is Holmes's position on use of the N-word? Summarize his point of view and quote a passage in which he states his position most clearly.

    Talking about ethnic slurs in general, Holmes expresses his belief that they should be recognized as hurtful and no longer used: "No one can argue that the reduction in the use of traditional racial and ethnic slurs means that American society has rid itself of all its prejudices. At the same time, it is undeniable that so many racial and ethnic slurs have been driven out of the public square by a general view that uttering such words is unacceptable. And that's a good thing" (p. 418). By extension, he is part of the group who "wish [the N-word] would go the way of the ethnic slurs of yesteryear" (p. 420) even though he is doubtful that this will happen.

5. Who are the members of what Holmes calls the "army of the N-word"?

    Entertainers, rappers, younger black people, some whites, and analysts form what Holmes calls the "army of the N-word" (p. 420).

Rose Bridges, "You Can Call Me 'Fag': American Teens Don't Find Offensive Slurs Offensive"

Blogger Rose Bridges weighs the impact of derogatory terms about the LGBTQ community, citing her own experience and observations, current campaigns to ban derogatory phrases, and a recent poll surveying teens' attitudes toward such language. She concludes that it is impossible to "control the context" in which such terms are used. In doing so, Bridges raises an issue that can be connected to Holmes's and Matthews's discussions of other problematic words.

Suggested Responses to "Mapping the Reading" Questions

1. According to Bridges, how do teens view the use of potentially homophobic slurs?

   They are not as concerned about the use of these words as are some adults. Bridges cites a poll that suggests teens see the terms used mostly in humorous and not offensive ways.

2. What is the goal of the campaigns by the Special Olympics and GLSEN?

   GLSEN's "Think B4 You Speak" and the Special Olympics' "Spread the Word to End the Word" campaigns want to convince people to stop using phrases like *fag*, *dyke*, *so gay*, and *retard* because they believe that these phrases are offensive.

3. Summarize the different environments Bridges experienced in her middle school and high school. What point(s) does this contrast help her make?

   The environment at Rose's middle school was hostile to gays and lesbians, with students frequently using homophobic slurs. At her high school, the environment was much more supportive; there was a Gay-Straight Alliance, for instance. Some students used homophobic slurs, but because the overall atmosphere was supportive, these words did not have as much effect.

4. Bridges observes, "When so many kids are being bullied for their actual or perceived sexual orientation, but they aren't too bothered with homophobic language—maybe these kids are telling us that GLSEN is missing the mark. Maybe language isn't the problem." What does she mean?

   Bridges raises the issue that other forms of bullying (beyond insults and name calling) might be what organizations like GLSEN should focus on instead of focusing on slurs.

5. What is Bridges's position on the use of slurs? As part of your answer, include a quotation of what you consider to be her clearest expression of her view.

   Bridges takes a middle ground: While she does not argue for banning the words, she does not suggest that they are unimportant. She believes that the context helps to shape how words are received, but she also believes that the context can't always be controlled. That is, speakers can't always be certain that their audience will hear the words being used in the friendly way they intend. "But part of the problem, and the reason I'm not comfortable completely dismissing the importance of language, is that you can't always control the context. You can't always know who else is listening besides your friends. Others could hear it and think you do mean it as a slur and be offended. Still others might actually be bigots themselves and take your use of offensive words as evidence that people out there agree with them" (p. 424).

Anna Munsey-Kano, "Why You Shouldn't Be Politically Correct"

Munsey-Kano, a college student from Atlanta, Georgia, argues that politically correct language hides real differences and conflicts that should be discussed instead of covered up. She implores her readers, "Please stop trying to be politically correct, and admonishing those who are not. Instead, consider earnestly the ways you think and act and have mindful, respectful conversations" (p. 428). Munsey-Kano provides one perspective on political correctness that can be used to explore the arguments made by the other writers in this cluster, Garcia and/or Shenker-Osorio.

Suggested Responses to "Mapping the Reading" Questions

1. According to Munsey-Kano, what does it mean to be "politically correct"?

   Being "politically correct" means trying to eliminate language that others might find offensive.

2. What point(s) does Munsey-Kano try to prove by looking at the dictionary definitions of *politically correct* and *offend*?

   Munsey-Kano uses the dictionary definitions in her attempt to prove that political correctness does not change how people think. She emphasizes that the word *offend* means to commit a moral transgression, not just hurt feelings. She believes that political correctness focuses too much on hurt feelings and not deeper mistakes.

3. What are the problems Munsey-Kano sees in current ideas about political correctness?

   She believes that political correctness is censorship that works to eliminate discussion; the effect is that real problems are not solved. Being politically correct, then, does not address problems but is a "Band-Aid" that covers them up. She believes that political correctness focuses on the wrong types of offenses (on hurt feelings instead of moral wrongs).

4. What does Munsey-Kano mean by being "mindful" of how we think and act?

   Munsey-Kano believes that rather than worry about our words, we should pay attention to how our words are influenced by our beliefs, stereotypes, and privileges. We should think about what is shaping our attitudes and focus our conversations on that rather than on word choice.

5. What are "social justice warriors," and what is Munsey-Kano's view of them?

   "Social justice warriors" (p. 427) jump into conversations and call out people for being offensive. Munsey-Kano says that they often are unaware of a humorous context or are just interested in showing off their moral superiority. She is annoyed by these people; they exemplify the wrong-headed nature of political correctness that she sees.

Charles Garcia, "Why 'Illegal Immigrant' Is a Slur"

Pointing to the ways in which the common term "illegal immigrant" criminalizes a person and not an action, Garcia argues that this phrase has the potential to bias people and policymakers against undocumented immigrants. Garcia's article can be used as part of the politically correct language cluster or the slur cluster. It can also be paired with Vargas's article in Chapter 6 to consider how it provides context for Vargas's decision to come out regarding his immigration status.

Suggested Responses to "Mapping the Reading" Questions

1. According to Garcia, why is it technically incorrect to use the term *illegal immigrant*?

    There are two main reasons: First, this term "criminalizes" a person rather than that person's action. Second, being in the country without documentation is technically not a crime.

2. What is Garcia's view of the Supreme Court's choice of terms in the ruling he mentions?

    He praises it for being "nonjudgmental" and for being "less likely to promote hatred and divisiveness" (p. 431).

3. Why is it important to Garcia's argument that undocumented immigrants would face civil rather than criminal action?

    Being undocumented is not a crime; in a civil deportation case, the judge has more leeway in deciding whether someone should be allowed to stay.

4. Why was the Associated Press's 2004 judgment that the term *illegal immigrant* is "accurate and neutral" so important? (The Associated Press has since changed its policy on the use of this term.)

    The AP Stylebook is used by many news organizations, and so its guidelines are very influential.

5. What point does Garcia make with the questions he raises in the third paragraph?

    These questions illustrate that we do not label people who commit the crimes of tax evasion, speeding, murder, and child molestation as "illegal." This allows Garcia to make his point that undocumented immigrants should not be called "illegal" either.

Anat Shenker-Osorio, "Do You Think the Poor Are Lazy?"

Shenker-Osorio argues that the words we use to describe the poor and the rich have helped stop lawmakers and the public from taking action on wealth inequality, despite alarming data that the rich are getting richer and the poor are getting poorer. The author proposes that we speak more directly and less euphemistically, in the hopes that new language will inspire action rather than present the unequal division of money and wealth as a natural, reasonable, and unchangeable "fact of life." Her article can be paired with Munsey-Kano's as well as with the chapter opening image to prompt students to find their own perspectives on whether words have the power to shape ideas and behaviors.

Suggested Responses to "Mapping the Reading" Questions

1. What do the statistics that Shenker-Osorio offers at the beginning of her article suggest?

    Shenker-Osorio presents the statistics to support her point that Americans do not have clear and correct ideas about wealth inequality. Americans tend to underestimate wealth distribution and also believe that some inequality is acceptable.

2. What is the problem that the author sees in using phrases like *wealth divide* and *income gap* to describe the difference in wealth between the rich and the poor?

    The terms suggest that the difference is natural and cannot be changed. The language suggests that the two groups' finances are separate from one another and not part of the same economy.

3. In Shenker-Osorio's view, how does the language of *up* and *down* and *top* and *bottom* influence our view of the morality of the rich and the poor?

    Up and *top* are associated with being good or good things, while *down* and *bottom* are associated with bad or negative things. *Upper class* suggests that people are better—in wealth and in morality. The language implies that they are good people who deserve what they have.

4. In the author's view, why would calling wealth inequality a "barrier" be more productive than calling it a "gap between rich and poor"?

    She argues that a *barrier* creates the image of someone trying to keep others out. A barrier is artificial, and steps can be taken to remove the barrier.

5. What does Shenker-Osorio think can happen as a result of changing the way we talk about the rich and the poor? As part of your response, include a statement that best expresses her view.

She believes that it will allow us to take steps to remove the barriers that block access to resources and opportunities. She mentions prenatal care, universal preschool, and wider access to healthy food as programs that could be developed. "The metaphor of inequality as a barrier, wall, or other obstruction highlights several critical truths about our economy. It tells us these objects are man-made. This conveys that inequality is not some God-given, inevitable, natural wonder. We have built these barriers, and we can bring them down. In other words, there's another way our economy can be structured if we elect and work for it" (p. 436).

Lexile® Measures

The following list contains Lexile® measures for each of the readings included in *Intersections*. A Lexile® measure helps match a reader's ability with a text's level of difficulty. The Lexile® scale ranges from below 0L for beginning readers and materials to above 2000L for advanced readers and materials. The readings are listed here from lowest Lexile® measure to highest.

Title	Author	Chapter	Lexile® Measure
"My Son Wears Dresses; Get Over It"	Matt Duron	8	800L
"'Overnight, Everything I Loved Was Gone': The Internet Shaming of Lindsey Stone"	Jon Ronson	10	840L
"How Social Media Is Having a Positive Impact on Our Culture"	Josh Rose	10	930L
"One Man Explains Why He Swears by Wearing Spanx"	Kevin Fanning	5	930L
"I Was Trapped in My Own Body"	Brian Eule	7	960L
"I Can Hardly Believe It's Legal"	Bob Ryan	9	980L
"What Happened When I Confronted My Cruelest Troll"	Lindy West	10	990L
"Derrick Gordon Finds His Freedom"	Cyd Zeigler	9	1000L

Title	Author	Chapter	Lexile® Measure
"My Life as an Undocumented Immigrant"	Jose Antonio Vargas	6	1030L
"The Letter That Went Viral"	Mike Matheny	9	1050L
"My Soul to Keep, My Weight to Lose"	Alice Randall	5	1060L
"Do You Think the Poor Are Lazy?"	Anat Shenker-Osorio	11	1070L
"Are Your Words Holding You Back?"	Ellen Welty	4	1090L
"The 'F Word'"	Firoozeh Dumas	6	1090L
"Why You Shouldn't Be Politically Correct"	Anna Munsey-Kano	11	1100L
"Escaping Digital Histories"	Julian B. Gewirtz & Adam B. Kern	10	1120L
"Autism and Visual Thought"	Temple Grandin	7	1130L
"Why We Need to Reimagine Masculinity"	Andrew Romano	8	1170L
"Why They Came"	John F. Kennedy	6	1170L
"Facebook Envy: How the Social Network Affects Our Self-Esteem"	Andrea Shea	10	1170L
"A Life in Two Genders"	Jennifer Finney Boylan	8	1170L
"On Living with Depression, and the Dangers of Our Culture of Silence"	Udoka Okafor	7	1170L

continued >

Title	Author	Chapter	Lexile® Measure
"Why the N-Word Doesn't Go Away"	Steven A. Holmes	11	1180L
"Why Do We Fear the Blind?"	Rosemary Mahoney	7	1190L
"Non-Spanish-Fluent Latinas: 'Don't Judge Us'"	Tracy López	4	1190L
"How Body Modification Ended the War against My Body"	Sharon Haywood	5	1210L
"Breaking Out the Broken English"	Arthur Chu	4	1210L
"Personal Errata"	Amy Tan	10	1210L
"The B-Word"	Shanelle Matthews	11	1220L
"Between Two Worlds"	Nadia Mustafa & Jeff Chu	6	1220L
"Cognitive Outlaws"	Joann Rodgers Ellison	7	1250L
"My Year of Modesty"	Lauren Shields	5	1260L
"Chivalry Isn't Dead, but It Should Be"	Hailey Yook	8	1270L
"What I Learned from Mo'ne Davis about Girls, Sports, and Success"	Hilary Beard	9	1270L
"The Way of the Dinosaurs"	Rafael Campo	4	1280L
"Athletic Blacks vs. Smart Whites: Why Sports Stereotypes Are Wrong"	Casey Gane-McCalla	9	1280L

Title	Author	Chapter	Lexile® Measure
"Field Guide to the Tomboy: High Heels and Pink? No Way"	Sarah Showfety	8	1310L
"Chivalry, Feminism, and the Black Community"	Theodore R. Johnson III	8	1310L
"Why 'Illegal Immigrant' Is a Slur"	Charles Garcia	11	1310L
"Linguistic Profiling: The Sound of Your Voice May Determine If You Get That Apartment or Not"	Patricia Rice	4	1310L
"You Can Call Me 'Fag': American Teens Don't Find Offensive Slurs Offensive"	Rose Bridges	11	1320L
"The Epic Story of America's Great Migration"	Isabel Wilkerson	6	1330L
"Sex Sells Sex, Not Women's Sports"	Mary Jo Kane	9	1350L
"Why We Diet"	Abigail Saguy	5	1380L
"The Creative Gifts of ADHD"	Scott Barry Kaufman	7	1440L
"Spoken Soul and Standard English"	John Russell Rickford & Russell John Rickford	4	1490L
"Targets of Caricature: Irish Immigrants in Nineteenth-Century America"	Joe DeGuzman	6	1520L

Suggested Writing Assignments

(Note: The following assignments are not in the student edition of the text.)

In this section, four or more essay questions are provided for each readings chapter. Essay questions are developed with the following writing genres in mind:

Reflecting on the Intersections: These questions ask students to write a reflection, frequently encouraging personal narratives.

Reporting and Informing: These questions direct students to summarize and report on a reading or an observed event.

Writing Analytically: These questions direct students to closely examine and analyze an issue, often by comparison and contrast or causal (cause-and-effect) analysis.

Making an Argument: These questions present students with a debatable issue and ask them to develop and defend a position.

Chapter 4, "Language and Identity: Are We Made with Words?"

1. **Reflecting on the Intersections.** Many of the writers in this chapter question how people's identity, or sense of themselves, is affected by the language they use. How are *you* made with words—by the language or languages that you use? Write an essay in which you explain the place of language in your life. How essential are the languages you speak—or don't speak—to your sense of self? To how others view you? What is the connection between your language(s) and your identity?

2. **Reporting and Informing.** According to Dennis Baron, a linguist, "Aside from a person's physical appearance, the first thing someone will be judged by is how he or she talks" (p. 170). Looking at two examples from this chapter in addition

to examples and observations from your own life, present at least three ways that people can be judged for their language, making sure you also discuss the consequences of these judgments.

3. **Reporting and Informing.** According to Dennis Baron, a linguist, "Aside from a person's physical appearance, the first thing someone will be judged by is how he or she talks" (p. 170). Drawing on readings from this chapter, summarize the key problems connected to being judged by one's language use, as well as the best advice for avoiding these problems.

4. **Writing Analytically.** Write an essay in which you consider how John Baugh's concept of "linguistic profiling" (discussed in "Linguistic Profiling: The Sound of Your Voice May Determine If You Get That Apartment or Not" on p. 187) might be used to understand the issues raised in another reading from this chapter. For example:

   ○ What kind of profiling might López's non-Spanish-fluent Latinas face?

   ○ What kind of profiling might Welty's women face?

   ○ How might Campo be seen as attempting to avoid linguistic profiling by "unlearning Spanish"?

   ○ How might Chu be seen as attempting to avoid linguistic profiling by developing a "neutral" accent?

   ○ How might African Americans be seen as attempting to avoid linguistic profiling by using both Black English and Standard English?

5. **Making an Argument.** Many of the writers in this chapter question how people's identity, or sense of themselves, is affected by the language they use. Choosing two authors from this chapter, develop your own argument about the connection between language and identity. Issues to consider might include the following: How essential is language in creating someone's identity? Can people remake their identities by changing their language? What happens when people don't fit into their assumed linguistic community? What happens when they don't *want* to fit into that community?

Chapter 5, "Appearance: Who Should Decide What We Look Like?"

1. **Reflecting on the Intersections.** If you have a body acceptance story to tell — how you grew to dislike, change, and/or accept your body — tell that story in a reflective paper, being sure to try to make meaning of your story. Alice Randall and Sharon Haywood provide two examples of approaches to this kind of narrative writing, and there are many other options available.

2. **Reflecting on the Intersections.** Select a reading that you found yourself responding to strongly — in agreement, in disagreement, or perhaps a mix of both. Using those strong feelings, write a response paper in which you directly respond to the author's essay with your own point of view.

3. **Reporting and Informing.** Select two readings from this chapter and compare and contrast the authors' points of views. How are they approaching the issue of appearances differently? How are they similar? What is important about any similarities or differences for understanding appearance issues?

4. **Reporting and Informing.** In this chapter, authors have written about personal challenges people face because of their appearances or because of social pressure put upon them because of their appearances. Find an article online written about another appearance issue; for example, you might look into the experiences of another group of people whose appearances are atypical, leading to stereotyping and possible discrimination. Read the article, summarize it, and explain how this is also an important appearance issue.

5. **Writing Analytically.** A fundamental human value is that a person should not be judged for his or her appearance. This is a value that is reflected in both clichéd sayings ("Don't judge a book by its cover"), popular culture (*Shrek*), and classic literature (*The Hunchback of Notre Dame* by Victor Hugo). However, while the value is widely upheld *in theory*, we seem to have a lot of trouble following the value in practice. For this writing assignment, your job is to analyze why people judge by outward appearance in particular cases (for example, in the case of the obese, the tattooed, the pierced, the ultra-thin, the revealingly dressed, etc.). You should choose your own case (or cases) to help you explain — not justify but simply explain — why it is that people violate this fundamental human value.

6. **Writing Analytically.** Kevin Fanning, Sharon Haywood, and Lauren Shields address body image or self-image problems by changing their appearances — not through weight loss but through clothing or tattooing and piercing. Write an essay in which you evaluate the value and effectiveness of two of these writers' methods. Things to consider include: What problems are these changes meant to address? How effective (or ineffective) are they in doing so? How lasting is the change? Do these changes address the problem or merely hide it?

7. **Making an Argument.** At the end of "Why We Diet," Abigail Saguy challenges readers to fight weight-based discrimination by "call[ing] for increasing tolerance and appreciation of diverse body types" (p. 212). Write an essay in which you consider if and how this goal can be achieved. Things to consider include: What needs to be done to meet this challenge? What obstacles stand in the way? You must draw on and refer to two readings from this chapter as you make your case.

8. **Making an Argument.** What is the standard of beauty in your community? Write an essay in which you identify and describe your community's standard of beauty and discuss and explain its effects on members of that community. How do people fit in? What happens if they don't fit in? What steps do people take to conform, defy, or reject that standard? Draw on two readings from this chapter.

Chapter 6, "Immigration: America's Great Story"

1. **Reflecting on the Intersections.** Tell your own family's immigrant or migrant story. How did your family come to the place where you grew up? From what places did they come, and what kinds of experiences did they have? There will be gaps in the story but talk to relatives to fill in what gaps you can. Questions to ask of a family member (or of yourself) might include:

   ○ Where did you immigrate or migrate from?

   ○ Where in the United States did you go first?

   ○ Why did you immigrate to the United States or why did you move within the United States?

   ○ What has been the best part about immigrating to the United States (or moving within the United States)?

   ○ What has been the hardest part about immigrating to the United States (or moving within the United States)?

   If your own family doesn't feel like a good possibility for you, select a friend or other family that you feel comfortable talking with and interviewing.

2. **Reflecting on the Intersections.** Select one of the readings that made you feel strongly, in agreement or disagreement, and write a response to the author. What do you want that author to know? What did he or she miss? How did his or her essay affect you?

3. **Reporting and Informing.** Write a descriptive essay in which you describe how a current immigrant group is represented in the media. Following Joe DeGuzman's example, search out images and headlines depicting this group in the media and describe recurring images, stereotypes, and beliefs.

4. **Writing Analytically.** This chapter offers historical perspectives on immigration to the United States, and you have likely observed that the same themes and conflicts come up again and again. For this assignment, your job is to take on *one issue* related to immigration and draw upon the readings to take a position on how that contemporary issue is informed or shaped by the past. The following

are specific issues that the readings have addressed; you may select one of these or design your own focus:

a. *Nativist Response to Immigrants:* Identify and discuss the response to immigrants by native-born Americans, historically and today. Consider the importance of any similarities and differences in these responses in terms of what they suggest we can learn from the past.

b. *Challenges for Immigrants:* What are the primary challenges for different groups of immigrants coming to America at different times? Identify and discuss the importance of any similarities and differences in these experiences in terms of what they suggest we can learn from the past.

Be sure to draw upon two (or more) readings. One should be historical — Kennedy, DeGuzman, or Wilkerson.

5. **Writing Analytically.** Opinions about immigration are often locally and geographically dependent. What are the current immigration issues in your community? Select a community you are connected to — a town, county, neighborhood, or state — and do some research on how immigration issues are affecting that community. Questions to consider include:

  ○ How is immigration an issue in proposed legislation, ordinances, or governmental policies? (Search a community website, local newspaper, or other news source.)

  ○ How is immigration impacting public resources such as education?

  ○ How is immigration affecting the diversity of the community? How is it changing the "identity" of the community?

6. **Making an Argument.** *Melting pot* and *salad bowl* are common metaphors that are used to describe the diversity of America. Which one is it? Those who think America is a melting pot believe that people come to the United States from all over the world and, as their distinctive cultures get added to the pot, they melt to form a blended culture that is uniquely American. Those who believe America is a salad bowl reject that idea of "melting" and "blending," imagining instead a salad bowl where each vegetable is still distinct and recognizable, despite being mixed with all the other vegetables. Drawing on readings from this chapter to help support your position, write an essay in which you argue for the metaphor you feel is most appropriate.

Chapter 7, "Abilities and Disabilities: Are They Linked?"

1. **Reflecting on the Intersections.** Write a narrative in which you discuss a disability/ability that you or someone close to you has. As part of your narrative, you might consider how the disability has shaped your (or your subject's) experiences and perspectives as well as how others treat you (or your subject).

2. **Reporting and Informing.** Write an essay that profiles a person with a disability, using the profile to examine the issue of disability, and in particular, to consider whether human *disabilities* can be linked to valuable special human *abilities*. Take the following steps:

   a. Select a "disability/ability" that you have learned about from the readings in this chapter or that you know about from personal experience or observations. Then choose a person to profile from the readings in this chapter or from your own research. (If you go to the blogosphere to find a first-person account of a disability, make sure the account is long enough, providing the personal and factual details that will enable you to understand the disability and how the writer has been advantaged and disadvantaged by it. If you choose a person to interview, be prepared to ask direct questions that will help you get this factual information and personal perspective.)

   b. Write a descriptive profile of this person and his or her disability and ability, including direct quotes. Make sure you:

      ○ Detail the ways that this person is disadvantaged by this disability.

      ○ Detail the ways that this person is advantaged by this ability.

      ○ Detail what is needed for this person to thrive.

3. **Writing Analytically.** Choosing two of the people profiled in this chapter, compare and contrast their experiences coping with and adapting to their disabilities. How are their experiences and responses similar? How are they different? As you consider their differences, reflect on why their experiences vary. What advantages or disadvantages did they face? How were they supported (or not) by their families, friends, and schools? What do their examples help us to understand about disabilities, abilities, and the experiences of the differently abled?

4. **Making an Argument.** Write an essay in which you argue in favor of using the term *differently abled*, *disabled*, or perhaps another term that you discover or create. For this assignment you will need to define your term, describe its value to individuals and the larger society, and support your argument with references to points made by the chapter's authors and points developed through your own reasoning and research.

Chapter 8, "Twenty-First-Century Gender: When It Matters and When It Doesn't"

1. **Reflecting on the Intersections.** How important is your gender *identity* to you? To answer this question, spend two or three minutes making a list of nouns that describe the various roles you play in your life (for example, co-author Emily's list

would begin like this: mother, child, teacher, leader, organizer, cleaner, reminder, driver, typist, writer . . .). When you have a list of about twenty nouns, take a look at that list as a way to begin to understand how important gender identity is to you. For example, do you see yourself as a son/daughter or more generally as a child? And what might that difference be? How many of your roles tend to be associated with a particular gender? Think about yourself—your habits, behaviors, preferences. To what degree do you follow gender stereotypes? To what degree do you break them? Write an essay in which you explain the importance that gender roles—whether you conform to or break them—play in your life.

2. **Reporting and Informing.** For this paper, select a person you know who has an interesting approach on gender—perhaps the person has a traditional role or nontraditional one, or perhaps he or she seems to resist having any specific role at all. Observe and describe the person and also develop a short set of interview questions to explore the topic more closely with your selected person. (An example of a gender profile can be found in "Field Guide to the Tomboy: High Heels and Pink? No Way!" on p. 321. Showfety includes a gender profile of Maryellen White that can be a useful model.)

    For your paper, your job is to describe your subject in terms of his or her approach to gender roles, and then, secondarily, to analyze how this person is affected by his or her assigned gender role. To conduct your analysis, you will find it useful to draw on the articles that discuss masculinity and/or femininity in this chapter (Romano, Johnson, Boylan, Yook, and/or Showfety). In what ways are expectations about gender roles helpful? In what ways are they limiting?

3. **Writing Analytically.** Some of the selections in this chapter take up the issue of whether gender roles are becoming blurred, revised, or replaced. While some people welcome these changes, others are upset by them. Write an essay in which you explore *how* and *why* some people feel uncomfortable with gender roles that are unclear or unfixed. Build on your findings to take a stance on which concept—rigid or blurred gender roles—has more value. You should refer to two readings from the chapter; you might wish to use one that presents an opposing viewpoint.

4. **Writing Analytically.** Throughout this chapter, writers argue their positions about gender using a variety of different methods, but mostly they provide either *personal, subjective* evidence (for example, personal experiences), or *impersonal, objective* evidence (for example, statistical research). (Sarah Showfety is an author who uses both methods.) Look closely at two of the essays and write an analysis of how they work similarly and differently, considering potential audiences for the essays. When does personal, subjective evidence work best? When does impersonal, objective evidence work best? What kinds of evidence are best for what kinds of writing situations? Which methods do you find most convincing when it comes to writing about issues related to gender? Why?

5. **Making an Argument.** While many of the authors collected here appear to argue that gender roles are limiting and should be abandoned, many other people celebrate gender roles. What's so great about gender roles? Make an argument for the value of gender roles: How does having specific gender roles support individuals, families, or social groups? To make this argument, you will need to consider those who disagree with you and use a counterargument to refute their claims.

Chapter 9, "More Than Just a Game: What Sports Say about American Society"

1. **Reflecting on the Intersections.** Many of the writers in this chapter raise questions about stereotypes in sports. How important do you think it is to eliminate stereotypes in sports? How can working to eliminate stereotypes in sports be important to society more generally? What lessons can sports offer us for combating stereotypes and discrimination in life?

2. **Reporting and Informing.** Interview a few student athletes, both male and female, and ask them about sports stereotypes, focusing on these questions: What stereotypes do athletes face? How have these stereotypes affected them? After you have completed your interview, write a report in which you compare and contrast stereotypes faced by male and female athletes. Consider your own experiences and observations as well, whether as a player or a spectator.

3. **Writing Analytically.** Some of the writers in this chapter allege that the media is biased in its coverage of athletes. To test claims made by these authors, you can do some outside research. Find a media article about an athlete; this article should be a fully developed profile (a story about the athlete) rather than a report about a particular game or match. (Save a copy of the article to submit along with your paper.). Examine the article closely for examples of stereotyping or combating stereotypes. Here are some of the questions you might consider in doing so: What does this article focus on in its coverage of the athlete (for example, performance on the field, appearance, behavior off the field, family, personality)? What doesn't it focus on? (That is, what doesn't get covered in the article?) How is the athlete described? What stereotypes are *used* or *rejected* in the description? After examining your example and considering the arguments made by two writers from this chapter, write an analysis of the article, arguing for how it does or doesn't reflect stereotypes.

4. **Writing Analytically.** Collect a series of three (or more) sports images either from one newspaper (for example, three weeks of your school's sports page), or from three different sources on the same day (for example, April 12 edition of *The Columbus Gazette*, *The LA Times*, and *The Miami Herald*) and print out or save

all the images — pictures, graphics, or cartoons — from that day. Examine them closely for portrayals of stereotyping or combating stereotyping. What patterns do you see? How do these images portray sports and athletes? What do these images tell readers about how the publications *see* sports and athletes? After examining your examples and considering the arguments made by two writers from this chapter, write an analysis of the images, arguing for how they do or do not reflect stereotypes.

5. **Making an Argument.** Drawing on two readings from this chapter, take a stance on the individual and/or societal value of sports. Why are or aren't sports valuable to American society and to individuals, and in what specific ways? You might include some personal experience, but the main focus of your argument should be examples from the readings. As part of your argument, you might consider what sports say about society and whether sports provide a useful lens for examining society.

Chapter 10, "The Digital Age: Risks and Rewards"

1. **Reflecting on the Intersections.** How important is social media to you? Over a period of two or three days, keep track of all the ways in which you use social media. When do you use it? What information are you sharing? What information are you getting? What kinds of connections do you have with people through social media? Write an essay in which you explain the place of social media in your life.

2. **Reporting and Informing.** Personal electronic devices from smart phones to tablets to laptops, and social networking tools like Twitter, Facebook, and Instagram, allow us to be connected at all times. News reports suggest that Americans spend a great deal of time online using social media. But what kinds of human connection do our devices and social media allow? Looking at two examples from this chapter, and also reflecting on your own experiences or observations, explain how social media affects the types of relationships and interactions people can have.

3. **Writing Analytically.** Toward the end of his essay, Josh Rose asserts, "[t]he Internet doesn't steal our humanity, it reflects it. The Internet doesn't get inside us, it shows what's inside us" (p. 379). Drawing on two other readings from the chapter, test this claim. As part of your analysis, explain what Rose means. You should also explain how the ideas or examples from the other articles help to illustrate, prove, challenge, or show the need to modify Rose's claim.

4. **Making an Argument.** The combination of social networking tools and personal electronic devices allows us to share thoughts, information, and pictures

quickly, frequently, and widely. Although some of this information is shared in the moment without considering any possible consequences, it combines to form a digital history that others may use to make judgments about an individual. A prospective employer, for example, may think twice before making an offer to someone whose social media posts suggest excessive partying. As more people use social media, the potential for possibly compromising posts increases. Drawing on two of the assigned readings and your own observations or experiences, develop a position on whether it is right for an employer to search and make judgments on a potential employee based on his or her digital history.

Chapter 11, "Words: Sticks and Stones?"

1. **Reflecting on the Intersections.** Describe a situation in which words you used or heard were considered to be offensive or politically incorrect, including the reactions of those involved. How do the ideas of any two of the writers in this chapter help you see or re-see what happened?

2. **Reporting and Informing.** Many of the writers in this chapter explore the ways in which the terms used can shape people's perceptions of and beliefs about an issue or a group of people. Drawing on two of the readings from this chapter, write an essay in which you compare and contrast their arguments about how words can affect the ways in which an individual, a group, a situation, or an issue is perceived.

3. **Writing Analytically.** Several of the articles in this chapter address attempts to reform language (such as by eliminating sexist, racist, or offensive or politically incorrect terms from speech and writing). Yet, as Bridges asks, "are slurs really such a big deal, or are there bigger issues we need to fix first before going after the language?" (p. 422). Write an essay in which you compare and analyze the arguments made by two of the authors in this chapter to determine whether language reform simply covers up a social problem or whether it can help solve a social problem.

4. **Making an Argument.** In their essays, Matthews, Holmes, and Bridges raise the issue of who gets to use certain words and in what situations, arguing that in some contexts the use of apparently derogatory slurs may be appropriate or acceptable. Analyzing two of these writers' positions, make an argument about whether it is possible to define the situations in which apparent slurs are not derogatory.

Teaching and Designing a Co-Requisite (or ALP) Writing Class

By Jamey Gallagher, Co-Director of the Accelerated Learning Program, Community College of Baltimore County

Teaching a Co-Requisite Writing Class

Whether or not you have experience teaching basic writing or composition classes, it is likely that you are at least relatively new to the idea of teaching co-requisite (or ALP) classes.[1] Most commonly, co-requisite classes are structured so that a credit course is combined with a companion course—the credit course having a mixed population of credit and developmental students, while the companion course includes only the developmental students. The same teacher generally teaches both classes. While the composition class remains identical to all other composition courses at the institution, requiring the same number of essays and holding students to the same standards, the basic writing or *cohort* class provides the developmental students with the additional support they will need to complete the composition course successfully.

Some institutions consider both courses one, creating a new course that might be labeled 100A or 101A, but by and large the two are separated. Some institutions consider the extra class a shorter "lab" portion, but for my purposes the cohort classes will be assumed to be a full, 3 credit-hour class.

---

[1] Many schools refer to them as ALP classes, because they are based on the model developed by Peter Adams at the Community College of Baltimore County for the Accelerated Learning Program there. For my purposes, ALP and *co-requisite* will be synonymous. While co-requisite lacks the poetry of *accelerated*, it has broader explanatory power.

What Is Different about Co-Requisite Classes?

So, what exactly is different about co-requisite classes? In traditional developmental writing classes, teachers would often tell their students, with varying degrees of accuracy, that what they were learning would be valuable to them when (or *if*) they took their next writing class. In co-requisite classes, the teacher is able to tell students that what they are learning will be valuable to them immediately, in the next class session. For that reason, students quickly come to appreciate the utility of the cohort class. All writing and learning activities done in the cohort class are designed to ensure that students will be able to perform at an acceptable level in the composition class.

There are several administrative issues that make co-requisite classes different, including scheduling, classroom space issues, and pre-requisites. But since these issues are unique to each institution, it would be unproductive to cover them here.

How Do Co-Requisite Classes Change How We Teach?

Co-requisite classes change how we teach in several ways. For one thing, since the cohort class is likely to be small (a subset of the larger composition class), we now have more time to spend with those students who need our assistance most. We have an opportunity to tailor the course to support the work these students are doing in the composition course. We also have time to attend to the nonacademic issues that frequently get in the way of success for students in the cohort class. I discuss in more detail below how the smaller class size and a tailored support class affect our teaching.

Smaller Cohort

At most institutions, the cohort class is considerably smaller than the composition class. In the most common example, twenty students in the composition class winnow down to ten students in the cohort class. Anyone who has ever taught a small class knows how different that experience is from the more typical experience of teaching twenty, or more, students at a time. In the cohort classes, students and teacher are able to get to know each other quickly. While it may take a number of weeks for instructors in a large composition class to recognize the writing issues that students need to work on most, a teacher in a cohort class can quickly recognize these issues. Because students get to know their teacher in a new way, students may also feel more attached to the institution and more likely to work on their own writing, which is important, as students are likely to come to us with a mistaken belief that writing is a one-and-done activity.

The smaller cohort makes certain activities in the classroom easier to facilitate. Pair work and small group work become easier to manage and monitor. While peer review groups can be challenging to manage effectively in large classes, in a class of ten, two peer review groups can be monitored with ease. Whole-class workshops — entire classes devoted to one student's paper — also become possible. Projects that require the use of video cameras or technology can be more simply facilitated as well.

Aligning the Two Courses

Some have argued that the small class size is the main cause of the benefits of co-requisite classes. While the small size of the cohort class is a contributing factor to success, it is not the only driver. Another important aspect of the class is that it is tied to a credit-bearing class. Even in schools that have decided not to keep cohort classes small, there are benefits to aligning a developmental class with a credit class.

Cohort classes answer the question of transferability: In the traditional model of developmental education, a mismatch often occurs between the teaching philosophy of the professors of the developmental and credit courses. For example, the teacher of a developmental course may focus exclusively on the five-paragraph essay, while the teacher of the credit course may actively discourage the form. Rather than helping students, the developmental instruction could act as a barrier. Since the credit class is ultimately the class that allows students to take other classes and to continue their education, it makes sense to privilege the outcomes of that course.

Integrated Reading and Writing

A popular trend in developmental education is the idea of integrating reading and writing instruction. Traditionally, reading has been regarded as a foundational skill, something that students needed to master in order to have any chance in college. This makes a great deal of sense, since so much college work revolves around the written word. But reading is not a skill that is divorced from other language skills, especially writing. There may be a small percentage of students who truly *cannot* yet read at a college level, but there is a much larger population that would benefit from some help in reading.

Why?

A recent study[2] has shown that high schools are requiring reading at a lower "grade level" than they ever have in the past. As a greater number of students come to school lacking wide experience in reading, especially in reading academic texts, the need to integrate reading instruction into writing classes becomes ever more

---

[2] www.huffingtonpost.com/2012/03/22/top-reading_n_1373680.html

vital. Often, a problem with writing actually stems from a problem with reading comprehension. Even those teachers — like myself — who believe that writing is the most important skill a college student can learn should realize that more reading instruction will benefit students.

How?

If you have a reading department at your institution, network with the faculty and get to know the pedagogy of the reading faculty better. Your textbook may also help you teach reading. *Intersections,* for example, improves students' reading skills in the following ways:

1. It provides overt reading instruction in Chapter 1, "Getting Active: An Approach to Successful College Reading," including definitions of reading terms and twelve academic reading strategies as well as detailed coverage of reading critically and actively.

2. "Before You Read," "As You Read," and "After You Read" questions surround every reading in Chapters 4–11, giving students the critical reading guidance they need to tackle texts.

3. Section 1 of Chapter 3, "Getting the Most Out of Reading," includes fourteen reading toolkits, featuring activities in annotation, outlining, vocabulary, reading visual texts, and overcoming reader's block.

4. Section 4 of Chapter 3, "Revising Writing," includes eight different types of peer review activities, teaching students how to effectively read and interpret feedback on their writing.

Below are some of the strategies that I emphasize.

Forecasting (covered on pp. 6–7 in *Intersections*)

Asking students what they think a text will be about before they read it can activate their schema and get them ready to receive new information. Teachers can get students to look at author headnotes, book covers, and other illustrations in the text; preview the introduction, conclusion, headings, and the activities and other apparatus following a reading assignment, and to make their best guesses as to what the piece will be about.

Introducing Concepts

Before discussing a piece of writing, students can be introduced to the concepts covered in the piece. For example, I often have students write about different "discourse groups" to which they belong before asking them to read a difficult James Paul Gee work entitled "What Is Literacy?" Before handing out this essay, students go to the cafeteria to study language use "in the wild." This prepares them to talk about language variety.

Reading Strategies (covered on pp. 5–12 in *Intersections*)

What do you do when you come across a difficult word or fail to understand a passage? As a teacher, you may use a variety of strategies, even if you don't do so consciously. Some students may be tempted to look up every difficult word, but that is often not the best solution. *Intersections*, pp. 5–12, offers some specific strategies for students to use to figure out the meaning of unfamiliar words as they read, including looking for context clues, saying the word aloud, and analyzing the word parts. Students may sleep-read through passages without any ability to grasp the concepts. Asking them to draw a graphic organizer for the reading or to summarize the reading can help encourage more active engagement. (Coverage of writing a summary appears in Chapter 3, pp. 39–40.) Using the students' preferred learning styles (independent or social, pragmatic or creative, verbal or spatial, rational or emotional, concrete or abstract) and the tips provided in the text may also help.

Annotating and Summarizing (covered on pp. 36–37 and 39–40 in *Intersections*)

Most writing teachers ask their students to do some kind of annotation. There are countless ways to do this. Some people use double-entry notebooks, others use Cornell notes. Getting students to put pen to paper is the important thing. Asking students to annotate before they write summaries — and to write the summaries based on their annotations — can lead to more complete work.

Levels of Reading

I encourage students to think about different ways that they read. These ways include metacognitive, intertextual, and imitative. Metacognitive reading deals with *how* a student reads, intertextual reading is how we put texts into dialogue with each other, and imitative reading centers on using other people's writing as models for our writing.

Quizzes That Drive Understanding

Too often, reading quizzes are designed only to prove that a student has (or, more often, has not) read a given selection. More meaningful quizzes can drive students toward a deeper understanding of a text, or toward asking better questions of a text.

Group Work Calling for Interpretation

The activities following the reading assignments in *Intersections* can be used as group activities. There are also many toolkits in Chapter 3 that can be used as group activities. Alternatively, ask students to come up with a position on a reading that can be questioned and debated. This may make them more willing to read and more engaged readers.

Role-playing

Many teachers have students play games in the class, including role-playing, to help their them better understand a text. Students can be asked to role-play one position while another role-plays the opposing position.

Reading and writing are reinforcing skills, and seeing them as reinforcing in the classroom is important, too. Since working with reading faculty at my own institution, I now rarely give a reading assignment without some kind of scaffolding activity to go along with it.

While all these techniques to integrate reading and writing are useful in composition classes, it may be difficult to give up time to discuss and work with *reading* in a composition class. Co-requisite classes allow more time to work with students, so we *have* time to work with them on developing reading skills.

Non-Cognitive Issues in the Classroom

Because of the small size of the cohort classes, and because many students drop out of college for reasons that have nothing to do with cognitive ability, a focus on issues beyond writing and reading—what many people call "non-cognitive" skills or issues—makes sense in the cohort class. Psychologists David Yeager and Angela Duckworth have made these ideas salient in education, with terms such as *grit* becoming common. The basic argument is that attitudes and strategies are every bit as important as cognitive ability.

Skill Levels

The fact that we DO have different skill levels in the classroom is something that has to be acknowledged. It can be difficult to deal with both the student who has major issues with putting a sentence together and the student who needs to be pushed in terms of thinking but has the mechanics down. In both cases, though, the student benefits from being treated as a college student with additional challenges beyond the classroom. Paying attention to non-cognitive issues moves us beyond "different skill levels" in the classroom and moves us toward treating students differently.

Building Community

One way to help all students is to build community in the small classroom. In a small cohort, this community forms almost regardless of what a teacher does. After spending this long with each other, in intense study, students can't help but become closer. Although I have had students whose close relationship became problematic because outside issues came into the classroom, by and large the community of a cohort class is strong and vital, and does a great deal to connect a student to the institution. It also becomes easier for students to admit that they're having troubles with issues beyond the classroom. Regardless of skill level, a student in these classes begins to feel more like a college student. In my institution, our cohort classrooms are small and feature a small table, giving the class a "seminar" feeling.

Issues in the Community College

While college-level work is what students should be doing, the small cohort class gives us an opportunity to informally address issues that students often struggle with outside of class. For example, if students have questions about financial aid or registration, we can answer them here. I have interacted with many different kinds of students in my classes, from pregnant young women who needed to figure out how to get back and forth to work, to fulltime workers who were struggling to juggle work, home, and school, to students who have been incarcerated or lost their homes. While English teachers are not counselors, we can provide a safe space for students to discuss these issues and direct them to appropriate resources. Using class time to talk about the life issues that students are going through is not a waste of time. Anything that connects students to the college will help students succeed in the class.

Some non-cognitive issues are more prevalent in community colleges than in four-year schools. In community colleges, we often teach students who are the first in their families to attend college and, therefore, don't have the support systems that other students may have. As a result, some students benefit greatly from even a little institutional direction. Many teachers in our program take students on tours of the campus, show them whom they need to contact if they have a problem, and even direct them to certain advisors on campus. Students benefit from learning to do things by themselves, so sometimes just a nudge in the right direction is sufficient.

A higher percentage of developmental students attend community colleges. It is not uncommon for eighty percent of all incoming students to place into developmental classes. These students are labeled *developmental* for all kinds of reason:

- Sometimes they didn't get the help they needed in high school.
- Sometimes they speak a nonstandard dialect of English.
- Sometimes they haven't taken school seriously until now.

Many teachers discuss the question of WHY students are in these classes to begin with and share data about developmental students with their classes, not to shame students but to suggest that their placement is not entirely their fault, or "society's" fault, to give them an idea that there is something that they can do from here.

Another issue common to students at community colleges, one that we can address in the cohort class, is transience. Many students work full time and struggle to find the time to take classes. Even full-time students are on campus only to attend their classes, so they don't feel connected to the institution. The structure of co-requisite classes helps to alleviate this problem because students are on campus for two classes in a row and form more of a connection to the institution.

Spending some time in cohort classes talking about the challenges students face, and, even better, using those challenges as the basis for short writing assignments, is time well spent. For instance, a short paper could focus on the challenges students face and how they can surmount those challenges. Reflections on these challenges can be ongoing journal or freewriting topics throughout the semester. One successful assignment I've used has students record videos giving other students advice about the home-school-work balance. By advocating for addressing non-cognitive issues, I am suggesting not that we do less writing in these classes but that the writing be focused on students' own lives.

Common Mistakes

A wide array of pedagogical approaches to the cohort class can be taken successfully, but a handful of mistakes are common. Listing them here may help some new teachers avoid the mistakes many of us have had to learn to avoid through hard experience.

1. **Treating the cohort class like any other traditional class.** The cohort class is not the old developmental class jammed onto the credit class, and the old outcomes and objectives do not necessarily apply. One of the most common mistakes teachers new to this approach make is to try to fit what they used to do in the traditional developmental class into this new format. The cohort class has to be completely rethought, re-conceptualized as a support class for the credit course.

2. **Failing to align the two courses.** One of my own early mistakes was failing to align the material in the cohort class with that in the first-year composition course and failing to show students how the two courses were related. Planning both courses side-by-side has helped in that effort. Students should be able to see, if not immediately then eventually, how what they are doing in the cohort class helps them in the credit course.

3. **Asking for too much, or too little, work in the cohort class.** The cohort class should not be treated like simply a lab or workshop. To get the most out of the class, students should do additional writing that reinforces the writing they are doing in the credit class. On the other hand, they should not be writing a series of major essays in the developmental class, because then they will become overwhelmed.

There are certainly other issues to work out — for instance, how the identity of the teacher changes from one class to the other — but these are three of the most common and important.

Final Thoughts

At this point, almost no one has a great deal of experience teaching co-requisite courses, because (as of this writing) they have been around for only the past six years or so, but we know that what teaching co-requisite classes takes is a combination of good composition pedagogy and good basic writing pedagogy.

If there is any cohering pedagogical principle, it is to view writing development as holistic. Co-requisite classes move away from the part-to-whole structure of earlier developmental education, toward a more integrated approach, one that suggests students learn to write essays by actually writing essays and by having teachers help them with what they need the most help with, *when* they need that help.

The great promise of co-requisite classes is that more students will be able to benefit from higher education — a promise that many schools have already delivered on. This is a social justice issue. The students most served by co-requisite classes are those students who have been traditionally underserved by higher education. Ensuring that they are able to continue their education is the most important thing we can do as educators.

Course Design for Co-Requisite Sections

One of the most common questions I hear is: What should we do in our cohort classes? One of the things that I value most about teaching co-requisite classes is the fact that there is no template for success, no blueprint to follow. These classes can be approached in a myriad of ways. Still, some practices are fairly common in co-requisite classes, including those I discuss below.

Writing Assignments That Support the Objectives of the Credit Course

Since helping students to pass the credit course is the goal, giving them practice with the kinds of writing they are doing in the co-requisite class makes sense. For example, if students are writing an analysis paper in the credit course, then they will benefit from doing additional analysis in the cohort class. This additional practice is the key to student success. In many cases, these ways of writing are new to students, and in all cases extra practice is helpful. (I spend a lot of time in both the credit and cohort classes talking about academic "moves" that writers make. For more on academic moves, see Joseph Harris's *Rewriting* or Graff and Birkenstein's *They Say/I Say*.)

Some teachers will also have students do writing in the cohort class that will help them build their final paper for the credit course. For example, a teacher who has assigned a cause and effect essay could get students started in the cohort class by asking them to write about one cause and one effect that they could then incorporate into their longer paper for the credit class. Other kinds of writing that might support the objectives of the co-requisite class are inquiry-based, informal assignments that ask students to clarify their thinking about a topic. If working with argument, students could be asked to defend their arguments in writing in the cohort classes. There is no limit to the kind of short writing assignments that teachers can devise for these cohort classes.

Workshops

Some teachers spend a good deal of time in the cohort class workshopping drafts with students. Workshops can be held as a whole class (this is especially easy in a smaller cohort class of eight or ten) or in groups. Workshops function best when students have been trained in workshopping each other's writing, so some time should be spent — ideally in the credit class — explaining and practicing the process. Teachers should be aware that left on their own, students tend to focus on grammar and give unhelpful general comments. It can help to instruct students to focus on one level of revision at a time — from broader global concerns all the way down to proofreading. It should become clear to students that their responsibility as responders changes at each stage of the process. I often model the workshop process with my own in-process writing, asking students to give me advice that I then act on in the next revision.

Conferences

Many teachers use some time in a cohort class to meet one-on-one with students. The other students may be assigned a writing task, and while they work the teacher can talk with one student at a time. This can be invaluable for a number of reasons. I've found that, especially in the cohort classes, after a few weeks students begin to recognize their own writing challenges, and they are able to articulate them orally, but the movement from realization to application often requires conversation. For instance, one student had an epiphany in a conference. She said, "Wait a second, I get it: I put too many ideas into one sentence, and she doesn't put enough." This kind of *a-ha* moment is best facilitated by conferences. Students with writing difficulties can be asked to read aloud; they will often fix their own mistakes as they read — or they can use conferences to clarify their thinking. (For more ideas on conferences, see the work of Donald Murray.)

Individual Work on Editing

The efficacy of assigning decontextualized grammar drills is doubtful, but anyone who teaches developmental writing knows that that doesn't mean teachers should throw up their hands and give up trying to help their students write grammatically correct sentences. Teachers can help students improve their grasp of grammar by getting them to work *with their own writing* in new ways. In the cohort class, the instructor can spend time getting students to work on issues that they now recognize as problematic.

One of the few decontextualized activities that has shown consistent results is the use of sentence combining, having students take three or four short sentences and combine them in different ways. Students for whom short sentences are endemic could be encouraged to combine their own sentences. One positive aspect of sentence combining is that it gets students to think about their own writing in strategic ways, asking themselves what effect their writing will have on an audience.

Other activities that get students to look at their own writing can be helpful, such as what Wendy Bishop calls *radical revision*. Radical revision asks students to revise a piece of writing into a new genre. I've also found that bringing in student writing from other classes and asking students to edit that writing can be productive. Given some distance from the writing — while also seeing someone who makes the same mistakes that they make — can lead to insights into writing.

Discussions of Non-Cognitive Issues

One of the greatest benefits of a co-requisite class is that it assists those students most in need of help with issues that get in the way of success in the classroom. Students who land in developmental classes are there for a variety of reasons, many of them non-cognitive. In the small classes, students form cohorts, bond with each other, and talk about issues that they may not talk about in larger classes, and it makes sense to open these issues up to class discussion.

One recurring problem in the community college is the difficulty of balancing home, school, and work life. In the cohort classes, instructors can design writing assignments that ask students to think about that balance and to devise ways in which to deal with the juggling more fruitfully, or instructors and students may simply use class time to discuss challenges that the students are facing. Teachers are not usually trained as social workers or counselors, but it is fairly easy to help a student navigate the bureaucracy of an institution, and often students provide the best advice to their classmates. Since the cohort class is typically more informal than the credit class, using time in this way can be valuable.

Reading

Many students entering our classrooms do not have extensive reading experience. Even those with reading experience may not have experience with the kinds of academic texts that we are asking students to read. Because we have more time in cohort classes, we have time for more overt reading instruction. I discuss integrating reading and writing below, so here I will simply claim that teaching students strategies for tackling academic texts — predicting, annotating, summarizing — can be fruitful in the cohort classes.

Best Practices: Backward Design

As you can tell from the above list, there is no single "correct" way to teach cohort classes. However, there are some practices that seem to make more sense in this setting than others.

Instructors are called upon to be flexible in the co-requisite model, always gauging the needs of the individual students in the cohort classes. In the traditional developmental model, very often the curriculum was set before the class began. Students would start by building different types of sentences. Next they would learn how to write various kinds of paragraphs. Then they would combine those sentence and paragraphs to form essays. A co-requisite class, on the other hand, takes the students in the class as its starting point. If most of the students need to work on sentence boundaries, then it makes sense to spend a class period on sentence boundaries. In most instances, the majority of students need to work on higher-level thinking and integrating information and ideas from sources. Individual sentence-level issues *should* be addressed, but they will vary from student to student. For this reason, flexibility is the most important attribute a teacher can bring to these classes.

Instructors should also be sure to align the cohort and credit courses, so that students can recognize that what they are doing in the cohort class is helping them in the credit course. There are various ways to align the two courses, but to the students in them, co-requisite classes should feel much more like one class than like two separate classes. I detail ways to align the classes below.

Finally, instructors should hold all students, both credit and developmental students, to high academic standards. In *The College Fear Factor*, which looks at writing instruction in community colleges, Rebecca Cox claims that "the most promising pedagogical approach accomplished three crucial goals: it (a) demonstrated the instructor's competence in the field of study; (b) clarified both the instructor's *expectations* for student performance and procedures for accomplishing the work; and (c) *persuaded* students that they were more than capable of succeeding"

(163 — emphasis added). Both the clear expectations of what students must do and the belief that they are capable of doing that work are important here. In a co-requisite model, students in the cohort class should be doing college-level work.

For this reason, one of the fundamental underpinnings of co-requisite classes is the idea of backward curriculum design. This term has been used by many people, including Katie Hern, who has defined it in a clear and practical way: "[B]ackward design involves thinking carefully about the outcomes we want for students — what should they know or do as a result of our work with them? Once the end goals are clear, a teacher plans backward for how to assess student performance on those outcomes, and finally, builds activities into the class to support students' learning. It's an alternative to a more traditional approach to planning, which begins with a list of topics to cover, or texts and activities to use in class" (9).

The important question is: what are we backward designing *from*? Every institution has its own approach to college composition, with textbooks aligned with one approach or another. The program's approach and goals should direct how the cohort class is designed. Below I look at three approaches:

- A modes-based approach
- An argument-based approach
- A writing about writing approach as taken in books such as Wardle and Down's *Writing about Writing: A College Reader*

This brief description of approaches to composition is by no means a primer on teaching composition, but it should demonstrate how instructors might apply backward design in practice. In all cases, teachers should think about the higher order outcomes they are looking for in the composition class and develop ways that they can encourage the learning of those outcomes in the cohort class.

The Modes

The classic modes, a staple of what has been called the "current-traditional" approach to composition, are Narrative, Exposition, Description, and Argumentation. Taking this approach in first-year composition means that students would be writing papers using one main pattern and drawing on various other patterns to develop supporting paragraphs.

To design backward taking a modes approach, teachers might use time in the cohort class to have students brainstorm ideas for developing the main pattern and drafting supporting paragraphs in one or more of the other modes. When working with comparison and contrast, for instance, students in the cohort class could be asked to devise pairs of items or ideas to compare or contrast. They could also build up a description of the items to be compared or contrasted in the essay or develop a definition of the items to make the comparison or contrast clearer. For instance, a student writing about the difference between Mexican and Southwestern cuisine could work on paragraphs defining Southwestern cuisine in contrast to its Mexican cousin or could work on paragraphs describing the ingredients, cooking techniques, or histories of the two cuisines as a way of developing the body of her essay. Students might also be asked to use tools like graphic organizers or outlines before and after they have written their essays, which can clarify their own thinking and demonstrate that writing can be not only a presentational tool but also a tool to facilitate thinking.

Argumentation

Many teachers focus on persuasive writing, central to academic writing, and so ask students to write a number of argumentative essays for their classes. Rather than focusing on thesis statements per se, these teachers might ask students to think in terms of claims. Rhetorical strategies—including the classic rhetorical appeals of *logos*, *ethos*, and *pathos*—might be emphasized within the context of persuading readers. Teachers focusing on argument may encourage students to write in topic areas such as education or technology.

A teacher backward-designing a class that focuses on argument may use the cohort section to help students think more deeply about the arguments they are making in their papers, to devise examples that use the rhetorical appeals, or to respond to alternative viewpoints, having students test their ideas in class.

Evidence can be built up over the course of a few class periods, leading students inductively to their own take on the issue. For instance, when I teach a unit on video games, I let students arrive at their own claims about whether the learning facilitated by video games is valuable or not. We have discussions that explore the ideas before students are ever asked to write.

Writing about Writing

Starting with Elizabeth Wardle and Douglass Down's article "Teaching about Writing, Righting Misconceptions," many instructors have embraced the idea that students can more effectively transfer the skills they develop in their first-year composition course if they think about and reflect upon the writing they do in class. So they have students read and write articles about writing and the writing process in order to encourage metacognition and reflection.

A teacher taking this approach might ask students in the cohort classes to track their own thinking about writing more closely. While writing, students could write reflectively, tracking their own process. Students could be asked to transform their drafts into other genres or for other disciplines, additional work that could be done in the cohort class, which would support work being done in the credit class. They could also study discourse groups to which they belong. Teachers could do some of the same things that other teachers would do—providing additional time to work on the kinds of skill needed in this paradigm.

A Sample Unit

To give a better idea of how the two classes can be aligned, I provide a sample unit below, starting with the major writing assignment that structures the unit.

Gaming Games
English 101
Spring 2016

I want us to think about video games as a topic for inquiry. (Reminder: inquiry is the art of figuring stuff out.) I don't want you to have your answers and then write about them; I want you to discover your answers as you write. That means that you have to have some good questions to begin with. You can take this topic almost ANYWHERE (except for the old "video games and violence" route). Here are some ideas with which you could work. You can either choose ONE of the topics below to write about, or you come up with your own topic related to video games:

- **What we learn from video games.** It's pretty clear that video games can be beneficial, that people can learn from them. You can't really argue that in a paper. You can argue for HOW games are good for learning, and what that means. You would definitely want to include examples of learning.

- **The cultural value of video games.** Do video games have any cultural value? Which games do? How? If they don't have cultural value, why not? Are video games a kind of literature?

- **A critical look at a video game you play or have played.** "Critical" here does not mean that you would look at the game negatively; it means that you will go beyond what you already know about games and make an interesting claim about the way a certain game deals with the world. You will read a student paper that takes this approach.

Your final paper will be 4–6 pages long, and it will make a sustained argument about video games.

You will have to quote the James Paul Gee essay and at least one other source in our Gaming Games Reading tab on Blackboard.

Due Dates:
Rough Draft: February 11
Final Draft: February 20

This assignment does a few things for me as a teacher:

1. It shows students that I give priority to thinking over formulaic writing, while also asking students to make a sustained argument.

2. While it is an argument essay, it also points us toward issues related to Writing about Writing. James Paul Gee's *What Video Games Have to Teach Us about*

Learning and Literacy makes an argument that video games are a new "semiotic domain." A semiotic domain describes how a specific group of people use language in similar ways. Some semiotic domains include health care, rap music, and Writing Studies. I use James Gee's concepts in this unit to talk about writing, explaining how students are entering a new "semiotic domain" when they enter a college writing class, and beginning to lay out and discuss the "inner grammar" of that domain, which includes how to make arguments.

The readings for this unit include the following:

- James Paul Gee, *What Video Games Have to Teach Us about Learning and Literacy*
- "Can Video Games Teach Us How to Succeed in the Real World?" *The Atlantic*, Lane Wallace
- Jane McGonigal TED Talk, "Gaming Can Make a Better World"
- Anna Sarkeesian, YouTube video, "Tropes vs. Women in Video Games"
- "Slavery as New Focus for a Game," *New York Times*, Chris Suellentrop
- A student paper on Grand Theft Auto

A teacher should align the two courses by first figuring out the goal(s) for the credit class, then determining how to help students in the cohort classes attain these goals. Here is an outline detailing how I align the two classes during my first unit of the semester:

	Credit Class	**Cohort Class**
WEEK ONE *Day 1*	• Introduction • First-Day Writing • Self-Directed Source-Driven Sample	• Writer Profile
Day 2	• Review First-Day Writing • Video Games and Learning • First Assignment Sheet • Read Gee and Student Paper	• Informal Writing on Video Games • Tearing Apart Gee • Kinds of Reading—Metacognitive, Intertextual, Imitative
WEEK TWO *Day 1*	• Kinds of Reading • Student Paper • Play "Limbo" Demo • Watch Sarkeesian Video • Reread Gee	• Sarkeesian Discussion • Watch TED Talk • Summary and Response

continued >

	Credit Class	*Cohort Class*
Day 2	• Discuss Cultural Aspect of Video Games • Inquiry • Claims • Focused Writing • Watch McGonigal TED Talk	• Close Reading of Article • Summary and Response • Good Student Papers
WEEK THREE *Day 1*	• Good Student Writing Discussion • Rough Draft Workshop	• Discussion of Workshop • Discussion of TED Talk • Working with Sources
Day 2	• Round Robin Video Games Ideas • Writing—Some Alternative Methods	• Work Time on Drafts • "Problem" Issues
WEEK FOUR *Day 1*	• MLA and Organization • Writing Workshop	• Additional Organization Work
Day 2	• Paper Due • Begin Unit 2	• Information Writing toward Unit 2

Rarely do I ever plan a co-requisite class for longer than four weeks at a time, because there are always issues that crop up—a writing issue that all students share or a need to work more intensely on incorporating sources, etc.

The first week of the semester is an important time for setting expectations and giving students an idea of what I value in writing. Therefore, instead of asking students to write autobiographical first writings or literacy narratives, as many teachers do, I ask my students to think about something that they are interested in, to find an Internet source about that topic, and to write a short, speculative essay using that source as a springboard for their own thinking. This task is neither purely personal nor purely academic but a mix of the two. From this first assignment, I am able to gauge how well students can integrate sources into their writing, what they're interested in, and their basic proficiency level. At my institution, we are required to assign a diagnostic essay during the first week, and though I question the validity of a one-time, timed writing task as a measure of students' writing, the task I've designed is more meaningful to me than others I've used, or been required to use, in the past.

This first week is also a time for community building, and we spend a lot of time talking about our interests and why we're in school. After the first credit class, in which I discuss the syllabus and have students write, the discussion continues in the cohort class as students talk about their experience writing the self-directed, source-driven sample. They also talk about their earlier experiences with English classes and why they think they landed in this cohort section. I then ask student to write profiles of each other, profiles that must include some element of their history with writing. This sets the stage for the class by letting students know that the cohort class is a *companion* to the credit course, that it will revolve around their experiences with writing, in a way that is similar to the studio model promoted by Grego and Thompson in *Teaching/Writing in Thirdspaces*, though the co-requisite class is slightly more formal than a "studio," in that it is a three-credit hour class.

On the second day of the credit class, we talk a little more about writing and I explain the video game assignment. I hand out the James Paul Gee piece, which is the most difficult piece of writing that students will read during the entire semester. In the cohort class following the credit class, we spend a lot of time talking about the reading, and I give the students terms that describe three different kinds of reading: metacognitive, intertextual, and imitative, an idea borrowed from Dan Keller's 2013 "A Framework for Rereading in First-Year Composition." This is the kind of extra work that co-requisite classes were designed for. It is not work divorced from the work done in the credit class, but rather an opportunity to give students the tools that they will need in order to be successful *in* the credit class.

During the second week, we dig into the reading and do informal writing about video games. The discussion is wide-ranging, since I want students to find their own way into the topic of video games. When I first taught this unit in Spring 2014, students were divided. Some thought that video games had both cultural value and could teach us things that could translate to the real world, while others thought that video games were a waste of time. In the credit class, we discussed the readings, watched one student play a video game that was new to him and, as a class, analyzed what he learned from the activity, before we started working toward the paper. In the cohort class, we did two things that week: during one class we started talking about incorporating sources into our writing, and students wrote one paragraph incorporating a source, and we read one of the papers and did a summary and response, a skill that will be essential for many other classes.

It should be evident from the first two weeks that what happens in the cohort class is additional college-level work on reading and writing. Around this time, I am also starting to become aware of the specific needs of the students in my cohort classes. For instance, in spring 2014, one student wrote too quickly and didn't go back to revise his work, believing that writing was a one-and-done activity. Another student took a painfully long time to get a single sentence onto the page. Two others had second language issues. And every student had problems with fused sentences.

During the third and fourth week of the course, I start to spend more time with individual students working on their specific writing challenges.

The third and fourth week also led us toward the due date for the first major paper, and we spent some time in class talking more about the process of writing academic papers, which included work with MLA citation style and workshops, both in the credit class and the cohort class. I hope this schedule makes the idea of backward design more tangible. All work done in the cohort class supports the work done in the credit class.

For an example of how the courses could be aligned using *Intersections* as a course text, see pp. 15–23 in this manual.

There is always an element of judgment involved in teaching a co-requisite class, as the instructor determines what the students need most. The alignment should be between the composition course and the basic writing class, as well as between the needs of the students and the class. It can't be said too often that the cohort class should feel to the student like part of the credit class, that they should recognize the alignment between the two. While I wouldn't necessarily share the week-by-week syllabus with students, a teacher should repeatedly explain how one class plays off the other.

Works Cited

Bishop, Wendy. *Released into Language: Options for Teaching Creative Writing.* National Council of Teachers of English, 1990.

Cox, Rebecca D. *The College Fear Factor: How Students and Professors Misunderstand One Another.* Harvard UP, 2011.

Gee, James P. *What Video Games Have to Teach Us about Learning and Literacy.* Palgrave Macmillan, 2003.

Graff, Gerald, and Cathy Birkenstein. *They Say/I Say: The Moves That Matter in Academic Writing.* W. W. Norton, 2008.

Grego, Rhonda C., and Nancy S. Thompson. *Teaching/Writing in Thirdspaces: The Studio Approach.* Southern Illinois UP, 2008.

Harris, Joseph. *Rewriting: How to Do Things with Texts.* Utah State UP, 2006.

Hern, Katie, and Myra Snell. *Toward a Vision of Accelerated Curriculum and Pedagogy.* LearningWorks, 2013, www.canadacollege.edu/cwd/reports/AcceleratingCurriculum_508.pdf.

Keller, Dan. "A Framework for Rereading in First-Year Composition." *Teaching English in the Two-Year College,* vol. 41, no. 1, Sept. 2013, pp. 44-55.

McGonigal, Jane. "Gaming Can Make a Better World." *TED Talks,* February 2010, www.ted.com/talks/jane_mcgonigal_gaming_can_make_a_better_world?language=en.

Murray, Donald M. *A Writer Teaches Writing: A Practical Method of Teaching Composition.* Houghton Mifflin, 1968.

Sarkeesian, Anita. "Ms. Male Character—Tropes vs. Women | Feminist Frequency." *YouTube,* 18 Nov. 2013, youtu.be/eYqYLfm1rWA.

Suellentrop, Chris. "Slavery as New Focus for a Game." *The New York Times,* 27 Jan. 2014, nyti.ms/1f7CVku.

Wallace, Lane. "Can Video Games Teach Us How to Succeed in the Real World?" *The Atlantic,* 15 Dec. 2010, www.theatlantic.com/technology/archive/2010/12/can-video-games-teach -us-how-to-succeed-in-the-real-world/67942/.